The IDG Books Bible Advantage

The *Office 97 Bible* is part of the Bible series brought to you by IDG Books Worldwide. We designed Bibles to meet your growing need for quick access to the most complete and accurate computer information available.

Bibles work the way you do: They focus on accomplishing specific tasks — not learning random functions. These books are not long-winded manuals or dry reference tomes. In Bibles, expert authors tell you exactly what you can do with your software and how to do it. Easy-to-follow, step-by-step sections; comprehensive coverage; and convenient access in language and design — it's all here.

The authors of Bibles are uniquely qualified to give you expert advice as well as to provide insightful tips and techniques not found anywhere else. Our authors maintain close contact with end users through feedback from articles, training sessions, e-mail exchanges, user group participation, and consulting work. Because our authors know the realities of daily computer use and are directly tied to the reader, our Bibles have a strategic advantage.

Bible authors have the experience to approach a topic in the most efficient manner, and we know that you, the reader, will benefit from a "one-on-one" relationship with the author. Our research shows that readers make computer book purchases because they want expert advice. Because readers want to benefit from the author's experience, the author's voice is always present in a Bible series book.

You will find what you need in this book whether you read it from cover to cover, section by section, or simply one topic at a time. As a computer user, you deserve a comprehensive resource of answers. We at IDG Books Worldwide are proud to deliver that resource with the *Office 97 Bible*.

Brenda McLaughlin
Senior Vice President and Group Publisher
Internet: YouTellUs@idgbooks.com

Office 97
Bible

Office 97 Bible

Edward Jones and Derek Sutton II

IDG Books Worldwide, Inc.
An International Data Group Company

Foster City, CA ✦ Chicago, IL ✦ Indianapolis, IN ✦ Southlake, TX

Office 97 Bible

Published by

IDG Books Worldwide, Inc.
An International Data Group Company
919 E. Hillsdale Blvd.
Suite 400
Foster City, CA 94404

www.idgbooks.com (IDG Books Worldwide Web Site)

Library of Congress Catalog Card No.: 96-78775

ISBN: 0-7645-3037-2

Printed in the United States of America

10 9 8 7 6 5 4 3 2 1

IE/TQ/RS/ZW/FC

Distributed in the United States by IDG Books Worldwide, Inc.

Distributed by Macmillan Canada for Canada; by Contemporanea de Ediciones for Venezuela; by Distribuidora Cuspide for Argentina; by CITEC for Brazil; by Ediciones ZETA S.C.R. Ltda. for Peru; by Editorial Limusa SA for Mexico; by Transworld Publishers Limited in the United Kingdom and Europe; by Academic Bookshop for Egypt; by Levant Distributors S.A.R.L. for Lebanon; by Al Jassim for Saudi Arabia; by Simron Pty. Ltd. for South Africa; by Pustak Mahal for India; by The Computer Bookshop for India; by Toppan Company Ltd. for Japan; by Addison Wesley Publishing Company for Korea; by Longman Singapore Publishers Ltd. for Singapore, Malaysia, Thailand, and Indonesia; by Unalis Corporation for Taiwan; by WS Computer Publishing Company, Inc. for the Philippines; by WoodsLane Pty. Ltd. for Australia; by WoodsLane Enterprises Ltd. for New Zealand. Authorized Sales Agent: Anthony Rudkin Associates for the Middle East and North Africa.

For general information on IDG Books Worldwide's books in the U.S., please call our Consumer Customer Service department at 800-762-2974. For reseller information, including discounts and premium sales, please call our Reseller Customer Service department at 800-434-3422.

For information on where to purchase IDG Books Worldwide's books outside the U.S., please contact our International Sales department at 415-655-3172 or fax 415-655-3295.

For information on foreign language translations, please contact our Foreign & Subsidiary Rights department at 415-655-3021 or fax 415-655-3281.

For sales inquiries and special prices for bulk quantities, please contact our Sales department at 415-655-3200 or write to the address above.

For information on using IDG Books Worldwide's books in the classroom or for ordering examination copies, please contact our Educational Sales department at 800-434-2086 or fax 817-251-8174.

For press review copies, author interviews, or other publicity information, please contact our Public Relations department at 415-655-3000 or fax 415-655-3299.

For authorization to photocopy items for corporate, personal, or educational use, please contact Copyright Clearance Center, 222 Rosewood Drive, Danvers, MA 01923, or fax 508-750-4470.

 is a trademark under exclusive license to IDG Books Worldwide, Inc., from International Data Group, Inc.

About the Authors

Edward Jones

Edward Jones is a leading author of computer books. He has written more than 30 titles, many about database, spreadsheet, and word processing programs. He has also served as a technical editor of many computer books and has written several magazine articles. Mr. Jones is an applications development analyst for Schulte, Roth & Zabel LLP, a major New York law firm. He has performed consulting services for major Washington, D.C.-based law firms and government agencies. He resides in the New York metropolitan area.

Derek Sutton II

Derek Sutton II is a college computer science student who minors in journalism. As a co-author with Mr. Jones, Mr. Sutton has published titles about Windows databases and Windows 95. Mr. Sutton also provides training and consulting services in Windows and Windows applications through his company, Derek Sutton and Associates, located in the Washington, DC area.

ABOUT IDG BOOKS WORLDWIDE

Welcome to the world of IDG Books Worldwide.

IDG Books Worldwide, Inc., is a subsidiary of International Data Group, the world's largest publisher of computer-related information and the leading global provider of information services on information technology. IDG was founded more than 25 years ago and now employs more than 8,500 people worldwide. IDG publishes more than 275 computer publications in over 75 countries (see listing below). More than 60 million people read one or more IDG publications each month.

Launched in 1990, IDG Books Worldwide is today the #1 publisher of best-selling computer books in the United States. We are proud to have received eight awards from the Computer Press Association in recognition of editorial excellence and three from *Computer Currents'* First Annual Readers' Choice Awards. Our best-selling *...For Dummies*® series has more than 30 million copies in print with translations in 30 languages. IDG Books Worldwide, through a joint venture with IDG's Hi-Tech Beijing, became the first U.S. publisher to publish a computer book in the People's Republic of China. In record time, IDG Books Worldwide has become the first choice for millions of readers around the world who want to learn how to better manage their businesses.

Our mission is simple: Every one of our books is designed to bring extra value and skill-building instructions to the reader. Our books are written by experts who understand and care about our readers. The knowledge base of our editorial staff comes from years of experience in publishing, education, and journalism — experience we use to produce books for the '90s. In short, we care about books, so we attract the best people. We devote special attention to details such as audience, interior design, use of icons, and illustrations. And because we use an efficient process of authoring, editing, and desktop publishing our books electronically, we can spend more time ensuring superior content and spend less time on the technicalities of making books.

You can count on our commitment to deliver high-quality books at competitive prices on topics you want to read about. At IDG Books Worldwide, we continue in the IDG tradition of delivering quality for more than 25 years. You'll find no better book on a subject than one from IDG Books Worldwide.

John J. Kilcullen

John Kilcullen
President and CEO
IDG Books Worldwide, Inc.

Eighth Annual
Computer Press
Awards ≥1992

Ninth Annual
Computer Press
Awards ≥1993

Tenth Annual
Computer Press
Awards ≥1994

Eleventh Annual
Computer Press
Awards ≥1995

IDG Books Worldwide, Inc., is a subsidiary of International Data Group, the world's largest publisher of computer-related information and the leading global provider of information services on information technology. International Data Group publishes over 275 computer publications in over 75 countries. Sixty million people read one or more International Data Group publications each month. International Data Group's publications include: **ARGENTINA:** Buyer's Guide, Computerworld Argentina, PC World Argentina; **AUSTRALIA:** Australian Macworld, Australian PC World, Australian Reseller News, Computerworld, IT Casebook, Network World, Publish, Webmaster; **AUSTRIA:** Computerwelt Osterreich, Networks Austria, PC Tip Austria; **BANGLADESH:** PC World Bangladesh; **BELARUS:** PC World Belarus; **BELGIUM:** Data News; **BRAZIL:** Annuario de Informática, Computerworld, Connections, Macworld, PC Player, PC World, Publish, Reseller News, Supergamepower; **BULGARIA:** Computerworld Bulgaria, Network World Bulgaria, PC & MacWorld Bulgaria; **CANADA:** CIO Canada, Client/Server World, ComputerWorld Canada, InfoWorld Canada, NetworkWorld Canada, WebWorld; **CHILE:** Computerworld Chile, PC World Chile; **COLOMBIA:** Computerworld Colombia, PC World Colombia; **COSTA RICA:** PC World Centro America; **THE CZECH AND SLOVAK REPUBLICS:** Computerworld Czechoslovakia, Macworld Czech Republic, PC World Czechoslovakia; **DENMARK:** Communications World Danmark, Computerworld Danmark, Macworld Danmark, PC World Danmark, Techworld Denmark; **DOMINICAN REPUBLIC:** PC World Republica Dominicana; **ECUADOR:** PC World Ecuador; **EGYPT:** Computerworld Middle East, PC World Middle East; **EL SALVADOR:** PC World Centro America; **FINLAND:** MikroPC, Tietoverkko, Tietoviikko; **FRANCE:** Distributique, Hebdo, Info PC, Le Monde Informatique, Macworld, Reseaux & Telecoms, WebMaster France; **GERMANY:** Computer Partner, Computerwoche, Computerwoche Extra, Computerwoche FOCUS, Global Online, Macwelt, PC Welt; **GREECE:** Amiga Computing, GamePro Greece, Multimedia World; **GUATEMALA:** PC World Centro America; **HONDURAS:** PC World Centro America; **HONG KONG:** Computerworld Hong Kong, PC World Hong Kong, Publish in Asia; **HUNGARY:** ABCD CD-ROM, Computerworld Szamitastechnika, Internetto online Magazine, PC World Hungary, PC-X Magazin Hungary; **ICELAND:** Tolvuheimur PC World Island; **INDIA:** Information Communications World, Information Systems Computerworld, PC World India, Publish in Asia; **INDONESIA:** InfoKomputer PC World, Komputek Computerworld, Publish in Asia; **IRELAND:** ComputerScope, PC Live!; **ISRAEL:** Macworld Israel, People & Computers/Computerworld; **ITALY:** Computerworld Italia, Macworld Italia, Networking Italia, PC World Italia; **JAPAN:** DTP World, Macworld Japan, Nikkei Personal Computing, OS/2 World Japan, SunWorld Japan, Windows NT World, Windows World Japan; **KENYA:** PC World East African; **KOREA:** Hi-Tech Information, Macworld Korea, PC World Korea; **MACEDONIA:** PC World Macedonia; **MALAYSIA:** Computerworld Malaysia, PC World Malaysia, Publish in Asia; **MALTA:** PC World Malta; **MEXICO:** Computerworld Mexico, PC World Mexico; **MYANMAR:** PC World Myanmar; **NETHERLANDS:** Computer! Totaal, LAN Internetworking Magazine, LAN World Buyers Guide, Macworld Netherlands, Net, WebWereld; **NEW ZEALAND:** Absolute Beginners Guide and Plain & Simple Series, Computer Buyer, Computer Industry Directory, Computerworld New Zealand, MTB, Network World, PC World New Zealand; **NICARAGUA:** PC World Centro America; **NORWAY:** Computerworld Norge, CW Rapport, Datamagasinet, Financial Rapport, Kursguide Norge, Macworld Norge, Multimediaworld Norge, PC World Ekspress Norge, PC World Nettverk, PC World Norge, PC World ProduktGuide Norge; **PAKISTAN:** Computerworld Pakistan; **PANAMA:** PC World Panama; **PEOPLE'S REPUBLIC OF CHINA:** China Computer Users, China Computerworld, China InfoWorld, China Telecom World Weekly, Computer & Communication, Electronic Design China, Electronics Today, Electronics Weekly, Game Software, PC World China, Popular Computer Week, Software Weekly, Software World, Telecom World; **PERU:** Computerworld Peru, PC World Profesional Peru, PC World SoHo Peru; **PHILIPPINES:** Click!, Computerworld Philippines, PC World Philippines, Publish in Asia; **POLAND:** Computerworld Poland, Computerworld Special Report Poland, Cyber, Macworld Poland, Networld Poland, PC World Komputer; **PORTUGAL:** Cerebro/PC World, Computerworld/Correio Informatico, Dealer World Portugal, Mac*In/PC*In Portugal, Multimedia World; **PUERTO RICO:** PC World Puerto Rico; **ROMANIA:** Computerworld Romania, PC World Romania, Telecom Romania; **RUSSIA:** Computerworld Russia, Mir PK, Publish, Seti; **SINGAPORE:** Computerworld Singapore, PC World Singapore, Publish in Asia; **SLOVENIA:** Monitor; **SOUTH AFRICA:** Computing SA, Network World SA, Software World SA; **SPAIN:** Communicaciones World España, Computerworld España, Dealer World España, Macworld España, PC World España; **SRI LANKA:** Infolink PC World; **SWEDEN:** CAP&Design, Computer Sweden, Corporate Computing Sweden, Internetworld Sweden, it.branschen, Macworld Sweden, MaxiData Sweden, MikroDatorn, Nätverk & Kommunikation, PC World Sweden, PCaktiv, Windows World Sweden; **SWITZERLAND:** Computerworld Schweiz, Macworld Schweiz, PCtip; **TAIWAN:** Computerworld Taiwan, Macworld Taiwan, NEW ViSiON/Publish, PC World Taiwan, Windows World Taiwan; **THAILAND:** Publish in Asia, Thai Computerworld; **TURKEY:** Computerworld Turkiye, Macworld Turkiye, Network World Turkiye, PC World Turkiye; **UKRAINE:** Computerworld Kiev, Multimedia World Ukraine, PC World Ukraine; **UNITED KINGDOM:** Acorn User UK, Amiga Action UK, Amiga Computing UK, Apple Talk UK, Computing, Macworld, Parents and Computers UK, PC Advisor, PC Home, PSX Pro, The WEB; **UNITED STATES:** Cable in the Classroom, CIO Magazine, Computerworld, DOS World, Federal Computer Week, GamePro Magazine, InfoWorld, I-Way, Macworld, Network World, PC Games, PC World, Publish, Video Event, THE WEB Magazine, and WebMaster; online webzines: JavaWorld, NetscapeWorld, and SunWorld Online; **URUGUAY:** InfoWorld Uruguay; **VENEZUELA:** Computerworld Venezuela, PC World Venezuela; and **VIETNAM:** PC World Vietnam.   10/1/96

Dedication

We want to dedicate this book to many people who have stood behind us.

Thanks Alberta, for sticking with me during one of the roughest years of my life. Thank you for being with me when I need a family member to be there for me. I will always love you for that. Hugs and kisses.

Jeanine, this one's for you, baby. Miss Vida, be strong, baby. Chris M, take care; you are a beautiful person and you are going to make someone very happy one day. Mrs. Z., once more I have to say thank you for looking out for me. And to all my other friends that I was so mean to during this book, you know how I get. A special thanks to John C. and Felicia S. for giving me the needed time to complete this. Finally thanks to Chaka for helping me get through those long work sessions.

— Derek Sutton II

To Timothous Mack-Jones, who knows full well what he's done to deserve the dedication. And this one is also dedicated to everyone that's a member of my extended family, wherever you may be.

— Ed Jones

Credits

Acknowledgments

As with any major work (and trust us, this was a major work!), this book is the combined result of the concerted efforts of many people.

First, the IDG Books Universe: We would like to thank Greg Croy, who entrusted us with this significant project. Sincere and well-deserved thanks to Hugh Vandivier, whose long hours in the editorial process were instrumental in making this book the best guide to Microsoft Office there is. Thanks to Erik Dafforn for leading in the early days of this project, and to Andy Cummings for his keeping an eye on the overall flow of things. Thanks to Paul and Mary Summitt for producing a thorough technical review. Thanks to everyone in the Production department at IDG Books — they played important roles in helping us bring this work to market. Finally, thanks to Accounting for getting the checks out (no one ever seems to remember the people who help you pay your bills!).

Thanks to America Online for making it possible for us to work from most parts of this planet and still manage to stay in contact with friends and family. Thanks to the sysops of the Microsoft Beta Support Team on CompuServe, for their fast answers to the many questions that inevitably arose during the software shakeout process.

(The Publisher would like to give special thanks to Patrick J. McGovern, without whom this book would not have been possible.)

Contents at a Glance

Table of Contents

Introduction

Welcome to *Office 97 Bible*. This is your personal guide to the applications that compose the Standard and Professional editions of Microsoft Office: Microsoft Word, Microsoft Excel, Microsoft PowerPoint, Microsoft Access, Microsoft Outlook, and Microsoft Binder. This book tells you everything you need to learn any or all of the Microsoft Office applications, regardless of how much you already know about Office. This book is first and foremost a comprehensive reference, but it also helps you learn by example, and it gives you special tips and techniques to get the most out of the Office applications. *Office 97 Bible* also tells you how to make the Office applications work in concert for maximum results. Using the techniques outlined in this book, you'll be able to integrate the use of the Office applications for maximum efficiency and share information between the applications to produce impressive documents and presentations.

Although each chapter is an integral part of the book as a whole, each chapter can also stand on its own. You can read the book in any order you want, skipping from chapter to chapter and from topic to topic. (This book's index is particularly thorough: rely on the index to find the topics that interest you.)

For each of the major applications (Word, Excel, PowerPoint, and Access), we've included chapters that answer the ten most common user questions, based on user feedback to Microsoft and support discussions on CompuServe and America Online. We've also included "At Work" chapters that show you how to accomplish common, everyday office tasks with Office. If you've never touched Word, Excel, PowerPoint, or Access, we've included appendixes that tell you the basics for each application.

Is This Book for You?

If you use (or will soon use) Microsoft Office, this book is for you. As we'll describe fully in just a minute, this book is divided into parts: each part describes one of the Office applications. If you're an Office beginner, start with the first chapter in each part and work to the end. (If you've never used *any* kind of word processor, spreadsheet, database manager, or presentation creator before, start with the appendixes!) If you have some Office experience, be sure to breeze through the chapters that cover topics you already know: we've added special tips and techniques throughout that will help you work better with Office.

How This Book Is Organized

We've divided this book into five parts: one that gives an overview of Office; one each for Word, Excel, PowerPoint, and Access; and one that describes Outlook (a time management and messaging application) and tools you can use to make Office applications work together.

Part I: Introducing Microsoft Office

This tiny, one-chapter part tells you about tools Office gives you to work more efficiently.

Chapter 1: About Microsoft Office starts you off. You'll learn about starting the Office Manager, launching applications, getting Office Manager tips, making appointments, adding tasks, adding contacts, and exiting the Office Manager.

Part II: Word

Ah, Word: the 800-pound gorilla of word processors. This part tells you what Word can do for you.

Chapter 2: Creating and Working with Documents is where you'll create your first document. You'll also be introduced to templates, Clipboard insertions, and Word's multiple views. This chapter also helps you tackle some everyday word-processing tasks: changing margins, setting tabs and line spacing, and moving and copying text. You'll also learn about using search and replace; using the thesaurus; using the spelling and grammar checkers; changing your hyphenation options; adding bullets and paragraph numbering; and creating and editing glossaries.

Chapter 3: Formatting Documents tells you the hows and whys of formatting, which is the way you specify what your document will look like. It helps you apply *character* and *paragraph* formatting, as well as *page* and *section* formatting. It tells you how to deal with tabs; create document summaries; make headers, footers, and page numbers; and handle complex documents.

Chapter 4: Previewing and Printing Your Documents discusses previewing documents; adjusting margins and objects in preview mode; printing documents; printing multiple documents; printing parts of a document; printing sideways; printing envelopes; and changing the printer setup.

Chapter 5: Working with Tables and Outlines tells you how to create, edit, and format tables; work with side-by-side paragraphs; and convert text to tables. It also describes Word outlines, telling you how to create and organize outlines; promote and demote headings; convert headings to body text and vice versa; and move headings.

Chapter 6: Working with Fields tells you all about working with fields and with Word's mail merge facility. It gives you great tips on embedding Excel data into a mail merge, and you'll also find information that helps you work with data from other programs, such as dBASE and Paradox.

Chapter 7: Building Tables of Contents and Indexes helps you create tables of contents. You can do this in two ways: by using existing headings in your document, or by embedding special codes called *TC* fields. The chapter also helps you add multiple levels to a table of contents. In addition, this chapter tells you how to build indexes, including creating multilevel index entries, and how to use page number ranges. It gives special tips for handling large indexes.

Chapter 8: Working with Styles and Templates helps you make your documents look better. You can use styles to format your documents. Word comes with some predefined styles, but you can create and apply your own, and even use styles from other documents. Templates are a way to collect styles you want to reuse: for example, creating a *memorandum* template that includes all the styles you typically use when you write a memo. The chapter tells you how to use templates to create documents; how to create and apply a template; and how to customize Word's default template.

Chapter 9: Working with Macros helps you reduce tedious tasks to a single keystroke (or toolbar button or menu choice). This chapter tells you how to record and play macros, and how to assign shortcut keys to macros. It even tells you how to create macros that run automatically. And you'll also find suggestions for real-world uses of macros in your work.

Chapter 10: Desktop Publishing with Word describes ways you can add desktop publishing-style flair to your documents. It discusses using columns and adding graphics. It tells you about Word's brochure and newsletter wizards — fast ways to look professional. It also tells you about Word's AutoFormat feature, which can make your plain-text document look pretty.

Chapter 11: Word and the Web describes how you can use Word with the Internet, to browse the web and to create web pages (also known as *HTML* documents) from directly within Word. The chapter also describes how you can add *hyperlinks* to Word documents which let you jump to locations in other Office documents.

Chapter 12: Word and Visual Basic for Applications details Visual Basic for Applications (VBA), the programming language that lies behind all Word macros that you create. As Word macros are based on Visual Basic for Applications, VBA can be used to automate many common tasks in Word.

Chapter 13: Word for Windows At Work provides step-by-step details of how you can perform various common office tasks with Word. It helps you create a fax cover sheet and an interoffice memos, using detailed instructions you can follow.

Chapter 14: The Word for Windows Top Ten answers the ten most burning questions Word users have.

Part III: Excel

This part describes Office's spreadsheet application, Excel.

Chapter 15: Making the Most of Workbooks tells you all about workbooks, which are collections of individual Excel spreadsheets. It tells you how to create, open, save, and close workbooks. It tells you how add, delete, rename, move, and copy sheets within a workbook. It also tells you about selecting cells and sheets, and about moving and copying data between sheets.

Chapter 16: Getting Information into Excel tells you how to get data into Excel. It describes entering numbers, dates, and times; text entry; building series; handling trends as a part of data entry; editing, moving, and copying cells; and adding and deleting rows and columns. It also details using and customizing AutoFill, a great way to make Excel do some work for you.

Chapter 17: Excel Formatting tells you how to customize the look of your spreadsheets. It details changing row heights and column widths; changing alignments and fonts; changing borders, patterns, and colors; modifying cell shading; working with number formats; using custom formats; using styles with formats; and using AutoFormat.

Chapter 18: Adding Graphics to Worksheets tells you how to embed graphics into your spreadsheets. (And you thought spreadsheets were only for crunching numbers!) It discusses drawing objects, adding text, selecting and grouping objects, and sizing and moving objects.

Chapter 19: Working with Excel Charts discusses Excel's chart feature, a quick way to turn your spreadsheet data into an easily understandable graphic. It tells you how to add *embedded*, *separate*, and *freestanding* charts. It helps you add titles and labels to your charts, change a chart's type after you've created it, and format charts.

Chapter 20: Printing with Excel tells you about the choices you have when printing your work in Excel. It describes working with printer setup and margins, using headers and footers, previewing print jobs, specifying what to print, dealing with complex print jobs, working with title layouts, working with fonts, and general printing tips.

Chapter 21: Working with Excel Databases tells you about using information from a database in Excel. It tells you how to create databases in Excel, how to find the information that you need, and how to print reports. You'll also find tips here on designing your databases for maximum efficiency, importing data, how to use Microsoft Query and ODBC, and how to work with query results.

Chapter 22: Working with Macros helps you reduce tedious tasks to a single keystroke (or toolbar button or menu choice). It tells you how to make and use macros and use the macro toolbar, and it gives useful examples of Excel macros.

Chapter 23: Excel and the Web helps you use Excel's powers to work with the Internet. The chapter describes how *hyperlinks* can be added to allow users to jump from any point in an Excel document to any other Office document, and how Excel worksheets and charts can be converted to HTML documents, for placement on an intranet or on the Internet.

Chapter 24: Excel and Visual Basic for Applications introduces you to Visual Basic for Applications, a programming language you can use to make Excel do more for you. Macros are a key to learning Visual Basic for Applications; this chapter tells you how. It also helps you understand Visual Basic for Applications code; tells you how to use comments, cell selection techniques, and control statements; tells you how to display input boxes and dialog boxes; and describes the editor you use to create Visual Basic for Applications programs.

Chapter 25: Excel at Work helps you use Excel in the office to create cash-flow management worksheets, IRA calculations, a break-even analysis, and an amortization schedule.

Chapter 26: The Excel Top Ten answers the ten most problematic questions Excel users have.

Part IV: PowerPoint

This part tells you how to use PowerPoint to create great presentations.

Chapter 27: Working in PowerPoint introduces you to PowerPoint basics: selecting and grouping objects; moving and copying objects; resizing, scaling, and aligning objects; using the grid; drawing lines, shapes, and curves; and drawing freeform shapes.

Chapter 28: Enhancing a Presentation tells you how to make your presentations look better. You can use AutoLayouts, which makes PowerPoint format the presentation for you. You can also use slides from other presentations. This chapter tells you how to do both. It also describes working with columns and lists; working with fonts, styles, and colors; working with color schemes; working with shading and fill; and adding sound to your presentation. Finally, it tells you how to add Excel worksheets and Word tables.

Chapter 29: Working with Charts in PowerPoint describes PowerPoint's chart feature. It tells you how to insert and edit graphs, and discusses using the various formatting options of PowerPoint to choose a graph's design. It helps you enhance a chart's appearance by giving tips on formatting; on sizing and positioning of objects; and on working with shadows, colors, and backgrounds.

Chapter 30: Producing Your Work tells you how to print presentations, produce on-screen slide shows, create speaker's notes, and create audience handouts.

Chapter 31: Working with PowerPoint Macros helps you reduce repetitive tasks to a single keystroke (or toolbar button or menu choice). It tells you how to make and use macros and use the macro toolbar, and it gives useful examples of PowerPoint macros.

Chapter 32: PowerPoint and the Web explains how to move PowerPoint presentations to the Internet or to an intranet. The chapter details how *hyperlinks* can be added to allow users to jump from any point in a PowerPoint document to any other Office document, and how slides from a PowerPoint presentation can be converted to HTML documents, for placement on an intranet or on the Internet.

Chapter 33: PowerPoint for Windows at Work tells you how to create an organization chart and a sales presentation using PowerPoint's AutoContent wizard.

Chapter 34: The PowerPoint Top Ten solves the ten most frustrating problems users have with PowerPoint.

Part V: Access

This part tells you how to use Access, the database manager that's included with the Professional edition of Office 97.

Chapter 35: Working with Tables gets you started creating tables; adding, editing, and deleting data into *datasheets*. It tells you about the Database Wizard, which creates the tables needed for a common database management task and automatically defines the default relationships required between the tables. This chapter also helps you add indexes to your database tables, and establish relationships between tables in your database.

Chapter 36: Working with Simple Queries tells you how to ask questions to get answers from your data. You'll learn how to design queries with the Query Design toolbar and the Query menu. You'll also learn about query criteria and about a query's *dynaset*, which is a dynamic set of records based on the query's design. For those of you familiar with SQL, this chapter will show you how to use SQL code in your queries.

Chapter 37: Working with Forms gives you another way to enter and view data. The datasheets you learned about in Chapter 31 are limited to rows and columns. Forms are more flexible, letting you show one record at a time in any arrangement. You'll learn how to create forms with the help of Access (via the Form Wizards or the New Object button), as well as manually. You'll also learn how to add graphics and controls to your forms.

Chapter 38: Working with Reports tells you how to manipulate your data to create reports. The chapter describes the available report types, and tells you how to plan and then implement each type. It also describes the Report Wizards, with which you can quickly and easily create reports. You'll learn how to add formatting and graphics to your reports.

Chapter 39: Working with Relational Queries expands on the discussion of Chapter 36 by describing queries that use data from more than one table at a time. This chapter tells you how to structure relational queries, and tells you what relational queries will and won't do. You'll learn about *relational* joins, which is how you tie two tables together, and about the kinds of data relationships these joins create.

Chapter 40: Working with Specialized Queries tells you about *action* queries, which manipulate the data they query; *crosstab* queries, which give you a spreadsheet-like view of your data, and *parameter* queries, which let you change query criteria each time you run them.

Chapter 41: Working with Relational Forms and Reports continues the discussions of Chapters 37 and 38, telling you how to create and use forms and reports that use more than one table at a time.

Chapter 42: Working with Macros tells you how to create and use macros in Access to simplify complex or routine tasks.

Chapter 43: Working with Charts in Access tells you how to create and display charts in your Access forms. You use Microsoft Graph, a Windows mini-application included with Office, to create the charts.

Chapter 44: Access and the Web details how you can use Access to produce database information in the form of Web pages (also known as *HTML* documents) that can then be uploaded to a Web server for access on an intranet or the Internet. You'll also learn how *hyerlinks* can be used to provide jumps from Access fields directly to other Office documents.

Chapter 45: Access and Visual Basic for Applications deals with the use of Visual Basic for Applications (VBA), the programming language that is a virtual requirement for taking Access applications beyond a level of what is possible with macros alone. Using VBA, you can not only perform the kinds of automated operations that are possible with macros, but you can exercise a much tighter degree of control over complete custom applications.

Chapter 46: Access for Windows at Work tells you how to use Access to maintain and manage your mailing list, and to track personnel assignments.

Chapter 47: The Access Top Ten answers the ten most Maalox-moment-making problems that users have with Access.

Part VI: Office Works Together

This part tells you about Outlook, Office's time management and messaging application. It also describes Object Linking and Embedding (OLE) and the Office Binder, two ways that you can make Office applications work together.

Chapter 48: Using Outlook helps you send and receive e-mail, create appointments and tasks, schedule meetings, and respond to meeting requests. Using Outlook as your planning assistant, you can track appointments, projects, meetings, personal and business contacts, and events.

Chapter 49: Using the Binder tells you how to group documents from the various Office applications into *binders*, which are collections of Word, Excel, and PowerPoint documents. Binders provide you with a central place to edit and print documents related to a single project.

Chapter 50: Sharing Data Between Applications with OLE tells you how OLE (Object Linking and Embedding) lets you place data from one Office application into another and have the data automatically stay up to date.

Appendixes

If you haven't installed Office on your computer yet, or if you've never used any of the Office applications, then bury your nose in the appendixes. They'll get you going.

Appendix A: Installing Office tells you how to install Microsoft Office.

Appendix B: Word Basics tells the new Word user how to start Word, how to create a document, how to open an existing document, how to navigate a document, how to enter and edit text, how to print a document, and how to save a document.

Appendix C: Excel Basics tells the new Excel user how to start Excel, what a *workbook* is, how to navigate a workbook, how to enter and edit data and formulas, how to do basic formatting, how to print your work, and how to save your work.

Appendix D: PowerPoint Basics tells the new PowerPoint user how to start PowerPoint; how to create, move around in, and save presentations; and how to enter text and graphics into presentations.

Appendix E: Access Basics tells the new Access user what a database is, how to start Access, how to create a table, how to create a basic form and a report, and how to use simple queries to get the data that's needed.

Conventions This Book Uses

We've written a thick book: there's a lot to say about Office! Therefore, we've used several devices that help you find your way.

You'll see eye-catching icons in the margin from time to time. They'll alert you to critical information, warn you about problems, tell you where to go for more information, and highlight useful tips.

Note This icon highlights a special point of interest about the current topic.

Hot Stuff This icon helps you work faster by pointing out shortcuts and killer techniques. If you've worked with the Office applications before and want to expand your knowledge quickly, skim the book for these icons.

Danger Zone Sometimes bad things can happen when you work in Office. This icon points out all of them that we found.

More Info This icon sends you to other places in the book for more information about something we mention.

Working Together The whole *point* of Office is that its applications work together. This icon highlights examples where we've used more than one Office application to accomplish a task.

Sidebars

We use sidebars to highlight related information, give an example, or discuss an item in greater detail. For example, one sidebar tells you where to get graphics you can add to documents, spreadsheets, and presentations — cool information, but not critical. If you don't want to delve too deeply into a subject, stick to the body of the text and skip the sidebars.

When we write command names, we use a convention that shows you the menus you need to use to execute the command. So, when we want you to execute the Print command from the File menu, we've written File⇨Print. When we want you to execute the Define command from the Name submenu of the Insert menu, we've written Insert⇨Name⇨Define.

Finally, we've taken great (tedious) pains to underline every single hotkey in this book. You can use hotkeys to execute menu commands from the keyboard. For example, you can execute File⇨Print by pressing Alt+F+P: that is, press and hold the Alt key, press F, press P, and release Alt. *F* and *P* are the Print command's hotkeys, and you use the Alt key to activate them. Remembering hotkeys isn't easy because they're not always the first letter of each command. So, from here on out, it's File⇨Print, it's Edit⇨Paste Special, and it's Format⇨Sheet⇨Hide.

Where Should I Start?

If you want to learn about Word, start with Chapter 2. If you've never used a word processor before, read Appendix B first.

If you want to work with Excel, go to Chapter 15. Appendix C teaches the basics of Excel, if you've never used a spreadsheet program.

If you want to create presentations in PowerPoint, start with Chapter 27 (or Appendix D, if you don't know the first thing about presentation creation software).

If you want to create a database using Access, start with Chapter 35. Appendix E teaches the basics of Access for those who are completely new to the term *database management*.

If you want to use Outlook, go to Chapter 48.

If you're fairly familiar with Office but want to know how to make its applications work together, go to Chapters 49 and 50.

✦   ✦   ✦

Introducing Microsoft Office

◆ ◆ ◆ ◆

In This Part

◆ ◆ ◆ ◆

About Microsoft Office and the Office Shortcut Bar

This chapter introduces Microsoft Office and the Office Shortcut Bar, giving you an overview of the parts of Microsoft Office. It details how you can work with the Office Shortcut Bar, a toolbar that provides easy access to the applications in Microsoft Office and to other applications and files that you can add by customizing the toolbar.

Getting to Know Microsoft Office

Microsoft Office consists of a group of applications developed over time by Microsoft to work together, both in terms of accomplishing things in a similar way and in terms of providing easy access to data shared between the individual applications. Office is designed to make you more productive with less hassle. With Microsoft Office, you can create business documents to meet virtually any need, handle complex financial analysis, and produce professional presentations. Microsoft Office includes the following applications:

◆ **Word** — Arguably the most popular Windows word processor on the market, Microsoft Word provides all the power you need in a word processor along with a range of tools that make complex formatting tasks easier.

The Office Shortcut Bar is designed to provide you with fast access to any of the Office Manager applications. Just click on the application's button to start the program. You can also start any of the applications by choosing Programs from the Start menu, selecting Microsoft Office, and then clicking on the desired application from the pop-up menu that appears.

Hot Stuff   By default, the Office Shortcut Bar does not contain buttons for Word, Excel, PowerPoint, or Access. You can easily add buttons for these applications, though. You do this by right-clicking on any blank space in the toolbar, choosing Customize from the menu that appears, clicking on the Buttons tab in the resulting dialog box, and turning on the desired buttons. For more details on adding buttons, see "Customizing the Office Shortcut Bar" later in this chapter.

Creating and opening documents

You can use the New Office Document button to create new documents, and you can use the Open Office Document button to open existing Office documents. (By "Office" documents, we mean any documents you create using Word, Excel, PowerPoint, or Access.) This is one convenient benefit of using the Office Shortcut Bar; rather than opening an application like Word or Excel and then using the File menu commands to open or create a document, you can simply use the buttons on the Office Shortcut Bar. When you use the Office Shortcut Bar to create or open a document, the appropriate application (Word, Excel, PowerPoint, or Access) starts automatically, if it isn't already running.

To create a new document, click the New Office Document button on the Office Shortcut Bar. When you do this, the New Office Document dialog box appears, as shown in Figure 1-2.

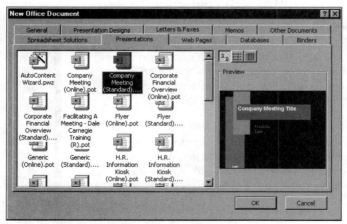

Figure 1-2: The New Office Document dialog box.

✦ **Excel** — In Microsoft Excel, you have a spreadsheet that is powerful yet simple to use. Besides offering powerful spreadsheet capabilities and the capability to work with multiple pages in the same spreadsheet file (the *workbook* concept), Excel provides powerful charting and graphing features and can readily use spreadsheets you have saved in other popular spreadsheet formats, such as Lotus 1-2-3.

✦ **PowerPoint** — PowerPoint is a presentation graphics program that can provide you with overheads for team meetings, slides for sales meetings, animated special effects for video presentations, and more. PowerPoint's tools combined with its simple approach make it easy for you to create presentations that clearly emphasize what you are trying to say.

✦ **Access** — With Microsoft Access (provided with the Professional edition of Microsoft Office), you get a database manager that provides all the power of a fully relational product with the capability to produce complex applications. At the same time, Access's design tools enable you to design databases that are easy for end-users to utilize. Access was designed from the ground up to make use of a wide variety of data from existing database sources.

✦ **Outlook** — Outlook is a desktop information management system you can use to manage your appointments, meetings, tasks, contacts, and events. You can also send and receive e-mail, manage your messages, view and open files, and share information with others. Outlook includes a message inbox and outbox, a calendar, a contact manager, a tasks list, a journal, and a notes page. Outlook replaces Schedule+, which was provided with earlier versions of Office.

Understanding the Office Shortcut Bar

When you install Microsoft Office for the first time, one of the default options causes the Office Manager to install. The Office Manager is automatically added to Windows setup routines — an option for Microsoft Office is added to the Windows Programs menu. Choose the Programs command from the Start menu at the lower-left corner of your screen and then choose the Microsoft Office Shortcut Bar option from the Microsoft Office pop-up menu. After you choose these commands, the Office Shortcut Bar appears as a toolbar at the upper-right corner of the screen. Figure 1-1 shows the Office Shortcut Bar. In the figure, the toolbar is arranged horizontally. However, you can change the location and shape of the toolbar, as detailed in "Customizing the Office Shortcut Bar" later in this chapter.

Figure 1-1: The Microsoft Office Shortcut Bar.

In this dialog box, you can click the tab for the overall type of document that you want to create, select the desired document in the list box, and click OK. For example, if you wanted to create a fax sheet, you might click the Letters and Faxes tab and then choose Contemporary Fax. Or, if you wanted to create a sales presentation using PowerPoint, you might click the Presentations tab and select one of the sales presentations in the list box. Once you make your choice, the appropriate program (Word, Excel, PowerPoint, or Access) starts, and you can proceed to create the document.

To open an existing document, click the Open Office Document button on the Office Shortcut Bar. When you do this, the Open Office Document dialog box appears, as shown in Figure 1-3.

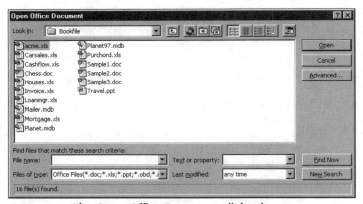

Figure 1-3: The Open Office Document dialog box.

Select the desired document in the dialog box, and click Open. The appropriate Office program will launch (if it isn't already running), and the document will appear.

You can use the remaining button on the Office Shortcut Bar to create new messages, appointments, tasks, contacts, journal entries, or notes. These are all features of Microsoft Outlook, a task management, contacts tracking, and messaging system that's provided with Office. You can find specifics on using the features of Outlook in Chapter 48.

Finally, two buttons that may be present on the Office Shortcut Bar (if you enabled these during your initial installation of Office 97) are buttons for Microsoft Book-shelf Basics and for the Getting Results with Office 97 publication. The Bookshelf Basics button provides information on the use of Microsoft Bookshelf, an optional reference product from Microsoft. (The Microsoft Bookshelf CD-ROM must be loaded into your CD-ROM drive before you can use this option.) The Getting Results button loads the Getting Results publication from the Office 97 CD-ROM: this is an on-line publication from Microsoft that provides examples on the use of Office 97.

Using the Office Shortcut Bar versus the Start menu

There can be a significant difference between launching one of the Office applications with the Office Shortcut Bar and launching that same application through the Windows 95 Start menu. The difference exists when a copy of the application is already running. When an application is running and you use the Office Shortcut Bar to start one of the Office applications, Windows switches to the application that is already running. When an application is running and you use the Start menu to start that same application again, you launch a second instance of the same Office application, one that now runs in Windows memory.

Danger Zone Running two instances of the same application uses Windows resources and slows overall system response time. If all you want to do is switch from one Microsoft Office application to another, click on the desired application on the Taskbar button at the bottom of the screen or use the Office Shortcut Bar (or the Alt+Tab key combination) instead of the Programs command on the Start menu.

Sizing and docking the Office Shortcut Bar

You can click on and drag any side of the Office Shortcut Bar to change its size and shape, and you can click on and drag the toolbar to a different location on-screen. When you drag the toolbar against any of the edges (the top, bottom, left, or right sides of the window), the bar takes on a narrow, rectangular shape and appears docked against the chosen edge. When the toolbar is not dragged against an edge, you can change the size of the rectangle that contains the toolbar by clicking on and dragging any corner of the toolbar. Figure 1-4 shows one possible shape for the Office Shortcut Bar when it is not docked against one side of the screen.

Figure 1-4: The Office Shortcut Bar shown as a floating bar.

Customizing the Office Shortcut Bar

You can customize the Office Shortcut Bar — or any toolbar, for that matter — by adding and deleting buttons, changing the size of the buttons, changing the toolbar's position on-screen, and making all sorts of adjustments. To customize the Office Shortcut Bar, right-click in any blank spot on the Office Shortcut Bar. From the menu that opens, choose Customize. The Customize dialog box appears. Notice its four tabs. You can make all sorts of changes to the toolbars by using these tabs.

The Buttons tab

If you regularly use other applications (such as Microsoft FoxPro) or other common Windows tools (such as Windows Paint), you can add buttons for these applications to the toolbar. You aren't limited to applications produced by Microsoft, either: you can add any Windows application to the Office Shortcut Bar. You may want to consider adding buttons for Explorer, My Computer, or for the MS-DOS prompt, if you regularly use any of these aspects of Windows. If the Buttons tab isn't already selected in your Customize dialog box, click on its tab to bring it to the front, as shown in Figure 1-5.

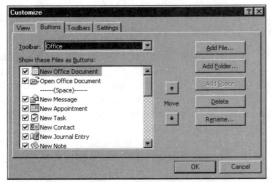

Figure 1-5: The Buttons tab in the Customize dialog box.

Moving buttons

To move the location of a button within the toolbar, first choose the toolbar that you want to change in the Toolbar list box, and then select the application that you want to move in the Show these Files as Buttons list box. Click on the up or down Move arrows to move the order of the selected application. (Moving it up places it closer to the left side or top of the toolbar; moving it down places it closer to the right side or bottom of the toolbar.)

Adding new buttons

To add a button to the toolbar for an existing item in the Toolbar list, select the item in the list and click on its check box. When you click on the check box, the item is added to the toolbar.

To add Windows software that isn't already in the Show these Files as Buttons list, click on the Add File button. The Add File dialog box appears, as shown in Figure 1-6.

In the Look in list box, you can select the drive or folder that contains the desired program. When you locate the desired program, click on it to select it and then click on the Add button in the dialog box. If you know the program's exact name and path, you can type it in the File name text box and then click on the Add button. After you click on Add, the icon for the new program is added to the Office Shortcut Bar.

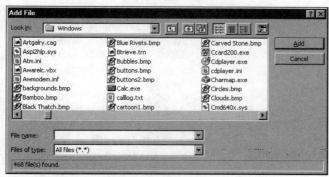

Figure 1-6: The Add File dialog box.

Removing buttons

To remove a button from the toolbar, first select the unwanted application in the applications list in the Buttons tab of the Customize dialog box, and then uncheck the option to remove it from the toolbar and from the applications list.

The View tab

To see the View tab, click on its tab to bring it to the front of the Customize dialog box, as shown in Figure 1-7. In this tab, you can do many things to make the toolbar stand out.

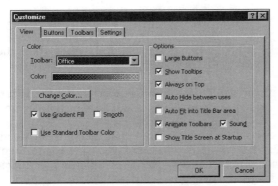

Figure 1-7: The View tab in the Customize dialog box.

In the Color section of the dialog box, you can change the color for the Office Shortcut Bar. Click on the Change Color button to display a Color dialog box, where you can select a desired color and click on OK. Checking the Use Gradient Fill option causes the chosen color to use a gradient fill pattern, and checking the Use Standard Toolbar Color option causes the Office Shortcut Bar to take on the default Windows color.

In the Options area of the View tab, you can turn on or off any of the options shown. Large Buttons switches between small and large toolbar buttons, Show Tooltips turns on the Tooltips feature, and Always on Top specifies that the toolbar should remain above other applications. When turned on, Auto Hide between uses hides the toolbar when it isn't in use (you can redisplay it by holding the mouse pointer over the side of the screen where the toolbar is docked). The Auto Fit into Title Bar area causes the toolbar automatically to fit into an area the width of the title bar when you drag the toolbar to resize it. Turn on Animate Toolbars if you want the toolbars to appear to grow and shrink as you open and close them, or turn on Sound to hear a noise when Office applications are launched. The Show Title Screen at Startup option, when turned on, causes the Microsoft Office Title screen to appear when the Office Shortcut Bar is started.

The Toolbars tab

Click the Toolbars tab to bring it to the front of the Customize dialog box (see Figure 1-8). You can use the Toolbars tab to add other folders or programs to the screen as separate toolbars. In the Show these Folders as Toolbars list box, you can check the folders that you want to appear as toolbars. You can move the folders in the list so that the toolbars produced by the folders that you add appear in a certain order on screen. To do this, click on a desired folder and use the up or down Move arrows to move the folder to the desired location in the list of checked folders. You can use the Rename button in the dialog box to rename any toolbar to a name of your choosing.

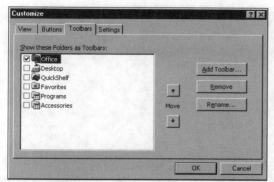

Figure 1-8: The Toolbars tab in the Customize dialog box.

For example, Figure 1-9 shows three toolbars that have been enabled in the Toolbars tab of the Customize dialog box. In addition to the Office Shortcut Bar, toolbars for the Favorites folder and for all programs have been enabled. If you look at the top of the resulting toolbar arrangement (at the right edge of the screen), you see three toolbar icons at the top. The first icon displays the Office Shortcut Bar, the second displays the Favorites folder toolbar, and the third displays the Programs toolbar. The three toolbars appear layered in this order because they were placed in the Customize dialog box in that order. If you choose one toolbar that hides the others, you always see icons for the hidden toolbars at the bottom or right edge of the visible toolbar. You can click on any of those icons to display the other toolbars.

You can create a new toolbar based on an existing folder. Click on the Add Toolbar button. An Add Toolbar dialog box appears. Use it to make a toolbar for a folder that you choose or to create a new, blank toolbar. (If you create a blank toolbar, you can then add buttons to that toolbar by using the steps shown under "Adding new buttons" earlier in the chapter.)

The Settings tab

Click on the Settings tab to bring it to the front of the Customize dialog box (see Figure 1-10). In this tab, you can change the default folder that stores the templates used by Microsoft Office or the default folder that stores the templates used by workgroups (on a local-area network). To change any of the settings, click on the desired setting in the dialog box and then click on the Modify button. If you are changing one of the file folder options, clicking on <u>M</u>odify displays a User Templates Location dialog box, in which you can choose the desired folder that is to contain the templates.

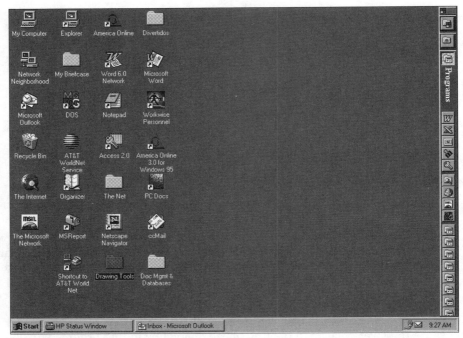

Figure 1-9: The Customize dialog box toolbar settings and three resulting toolbars.

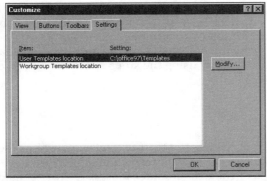

Figure 1-10: The Settings tab in the Customize dialog box.

Closing the Office Shortcut Bar

If you don't want the Office Shortcut Bar on-screen all the time and you seldom switch between applications, go ahead and close the Office Shortcut Bar. You can still use the Microsoft Office applications, but you have to launch them from the Windows Start menu or by using shortcuts that you've added to your Windows environment. You can close the Office Shortcut Bar by performing these steps:

1. Right-click on the title bar of the Office Shortcut Bar.

2. From the menu that appears, choose Exit.

You can redisplay the Office Shortcut Bar at any time by choosing the Programs command from the Start menu. Then choose the Microsoft Office Shortcut Bar option from the menu of available programs. (If this option doesn't appear on your Programs menu, you will need to enable it. Open the Windows 95 Start menu, choose Settings, and Taskbar. In the Taskbar Properties dialog box that appears, click Add. In the Create Shortcut dialog box that appears, click Browse. Go to the folder containing your Office 97 files, choose Microsoft Office Shortcut Bar, and click Open. When the Create Shortcut dialog box again appears, click Next twice, and click Finish.)

Adding and Removing Office Programs

After you've installed Microsoft Office, you can add or remove one of the applications or a part of an application. You can also remove any previously installed Office applications and their components. For example, you may want to add text converters for Word if you didn't originally install them with Word, or you may want to remove clip art if you're running short on hard disk space. You can add and remove Office programs by performing the following steps:

1. On the Office Shortcut Bar, right-click on the title bar to open the Office menu.

2. From the menu, choose Add/Remove Office Programs. You will see the Office Setup and Uninstall dialog box. Select the application that you want to modify, reinstall, or remove and then click on OK.

3. You will be prompted to insert your CD-ROM or the first system diskette. When you do this and click OK, the Welcome screen for the Setup program appears. The screen contains choices that enable you to add or remove parts of the application, repeat the previous installation, or remove all installed applications and their parts. Follow the instructions that appear on-screen to add or remove the desired parts of Microsoft Office.

Summary

This chapter showed how you can work with the Office Shortcut Bar to provide fast access to the Microsoft Office applications. The Office Shortcut Bar is easily customizable — you can add your favorite programs and files to this toolbar to make performing your tasks much easier. This chapter covered these points:

✦ Microsoft Office includes Word (for word processing), Excel (for spreadsheets), PowerPoint (for presentations), and Outlook (for managing messages and tracking time-related tasks). The Professional version of Office includes all these applications and Access (for database management).

✦ You can use the Office Shortcut Bar to launch different Microsoft Office applications quickly.

✦ You can customize the Office Shortcut Bar by adding applications and files to the toolbar, changing the position of the toolbar, enlarging its buttons, and doing other things to the toolbar to make it stand out.

The remainder of this book will detail how you can get the most out of the different applications of Microsoft Office.

Where to go next...

✦ If you want to work in Word, go to Chapter 2. If you're a Word neophyte, Appendix B gets you started.

✦ If you want to use Excel, go to Chapter 15. Appendix C gives you Excel basics, if you've never used a spreadsheet before.

✦ If you want to create presentations in PowerPoint, see Chapter 27. Rank beginners, see Appendix D.

✦ If you want to use Access to manage your data, see Chapter 35. If the mere mention of the word *database* makes you break out in a cold sweat, you'll find Appendix E comforting.

✦ If you've yet to install Office, hie thee directly to Appendix A.

✦　　✦　　✦

Word

◆   ◆   ◆   ◆

In This Part

◆   ◆   ◆   ◆

Creating and Working with Documents

Because the first thing you will do in Word is create documents, it makes sense to cover creating documents in the first Word chapter. You also need to know about the many techniques that you can use to edit the documents that you create. These techniques will help you find mistakes in your documents so that you can create the best documents possible.

Creating New Documents

You can start Word by opening the Windows 95 Start menu, choosing Programs, and then Microsoft Word from the submenu that pops up. A blank document screen appears in which you can begin typing your new document.

Hot Stuff If you already have some documents created and saved, you can launch Word and open a document simultaneously by finding the document in My Computer or in the Windows Explorer and double-clicking on the document.

Understanding Templates

Word gives you two ways to create your documents: you can use the Normal.dot template or a template of your choosing. You will probably use both methods in your work. *Templates*, or document models, help you streamline the creation of documents that you produce on a regular basis.

Making Word easier to start

If you regularly start Word by choosing Word from the Windows 95 menus, you can save yourself considerable time by adding an icon to your Windows desktop. This icon represents a shortcut to the program. To add the icon to the desktop, open Explorer, click on the drive in which you have installed Office and choose the folder in which it is installed. Next choose Program files and the Office folder. (If you accepted the default settings, it will be installed within the MSOffice Folder.) After opening the MSOffice folder, you will see the Word program file. Choose the Word Shortcut and drag it onto your desktop. You can now start Word from your desktop.

From now on, you can start Word by double-clicking on the Shortcut to Winword icon on your desktop. If you don't like the icon's default name, you can change it by right-clicking on the icon, choosing Rename from the menu that appears, and entering a new name. Alternately, you can click on the icon, click on the name portion of the icon to select it, and type a new name.

Do *not* be tempted to skip the creation of a shortcut by simply dragging the Winword icon from the Winword folder onto the desktop. If you do this, you are literally moving the program file from the Winword folder (where it is designed to work well) into a folder called Desktop, which Windows 95 uses to manage the desktop. The result is that Word suddenly has a hard time finding its files.

When Word is first opened, it contains a document with default settings ready for you to use. This is the Normal.dot template (stored as Normal.dot in the Templates folder), which contains a set of standard margins and no formatting. Keep in mind that clicking on the New button in the Standard toolbar always creates a new document based on the Normal template. After you begin to enter text, you can change all these settings to anything you want.

If you do not want to use the default Normal.dot template, you can use one of the other templates in Word that may be better suited to your needs. To open one of these templates, choose New from the File menu. The New dialog box appears, in which you can make the selection that is best for your needs (see Figure 2-1). The dialog box is divided by a series of tabs, and each tab contains one or more templates appropriate to a specific task. For example, if most of the documents that you create are memos, you can click on the Memos tab to display a group of templates appropriate for creating memos. (The tab also lists one wizard; see the heading "Looking at template wizards" a little later in this chapter for information about using wizards.) After you create a document based on a template, the template controls the appearance of the document.

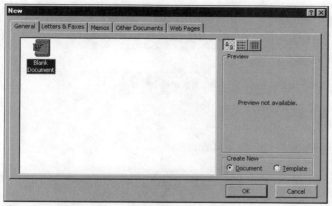

Figure 2-1: The New dialog box.

Many documents are made up of standard parts. For example, an interoffice memo often contains a company name and address heading; To, From, Date, and Subject headings; and closing information, such as a routing list of persons receiving the memo. Assuming that a template is designed for your interoffice memos, you can let the template fill in the *boilerplate,* or standard text, for you. Templates can also be designed to prompt you for the specific information (such as the recipient's name) needed each time the template is used. The information you enter is automatically inserted into the proper place in the document, based on the template.

Exploring template categories

Table 2-1 lists the template categories that the New dialog box contains, and the templates in each category. The names of the templates explain their functions.

Table 2-1 Templates available in Microsoft Word	
Template Category	**Name of Template**
General	Blank Document (uses Normal template)
Other Documents	Contemporary Resume
	Elegant Resume
	More Templates and Wizards
	Professional Resume
Letters & Faxes	Contemporary Fax
	Contemporary Letter
	Elegant Fax
	Elegant Letter
	Professional Fax
	Professional Letter
Memos	Contemporary Memo
	Elegant Memo
	Professional Memo
Web Pages	Blank Web Page
	Web Page Wizard
Office 95 Templates (These are available only if you installed Office 97 over the previous version.)	Brochure
	Contemporary Letter
	Contemporary Memo
	Contemporary Press Release
	Contemporary Report
	Contemporary Resume
	Directory
	Elegant Fax
	Elegant Memo

Template Category	Name of Template
Office 95 Templates	Elegant Press Release
	Elegant Report
	Elegant Resume
	Invoice
	Manual
	Newsletter
	Blank Document
	Professional Fax
	Professional Letter
	Professional Memo
	Professional Press Release
	Professional Report
	Professional Resume
	Purchase Order
	Thesis
	Weekly Time Sheet

Looking at template wizards

Word 97 also includes template wizards, which help you create a document when you may not be sure of its layout or even its content. To activate any one of these wizards, choose New from the File menu. Scroll through the Template list and click on the wizard that best fits the document that you want to create. Then click on OK.

Use the Resume Wizard, also found under the Other Documents tab, to create résumés in record time tailored to your experience (see Figure 2-2). The Resume Wizard can create a résumé in various forms. You may need a contemporary, classic, or professional résumé. The Resume Wizard also provides some tips on the best way to lay out a résumé. You can choose to create a professional, chronological, entry-level, or functional résumé. Finally, you can omit any elements you don't want to include.

Figure 2-2: A résumé created with the Resume Wizard.

For example, the Resume Wizard found in the Other Documents tab can create a résumé in various forms. It may be an entry-level, chronological, functional, or professional résumé in a contemporary, professional, or elegant style. As you step through the dialog boxes in the Resume Wizard, you are prompted to add elements to the résumé that may be included in a résumé for the type that you have chosen. For example, you are prompted to add your phone number, e-mail address, fax number, and physical address. Next, you are prompted for the categories that you wish to include in your résumé, such as your work experience, volunteer history, and educational background. The wizard next gives you the chance to add any additional heading you would want in the résumé and change the order in which they appear. Finally, you can choose a style for your résumé, such as professional or contemporary. Figure 2-2 shows a résumé created by the Resume Wizard; one that you create may differ based on the choices you make in the wizard.

More Info You'll find the Envelope Wizard on the Letters and Faxes tab. When you choose this wizard, the animated help is activated and you are asked to choose between creating a single envelope or using the Mail Merge feature of Office (Chapter 6 will cover that in detail). If you choose to make a single envelope, the Envelopes and labels box is opened with the Envelope tab selected, and you can enter To and Return addresses for the envelope. If you choose the Mailing list option from the animated help, you will see the Mail Merge helper appear, which will aid you in creating envelopes from a mailing list. This is covered in detail in Chapter 6.

The Fax Wizard, found under the Letters & Faxes tab, creates a fax sheet that you can customize. The fax sheet can be a contemporary, modern, or jazzy fax sheet. In the Fax Wizard, you also have the luxury of not having to look for your names and addresses. If they are stored in Microsoft Exchange (a feature of Windows 95, see Alan Simpson's *Windows 95 Uncut*, IDG Books Worldwide [1995], for details), you can click on Address book and pull the name of the person to which you want to send the fax into the address and phone number boxes. Figure 2-3 shows a fax sheet created by the Fax Wizard. (See Chapter 48 for more information on Microsoft Outlook.)

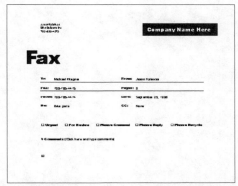

Figure 2-3: A fax sheet created with the Fax Wizard.

The Award Wizard, also found under the Other Documents tab, creates a customized award for any occasion by providing the art for the award certificate (which avoids the annoyance of finding clip art and then appropriately inserting it). The wizard lets you choose award certificates of a more modern, formal, or decorative manner. Each one of the styles has corresponding art for the certificate. Figure 2-4 shows a document created with the Award Wizard.

Figure 2-4: A document created with the Award Wizard.

The Calendar Wizard, found under the Other Documents tab, creates a monthly calendar in various styles, such as the one shown in Figure 2-5. You can design the calendar in either a portrait or a landscape orientation. You can show the month name in different formats, such as a banner or box-and-border. You can add pictures to the calendar if you want. Finally, one of the Calendar Wizard's most impressive features is that it can create a calendar that starts and ends with the months that you specify.

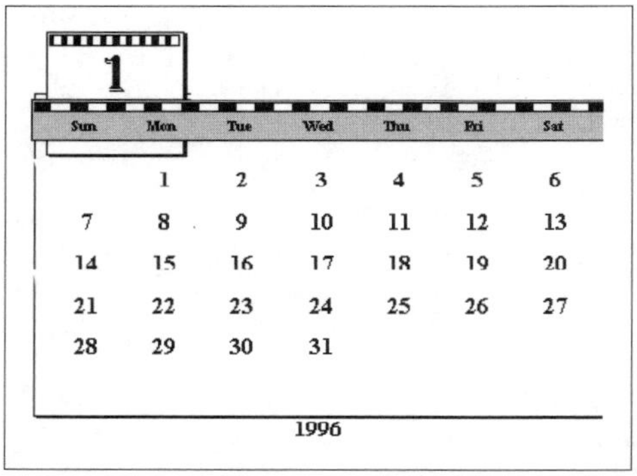

Figure 2-5: A calendar created with the Calendar Wizard.

The Letter Wizard, located under the Letters & Faxes tab, can create prewritten letters or help in the design of your own letters. Again you have the choice of creating a letter via a mailing list or just one letter. You also have the option of choosing a page design for your letter, be it professional, newsletter, or elegant. You can also choose different styles for your letters, block or semi-block. The letter wizard ends with a choice to enter sender information. Yes, that would be you. Figure 2-6 shows a letter created using the letter wizard.

Figure 2-6: A letter created with the Letter Wizard.

The Memo Wizard, found under the Memos tab, helps you create customized memos (see Figure 2-7). You can create office memos (the default setting) or any other kind of memo. Addresses here can also be drawn from the Address book in Microsoft Exchange.

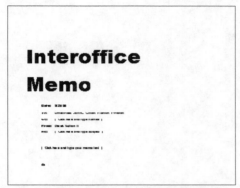

Figure 2-7: An office memo created with the Memo Wizard.

The Newsletter Wizard, found under the Publications tab, helps you create an attractive newsletter. You can create the newsletter in a classic or modern style with the number of columns and pages that you specify. You can also include the date, table of contents, and volume number. Figure 2-8 shows a newsletter created with the Newsletter Wizard. As you can see, the wizard handles what would manually be a challenging task by creating a professional-looking newsletter in a short amount of time.

Figure 2-8: A newsletter created with the Newsletter Wizard.

The Pleading Wizard, found under the Other Documents tab, provides a quick and easy way to create a legal pleading (see Figure 2-9). The legal pleading that results includes the name of the court, inserted in the correct location in the document for the style you choose. The alignment and style can all be modified by using the various options presented as you move through the Pleading Wizard. Footnotes can also be added to the pleading.

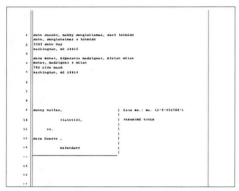

Figure 2-9: A legal pleading created with the Pleading Wizard.

More Info   Use the Mailing Label Wizard, located on the Letters & Faxes tab, to create mailing labels for letters that you have created. After you activate this wizard, you have the option of creating a sheet of mailing labels or doing so via the Mail Merge helper. For additional details on the topic of mail merges, see Chapter 6.

More Info   The Table Wizard is a quick and easy way to create new tables in Office 97. This wizard is located under the Other Documents tab and steps you through the process of creating a tab. Along the way, it asks you for the number of columns you want, headings (if any), layout, and the style of table you want to create. For more specifics on creating tables, see Chapter 5.

The Web Page Wizard, located on the Web Pages tab, lets you painlessly create a web page. You can create various types of web pages. Among them are simple layout pages, centered (which causes the text of the page to appear centered on the web page), and survey pages to name a few. Chapter 11 discusses the use of the Web Page Wizard in detail.

Editing templates

You can change the different templates so that they can better fit your needs. To change the templates, choose the File⇨Open menu to get to the Open dialog box. Move to the Templates directory and in the Files of type drop-down menu, select Document Templates. Select the folder that continues the template. Then type or select the name of the template that you want to modify and click on OK. Edit the template as though it were a document. When you have finished the modifications, choose Save from the File menu to save the template and give it the name of your choice.

More Info You'll find additional information on working with templates in Chapter 8.

Working with Text

To create text, type on the keyboard. The text is then entered at the insertion point. You shouldn't press Enter at the end of each line — Word automatically moves from line to line as you type. This feature is called *word wrap*. Press the Enter key only when you want to create a new paragraph. After you press Enter, previously entered text is moved up to keep the insertion point visible.

Deleting text

You can delete text in several ways. One method is by using the Backspace key. When you use the Backspace key, the text to the left of the insertion point is removed. Another method is using the Delete key. Use the Delete key to delete text that appears to the right of the insertion point.

You can also delete blocks of text in Word. First you should highlight the block of text that you want to delete. (You can click on and drag across a desired selection with the mouse, or you can hold the Shift key down and use the arrow keys to highlight a section of text.) After selecting the text, press the Delete key to remove the text from the document.

Inserting text from the Clipboard

You can paste text or graphics from the Clipboard into a document. The Clipboard, a standard Windows 95 feature, is an area of memory that stores temporary information (see your Windows 95 documentation for additional information about the Clipboard). Edit⇨Paste, or Ctrl+V, pastes whatever is in the Clipboard into the current document at the insertion point. (Of course, the Clipboard must contain something before you can paste it into your document.)

To insert text into the Clipboard, select the desired text and choose the Edit⇨Copy command (Ctrl+C), or click on the Copy button on the Standard toolbar. Then move the insertion point to the desired position for the text and choose Edit⇨Paste (Ctrl+V), or click on the Paste button on the Standard toolbar. The text stored in the Clipboard appears at the insertion point.

You can also use the Clipboard to move text from one place in a document to another. To move text, use Edit⇨Cut (Ctrl+X). First, highlight the text that you want to move. Next, click on the Cut button on the Standard toolbar or press Ctrl+X. This action places the selected text on the Clipboard. Move the insertion point to the desired location and click on the Paste button on the Standard toolbar or press Ctrl+V. The text is then inserted at the insertion point location.

Inserting graphics

If you want to paste graphics, first get into the drawing or graphics program (such as Paint) that contains the image you want to use in your Word document. Use the selection tool within the drawing or graphics program to select the desired image; then choose Edit⇨Copy (or press Ctrl+C) to copy the selection into the Clipboard. Exit from the drawing or graphics program and get into your document. With the insertion point at the desired location, choose Edit⇨Paste (or press Ctrl+V). The graphic appears at the insertion point.

Hot Stuff If you are running Word and your graphics program simultaneously, you can easily switch from the graphics program to Word by pressing Alt+Tab, or by clicking on the desired program's name in the Windows 95 Taskbar.

Avoiding bad typing habits

If you are upgrading to the world of Word from a very old environment (such as a typewriter or a very early generation word processor), you may have accumulated some habits that won't do you any good in Word. First, and probably the most obvious, is that you don't have to press Enter at the end of every line because of Word's automatic word wrap feature. Second, don't use spaces (inserted with the Spacebar) to center or indent text. To center text, use the Center button on the Formatting toolbar (discussed in Chapter 3). To indent, use tabs or indented paragraphs (also discussed in Chapter 3). If you need to create columns, don't use spaces or tabs — use Word's *columns* feature (see Chapter 3), or use tables (see Chapter 5).

You can also add graphics to your documents by means of clip art. Word for Windows 95 includes a great deal of clip art that can be added to documents. Simply choose Picture from the Insert menu to open the Insert Picture dialog box, as shown in Figure 2-10. After you select one of the clip art files, you can see it in the Preview box. To insert the selected clip art into your document, position the insertion point where you want the clip art to go and click on OK. The clip art appears at the insertion point in your document.

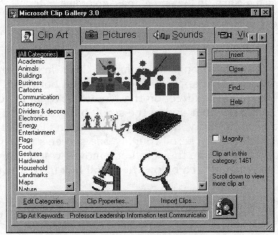

Figure 2-10: Preview the clip art file before you insert it into your document.

Navigating within a document

For basic navigation within a Word document, you can use the arrow keys and the navigation keys on the keyboard. Table 2-2 lists the keyboard combinations that help you move around in your document.

Table 2-2 Navigation shortcuts	
Keyboard Combination	**What it Does**
Ctrl+Up Arrow key	Moves the cursor up one paragraph
Ctrl+Down Arrow key	Moves the cursor down one paragraph
Alt+Left Arrow key	Moves the cursor one word to the left
Alt+Right Arrow key	Moves the cursor one word to the right
Page Up key	Moves the cursor up one screen page
Page Down key	Moves the cursor down one screen page
Home key	Moves the cursor to the beginning of the current line of text
Ctrl+Home key	Moves the cursor to the beginning of the document
End key	Moves the cursor to the end of the current line of text
Ctrl+End key	Moves the cursor to the end of the document

You can also use the scroll bars to move through a document. Click on the scroll box (scroll boxes are the square boxes that appear inside the scroll bars) and drag it up or down or left or right to move in the direction that you want to go in your document. Or click the arrow blocks at either end of the scroll bars to move a preset amount of space in the direction that you want to go. You can also click within the shaded areas of the scroll bars to scroll roughly one screen's worth of document. Clicking on the shaded area above the scroll box moves you upward in the document, and clicking on the shaded area below the scroll box moves you downward in the document.

Hot Stuff If you click on the scroll box, drag it, and hold the mouse button down for roughly a half-second or more, a small window will appear showing the page number of the document represented by that position of the scroll box. In a large document, this can provide an easy way to quickly reach a desired page.

Hot Stuff If you want to jump to a specific page number in a document, press F5 and enter a page number in the dialog box that appears.

Document Map

The Document Map view provides another useful way of navigating in a document. This view is especially useful when you are working with long documents. You activate this method of navigation by choosing Document Map from the View Menu. Document Map will analyze a document, find the patterns for the headings you have included, and place them in a window to the left of the original. This will give you a quick view of your entire document without the use of the scroll bar. As you look at the headings, you can click on them and move to that heading in your document.

More Info Right-clicking the heading on the right acts as a way for you to show the different types of headings in that particular section. This feature is much like the Outline View, which is discussed in detail in Chapter 5.

Selecting text

After you've typed large amounts of text, you need ways to select it so that you can work with it. For most users, clicking and dragging with the mouse is the most common way to select text. If you're not proficient with a mouse, spend time practicing. In the long run, the time that you spend practicing with the mouse will regularly save you hours of time at the keyboard. The following list contains practical techniques for selecting text:

✦ To select entire words, double-click anywhere in the word. You can then select adjacent words by holding down the mouse key after the second click and dragging through the additional words.

✦ To select entire lines, move the mouse pointer to the left of the line (where it changes into the shape of an arrow) and click on it once.

✦ To select entire sentences, hold down the Control key while you click anywhere in the sentence.

✦ To select entire paragraphs, triple-click anywhere within the paragraph.

✦ To select the entire document, press Ctrl+A.

✦ To select a large portion of a document, click on the start of the portion that you want to select. Then move to the end of the desired portion, hold down the Shift key, and click again.

Saving

Saving is a fundamental part of working with documents. (Your documents won't be very permanent if you can't save them for later use.) Choosing File➪Save lets you save an existing document under the same name or under any name you choose if you've never saved the document before. You can choose File➪Save As to save an existing document under a new name or to save a document under a file format different than Word's native file format. In addition to the normal Save and Save as commands which allow you to save a document or change the name and file extension, Word 97 offers additional options for saving documents.

You can choose File➪Save as HTML to save a Word document as an HTML file. (*HTML*, or *HyperText Markup Language*, is the language used to store information on the World Wide Web.) The HTML files that you create using Word can be uploaded to a Web server for availability on the Web or to a corporate intranet. When you save a word document as an HTML file, the document is closed by Word and then reopened in HTML format with Word acting as a Web browser. Note that formatting not supported by HTML is simply removed from the document. Here are examples of formatting that would be dropped from a document when you save it as HTML:

✦ Comments

✦ Paragraph Formatting

✦ Tabs

✦ Fields

✦ Tables of Contents and Authorities

✦ Indexes

✦ Drawing Objects

✦ OLE Objects

✦ User-Defined Styles

More Info   For more specifics on working with Word and the Web, see Chapter 11.

You can also save multiple versions of the same document to a single file. By choosing File⇨Versions, you can display a dialog box that lets you save a new version of the same document. When you use this version control feature of Word, each additional version that you create is saved to the same file. The versions are identified within the dialog box by the date of creation and the author of the version.

When you choose File⇨Versions, you see a listing of the existing versions of the document, the date they were last saved, and the modifier of that version. After clicking on the Save now button in the dialog box, you can add comments about the particular version of the document that can further aid as an identifier of the document.

Looking at Word's Views

Word lets you view a document as you edit it in one of four possible views: Normal, Outline, Page Layout, and Master Document. You can access these views by clicking on the appropriate command on the View menu. These commands work like toggle switches, so you can turn the view on and off by clicking on the command. A bullet appears beside the command in the View menu if it is turned on. If you don't see a bullet by Outline, Page Layout, or Master Document in the View menu, you are in Normal view (the default view). You can also switch among all views except Outline Document by clicking on the View buttons at the bottom left of the screen. (At the bottom left corner, the leftmost button is Normal View, the next button is Online Layout View, the center button is Page Layout View, and the rightmost button is Outline View.) Master Document view must be activated by the View menu.

Use Normal view for basic typing and editing. Normal view shows a simple version of the document and is the best all-purpose view for typing in Word. Normal view is the default setting for Word for Windows 95. After you change views, you can return to Normal view any time by clicking on the Normal View button in the lower-left corner of the screen.

More Info   If line numbering is on, you must be in Page Layout view to see the line numbers. See Chapter 3.

More Info   Use Outline View for outlining and organizing a document. Outline View lets you see only the main headings of a document or the entire document. In this view, you can easily move text over long distances or change the order of your topics, as detailed in Chapter 5. To change to Outline View, choose View⇨Outline.

More Info You control how much you see of the document in Outline View by clicking on the plus signs located next to the headings for each section. When you double-click on the plus sign, the text under the heading is hidden to show only the heading. Chapter 5 discusses outlines in detail.

Use Page Layout View to "see the printed page," while still allowing for editing. This view lets you see how the different elements of the document will appear when they are printed. This view is very useful in checking the final appearance of your document. (This differs from Print Preview in that you can't edit a document in Print Preview.) To switch to Page Layout View, click on the Page Layout View button on the lower-left corner of the screen, or choose Page Layout from the View menu.

Use Master Document View to work with long documents. This view helps you divide long documents into several shorter documents to make them easier to work with, because you can see all the components of a document when you are in Master Document View. To switch to Master Document View, click the Master Document View button at the lower left corner of the screen.

Word 97 also lets you change options in each of the views. To change the default settings, choose Options from the Tools menu. An Options dialog box appears, from which you can change options for the current view. The Options dialog box contains 10 tabs, each with its own set of options, as shown in Figure 2-11. Click on a tab to bring it to the front of the dialog box so that you can view and make changes to its options. Make whatever changes that you want in the tabs. The new settings take effect in all the tabs that you have changed after you click on the OK button.

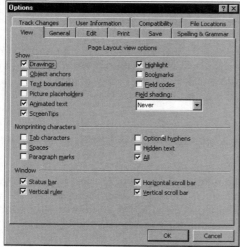

Figure 2-11: The Options dialog box.

Examining the Vital Three: Margins, Tabs, and Line Spacing

The three most elementary aspects of formatting — margins, tabs, and line spacing — can be found even on the most basic typewriters. These elements are very important to setting up your pages appropriately in Word for Windows. This section shows you how to apply these formatting elements to all or part of a document. To control page margins, you use the Page Setup command from the File menu; to set default tab stops, you use the Tabs command from the Format menu; and to change line spacing, you use the Paragraph command from the Format menu. Keep in mind, however, that these commands are not the only ways to change parameters that affect margins, tabs, and line spacing in Word, as you'll discover shortly.

Changing margins

When you start a new document in Word for Windows 95, default margins are already set at 1 inch for the top and bottom margins and 1.25 inches for the left and right margins. If you want to change the default settings, choose File⇨Page Setup. The Page Setup dialog box appears, with its four tabs. The Margins tab lets you set the top, bottom, right, and left margins to your desired measurements. You also can click on the Mirror Margins check box to force the left-facing and right-facing pages to have the same margins between the edge of the text and the center of the binding.

Applying tabs

Using tabs is a common method for aligning text in columns; therefore, Word has tab stops set to every 0.5 inch by default. You can identify these tab stops by looking for the gray tick marks that appear at the bottom of the ruler. To turn on the ruler, click on the Ruler command on the View menu so that it has a check mark beside it. Use the Tabs command from the Format menu to change the default tab stops. In the Tabs dialog box, change the measurement in the Default Tab Stops box to any desired value in inches or centimeters.

In addition to the default tab stops, Word lets you set custom tab stops for each paragraph. Custom tab stops take precedence over the default tab stops; therefore, whenever you set a custom tab stop, Word clears all default tab stops that occur to the left of the custom tab stop. When you set one or more custom tab stops, these remain in effect until you change the tab setting. Each paragraph in Word can have its own tab settings, so remember to use the newline command (Shift+Enter) between lines of text if you want the same set of tabs to apply to all the lines.

Types of tabs

In Word, you can use any of five types of tabs; left, center, right, decimal, and bar. The type of tab that you choose indicates precisely where the text aligns with the tab. When you use a left tab, the left edge of the text aligns with the tab stop. With right tabs, the right edge of the text aligns with the tab stop. When you use centered tabs, the text centers at the tab stop. Decimal tabs are used when the decimal point in numbers must align with the tab stop. Finally, bar tabs are thin vertical bars that can be used to separate columns created by tabs within a document.

Setting custom tabs

You can set custom tabs with the mouse and the Tab button on the ruler (the easier method) or with the Tabs command on the Format menu. To set tabs with the mouse, first click on the Tab button on the ruler (the button to the far left of the ruler) until you get the tab alignment that you want and then click just under the ruler at the desired location. For example, to set a center tab at the 2-inch location on the ruler, you would first click on the Tab button until the one for the center tab appears and then click just under or on the 2-inch marker on the ruler. To verify the position of the tab stop, choose Format⇨Tabs to open the Tabs dialog box (see Figure 2-12).

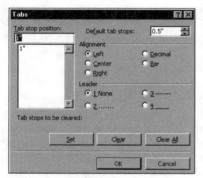

Figure 2-12: The Tabs dialog box.

If the 2-inch tab stop isn't in the exact position that you want, you can click on it and drag it to whatever position you want on the ruler. After you drag it to its new location, verify the new position of the tab stop by opening the Tabs dialog box again. If you are still not satisfied with the position of the tab stop, you can manually enter a measurement in the Tab Stop Position text box. The Tabs dialog box gives you unlimited control of how you want to position the tabs in your documents.

Figure 2-13 shows some of the different tab alignments in Word. In the figure, a left tab stop has been set at the 1.0 inch position, a center tab at the 2.0 inch position, a right tab at the 4.0 inch position, and a decimal tab stop at the 5.0 inch position.

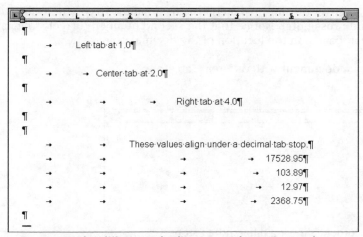

Figure 2-13: The different Tab alignments shown in Word.

To set tabs with the Tabs command, choose Format⇨Tabs. The Tabs dialog box (Figure 2-12) appears. In this dialog box, you can enter or clear tab stops. Enter the desired location for the tab stop in the Tab Stop Position text box and then choose the type of tab that you want (Left, Center, Right, Decimal, or Bar) from the Alignment options. If you have additional tabs to set, click on the Set button to set the tab and then go back to the Tab Stop Position box to enter the location for the next tab and to choose its alignment. After you finish setting the tabs, click on the OK button.

Try experimenting with the tab stop techniques to find the one that suits you best. You can use the following steps to see the effects of the different tab stops that you can set in Word:

1. Create a new document with a left tab at 1.0 inch, a center tab at 2.5 inches, a right tab at 3.5 inches, and a decimal tab at 5.0 inches.

2. Press the tab key once (to reach the left-aligned tab at the 1-inch mark), and type the words **left-aligned**. Then, press Enter.

3. Press the tab key twice (to reach the center tab at the 2.5-inch mark), and type the word **centered**. Notice that as you type, the word remains centered at the tab stop. When done, press Enter.

4. Press the tab key three times (to reach the right-aligned tab at the 3.5-inch mark), and type the words **right-aligned**. Notice that as you type, the words remain right aligned with the tab stop. When done, press Enter.

5. Press the tab key four times (to reach the decimal tab), type the value **103.99**, and press Enter.

6. Press the tab key four times (to reach the decimal tab), type the value **1342.23**, and press Enter. Notice that the second number correctly aligns with the first, based on the location of the decimal point.

Figure 2-14 shows a document with different tab stops.

Figure 2-14: A document showing different tab stops

Moving and clearing tabs

As with setting tabs, you can move tabs and clear tabs with the ruler and the mouse or with the Tabs command on the Format menu. Again, the mouse excels in ease of use. To move a tab, simply click on the tab and drag it to the desired location. To clear a tab, simply drag the tab up or down off the ruler.

You can also use the Tabs command from the Format menu to move or clear tabs. The Tab Stop Position area of the Tabs dialog box displays all tab settings for custom tabs in the document. From the list of tab positions, select the tab that you want to delete and then click on Clear. To clear all custom tabs, click on Clear All and then click on OK. To move a tab stop, select it in the dialog box, click on Clear, and then enter a new location for the tab.

Creating leader tabs

Some documents, such as tables of contents, make use of *leader tabs,* characters that fill the space left by the tab. To set a leader tab, set the tab as you normally would and then open the Tabs dialog box with the Tabs command. Word offers three kinds of leader tabs: periods, hyphens, and underlines. After you select the desired type of leader, click on OK to set the tab.

Line spacing

Line spacing affects the amount of space between lines of a paragraph. You can also change the spacing between paragraphs. To change the line spacing, place the insertion point anywhere within the desired paragraph and then choose

Format⇨Paragraph. The Paragraph dialog box appears, with the Indents and Spacing tab visible, as shown in Figure 2-15. Use the options in this tab to enter the desired line and paragraph spacing. In the Line Spacing list box, select the kind of spacing that you desire: Single, Double, 1.5, At Least, Exactly, and Multiple. You can adjust the preset spacing of these options by clicking on the arrows in the At box. The Exactly option makes the spacing only the specified amount. The At Least choice can be used to set the spacing to a specified amount or greater.

In the Indentation area, you can specify the amount of indentation that you want to apply to the left and right margins of the document. The Special box also allows for the addition of a hanging indent or other custom indent.

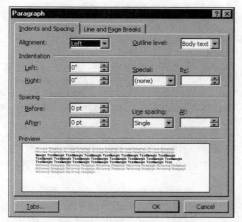

Figure 2-15: The Indents and Spacing tab of the Paragraph dialog box.

If you don't want to use the default measurements, be sure that you enter one of the abbreviations. In the At box to the right of the Line Spacing list box, enter any value that Word understands: inches (in.), centimeters (cm.), picas (pi.), points (pt.), or lines (li.). Picas and points are units of measurement used by typesetters: 6 picas equal 1 inch, and 72 points equal 1 inch. If you enter a numeric value alone, Word assumes that the value is in points.

You can use various Control key combinations to set the three commonly used variations of line spacing. With the insertion point anywhere in the desired paragraph, press Ctrl+1 for single line spacing, Ctrl+2 for double line spacing, or Ctrl+5 for one-and-a-half line spacing.

If you want to apply spacing to a specific paragraph only, first select the paragraph and then choose Paragraph from the Format menu. In the Paragraph dialog box, select the desired spacing and click on OK. You may also use the Control key combinations to change the spacing in the paragraph.

Paragraph spacing

Word also lets you control the amount of space that appears before or after paragraphs. In the Paragraph dialog box, you may have noticed the Before and After text boxes in the Spacing area of the dialog box. You can enter numeric values in the Before or After boxes to indicate a desired additional spacing before or after a paragraph. As with line spacing, you can enter any value for paragraph spacing that Word understands: inches (in.), centimeters (cm.), picas (pi.), points (pt.), or lines (li.). Word assumes points as a default value of measurement (one point being $\frac{1}{72}$ of an inch).

Moving and Copying Text

Word 97 provides a way to move and copy information without using the Clipboard if you want to save what you may have stored there. You can use the drag-and-drop method to move text: after you select the text, click on it and drag it with the mouse to the desired position.

If you want to copy information without using the Clipboard, simply select the text that you want to copy, hold down the Control key, click on the selected text, and drag it to the new location where it is copied.

You can also use the Clipboard to copy and move information. If you want to make a copy of information to place in another application or in another section in Word, select the text that you want to copy and click on the Copy button on the Standard toolbar, or choose Edit⇨Copy. Then move the cursor to the desired position and click on the Paste button, or choose Edit⇨Paste, to copy the information.

You can also use the Clipboard to move information. Select the desired text and click on the Cut button on the Standard toolbar, or choose the Cut command from the Edit menu. The text is then placed in the Clipboard. Then move the cursor to the desired position and click the Paste button, or choose Edit⇨Paste to place the text in the desired position.

Because Word lets you work on multiple documents at the same time, it is easy to move or copy text from one document to another. If you use the Open command from the File menu to open more than one document, you can then open the Window menu and choose Arrange All to see all your open documents in multiple windows. Then you can select the desired text in one document and choose the Move or Copy command. Place the insertion point at the desired location in the other document and choose the Paste command.

Hot Stuff Word also lets you move text from one location to another by using a feature called *drag and drop*. With drag and drop, you select the desired text and then you click on and drag it to the desired location by holding down the mouse button as you drag. As you drag the selection, the mouse pointer consists of the usual pointer arrow and a small rectangle; the rectangle indicates that you are dragging text. After you release the mouse button, the selected text appears in the new location. You can also copy text with drag and drop; just hold down the Control key as you perform the drag-and-drop operation.

Using Search and Replace

Like all full-featured word processors, Word 97 offers a search-and-replace capability through the Find (Ctrl+F) and Replace (Ctrl+H) commands from the Edit menu. These commands may offer more search capability than you are accustomed to because you can look for more than just text. You can search for specific formatting as well as for special characters, such as paragraph marks, newline characters, and tabs.

Searching for regular text

To search for text, choose Edit⇨Find. In the Find dialog box (see Figure 2-16), enter the desired word or phrase in the Find What text box. Click on the Find Next button or press Enter. Word finds the first occurrence of the text. You may continue the search for subsequent occurrences by pressing Enter or the Find Next button.

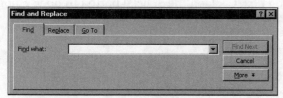

Figure 2-16: The Find tab of the Find and Replace dialog box.

Clicking on the More button gives you more choices to aid you in your search. The choices in the dialog box are fairly self-explanatory. The Match case option tells Word whether you want the search to be case-sensitive. If the option is checked, Word searches for a match that uses the same case as the letters you entered. When the option is not checked, case does not matter during the search. The Use wildcards option tells Word to let you use wildcards, such as a question mark, for any single character and an asterisk for any combination of characters within the search text.

The find whole words only option specifies that only whole words matching the search text will be found. For example, if you search for the word *move* in the sample document and the Find whole words only option is not checked, Word finds occurrences of *move, moves,* and *moved* in the document. If Find whole words only is checked, only occurrences of the word *move* are found. The Sounds like option finds words that sound like the word entered but are spelled differently. The Find all word forms option, when checked, tells Word to locate all matching noun forms or verb tenses. (Word is able to do this based on logic built into its grammar checking.) The Search list box lets you set the direction of the search. The default choice is All, which tells Word to search through the entire document. If you select Up or Down from this list box, Word begins its search at the current insertion point location and searches up or down in the document for the desired search term. If the end of the document is reached and the search term has not been found, Word displays an alert box telling you that a match has not been found.

If you have text stored in the Clipboard, you can search for that text by pressing Shift+Insert when the Find dialog box appears. First select the desired search text and use the Copy command to copy it into the Clipboard. Then choose Edit⇨Find, press Shift+Insert, and click on the Find Next button to begin the search.

Searching for special characters

If you want to find special characters, such as paragraph marks or tab characters, you can also use the Find dialog box. Click on the Special button to open a pop-up menu (see Figure 2-17) for special characters that you want to search for and select the desired character from the menu.

If you want to search for a format, click the Format button and select the format that you want to find. This option lets you search for fonts, paragraph formats, languages, styles, tabs, frames, and highlighting.

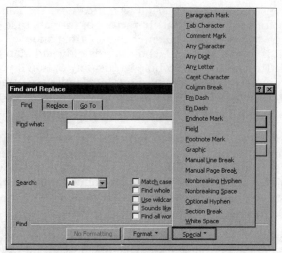

Figure 2-17: The pop-up menu for special characters.

Replacing text

You can use the same search techniques to replace the search text with other text as well. For example, you may want to replace every occurrence of the word *version* with the word *level* throughout a document. Or perhaps a certain word has been underlined at every occurrence in a document and you want to replace it with the same word without the underline. To replace text, you use Edit⇨Replace (Ctrl+H), which displays the Replace dialog box, as shown in Figure 2-18.

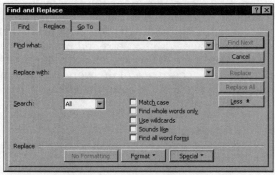

Figure 2-18: The Replace tab of the Find and Replace dialog box.

As with searches, you enter the search text in the Find what text box. You can also use the Format and Special buttons to find special characters or formats that you want to replace. In the Replace with text box, you enter the text that should replace the search text when it is found. The Find whole words only and Match case options can also be used. Turn on the Find whole words only option if you want the search to find only complete words, and turn on the Match case option if the case of the letters found must match that of the search text. The Use Pattern Matching and the Sounds like option works just as it does in the Find dialog box.

After you click on the Find Next button, Word stops and asks for confirmation when the search term is located. Click on the Replace button to make only the change that Word has currently found. Click on the Replace All button if you want Word to make automatically all the subsequent changes for you without asking for confirmation. After the changes are made, Word tells you the number of replacements it made.

Danger Zone Be careful when using the Replace All button because it may cause you to make some replacements that you do not care to make. For example, if you want to replace the word *Figure,* as in *Figure* 2-18 with the word *Item,* and you choose Replace All, then the phrase "Figure out the answer" also gets changed, to "Item out the answer." Oops! Not exactly what you intended. Therefore, if you are not sure that the word is used only in the one context that you want to replace, click on the Replace button to make the first replacement and then use the Find Next button to find the next occurrence of the word and decide if you want to replace it.

If you choose the Replace button, the replacement of the word is then made. If you do not care to replace that particular word, skip it by using the Find Next button. Word then finds the next occurrence of the word and again you have the option of replacing it if you want.

More Info In Chapter 3, you will learn more about formatting documents, so you should know that you can search for and replace formatting in the Replace dialog box. For example, you can replace all instances of a word in bold formatting with the same word in italic formatting. With the cursor in the Find What text box, press Ctrl+B (for Bold formatting). Then tab to the Replace With text box and press Ctrl+I (for Italic formatting). Figure 2-19 shows an example of this search procedure. After you click on Find Next, Word finds the first occurrence of the word *Figure* in Bold formatting. You can click on Replace or Replace All to make the change to Italic formatting.

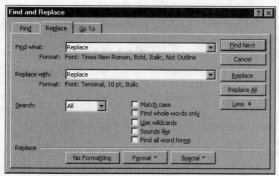

Figure 2-19: Replacing formatting in the Replace dialog box.

If you are searching for an occurrence of a word or format by using the Find dialog box, and you decide to change the word or format, Word provides an easy way to make the change. Simply click on the Replace button, which brings up the Replace dialog box. In the Replace dialog box, you can replace what you are looking for in your search by entering text in the Replace With text box.

Using the Spelling and Grammar Checker

You can use Word's Spelling and Grammar Checker to check your documents for spelling errors or for proper grammatical construction. Word offers multiple dictionaries, allows you to create your own custom dictionaries, and permits you to use different dictionaries for special uses. You can check the spelling of a single word or of entire documents. As part of the grammar-checking process, Word checks the selected section or the entire document for grammatical errors. If Word finds an error, it often suggests ways to correct the sentence containing the error. You can make changes based on Word's suggestions, you can make changes based on your own preferences, or you can bypass the error altogether (the "error" may be okay as is).

Word's Spelling and Grammar Checker uses a main dictionary and a custom dictionary to check for potential misspellings. The main dictionary is supplied with the program and cannot be changed. The custom dictionary, called Custom.dic, is the default supplemental dictionary. When you add new words to the dictionary (which you can do when the Spelling Checker finds a word it does not know, but you know is spelled correctly), you are adding them to Custom.dic unless you specify a different dictionary.

The Spelling Checker in Word lets you check a selected portion of a document or the entire document. To check the spelling or grammar in only part of a document, first select the part that you want checked and then choose the Spelling and Grammar command from the Tools menu. If no selection has been made, Word assumes that you want to check the entire document.

After you choose the Spelling and Grammar command from the Tools menu, or you click on the Spelling button on the Standard toolbar, Word checks all words and grammar constructions against those in the dictionaries. If a suspected misspelled word or improper use of grammar is found, Word stops, and the Spelling dialog box shown in Figure 2-20 appears. After Word finds a misspelling or misuse of grammar, it tries to provide a number of options for a correct spelling of the word, or offers an alternate grammar construction that can be used.

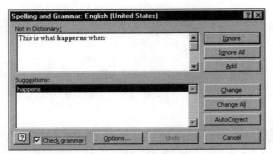

Figure 2-20: The Spelling and Grammar dialog box.

Often, Word offers suggestions for the misspelled word in the Suggestions list. If one of the suggestions is the desired spelling, select it in the list box and then click on the Change button. The Ignore button lets you leave a word as is; the Cancel button cancels the entire spell-checking operation. The Add button lets you add a word to the selected user dictionary (Custom.dic by default).

Hot Stuff You can use the Spelling key (F7) to start checking the spelling of a selection or a document. Pressing F7 is the equivalent of choosing the Spelling and Grammar command from the Tools menu or clicking on the Spelling button on the Standard toolbar. The same applies for the Grammar checker. If you wish to keep the grammar construction that you presently have, you can again simply choose Ignore from the dialog box, and Word will leave the sentence as it is.

Hot Stuff When checking large documents, you can increase the speed of the Spelling and Grammar Checker by reducing the overhead needed by Windows for other operations. To improve performance, close any other documents that are open under Word and close any other Windows applications that you are not using.

Make sure that you are in Normal View and turn off the Formatting toolbar (Alt+V+T and click on the Formatting toolbar check box), ruler (Alt+V+R), and status bar (Alt+T+O and click on the Status Bar check box in the Window section of the View tab).

Checking grammar

To check grammar in a document, first select a passage of text or make no selection to check the entire document. Then choose Spelling and Grammar from the Tools menu. If an error is found, Word displays the Grammar dialog box and the animated help, if you haven't turned it off. A suggestion may appear that explains the error or that offers a way to fix it. If you agree with the suggestion to fix the error, click on the Change button. You can ignore the error by clicking on the Ignore button. Sometimes you may want to edit the sentence yourself. Click in the Sentence text box and edit the sentence as you normally would. Then click on the Change button. You can also start the Grammar checker by clicking on the Spelling button on the Standard Toolbar.

The Suggestions box contains alternatives to the construction that you used in your sentence. Your animated help will provide you with some explanations as to why the grammar construction is incorrect. The Explanation will appear in the automated help windows as shown in Figure 2-21. After reading the rule, close the Grammar Explanation window by double-clicking on the close box in the upper-right corner of the window. You can ignore this rule in the rest of the grammar check by clicking on the Ignore Rule button in the Grammar dialog box.

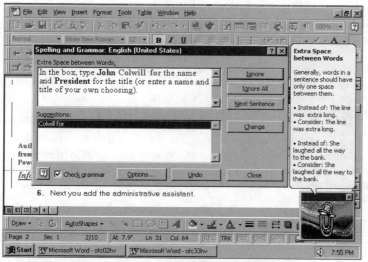

Figure 2-21: The Spelling and Grammar dialog box with the Grammar Explanation window open.

To see the options that are available to you for the Grammar Checker, click on the Options button. The Grammar tab of the Options dialog box appears, as shown in Figure 2-22. The Writing Style box allows you to choose the rules group that you want to use. The default setting is Standard, but you can change this choice by selecting the writing style that you will be using, be it casual, technical, formal, or a custom style that you create by removing or changing the settings. By clicking on the Settings button, you can customize the type of grammar checking you want for your documents.

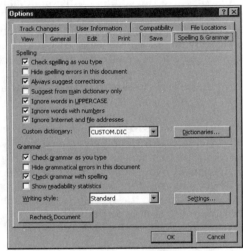

Figure 2-22: The Spelling and Grammar tab of the Options dialog box.

As mentioned earlier, Word 97 also checks your spelling as it checks your grammar. This feature slows down Word, however. You can turn off this feature by removing the check mark from the Check Spelling box on the Grammar tab of the Options menu to increase the speed of your grammar checking.

You can also obtain readability statistics on your document. After Word has completed the grammar check, it analyzes the document and provides a summary of readability statistics. These statistics let you evaluate whether an adult reader can easily understand your document. You can turn this analysis on and off through the Grammar tab of the Options menu.

Changing Dictionaries

As mentioned, Word always uses the main dictionary and at least one supplemental dictionary. You normally add words to the Custom.dic supplemental dictionary when you click on the Add button in the Spelling dialog box, but you can add words to any supplemental dictionary that you have created or intend to create.

To change supplemental dictionaries, click on the Options button in the Spelling and Grammar dialog box. The Spelling and Grammar tab of the Options dialog box appears, as shown in Figure 2-23. In the Custom Dictionaries area, you should see CUSTOM.DIC, the default custom dictionary, already chosen. After you click on the Dictionaries button, the Custom Dictionaries dialog box appears. Click on the New button to create a new custom dictionary. For example, if you work with medical documents that use many medical terms that are not found in your regular custom dictionary, you can create a medical dictionary, called Med.dic. Then you can add the medical words to this new dictionary as they are found in the Spelling Checker. But remember to tell Word to use that dictionary via the Options button in the Spelling dialog box.

Figure 2-23: The Custom Dictionaries dialog box.

Click on the Add button in the Custom Dictionaries dialog box to add a custom dictionary that you have on a disk. The Add Custom Dictionary dialog box opens (see Figure 2-24), where you can enter the name and location of the dictionary that you want to install. Select the dictionary that you want to add, and then click on the OK button.

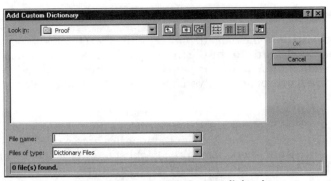

Figure 2-24: The Add Custom Dictionary dialog box.

Checking spelling and grammar as you type

One new feature of Word is its ability to do automatic or "on-the-fly" spelling and grammar checking; you can check spelling and grammar as you type. You can turn on automatic spelling and grammar checking with these steps:

1. Choose Tools⇨Options.

2. In the Options dialog box that opens, click on the Spelling and Grammar tab.

3. Turn on the Check spelling as you type check box or the check grammar as you type check box as desired and then click on OK.

When Word checks spelling as you type, red wavy lines appear underneath any words that Word thinks you have misspelled. Green wavy lines appear underneath any suspected misuse of grammar. You can get help correcting your mistakes by right-clicking on any word so underlined. A pop-up menu appears, containing alternate spellings or suggestions for proper grammar (assuming Word can find any in its dictionaries). You can choose the desired word from the list. In addition to a list of alternate words, the pop-up menu also contains three options: Ignore All, Add, and Spelling. Use Ignore All to tell Word to ignore all occurrences of the word, or use Add to add the word to the default custom dictionary. Use Spelling to open the Spelling dialog box, discussed earlier.

Why should you use more than one custom dictionary?

Many Word users leave Word set to the default custom dictionary, called CUSTOM.DIC. But, depending on your needs, you may have good reason to create and use more than one custom dictionary. If you tend to bounce back and forth between projects that involve a good deal of technical lingo or other nonstandard terms, you can make the overall process of spell checking a bit faster by using different custom dictionaries, with each one specific to the task you are working on. Word spends less time searching a smaller, specific custom dictionary than a large custom dictionary that contains terms for lots of subjects. Just remember to turn on the custom dictionary of your choice when it's needed by using the Spelling tab available through the Tools⇨Options command.

Using the Thesaurus

Word's Thesaurus lets you find synonyms for specific words in your documents. To find a synonym, first select the desired word (remember, you can double-click on anywhere in a word to select it) and then choose Language from the Tools menu (Shift+F7). The Thesaurus dialog box appears, as shown in Figure 2-25.

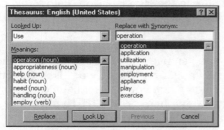

Figure 2-25: The Thesaurus dialog box.

The dialog box shows any synonyms found for the selected word in the Replace with Synonym list box. To replace the selected word with a synonym, select the desired synonym from the list box and then click on the Replace button.

In the Meanings list box, you can find one or more definitions for the selected word. The list of available synonyms changes when you select a different meaning. You can use the mouse to move between the Replace with Synonym and the Meanings list boxes. If you want to look up one of the words in the Meanings list box, simply select the word and click on the Look Up button.

Using Hyphenation

Word provides different ways to handle *hyphenation,* the process of adding hyphens to reduce the ragged appearance of a document's right margin. If the text is justified, hyphens reduce the space between words to fill out a line. In Word, you can add hyphens manually or automatically.

To enter hyphens manually, you must choose Tools Language Hyphenation. This displays the Hyphenation dialog box (see Figure 2-26). After you click on the Manual button, Word switches to Page Layout View and stops to let you confirm the desired location for each hyphen. If you don't want to add a hyphen to the word, or you want to skip it, click on No, and the word is skipped.

Figure 2-26: The Hyphenation dialog box.

With automatic hyphenation, Word adds hyphens automatically, making its best guess as to where hyphenation should occur. In the Hyphenation dialog box, click on the Automatically Hyphenate Document check box to activate automatic hyphenation.

If you choose to hyphenate as you type, you can use one of two types of hyphens: optional or nonbreaking. Optional hyphens appear only if the word is at the end of the line. Word also inserts an optional hyphen when you use semiautomatic or automatic hyphenation. To insert an optional hyphen, press Ctrl+Hyphen. Use nonbreaking hyphens (also called *hard hyphens*) when you do not want a hyphenated word to be broken at the end of a line. To insert a nonbreaking hyphen, press Ctrl+Shift+Hyphen.

Adding Bullets or Paragraph Numbers

With Word, you can automatically add paragraph numbers to your documents or bullets to each paragraph. This feature can be very useful when you are working with legal documents. Also, documents that are numbered are easy to edit and revise. As you add or delete paragraphs, Word maintains the correct numbering for the paragraphs.

To add paragraph numbering or bullets, open the document and select the paragraphs or section to which you want to apply the numbering or bullets. Next, choose Format⇨Bullets and Numbering. The Bullets and Numbering dialog box appears, from which you can choose from seven different bullet layouts on the Bulleted tab. On the Numbered tab, you can choose from seven different numbering layouts. The Outline Numbered tab lets you create outline style numbering with numbers and letters. Each of the tabs contains diagrams of the different layouts.

If you want to add bullets or numbers to the paragraphs as you type, use the buttons on the Formatting toolbar. Select the paragraphs or section to which you want to add numbers or bullets and then click on the Bullets button to add bullets or the Numbering button to add numbers. When you want to add numbers, Word automatically checks the preceding paragraph for its numbering style. If it is numbered, Word uses the same style of numbering for the selected paragraph. If the paragraph is not numbered, Word applies the style of numbering that you selected last.

Using AutoText Entries

AutoText entries are stored entries of text that you frequently use but that you don't want Word to insert automatically. For example, closings to business or personal letters can be stored as AutoText entries. To store an AutoText entry, type the text that you want or import the graphic and then select it. Next, choose Insert⇨AutoText⇨New. The Create AutoText box appears, with the entry as the default name. If you want to keep the suggested name, simply click on the OK button. If you want to change the name, type the name that you want to give the entry in the Name text box and click on OK. Word keeps track of the entries on the submenu that appears after choosing Insert⇨AutoText⇨AutoText.

You can view some default entries by choosing Insert⇨Auto Text. These entries cover things such as common openings and closings to letters, signatures, and filenames. Figure 2-27 shows the AutoText tab of the AutoCorrect dialog box. (This is the dialog box that appears after choosing Insert⇨AutoText⇨AutoText.) The AutoText tab of this dialog box shows the default entries that are available for your use.

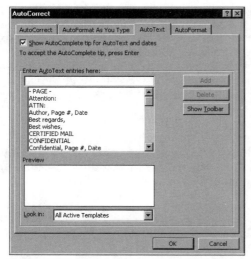

Figure 2-27: The AutoText dialog box.

To insert an AutoText entry, put your cursor in the place where you want the entry to go and then choose Insert⊏>AutoText⊏>AutoText. In the dialog box that appears, click the AutoText tab and select the desired AutoText entry from the list box.

Word also gives you the option of assigning an AutoText entry to a toolbar, which allows you to insert the AutoText entry by clicking on that toolbar button. If you want to assign an AutoText entry to a toolbar, perform the following steps:

1. From the View menu, choose Toolbars and choose Customize from the submenu.

2. In the Customize dialog box, click on the Commands tab. (see Figure 2-28).

Figure 2-28: The Commands tab of the Customize dialog box.

3. In the Categories list box, scroll down to the AutoText entry. When you click on this category, the adjacent box becomes the AutoText box, which displays the name of all AutoText entries that you have stored.

4. Click on the name of the entry to which you want to assign a button. You will see the outline of a toolbar button appear.

5. Next, drag the button to the toolbar to which you want to assign the AutoText button.

6. The name of the AutoText entry appears as the default name for the button, but you can change the name to whatever you want. With the Customize window open, right-click on the button you created and choose Change Button Image. This will provide you with a list of default choices.

7. If you choose to create your own button, the Button Editor dialog box opens (see Figure 2-29), where you can use the grid to draw a text button as you desire.

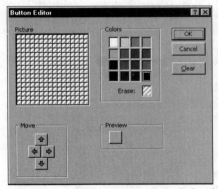

Figure 2-29: The Button Editor dialog box.

Changes can be made to an AutoText entry at any time. Type the name of the AutoText entry and make the revisions. After making the revisions, select the entry and, in effect, redefine it by giving it the same name.

If you no longer need an AutoText entry, you can delete it. Open the AutoText dialog box by selecting any word in the document and then clicking on the Edit AutoText button on the Standard toolbar. Select the name of the AutoText entry that you want to delete and click on the Delete button. The entry is removed.

You can also print your AutoText entries. To print them, select Print from the File menu. The Print dialog box appears. Next, select AutoText Entries from the Print what list box. After you click on OK, the AutoText entries will be printed.

Creating Comments

You can easily create and edit *comments,* a form of notes regarding your document, as a part of a Word document. Think of comments as annotations added to a document: they are not normally visible in the document, but they can easily be seen by using the Comments command from the View menu. Comments are very useful when multiple Word users want to make comments on a proposed document. Because each comment includes the initials of the person making the comment, you can view the comments and contact the persons who have made the comments for help in incorporating the changes. Even when you are working on documents alone, you may find comments useful for reminding yourself about revisions that you plan to make to the document.

To create a comment, place the insertion point at the desired location for the comment and choose the Comment command from the Insert menu (ALT+I+M). Word splits the current window and inserts your initials within a bracket at the comment point, as shown in Figure 2-30. In addition to your initials, Word provides an annotation number so that you can add more comments later. Each comment is assigned a number in sequential order.

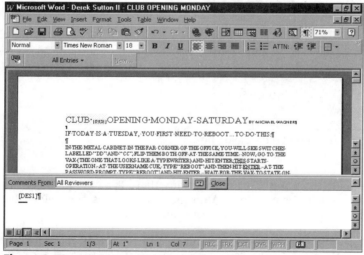

Figure 2-30: The Comments window.

The active insertion point is automatically placed in the Comments pane, which is the lower half of the split window. You can type your desired comments here — there is no limit to the length of an annotation. You even have the option of adding sound as part of your comment. This can be especially useful in giving specific instruction that should be delivered with the touch of a human voice. You can do this by clicking on the insert sound object button in the comments window. Figure 2-31 shows the sample document with two comments added.

When you finish writing the comments, close the Comments pane of the window by choosing the Comments command from the View menu or by dragging the split bar within the right scroll bar to the bottom of the window.

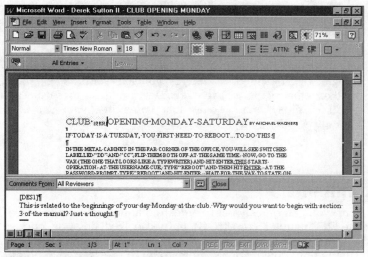

Figure 2-31: A document with comments.

To view comments that you have added to a document, use the Comments command from the View menu. The command is a toggle, so choosing it repeatedly will turn comments viewing on or off. To edit the text of an existing comment if the Comments pane is not already open, choose the Comments command from the View menu or right-click on the comment back highlight that indicates a comment in the documents, and then edit the text as you would edit any other text.

To delete a comment, go to that comment's marker in the document (the yellow back-shading right-click on the highlighted word) and choose Delete Comment from the shortcut menu. You can also print all the comments in a document by choosing the Print command from the File menu, selecting the Options button, and turning on the Comments check box.

Remember that you can use the Cut and Paste commands to move text from the Comments pane into the document. This technique is particularly helpful when some of the comments that have been added to your documents by other people should be incorporated into the document itself.

Multimedia? Why not?

In adding sound comments to documents, Word is making use of the multimedia features that are built into Windows. Multimedia is increasingly a feature of business applications — you can drop sound notes into Word documents, into PowerPoint presentations, and into records of an Access table. (Video is a feature of multimedia as well, but it demands a whole new level of hardware capabilities that we don't get into here.)

If your system isn't yet multimedia-capable, you should consider upgrading. For sound, all you'll need is a sound card that supports the MPC-2 standard (and these days, most do). Cards manufactured by the major

companies (like Creative Labs' popular Sound Blaster series) come with fairly clear documentation to help you get the card installed. After installing the card, you'll need to run the Windows 95 Hardware Installation Wizard to tell your system about the sound card (see your Windows documentation for details). Then, connect your microphone and speakers to the card, and you're in business.

Oh, and do yourself a favor — run down to Radio Shack or another electronics store, and get yourself some nice, amplified speakers. Don't settle for those cheesy little ones that come free with some sound cards.

Finding comments

In a large document, you can quickly get to a desired annotation with the Go To command from the Edit menu (F5 or Ctrl+G). In the Go To dialog box, choose Annotation in the Go to What list box, followed by the name of the reviewer, or Any Reviewer if that is not known. For example, to go to the second annotation in the document, press the Next button. You are then moved to the next annotation in the document by the specified reviewer or any reviewer based on what was entered in the Enter Reviewer's Name box.

After you have reviewed all the changes to a document, you can track the changes to your document using the track changes feature. To track the changes to a document, choose Track Changes from the Tools menu. You will then have three choices: to highlight the changes, to accept or reject the changes, or to compare different versions of the same document. If you wish the changes to be highlighted on screen, choose Highlight Changes from the Track Changes submenu. This will then open the Highlight Changes dialog box as shown in Figure 2-32. There, you have the choice of tracking the changes as you edit, much like revision marks. You also may have the changes highlighted on screen or in printed form. This can be extremely beneficial in seeing how a document changes as it goes through the editing process.

Figure 2-32: The Highlight Changes dialog box.

By using the Accept or Reject Changes options of the Track Changes submenu, you can go through your document and look for the changes. After the you have read the tracked changes, you have the choice of accepting or rejecting the changes that were made to the document. Again, this can prove to be very useful in cases where a document goes through stages of editing, possibly by several persons.

Locking the document

When multiple persons are commenting on a document, you may find it helpful to lock the document so that no one but the author can change the document itself — others can only add or edit comments. If you lock a document for comments only, you can then safely pass the file around for comments, while ensuring that others cannot make any changes to the document.

To lock a file for comments only, choose the Save As command from the File menu when you next save the file and then click on the Options button in the Save As dialog box. In the Save tab, you can enter a Password for Modification that prevents changes from being made to a document. You can also restrict the editing of your document by clicking on the Read-Only Recommended box.

Document Summaries

While not directly related to the formats of your document, document summaries are an important aid to the editing process. If you customarily press Enter to bypass the document summary screen every time you are creating a new document, you are missing out on a flexible way of storing information relating to a document. And you can use the information stored in the document summaries as a way to search for desired documents.

Hot Stuff If you can't recall a filename, you can find the file by searching document summaries. Choose File⇨Open, click on the Advanced button in the Open dialog box that appears, set the desired search criteria for the document summaries, and click on the Find Now button.

To view or edit the document summary, make sure that the document is open, choose File⇨Properties, and then click on the Summary tab in the dialog box that opens. The Summary tab is shown in Figure 2-33.

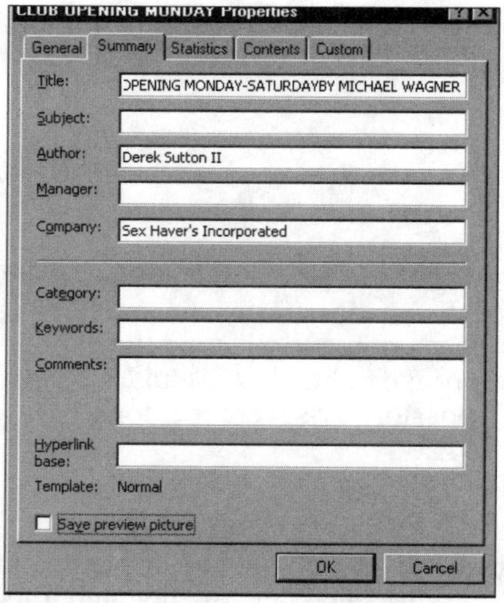

Figure 2-33: The Summary tab of the Properties dialog box.

The fields are self-explanatory — you can enter the desired document title, subject, and keywords that may help you identify the document later. Word inserts the author's name, based on the name that is stored in the dialog box on the User Info tab of the Options dialog box (accessed from the Tools menu). When you change the author's name in the Summary dialog box, the change takes effect only for the current document.

The Statistics tab in the Properties dialog box can be useful for getting information about the productivity of the document. After you click on this tab, you see all sorts of useful information regarding your document (see Figure 2-34).

The Statistics tab shows the document's creation date, when it was last saved, how many times it has been revised, the total time you have spent editing it, and how many characters, words, and pages are in the document.

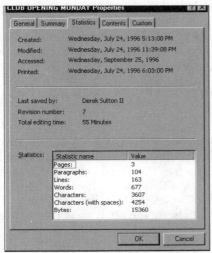

Figure 2-34: The Statistics tab of the Properties dialog box.

If you fill in the fields of the Summary tab of the Properties dialog box for all your documents, you can later find documents based on those fields. This is often helpful when you need to retrieve a document but can't remember the filename. To search for a document based on the summary information, choose File➪Open. From the Open dialog box that appears, choose Advanced. From the Property portion of the dialog box, choose the summary information that you want to use in the search. The Advanced Find dialog box, used for advanced searches, is shown in Figure 2-35.

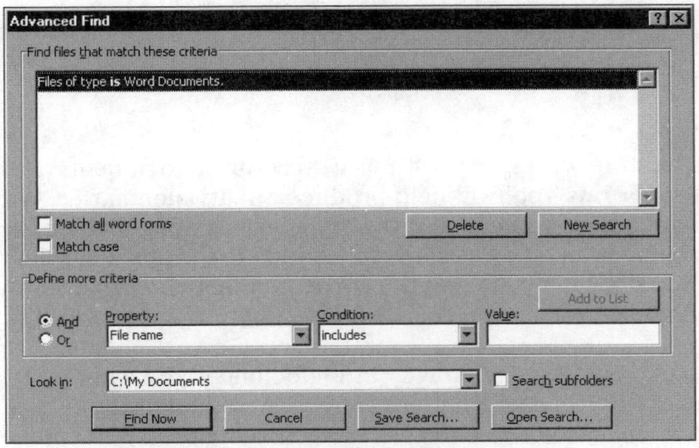

Figure 2-35: The Advanced Find dialog box.

After specifying the location of your search, use the condition and value portions of the dialog box to specify the information that you want Word to use in the search. Special characters may also be used to create approximate criteria (see "Searching for special characters" earlier in this chapter). After you have entered the information, click on Find Now to carry out the search.

AutoSummarize

The AutoSummarize feature is a tool at your disposal in Office 97. This feature will allow you to summarize the key points in a document. The AutoSummarize feature analyzes documents and assigns scores to each of the sentences in a document by analyzing the frequency of words in sentences. You are also allowed to choose a percentage of the high scoring sentences that you wish to display in your summary. Figure 2-36 shows the AutoSummarize window that appears when you choose Tools⇨AutoSummarize.

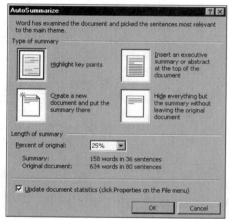

Figure 2-36: The AutoSummarize dialog box.

You will find that this feature works best with well-structured documents. Also, the use of the Find All Word Forms Tool will help produce quality summaries. With your well-structured document you can add the summary as a highlighted section at the top of your document, in a new document, or hide the original and just show the summary. You do this by making the corresponding choices from the AutoSummarize dialog box.

Next you will want to choose the percentage of the document you want to summarize, using the options in the Length of Summary section of the AutoSummarize box. There, you have choices between sentences, percentages, or number of words in your document on which you wish to base the summary. This gives you the power to control the length of the summary Word creates for you.

After the summary is created, the results will appear based on the selection you made in the Type of Summary section of the AutoSummarize dialog box. The AutoSummarize box will also by default update the Document statistics automatically.

Summary

This chapter provided you with techniques that are useful in your start with Word. The following points were covered:

✦ Word's File➪New command displays a dialog box containing tabs that you can use to create new documents. New documents are based on a blank document or on one of Word's predefined templates. In Word, you can base your documents on different templates containing certain formatting and, in many cases, boilerplate text.

✦ Word includes a number of wizards that ask you a series of questions and then create a basic document based on your responses.

✦ You can work with text in Word through one of four possible views: Normal, Outline, Page Layout, and Master Document.

✦ You can change your margin settings with the File➪Page Setup command; your tabs with the Format➪Tabs command; and your line spacing with the Format➪Paragraph command.

✦ You can search for text with the Edit➪Find command, and you can search for and replace text with the Edit➪Replace command. Word provides a full-featured search-and-replace capability that lets you search for text, formatting, and special characters such as paragraph marks and tabs.

✦ You can use Word's spell-checking feature to find and fix misspellings, and you can have Word check spelling as you type. And Word also provides a grammar checker that can check your documents for proper grammar and style.

✦ You can use the Insert➪Comments command to add comments to a document.

Chapter 3 takes you to the next step: Formatting Documents.

Where to go next...

✦ If you're ready to print your work, Chapter 4 tells you how.

✦ If you need to create tables, outlines, tables of contents, or indexes, see Chapters 5 and 7 for help.

✦   ✦   ✦

Formatting Documents

As you create and refine your text, you will need to control
the appearance of the document. You can do so by using
Word's formatting features. In Chapter 2, you were introduced
to some of the basic ways of formatting your text. This
chapter will detail formatting as it applies to characters,
paragraphs, pages, and sections of a document.

Formatting Levels

Word provides formatting options for different levels of text,
including characters, paragraphs, sections, and documents.
Later in this chapter, you'll use many of the options on
Word's Format menu, which offers many of the features that
control Word's formatting:

+ The smallest unit of formatting is the character. With
  character formatting, any formatting that you apply
  affects all the characters within a selected area of text
  or all the characters that you type after you select the
  formatting. Here's a case where you're applying
  character formatting and you may not even realize it:
  when you select a sentence and then click on the Bold
  button in the Formatting toolbar to transform the
  sentence into bold text. Character formatting is often
  used to make a word or group of words in your
  document stand out.

+ The next size up in the formatting arena is *paragraph
  formatting.* With paragraph formatting, the formatting
  that you apply controls the appearance of the text from
  one paragraph mark to the next. Paragraph marks
  appear whenever you press the Enter key. If you press
  Enter once, type seven lines of text, and then press
  Enter again, those seven lines of text are one paragraph.

After you select a paragraph, you can change the formatting for that particular paragraph. For example, you can change its alignment or its line spacing.

Because characters comprise paragraphs, it is easy to confuse character and paragraph formatting. It may help to remember that paragraph formatting generally controls the appearance of lines because a group of lines typically makes up a paragraph. Paragraph formatting controls the alignment of lines, the spacing between lines, the indents in lines, and borders around the paragraph.

✦ Next, there is *page formatting*. With page formatting, you control the appearance of every page for the entire document. Page formatting affects such settings as page size, default tab stops, and margins for the document.

✦ Optionally, you can apply *section formatting* to entire sections of a document. (A document can consist of a single section, or you can divide a document into multiple sections.) When you format a section of a document, you change certain formatting aspects for pages within that section. For example, you may want to change the number of columns in a portion of the document, or you may want to change the look of the headers and footers in another section. After you divide a document into sections, you can use many formatting commands to format each section individually.

Choosing your weapon

Although Word divides formatting into four levels that control Word's behavior, these levels do not need to control your formatting choices. Where you start and end a particular type of formatting depends entirely on how you want the document to appear. For example, suppose that you want to display all the text of two paragraphs in italic. Even though you are applying formatting to two *paragraphs*, you can select these paragraphs and click on the Italic button on the Formatting toolbar to apply *character* formatting. Remember that *you* are in control of formatting options. This chapter explains the levels of formatting in Word for Windows because that is how Word provides access to the formatting options within its menus. You can, however, choose to apply formatting by using any combination of methods that suits your needs.

Character Formatting

As mentioned earlier, character formatting is the smallest level of formatting. Character formatting governs how your characters look on-screen and in print. When you apply character formatting (the most common type of formatting), you are changing the format for each character. When you look at a newspaper or a book, character formatting is evident. Headlines appear in boldfaced characters and in large fonts. Secondary headlines, however, are in smaller fonts and may not be in bold print. The role of character formatting, therefore, is to emphasize text:

Characters and lines

<u>can be produced</u>

in a number of ways,

<u>even in combination,</u>

TO HELP MAKE

a different point.

Also, you can add color formatting to the characters in your document. Whether you can view or print the colors that you select depends on the type of printer you have and the display hardware.

Using character formatting options

We can further divide character formatting into specific areas that are controlled by the options in the Font dialog box, which appears after you choose the Font command from the Format menu. Table 3-1 explains the formatting options available in the Font dialog box.

The quickest way to apply character formatting is to use the Formatting toolbar. You can choose the font and point size that you want to use and apply bold, italics, and underlining. These choices are the most frequently used character formats in documents.

If you need to make adjustments or change several formats at one time, choose the Format⇨Font command. The Font dialog box appears. Click on the Font tab to reveal the options available in Figure 3-1. Here you can choose from the many fonts, select a style, change text color, specify the type of underlining you desire, and add effects such as strikethrough, all caps, or small caps.

Table 3-1
Formatting options

Option	Description
Font	A character set with a consistent and identifiable typeface, such as Times New Roman, Courier, or Arial.
Font Style	Defines a style for the chosen font, such as regular text, italic, bold, or bold italic.
Size	Specifies what *point size* to use — essentially, how big the text should be. Strictly speaking, point size measures character height, but characters proportionally increase in width as they increase in height. A point is ½ of an inch, so a 72-point font can take up an inch from top to bottom. (Not counting *descenders,* which dangle from the bottom of *y, g, q,* and so on.) This does not mean, however, that a 72-point *P* is always an inch tall. Each font has other characteristics that determine its actual size. (This is why a *P* in one font may look bigger than a *P* in another font, even when they're at the same point size.)
Color	Offers 16 possible colors that can be viewed in the list box.
Underline	Specifies a type of underlining (single, double, dotted).
Effects	Specifies appearance attributes such as ~~strikethrough~~, hidden (which means the text does not appear, but is actually still there), superscript, subscript, SMALL CAPS, and ALL CAPS.
Spacing	Controls the amount of space that appears between characters (found on the Character Spacing tab of the Font dialog box). Word allows a default amount of space between characters, but you can expand or condense this allowance.
Position	The position of the characters on a line, such as normal, raised (the characters appearing above the baseline by half a line), or lowered (the characters appearing below the baseline by half a line).
Drop Caps	Inserts an oversized "drop capital," a large first letter as in the following example: **O**nce upon a time there was a boy named George. George was a very good boy and lived in Idaho. George was very curious.
Animation	Controls different animating effects to your document such as a Las Vegas lights effect, blinking, and moving borders.

Figure 3-1: The Font tab of the Font dialog box.

You can use the options in the Font and Font Style list boxes to choose a desired font and font style, and you can choose a desired size in the Size list box. You can select a type of underlining (Single, Words Only, Double, or Dotted) in the Underline list box, and you can select a color for the text in the Color list box. In the Effects portion of the tab, you can turn on as many of the special effects at one time as you want.

The Character Spacing tab of the Font dialog box (Figure 3-2) provides options for changing the amount of spacing between characters (Normal, Expanded, or Condensed), the position (whether text appears raised or lowered relative to the baseline of normal text), and *kerning* (the precise amount of space between characters, as detailed shortly).

The Animation tab of the Font dialog box applies animation to the characters in your document. You may find this option useful when you want to draw attention to certain words in your document. Select the text you wish to animate using your preferred selection method, choose Font from the format menu to open the Font dialog box. Next choose the Animation tab of the Font dialog box. (The Animation tab is shown in Figure 3-3.) Select the type of animation you wish to insert and click on OK, and you will see the animation applied to your text. The preview box at the bottom of the animation tab gives you the opportunity to see how the text will appear in your document.

Figure 3-2: The Character Spacing tab of the Font dialog box.

To remove or apply character formats, simply select the text that you want to format, or position the cursor where you want to begin typing the formatted characters. Then, using the Formatting toolbar, click on the formatting option that you want to apply to the characters.

Using character formatting shortcuts

You can apply most of these character formats with shortcut keys, which are easier to use when you are typing than removing your hands from the keyboard to use the mouse. The shortcut keys act as switches to turn the various Format commands on and off. Table 3-2 contains several shortcut keys that you can use to apply character formatting.

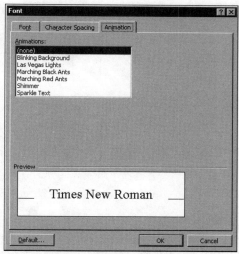

Figure 3-3: The Animation Tab of the Font dialog box.

Table 3-2
Shortcut keys for character formatting

Format	Shortcut Key
Bold	Ctrl+B
Italic	Ctrl+I
Underline	Ctrl+U
Word underline	Ctrl+Shift+W
Double underline	Ctrl+Shift+D
Subscript (H_2O)	Ctrl+Equal Sign
Superscript (X^2)	Ctrl+Shift+Equal Sign
Small caps	Ctrl+Shift+K
All caps	Ctrl+Shift+A
Change case of letters	Shift+F3
Hidden text	Ctrl+Shift+H

(continued)

Table 3-2 *(continued)*	
Format	**Shortcut Key**
Remove formats	Ctrl+Spacebar or CTRL+Z
Font	Ctrl+Shift+F
Symbol font	Ctrl+Shift+Q
Point size	Ctrl+Shift+P
Next larger size	Ctrl+SHIFT+>
Next smaller size	Ctrl+SHIFT+<
Up one point	Ctrl+]
Down one point	Ctrl+[

Hot
Stuff

You can turn off all character formatting for a selection by pressing Ctrl+Spacebar. This is especially useful when you've used several key combinations to turn on various formatting features for a selection, and you want to turn them all off.

Changing character fonts and point sizes

One significant advantage of using Word for Windows is your ability to see and use various fonts within your document. The font used as the default is initially Times New Roman, but you can change this to whatever you wish. The fonts available to you depend on the type of printer that you are using and the fonts that were installed as a part of your Windows installation. You can use the following steps to change the default font used for your documents:

1. From the menus, choose Format⇨Font.

2. Click on the Font tab in the Font dialog box (if it isn't already visible).

3. Choose the desired font, font style, and size you want to use as the default.

4. Click on the Default button in the dialog box.

5. When asked for confirmation that you want to change the default font, click on Yes.

The hows and whens of formatting

Word provides a great deal of flexibility by offering many formatting options. You can apply formatting as you are creating a document, which changes the appearance of the document as you go along, or you can enter all the new text in a single format and then change the formatting in selected areas of the document, or you can use both methods in combination.

If you choose to format as you go along, remember that many options of formatting (particularly for characters and paragraphs) can be turned on and off as you work. For example, when you turn on underlining, everything that you type from that point is underlined. To stop underlining, turn underlining off. This is true whether you apply formatting with commands, shortcut keys, or buttons on the toolbars.

If you want to enter the text of a document first and then apply formatting to specific areas later, you can use the *select and act* technique common to Word for Windows. That is, you first select the affected text and then you execute an action (by choosing a formatting command or button) that applies to the selection.

In addition to choosing appropriate fonts, you can also select various point sizes with the Formatting toolbar or the Font dialog box. Each point is $1/72$ of an inch, so in a 10-point font size, the characters would be roughly $10/72$ of an inch high. The following lines demonstrate the effects of various point sizes:

This is 12-point Times New Roman.

This is 14-point Times New Roman.

This is 16-point Times New Roman.

This is 18-point Times New Roman.

With varied fonts and font sizes, you can very easily get carried away. A document with too many different fonts and font sizes can take on a busy look and be visually distracting to the reader.

Applying superscript and subscript

You can create raised, or *superscripted,* text, and lowered, or *subscripted,* text, by selecting the Superscript or Subscript options on the Font tab of the Font dialog box. Most formatting of this type is applied while you type the information, although as with other formatting in Word, you can apply the formatting later by selecting the desired characters and then choosing the Superscript or Subscript options. Examples of both types of text are as follows:

This is $^{superscripted\ text}$, and this is back to normal.

This is $_{subscripted\ text}$, and this is back to normal.

You can apply super- or subscripting to text by using either the Font dialog box or the shortcut keys (see Table 3-2). One advantage of using the Font dialog box is that you can change the measurement amount that you use for the superscript or the subscript. Click on the Font tab, and turn on the Superscript or the Subscript option as desired for the selected text.

Adjusting kerning

You can also control kerning from the Character Spacing tab of the Font dialog box. Kerning is the adjusting of the space between characters, relative to the specific type of font used. Kerning can be useful in giving a document a better appearance, although you need a high-resolution printer (a 600-dpi laser printer or better) for the effects of minor changes in kerning to be noticeable. Kerning can be used only with proportionally spaced TrueType fonts or with similar scalable fonts that are larger than a minimum size you specify.

Copying character formatting

If you are using a particular type of formatting often in a document (but not in all places), you can save time by copying the format from one place in the document to another. Word for Windows makes this a simple task when you use the Format Painter button on the Standard toolbar. To copy a character format, first select the characters with the format that you want to copy. Next click on the Format Painter button on the toolbar. (It's the button with the small brush.) Then choose the characters or section to which you want to apply the format. The formatting is automatically applied to the new characters.

Paragraph Formatting

Word lets you apply paragraph formatting to any area that is considered a paragraph. Word considers any amount of text that you enter between one paragraph mark and the next to be a single paragraph. If you want to see the paragraph marks in a document (see Figure 3-4), press the Show/Hide button on the Standard toolbar (it's the button containing the paragraph symbol, which looks sort of like a backwards *P*).

This·is·an·example·of·what·paragraph·marks·look·like·in·a·document.·If·you·
press·Enter,·you·will·see·a·paragraph·mark·appear·at·the·end·of·the·sentence.·¶
¶
As·you·can·see,·a·paragraph·mark·appears·each·time·you·press·Enter.·¶
¶

Figure 3-4: Paragraph marks in a document.

When deciding where paragraph formatting is necessary, remember that
paragraphs are basically collections of lines. Paragraph formatting affects the
appearance of a collection of one or more lines that end with a paragraph marker,
which appears when you press Enter. Paragraph formatting lets you control the
length of lines, the alignment of lines at the left and right edges, the space between
lines, and the space between paragraphs. You can also control the placement of
tab stops and how text is aligned at the tab stops.

 Hot Stuff Using the newline command (Shift+Enter) rather than pressing the Enter key can
make paragraph formatting easier because Word does not consider the newline
character (a left-pointing arrow) to be the start of a paragraph.

Applying paragraph formatting

As with character formatting, you can apply paragraph formatting in different
ways. You can use the Format⇨Paragraph to bring up the Paragraph dialog box
shown in Figure 3-5. Or you can use the buttons that apply to paragraphs on the
Formatting toolbar. The Formatting toolbar also displays important information
regarding the existing formats for the current paragraph. Look at the alignment
buttons (Align Left, Center, Align Right, and Justify). The one that looks pressed in
reflects the alignment of the paragraph that contains the cursor.

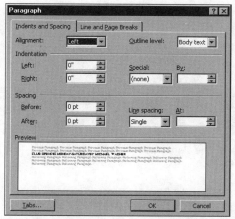

Figure 3-5: The Indents and Spacing tab of the Paragraph dialog box.

The Paragraph dialog box contains two tabs. On the Indents and Spacing tab, you can choose the amount of left and right indentation and whether there should be a first-line or a hanging indent (and the corresponding amount of indentation). In the Spacing area, you can choose the amount of spacing before and after each line and the line spacing for the line itself.

The Line and Page Breaks tab of the Paragraph dialog box (see Figure 3-6) contains options that control how text flows within a paragraph. You can turn on the following options:

✦ The Widow/Orphan Control option prevents a widow (a single line at the bottom of the page) from appearing by itself at the bottom of the page, and it prevents an orphan (a single line at the top of a page) from appearing by itself at the top of the page.

✦ The Keep Lines Together option prevents a page break within the paragraph.

✦ The Keep with Next option prevents a page break between the paragraph and the one that follows.

✦ The Page Break Before option inserts a page break before the paragraph.

✦ The Suppress Line Numbers option suppresses line numbers for the selected paragraph when line numbering is turned on in a document.

✦ The Don't Hyphenate option excludes the paragraph from automatic hyphenation.

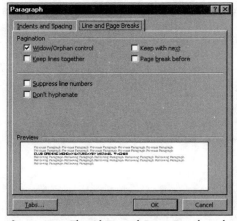

Figure 3-6: The Line and Page Breaks tab of the Paragraph dialog box.

You can also click on buttons on the Formatting toolbar and drag items on the ruler to indent paragraphs, align text, or set tab stops in a document. Many of these paragraph formats can also be applied by using shortcut keys. Table 3-3 provides a list of the paragraph formatting shortcut keys.

What are first-line indents and hanging indents?

In some paragraphs, you might want to align the first line of the paragraph differently than the remaining lines.

A *first-line indent* begins a paragraph's first line to the right of the paragraph's margin. You probably remember the *two-finger* first-line indent you learned in elementary school: this is the high-tech version.

A *hanging indent,* sometimes called an *outdent,* begins a paragraph's first line to the *left* of the paragraph's margin. You can use a hanging indent to create a bulleted list, for example. Use Format⇨Paragraph to bring up the Paragraph dialog box. In the Special list box of the Indents and Spacing tab, choose Hanging. In the By entry, type **.25"**. Click on OK. Now, type a bullet symbol, a tab, and then type the text of the bullet item. The text wraps cleanly along that quarter-inch margin.

Table 3-3
Shortcut keys for paragraph formatting

Format	Shortcut Key
Left-align text	Ctrl+L
Center text	Ctrl+E
Right-align text	Ctrl+R
Justify text	Ctrl+J
Indent from left margin	Ctrl+M
Decrease indent	Ctrl+Shift+M
Create a hanging indent	Ctrl+T
Decrease a hanging indent	Ctrl+Shift+T
Single-space lines	Ctrl+1
Create 1.5-line spacing	Ctrl+5
Double-space lines	Ctrl+2

(continued)

Table 3-3 *(continued)*	
Format	*Shortcut Key*
Add or remove 12 points of space before a paragraph	Ctrl+0 (zero)
Remove paragraph formats not applied by a style	Ctrl+Q
Restore default formatting (reapply the Normal style)	Ctrl+Shift+N
Display or hide nonprinting characters	Ctrl+*(asterisk)

Word for Windows also provides a shortcut menu to do character and paragraph formatting. You can open this menu by clicking on the right mouse button over any location in your paragraph. Figure 3-7 shows the formatting shortcut menu that appears. Here you can choose Cut, Copy, Paste, Font, Paragraph, or Bullets and Numbering to accomplish their different formatting tasks. Along with those, you can choose Draw Table, which will be discussed in Chapter 5.

Another new option experienced Office users will find is the Define option. This option is used in conjunction with Microsoft Bookshelf, to provide you with a definition based on information found in Microsoft Bookshelf. (Microsoft Bookshelf is a collection of references that includes a Thesaurus, Dictionary, Encyclopedia, Dictionary of Quotations, and a World Atlas.)

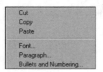

Figure 3-7: The formatting shortcut menu.

Indenting paragraphs

A common change to paragraphs involves setting the indents. When indenting paragraphs, remember that all paragraph indents are relative to any page indents that you may also have specified. Word lets you indent paragraphs from the left or right sides. You can also indent the first line of a paragraph. For practice, type the following text (or use text from a paragraph of your own devising) and follow the steps for applying different kinds of paragraph formatting:

1. Type the following text:

Bungee Jumping

Bungee jumping is considered by many a high-risk sport. The sport entails tying a giant rubber band to your legs and jumping from a high object, usually a crane of some kind.

The sport has become increasingly popular over the years since its introduction. At present, you can take vacations that include trips to practice these high-risk sports. Bungee jumping has become so popular that it is now a sport at the Extreme Games. There are now professionals who make their living much like platform divers do. There are many similarities between platform diving and bungee jumping. The grading is much the same and the tricks that the jumpers do are very reminiscent of diving.

2. Place the insertion point anywhere on the first line, and click on the Center button in the Formatting Toolbar. When you do this, the first paragraph (containing just the word *Bungee*) takes on a centered alignment.

3. Place the insertion point anywhere within the first full paragraph of text. Choose Format➪Paragraph. The Paragraph dialog box appears. You will use the Indentation area on the Indents and Spacing tab to control the paragraph indents.

4. Enter **0.5** as a value in the Left box, and then enter **0.5** as a value in the Right box. Click on OK. The paragraph appears indented by one-half inch on both sides.

5. In the Paragraph dialog box, choose the Indents and Spacing tab. In the Special list box, select the First Line option. Enter **1** in the By entry. Click on OK. The first line of the paragraph is now indented by 1 inch.

Figure 3-8 shows the results of all this paragraph formatting.

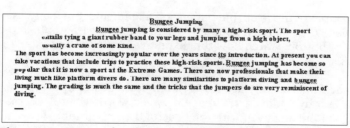

Figure 3-8: Paragraphs after formatting has been applied.

Mouse users can also use the ruler to set the left indent, right indent, and first line indent values. You may have noticed that when you changed the values by using the Paragraph command, the triangle-shaped symbols on the ruler moved accordingly. You can set the indentations by dragging the appropriate symbol on the ruler to the desired location. If you drag the left-indent symbol (the lower of the two triangles) of the first full paragraph back to the zero mark on the ruler, the left edge of the paragraph realigns with the zero marker on the ruler. Now the paragraph is no longer indented from the left, although the first line remains indented by one inch. Next, drag the first-line indent symbol back to the zero mark on the ruler and drag the right-indent symbol ½ inch to the right. The paragraph now takes on the appearance it had before you changed any of the indentations.

When you set indentations by dragging the symbols in the ruler, keep in mind that the measurement set by the first-line symbol is always relative to that set by the left-indent symbol. Therefore, if you want to indent an entire paragraph by ½ inch and the first line by another ½ inch, you should drag the left-indent symbol to the right by ½ inch and then drag the first-line symbol to the right another ½ inch past the left-indent symbol. To drag the first-line symbol without dragging the left-indent symbol, be sure that the mouse pointer is on the top of the two triangles.

Aligning paragraphs

Paragraphs in Word can be aligned in four ways: left, right, centered, and *justified* (aligned on both sides). Most of the text that you typed in the exercise has been left aligned, meaning that the left edge of the paragraph is even and the right edge is ragged. By comparison, there may be times that you need justified text (where both edges of the paragraph are aligned), or centered paragraphs (as in titles or headings). In rare instances, you may need to right align a paragraph; in such cases, the right side aligns flush, and the left edge of the paragraph is ragged. You can change these settings in the Alignment box of the Indents and Spacing tab in the Paragraph dialog box or by clicking on the alignment buttons on the Formatting toolbar.

To see an example of the available paragraph alignments, open any existing document, place the insertion point anywhere within a paragraph, and click on each alignment button. Watch how the text moves from left to center to right to justified.

Books and magazines usually use justified text for a neater appearance. Word justifies your text by adding extra space between words where necessary to make the right edge of the line even with the edge of the paragraph.

Note   Depending on the type of document, the appearance of justified text may be improved by hyphenation. To enable Word to hyphenate automatically, choose Tools⇨Language, Hyphenation and turn on the Automatically Hyphenate Document option in the Hyphenation dialog box, and then click on OK.

To justify, or not to justify?

Many people consider the look that results from fully justified text (that is, justified both left and right) to have a professional and "typeset" quality. Justification also provides an appearance of formality. And in multicolumn text, the justified right edge creates a line that serves as a clear delimiter between columns. On the other hand, if you want your document to appear more "friendly," avoid full justification. Also, bear in mind that full justification can cause uneven spacing and vertical "rivers" of white space in paragraphs. If you don't allow hyphenation, full justification creates some lines that are excessively *loose* (lots of space between words), and some lines that are excessively *tight* (too little space between words). If you allow hyphenation when you use full justification, Word hyphenates lots of words to create evenly spaced lines — far more than if you left the right margin ragged.

Applying line spacing

Line spacing affects the amount of space between lines in a paragraph. To change the line spacing, place the insertion point anywhere within the desired paragraph and then choose the desired line spacing by using shortcut keys (see Table 3-3) or by setting the Line Spacing option in the Indents and Spacing tab of the Paragraph dialog box.

The common choices for line spacing are Single, 1.5 Lines (for 1½ times single spacing), and Double. You can also select At Least, Exactly, or Multiple. (When you choose any of the last three options, you must enter or select a corresponding amount in the At box.) The At Least choice sets a minimum line spacing that Word adjusts when needed to allow for larger font sizes or graphics. The Exactly choice sets a fixed line spacing that Word cannot adjust. The Multiple choice lets you enter incremental values (such as 1.2) to increase or decrease spacing by a fractional amount. For example, choosing Multiple and entering 1.2 in the At box results in line spacing that is 120 percent of single spacing.

Applying paragraph spacing

Word also lets you control the amount of space that appears before or after paragraphs in the Spacing area on the Indents and Spacing tab of the Paragraph dialog box. You can enter numeric values in the Before or After boxes to indicate the additional space that you want. As with line spacing, you can enter the value in points (pt.), each point being ½ of an inch.

Applying borders to paragraphs

You may find borders useful for emphasizing a particular portion of text. Borders are also commonly used in newsletter layout. You can apply a border to paragraphs by using the Borders and Shading command from the Format menu. If you apply borders often, click on the Show Toolbar button in the Borders and Shading dialog box. (Alternatively, you can right-click in any blank area of the toolbar, and choose Borders from the shortcut menu that appears.) The Borders toolbar that appears makes adding borders to your documents much easier.

Word offers several border choices:

- ✦ **Top Border** — a line above the paragraph
- ✦ **Bottom Border** — a line below the paragraph
- ✦ **Left Border** — a line to the left of the paragraph
- ✦ **Right Border** — a line to the right of the paragraph
- ✦ **Inside Border** — a line within the paragraph
- ✦ **Outside Border** — lines that surround the paragraph
- ✦ **Box Border** — a line around all sides of the paragraph
- ✦ **Shadow Border** — a shadowed line around the paragraph
- ✦ **3-D** — a 3-D line around the paragraph
- ✦ **Custom** — a custom line of your choice around the paragraph
- ✦ **No Border**

Keep in mind that after you select the type of border that you wish to have for you paragraph, you still need to make a selection as to where you want the border to appear, On the right side of the Borders tab in the Preview box, you can click on the side of the paragraph that you want the border to appear on. This will give you a general idea of what the border will look like, once it is applied to your paragraph.

You can even change the line size that you use for the different borders in your document. Click on the down-pointing arrow in the Border toolbar to drop down the line-size options. Or you can select these same options in the Style section of the Borders tab of the Paragraph Borders and Shading dialog box (see Figure 3-9).

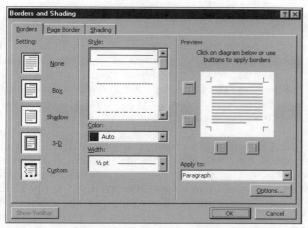

Figure 3-9: The Borders tab of the Borders and Shading dialog box.

The Shading tab of the Borders and Shading dialog box (Figure 3-10) lets you add various kinds of shading to your text. The shading can range from a light gray to a solid black. Click on the Custom radio button to apply a shading and then select the desired level of shading from the list box. The color options in the Fill and Style and Color sections of the Patterns area allow you to provide a background for the text that you are coloring and a style of pattern to the background color. The Preview area to the right will give you a general idea of how that will appear in your document.

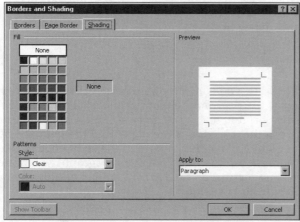

Figure 3-10: The Shading tab of the Borders and Shading dialog box.

Page Formatting

In Word, you use page formatting to control the appearance of each page for the entire document. Page formatting controls such settings as page size, orientation, and page margins. To change most aspects of page formatting, you use the File⇨Page Setup command, which produces the Page Setup dialog box with its four tabs: Margins, Paper Size, Paper Source, and Layout. All tabs have a Default button, an Apply To list box, and a Preview window.

The Default button can be used to apply your changes to Word's default settings. (If you are using a template other than the default Normal.dot template, the changes are applied to the template that you are using.) The remaining choices you make apply to the rest of your document as you specify in the Apply To list box. You can choose Whole Document (applies your changes to the entire document) or This Point Forward (applies your changes to the current page and all pages that follow). The Preview window provides a visual representation of how the formatting changes appear when applied to the printed page.

Backgrounds are an aspect of formatting that can enhance the appearance of your documents. Word allows you to choose a color that you want to appear as the background for the entire document. This can come in handy if you wish to save your file as an HTML file for the creation of a web page. (For more on Word and the Web, see Chapter 11.)

To add a background to your document, choose Background from the Format menu. You are then presented with a pallet from which you can make your selection to apply the color as a background for the entire document.

The options that appear in the Layout tab of the Page Setup dialog box are covered in detail in the "Section Formatting" section. The next few sections describe the other tabs in this dialog box.

The Margins tab

In the Margins tab (see Figure 3-11), you can enter a numeric value to determine the distance between the top of the page and the first printed line or between the bottom of the page and the last printed line. You can also enter a numeric value to determine the distance between the left edge of the paper and the left edge of the printed lines, or between the right edge of the paper and the right edge of the printed lines. (Remember that any indents that you give paragraphs will be added to this amount.) Note that when you turn on the Mirror Margins option, the names of these options change to Inside and Outside.

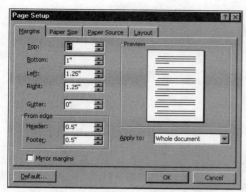

Figure 3-11: The Margins tab of the Page Setup dialog box.

Turn on Mirror Margins to force margins on facing pages to mirror each other. You should use this option when you want to print on both sides of a page. With this option turned on, inside margins will have the same width as outside margins. You can also enter a numeric value to determine the width of an optional gutter, an additional white space that is allowed when a document is to be bound.

If you choose the From Edge option, you can enter or choose the distance from the top and bottom edge of the page to the header and footer. Word measures the distance from the top edge of the header and the bottom edge of the footer to the page edges.

In the Apply To list box, you can choose Whole Document to apply the changes to the entire document, or you can choose This Point Forward to apply the changes to all text following the current location of the insertion point.

The Paper Size tab

In the Paper Size tab (see Figure 3-12), you can select a desired paper size from the list box. The available choices are Letter, Legal, Executive, A4 (European), No. 10, DL, six different envelope sizes, or Custom Size. When you use Custom Size as a paper size, you can enter the desired width and height for the paper size in the Width and Height boxes, or you can use the arrow buttons at the right edge of the text boxes to dial in the desired values. In the Orientation list box, you can choose the orientation desired (Portrait or Landscape).

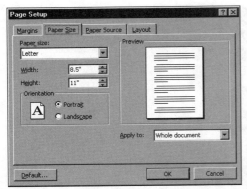

Figure 3-12: The Paper Size tab of the Page Setup dialog box.

The Paper Source tab

The options that appear in the Paper Source tab of the Page Setup dialog box are First Page and Other Pages (see Figure 3-13). Use either of these options to determine which bin of your printer is used to supply paper for the first printed page and for remaining pages. (If your printer does not support multiple-bin printing, you will not be able to select these options.)

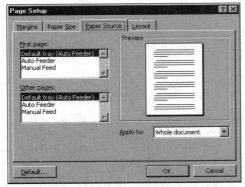

Figure 3-13: The Paper Source tab of the Page Setup dialog box.

A word about styles

Like most programs under Windows, Word gives you more than one way to accomplish the same task. Character, paragraph, and page formatting are known as *direct formatting* options. Another way to control formatting is with *styles*. When you use styles, you apply a group of formatting settings to an entire document. As an example, if a certain style defines indented paragraphs, and you apply that style to a document, that document's paragraphs will be indented. Chapter 8 explores the use of styles.

Section Formatting

Sections are portions of documents that carry formatting characteristics independent of other sections in the same document. Section formatting isn't required; by default, Word treats an entire document as a single section. By giving you the power to add multiple sections to a document, Word gives you a way to apply different formatting settings to each section. At first, the concept of sections may be difficult to understand because so many word processors apply formatting to characters, lines, or entire pages. Knowledge of how sections operate in Word is worth the effort because sections add flexibility to how a document can be formatted. If you have used older versions of Word for DOS or powerful desktop publishing software such as Corel's Ventura Publisher or Aldus's PageMaker, the concept of formatting in sections will be more familiar to you. (Older versions of Word for DOS use *divisions,* which are equivalent to sections under Word for Windows. Like Word for Windows, the last versions of Word for DOS use sections.)

Typically, you use section formatting when you want to change the number of columns or the style of page numbering for a section of the document. Changes that affect all pages of a document, such as page margins, are part of page formatting.

Even in a very short document, you are still using sections, although you may not give them any thought. In a short document (such as a one-page memo), the entire document consists of a single section, so you can use Word's section formatting commands to control certain elements of its layout.

If you want to apply a specific set of formatting to a section, select the text and choose File⇨Page Setup. In the Page Setup dialog box, click on the Layout tab (see Figure 3-14). In the Apply To list box, you can see Selected Text, the default option. In this tab, you can control the section breaks for a document, headers and footers, and vertical alignment.

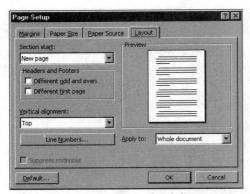

Figure 3-14: The Layout tab of the Page Setup dialog box.

To control the section breaks in a document, select an option in the Section Start list box. Here, you can control where you want the section to begin and where the preceding section should end.

✦ **Continuous** — This option causes the selected section to immediately follow the preceding section, without a page break.

✦ **New Column** — This option starts printing the selected section's text at the top of the next column.

✦ **New Page** — This option breaks the page at the section break.

✦ **Even Page** — This option starts the selected section at the next even-numbered page.

✦ **Odd Page** — This option starts the selected section at the next odd-numbered page.

The Layout tab also lets you control vertical alignment. *Vertical alignment* is the spacing of a document from the top to the bottom of the page. The document can be vertically centered to the top, centered, or justified. You can also add line numbers by clicking on the Line Numbers button and turning on the Add Line Numbering option in the dialog box that appears (see Figure 3-15). You can apply line numbers to the whole document or only to a selected section.

You can apply line numbers in various ways: they can start at the beginning of the document and go to the end, they can start at a specified line or section, they can begin from line 1 at the start of each new page, or they can begin at a specified number on the selected page. Line numbers are useful in legal documents where you may need to examine a specific line of a contract or other legal document.

Figure 3-15: The Line Numbers dialog box.

Headers and Footers

Word for Windows also makes it easy to add headers and footers to a document. A *header* is text or a graphic that is printed at the top of every page in a document; a *footer* is text or a graphic that is printed at the bottom of every page. Headers and footers can also be different for odd and even pages.

You can create headers and footers by choosing the View⇨Header and Footer command. Word switches to Page Layout view, and the Header and Footer toolbar appears, as shown in Figure 3-16. You can switch between headers and footers by clicking on the Switch Between Header and Footer button (the first button) on the toolbar, or you can scroll up or down the document with the vertical scroll bar.

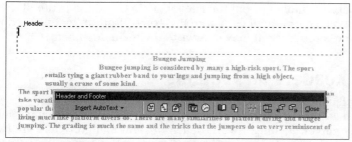

Figure 3-16: The Header and Footer toolbar in Page Layout view.

You type and format text in headers and footers the same way you type text in a normal document. After entering the characters that you want for your header or footer, click on the Close button, and Word displays the dimmed entry in Page Layout view.

You can also enter page numbers, the date, and the time as a header or footer in a document. Click on the Page Numbers, Date, and Time buttons on the Header and

Footer toolbar. Remember, you can format the header or footer the same way you format normal text; therefore, if you want the time, page number, or date centered, you can do so just the way you center text in a document.

You may also want to use a different header or footer for the first page and for the odd and even pages. On the Layout tab of the Page Setup dialog box, click on the Different Odd and Even check box if you want to create different headers and footers for the odd and even pages of a document. If you want to create a different header or footer for the first page in a document, click on the Different First Page check box.

Deleting a header or footer

Deleting a header or footer is also a simple task. Choose the Header and Footer command from the View menu and then select the text that you want to delete in the header or footer. Press Delete or the Backspace key to remove the text. If you want to delete other headers or footers, click on the Show Next button on the Header and Footer toolbar to display the next header or footer. Then follow the steps to delete the text.

Adjusting margin settings

Headers and footers are printed in the top and bottom margins. If the header or footer is too large to fit in the margin, Word adjusts the top or bottom margin so that the header or footer will fit. If you don't want Word to adjust the margins, choose the Page Setup command from the File menu. In the Margins tab of the Page Setup dialog box, enter a hyphen before the Top or Bottom margin setting. If the header or footer is too large, it may overwrite the main document.

Positioning headers and footers

You may want to adjust the position of your headers and footers in your document. You can adjust the horizontal position by centering it, running it into the left or right margin, or aligning it with the left or right margin. There are two preset tabs in the header and footer areas. One is centered between the left and right margins, and one is right aligned at the default right margin. You can use these tabs to place a page number flush right and to center text in the headers and footers. (If you change the margins, you may also want to adjust the tab stops.)

For a left-aligned header or footer, type the text where the cursor first appears in the text box. For a centered header or footer, tab once to the center and begin typing. You may also use the alignment buttons on the Formatting toolbar to center, left align, right align, or justify your headers or footers. If you want to add a negative indent to your header or footer, drag the indent markers on the ruler or use the Paragraph command from the Format menu to place a negative indent in your header or footer. (Remember, you need to select the header or footer before using the Paragraph command.)

You can adjust the vertical position of the header or footer by adjusting the distance of the footer from the top or bottom of the page. Simply click on the Page Setup button on the Headers and Footers toolbar. Then select the Margins tab and make the necessary changes by typing or selecting the distance that you want from the edge of the paper.

You can also adjust the space between the header or footer and the main document. Go to the header or footer that you want to adjust. Move your pointer to the vertical ruler at the left of your screen and point to the top or bottom margin boundary. The pointer becomes a double-headed arrow. If you want to reduce the space between the top of the document text and the header, simply drag the top margin boundary up or down. To adjust the space between the bottom of the document text and the footer, drag the bottom margin boundary up or down.

Page Numbers

Inserting page numbers is one of the easiest of all formatting jobs. Choose Insert⇨Page Numbers to bring up the Page Numbers dialog box shown in Figure 3-17.

Figure 3-17: The Page Numbers dialog box.

In this dialog box, you can change the position and the alignment of page numbers by using the corresponding list boxes. If you press the Format button, you open the Page Number Format dialog box. This dialog box lets you change the number format. For example, you may want to use letters instead of numbers or roman numerals. You also can add chapter numbers to your document, but you have to tell Word where a new chapter begins. To indicate where a new chapter begins, use the Chapter Starts With Style list box, which causes Word to look for the style that is designated as the chapter heading for each chapter. You also have the option of numbering from a previous section if you don't want to number the entire document. And finally, you can ask Word to start numbering from a specific page.

Footnotes

Word's capability to display multiple portions of a document simultaneously makes adding footnotes to a Word document a simple matter. You can look at and work with the text of a footnote in a separate pane, while the related portion of your document remains visible. Word, like most word processors, lets you position footnotes either at the bottom of each page or collectively at the end of the document. (When footnotes are placed at the end of a document, they are called endnotes.) However, in Word you can also put a footnote directly beneath the text to which it applies or at the end of a section.

To add a footnote, first place the insertion point where the footnote reference mark (such as a superscript number) is to appear in the text. Then choose the Insert⇨Footnote command to bring up the Footnote and Endnote dialog box shown in Figure 3-18.

Figure 3-18: The Footnote and Endnote dialog box.

In this dialog box, you can specify whether you want the footnote to be automatically numbered by Word (the default), or you can enter a reference mark of your own choosing, such as an asterisk or a number in parentheses. The Options button displays another dialog box that lets you control the placement of footnotes and the number format that you want.

Word also has the option for choosing the symbol you wish to appear as your default foot or endnote indicator. At the Footnote and Endnote dialog box select the Symbol button. This opens the Symbol dialog box shown in Figure 3-19. Here you can select a font for the symbol. If there is a subset for the font, the Subset list box will appear and provide you more choices for the symbol you wish to use to indicate a foot or endnote.

Figure 3-19: The Symbol dialog box.

After you click on OK, a footnote pane opens in the bottom portion of the screen (Figure 3-20) where you type the desired footnote. When the footnote pane is open, a split bar appears in the vertical scroll bar. Mouse users can drag the split bar up or down to change the size of the pane. At any time when you are working with footnotes, you can return to the main part of the document while leaving the footnote pane open. Press F6 (Next Pane). When you are finished typing the footnote, you can drag the split bar to close the footnote pane or click on the Close button. You can see footnotes in your document only if you are in Page Layout view.

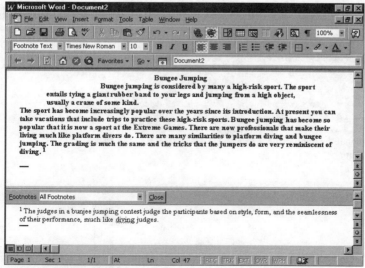

Figure 3-20: The footnote pane.

Try adding a footnote to the sample document that you created earlier in the chapter or to a paragraph of your own choosing. After you create the footnote, the following sections will show you how to edit and delete the footnote text, position both the reference marks and the footnotes themselves, and define the separator line at the bottom of the page. Follow these steps to add a footnote to a document:

1. Switch to Normal view and put the insertion point at the end of a paragraph. You can use the bungee jumping document you created earlier, or you can use a document of your own choosing. If you use the chess document, place the insertion point at the end of the second full paragraph of text.

2. Choose Insert⇨Footnote.

3. To accept automatic numbering for footnotes, choose OK from the dialog box. Word places a superscript reference number at the end of the paragraph in the document and opens the footnote pane for the footnote text.

4. Type the following text in the footnote pane:

   The judges in a bungee jumping contest judge the participants on style, form, and the seamlessness of their performances, much like diving judges.

5. Click on the Close button or use the Alt+V+F shortcut to close the footnote pane. (This shortcut acts like a toggle switch to open and close the footnote window.)

If you have used the sample document for your exercise, your footnote should look like the one in Figure 3-21.

Hot Stuff You can return to the document and keep the footnote pane open by pressing F3.

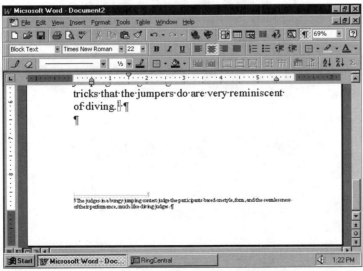

Figure 3-21: A footnote added to end of a sample document in Page Layout view.

Editing existing footnotes

To edit an existing footnote, open the footnote pane with the View⇨Footnotes command. Scroll within the footnote pane to find the desired footnote and edit it as you would regular text.

Hot Stuff
You can quickly jump from footnote to footnote with the Go To key (F5). Press F5 and click on Footnote in the Go to What list box. Then use the Next and Previous buttons to jump through the footnotes until you find the one that you want, or enter the footnote number in the Footnote Number box and click on OK to go to that footnote.

Moving and deleting footnotes

Footnotes are indicated by the reference marks in the document, so moving or deleting a footnote is as easy as moving or deleting the reference mark.

✦ To move a footnote, select the reference mark within the document and move it to the desired new location.

✦ To delete a footnote, select the reference mark and press Delete or use Edit⇨Cut. If you used Word's automatic footnote numbering, the footnotes are renumbered accordingly. If you numbered footnotes manually, you need to renumber them yourself as necessary.

Exploring footnote options

In the Footnote and Endnote dialog box is the Options button. After you click on this button, the Note Options dialog box appears, as shown in Figure 3-22. Click on the All Footnotes tab to choose options that apply to footnotes, or click on the All Endnotes tab to choose options that apply to endnotes.

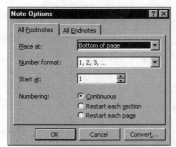

Figure 3-22: The Note Options dialog box.

The Place At list box in the All Footnotes tab lets you determine the placement of the footnotes. You can choose between Bottom of Page or Beneath Text. Select Bottom of Page to place the footnotes for a given page at the bottom of that page. The Beneath Text choice places the footnote directly after the text containing the footnote reference mark.

The Number Format list box lets you choose the type of numbers that you want to use for the footnotes. The Start At box lets you change the starting number for automatically numbered footnotes. If you want Word to restart the automatic numbering each time a new section begins, turn on the Restart Each Section option in the Numbering area.

Changing footnotes to endnotes

Changing all your footnotes (or just one footnote) to endnotes is easy. Activate the footnote window by choosing the Footnotes command from the View menu. Select the footnotes that you want to convert to endnotes by moving the cursor to the beginning of each. Right-click in the footnote pane to open the shortcut menu. You will notice two new menu options: Go to Footnote and Convert to Endnote. Choose Convert to Endnote to convert the footnote to an endnote. Now, to see the kind of note you want, choose it from the Notes box in the footnote window.

You can also copy and move a footnote by using the regular Cut, Copy, and Paste commands or by clicking and dragging it to its new location. You can delete a footnote by highlighting the reference mark and pressing Delete.

Summary

In this chapter, you have read about all sorts of formatting techniques that you will use often if you work in Word on a regular basis. The chapter covered these points:

- ✦ In Word, you can apply formatting to characters, paragraphs, pages, or sections of a document.

- ✦ To apply formatting to characters, you can use the various buttons of the Formatting toolbar that apply to character formatting, or you can use the Format⇨Font command.

- ✦ To apply formatting to paragraphs, you can use the various buttons of the Formatting toolbar that apply to paragraph formatting, or you can use the Format⇨Paragraph command.

- ✦ You can apply borders and shadings to paragraphs by using the Format⇨Borders and Shading command.

✦ You can change most aspects of page formatting through the various tabs of the Page Setup dialog box. To display the dialog box, use the File➪Page Setup command.

✦ Section formatting can also be applied through the use of the File➪Page Setup command, by using the options that appear under the Layout tab of the resulting Page Setup dialog box.

✦ You can add headers and footers to a document with the View➪Header and Footer command.

✦ You can add footnotes and endnotes to a document with the Insert➪Footnote command.

Where to go next...

✦ Now that you've explored so many aspects of document formatting, you're probably anxious to try printing some examples of your work. Chapter 4 will set you right up.

✦ You can make many common formatting tasks easier by applying *styles* to portions of your document. You'll find details in Chapter 8.

✦   ✦   ✦

Previewing and Printing Your Documents

T his chapter details how you print your documents and how you can preview them prior to printing. Keep in mind that your printer must be set up and ready before you can print documents — an obvious point, maybe, but many printer problems can be traced to an incorrect printer setup or to a printer that was never turned on.

Printing in the Background

If you just have one printer connected to your computer (and you know it works with other Windows applications), you can print a single copy of any document in Word with one simple action: a mouse click on the Print button on the Standard toolbar. (The Print button is ridiculously easy to find: it's the only one with a picture of a printer on it.) When you open any document and click on the Print button, Word sends one copy of the document to the printer. As the document is processed by the built-in Windows Print Manager, the status bar in Word displays the progress of the printing process. Note that by default, Word prints in the background and creates an image of the document on disk that can be sent to the printer when the printer is ready to receive data. So unless you're printing to a network laser printer that is the size of a compact car (one of those big, *fast* models), Word is likely to finish the printing process long before your printer does.

If your system doesn't print in the background — instead, it waits until the printing is finished before it frees Word to do something else — you can change the system. Choose Tools⇨Options, click on the Print tab, turn on the Background Printing option, and click on the OK button. Your system will print in the background.

Previewing Documents

The Print Preview command from the File menu (and the Print Preview button on the Standard toolbar) lets you see on your screen what a document will look like when you print it (see Figure 4-1). Print Preview saves trees: you don't waste paper printing draft copies before printing a final copy. Print Preview shows footnotes, headers, footers, page numbers, multiple columns, and graphics. You can view more than one page at a time by clicking on the Multiple Pages button on the Print Preview toolbar and selecting the number of pages that you want to see at one time. You can easily move between pages, but you cannot edit a document while in Print Preview mode.

Figure 4-1: A document as it appears in the Print Preview window.

Understanding the Print Preview toolbar

After entering Print Preview mode, the Print Preview toolbar (Figure 4-2) appears. It provides useful options when you are in Print Preview mode. Click on the appropriate button to perform a task, as outlined in Table 4-1.

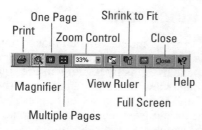

Figure 4-2: The Print Preview toolbar.

Table 4-1	
Print Preview toolbar buttons	

Button	Function
Print	Click on this button to print the document.
Magnifier	Lets you magnify a certain section of your document that you may want to make larger.
One Page	Lets you see the current page in Print Preview mode.
Multiple Pages	Lets you see up to six pages at once on-screen. These pages appear so that you can see the layout of each page.
Zoom Control	Lets you control the distance at which you see the pages on the Print Preview window.
View Ruler	Lets you see a ruler for each of the pages that you have on-screen so that you can move the margins in Print Preview mode.
Shrink to Fit	Lets you shrink information so that it will all fit on one page. This feature helps you keep paragraphs together.
Full Screen	Lets you see your document in Full Screen mode.
Close	Returns you to Normal view.
Help	Provides online help for your printing questions.

Hot Stuff A quick way out of Print Preview mode is to press the Esc key.

Many commands from the normal Word menus are not available when you are in Print Preview mode. These commands appear dimmed on the menus. Remember that you cannot open files or change windows while you are in Print Preview mode.

Adjusting margins and object locations

Although you cannot edit documents in Print Preview mode, you can make changes to some aspects of the document, such as the location of page margins, headers, and footers. You can easily make changes to page margins by turning on the ruler. Choose View➪Ruler. (Note: If you are in Full Page view, moving the mouse to the top of the screen will bring the menu choices into view.) Then select the text by clicking on the Magnifier icon to change to the arrow. Next, click and drag to select the text you wish to highlight. Now, move the triangles on the ruler until the document takes on the appearance that you want. You can also use clicking and dragging techniques to move graphics in your document while you are in Print Preview mode. Don't forget that you can also right-click on the highlighted text to see a shortcut menu that will allow you to cut, paste, make font changes, add paragraph modifications, add bullets and numbering, and draw tables.

If you inserted an object, such as a picture, into your document, you may want to frame it so that you can drag it to any location while you are in Print Preview. To frame the object while you are in Print Preview, first click on the Magnifier button to turn off the magnifier and then right-click on the picture that you want to frame. Choose Format Picture from the shortcut menu. From the Format Picture dialog box, shown in Figure 4-3, choose the Colors and Lines tab. Choose the type of frame lines desired. When you do so, the frame appears around the picture.

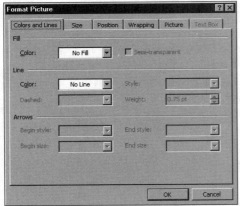

Figure 4-3: The Colors and Lines tab of the Format Picture dialog box.

If the text does not wrap around the frame, it means that text wrapping is not turned on. Right-click on the frame and choose Format Picture from the shortcut menu. Next, choose the Wrapping tab as shown in Figure 4-4. Choose the type of wrapping desired from the diagrams, and the text then will wrap accordingly.

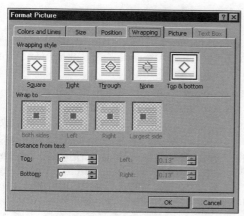

Figure 4-4: The Wrapping Tab of the Format Picture Box.

You can use the Distance from text section of the Wrapping tab to control the distance of the text from the picture. This section of the tab will allow you to adjust the distance from all sides of the picture. Simply adjust the numbers in the top, bottom, left, and right sections of the Distance from text section.

Printing a Document

Any word processor lets you print a document, but Word gives you more: you can print selected portions of a document; multiple copies of a document; and other information related to a document, such as summary information, annotations, AutoText entries, or style sheets. You can print documents by choosing File⇔Print. The Print dialog box appears, as shown in Figure 4-5.

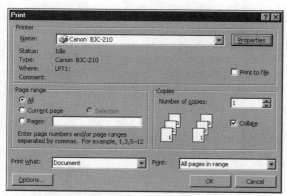

Figure 4-5: The Print dialog box.

The available options in the Print dialog box include:

Note✦ **Printer** — The Printer list box lets you choose the default printer that you want to use by selecting it from the entries. After making a selection, Word provides you with the status and location of the printer.

If you don't see the printer that you want to use in the list box, you need to install it. Consult your Windows documentation for the steps.

✦ **Copies** — In the Copies area, you can enter the number of copies that you want printed in the Number of copies list box (the default is 1). This area also lets you collate copies. When you check the Collate option for more than one copy of a document, Word prints all the pages of each document before it goes on to the next set. If you do not check this option, Word prints all needed copies of page 1, followed by all copies of page 2, followed by all copies of page 3, and so on.

✦ **Page range** — In the Page range area, you can choose which portion of the document should be printed. To print the entire document, choose All; to print a selection of text, choose Selection; to print just the current page, choose Current page; or to print selected pages of a document, choose Pages to print.

Hot Stuff You can print a range of pages by separating the starting and ending pages with a hyphen. For example, entering **7-12** in the box will print pages 7 through 12 of the document. You can also separate numbers by commas to print individual pages. For example, entering **3,5,8,10-12** in the box will cause pages 3, 5, 8, and 10 through 12 to print.

✦ **Print** — In the Print list box, you can choose All Pages in Range to print all the pages in the chosen print range (as selected in the Page range area of the dialog box). You can also choose to print only the odd pages or only the even pages in the range.

✦ **Options** — You can click on the Options button to display additional options relating to printing (see the "Using the Print Options" section later in this chapter).

✦ **Properties** — The Properties button opens the Printer Properties dialog box shown in Figure 4-6 (the dialog box in this figure will look a little different from yours unless you have the same printer we do). In this dialog box, you can set different options for your printer. The properties in this dialog box will be different for each printer.

✦ **Print what** — Use this box to choose what to print. You can print key assignments, style sheets, summary information, annotations, AutoText entries, and other items related to your documents.

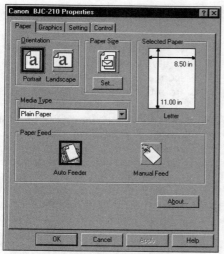

Figure 4-6: The Printer Properties dialog box for Canon BJC-210.

Note You can use the Print key combination (Ctrl+Shift+F12) rather than File ⇨ Print to open the Print dialog box and to make your printing selections. You can also press Ctrl+P to activate the Print dialog box; this is a useful time-saver if you wish to print quickly.

After you have chosen your desired options in the Print dialog box, click on the OK button to start printing.

Printing a portion of a document

You will encounter times when you want to print only a section of a document. You can choose between two methods to print a section of text. First, you can choose a starting and ending page number to print and enter the page numbers in the Pages text box in the Page range area of the Print dialog box. Word prints the starting and ending page and all pages in between. Or, you can first select a portion of text and then turn on the Selection option in the Page range area of the Print dialog box to print just that selection.

For a more detailed look at the steps involved in printing a section of a document, take a look at the steps that follow. To print selected pages of a document, perform the following steps:

1. With the document open, choose File⇨Print.

If you have problems...

If you have difficulty printing or if the printer name in the dialog box doesn't match the printer that is connected to your computer, choose File⇨Print and click on the name list box in the Printer field of the dialog box that appears. This opens the list of printers installed under Windows 95. Select the troublesome printer and then click on the OK button. Try the Print command again. If the correct printer is selected and you still can't print, the problem is either inside the printer itself, with how Windows 95 is set up on your system, or that the printer you wish to use is not installed under Windows 95.

If the printer you wish to use is not installed under Windows 95, perform the following steps:

1. From the Taskbar's Start menu, choose Settings, and then Printers.

2. In the window that appears, double-click on the Add Printers icon and follow the instructions from the Add Printer Wizard.

Word uses the Windows 95 Print Manager to manage all printing. If you can't print from another Windows application (such as WordPad), you can't print from Word, either. If you can't print from Windows, refer to your Windows documentation or the *Microsoft Word for Windows Printer Guide* (supplied with your Word documentation). Also, be sure to check the obvious: make sure that the printer is properly connected, turned on, and online. If you still can't find the source of the problem, you can find many helpful troubleshooting tips in the *Printer Guide*.

2. In the Page range area, click on the Current page radio button to print the current page, or click on the Pages radio button and enter the starting page number that you want to print. If you want to print consecutive page numbers, separate them with a hyphen. Nonconsecutive page numbers should be separated by a comma.

3. Click on the OK button. The selected pages of the document print.

To print a selection of text, perform the following steps:

1. Select the text that you want to print by using the usual methods for selecting text.

2. With the document open, choose File⇨Print.

3. Click on the Selection radio button.

4. Click on the OK button to print the selected text.

Printing more than documents

To print something other than the document itself, click on the down arrow of the Print what list box in the Print dialog box to reveal the list of options that you can print (see Figure 4-7). If you choose Document (the default), Word prints the document. If you choose Summary Info, Word prints just the summary information for the document. If you choose Annotations, Word prints all annotations stored in a document. If you choose Styles, Word prints the style sheet for the document. If you choose AutoText Entries, Word prints the template AutoText entries. If you choose Key Assignments, Word prints the names of macros and the keys to which they are assigned.

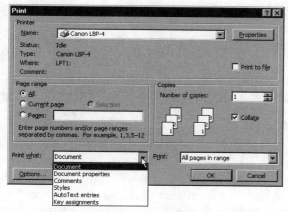

Figure 4-7: The Print what list box in the Print dialog box.

You can print summary information or annotations simultaneously with the printing of the document. See the "Using the Print Options" section later in this chapter for more information on how to print these items simultaneously.

Printing sideways

On occasion, you may want to print a document sideways, or in what is known as *landscape orientation*. Such a technique is particularly useful with very wide documents, such as those that contain a table of numbers or documents containing pictures. If your printer supports landscape printing, you can easily print documents that use landscape orientation.

To print a document in landscape orientation, choose File➪Page Setup and click on the Paper Size tab of the Page Setup dialog box. In the Orientation area, click on the Landscape radio button and then click on the OK button. Now you can print the document by choosing File➪Print. If no Landscape option appears in the Page Setup dialog box, your printer does not support landscape printing, and you cannot print sideways under Windows.

Hot Stuff When you are finished printing in landscape orientation, be sure to change your paper orientation back to normal (portrait) mode. If you do not make the change, all successive printings will be in landscape mode. To change back to portrait mode, choose File➪Page Setup and click on the Paper Size tab. Then click on the Portrait radio button in the Orientation area of the dialog box.

Using the Print Options

You can find additional printing options in the Print dialog box. These options enable you to include annotations or summary information with documents, to print in reverse order, and to print draft versions of documents. To use these options, choose File➪Print and then click on the Options button. The Options dialog box appears with the Print tab activated, as shown in Figure 4-8. To choose any of the desired options, click on the option or press the Alt key plus the underlined letter of the option name.

The Print tab options include the following:

✦ **Draft output** — When you choose the Draft Output option, Word prints a draft of your document. A *draft* is a document that is printed with minimal formatting. This would be a document where the character formatting is removed. This allows you to print your documents faster.

✦ **Update fields** — The Update Fields option makes Word update any fields that are in a document before it is printed.

✦ **Update links** — When you choose the Update Links option, Word updates any fields that are in a document before it is printed.

✦ **Background printing** — The Background Printing option lets you work in Word while you're printing. However, this option uses memory, so you may want to turn it off to speed up printing.

✦ **Reverse print order** — The Reverse Print Order option causes the document to be printed last page first. This option is helpful with laser printers that are based on the first-generation Canon engine (like the original Hewlett-Packard LaserJet). The design of such printers causes printed pages to come out face up, so a multiple-page document would be stacked with the last page on top (which is usually not where you want it). If you turn on the Reverse Print Order option, however, the print run starts with the last page and ends with the first page so that the printed document ends up in the proper order.

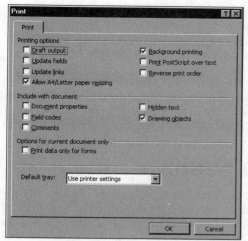

Figure 4-8: The Print tab of the Options dialog box.

✦ **Include with document** — Use the Include with Document options to specify which information should be included with the printed document. If you turn on Summary Info, a summary information sheet is printed along with the document. Turn on Field Codes to print field codes instead of the results of the fields. If you turn on Annotations, Word prints the document and any annotations added to the document. Turn on Hidden Text to print the document and any text that you hid with the Hidden option from the Character dialog box. Also, you will see the Drawing Objects check box. This will print the drawing objects you may have included in your document.

✦ **Options for current document only** — This area applies the options that you select to the current document but returns to the default options for the next print job. Print Data Only for Forms is used to print just the data for forms that may be in your documents.

✦ **Default tray** — The Default Tray list box lets you select different paper feed bins (assuming that your printer allows feeding from different paper bins). Actual choices depend upon the printer you have installed. Typical choices are these:

  • **Manual** — Choose Manual to make the printer draw paper from its manual bin.

  • **Auto** — Choose Auto for automatic paper feed.

  • **Bin 1, Bin 2, Bin 3** — Choose Bin 1, 2, or 3 to draw paper from a specific bin.

- **Mixed** — Choose Mixed to feed the first sheet from bin 1 and successive sheets from bin 2. Mixed feeding is a common technique with high-production office laser printers, which may have company letterhead stored in one bin and bond paper stored in another bin.

If the Default Tray option appears dimmed in your dialog box, your printer does not support feeding from multiple paper bins. From Print Manager is the default setting for this option. If you wish to change it, click on the arrow and choose one of the feeding options from the list.

Changing Your Printer Setup

Word provides access to the printer setup facility of Windows through File⇨Print. You can choose the default printer from among different printers. The Print dialog box lets you select a printer that is already installed under Windows in the name list box; however, you cannot use this dialog box to choose a printer that is not yet installed under Windows. (See your Windows documentation if you need to add a new printer to your Windows configuration.)

Note   Only one printer can use the same connection (*printer port*) at a time. If you change printers and the new printer is connected to the same printer port, you must use the Windows Control Panel to change the printer connection. To change the setting, choose Settings from the Start menu and then choose Control Panel. Double-click on the Printers icon. Right-click on the printer for which you want to change the port. Then choose Properties from the shortcut menu and select the Details tab (see Figure 4-9). In this tab, you can change the port for the printer. See your Windows documentation for more details. (Remember that the actual appearance of this dialog box depends upon the printer you're using.)

If you want only to change printers, you can do so from the Print dialog box if the printer is already installed. Choose File⇨Print. In the Print dialog box, click on the arrow in the Name list box to open the menu of available printers. Choose the printer that you want and then click on the OK button to print the document. If you click on the Properties button in the Print dialog box, you will see the printing options for the new printer. Figure 4-10 shows the Paper tab, which shows some of the printing options for a Canon BJC-210 printer. These options vary, depending on the type of printer that you have installed. Because literally hundreds of printers are on the market, it is impossible to explain all the possible settings here. Each printer's dialog box contains the options that are applicable to that particular printer. What's more, most dialog boxes contain buttons for choosing between portrait (the default) and landscape printing.

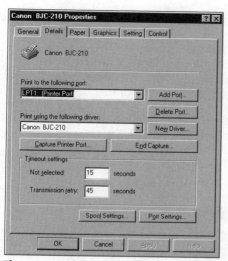

Figure 4-9: The Details tab of the Printer Properties dialog box.

Figure 4-10: The Paper tab options for a Canon BJC-210.

If you are using a laser printer that employs font cartridges, you can select the fonts from a list box in the Print Setup dialog box. Refer to the *Microsoft Word for Windows Printer Guide* to determine the fonts that you can use with your particular laser printer.

Printing Envelopes

Word has an envelope-printing feature that makes printing envelopes a very simple matter if your printer is able to handle envelopes. Choose Tools⇨Envelopes and Labels to open the Envelopes and Labels dialog box (see Figure 4-11). In this dialog box, you are provided with two text boxes where you can enter a delivery and return address. In the Return Address text box, Word enters, by default, the name stored under the User Info tab of the Options dialog box. If you want to change the kind of envelope that you are printing, click on the envelope in the Preview window, or click on the Options button to open the Envelope Options dialog box shown in Figure 4-12.

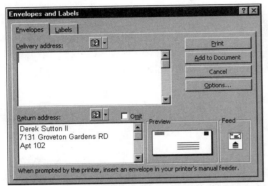

Figure 4-11: The Envelopes and Labels dialog box.

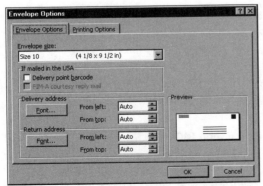

Figure 4-12: The Envelope Options dialog box.

The Envelope Options dialog box contains two tabs. The Envelope Options tab lets you change the kind of envelope that you are printing, add delivery point bar codes and courtesy facing ID marks, format the delivery and return addresses, and control the positioning of the text on the envelope. The Printing Options tab of the Envelope Options dialog box lets you control the way envelopes are printed (see Figure 4-13). You can choose either a horizontal or a vertical feed method. You can also change the way envelopes are fed into your printer, whether you use a manual tractor, an upper or lower tray, and so on.

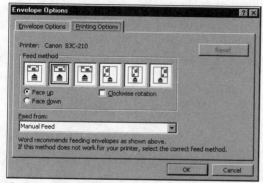

Figure 4-13: The Printing Options tab of the Envelope Options dialog box.

After you have made all the necessary formatting changes and you have specified the size of the envelope that you want to print, you are ready to print the envelope. Click on the Print button in the Envelopes and Labels dialog box, and your envelope prints.

Summary

In this chapter, you learned how to examine the appearance of documents before you print them and then how you can print the documents in Word. The following points were covered:

✦ Choosing File⇨Print Preview provides a useful way to see what a document will look like before it is printed.

✦ You can quickly print one copy of any document by clicking on the Print button on the Standard toolbar.

✦ Using the options shown in the Print dialog box, you can print portions of the document, and you can print other items (such as annotations, styles, macros, and keyboard assignments).

In the next chapter, you will learn how to work with tables and outlines in Word.

Where to go next...

✦ Macros let you automate the printing of documents you print regularly. Chapter 9 gives you the lowdown on macros.

✦ The appearance of your printed document depends on how your document is formatted. Chapter 3 helps you format your documents.

✦   ✦   ✦

Working with Tables and Outlines

Tables are a common feature of business correspondence, but tables in word processing documents have had a reputation for being hard to implement and extremely difficult to modify. These negative characteristics of tables are no longer true with Word's Table feature. Word's Table feature makes it a simple matter to insert tables containing varying amounts of text or graphics.

Outlines are also an important organizational aid in Word. For many who work with words, creating an outline is the first step in putting their thoughts on paper. If you've been working with something less than the power of Word in the past, you may be accustomed to creating outlines by means of tabs and manually typed headings. With Word, there's no need to stay in the Stone Age: Word's automatic outlining enables you automatically to number headings and create tables of contents based on the outline headings.

Understanding Tables in Word for Windows

A *table* is any grouping of information arranged in rows and columns, as illustrated in Figure 5-1. Tables have two or more columns and one or more rows. Each intersection of a row and a column is a *cell* of the table. If you are familiar with computer spreadsheets, such as Excel, you should easily understand the concept of a cell.

Group 1	Group2	Group3
Michael Wagner	Dirk Johnson	John Colwill
Dianne Sharp	Mary Richard	Nicole Morgan
Jason Comer	Robert Moore	Falicia Schlick

Figure 5-1: A sample table.

Before Word's Table feature came along, people typically set up tables by using tabs or indented paragraphs. Although this method works, it is very cumbersome and, well, just awkward. A table set up with tabs can be tricky to design when some cells in the table contain more than one line of text. You have to add all sorts of manual tabs to line up the information on-screen, and then you have no guarantees that the table will line up when you print it! Worse, any changes that you make to the table's text will also throw off the alignment of the tabs so that you have to constantly rework the table. Manually creating a table is more trouble than it is worth.

In comparison, Word's Table feature creates a group of cells that expands as needed to fit all your required text or graphics. The only limit to the size of your table is that a single cell cannot be larger than a page. You can resize columns and cells, and you can add rows, columns, and cells. Word also provides useful commands that make life easier when you need to edit the tables. All in all, Word's Table feature is the best way for you to create a table.

By default, a table appears with gridlines surrounding the cells. If you do not see the gridlines surrounding the tables that you create, choose Table⇨Gridlines to turn on the gridlines. Gridlines do not print in your document; they are simply an aid for entering and editing text in tables. You can also add borders (which do appear when printed) to cells or to an entire table (see "Formatting Tables" later in the chapter).

Creating Tables

You can add a table to a document by choosing Table⇨Insert Table or by clicking on the Insert Table button on the Standard toolbar. When you choose the Insert Table command, the Insert Table dialog box appears, as shown in Figure 5-2.

In the Number of Columns text box, you enter the desired number of columns for the table. Word proposes 2, but you can enter any value up to 31. If you are not sure how many columns you will need, don't worry. You can add columns at any time by selecting the column to the right of the table and then choosing the Insert Columns command from the Table menu or clicking on the Insert Columns button on the Standard toolbar.

Figure 5-2: The Insert Table dialog box.

In the Number of Rows text box, enter the desired number of rows for the table. It is very easy to add rows as you need them by choosing Table⇨Insert Rows, or by clicking on the Insert Rows button on the Standard toolbar. (When the insertion point is in a table, the Insert Table button on the toolbar changes to an Insert Rows button. When a column is selected, the button changes to an Insert Columns button.) Thus, if you are not sure how many rows you need, you should enter the minimum number of rows because you can always add more later.

In the Column Width text box, you can leave the setting at Auto, which is the default, or you can enter a decimal measurement for the width of the columns. If you use Auto, Word makes all columns an equal width. How to make columns of differing widths is discussed later.

You may have noticed that this dialog box contains a Wizard button. The Table Wizard takes you through a series of dialog boxes that help determine the table that you need. The wizard then adds the table to your document. Using the Table Wizard is a nice, quick, and easy way to make standard tables with attractive formatting in them.

You can create a table by following these steps:

1. Place the insertion point at the desired location for the table in your document.

2. Choose Table⇨Insert Table or click on the Insert Table button on the Standard toolbar.

3. Enter the number of columns desired in the Number of Columns text box and enter the number of rows desired in the Number of Rows text box.

4. Enter the desired column width in the Column Width text box (or accept the Auto default).

5. If you want to have borders or other formatting added to your table, you can click on the AutoFormat button in the dialog box. In the Table AutoFormat dialog box, you can choose from a wide range of effects for your chart (see "Formatting Tables" later in this chapter). You can apply predefined lines, borders, and shading to different sections of the table.

6. When you are finished making your selections, click on the OK button in the dialog box to add the table at the insertion point location.

After you have created a table, you can type the desired data into each cell. You can move forward from cell to cell in the table by using the Tab key; you can move in reverse by using the Shift+Tab combination. If you reach the end of a table and press Tab, you add a new row to the table. The arrow keys will also move the insertion point within the table, and you can use these keys to move into and out of a table. With the mouse, you can click in any cell to place the insertion point in that cell. For a complete summary of the keys used for navigation in tables, see the section "Navigating with the keyboard."

A second way to create a table is by the use of Word's intuitive Draw table feature. This actually allows you to draw a table in your document using the mouse. Word will do its best estimate of the measurements for the cell sizes. To create a table using the Draw table feature of Word, click on the Tables and Borders Button on the Standard Toolbar, or choose Draw Table from the Table menu. The mouse pointer then becomes a pencil. Click and drag to draw the table as you wish it to appear. You can create the cells within the table by drawing horizontal and vertical lines where desired. Again keep in mind that if you are not sure how many cells you will need, you can always add cells and columns to the table as needed by drawing additional lines. If you find after you have drawn the table that you need to remove some of the cells or lines, you can press and hold the Shift key and then use the mouse to erase the lines in the table. Keep in mind that if you use the draw table feature you will not see the Insert Table dialog box shown earlier in Figure 5-2.

Navigating with the mouse

Navigating inside a table with the mouse works in the same way as navigating in regular text: you point and click at the location where you want the insertion point to be. However, you need to know some additional mouse techniques beyond the obvious. Tables provide special selection areas for mouse use. At the left edge of each cell is a selection bar, an area where the mouse pointer changes to an arrow pointing upward and to the right. If you click on the left edge of a cell while the pointer is shaped like this arrow, you will select the entire cell. You can also double-click in any cell's selection bar to select the entire row of the table. You can also click and drag across cell boundaries to select a group of cells.

At the top of a table is a column selection area. If you place the mouse pointer above the border at the top of the table, the pointer changes to the shape of a downward-pointing arrow, which indicates the column selection mode. If you click while the pointer is shaped like the downward-pointing arrow, you select the entire column below the pointer.

So, how can I type a tab?

Because you use the Tab key to move around within a table, you can't use the Tab key to enter a Tab character. In some ways, this is good because tabs inside tables are dangerous. In the first place, you don't have much horizontal space in the cells to play with. In the second place, the tabs may mess up your overall formatting for the table. Nevertheless, if you must have a tab character inside a table, you can add one by pressing Ctrl+Tab.

Hot Stuff

Easily selecting rows and columns with the mouse is a handy technique to know when you have to format portions of your table. You can select the desired cells, rows, or columns and then use Format⇨Font and Format⇨Paragraph to format your text in those selected cells as desired.

Navigating with the keyboard

To move from cell to cell within a table, you can click on the desired cell with the mouse, or you can use the Tab key (to move forward through cells) or the Shift+Tab combination (to move in reverse). Within a single cell, you can use the same keys that you use to navigate in any Word document. Table 5-1 summarizes the keys that you use to navigate within a table.

Table 5-1
Navigation keys to use within tables

Key	Purpose
Tab	Moves the cursor to the next cell in the table. If the cursor is in the last cell in the table, the Tab key adds a new row and moves the cursor to the first cell of the new row.
Shift+Tab	Moves the cursor to the preceding cell.
Alt+Home	Moves the cursor to the first cell in a row.
Alt+End	Moves the cursor to the last cell in a row.
Alt+PgUp	Moves the cursor to the top cell in a column.
Alt+PgDn	Moves the cursor to the bottom cell in a column.
Alt+NumLock+5	Selects the entire table.

(continued)

Table 5-1 *(continued)*

Key	Purpose
Shift	Activates the eraser if you used the draw table feature, and you can then use the eraser to erase unwanted lines.
Arrow keys	Moves the cursor within the text in a cell and between cells. If the insertion point is at the edge of a table, you can use the arrow keys to move in or out of the table.

If you press Tab while the insertion point is in the last cell of a table, a new row is automatically added, and Word places the insertion point in the first cell of the new row. You can add new rows by choosing Table➪Insert Rows or by clicking on the Insert Rows button on the Standard tool bar, but it is generally easier to add new rows as needed by using the Tab key.

Cells can contain mucho texto . . .

One useful aspect of cells that may not be readily apparent is that you can have more than a single paragraph of text in a cell. At the end of any paragraph in a cell, you can press Return and keep right on typing. The cell expands as needed to accommodate the text. Longtime users of Word for Windows have often taken advantage of this design trait to create side-by-side columns of unequal size, even though newer versions of Word (like yours) offer specific commands for handling multiple-column documents. You can also format every paragraph in a table just like paragraphs that are not in cells of a table; you can assign your paragraphs indentation settings, alignments, line spacing, and the like.

Creating your own table

To get some practice in setting up a table, entering information, and revising a table, follow along with this next exercise. You can also create your own table with your own data if you want. Follow these steps to create a sample table:

1. Begin a new document by clicking on the New button on the Standard toolbar. Type the following phrase and press Enter to begin a new paragraph:

   Food arrangements for Paul's visit with us

2. Choose Table➪Insert Table (or click on the Tables and Borders button, or choose Draw Table from the Table menu).

3. In the Number of Columns text box, enter **4**. (Again, if you use the Draw table method you will not see this dialog box.)

4. Tab to or click in the Number of Rows text box and enter **6**. For now, you can leave the remaining options as they are.

5. Click on the OK button. The new table containing six rows and four columns appears. The insertion point is in the first cell.

6. Enter the information shown in Figure 5-3. Use the Tab key to advance to each new cell. (Do not press the Enter key to advance to a new cell because the Enter key cannot move you out of a cell.)

Notice that as you enter the information shown in the table, the text in the rightmost column will often be too long to fit on a single line. When this happens, the cell expands in size automatically. This example illustrates one advantage of Word's Table feature: you do not need to calculate the space that you need between rows of a table because Word does this automatically. You can enter as little or as much text as you want in a cell (up to the limit of one page in size).

Day	Who	What	Where
Monday	Gina and Kitty	Salads	Garden Oasis of Mill Valley
Tuesday	Brandon & Dirk	Mexican	Las Casas Grandes
Wednesday	Brad	Chinese	China Wok
Thursday	Shawn	Pizza	Programmers Pub
Friday	Jacob & Donna	Thai	Former Job holder's Pub

Figure 5-3: A sample table containing lunch arrangements.

7. After you have finished entering the information in Step 6, move your cursor into the cell containing the text "Programmer's Pub." Use the End key to get to the end of the existing text and then press Enter to begin a new paragraph. Type the following text:

(reservations will need to be made in advance if we want to obtain the best seating)

Notice how Word expands the table as necessary to accommodate all the necessary information (see Figure 5-4).

Day	Who	What	Where
Monday	Gina and Kitty	Salads	Garden Oasis of Mill Valley
Tuesday	Brandon & Dirk	Mexican	Las Casas Grandes
Wednesday	Brad	Chinese	China Wok
Thursday	Shawn	Pizza	Programmers Pub (reservations will need to be made in advance if we want to obtain the best seating)
Friday	Jacob & Donna	Thai	Former Job holder's Pub

Figure 5-4: Word expands the table to accommodate more information.

Remember that you can insert graphics into the cells of a table. To do so, use the cut-and-paste technique for graphic images that is detailed in Chapter 10.

Editing Tables

You can edit a table in many ways after you have created it and added text. You can add or delete columns and rows, you can merge the information from more than one cell, and you can split your table into more than one part. This section looks at how to do all these things in a table.

Before you can edit a table, though, you must learn how to select the cells in a table. To select cells in a table, use the same selection methods that you use in regular text. Briefly, you can click and drag across text in one or more cells with the mouse, or you can hold down the Shift key while you use the arrow keys. You can also use any of the Alt key combinations shown in Table 5-1. While selecting, as you move the insertion point past the end of text in a particular cell, text in the adjacent cell is selected. If no text is in a cell, the entire cell is selected as you move through it while dragging.

Inserting and deleting cells

When you need to remove rows, columns, or cells from a table, first select the cells that you want to delete and then choose Table⇨Delete Cells. The Delete Cells dialog box (see Figure 5-5) lets you shift the cells left after deletion, shift the cells up after deletion, or delete entire rows or columns.

Figure 5-5: The Delete Cells dialog box.

You can use the Insert Cells command to insert a cell or a group of cells. First select the cell next to where you want to insert the cell or group of cells. Then choose Table⇨Insert Cells, or click on the Insert Cells button on the Standard toolbar. The Insert Cells dialog box shown in Figure 5-6 asks whether you want to insert a row of cells or whether you want the cells to shift after you add them to the table.

Figure 5-6: The Insert Cells dialog box.

How the insertion or deletion of cells affects the table depends on what you delete or add and whether you choose to shift the cells horizontally or vertically. As an example, Figure 5-7 shows a table measuring 5 rows by 2 columns: 10 cells.

FIRST	SECOND
THIRD	FOURTH
FIFTH	SIXTH
SEVENTH	EIGHTH
NINTH	TENTH

Figure 5-7: A 5 × 2 table.

If you select a cell or a group of cells *and not the entire row* (in the first two examples that follow, the third and fourth cells are selected), choose Table ➪ Insert Cells and then choose Shift Cells Right in the dialog box. The new cell or cells are inserted at the selection location, and the existing cells are moved to the right, as shown in Figure 5-8.

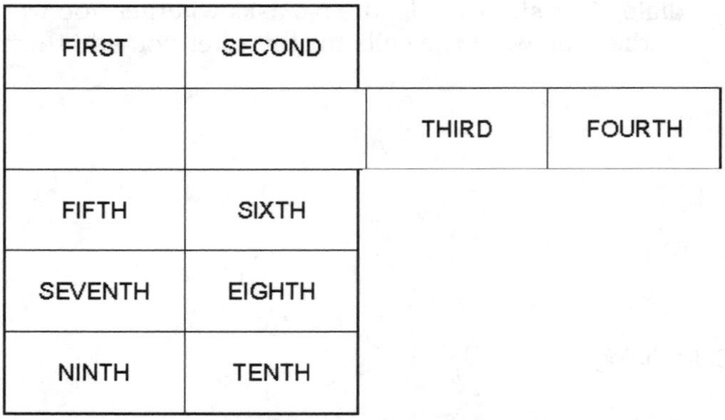

FIRST	SECOND		
		THIRD	FOURTH
FIFTH	SIXTH		
SEVENTH	EIGHTH		
NINTH	TENTH		

Figure 5-8: The table from Figure 5-7 after choosing Shift Cells Right from the Insert Cells dialog box.

If you select a cell or a group of cells (not the entire row), choose Table⇨Insert Cells and then choose Shift Cells Down in the dialog box. The new cell or cells are inserted at the selection location, and the existing cells are moved down, as illustrated in Figure 5-9.

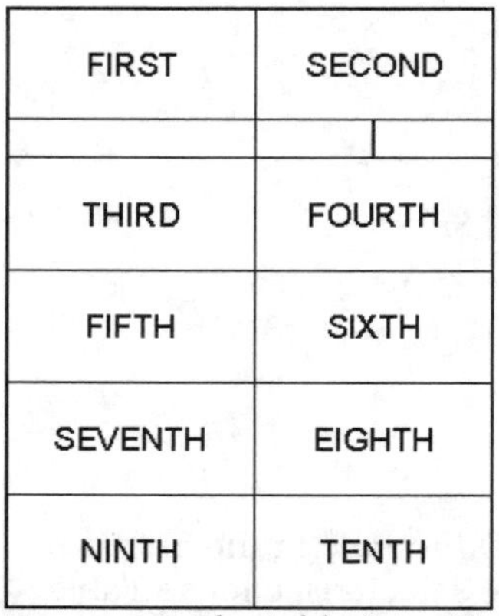

FIRST	SECOND
THIRD	FOURTH
FIFTH	SIXTH
SEVENTH	EIGHTH
NINTH	TENTH

Figure 5-9: The table from Figure 5-7 after choosing Shift Cells Down from the Insert Cells dialog box.

If you select a cell or a group of cells (not the entire row) and choose Table⇨Delete Cells, you again have the choice of choosing to shift the cells up or to the left. Figure 5-10 shows the example table if the fifth and seventh cells were selected and the Shift Cells Left option was chosen.

FIRST	SECOND
THIRD	FOURTH
SIXTH	
EIGHTH	
NINTH	TENTH

Figure 5-10: The table from Figure 5-7 after choosing Shift Cells Left from the Insert Cells dialog box.

Merging cells

Once in a while, you may need to merge information from one group of cells into one cell. You can merge a group of horizontally adjacent cells into a single cell by first selecting the cells that you want to merge and then choosing Table⇨Merge Cells. After choosing the command, the information merges into one cell. As an example, consider the simple table shown in Figure 5-11.

Group 1	Group 2	Group 3	Group 4
Alberta Sutton	Selita Sutton	Epey White	Felton White
Alice Royals	Jim Royals	Ricky Stephens	Kirk Stephens
Leona Sutton	Michael Whitfield	Eric Whitfield	Vanessa Williams

Figure 5-11: A table before cells are merged.

If you were to select the two cells at the right end of the top row of the table and choose Table⇨Merge Cells, the result would resemble that shown in Figure 5-12, where the adjoining cells are merged into one cell. Note that any text in the cells is also merged into a single entry, as demonstrated in the example.

Group 1	Group 2	Group 3 Group 4	
Alberta Sutton	Selita Sutton	Epey White	Felton White
Alice Royals	Jim Royals	Ricky Stephens	Kirk Stephens
Leona Sutton	Michael Whitfield	Eric Whitfield	Vanessa Williams

Figure 5-12: The same table after cells are merged.

If you merge cells and you don't like the result, keep in mind that you can undo the operation by immediately choosing Edit⇨Undo Merge Cells.

Splitting a table

You can also split a table in two horizontally at a point between any given rows. When you choose Table⇨Split Table, the table splits in two just above the insertion point. (You can also use the Ctrl+Shift+Enter key combination to split a table.) This option is very useful in cases where you need to separate groups in a table. Splitting the table makes the groups more visible. Splitting a table is also useful if you want to insert text between the rows of an existing table, and you do not want the text to be a part of the table.

Formatting Tables

In Word, you can format the contents of your tables (usually text), and you can format the tables themselves. You can apply formatting to the contents of tables in the same way that you apply formatting to characters or paragraphs in Word. (See Chapter 3 for more on character and paragraph formatting.) For example, if you want to apply bold character formatting to a portion of text in a table, you can select the desired text and then click on the Bold button in the Standard toolbar, or press Ctrl+B to apply the formatting.

If you want to format aspects of the table itself (as opposed to its contents), you use Table⇨Table AutoFormat to open the Table AutoFormat dialog box (see Figure 5-13). In this dialog box, you see a selection of various formats that you can apply to your table. Choose the format that you want to use and select the areas to which you want to apply the format by clicking on as many check boxes as you want. The Preview box lets you see what the table will look like after the formatting is done. When you are finished making your selections in the dialog box, click on the OK button to apply the formatting to the table.

Setting column widths

Choose Table⇨Cell Height and Width to open the Cell Height and Width dialog box (see Figure 5-14) where you can specify the width of one or more cells of the table. In the Row tab of the dialog box, you can change the row height, the indentation from the left, and the alignment. You can also tell Word whether to allow rows to break across the ends of pages. In the Column tab, you can set the width of the columns and the amount of space between columns.

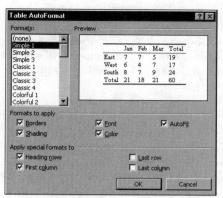

Figure 5-13: The Table AutoFormat dialog box.

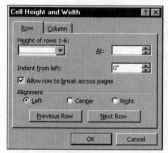

Figure 5-14: The Cell Height and Width dialog box.

You can also adjust column and cell width by placing the mouse pointer on the gridline of the desired cell or column. When you do so, the pointer changes into a two-sided arrow that you can click and drag to the desired width.

After you have adjusted the column width, all the columns to the right of the adjusted column are resized in proportion to their previous widths, but the overall width of the table is not changed when you drag the gridline or the column marker. The following list contains the options that you have for adjusting your current column:

✦ To adjust the current column and one column to the right (the overall table width remains unchanged), hold down the Shift key while you drag.

✦ To adjust the current column and make all columns to the right equal in width, hold down the Ctrl key while you drag.

✦ To adjust the current column without changing the width of the other columns (the overall table width changes), hold down the Ctrl and Shift keys while you drag.

Hot
Stuff
From time to time, the use of the draw table feature to create your tables will result in cells or columns that are not of the same height. If you find this to be the case, you will need to make adjustments choosing either Distribute Rows Evenly or Distribute Columns Evenly from the Table menu. These options will even out the columns and the rows with an average of the size. This will give a drawn table a more refined look, even when it is drawn freehand.

Adjusting the space between columns

You can adjust the spacing between columns by choosing the Cell Height and Width command from the Table menu and clicking on the Column tab in the Cell Height and Width dialog box (see Figure 5-15). In this tab, you can use the Space Between Columns box to adjust the horizontal space that Word places between the text of adjacent cells. (The default value is 0.15 inches.) If you click on the AutoFit button, Word automatically sizes the columns to best fit the text contained in them.

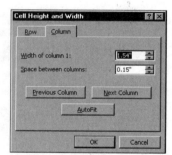

Figure 5-15: The Column tab of the Cell Height and Width dialog box.

Making row adjustments

To set the height of a row, choose Table⇨Cell Height and Width and click on the Row tab in the dialog box. Use the Height of Rows list box to set the minimum height of one or more rows. By default, this value is set to Auto, which means that the row will be high enough to contain any text in the row. If you choose the At Least option from the Height of Rows list box, Word makes the row at least as tall as the value that you enter. If any text within a cell is larger than the minimum height, Word increases the height as needed to accommodate the text. You can also choose the Exactly option from the list box, which causes Word to make the cell exactly the height that you enter in the box.

To add indents to your cells, click on the Indent From Left box on the Row tab. The row will be indented from the left page margin by the decimal amount that you enter. For example, if you enter **0.5 in.**, the row will be indented one-half inch from the left page margin. You can enter a negative value to shift the row to the left, past the left margin. If you want to apply the indent to one row, select the entire row or just one cell in the row before you open the dialog box. Then, after you make your entries on the Row tab of the Cell Height and Width dialog box, they are applied to the entire row. If you don't make a selection first, the changes are applied to the entire table.

To determine the alignment of rows with respect to the page margins, choose from among the Left, Center, or Right options in the Alignment area of the Row tab. These options are comparable to the ones found in the Paragraph dialog box from Format⇨Paragraph. As with paragraphs, you can left-align, center, or right-align rows horizontally on a page. By default, the selected row is left-aligned, which causes the left edge of the row to be aligned with the left margin (assuming that you have not specified an indentation). Choose Center to center the row or choose Right to align the right edge of the row with the right page margin.

For the Row Alignment options to have any visible effect, your table must be smaller than the width of the page margins. If you used the default options in the Insert Table dialog box when you created the table, the table is already as wide as the page margins, and choosing an alignment option will have no visible effect. The alignment options are useful when you specify your own widths for the table columns rather than letting Word automatically size the table.

Remember that adjusting the Alignment options in the dialog box moves the horizontal position of the entire row, not the text within the row. If, for example, you choose the Center option from the Alignment area, Word will center the row within the page margins, but individual text within the cells will not be centered. If you want to left-align, center, or right-align text within a cell, you have to select the desired text and then use the alignment options of the Format⇨Paragraph command (or the alignment buttons on the Formatting toolbar).

If you don't select any text to which to apply the text alignment, the alignment that you choose applies to the specific cell that contains the insertion point. To apply the alignment to the current row, select the row and then choose one of the alignment buttons on the Formatting toolbar.

Applying borders

You can use the various options within the Cell Borders and Shading dialog box (see Figure 5-16) to place borders around a cell or a group of cells in the table. You select one or more cells and open this dialog box by choosing Format⇨Borders and Shading while the insertion point is in a table. The borders that you insert by using this dialog box will be printed, unlike the table gridlines that are visible by default. The borders that you specify are added directly on top of the table gridlines.

How Word applies the borders depends on the selections that you make in the Cell Borders and Shading dialog box. As with other options in this dialog box, Word applies borders and shading according to the cell or cells that you select in the table.

From the Borders and Shading Toolbar, you can also select the Line Style list box. Doing so gives you a list of choices for line styles that you can use for the table you have created. After selecting the line style, the cursor becomes a pencil. Simply draw on the line you wish to change the style of, and Word will apply the style to the line. If you choose a style that you do not like after it is applied, simply click on the Undo button and the style will be removed.

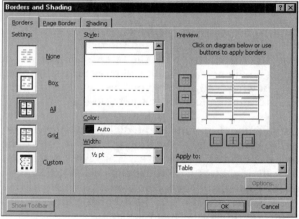

Figure 5-16: The Borders tab of the Cell Borders and Shading dialog box.

You can also use Table⇨Table AutoFormat to add borders and shading to a table. When you choose this command, Word provides you with a list of different formats for shading and borders that you can use (see "Formatting Tables" earlier in this chapter). Simply select the format that you want in the Table AutoFormat dialog box and click on the OK button.

Besides specifying the presence of a border, Word lets you select from among different types of borders. After you choose the desired option (Outline, Inside, Top, Bottom, Left, or Right) in the Cell Borders and Shading dialog box, you can select the style of borders that you want and the colors to be used for the border.

Exploring Other Uses for Tables

You can do more with tables than just create them and type in text. You can use tables to lay out large amounts of textual data in the form of side-by-side paragraphs. You can also convert existing text to table form, and you can sort information stored in your tables.

Creating side-by-side paragraphs

Word's capability to store up to one page length of text in any column of a table makes it easy to set up side-by-side paragraphs by using the Table feature. (Side-by-side paragraphs are one way to create newspaper-style columns. You can create side-by-side paragraphs in other ways as well, and Chapter 10 provides additional details regarding this and other desktop publishing topics.) To create side-by-side paragraphs, simply insert a table with two or more columns into your document and use the Cell Height and Width dialog box to size the columns as desired. Remember that you can use the mouse to set the column widths by clicking on the gridlines and dragging them to the appropriate width. Then type as much text as you want in the columns, but keep in mind the rule that a table cannot extend beyond the length of a single page. The table will automatically display the paragraphs of text side-by-side on-screen. You can add borders to differentiate the text.

Converting text to tables

Rest easy. Word lets you convert all the old tables that you created — by inserting tabs, spaces, and other characters to separate your columns — into brand new, usable, and up-to-date Word tables. Therefore, if you have old tables that you still need, you can "clean them up" by using Table⇨Convert Text to Table.

This feature is also helpful if someone else has created an old-fashioned table, and you want to work with it in the new table format. You can also use this feature to convert data from databases in a comma-delimited format into the table form in Word. (See your database management software documentation for directions on creating comma-delimited files.) Text that is separated either by tabs, by commas, or by paragraph marks can be converted into a table.

To convert text into a table, first select the text and then choose Table⇨Convert Text to Table. When the Convert Text to Table dialog box appears, choose the Paragraph, Tabs, or Comma option (as appropriate, based on the text to be converted) from the Separate Text At area of the dialog box. Then click on the OK button. Word will recommend a number of columns and a number of rows, based on the appearance of the text that you are converting to table form. (You can change the recommendations by entering any desired values in the Number of

Columns and Number of Rows text boxes.) To complete the conversion of the text to a table, click on the OK button.

For example, consider the text shown in Figure 5-17. (You can easily duplicate this example by opening a new document, typing the text shown, pressing tab once between columns, and pressing Enter at the end of each line.)

```
¶
¶
¶
¶
Alberta·Sutton → Selita·Sutton → Epey·White → Felton·White¶
Alice·Royals → Jim·Royals → Ricky·Stephens → Kirk·Stevens¶
Leona·Sutton → Michael·Whitfield → Erick·Witfield → Dirk·Johnson¶
¶
```

Figure 5-17: Text separated by tab marks can form the basis of a table.

To convert this text into a table, select all three rows of text and choose the Convert Text to Table command from the Table menu. In the Convert Text to Table dialog box, accept Word's suggestions for a table measuring 4 columns by 3 rows by clicking on the OK button. The table shown in Figure 5-18 is the result of Word's efforts. (In the figure, we've added borders to the table to make the effects of the table more visible.)

Alberta Sutton	Selita Sutton	Epey White	Felton White
Alice Royals	Jim Royals	Ricky Stephens	Kirk Stevens
Leona Sutton	Michael Whitfield	Erick Witfield	Dirk Johnson

Figure 5-18: A newly created table based on the text in Figure 5-17.

Sorting information

You may encounter times when you want to arrange a list of data (often within a table) in alphabetical or numerical order. You can use Word's Sort command for this task.

Keep in mind, however, that the Sort command is by no means limited to tables. You can use the Sort command to sort any list of data, whether the information is in a table or in a simple list with paragraph marks separating the lines.

When Word sorts a list, it rearranges the list entries in alphabetic or numerical order. You can choose whether to sort in ascending or descending order or whether to sort by date, text, or number. Follow these steps to sort the data in a table:

1. Select the column or row or the items in the table that you want to sort.

2. Choose Table⇨Sort. (If the selected information is not a table, the command is Sort Text.) The Sort dialog box appears, as shown in Figure 5-19.

3. If you have headings that you do not want sorted, click on the Header Row radio button in the My list has area of the dialog box.

4. In the Sort by area, make your selection for the column that you want to sort by.

5. In the Type list box of the Sort by area, choose the Text, Number, or Date option and then click on either the Ascending or the Descending radio button. To choose additional columns to sort by, repeat Steps 4 and 5.

6. Click on the OK button to sort the data.

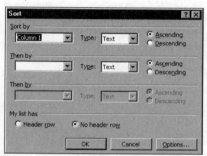

Figure 5-19: The Sort dialog box.

Understanding Outlines in Word for Windows

For many who work with words, an outline is the first step to putting cohesive thoughts down on paper. With even the earliest of word processors, simple outlining was possible with the use of tabs and manually typed headings. Word, however, offers automatic outlining and its significant advantages. In addition to aiding the organizing process, Word's outlining lets you number headings automatically and create tables of contents based on an outline. When you create an outline in Word, you can easily rearrange parts of the outlining without giving thought to precise formatting.

In Word, outlining is built into a document. As you create a document, you can create an outline at the same time. With Word, the only difference between a normal document and an outline is the view that you use to examine the document. When you are in Normal view, Draft view, or Page Layout view, you are looking at the document in its normal (nonoutline) form. When you turn on Outline view, however, you look at the document in the form of an outline. Figure 5-20 shows an example of a document in outline form (you will duplicate this document later in an exercise).

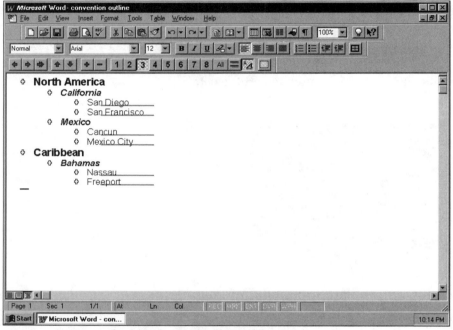

Figure 5-20: A sample document viewed in outline form.

Outlines consist of headings and body text. A *heading* is any paragraph that has been assigned a special paragraph style. Word provides these styles specifically for the creation of outlines. There are eight of these predefined styles, from Heading 1 through Heading 8. The numbers define the importance of headings in an outline: a top-level heading is assigned the Heading 1 style, the next level heading is assigned the Heading 2 style, and so on. Word automatically places all top-level headings at the left margin by default, and each lower-level heading style is successively indented (placed farther to the right than the preceding heading level).

Body text is any text within an outline that hasn't been given a heading style. Word also uses the term *subtext* to refer to all headings and body text that appear below a particular heading.

Selecting text

When you are in Outline view, selecting text is basically the same as selecting text in other areas of Word. However, you should be aware of some differences. The most significant one is that you lose the capability to select a full paragraph along with only part of another paragraph. If you use the mouse or keyboard methods to select past the boundary of a paragraph and into the following paragraph, the entire second paragraph becomes selected. As you drag across additional paragraphs, each paragraph becomes selected in its entirety. This feature makes editing more difficult in Outline view. (You can, of course, get around this by turning off Outline view while you do your editing.)

You can select a heading and all the subtext below it by double-clicking in the selection bar area beside the heading. Unfortunately, you have no equivalent for this mouse action from the keyboard, but you can accomplish the same result by selecting the desired heading and subtext with a combination of the Shift and arrow keys.

Changing the structure of an outline

To work with a document in Outline view, choose View⇨Outline. In Outline view, Word gives you additional tools to help structure the outline. A different toolbar, called the Outlining toolbar, appears at the top of the screen when you choose the Outline command. Figure 5-21 shows the Outlining toolbar. In addition to the Outlining toolbar, small icons appear to the left of each paragraph.

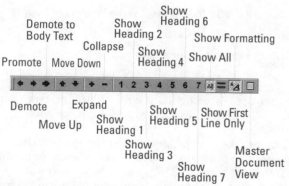

Figure 5-21: The Outlining toolbar.

A flexible feature of Word's outlining is that you can use it with a document at any time. You can create a document and later come back to it and structure the document in outline form, or you can create the document in outline form as you go along. You can add additional portions of a document, whether they are headings or body text, to the document at any time.

You can change the structure of the outline by promoting a paragraph to a higher level or by demoting it to a lower level of importance. When changing the structure of an outline in Word, you generally select the desired paragraph and then click on a button from the Outlining toolbar to change a feature of the outline. Table 5-2 explains the function of the Outlining toolbar's buttons.

Table 5-2
The Outlining toolbar's buttons and their functions

Button	*Function*
Promote	Promotes a paragraph to a higher level
Demote	Demotes a paragraph to a lower level
Demote to Body Text	Demotes a heading to body text
Move Up and Move Down	Moves a heading up or down to a new location in the outline
Expand	Expands all text within a heading
Collapse	Collapses a paragraph so that only the heading shows
Show Heading	Controls how many levels of the outline are displayed
All	Expands or collapses entire outline
Show First Line Only	When All is selected, shows just the first line of body text
Show Formatting	Shows or hides character formatting
Master Document View	Switches to Master Document view

Keyboard users should note that there are keyboard equivalents for every button on the Outlining toolbar. Table 5-3 summarizes the keyboard equivalents.

Although Alt+Shift+5 on the numeric keypad is specified as the keyboard equivalent for converting headings to body text, laptop users should note that this keyboard combination does not work on many laptop keyboards (or other keyboards, too) because of the compromises made in designing laptop keyboards. These keyboards often give up the numeric keypad and combine all numbers with the character keys. If you are using a laptop and you plan on doing a lot of work with outlines, consider adding a mouse so that you can use the Outlining toolbar.

Table 5-3
Keyboard equivalents for the Outlining toolbar

Keyboard combination	Function
Alt+Shift+left arrow or Tab	Promotes a paragraph
Alt+Shift+right arrow or Tab	Demotes a paragraph
Alt+Shift+up arrow	Moves a paragraph up
Alt+Shift+down arrow	Moves a paragraph down
Alt+Shift+plus sign	Expands body text
Alt+Shift+minus sign	Collapses body text
Alt+Shift+5 (on numeric keypad)	Converts heading to body text
Alt+Shift+1 through Alt+Shift+9	Expands or collapses headings to specified levels (on numeric keypad) (1 through 8), or to show body text (9)
Alt+Shift+A	Shows all headings and body text
Alt+Shift+L	When All is selected, shows just the first line of body text
Slash (/ on numeric keypad)	Shows or hides character formatting

Changing Outline Headings

You can use the Promote and Demote buttons, or the equivalent keyboard combinations, to change heading levels, to convert body text to headings, or to convert headings to body text. To promote a heading level with the mouse, select the heading and click on the Promote button on the Outlining toolbar or drag the heading's icon to the left. To demote a heading level, select the heading and click on the Demote button on the Outlining toolbar or drag the heading's icon to the right.

When you promote a heading, it is assigned the next highest heading level, and it is outdented farther to the left. The opposite happens when you demote a heading: it is assigned the next lower level, and it is indented farther to the right.

Converting body text

To demote a heading to body text, click on the double-right arrow in the Outlining toolbar. This action causes the selected text to appear as body text in the document rather than as a heading.

You can convert body text to a heading simply by promoting the body text. Select the body text and click on the Promote button. When body text is promoted, it is converted to a heading that has the same level as the heading above it.

Expanding or collapsing outline headings

As an aid in organizing your thoughts, Word lets you expand or collapse outline headings. When you expand a heading, all the subtext (lower-level headings and body text) below the heading are made visible. On the other hand, when you collapse a heading, all subtext below the heading is hidden from view. Figure 5-22 shows an outline with its body text collapsed; it then shows the same outline with its body text expanded.

Figure 5-22: At left: An outline with collapsed body text. At right: The same outline with body text expanded.

To expand a heading, select the desired heading and then click on the Expand button on the Outlining toolbar. To collapse a heading, select the heading and then click on the Collapse button.

Many keyboards have two minus keys and two plus keys (one set located on the numeric keypad). Word recognizes either set — it doesn't matter which set you use with the Alt+Shift keyboard combinations.

You can also use the Show buttons on the Outlining toolbar to collapse or expand an entire outline. The numbered buttons correspond to the possible heading levels within an outline: clicking on the 1 button causes level 1 headings to be visible; clicking on the 2 button causes all headings that are level 1 or level 2 to be visible; clicking on the 3 button causes all heading levels of 1, 2, or 3 to be visible; and so on. Clicking on the All button causes all headings and all body text in an outline to be visible.

Moving headings

Word provides considerable flexibility regarding the movement of headings and associated subtext. You can move headings around in an outline, you can move associated subtext with or without the headings, and you can move multiple headings and associated subtext by selecting more than one heading prior to the move operation.

To move a heading, first select it. This is not quite as simple as it sounds, however. If you select only a heading in an expanded outline (the subtext is visible), Word moves only the heading and leaves the subtext in its current position. If the heading is collapsed, however, any movement of the heading causes the associated subtext to be moved, even if only the heading is selected.

After you have selected the heading that you want to move, click on the up arrow or down arrow on the Outlining toolbar to move the heading up or down in the outline. You can also use the click-and-drag method to move the headings. Simply click on the heading that you want to move and drag it to its new location.

Applying numbering to outlines

You may want to apply numbering to the headings of an outline. Of course, you could manually number an outline by typing the numbers as you type the headings, but a major drawback to this technique is evident if you later rearrange the outline by adding, deleting, or moving headings. If you make these changes, you must then manually renumber the headings. You can avoid this problem if you use Word's Format⇨Bullets and Numbering command to apply numbering to your outline headings.

To number an outline, perform the following steps:

1. Collapse or expand the outline so that only those headings that you want to number are visible. Word will number any visible paragraphs, so if all headings and body text are visible, the entire contents of the outline will be numbered, which is probably not what you want.

2. Select the paragraphs that you want to number. If you want to number the entire document, select the entire document by pressing Ctrl+A.

3. Choose Format⇨Bullets and Numbering to open the Bullets and Numbering dialog box. (See Chapter 3 for a more detailed discussion of this dialog box.)

4. Leave the default settings as they are.

5. Click on the Outline Numbered tab and then click on one of the six possible number formats shown in the tab.

6. Click on the OK button. Paragraph numbers will appear beside each visible topic in your outline.

Remember that you can remove paragraph numbering from the outline at any time by choosing Format⇨Bullets and Numbering and clicking on the Reset button on the Outline Numbered tab.

Creating Your Own Outline

To demonstrate the concepts that you can use in building outlines, you need to create an outline of your own on which to experiment. Follow along with this exercise to create an outline:

1. Choose File⇨New and click on the OK button in the New dialog box to create a new document.

2. Choose View⇨Outline to switch to Outline view.

3. To form the headings for your outline, type the following text and press Enter after each line:

North America

California

San Diego

San Francisco

Mexico

Cancun

Mexico City

Caribbean

Bahamas

Nassau

Freeport

4. To create a second level in your outline, move the cursor to the California heading and click on the Demote button. Repeat this step for the Mexico and Bahamas headings.

5. To create a third level in your outline, move the cursor to the San Diego heading and demote this line twice by clicking on the Demote button twice. Repeat this step for the San Francisco, Cancun, Mexico City, Nassau, and Freeport headings.

At this point, the structure of the sample outline is apparent. If you have been following the directions, your outline should resemble the example shown in Figure 5-23.

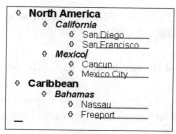

Figure 5-23: The structure of the sample outline.

Now you can begin adding body text to the various parts of the outline. Keep in mind that Word's flexibility means that you do not necessarily have to create your outlines in this same manner. This example follows the common technique of creating outline headings first and then filling in the details; however, you can create headings and body text as you go along. To add some body text to the sample outline, perform the following steps:

1. Move the cursor to the end of the San Diego line. Press Enter to begin a new line. Note that the icon aligns with the existing lines; hence, the new line is initially a heading. Before you begin typing, convert this new line to body text.

2. Click on the Demote to Body Text button on the Outlining toolbar and then type the following text:

   Great meeting facilities, accommodations, and restaurants all centrally located in downtown area.

3. Move the cursor to the end of the San Francisco line. Press Enter to begin a new line and click on the Demote to Body Text button on the Outlining toolbar. Then type the following text:

   Proximity to company offices will reduce transportation costs. Excellent dining and attractions in Fisherman's Wharf area.

4. Move the cursor to the end of the Cancun line. Press Enter to begin a new line and click on the Demote to Body Text button on the Outlining toolbar.

Then type the following text:

Convention center and hotels located on the beach. Cancun offers first-rate water sports all year.

5. Move the cursor to the end of the Mexico City line. Press Enter to begin a new line and click on the Demote to Body Text button on the Outlining toolbar. Then type the following text:

Business hotels near Chapultepec Park provide meeting accommodations and computer fax lines.

6. Move the cursor to the end of the Nassau line. Press Enter to begin a new line and click on the Demote to Body Text button on the Outlining toolbar. Then type the following text:

Great hotels with meeting facilities located on the beach, in Cable Beach area.

7. Move the cursor to the end of the Freeport line. Press Enter to begin a new line and click on the Demote to Body Text button on the Outlining toolbar. Then type the following text:

Shopping, excellent golf, and water sports readily available.

8. Choose File⟹Save to save the document with the name Sample Outline #1. At this point, your outline should resemble the one shown in Figure 5-24.

Figure 5-24: Adding body text to the sample outline.

Collapsing and expanding the sample outline

As mentioned earlier, it's often helpful to collapse an outline so that you can look at the major points without being distracted by the less important points or by the body text. An easy way to collapse an entire outline is by using the numbered Show buttons on the Outlining toolbar or their keyboard equivalents.

To experiment with collapsing your own outline, open the Sample Outline #1. Click on the 1 button on the Outlining toolbar to show only level-1 headings in your outline. At this point, only the North America and Caribbean lines should be visible. To expose the next level of headings, click on the 2 button. Now you should also be able to see the California, Mexico, and Bahamas lines. When you click on the 3 button, the level 3 headings (the names of the cities) become visible beneath the level 2 headings. Finally, click on the All button. The body text becomes visible along with all headings of the outline.

Of course, you can also individually expand or collapse headings by using the Expand and Collapse buttons on the Outlining toolbar. To see how these buttons work, place the cursor anywhere in the Mexico heading and click on the Collapse button. Notice that the Cancun and Mexico City headings collapse underneath and hide the body text. If you click on the Expand button, the subheadings expand to reveal the body text underneath.

Changing headings in the sample outline

You can use the Promote and Demote buttons on the Outlining toolbar to promote and demote headings. Remember that body text for a heading is promoted or demoted along with the heading, but subheadings do not. To see how this concept works, select the San Francisco heading and the subtext below the heading and then click on the Promote button. Notice that the San Francisco heading is promoted to the same level as the California and Mexico headings. While the heading and subtext remain selected, click on the Demote button to demote the heading and subtext back to its original level.

Use the Move Up and Move Down buttons on the Outlining toolbar (or their keyboard equivalents) to move headings up or down within an outline. Remember, if any subtext is collapsed, subtext moves with the heading. If subtext is not collapsed, it moves with the heading only if you have selected it with the heading. To demonstrate this concept, place the cursor in the Mexico City heading and click on the Move Up button (or press Alt+Shift+up arrow). The Mexico City heading moves up in the outline. However, the body text associated with the heading remains in its original location. While Mexico City is still the selected paragraph, click on the Move Down button (or press Alt+Shift+down arrow) to restore the heading to its proper location.

Next, select the Mexico City heading and the subtext underneath the heading. Click on the Move Up button twice. This step moves the heading and its subtext above the Cancun heading and its subtext, as shown in Figure 5-25.

In most cases you'll want the body text to move with the headings. To make this move easier, first collapse the outline to the level of the heading to be moved (with the numbered Show buttons or their keyboard equivalents). After you have collapsed the outline, you can move headings without worrying about selecting the subtext because the subtext will automatically follow the headings.

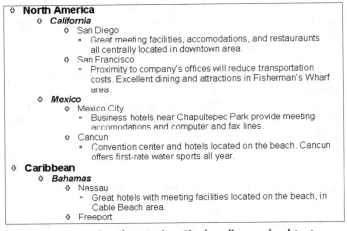

Figure 5-25: Moving the Mexico City heading and subtext.

Creating a Table of Contents from an Outline

One powerful feature that Word provides is the capability to generate a table of contents quickly based on the headings within an outline. Use Insert⇨Inde<u>x</u> and Tables command to insert a table of contents at the location of the insertion point.

After your document exists in outline form, perform the following steps to create a table of contents:

1. Place the insertion point where you want to insert the table of contents.

2. Choose <u>I</u>nsert⇨Inde<u>x</u> and Tables command to open the Index and Tables dialog box.

3. Click on the Table of Contents tab and then choose the type of format that you want for the table of contents from the Formats list box. The Preview box gives you an idea of how the format will look before you apply the style.

4. Click on the OK button. Word inserts a table of contents at the insertion point.

You can see how easy it is to create a table of contents by using the sample outline that you created earlier. Perform the following steps to add a table of contents to the sample outline or to any existing outline that you have created.

1. Choose View⇨Normal to turn off the Outline view. (You want to turn off Outline view so that you can add a page break to put the table of contents on the first page. You cannot add page breaks while you are in Outline view.) Otherwise, it doesn't matter whether you are in Outline view or not if you want to insert a table of contents, as long as the headings are in the document.

2. Press Ctrl+Home to get to the start of the document. Press Enter once to add a new line and then press Ctrl+Enter to insert a page break. Press Ctrl+Home again to get back to the start of the document. You will add the table of contents on what is now page 1 of the document, with the remainder of the document appearing on page 2.

3. Choose Insert⇨Index and Tables, and click on the Table of Contents tab.

4. Leave the default options set as they are.

5. Click on the OK button. Word creates your table of contents.

Because the entire outline is on page 2, all topics of the outline are shown in the table of contents as being on page 2. If your sample document were longer, Word would assign the proper page numbers automatically. If you later change the contents of the outline so that page numbers change, the table of contents is not updated automatically. You must update the table of contents by selecting the entire document and then pressing F9 (Update Fields) because the entries in the table of contents are based on fields. (For more information on fields, see Chapter 6.) Note that Word can do a lot more when it comes to tables of contents and indexes. See Chapter 7 for additional details on these subjects.

Printing Outlines

Although you print outlines in the same way that you print any other document, keep in mind that what you get will vary depending on what view you are using when you print. Just as the document looks different on-screen in the various views, the document also prints differently in the different views. If you are in Outline view, the document prints much like it appears on-screen in Outline view. The only items that don't appear on the printed copy are the outline icons. Word uses whatever tabs are in effect for the document to indent the headings and body text.

If you are not in Outline view, Word prints the document somewhat differently. The headings are still indented, but they are indented by a smaller amount, and body text is printed at the left margin, without any indentation. You may want to try printing the sample outline that you created with Outline view turned on and then with it turned off so that you can examine the differences in appearance of the printed copy.

Summary

This chapter covered topics related to tables and outlines:

✦ You learned how to create tables by using Word's Table feature.

✦ You learned how to edit the contents of a table and how to delete, insert, and merge cells.

✦ You were armed with the tools needed to add borders, control table alignment, and sort table contents.

✦ You learned how to convert text to a table.

✦ You were introduced to the Outlining toolbar.

✦ You learned how to promote, demote, and move headings in an outline.

✦ Finally, you learned how to create a table of contents from your outline.

In the next chapter, you will learn how to work with fields and form letters in Word.

Where to go next...

✦ Tables are a routine part of documents that demand a "desktop-published" appearance. For more tips and techniques on performing desktop publishing tasks, you'll find Chapter 10 devoted to the topic.

✦ If you regularly use outlining in complex documents, keep in mind that you can quickly create tables of contents based on your outline. For details on using an outline to create a table of contents, see Chapter 7.

✦   ✦   ✦

Working with Fields

This chapter covers topics that are related to working with fields, or special codes that can be inserted in documents to perform various tasks. You will learn some of the common uses for fields when working in Word and how to create form letters.

In Word, a *field* is a special set of instructions that tells Word to insert certain information at a given location in a document. The basic difference between fields and normal text is that with fields, the computer provides the information for you. However, using fields does more than just save the effort of typing in the information. Fields are *dynamic:* they can change as circumstances change. You already may have used fields at various times in your work with Word for Windows; for example, when you insert the current date or page numbers in a document, you are inserting a certain kind of field.

Think of fields as special codes that you include in documents. The codes tell Word to insert information at the location where the code appears. The codes can automatically update the text of your document, or you can tell Word to update the information produced by the fields only when you want it to. Typically, you will use fields to add text or graphics to a document, to update information that changes on a regular basis, and to perform calculations.

Word has dozens of types of fields. Some, like page numbers and the current date, are simple to understand and use. Others are more complex and are beyond the scope of this book. But all fields can be inserted into a document and updated by using the same procedures, and this chapter will detail those procedures.

You can effectively work with fields after you learn four skills: how to insert fields in a document, how to update fields so that they show the most current results, how to view fields, and how to move between fields.

How to Use Fields

A field consists of three parts: field characters, a field type, and instructions. As an example, consider the following date field:

```
{ Date \@ M/d/yy }
```

The *field characters* are the curly braces that enclose the field. The curly braces indicate the presence of a field in Word to the user. Inside the curly braces you find the special code or instruction that tells Word what is to appear in this area. Note that although curly braces are used to indicate the presence of a field, you cannot insert a field in a document by typing curly braces. You must use a command or a key combination specifically designed to insert fields, such as the Insert⇨Field command.

The *field type* is the first word that appears after the left field character. In the preceding example, the word *date* is the field type; this particular field type tells Word to insert the current date — based on the computer's clock — into the document.

The *instructions* follow the field type. Instructions are optional, depending on the field type, but most field types have instructions. The instructions tell Word exactly how the information specified by the field type will be displayed. In this example, \@ M/d/yy is an instruction that tells Word to display the current date in the American numeric format with the month, day, and year separated by slashes. The contents of the instructions may appear somewhat cryptic, but you need not be concerned with what they mean because Word inserts the proper instructions for you automatically.

Inserting fields

Many commands in Word insert fields indirectly. When you insert page numbers or a table of contents, for example, you are inserting fields to produce the page numbers or the table of contents. But when you specifically want to insert fields into a document, you use a special command or key combination that is designed to insert fields, such as Insert⇨Field. Follow these steps to use the Field command to insert a field into your document:

1. After placing the insertion point where you want to insert the field, choose Insert⇨Field. The Field dialog box appears, as shown in Figure 6-1.

2. From the Categories list box, select the field category that you want to insert. The All category enables you to see all the fields in alphabetic order in the Field Names list box. You can use the scroll bars or the arrow keys to navigate among the possible field types.

3. From the Field Names list box, select the field that you want to insert. The Field Codes text box at the bottom of the dialog box displays whatever field you have selected. (You can also use this text box to enter the name of the desired field; however, it's generally easier to pick the field by name from the Field Names list box.)

Figure 6-1: The Field dialog box.

4. Click on the Options button if you want to add switches or formatting to the field. When the Options button is clicked, the Field Options dialog box opens, as shown in Figure 6-2. To add switches or formatting, click on the Add to Field button. If you change your mind and decide to remove the formatting or switches, click on the Undo Add button.

5. Click on the OK button to insert the field into the document.

Hot Stuff Word also provides an Insert Field shortcut key combination (Ctrl+F9). This shortcut inserts the field characters (curly braces) into the document, which enables you to type the field name and instructions manually. This method for entering fields is typically used by programmers who are familiar with the Visual Basic programming language that is built into Word. Unless you are very familiar with field types and their instructions, you will probably find it much easier to add fields with Insert⇨Field.

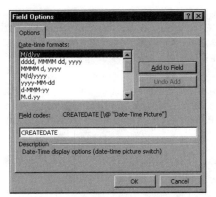

Figure 6-2: The Field Options dialog box.

Viewing field codes

By default, when you insert a field, you see the results of that field. For example, when you insert a date field, you see the current date. When you are editing documents, however, you may find it useful to see the actual contents of the fields rather than the results. Here's how to see a field's contents, instead of its results:

1. Place the pointer in the field and right-click with the mouse. Word displays a shortcut menu.

2. Choose Toggle Field Codes to turn on the codes for the field. Perform the same steps if you want to turn off the codes again.

Note that you can also view an individual field by using the Toggle Field shortcut key combination (Shift+F9). This shortcut switches between a field's results and its actual contents. Place the insertion point anywhere in the desired field and press Shift+F9. If you are working with a large document that contains a number of fields, you may find it helpful to split the document into two panes. You can then turn on Field Codes in one pane by selecting the entire document and right-clicking to open the shortcut menu. From the shortcut menu, choose Toggle Field Codes.

Updating fields

You can update fields by selecting the text containing the field, right-clicking the text, and choosing Update Field from the shortcut menu that appears. Some fields, like those used in page numbering, are automatically updated whenever you print or repaginate a document; others are not updated until you tell Word to update the fields.

To update fields in the entire document, select the entire document (Ctrl+A) and then right-click anywhere in the document. Choose Update Field from the shortcut menu that appears.

Moving between fields

To move to the next field, use F11 or Alt+F1. To move to a previous field in a document, use Shift+F11 or Alt+Shift+F1. If you're more comfortable with the mouse, just click on the field that you want to move to.

Formatting fields

You can format the field results or the field codes, and you can add switches to the field codes. To format the field when it displays its result, right-click the field and choose the desired formatting option from the shortcut menu. (Choose Font to format the fonts used or Paragraph to apply paragraph formatting.)

To format the field when it displays its code, perform the following steps:

1. Choose Tools⇨Options, click on the View tab of the Options dialog box that appears, check the Field Codes option, and click on OK. (If you just need to see the field codes for one field, place the insertion point in the field, right-click the field to open the shortcut menu, and choose Toggle Field Codes.)

2. After the fields are displayed, right-click the field and choose the appropriate option (Font or Paragraph) from the shortcut menu. Fill in the options in the dialog box that appears to apply the desired formatting.

Adding switches to field codes so that you can format the fields is not a "user-friendly" process, to say the least. You can add switches to the field codes by typing them into the code. Switches are options that change certain characteristics of the field results, such as displaying characters as uppercase, or converting numbers to roman numerals. For example, a simple DATE field looks like this:

```
{ DATE }
```

However, a field with the DATE code and a switch that tells Word how to display the date looks like this:

```
{ DATE \@ d-M-yy }
```

Table 6-1 lists some of the general switches and their functions.

Table 6-1
Commonly used switches and their functions

Switch	Function
* caps	Capitalizes the initial letter of each word in the result.
* firstcap	Capitalizes the initial letter of the first word in the result.
* lower	Makes all letters in the result appear as lowercase.
* upper	Makes all letters in the result appear as uppercase.
* arabic	Converts a number to Arabic (standard) format, overriding any default set elsewhere in Windows.
* dollartext	Spells out a number with two decimal places as words with initial capital letters, the word and, and the numbers that follow the decimal places (suitable for producing checks with currency amounts spelled out).
* roman	Converts a number to lowercase roman numerals.
* Roman	Converts a number to uppercase roman numerals.
\@ dddd,MMMM,d,yyyy	Displays a date as spelled out, as in Wednesday, May 24, 1995.
* mergeformat	Preserves manual formatting in the fields, such as character and paragraph formatting in text, and scaling and cropping dimensions in graphics.
* charformat	Applies the formatting on the first character of the field name to the entire field result.

Locking a field's contents

At times, you may want to prevent the results of a field from being updated. You can *lock* a field to prevent it from being updated until you unlock it. To lock a field, place the cursor anywhere in the desired field and press Ctrl+F11. To unlock the field, place the cursor anywhere in the field and press Ctrl+Shift+F11.

Using fields in an example

To see how fields can be used within a document, first open a new document in the usual manner and then perform the following steps:

1. Choose Insert⇨Field to display the Field dialog box. In the Categories list box, choose Date and Time. Then click on Date in the Field Names list box

and click on OK. The current date, as measured by your PC's clock, appears at the insertion point. (If you see the actual field type and instructions for the field instead of the current date, choose Tools⇨Options, click on the View tab in the Options dialog box, turn off the Field Codes option, and then click on OK).

2. Press Enter twice and then type the following words:

This document was written by:

Add a space after the colon and then choose Insert⇨Field. In the Categories list of the Field dialog box, choose Document Information. In the Field Names list box, choose Author. Click on OK to insert the author's name into the document. (The name that appears is based on what you entered for a user name when Word was installed; you can change the author's name by choosing the Options command from the Tools menu and clicking the User Info tab of the dialog box.)

Printing field codes

When you print a document containing fields, Word prints the results of the fields by default and does not print the actual field codes themselves. At times, you may want to print the field codes themselves so that you can get a concrete idea of what codes are actually in your documents. You can print the field codes by choosing File⇨Print and then clicking the Options button in the Print dialog box that appears. In the Print tab of the Options dialog box, turn on the Field Codes check box and click OK. Then click OK in the Print dialog box to begin printing.

3. Add a period after the author's name and then start a new sentence by typing the following:

The document contains

Add a space after the last letter and then choose Insert⇨Field. In the Categories list box, choose Document Information. In the Field Names list box, choose NumChars (an abbreviation for "number of characters") and click on OK.

4. Add a space after the number that was just inserted and then finish the sentence by typing the following:

words, and the time of day is now:

5. Add a space after the colon and choose Insert⇨Field. In the Insert Categories list box, choose Date and Time. In the Field Names list box, choose Time. Then click on OK to place the field.

At this point, your document should resemble the one shown in Figure 6-3. Of course, the date and time will be different from the date and time in the figure, and if you have varied the example text, the word count may differ, as well.

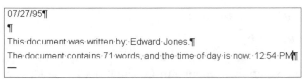

07/27/95¶

¶

This·document·was·written·by:·Edward·Jones.¶

The·document·contains·71·words,·and·the·time·of·day·is·now:·12:54·PM¶

Figure 6-3: The sample document containing fields.

How to Create a Mail Merge

One way to take advantage of fields in your documents is to use them in mail merges to create personalized form letters. You can also create mailing labels and put together legal documents, data sheets, catalogs, and other documents of this kind. Mail merges let you print multiple copies of a document, where certain information (such as a name or address) changes for each document. The form letters that you receive from businesses are examples of mail merges at work.

Mail merges combine two kinds of documents: a *main document,* which contains the text that is identical for each printed copy, and a *data source,* which contains the text that is specific to each copy printed. The main document also contains fields that tell Word where to find the information that is stored in the data source. These fields are referred to as *merge fields.* As you type the main document, you can insert the fields at any desired location.

In the data source, you type the information that Word needs to fill in the fields inserted in the main document. For example, if your main document contains a name field and an address field, your data document should have names and addresses of all the people who should receive the letter. The first line of a data document normally contains a *header record,* a single line that identifies the order in which you place the data in the data document.

Hot Stuff The easiest way to store the information in a data source is to set up a table. If you do not use a table, the data must be separated either by tabs or by commas. You can create a data source by typing the desired information into a Word document. You can also create a data source by using information stored in database form within spreadsheet programs (such as Excel or Lotus 1-2-3) or database management software (such as dBASE or Paradox). In the next section of this chapter, under "Creating a data document," you'll learn how to create a data source by using data stored in a spreadsheet or in a database.

How to finish your mail merge

After the data source and the main document both exist, you can print multiple copies of the main document, based on the data contained in the data source. When you print the file, Word reads the first record in the data source, inserts the fields of that record into the main document, and prints a copy. It repeats this process for as many records as are contained in the data source; therefore, if a data source has five entries that contain the name and address for five individuals, a mail merge operation would print five copies of the document, each addressed to a different individual.

Specifying a main document

In the process of creating a form letter, the first step is to choose the main document that you intend to use. To choose the main document, perform the following steps:

1. Choose Tools⇨Mail Merge to activate the Mail Merge Helper dialog box shown in Figure 6-4.

2. Click on the Create button and choose Form Letters from the list box that appears. Word then asks you whether you want to use the active document or to create a new document as your main document (click on the Active Window button to use the active document).

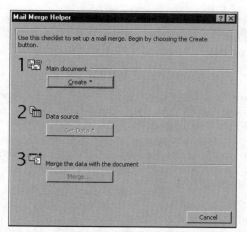

Figure 6-4: The Mail Merge Helper dialog box.

Creating a data source

Now that you have created your main document (the document that will be your actual form letter), you need to create a source from which you will get the data to use in the form letter's fields.

Follow these steps to create a data source:

1. After opening the main document or creating it, choose Tools➪Mail Merge to activate the Mail Merge Helper dialog box (see Figure 6-4).

2. Now click on the Get Data button and choose Create Data Source. This activates the Create Data Source dialog box shown in Figure 6-5. This dialog box aids you in the creation of the fields that you are going to use in your form letter. The Field Names in Header Row box lists commonly used fields for form letters.

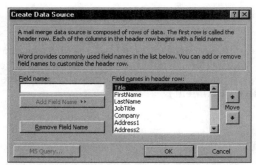

Figure 6-5: The Create Data Source dialog box.

3. In the Field Names in Header Row box, highlight the names of the fields you do not need. Remember Word includes all data fields by default. One by one, you click on the Remove Field Name box to get rid of the fields that you don't need. If you have a field that you want to use that is not included in the list, type the name in the Field name entry and click on the Add Field Name button. Click on the OK button. The Save as dialog box then opens. Enter a name for your data source and save it.

4. Word then displays a message telling you that your data source has no data. Click on the Edit Data Source button to open a data source in which you can enter information for your mail merge. If you have no information for one of the fields, press Enter to skip it. Don't enter any spaces in the boxes. To add a new record, click on the Add New button. Do this until you have entered all the information needed in your data source.

5. Now that you have created your data source, return to your main document by clicking on OK.

6. If you later decide that you want to add information to your data source, click on the Mail Merge Helper button on the Mail Merge toolbar. You will then see the Mail Merge Helper. Under Data Source, click on the Edit button and choose the data source that you created, or you can use the Edit data source button on the Mail Merge toolbar. You will then see the Data Form used to enter information in you data source. Click on the Add New button to add a new record.

Adding merge fields to the main document

After finishing the process of creating a data document or opening the one that you want to use, you can finish the main document.

First, add any text or graphics that you want to complete your document. Then add the fields. Insert a merge field where you want each category of information to appear in printed form. You can format the information in any way you want by using the Formatting toolbar. When the information is placed in the main document, the formatting that you applied appears.

To add merge fields to your main document, follow these steps:

1. Enter the graphics and text that you want in each version of the form letter.

2. Click on the Insert Merge Field button on the Mail Merge toolbar and choose the appropriate merge field. Be sure to add any spaces or punctuation that you want to include between merge fields. (A merge field cannot be typed directly into a document.)

3. Save the main document to complete your work.

Merging data

Now you come to the part where you actually merge the data with the main document. Before continuing, be sure that you have completed the following:

✦ You have entered all the information into the data document.

✦ You have inserted all the merge fields into the main document.

You can use the Mail Merge toolbar to see the form letter on-screen so that you can be sure that the records contain everything you want to have in the form letter. This is done by clicking on the View Merged Data button on the Mail Merge Toolbar. When you have completed your inspection, you can print each letter by using the Print command from the File menu.

Follow these steps to merge the data document with the main document:

1. Be sure that the main document is active and click on the View Merged Data button on the Mail Merge toolbar. You see the information from the first data record inserted into the fields in the main document. Click on the Next Record button on the Mail Merge toolbar to see the information inserted from the next records. You can print the current form letter by choosing File⇨Print.

2. Merge the data document into the main document by doing one of the following:

   If you want to place the resulting form letters or other merged documents into a new document, click on the Merge to New Document button on the Mail Merge toolbar.

   To print the form letters, click on the Merge to Printer button.

How to Print Envelopes and Mailing Labels

Word also provides a way to print mailing labels and envelopes by using the Mail Merge command. You can either create a new data document or use an existing one. This feature can prove invaluable: it prevents you from having to address lots of envelopes by hand.

Printing envelopes

The steps for printing envelopes and mailing labels are similar to the steps used to create a form letter. Follow these steps for printing envelopes:

1. First you need to set up the main document, the one that represents the face of the envelope. Keep in mind that Word uses the information from the currently selected printer. If you want to print on a different printer, you need to know which type of envelope and feeder the printer uses so that you can size the envelope correctly.

2. Choose Tools⇨Mail Merge and click on the Create button in the Main Document area. Select the Envelopes option.

3. In the Microsoft Word message box, click on the Active Window button.

4. You have an option for this step. In the Data Source area, you can click on the Get Data button and choose Open Data Source. Select the data document that you want and click on OK. Then click on the Set Up Main Document button.

   Your other option is to choose Create Data Source from the Get Data menu. Be sure that all the field names you want to include are listed in the Field

Names in Header Row list box and then click on OK. Next, you need to provide a file name to save the data source under and click Save.

5. The Envelope Options tab then appears; select the envelope size that you want from the Envelope Options tab. You can format the appearance of the address by using the font buttons on the Formatting toolbar. You can also adjust the position of the address. Then select the Printing Options tab.

6. Click on the OK button to close the dialog box. The Envelope Address dialog box appears (Figure 6-6).

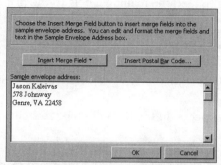

Figure 6-6: The Envelope Address dialog box.

7. In the Envelope Address dialog box, place the insertion point in the Sample Envelope Address box and insert the appropriate merge fields by clicking on the Insert Merge Field button on the Mail Merge toolbar. Enter all the punctuation that you want and press Enter at the end of each line. You can add a postal bar code to identify the delivery address by clicking the Insert Postal Bar Code button.

8. Click on OK to close the Envelope Address dialog box.

9. Click on the Edit button in the Main Document area and select the envelope document from the list of envelope documents.

10. The envelope is now displayed in Page Layout view in a frame. If an address is specified in the mailing address area, check the printer to be sure it is ready to print. Click on the Merge to Printer button.

After all of the steps have been performed, the envelope should zip right through your printer.

Printing mailing labels

You can also use Word to print mailing labels. If you have used the Merge command from the Print menu in earlier versions of Word, you can reuse your main document. If this is the first time you are printing labels or you want to change the size of the labels, use Tools⇨Mail Merge and set up a new main document. A document is automatically set up for most Avery brand labels. If you need to use another brand, specify an Avery label of the same size or specify a custom label. Keep in mind that it is important to know what printer you are using. Each printer feeds labels differently; therefore, you may need to look at your printer's documentation to see how to feed the mailing labels to the printer.

To print mailing labels, perform the following steps:

1. Choose Tools⇨Mail Merge and click on the Create button.

2. Choose the Mailing Labels option. In the Microsoft Word message box, click on the Active Window button.

3. The Mail Merge Helper dialog box appears. In the Data Source area, click on the Get Data button.

4. In this step, you have four options. You can choose Open Data Source, select the desired file in the dialog box, and click on Open. When the Word message is displayed, choose the Set Up Main Document button.

   Or you can create your own data document by choosing Create Data Source. In the dialog box that is displayed, save the new data document. When the next message is displayed, click on the Edit Data Source button. Enter the address information in the Data Form dialog box. Click on the OK button and then click the Mail Merge Helper button on the Mail Merge toolbar. Then click on the Setup button in the Main Document area.

   When you choose Use Address Book, the Use Address Book dialog box appears. Choose which address book you want to use.

   You can also choose Header Options. When you do, the Header Options dialog box appears. Choose the Create button to create a header. You can also use a current data source as a header if you want by clicking on the Open button and choosing the file you want to use.

5. Select the printer type and label feed method in the Label Options dialog box. Before choosing OK, enter the type of label and label product number you are using.

6. Enter the merge fields in the Sample Label text box, as shown in Figure 6-7. Simply move the cursor to the text box, click on the Insert Merge Field button, and select the fields that you want to include. Again, enter any spaces or punctuation that you want between the fields. Press Enter at the end of each line.

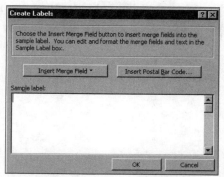

Figure 6-7: The Create Labels dialog box.

7. You can insert a postal bar code by clicking on the Insert Postal Bar Code button, selecting the fields that contain the ZIP code and delivery address, and clicking on OK.

8. Click on OK to close the Create Labels dialog box after you have inserted the merge fields.

9. Be sure that the printer is ready to print and then click on the Merge to Printer button on the Mail Merge toolbar.

How to Use Other Software to Create Data Documents

So far in this chapter, you've used data documents that were created by typing the data directly into a Word table. While this method has its advantages, you may want to set up a data document by using tabs or commas, especially when the data is already stored in another software package, such as in a spreadsheet or in a database manager. Most spreadsheets and nearly all database managers can export a file in a file format known as *comma-delimited*. This common file format can be imported as text into a Word document, and the document can then be used as the data document in a mail merge operation. (See your spreadsheet or database manager documentation for details on how to create a comma-delimited file.)

When setting up a data document where the data is not stored in table form, you must use either tabs or commas to separate the fields. A paragraph mark (at the end of the line) indicates the end of each record. If you use commas as field separators, you can also include quotation marks around each field. The quotation marks are not required, but many database managers automatically add quotation marks around each field when they produce comma-delimited files. All versions of dBASE and most dBASE-compatible database managers, for example, produce comma-delimited files resembling the following example:

```
"Johnson","Linda",2890.30,"Carrollton","TX"
"Ford","Brandon",2495.00,"Fort Worth","TX"
"Fairfield","Jason",2075.40,"Dallas","TX"
"Johnson","Mark",1890.50,"Arlington","TX"
"Sutton","Alberta",1775.00,"Carrollton","TX"
"Laveina","Chrissy",1740.00,"Dallas","TX"
"Carrol","Sarita",1534.60,"Garland","TX"
"Tellado","Carlos",1390.00,"Fort Worth","TX"
"Tatiem","Ryan",1170.20,"Dallas","TX"
```

In this database, all character fields are surrounded by quotation marks. Word can work with this file as a data document with no modifications, other than the addition of a header to indicate the names of the fields.

Working with Excel worksheets

Working Together

You can use Excel to create data documents, which is useful when you want to pull information from Excel for your mail merge. If you have a database stored as an Excel worksheet, you can easily create a table in Word based on that data. The process is much easier with Excel than with most other software. When a portion of an Excel worksheet is selected and copied to the insertion point in a Word document, the Excel data appears in the form of a table. You can then add a header and save the table as a Word document. Then you use the Mail Merge commands to do the merge.

To transfer data from an Excel worksheet into a Word document, perform the following steps:

1. Start Excel and open the desired worksheet.

2. Using the selection techniques common to Excel, select the worksheet range that contains the desired data.

3. Choose Edit⇨Copy to copy the selection to the Clipboard.

4. Start Word (if it's not already running) and open a new document.

5. Choose Edit⇨Paste. The data that was selected in the Excel document appears as a table in Word.

6. Choose Table⇨Insert Rows to add a new row to the start of the table and enter the header information into this row. (This step may not be necessary if the worksheet range you copied had column names in the first row. You can use the existing column names as the header.)

After the data exists in table form in Word, you can use the techniques outlined earlier in this chapter to complete the mail merge process.

Embedding data

Sometimes you will want to use data that already exists in Access or Excel for your merge. By establishing an OLE link to existing data in Access or Excel, you gain the advantage of having your mail merge information automatically updated when the data in Access or Excel changes. You can use this data by choosing between two methods: you can insert field codes that provide a link from your data document to the database file, or you can use the less complicated way and insert the data directly into the data document.

For more information about OLE (Object Linking and Embedding), see Chapter 50.

If you think you will regularly update the information in your data document, you will want to use the field code method. If you won't be updating the information, insert it directly into the data document. In both cases, click on the Insert Database button on the Database toolbar to open the Database dialog box shown in Figure 6-8.

Next click on the Get Data button to open the Open Data Source dialog box shown in Figure 6-9. This box looks like the Open dialog box from the File menu. Choose the data document that you want to use from the list by clicking on the Files of type list box. You can choose an Excel worksheet, an Access database, another Word document, or a number of other types.

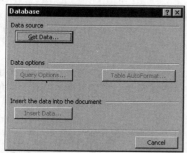

Figure 6-8: The Database dialog box.

The application corresponding to the file that you have opened is launched. For example, if you open an Excel file, Excel is launched in the background. You now see a dialog box that allows for the selection of a range if you are importing a worksheet. (You will learn how to import selected records for a database file later.) If you want to enter a range, press the Backspace key and enter a range. If not, choose OK.

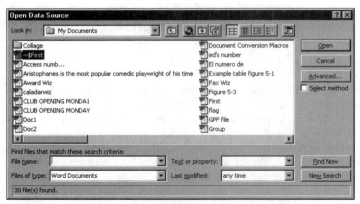

Figure 6-9: The Open Data Source dialog box.

After you have selected the range or the entire worksheet, you have the option of performing a query on the information that you are importing. Click on the Query Options button in the Database dialog box to open the Query Options dialog box, where you can filter records by entering conditions in the Filter Records tab, or you can sort records by choosing the desired sort fields in the Sort Records tab.

If your goal is to limit the number of imported records, click on the Filter Records tab and choose a field from the drop-down list. Next, move to the Comparison box and enter a comparison, such as equal to, not equal to, greater than, less than, and so forth. The final part of the query is to enter a value to which the field can be compared in the Compare to box. If you care to enter additional conditions for the query, accept And as the relationship and enter the rest of the conditions that you want to use in the query on successive lines of the dialog box (see Figure 6-10).

The records can also be sorted. Click on the Sort Records tab of the Query Options dialog box (see Figure 6-11). You can choose a field to sort by, and if there are additional conditions to your sort, you can enter the field names in the Then By boxes. Then choose between sorting in ascending or descending order.

After you have finished, click on OK, and you are returned to the Database dialog box. Before you click on the Insert Data button, you can format the table by choosing the Table AutoFormat command from the Table menu. The Preview window lets you see what the data will look like after the formatting is applied.

After choosing the format that you want for the table, click on OK and then click on the Insert Data button in the Database dialog box. The Insert Data dialog box appears, as shown in Figure 6-12. This dialog box gives you one more opportunity to choose a range for the information being imported. If you want to choose the entire worksheet, click on OK to import the information.

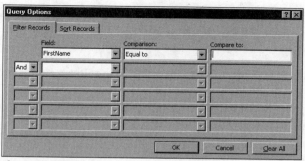

Figure 6-10: The Filter Records tab of the Query Options Dialog box.

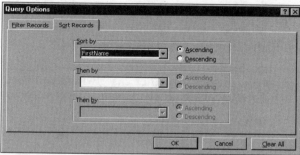

Figure 6-11: The Sort Records tab of the Query Options dialog box.

Figure 6-12: The Insert Data dialog box.

If you want the information to be linked, activate the Insert Data as a Field check box in the Insert Data dialog box. The information can be updated by selecting the text containing the fields, right-clicking the selected text, and choosing Update Fields from the shortcut menu that appears.

Summary

This chapter has detailed the following topics related to working with fields:

✦ Fields are instructions that Word uses to insert certain information, such as the current date, into a document.

✦ You can insert fields by choosing Insert⇨Field, or by using the Insert Field shortcut key combination (Ctrl+F9).

✦ You can update a field's results by right-clicking on the field and choosing Update Fields from the shortcut menu.

✦ Fields can be formatted like other text.

✦ A major use of fields in Word is in the creation of form letters, which can be handled with the Mail Merge Helper built into Word.

✦ Fields can also be used in the creation of envelopes.

✦ We also covered the creation of data sources in other software applications. This is very useful for large mailing lists or other cases where you need to work with large amounts of data that would be better handled in Access.

Where to go next...

✦ Embedding data in a document makes use of OLE. For more information on OLE, see Chapter 50.

✦ After you have created your form letters, you will want them to look the best that they can. This will require some formatting work. For more information on formatting, see Chapter 3.

✦   ✦   ✦

Building Tables of Contents and Indexes

This chapter covers two elements of a document that are similar in many ways: tables of contents and indexes. Both are essentially lists that are arranged in slightly different ways. A table of contents is a list of the major portions of a document (such as sections of a report), including the page numbers for each section. By comparison, an index is a list of important words or subjects in a document with page numbers where the subjects can be found.

Word lets you avoid much of the work in preparing both tables of contents and indexes. With the Index and Tables command from the Insert menu, you can automatically create tables of contents and similar lists or indexes based on special fields that you insert while writing your document. Besides saving you all that typing and formatting time and labor, you can easily update the table of contents and index to reflect changes that you make to the document.

Building Tables of Contents

You can use several methods for building a table of contents: you can base the table of contents on built-in heading styles or outline headings, you can change the default styles so that Word creates the tables of contents based on your chosen styles, or you can build the table of contents by using *TC fields,* a special type of field that you insert into a document by using the steps outlined in this chapter. The easiest method for creating a table of contents requires that you structure your document in outline form. Figure 7-1 shows an example of a typical table of contents in Word. In this case, the table of contents was generated on the default Heading styles used throughout the document.

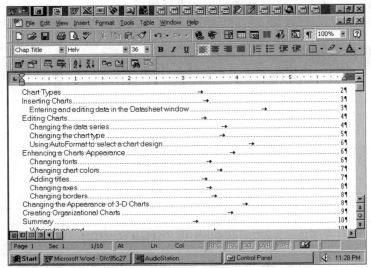

Figure 7-1: A typical table of contents generated in Word.

Hot Stuff   If you need both a table of contents and an index in the same document, create the index first (use the techniques discussed in the second part of this chapter). In this way, you can include an entry for the index in your table of contents.

Using style and outline headings

In any document, Word includes the default styles of Normal, Heading 1, Heading 2, Heading 3, and Heading 4. You can apply these styles (or outline headings, if you've added these to your documents) to lines of text in your document to make the creation of tables of contents a simple matter. Follow these steps:

More Info

1. Check the headings of your document to be sure that they are formatted in one of the Heading styles. To apply a Heading style, place the insertion point anywhere within the heading, open the Style list box at the left side of the Formatting toolbar, and choose one of the Heading styles. (For more about the use of styles, see Chapter 8.)

2. Move the insertion point to the place where you want the table of contents.

3. Choose Insert⇨Index and Tables and then click on the Table of Contents tab in the Index and Tables dialog box (see Figure 7-2).

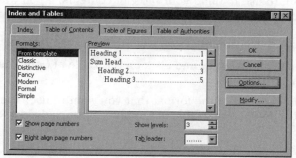

Figure 7-2: The Table of Contents tab of the Index and Tables dialog box.

4. In the Formats list box, select the format that you want to use in your table of contents. As you click on the different formats, a representative sample of what the table of contents will look like appears in the Preview area of the dialog box.

   Along with the format, you can include page numbers by leaving the Show Page Numbers check box turned on. You can also specify the number of heading levels by entering the desired value in the Show Levels box. (When you select 1, only Heading 1 styles are included in the table of contents; when you select 2, Heading 1 and Heading 2 styles are included in the table of contents; and so on.) Clicking on the Options button displays the Options dialog box that lets you designate styles (other than Word's default Heading styles) that Word should use to build the table of contents.

5. After you select the options that you want, click on the OK button. Word constructs the table of contents at the insertion point location.

Why does my table of contents contain funny codes instead of real text entries?

If you see a series of codes, such as {TOC}, rather than actual text after you generate your table of contents, your table of contents is displaying field codes. If you want to see the actual text of the table of contents, place the cursor in the field code and press Shift+F9. You can also choose Tools⇨Options, select the View tab in the Options dialog box, and then clear the Field Codes check box in the Show area.

Using nonstandard styles

Sometimes you may find that the heading styles that are built into Word are not the styles that you want to use to build your table of contents. If you want to base the table of contents on different styles, you can do so by performing these steps:

1. Position the cursor in the area that you want to insert the table of contents.

2. Choose Insert➪Index and Tables and click on the Table of Contents tab in the Index and Tables dialog box.

3. In the Formats list box, select the format that you want to use. Then click on the Options button to open the Table of Contents Options dialog box (see Figure 7-3).

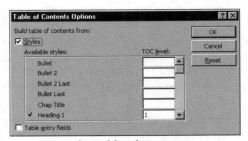

Figure 7-3: The Table of Contents Options dialog box.

4. Type a number from 1 to 9 in the TOC Levels entry to the right of the style name. This number is the level in the table of contents that you want headings that use this style to represent.

5. Scroll down in the Available Styles list box to find the style that you want to use for the table of contents. Click on the check box beside the name to turn it on. Repeat Steps 4 and 5 for all styles that you want to compile in the table of contents. Delete all level numbers that you will not use in your table of contents.

6. Click on the OK button in the Table of Contents Options dialog box to see the preview of what the table of contents will look like in the Index and Tables dialog box.

7. Click on the OK button in the Index and Tables dialog box. Word compiles the table of contents at the insertion point location.

Using TC entries

Another method for building a table of contents involves adding fields called *TC entries* (an abbreviation for table of contents entries) to your document. You can use the Ctrl+F9 (Insert Field) key combination because it takes fewer mouse actions than its equivalent of using Insert⇨Field. The overall technique involves two main steps: identifying and marking the items that should be included in the table of contents and then generating the table of contents itself.

How can I make the strange codes go away?

By default, TC entries are stored as hidden text. If you cannot see them, however, they become difficult to enter because you cannot see what you're typing. If you do see the codes, they may become annoying to look at when you are trying to proof your text. You need a way to turn these codes on and off easily. You can make hidden text visible while you are entering the TC entries by clicking on the Show/Hide button on the Standard toolbar. After you have finished inserting the TC entries, you can turn them into hidden text by clicking on the Show/Hide button again.

You can insert TC entries in a document and generate the table of contents by performing the following steps:

1. Be sure that hidden text is showing on the screen. (If you can see paragraph markers at the end of your paragraphs, then hidden text is showing.) If not, click on the Show/Hide button on the Standard toolbar.

2. Place the insertion point at the location in the document where you want to insert a TC entry. (A good place for TC entries is right after the section titles or headings in your document.)

3. Press Ctrl+F9 to insert an empty field. You will see the field braces with the insertion point placed between them. The field code resembles the following: {_}

4. Type the letters **TC** and then a space. Then type a quotation mark and then the entry that you want to appear in the table of contents and then another quotation mark. (The letters *TC* can be either uppercase or lowercase.) For example, if you want to add a table of contents entry that reads *Unpacking your new lawn mower*, your entry would resemble the following:

   {tc "Unpacking your new lawn mower"}

5. Repeat Steps 2 through 4 for each table of contents entry that you want to add.

6. When all the TC entry fields have been placed in the document, move the insertion point to the desired location in your document for the table of contents.

7. Choose Insert⇨Index and Tables and click on the Table of Contents tab. Next click on the Options button and, in the dialog box that appears, turn on the Table Entry Fields check box. This action tells Word to base the table of contents on the TC entries that you have added to the document. Click on the OK button.

8. Click on the OK button in the Index and Tables dialog box. Word builds the table of contents at the insertion point location.

   If the Field Codes option is turned on, you will see field codes in the table of contents rather than text. You can turn off the field codes by choosing Tools⇨Options, clicking on the View tab in the Options dialog box, and turning off the Field Codes option. (Another easy way to turn off the field codes is to right-click in the field code, and choose Toggle Field Codes from the shortcut menu that appears.)

Remember that the table of contents is based on a Word field. If you make changes to the document that changes the page count, you need to update the table of contents if it is to reflect those changes. To update a table of contents, place the insertion point anywhere within the table of contents and right-click. Choose Update Field from the shortcut menu that appears.

Hot Stuff Remember that TC entries are fields. If you want to delete or move a TC entry to another location, select the entire field and move it or delete it as you would move or delete any text in Word.

Creating Your Own Table of Contents

To see how to build a table of contents by inserting TC fields, you can follow the steps in the next exercise. Or if you have a sizable document of your own, you may want to apply these steps to create a table of contents based on your own document:

1. Choose File⇨New and then click on the OK button to create a new document.

2. Type the following lines (press Enter after each one) and press Ctrl+Enter after each line to insert a page break between each line and the next:

   Principles of Flight

   Aircraft and Engines

   Flight Instruments

   Navigation

Formatting your table of contents and indexes on the fly

Probably the easiest way to make a quick format change to your table of contents or index is to right-click anywhere within the table of contents or index. Then choose the Font, Paragraph, or Bullets and Numbering command from the shortcut menu that appears. Depending on which menu option you select, you can then make appropriate changes in the dialog box that appears.

3. If the hidden text option is not turned on, click on the Show/Hide button on the Standard toolbar (it's the button containing the paragraph symbol, which sort of looks like a backwards letter *P*) to show the hidden characters.

4. Place the insertion point at the end of the first line of text. Press Ctrl+F9 and then type the following inside the braces:

   tc "Principles of Flight"

5. Move the insertion point to the end of the next line of text. Press Ctrl+F9 and then type the following inside the braces:

   tc "Aircraft and Engines"

6. Move the insertion point to the end of the next line of text. Press Ctrl+F9 and then type the following inside the braces:

   tc "Flight Instruments"

7. Move the insertion point to the end of the next line of text. Press Ctrl+F9 and then type the following inside the braces:

   tc "Navigation"

8. Press Ctrl+Home to get back to the start of the document. Press Enter once to add a new line and then press Ctrl+Enter to insert a page break. Press Ctrl+Home again to get back to the start of the document. You will add the table of contents on what is now page 1 of the document, with the remainder of the document appearing on the following four pages.

9. Choose Insert⇨Index and Tables. Then click on the Table of Contents tab in the Index and Tables dialog box.

10. Click on the Options button to open the Table of Contents Options dialog box and turn on the Table Entry Fields check box. Click on the OK button.

11. Click on the OK button in the Index and Tables dialog box. Figure 7-4 shows the resulting table of contents that is inserted into the document.

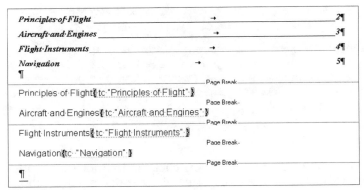

Figure 7-4: The sample table of contents.

Building Tables of Figures

A table of figures is another type of list that you can easily create in Word. Like a table of contents and an index, a table of figures is a list of items. In this case, the items are figure captions, shown in the order in which the figures appear in the document. A table of figures can include such items as illustrations, figures, charts, or graphs. Examples of figure captions appear throughout this book: every figure in this book includes a caption that describes the figure. You can do the same kind of thing in your Word for Windows documents.

All the captions that you create in your documents can be easily included in a table of figures that you can place at any location within your document. You first create the document, and then you insert the captions in your document by choosing Insert⇨Caption. In the Caption dialog box, you type the name of the caption. You repeat this process for every caption that you want to insert.

After inserting all your captions, you can perform the following steps to insert the table of figures:

1. Position the cursor where you want to place the table of figures.

2. Choose Insert⇨Index and Table and click on the Table of Figures tab in the Index and Tables dialog box (see Figure 7-5).

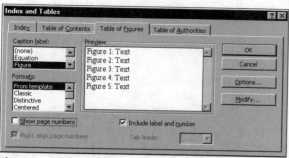

Figure 7-5: The Table of Figures tab in the Index and Tables dialog box.

3. Choose the kind of caption label that you want for your table of figures.

4. Select the format that you want for your table. As with tables of contents, you can choose to do your table of figures from a template, use a Classic, Distinctive, Centered, Formal, or Simple style. (These formats are displayed in the Preview portion of the dialog box.) The Show Page Numbers option, when checked, causes page numbers to be included with the table of figures. The Right Align Page Numbers option, when checked, causes the page numbers to be aligned with the right margin.

5. After making your choices, click on the OK button to insert the table of figures at the insertion point.

Building Indexes

Word lets you build indexes in a manner very similar to the one for building tables of contents. You again insert special fields, called *index entries*, into the document at locations where you mention the indexed topics. In the case of index entries, Word provides a command just for this purpose, or you can use the Insert Field key (Ctrl+F9). After you mark all the index entries, you use Insert⇨Index and Tables to place the index at the insertion point. As with a table of contents, the index that Word generates is based on a field, which you can easily change by updating the field as the document changes.

Word offers considerable control over the index. You can generate an index for the entire document or for a range of letters in the alphabet. Index entries can all appear flush left in the index, or they can be indented to multiple levels. And you can easily add bold or italics to the page numbers of the index entries.

Marking the index entries

Every item that is to appear in the index must have an index entry. You can mark index entries by performing the following steps:

1. Select the text in the document that you want to use for an index entry or place the insertion point immediately after the text.

2. Choose Insert⇨Index and Tables and then click on the Index tab in the Index and Tables dialog box. Click on the Mark Entry button to reveal the Mark Index Entry dialog box (see Figure 7-6). By default, any selected text appears in the Main Entry text box. If you want the text to appear in the index as a subentry (a secondary-level index heading), delete any entry in the Main Entry text box and enter the entry in the Subentry text box.

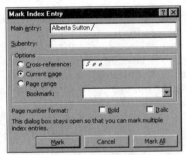

Figure 7-6: The Mark Index Entry dialog box.

3. After entering the desired entry, click on the Mark button. Word inserts the index entry at the insertion point location. (Like the fields that you use to insert tables of contents, index entries are stored as hidden text. You will not see them in the document unless you click on the Show/Hide button on the Standard toolbar.

The Mark Index Entry dialog box contains various options that you can use to determine how Word should handle the index entries. In the Cross-reference text box, you can type the text that you want to use as a cross-reference for the index entry. You can also specify a range of pages in an index entry by turning on the Page Range option and typing or selecting a bookmark name that you used to mark a range of pages. And you can use the Page Number Format options to apply bold or italic formatting to page numbers in the index.

For those who despise menus and dialog boxes, an alternative way of inserting index entries exists. Because an index entry is a field, you can use the Insert Field key (Ctrl+F9) to insert an index entry. To do so, press Insert Field (Ctrl+F9), type the letters **xe** and then a space, and then type the index entry surrounded by quotation marks. If you want the page number of the index entry to be in bold or italic, you must also add a \b or \i switch; type **\b** for bold or **\i** for italic (you can add both options in the same field). With hidden text showing, a sample index entry may resemble the following:

{xe "Adding Oil to the Lawn Mower" \b}

One important note: an index entry should follow the topic to which it refers in the text; that is, the index entry should be placed immediately *after* the sentence that concludes the subject that is indexed. (If you select the text before you use the Index and Tables command — rather than typing the index entry yourself — Word automatically places the index entry immediately after the selection.) This rule of thumb is important because if you place the index entry before the subject being indexed, and the subject is near the bottom of the page, Word may add a page break between the index entry and the text. The result would be an index with an incorrect page number.

Inserting the index

After you mark all the index entries, you can use Insert⇨Inde_x_ and Tables to place the index in the document. To insert the index, perform the following steps:

1. Place the insertion point at the desired location for the index. (With most documents, indexes are customarily placed at the end of the document.)

2. Choose _I_nsert⇨Inde_x_ and Tables and click on the Index tab of the Index and Tables dialog box, as shown in Figure 7-7.

Figure 7-7: The Index tab of the Index and Tables dialog box.

3. Choose the type of index (Indented or Run-in) that you want and choose the desired format for the index. As you select among the available formats, a preview of each format appears in the Preview area of the dialog box.

4. After you click on the OK button, Word generates the index. Note that if Field Codes is turned on, you will see the fields that built the index and not the index itself. You can turn off the field codes by choosing the Options command from the Tools menu and clicking on the View tab of the Options dialog box. Then turn off the Field Codes option in the Show area of the tab.

Creating multilevel index entries

You can insert index entries that indicate multiple levels. As an example, the following part of an index is designed with two levels:

Data
> Copying, 104
> Definition, 251
> Deleting, 92
> Editing, 91
> Linking, 216
> Reporting, 251

Data Menu, 64, 216

Database
> Attributes of, 251
> Creating, 216
> Criteria, 230

To create an index based on multiple levels, you enter the text of the secondary entry in the Subentry text box rather than in the Main Entry text box of the Mark Entry dialog box. If you are typing the entries manually, you simply add a colon (:) when you type the index entry into the dialog box to separate the levels. You can create a multilevel index by performing the following steps to mark your index entries:

1. Place the insertion point at the desired location for the index.

2. Choose Insert⇨Index and Tables and click on the Index tab of the Index and Tables dialog box. Then click on the Mark Entry button.

3. In the Main Entry text box, type the first-level entry. In the Subentry text box, type the second-level entry.

4. Click on the Mark button to place the index entry.

When you specify multiple levels, keep in mind that you now have a choice of how Word structures a multilevel index when you use the Index and Tables command. You can choose either the Indented or the Run-in type of Index on the Index tab. The default option is the Indented type of index, which results in an index where sublevel entries are indented, as shown in the following example:

Database
    Attributes of, 251
    Creating, 216
    Criteria, 230

On the other hand, if you choose the Run-in option in the dialog box, Word inserts all sublevel entries in the same paragraph as the main entry in the index. The main entry is separated from the subentries with a colon, and all remaining subentries are separated by semicolons. The preceding indented example now appears as a run-in example in the following:

Database; Attributes of, 251; Creating, 216; Criteria, 230

Using page number ranges in indexes

In those cases where a subject covered by an index entry spans several pages in a document, you may want the reference in the index to include the range of pages in the document. In the following example, the entries for the Go To command and Hardware both contain a range of pages:

Get Info command, 41

Go To command, 62-65

Gridlines command, 145

Hardware, 19-20

Help menu, 12

With the methods described so far for inserting index entries, you get only the first page of the subject referred to by the index, even if you make a selection that spans multiple pages. If you want page numbers that span a range of pages, you must do things a little differently. First you must select the range of text and insert a bookmark that refers to the selection by following these steps:

1. Use your preferred selection method to select the range of text that you want to index.

2. Choose Insert⇨Bookmark. In the Bookmark dialog box, type a name for the bookmark and then click on the Add button.

3. Choose Insert⇨Index and Tables, click the Index tab, and click on the Mark Entry button. In the Mark Index Entry dialog box, click on the Page Range Bookmark radio button and enter the bookmark name in the list box. When you create the index using the steps described earlier in this chapter, your entry includes your specified range of pages.

Using additional index options

Additional switches are available for you to use in index fields in Word to add sophistication to your indexes. These features include changing the separator character that is used between ranges of page numbers (normally a hyphen) and restricting an index to include only index items that begin with a certain letter. These special index switches are beyond the scope of this book, but you can find out more about them in your *Microsoft Word User's Reference*.

Building Large Indexes

If you are generating a large index (one with 4,000 entries or more), Word may run out of memory when you attempt to use the Index and Tables command. Microsoft recommends that you generate indexes for very large documents in multiple steps. For example, first you build an index that contains entries only for the letters A through L, and then you build an index for the letters M through Z. You choose the Field command from the Insert menu rather than the Index and Tables to insert a separate field for each portion of the index after you have marked all the entries that you want in the document.

To create a separate field for each portion of the index, do the following:

1. Place the insertion point at the location in the document where the index is to appear.

2. Choose Insert⇨Field.

3. Type the word **index** followed by a space, a backslash, the letter **p**, a space, and a range of letters (such as A - L).

4. Click on the OK button to insert the first index field into the document. If the hidden text option is turned on, the field may resemble the following:

    {index \p A - L}

5. Move the insertion point to the right of the existing index field and press Enter to start a new line.

6. Repeat Steps 2 through 5 for each additional range of letters that you need.

Summary

In this chapter, you learned how to use Word's capabilities to generate tables of contents and indexes. The chapter covered the following topics:

✦ Tables of contents can be based on heading styles, outline headings, or TC fields (a special kind of field inserted into a document).

✦ If you use Word's default heading styles or outlining in your document, you can quickly generate a table of contents by choosing Insert⇨Index and Tables, clicking the Table of Contents tab, and selecting the desired format in the dialog box.

✦ You can create tables of contents based on any text in your document by adding fields called TC Fields to your document. After adding the fields, you can generate a table of contents with the Table of Contents tab which appears in the dialog box when you choose Insert⇨Index and Tables from the menus.

✦ You can create indexes by adding fields called Index Entries to your document. After adding the Index Entries, you can generate an index with the Index tab which appears in the dialog box when you choose Insert⇨Index and Tables from the menus.

In the next chapter, you'll learn how to work effectively with styles and templates to govern the overall appearance of your document in Word.

Where to go next...

✦ If you make full use of Word's predefined styles or of outlines in your documents, the creation of tables of contents becomes an easy task. You can find more information on working with Word's predefined styles in Chapter 8. For the lowdown on using outlines in Word, see Chapter 5.

✦ Also, an important part of any complex document will be page number formatting, and possibly the inclusion of headers and footers. These topics are detailed in Chapter 3.

✦ ✦ ✦

Working with Styles and Templates

Word provides *styles* and *templates:* tools that you can use to easily mold the appearance of routinely produced documents. The first part of the chapter deals with styles; the second part of the chapter deals with templates. As you will learn, the two concepts are closely related.

What Are Styles and Templates?

Too many users of Word find styles and templates to be an esoteric subject, and they avoid it. It is quite possible to use Word for Windows day after day and never learn about the flexibility of styles or about any templates other than the default template Word uses. You're doing yourself a disservice if you avoid these tools — styles and templates can be major time-savers.

If you're a new Word user, you might be confused about what a style is and what a template is and how the two concepts are different. A *style* is a collection of character formatting and paragraph formatting settings that are stored under different names. Word already has a number of built-in styles, but you can also create your own. Figure 8-1 shows a letter that contains a number of different styles. Notice the names of the styles to the left of the document. (You can display style names at the far left like this by choosing Tools ➪ Options, clicking the View tab, and changing the Style Area Width value in the dialog box that appears.) You can use the drop-down Style list on the left side of the Formatting toolbar to view all the available styles as you are creating a document.

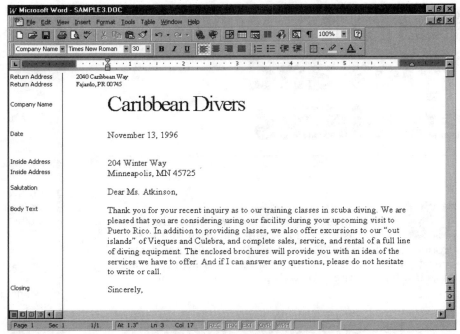

Figure 8-1: An example of a letter containing various styles.

If you use styles, you can save time that you might otherwise spend formatting your documents, and you can give your documents a consistent look. For example, you may routinely apply a 1/2-inch left indent, a first-line indent, and Times Roman font to paragraphs in a document. You can define this set of formatting aspects to a style. After the style has been defined, you then can apply all these formatting aspects to any paragraphs in a document with a single operation.

Besides making formatting easier to apply, styles also offer an advantage when you revise document formats. When you change the formatting in the style, all paragraphs that are formatted with this style will automatically change. For example, you may decide to apply a border and shading to all paragraphs with a particular style. By changing the definition of the style to include the border and shading, you automatically add the border and shading to all paragraphs in all documents that use that particular style.

Word offers two overall kinds of styles that you can use to format your documents: *character styles* and *paragraph styles*. Character styles apply a variety of formatting to the individual letters and punctuation in a document. You apply character styles with the Font command from the Format menu. In the Font dialog box, you can choose formatting that includes font size and style; bold, italics, or underlining; small caps; and other text-related settings. Paragraph styles govern the overall appearance of the paragraph. You apply paragraph styles with the Paragraph command from the Format menu. In the Paragraph dialog box, you can choose formatting that includes indentation, line spacing, and paragraph alignment.

Word normally saves styles along with the active document, but you can easily copy styles that you create to a specific template. A *template* is a collection of styles, keyboard and toolbar assignments, and macros that have been saved to a file with a .DOT extension. By storing styles in templates, you can make these styles available for use whenever you are using that template. When you click on the drop-down arrow in the Style list on the Formatting toolbar, the different styles that you see are all stored in the template that you are using at the present time.

Templates also provide a way to tailor a document quickly, but templates can encompass much more than just character and paragraph formatting. Think of a template as a model that governs the overall format of the document that you create. Templates can contain any boilerplate text that you want included in each variation of a document that you create. For example, in the case of an interoffice memo, you can create a template that has the same text for a company name, date, to, from, and subject headings. In addition to boilerplate text, templates can also contain styles, macros, and custom keyboard, menu, or toolbar assignments.

You select a template whenever you create a new document, as the second part of this chapter explains in more detail. Because templates include collections of styles, it's important to understand styles before you begin working with templates.

Applying Styles

You can apply styles throughout your Word documents in two ways. You can use the drop-down Style list that's in the Formatting toolbar, or you can use keyboard shortcuts.

Using the Formatting toolbar

Because Word comes with a number of default styles, putting them to work is as easy as choosing the desired style from the Style list on the Formatting toolbar. Follow these steps to apply any of the available styles to paragraphs in your document:

1. If the Formatting toolbar isn't already available, choose View⇨Toolbars and click on the Formatting option in the Toolbars dialog box.

2. If you want to apply the style to an entire paragraph, place the insertion point anywhere in that paragraph. To apply the style to a specific portion of a paragraph, select the desired portion of text. To apply the style to more than one paragraph, select all the desired text.

3. Click on the arrow to the right of the Style list in the Formatting toolbar to open the list of available styles (see Figure 8-2).

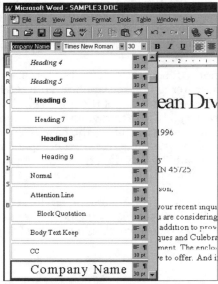

Figure 8-2: The drop-down Style list on the Formatting toolbar.

4. Click on the desired style to apply it to the selected paragraphs.

Hot Stuff If you don't like the effects of style that you apply, remember that you can undo its effects by immediately choosing Edit⇨Undo Style.

Using the keyboard

If you are using a document that is based on Word's default or Normal template, you can use keyboard shortcuts to apply the available styles. Table 8-1 shows the available styles in the Normal template and the keyboard shortcuts that you can use to apply the styles.

Why don't I see all the styles that you show here?

If you look at the available styles shown in Figure 8-2 and compare them to the styles shown in your own Style list, you may find that the lists don't exactly match. "Where are all these styles?" you may ask. Remember that a template is a collection of styles. When you look in the Style list, the styles that you see are part of the template that you are using. I may be using a different template, so my styles will be different. For now, keep in mind that you can choose different templates in the New dialog box that appears when you start a new document. Each template in the New dialog box has its own list of styles that are useful for that particular type of document.

Table 8-1
Styles that have keyboard shortcuts

Style name	Formatting applied	Keyboard shortcut
Normal	Font: Times New Roman 10 point; Language: English (US); Flush Left	Ctrl+Shift+N
Heading 1	Normal; Arial 14 point; Bold; Space Before 12 pts; After 3 pts	Alt+Ctrl+1
Heading 2	Normal; Arial 12 point; Bold; Italic; Space Before 12 pts; After 3 pts	Alt+Ctrl+2
Heading 3	Normal; Arial 12 point; Space Before 12 pts; After 3 pts	Alt+Ctrl+3

Hot Stuff
You can quickly apply the same style to a number of items in your document. After applying the style to the first selection, select the additional text that you want formatted with the same style and press Ctrl+Y.

I applied a style, and my italicized words are now normal text. Why?

If you apply a style that includes bold or italics to selected text that already contains bold or italic formatting, the existing bold or italicized text in the selection will change back to normal text. This change happens because in Word, bold and italic character formatting is a "switch" that is either on or off for a given selection, so any bold or italic formatting applied by a style will toggle that switch, which will remove any bold or italic formatting that was previously applied to the selection.

Defining a Style

Word provides two overall methods for creating, or defining, styles. In the first method, you choose Format⇨Style and then click on the New button in the Style dialog box. In the New Style dialog box that appears, you enter a name for the new style and then click on the Format button to define the style. Then you can choose any of the choices from the Format menu to lay out the aspects of the style. (Yes, this is a lot to describe in one paragraph, but the next section gives you the complete scoop.)

Styles can also be defined by example. In plain English, this means that you can define a style based on an existing paragraph that already has all the desired formatting. This method is easier, but you can be sure of exactly what you are getting only if you use the first method.

Using the Style command

The more powerful (and, yes, more complicated) method of defining a style is using Format⇨Style. This command opens the Style dialog box, as shown in Figure 8-3. Click on the New button in the dialog box to reveal the New Style dialog box, as shown in Figure 8-4.

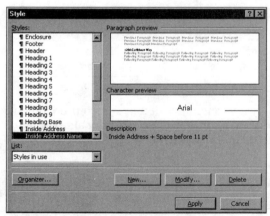

Figure 8-3: The Style dialog box.

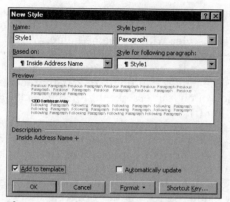

Figure 8-4: The New Style dialog box.

You can change the formatting for the style by clicking on the Format button and selecting the appropriate area that you want to format. Each of the menu choices displayed by the Format button (Font, Paragraph, Tabs, Border, Language, Frame, and Numbering) takes you directly to the dialog box that the particular formatting command uses. For example, choosing Font displays the Font dialog box that is displayed with Format⇨Font, choosing Paragraph displays the Paragraph dialog box that is displayed with Format⇨Paragraph, and so on. The Style Type list box offers two choices — Character or Paragraph — where you indicate whether your new style is a character style or a paragraph style.

Make the desired changes in the respective dialog boxes and then click on the OK button to get back to the New Style dialog box. (The only formatting option not covered elsewhere in this text is the one provided by the Language option. This menu option brings up a dialog box that lets you change the language used by the Spelling Checker, Thesaurus, and Grammar Checker.)

You can use the Based On list box in the New Style dialog box to base a style that you are creating on an existing style. (If the style that you are defining is not based on any other style, this box will be blank.) To base a new style on an existing one, type the name of the existing style into this text box or choose an existing style name. (This technique is covered in more detail in the "Basing a style on another style" section later in the chapter.)

You can turn on the Add to Template check box at the bottom of the New Styles dialog box if you want to add the style that you've defined to the current template. (If you are using the default Normal template, the style will be added to that template and will therefore be available in all documents that you create in Word.)

After you have made all the desired changes to the formatting, you enter a name for the style in the Name box. Remember that each style name must be unique. Because it doesn't make sense to have two styles with the same name, Word doesn't let you make this mistake. Style names are case sensitive, however, so you can use *Figures* and *figures* as two different style names (although to do so would be terribly confusing to most people). Style names can be up to 253 characters in length, and they can use any combination of characters except for the backslash (\), the curly braces ({}), or the semicolon (;).

After giving your style a name, click on the OK button to return to the Style dialog box. From here you can apply the style to the current paragraph or selection by clicking on the Apply button. When you do, the dialog box closes and you are back in your document. After the style has been defined, you can apply that style to the desired paragraphs of the document by using the techniques covered under the "Using the Formatting toolbar" section earlier in this chapter.

The Style dialog box also contains other interesting buttons in addition to the Apply button. Use the Modify button to change the formatting of an existing style that you have selected in the Styles list box. Use the Delete button to remove an unwanted style from the Styles list box. Click on the Organizer button to display the Organizer dialog box, which lets you rename and copy a style (see the "Copying, deleting, and renaming styles" section later in this chapter for more information).

Defining styles by example

The easy way to define a new style is to base it on an existing paragraph and then use the buttons on the Formatting toolbar. You can create a new style based on an existing paragraph by performing these steps:

1. Be sure that the Formatting toolbar is displayed. Then place the insertion point anywhere in the paragraph on which you want to base the style. Make any desired changes to the formatting for that paragraph. (Any changes will be reflected in the new style.)

2. Click *once* in the Style list box on the Formatting toolbar to display the current style of the paragraph. The style is highlighted (see Figure 8-5), indicating that you can type a new name.

3. Type a name for the style and press Enter. Word will add the new style name to the list of styles for the document.

Style list box

Figure 8-5: A highlighted entry in the Style list box.

Assigning a shortcut key to a style

As a time-saving feature, Word lets you assign shortcut keys to styles. Then anytime you want to apply a style that you use regularly, all you have to do is press a key combination to apply the style to the selected paragraphs. To assign a shortcut key to a style, perform the following steps:

1. Choose Format⇨Style.

2. In the Style dialog box (refer to Figure 8-3), select the desired style and then click on the Modify button to open the Modify Style dialog box.

3. Click on the Shortcut Key button to open the Customize dialog box (see Figure 8-6). In this dialog box, you can assign a shortcut key to the style that you have created.

4. Press the desired shortcut key combination. The Currently Assigned To prompt appears in the dialog box.

5. The Currently Assigned To area tells you whether the key combination that you have chosen is currently selected for another use in Word. If you see an existing description for that particular key combination, you can overwrite the existing key assignment or choose another.

6. Click on the Assign button to assign the shortcut key to the style.

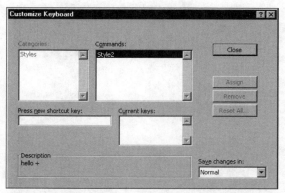

Figure 8-6: The Customize Keyboard dialog box.

Hot Stuff Before you create a large number of styles on your own, first take the time to become familiar with the styles that are already built into Word's templates. Word may already have a style that will accomplish what you want.

Basing a style on another style

In Word, you can base a new style on an existing style. Suppose that you have an existing paragraph of text that uses the Normal style. If you indent that paragraph by 1/2 inch, click once in the Style list box, and type a new name (to define a new style based on the way that the paragraph now appears). The new style that you have just created is based on the Normal style. If you then change the font used for the Normal style, the font used for your new style would also change. In such a case, the Normal style would be the *base style* for the new style that you created.

You can see which (if any) style is used as a base style by opening the Style dialog box (by choosing Format⇨Style). As you select any style in the Styles list box at the left, the Description area at the bottom of the dialog box shows whether that style is based on another style. For example, Figure 8-7 shows the Style dialog box with the Body Text style selected. The Description area tells you that the Body Text style is based on the Normal style with 6-point line spacing after paragraphs are added.

Danger Zone Be aware that this capability to base a style on another style can create quite a chain of interdependencies. For example, in a document that is based on Word's built-in Letter1 template, the Signature Name style is based on the Signature style, which is based on the Body Text style, which is based on the Normal style. A change to the paragraph indentation used by the Normal style would affect all the other styles named.

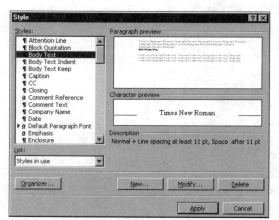

Figure 8-7: The Body Text style is based on the Normal style, according to the Description area in this dialog box.

You can change the base style for any style by using the options found in the Modify Style dialog box. To change a style's base style, follow these steps:

1. Choose Format⇨Style to display the Style dialog box.

2. In the Styles list box, select the style for which you want to change the base style.

3. Click on the Modify button to reveal the Modify Style dialog box, as shown in Figure 8-8. In the Name text box, you should see the name of the style that you want to change. In the Based On list box, you should see the base style that is currently used.

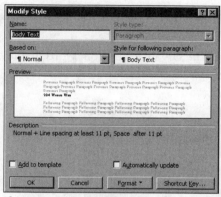

Figure 8-8: The Modify Style dialog box.

4. Click on the arrow at the right side of the Based On list box to display all available styles in the document.

Watch out when redefining the Normal style

Word takes advantage of the fact that styles can be based on styles by basing many of its built-in styles on the Normal style. Therefore, redefining the Normal style can cause major repercussions elsewhere, some of which may prove undesirable. For example, if you redefine the Normal style to use 12-point Arial font, every style based on the Normal style will use 12-point Arial, whether you like it or not. (In your headers and footers, 12-point Arial will look pretty silly.)

5. Choose a desired style to serve as the base style and then click on the OK button.

Note   If you turn on the Add to Template check box before clicking on the OK button, the changes to the base style are recorded in the template that you used to create the document.

Copying, deleting, and renaming styles

Word lets you copy styles from one document to another. In many cases, this capability helps you to avoid the work necessary in creating the same style twice. You can copy styles from one document to another and you can delete and rename styles by performing the following steps:

1. Choose Format⇨Style.

2. In the Style dialog box, click on the Organizer button. Word displays the Organizer dialog box, as shown in Figure 8-9.

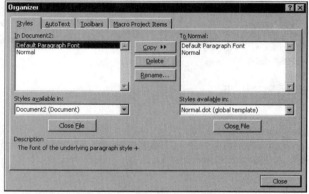

Figure 8-9: The Styles tab of the Organizer dialog box.

3. To copy a style to or from a different document or template, click on the Close File button and then click on the Open File button to open the desired document or template that contains the style. Select the desired style in the list box to the left and click on the Copy button to copy the style to the other document or template.

4. To delete a style, click on the desired style in the list box to the left and then click on the Delete button. (Note that Word will not let you delete its built-in styles; you can delete only custom styles that you or others have created.)

5. To rename a style, click on the desired style in the list box to the left and then click on the Rename button and enter a new name in the dialog box that appears. Then click on Close.

Finding Styles When You Need Them

Word provides two different ways in which you can find and use the various styles. You can display information about your styles as you work, using Word's Help feature and you can use Format⇨Style Gallery.

Displaying style names as you work

You can see which styles are in effect in your documents in two ways. One surprisingly simple way is to use the context-sensitive help that is built into Word to display a dialog box that shows the style information for any text in the document. Press Shift+F1, or choose Help then What is This? from the drop-down menu. The mouse pointer now includes a question mark along with the usual arrow. Then click on any place within the text that you are curious about. After you click, a balloon appears that contains the style and formatting information (see Figure 8-10).

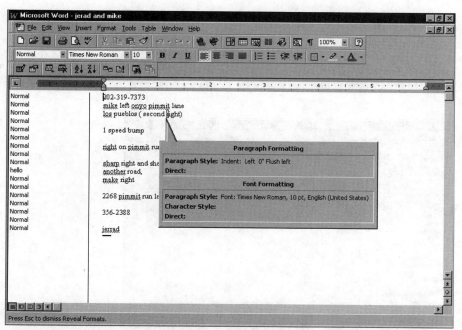

Figure 8-10: A balloon that displays formatting and style information.

The information in the dialog box includes the styles that are applied to the paragraph and the paragraph and font settings. As long as the mouse pointer includes the question mark, you can click on any other text in the document to see its formatting. To turn off the help, again click on the Help button on the Standard toolbar.

Another way to see the styles that you have used in your document is to display them on-screen in the left margin area. In Figure 8-1, you can see the styles displayed in such a manner. To see your styles to the left of the screen, first make sure that you are in either Normal or Outline View (you can't show styles in the margin in any of the other views of Word). Then perform the following steps:

1. Choose Tools⇨Options.

2. Click on the View tab in the Options dialog box.

3. In the Style Area Width box, enter or select a desired width. (One inch works well for showing the names of most styles, unless you've added very long style names to your document.)

4. Click on the OK button. After you do so, the style names in your document appear to the left of the document. You can remove the style names from view by opening the Options dialog box again and changing the Style Area Width setting to zero.

Using the Style Gallery

With Word's plethora of built-in styles scattered across numerous templates, it can be challenging to find where a useful style is located. To help you find the styles that you are looking for, use Word's Style Gallery dialog box (see Figure 8-11). To open this dialog box, choose the Style Gallery command from the Format menu.

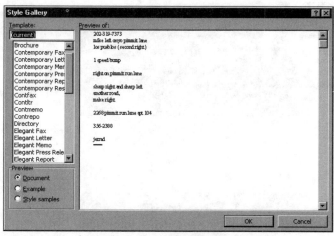

Figure 8-11: The Style Gallery dialog box.

The Template list box contains all the available templates. You can click on any template name in the list box to see a preview of the existing document that uses the styles contained in that particular template. At the lower-left corner of the dialog box, you can click on the Style Samples radio button to view samples of the different styles instead of viewing a preview of the document and you can click on the Example radio button to see an example document formatted with the various available styles. The Style Gallery is often helpful when you're trying to locate a style that will work in a given situation.

Defining and Applying Styles: An Exercise

Try your hand at creating new styles and applying them to a document by performing the following exercise:

1. Open any existing document that contains two or more paragraphs and place the insertion point anywhere in the first paragraph.

2. From the Format menu, choose the Style command. When the Style dialog box appears, click on the New button.

3. In the Name text box, type **My Style** as a name for the new style.

4. Click on the Format button and choose Font from the list to display the Font dialog box (see Figure 8-12). In the Font list box, choose any font other than the one you are currently using and then click on the OK button.

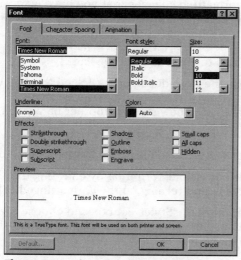

Figure 8-12: The Font dialog box.

5. Press the Format button again and choose Paragraph to display the Paragraph dialog box (see Figure 8-13). In the Indentation area, set the Left value to 0.5 inches; then click on the Special list box, choose First Line, and set the First Line indentation to 0.5 inches. Set the Line Spacing to 1.5 lines and then click on the OK button.

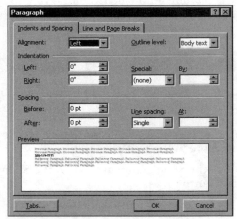

Figure 8-13: The Indents and Spacing tab of the Paragraph dialog box.

Note   The Preview box lists the formatting changes that you have made, including your selected font, the new paragraph indentations, and the new line spacing.

6. Click on the OK button to add the new style to the list.

7. To apply the style and close the Style dialog box, click on the Apply button.

Perform the following steps to apply the new style to another paragraph in the document:

1. Place the insertion point anywhere in a different paragraph of the document.

2. If the Formatting toolbar is not visible, turn it on by choosing the Toolbars command from the View menu and turning on the Formatting check box.

3. Click on the arrow to the right of the Styles list box and choose My Style from the list. When you choose the style, the paragraph assumes the style's formatting, as shown in Figure 8-14.

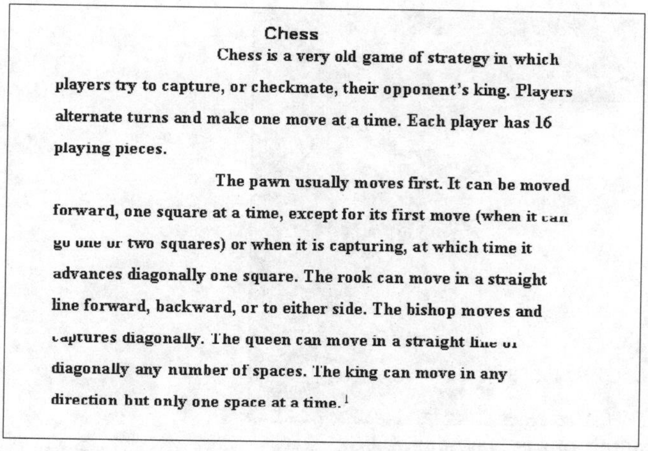

> **Chess**
>
> Chess is a very old game of strategy in which players try to capture, or checkmate, their opponent's king. Players alternate turns and make one move at a time. Each player has 16 playing pieces.
>
> The pawn usually moves first. It can be moved forward, one square at a time, except for its first move (when it can go one or two squares) or when it is capturing, at which time it advances diagonally one square. The rook can move in a straight line forward, backward, or to either side. The bishop moves and captures diagonally. The queen can move in a straight line or diagonally any number of spaces. The king can move in any direction but only one space at a time.[1]

Figure 8-14: The results of applying the styles to sample paragraphs.

Understanding Templates

If you want to carry your consistency of document design even further than character and paragraph formatting, you'll want to make use of templates. As mentioned earlier in the chapter, templates are collections of styles that are saved to a file. They are models that serve as molds for your documents.

When you create a new document with the New command from the File menu, Word always asks which template you want to use by displaying the available templates on several tabs in the New dialog box (see Figure 8-15). The tabs group Word's predefined templates according to their styles. Any new templates that you create appear under the General tab. If you click on the OK button in this dialog box without making a selection, Word uses the default Normal template to create the new document.

When you select a template from this dialog box, your new document takes on all the features belonging to that template — including any text stored in the template; any character, paragraph, and page layout formatting; any preset styles; and any new styles that you have added to the document. Any macros, AutoText entries, or keyboard, menu, or toolbar definitions stored in the template are also available to the document.

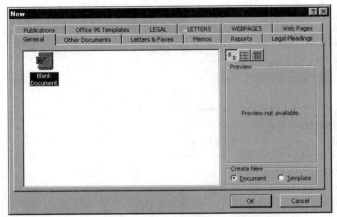

Figure 8-15: The General tab of the New dialog box.

You can use any of Word's predefined templates, or you can create and save your own templates. If you take the time to examine the templates provided with Word, you may find many that can be useful in your work. Word comes with several templates, including

- ✦ Contemporary fax
- ✦ Contemporary letter
- ✦ Elegant fax
- ✦ Elegant letter
- ✦ Professional fax
- ✦ Professional letter
- ✦ Contemporary memo
- ✦ Elegant memo
- ✦ Professional memo
- ✦ Contemporary resume
- ✦ Elegant resume
- ✦ Professional resume
- ✦ Blank web page

Because a template is a document, you use the same procedure to create and save a template as you use for a document. Word lets you specify whether you want to create a document or a template when you use the New command from the File menu. At the lower-right corner of the New dialog box, simply click on the Template radio button to make the new document a template and then click on the OK button. When the new document appears on-screen, you can add whatever boilerplate text, formatting, and styles that you want and then save the file with the Save command from the File menu.

You can also specify that a file be saved as a template after you have created it. For example, if you have created a boilerplate document, and you want to store that document as a template, you can do so with the Save As command from the File menu. In the Save As dialog box, choose Document Template from the Save as Type list box. The file will be saved as a template with the .DOT extension.

Working with Templates

When you need to set standards for more than just the character and paragraph formatting of your documents, you can use templates. As mentioned earlier in this chapter, templates can contain styles, and they can also contain boilerplate text or graphics, macros, and even custom menu, keyboard, and toolbar assignments.

What's "Normal"?

Some new users of Word get confused about what "Normal" refers to. Word has both a Normal *style* and a Normal *template*, and the two don't mean the same thing. The Normal style refers to one particular style (available in all Word's default templates) that defines the character and paragraph formatting for ordinary text. The Normal template, on the other hand, is a template file (saved as Normal.dot) that contains Word's default styles along with the default keyboard, menu, and toolbar macro assignments. All styles and default keyboard, menu, and toolbar macro assignments that are saved to the Normal template are available for use from anywhere within Word.

Applying templates

To apply a template, you simply choose that template by name when you use Word's New command from the File menu. Any template (with a .DOT extension) that you create will appear in the General tab of the New dialog box.

Creating a template

You can create a new template for use with Word by performing the following steps:

1. From the File menu, choose the New command.

2. In the New dialog box, click on the Template radio button and then click on the OK button.

3. Design your template as desired. Word will automatically insert the text and graphics in the same location whenever a new document is created based on that template.

4. Add any desired character, paragraph, section, or page layout formatting and create any desired styles. Define any desired AutoText entries or desired macros.

5. From the File menu, choose the Save command.

6. In the File Name text box, enter a name for the template. By default, Word saves all template files to a folder named Templates, which is stored in the Msoffice folder.

7. Click on the Save button to save the template.

Basing a new template on an existing template

You can use a simple variation of the steps in the preceding section to create a new template based on an existing template. In the New dialog box, click on the Template radio button. Then, click on the desired tab under which the existing template is stored, or choose the name of the template on which you want to base the new template, and then click on the OK button. When you save the template, be sure to save it under a different name than the original template.

Modifying an existing template

To modify an existing template, you simply open the template in a way similar to the way you open a document. From the File menu, choose the Open command. In the Open dialog box, select Document Template from the List Files of Type list box. The list box then shows only those files with a .DOT extension, and you can choose the desired template by name, or you can enter the name in the File Name text box. Make the desired changes to the template and save the template with the Save command from the File menu.

Changing the default template

Word uses its default template, Normal.dot, to store all its *global settings*, those settings that are available no matter what document you are using. Because Normal.dot is the default template, it is worth the time you may need to spend to customize it so that it meets the needs of the work that you do. And because the Normal template is a template like all other templates, you can modify it (and save the changes) as you would any other template. Keep in mind that the Default button present in some dialog boxes also lets you change the default settings in the Normal template. You can change the defaults for the character font, the page setup, and the language used by the proofing tools.

To open the Normal template, choose the Open command from the File menu and select Document Templates from the List Files of Type list box. Then look in the Templates folder (by default, it's stored in the \Program Files\Microsoft Office folder, unless you have customized the storage locations during Office installation). Select the Normal template.

To change the default font, choose the Font command from the Format menu, select the desired font and point size in the Font dialog box, and then click on the Default button. Click on the Yes button in the next dialog box to verify that the changes should be stored in Normal.dot.

To change the default page setup, choose File⇨Page Setup and select the desired options in the Page Setup dialog box. You will have a choice of four tabs: Margins, Paper Size, Paper Source, and Layout. Click on the desired tab and make the appropriate choices in that tab. Click on the Default button and then click on the Yes button in the next dialog box to verify that the changes should be stored in Normal.dot. Click on the OK button to close the Page Setup dialog box.

To change the default language used by the proofing tools, choose the Language command from the Tools menu and Set Language from the submenu to open the Language dialog box shown in Figure 8-16. Select the desired language in the dialog box and then click on the Default button. Then click on the Yes button in the next dialog box to verify that the changes should be stored in Normal.dot. Click on the OK button to close the Language dialog box.

You may need to purchase optional dictionaries to use a language other than the one supplied with the version of Word for your country.

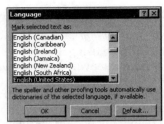

Figure 8-16: The Language dialog box.

Note When you are finished making changes to the Normal template, save the changes by using the Save command from the File menu.

Creating and Applying a Template: An Exercise

To give you practice in creating templates, create your own business letterhead as a template. You can later create documents based on that template, and the documents will automatically include your letterhead. Perform the following steps to create your own template:

1. Choose File⇨New.

2. In the New dialog box, click on the Template radio button and then click on the OK button. A blank document appears with the title Template1.

3. On the first three lines of the document, type your name and address. Add a blank line after the last line of your address.

4. Select all three lines and press Ctrl+E to center the text.

5. With the three lines still selected, choose the Font command from the Format menu. In the Font dialog box, select a font that you like and a larger point size (our example uses Century Gothic, 14 point). Click on Bold in the Font Style list box and then click on the OK button.

6. Press Ctrl+End to move to the end of the document and press Enter twice.

7. From the File menu, choose the Save command. When the Save As dialog box appears, you will notice that any filenames shown are all existing template files.

8. Enter **My Letter** in the File Name text box and then click on the Save button to save the template.

9. Close the document by choosing File⇨Close.

You can now create documents based on the template that you saved. Choose File⇨New, select My Letter from the General tab of the New dialog box, and then click on the OK button. The result will be a new document that already contains your letterhead, such as the example shown in Figure 8-17.

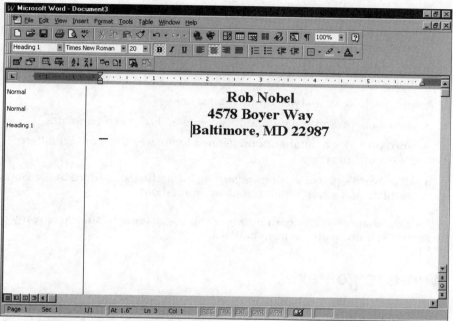

Figure 8-17: A sample letterhead produced with the new template.

This chapter gives you an idea of what you can do with styles and templates — a detailed discussion of the possibilities could fill a book of its own. You can obtain more ideas about creating styles and templates of your own by examining the sample templates provided with Word.

Summary

In this chapter, you learned how you can use styles and templates to mold the appearance of your documents to suit your needs. The following points were covered:

✦ Styles are collections of character and paragraph formatting decisions; templates are collections of styles, macros, and keyboard and toolbar assignments.

✦ You can choose a variety of styles from the Style list on the Formatting toolbar.

✦ You can base new styles on existing styles.

✦ You can copy styles between documents and between templates.

✦ Word provides a number of predefined templates that contain different collections of styles.

✦ All of Word's global settings regarding formatting are stored in the Normal template and saved under the name Normal.dot.

In the next chapter, you'll learn how you can use macros to automate many of the tasks that you normally perform in Word.

Where to go next...

✦ Because styles are, in effect, collections of character and paragraph formatting, it makes sense to be familiar with the mechanics of formatting when you want to put styles to work in your Word documents. You can find more details about those formatting specifics in Chapter 3.

✦ The complexities offered by styles and templates are naturals to use when you want to do desktop publishing in Word. Chapter 10 has the lowdown on desktop publishing.

✦   ✦   ✦

Working with Word Macros

Macros have always had a bad reputation. Macros were first made popular in DOS-based spreadsheet programs where you had to be a borderline programmer to use them. Because things are no longer dismal from an ease-of-use point of view, you do not need to fear macros in Word. Macros are easy to create, and they can accomplish a great deal by saving you time in your everyday work. In this chapter, you will learn what macros are and how you can create them. You can then take a look at step-by-step examples that illustrate how you can use macros to automate your common tasks in Word.

Defining Macros

Macros are recorded combinations of keystrokes and certain mouse actions. Macros can automate many of the tasks that you normally perform manually, keystroke by keystroke, within Word. In a macro, you can record a sequence of keyboard and mouse entries and link them to a single key combination or to a menu option or to a toolbar button. Later, you can "play back" the recorded sequence by pressing the assigned key combination or clicking the toolbar button or choosing the menu option. When the macro plays back, Word performs as if you had manually executed the operations contained within the macro. When your work involves highly repetitive tasks, such as the production of daily reports or the repeating of certain formatting tasks, you can often save many keystrokes by creating a few macros.

More
Info   At first glance, macros may seem similar to AutoText entries (see Chapter 2), but there are significant differences. AutoText entries can reproduce text at any location in a document. Macros can do much more than simulate typing. Macros can

perform menu and dialog box selections — something that you cannot do with AutoText entries. For example, if you routinely print two copies of a certain weekly report, you can create a macro that opens the document, chooses File, prints from the menus, and marks the dialog box options needed to send two copies of the report to the printer.

Word records your macros as instructions in the programming language used by the Microsoft Office applications: Visual Basic for Applications (or VBA for short). Don't panic at the sound of the name (or the implication that you need to learn programming). You can create macros in Word without knowing one iota about Visual Basic for Applications. You can create macros in the following two ways in Word:

✦ You can record a series of keyboard and mouse actions (the most commonly used method). This method requires no knowledge of Word's programming language.

✦ You can type a macro directly into a VBA Editor window. This method enables you to accomplish some advanced tricks by means of VBA commands that you can't do by recording actions, but it requires you to "get your hands dirty" to some extent with VBA.

Not only can you use a macro to combine a sequence of commands that you use regularly, but you can also use a macro to perform routine editing and formatting tasks faster. You can also create a macro to reach those well-buried Word features more quickly, such as the dialog box that you use to change printer options.

Macros are especially useful when you format documents. You may have to change a document's font and spacing, enter heading styles, change margins, and check spelling and grammar. If you make these changes regularly, create a macro so that you don't have to invoke the same commands over and over again. The following sections show you how to make your life easier with macros.

Alternatives to macros

After spending this much time touting the benefits of macros, you should know that sometimes a macro may not be the most effective solution to a specific need. Before you jump into the task of designing macros for any task that you handle often, consider whether another feature of Word can handle the task with less effort on your part. If you want to use a macro to apply many character or paragraph formatting options to selected text, consider using a style sheet instead. If you want to use a macro to type long, repetitive phrases, you can use AutoCorrect instead to designate an abbreviation of your choices to serve as the phrase. And if you are trying to use a macro to automate the process of filling out a form, you can use fields to make this task easier.

Storing Macros

Where you store macros depends on two things: the settings in the Template and Add-ins dialog box (which appears when you choose Tools⇨Templates and Add-Ins) and whether you are using the default template (Normal.dot). If you are using the default template, macros are stored in Normal.dot.

When you exit Word, you are asked whether you want to store the macros you've created during a session to the Normal.dot template; you can answer Yes to store the macros or No to discard the macros.

When you choose Tools⇨Templates and Add-Ins, the Templates and Add-Ins dialog box appears, as shown in Figure 9-1.

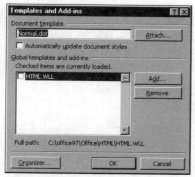

Figure 9-1: The Templates and Add-Ins dialog box.

If you are using a template different from Normal.dot, the storage location for new macros depends on the settings in the Templates and Add-ins dialog box. If you turn on the check box for the template you are using, Word saves macros in that template. You can click on the Add button to display all your templates and double-click on any template to add it to the list in the Templates and Add-ins dialog box. In addition to saving Macros to templates you've checked in the Templates and Add-ins dialog box, on exit Word will ask if you want to save the new macros to the Normal.dot template file. All macros saved to Normal.dot are *global* in nature, which means that they are available from any document in Word.

Creating Macros

The easiest way to record a macro is to turn on Word's macro recorder with Tools⇨Macro and then follow the steps in the dialog boxes that appear. You then perform the desired actions with your keyboard and mouse and tell Word to stop recording.

Note   You can also create macros manually by using Visual Basic for Applications, the programming language used with Word. Using Visual Basic for Applications to write and edit macros is beyond the scope of this chapter, but in short, you open a window into the VBA Editor and type macro instructions using VBA code. (You can learn more about Word and VBA programming in Chapter 12.)

Hot Stuff   The macro recorder is limited in an important way: You cannot record mouse actions within a document, such as selecting text with the mouse. If you try to use the mouse within a document, Word just beeps. You *can* use the mouse to select menu options and choose dialog box settings, however. If you want to select text as part of a macro, use the keyboard. (You can hold down the Shift key and use the arrow keys to select large amounts of text, and you can use the Ctrl+A key combination to select all text in a document.)

Preparing to create your macro

Before you record your macro, you need to make some decisions about how you will invoke your macro, in what kinds of documents you will use your macro, and so on. Keep the following points in mind:

✦ Give some thought to the overall workspace and how it should appear when the macro runs. You want to organize the workspace in the same manner as it should appear when the macro runs. For example, if you will use the macro in a blank document, you should have a blank document on-screen before you begin recording the macro.

✦ Think about all the steps you need to take to accomplish the task for which you are creating the macro. Write the steps down if this will help you remember them. You don't want to forget an important step as you are recording the macro.

✦ If you want the macro to apply to a selected piece of text, select the text before you begin to record the macro.

✦ Think of a name for the macro that reminds you of the macro's function. For example, if you have a bad habit of typing two periods at the end of a sentence and you want a macro that deletes the extra period, you can call the macro DELETE_PERIOD.

✦ Decide how you want to invoke your macro. You can assign a shortcut keystroke to your macro, place it in a menu in the menu bar, or create a button for it in a toolbar.

✦ When you choose to assign a shortcut keystroke to a macro, you can use Shift keys, Ctrl keys, or a combination of Ctrl and Shift keys along with all letters, numbers, and function keys F2 through F12. Word also lets you use the Insert and Delete keys alone or with the Ctrl or Shift keys. When you assign the keystroke, simply press it to execute the macro. So if you assign Ctrl+Alt+P to a macro that prints two copies of the document that's currently open and then you open a document and press Ctrl+Alt+P, the document prints twice.

It's not a good idea to assign a macro to the Insert or Delete key because doing so disables the normal editing function of these keys. Also, be aware that Word has several shortcut keys that have already been assigned to execute other functions. You can assign a macro to these pre-assigned keystrokes, but if you do, their pre-assigned function will be lost. For example, Ctrl+B makes typed or selected text appear in bold font. If you assign Ctrl+B to a macro, you would not be able to use that key combination to apply bold to any text. Don't worry about accidentally overwriting a keystroke, however, because Word tells you whether it's already assigned to another function.

Recording the macro

To record a macro, follow these steps.

1. Choose Tools⇨Macro⇨Record New Macro. In a moment, the Macro dialog box appears, as shown in Figure 9-2.

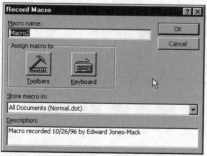

Figure 9-2: The Record Macro dialog box.

2. Type a name for your macro in the Macro Name text box. (Macro names cannot contain spaces, commas, or periods.) Word creates a new macro, saves it in the Normal.dot template, and makes the macro available to all active templates unless you choose a different template in the Store macro in list box.

3. If desired, add an optional description in the Description text box.

4. To assign the macro to a toolbar button or to a key combination, click the Toolbars button or the Keyboard button, as desired. (Which you use is up to you, and one isn't necessarily better than the other. People who aren't wild about the use of the mouse generally prefer keyboard shortcuts.)

5. After you choose how you want to activate the macro, the Customize dialog box appears.

If you choose to add the macro to a toolbar, click the Toolbars tab of the Customize dialog box (see Figure 9-3). Turn on the desired toolbar if it isn't already visible. Then click the Commands tab and drag the name of the macro to the area on the toolbar where you want to place the button.

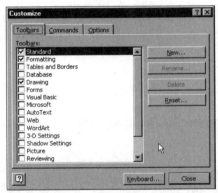

Figure 9-3: The Toolbars tab of the Customize dialog box.

Hot
Stuff

If you choose to assign your macro to a shortcut keystroke, the Customize Keyboard dialog box appears (see Figure 9-4). Click in the Press new shortcut key text box and press the keystroke that you want to assign to the macro.

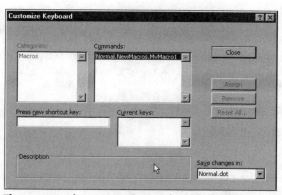

Figure 9-4: The Customize Keyboard dialog box.

6. When you have finished, click on the Close button to implement the changes and start recording the macro.

7. The Macro Recorder toolbar appears (see Figure 9-5). This toolbar contains just two buttons: a Stop button (the one on the left) and a Pause button (the one on the right). Perform the steps that you want to record in the macro.

   If you want to pause the recording of the macro while you carry out actions that you don't want recorded, click on the Pause button. When you want to start recording again, click on the Pause button again.

Figure 9-5: The Macro Recorder toolbar, with the Stop button on the left and the Pause button on the right.

What's recorded? What isn't?

Word's Macro Recorder doesn't actually record your *actions*; instead, it records the commands and the keystrokes that you enter. Remember that the Macro Recorder doesn't record mouse movements. If you want to create a macro that depends on selecting text, select the text by using the keyboard and not the mouse. Clicking the OK button in a dialog box while you are recording a macro records the state of every option in the tab that is visible in the dialog box. If you want to select options in another tab of the same dialog box, you must click OK to accept the options in the first tab and then reopen the dialog box. Click the new tab, select the options on it, and click OK to accept the options in the second tab. You do all these steps while you are recording the macro.

8. After you finish recording, click on the Stop button on the Macro Recorder toolbar. (Alternately, you can choose Tools➪Macro➪Stop Recording.)

Now you can activate the macro in the way you chose in Step 4: from the toolbar, or by pressing the shortcut keystroke. You can also choose Tools➪Macro➪Macros, as detailed in the following section.

Running Macros

If you assigned your macro to a shortcut keystroke, a menu, or a toolbar, you can execute the macro by using the appropriate method. You can also run macros with Tools➪Macro➪Macros. Follow these steps:

1. Choose Tools➪Macro➪Macros. The Macro dialog box appears, as shown in Figure 9-6.

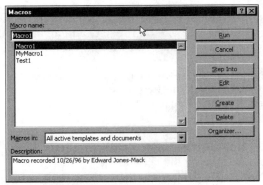

Figure 9-6: The Macros dialog box.

2. Type the name of the macro in the Macro Name text box or choose a macro from the list.

If the macro you want to execute isn't listed, Word may not be configured to run macros from all active templates. If the Macros in list box does not contain either All active templates and documents or the name of the template in which you created the macro, select either of those values. This list box controls available macros based on the templates in which they were created.

3. Click on the Run button. Word executes the chosen macro.

If you try to run a macro and you can't find it, chances are that your document is using a different template from the one to which your macro was originally saved.

Deleting Unwanted Macros

If you create a macro and later decide that you no longer need it, you can delete it. To delete a macro, choose Tools⇨Macro⇨Macros. In the Macros dialog box that appears, click the unwanted macro to select it and click Delete. Finally, click Yes in the confirmation dialog box that appears, and the macro will be deleted.

Understanding the Macro Dialog Box

As noted earlier, you enter the name of the desired macro in the Macro Name text box. After a name has been entered (or chosen from the list box), all the buttons at the right side of the dialog box are made available. Also, if you entered a description when you created the macro, the description appears in the Description text box at the bottom of the dialog box. The buttons in the dialog box perform the functions shown in Table 9-1.

Table 9-1 Macro dialog box buttons	
Button	*Purpose*
Run	Runs the selected macro
Cancel	Closes the dialog box without running the macro
Step Into	Opens the selected macro in the VBA Editor and runs the macro one step at a time
Edit	Opens the selected macro in the VBA Editor, where you can edit the code
Create	Creates a macro by using the Visual Basic for Applications program code
Delete	Deletes the selected macro
Organizer	Displays the Organizer dialog box, which can be used to copy macros between templates

After you click on the Organizer button in the Macro dialog box, you can use the Macros tab of the Organizer dialog box to copy macros from one template to another. This dialog box is very useful when you have created a macro in one template that you want to use in another template. Follow these steps to copy a macro from one template to another:

1. Choose Tools⇨Macro⇨Macros to bring up the Macro dialog box.

2. Click on the Organizer button to bring up the Organizer dialog box, as shown in Figure 9-7. The Macro Project Items tab should be in the front of the dialog box.

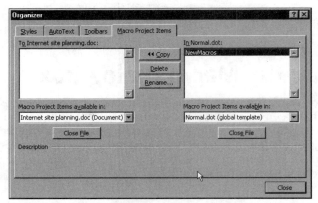

Figure 9-6: The Macro Project Items tab of the Organizer dialog box.

3. You may need to close the open file. If so, click on the Close File button on the left side of the dialog box. Then click on the Open File button and choose the template in which you created the macro that you want to copy. On the right side of the dialog box, do these steps again: Click on the Close File button, click on the Open File button, and then choose the template to which you want to copy the macro.

4. The Copy button now appears active so that you can copy the macro to the other template. You can also rename the macro by clicking on the Rename button and entering a new name in the Rename dialog box.

Note Word stores your macros in the Normal.dot default template so that you can use them with every document. You can use the Organizer dialog box to sort out your macros by putting them into the templates in which you will use the macros most often.

Using Macros in an Example

To show you that macros aren't intimidating, try your hand at creating the following example. After following these steps to create the macro, you can then try one of your own that will help you speed up operations at work or at home.

In this example, let's assume that you regularly switch to Page Layout view from Normal view so that you can see as much of your document as possible. You routinely choose View⇨Page Layout menu and then turn off the ruler. These steps are time-consuming if you do them a lot during a day, so you can save time by creating a macro to carry out the commands for you. To set the stage, first turn on your ruler (if it is not already on) by choosing the Ruler command from the View menu and be sure that you are in Normal view. Now you can record the macro by following these steps:

1. Choose Tools⇨Macro⇨Record New Macro to bring up the Record Macro dialog box.

2. In the Macro Name text box, enter **MoreSpace** as the name for this macro.

3. Click on the Keyboard button to assign the macro to a keyboard combination. The Customize Keyboard dialog box appears.

4. Because Word doesn't use Ctrl+Period for anything, it makes a good shortcut key. Press Ctrl+Period and then click on the Assign button to assign this key combination to the MoreSpace macro.

5. Click on the Close button to begin recording the macro.

6. Choose the Ruler command from the View menu to turn off the ruler.

7. Choose View⇨Page Layout to activate this view.

8. End the recording by clicking on the Stop button (the one on the left) on the Macro Recorder toolbar.

To try out the macro, go back to the Normal view and redisplay the ruler. Then run the macro by pressing Ctrl+Period. Word turns off the ruler and switches to Page Layout view. Now you can create a macro that switches it back!

Creating Macros That Run Automatically

You can assign specific names to macros that cause them to run automatically when you perform a certain action. For example, if you want a macro to run whenever you start Word, you would name that macro AutoExec. If you want a macro to run each time you open a new document, you would name that macro AutoNew. Table 9-2 lists the names that you can assign macros to make them run when you perform the related action.

You can have only one AutoExec macro for your copy of Word. However, you can have a different AutoOpen macro for each template. For example, a good use of an AutoOpen macro would be to activate a special toolbar that you need in that template or to add a special message to the screen. Note that an AutoClose macro, which runs whenever you close a document, will also run whenever you exit Word before closing a Word document (because Word automatically closes documents when you attempt to quit Word).

Table 9-2 Macros that run automatically on their related actions	
Macro name	Action that triggers the macro
AutoExec	Runs when you start Word
AutoExit	Runs when you quit Word
AutoOpen	Runs when you choose File⇨Open
AutoNew	Runs when you choose File⇨New
AutoClose	Runs when you close the current document

Hot Stuff An excellent use for an AutoOpen macro is one that automatically changes to your favorite subdirectory for your Word files. When you create this macro, name it AutoOpen, and while recording, use the usual selections in the Open dialog box from the File menu to switch to your favorite directory. After switching directories, click on Stop to stop recording the macro.

Summary

In this chapter, you've learned how to use macros in Word:

✦ Macros are actually Visual Basic for Applications programs, but you don't need to know programming to create a macro. You can *record* a series of keystrokes and mouse actions as a macro.

✦ You can assign macros to toolbar buttons and key combinations.

✦ Some macros can be associated with starting Word, exiting Word, creating a file, opening a file, or closing a file. Such macros execute automatically when the event occurs.

Where to go next...

✦ Macros can perform a number of tasks. Printing is one of them. Chapter 4 has the details.

✦ You may also create macros for formatting that you do on a regular basis. For some ideas on the different formatting options you have and how you can go about implementing them, see Chapter 3.

✦   ✦   ✦

Desktop Publishing with Word

This chapter explains how you can use several different techniques to take advantage of Word's desktop publishing capabilities. You will learn to create documents that contain graphic images, text boxes, frames, columns, newsletters, and other documents that contain headlines.

Word also provides significant drawing and charting tools that you can use to create business graphs (also called charts). You can easily insert the graphs you create — with such built-in Microsoft programs as Microsoft Graph or with many other programs, such as Harvard Graphics or CorelDRAW! — into a Word document.

Using Columns

When you get into desktop publishing, you will often want to insert columns into your documents, so this section explains just how to do that. You can add columns to only a section of your document, or you can set up the entire document in newspaper-style columns. To insert columns into a document, follow these steps:

1. Select the text that you want to place in columns.

2. Click on the Columns button on the Standard toolbar and choose the number of columns that you want for your text, or choose Format⇨Columns. The Columns dialog box (Figure 10-1) appears.

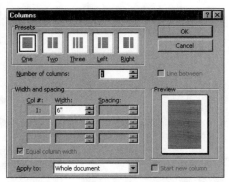

Figure 10-1: The Columns dialog box.

In this dialog box, you can choose one, two, or three columns for your document. You can also choose to have two columns, one smaller than the other, with the smaller column on the left or the right side of the page. You can also control width and spacing for the columns by adjusting the settings in the Width and Spacing area of the dialog box. The Preview area lets you see the layout of the document with the settings that you have chosen.

When you click on the Columns button on the Standard toolbar, a drop-down box lets you choose the number of columns that you want in your document. These columns are preset in width, but they can be adjusted, as explained in the next section.

After you have chosen the number of columns that you want for your document, you may need to change the preset column widths. There are two ways of changing the width of the columns. If you want to adjust the column width by using the Columns dialog box, you must first select the text that you have formatted for columns and then choose Format⇨Columns to open the Columns dialog box. In the Width and Spacing area, choose the desired width for the columns and click on the OK button to make the changes to your document.

You can also adjust the column width in the document itself. This method is very useful if you are not sure of the width that you want your column to be. To change the column width in the document, move your mouse pointer to the column marker on the ruler until the pointer turns into a double-sided arrow. Then click and drag to make the columns the width that you want.

So where are my columns?

If you add columns to a document and they aren't visible, don't think that you've done something horribly wrong. You are probably in Normal view. Columns aren't visible side-by-side in Normal view. To see your columns in a side-by-side format (the way they will actually appear when printed) you have to switch to Page Layout view (choose View⇨Page Layout). Keep in mind that many desktop publishing features of Word are not really evident unless you are in Page Layout view. So if you are doing a lot of desktop publishing work in Word, you may want to switch to Page Layout view after you have entered the basic text.

Using the AutoFormat Command

Automatic formatting is a relatively new feature, first introduced to Word with version 6.0. Word's AutoFormat command provides a quick and easy way to format a document that you have created. AutoFormat makes Word analyze each of the paragraphs in your document to determine how the paragraph is used. Even though you may have formatted the text, the AutoFormat command may change the formatting to improve the overall appearance of the document. The styles that you have applied while formatting the document are not changed unless you permit Word to do so. To accept the changes that Word makes, choose Accept from the AutoFormat dialog box.

AutoFormat removes extra returns or paragraph marks at the end of each line of body text. AutoFormat also replaces straight quotes and apostrophes with "smart" (curly) quotation marks and apostrophes. You can program AutoFormat so that it adds copyright ©, ™ trademark, and registered trademark ® symbols to a document.

AutoFormat can also replace hyphens, asterisks, or other characters that you have used in a bulleted list with another kind of bullet character. Finally, AutoFormat indents your paragraphs to replace horizontal spacing that you have inserted with the Tab key or the Spacebar.

To use AutoFormat, open the desired document and then choose Format⇨AutoFormat, or click on the AutoFormat button on the Standard toolbar. Before moving on, keep this in mind: if you use the AutoFormat button, you will not have the opportunity to review your changes. When you use this button it makes the changes; if you don't agree with any of them, you will need to go back and manually change them. Click on the OK button in the AutoFormat dialog box to begin the formatting process. When Word is finished formatting the document, it presents another dialog box that gives you the opportunity to accept all changes, reject all changes, or review the changes. You simply select the option that you want.

Some people may not be comfortable with permitting Word to make such global changes to their documents. However, you can control the changes that the AutoFormat command makes by adjusting the options on the AutoFormat tab of the Options dialog box (see Figure 10-2). To open this dialog box, choose Format⇨AutoFormat⇨Options. The AutoFormat tab lets you control the changes that Word makes to your document when you select the AutoFormat command. You can control whether Word preserves the styles that you apply or whether Word applies styles to lists, headings, and other paragraphs. You can also control whether Word makes adjustments to paragraph marks, spaces, tabs, and empty paragraphs. And in the Replace area of the AutoFormat tab, you can control the replacements that Word makes as it formats. It is a good idea to review these options before you begin the AutoFormat process to prevent unwanted changes.

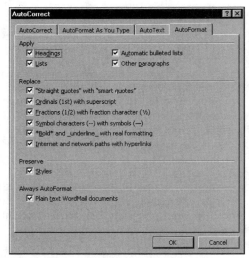

Figure 10-2: The AutoFormat tab.

You also have the option of reviewing the formatting results. When the formatting is complete, the second AutoFormat dialog box (Figure 10-3) appears. It contains the Review Changes button. Click on this button to review the changes made. Next you will see the Review AutoFormat Changes dialog box. In this box you can make changes one by one by clicking on the Find right arrow button to move forward, or clicking on the Find left arrow button to move back, to make changes. Each change is explained in the description area of the AutoFormat dialog box.

Hot Stuff Keep in mind the differences between the AutoFormat button and Format⇨AutoFormat. If you wish to format your document quickly, you can click on the AutoFormat button and review the changes after they are made. Remember, though, that if you use this method, you must review the changes manually. If you're at all worried about having Word wantonly reformat your text, and you wish to review each of the changes that AutoFormat makes, you will want to use Format⇨AutoFormat. This will give you the chance to review each of the changes that you were made to your document.

Figure 10-3: The Review AutoFormat Changes dialog box.

Word uses temporary revision marks and color to indicate the changes that it has made in the document. You can turn off these marks by clicking on the Show/Hide button on the Standard toolbar.

More Info The AutoFormat command is very valuable. It can take the monotony out of formatting documents for those of you who don't do it along the way. If you want more information about the styles that Word uses as it formats your documents, see Chapter 8.

When *not* to use AutoFormat

Word's AutoFormat command shares an interesting trait with that of Excel's: they both work well with documents (in Excel's case, *worksheets*) that follow a conventional format. If your document is very unusual in terms of how it is structured, you may not like the kind of changes that AutoFormat applies. If you happen to click on the Accept button in the AutoFormat dialog box, and you don't like what Word does to your document, remember that you can reverse the changes by choosing Edit⇨Undo.

Understanding Graphic Images

Word's capability to import graphic images from other software adds much to your desktop publishing capabilities. Word can import any of the image types in Table 10-1.

Table 10-1
Image types that you can import into Word

File type	Extension
AutoCAD 2-D Format	.DXF
CompuServe GIF	.GIF
Computer Graphics Metafile	.CGM
WordPerfect Graphics	.WPG
Encapsulated PostScript	.EPS
Hewlett-Packard Graphics Language	.HGL
JPEG	.JPG
Macintosh PICT	.PCT
Micrografx Designer/Draw	.DRW
PC Paintbrush	.PCX
Tagged Image Format	.TIF
TARGA	.TGA
Windows Bitmap	.BMP
Windows Metafile	.WMF

Word uses *graphic filters* to convert these image file formats to an image that appears in your document. When you install Word, it is possible to omit graphic filters that you don't need to save disk space. If you try to import a picture (with Insert⇨Picture) that has been captured in a file format that you don't have on your list, you have to run Word's installation program to re-install the graphic filter for that image file format. See your Word documentation for details.

Hot Stuff As programs grow in popularity, new graphic filters are added to Word, so your version of Word may be able to import more file types than those shown here. Refer to your Word documentation to see which file types your version of Word can import.

In Windows, there are two kinds of graphic images: *bitmapped images*, which are created in painting programs, and *object images*, which are created in drawing programs. Because both types of images have definite advantages and disadvantages, you should be familiar with both.

Bitmapped images

Bitmapped images are images that are composed of a collection of dots, or *pixels,* on-screen. These images are called bitmaps because the image is literally defined within the computer by assigning each pixel on-screen to a storage bit (location) within the computer's memory. You can use painting programs to create bitmapped images. Your copy of Windows comes with a painting program called Paint. (See your Windows documentation for information about how you can use Paint to create your own bitmapped images.) You can purchase bitmapped images from various software suppliers, or you can find them on computer bulletin boards. Disks of bitmapped images typically contain collections of useful graphics, such as business cartoons, sports illustrations, or images of animals and nature settings. You can import bitmapped images that are stored under any of the file formats into a Word document. Figure 10-4 shows an example of ready-to-use bitmapped images from a clip-art collection.

Figure 10-4: Example of a bitmapped image inserted into a Word document.

Some clip art is provided free with Paint. The art files have .BMP extensions and are stored in the same directory as your Windows program files. Computer bulletin boards and PC users groups are also excellent sources for clip art collections on disk.

Photographs are also stored as bitmapped images. If you have access to a scanner, you can scan photographs and store them on disk as bitmapped images by using the directions supplied with your scanner. You can then import the bitmapped image of the photo into your Word document. Note that black-and-white photos typically scan with greater clarity than color photos. Figure 10-5 shows an example of a photograph scanned into a bitmapped image.

The Giant Panda

A Report by Jarel M. Jones

The giant panda dwells in the mountains of central China near the Tibetan border in cool, damp bamboo forests. The animals are often found at elevations of 5,000 to 13,000 feet. The pandas' thick, wooly coat is typically brownish black interspersed with white.

The panda population has dropped significantly in the last decade. This trend has been caused by human invasion of the animal's natural habitats. Efforts by environmentalists and by the Chinese government to safeguard the natural habitats of the pandas have resulted in some overcoming of the

Figure 10-5: A scanned photo inserted as a bitmapped image in a Word document.

Bitmapped images have one major advantage and one major disadvantage. The strength of bitmapped images is that you can easily modify them. Most painting programs (including Paint) enable you to modify existing parts of a bitmapped image by selectively adding or deleting bits. You can "zoom in" on the image as if it were under a magnifying glass, and you can turn individual pixels black, white, or any one of a range of colors. The disadvantage of bitmapped images is that you typically cannot modify their size by *scaling* (stretching or shrinking the image in one or more directions).

Object images

Object images are images that are based on a collection of geometric objects, such as lines, arcs, circles, or rectangles. Object images are created by drawing packages. Some of the popular drawing packages that run under Windows include CorelDRAW! and Micrografx Draw (you may be using one of these). Drawing programs work better than painting programs for creating line drawings, such as company logos, maps, and images of constructed objects (houses, cars, planes, bridges, and so on). Painting programs work better than drawing programs for projects where you would sketch on a piece of paper without using a ruler, such as drawing a portrait of a person's face.

Where can I get some of those neat stock pictures and graphics?

You've probably seen documents created in Windows word processors (such as Word) that contain snazzy graphics and clip art. Many users who haven't done much work with graphics want to know where artwork like this can be found. There's no shortage of artwork available, and you may need to look no farther than your own PC. If you performed a complete installation of Office (or if you at least included the ClipArt files in the options list when you installed the program), you can find many clip art files in the ClipArt folder that is stored inside the **Microsoft Office** folder. In addition to these files, you can find clip art and stock photos in many inexpensive commercial disk packages that are available through computer and software retailers. You can also use mail-order libraries of photos and art — there are plenty of advertisements in the back pages of magazines such as *PC World*. And you can find clip art in the libraries of online services such as America Online and CompuServe.

The disadvantage of painting programs becomes the advantage of drawing programs, and vice versa. For example, object images can easily be scaled, which means that you can change the size of the object by stretching it or shrinking it in one or more directions. Because the object is based on a collection of straight or curved lines, the software simply expands or contracts the lines to expand or contract the entire image. The disadvantage of object images, however, is that you cannot modify them as easily as you can a bitmapped image. You can select any of the objects that make up the image (such as one line in a drawing of a building) and individually stretch, shrink, or redraw that line. But this is a tedious process, and with complex drawings, it may be difficult to get the results that you want when you are modifying an existing image.

Note Most drawing programs have the capability to load a bitmapped image and convert it to an object image. However, the differences between the way the images are stored means that the results of the conversion may be less than spectacular. Curved lines in a bitmapped image are stored as jagged or "stepped" patterns of light and dark pixels, and if you bring a bitmapped image into a drawing program and then try to scale the image, the jagged patterns will change disproportionately. The result is often an image with some distortion.

Using Graphic Images

As you begin your work in desktop publishing, you will find the addition of graphic images to your documents very useful. After you have inserted the images, you will need to perform various tasks to make the object look presentable in your document. This would include tasks such as cropping, adding borders, or even callouts to your graphic image.

Inserting images into Word

To import images from a wide range of software, you need to use Insert⇨Picture. To insert a picture into your document, perform the following steps:

1. Place the insertion point where the image is to appear.

2. Choose Insert⇨Picture⇨From file to open the Insert Picture dialog box, as shown in Figure 10-6.

Figure 10-6: The Insert Picture dialog box.

3. In the File name list box, you can enter the name of the image file, or you can select the desired filename from the list. To see files of a particular type, click on the arrow to the right of the Files of type list box and choose your image file format from the list. Use the Look in list box and the Up One Level button to change to a different folder or to a different drive.

   After you select a file in the Name list box, you can click on the Preview button at the top of the dialog box to see the image in the Preview box of the Insert Picture dialog box. The Preview box provides a handy way to examine collections of clip art. You can highlight each filename in the File name list box and click on the Preview button to see the image that's stored in the file.

Hot
Stuff

If you want to link the image in Word to the original graphic file, turn on the Link To File check box. Word then inserts the image as a field, and you can later use the Update Field key (F9) to update the picture if you later change the picture in the program that was used to create the image.

4. Click on the Insert button (or press Enter) to close the dialog box and to insert the image into your Word document. The image appears at the insertion point location. Figure 10-7 shows an example of a clip art image pasted into a Word document by using this technique.

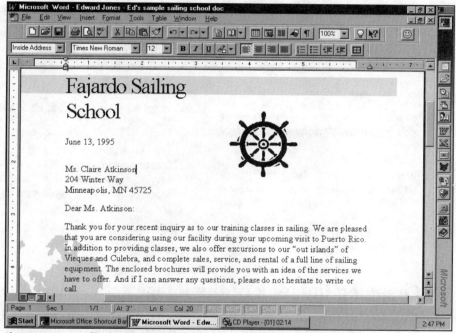

Figure 10-7: A clip art image inserted into a Word document.

Normally, you can think of an image that you insert into a document as a single large character, such as a giant letter *A*. As such, you cannot place text around the image because the image takes up one giant line of text. However, you can insert a frame that surrounds the image, and then you can position the frame containing the image anywhere in your document. Text will then automatically reposition itself around the frame (although this will be visible only in Page Layout view). See "Working with Frames" later in this chapter for details about using frames in Word.

In addition to importing graphics, you can also create graphics directly from Word. Word includes a Drawing toolbar that you can use to create graphics. If the Drawing toolbar isn't visible, choose View➪Toolbars, click on the Drawing check box in the Toolbars dialog box, and click on the OK button. After the Drawing toolbar is visible, you can click on any of the toolbar buttons or you can use the mouse to draw the shapes that you want to add to your document.

Don't forget your trusty Clipboard

If the software that you are using to produce the image runs under Windows, remember that you can also use the Windows Clipboard to copy images into a Word document. You can do so by performing the following steps:

1. Use the Start menu of Windows 95 to start your painting or drawing program under Windows in the usual manner.

2. After you have the desired image within your program, use whatever selection tool is provided by your program to select the desired portion of the image.

3. Choose Edit➪Copy (all programs that conform to Windows standards will have this command).

4. Press Alt+Tab to switch back to Word.

5. Open your desired document, place the insertion point at the desired location, and choose Edit➪Paste. The image from the other program is inserted into your Word document at the insertion point location.

Changing the look of the image

After you have inserted an image into a Word document, you can change the size of the image by *scaling* (resizing) and *cropping* (trimming) the images. It is easier to use the mouse than the keyboard to change the size of the image. Mouse users scale images by selecting the image and dragging the sizing handles that appear; keyboard users must use Format➪Picture and then enter dimensions in the dialog box that appears.

You can also apply borders to an image by using Format➪Borders and Shading or by clicking on the Borders button on the Formatting toolbar. You cannot apply shading to an image as you can to a paragraph. Notice that when you select a picture and then choose Format➪Borders and Shading, the Shading tab is dimmed in the dialog box.

Scaling an image

To scale an image, you must first select it. When you click on an image, Word selects the image and displays sizing handles. Keyboard users can select an image by placing the insertion point anywhere inside the image, holding down the Shift key, and pressing the right-arrow key once.

To scale (resize) a graphic with the mouse, you drag one of the handles until the image reaches the desired size. Dragging a handle on either center side resizes the width of the image. Dragging a handle on the center top or the center bottom resizes the height of the image. Dragging any of the corner handles resizes both the width and height of the image. To scale an image with the keyboard, select the image and choose Format➪Picture to open the Format Picture dialog box, as shown in Figure 10-8.

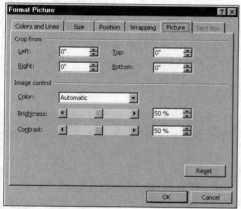

Figure 10-8: The Picture tab of the Format Picture dialog box.

You can change the scaling in one of two ways: either you can enter a percentage in the Width and Height text boxes in the Scaling area (in which case the Size measurements change accordingly), or you can enter a measurement in the Width and Height boxes in the Size area (in which case the Scaling percentages change accordingly). Use the Reset button to restore an image that you have scaled to its original size. (Word remembers the original size of an image, regardless of how you scale or crop it, so that you can later undo your modifications with the Reset button.) After you have made your desired changes, click on the OK button or press Enter.

Cropping an image

To crop a graphic by using the mouse, hold down the Shift key while you drag one of the handles. Dragging a handle on either center side crops the image on that side; dragging a handle on the center top or the center bottom crops the image from the top or the bottom; and dragging any of the corner handles crops from both the side nearest that corner and the top or bottom nearest that corner.

To crop a graphic by using the keyboard, select the image and then choose Format⇨Picture. In the Picture dialog box, use the measurement boxes in the Crop From area to enter the amounts by which you want to crop the image. A measurement in the Left and Right text boxes specifies how much the image should be cropped on the left and right sides, and a measurement in the Top and Bottom text boxes specifies how much the image should be cropped on the top and bottom. Use the Reset button to restore an image that you have cropped to its original size. After you have made your desired changes, click on the OK button or press Enter.

Adding borders

To apply a border to an image, first select the image and then choose Format⇨Borders and Shading. In the dialog box that appears, select the type of border that you want. (You can also add borders by using the Borders toolbar.)

You can add callouts to your art, too!

You may want to add callouts to the images that you insert into your documents. You can insert callouts in several ways, but one easy way is to use Word's Table feature. Add a table with the Table⇨Insert Table command and insert the image into one cell of the table. Then type the text of your callout into an adjacent cell of the table and format the table so that the text appears where you want it. You can also use the Drawing toolbar. After you select the image, click on the Format Callout button and then click and drag to place a callout of the desired size and type the desired text into the callout.

Editing images

After you have placed an image into Word, you can edit it. To edit an image, double-click on that image or right-click and choose Open Picture from the shortcut menu. Then you can edit the picture by using the Drawing toolbar.

After you are finished editing the image, click on the Close Picture button on the Picture toolbar located in the upper-left corner of the screen.

Note Remember that the drawing capabilities of Word are object based, so you may get unsatisfactory results if you import a bitmapped image into a Word document and then modify it with the Drawing toolbar.

Inserting Graphs into Word

You can insert graphs (charts) into Word by using Microsoft Graph, a program designed for creating business graphs. You can also insert graphs from spreadsheets, such as Lotus 1-2-3, Excel, and the spreadsheet module of Microsoft Works. To insert a graph from Microsoft Graph into a Word document, perform the following steps:

1. Choose Insert⇨Object to open the Object dialog box and click on the Create New tab. In the Object Type list box, select Microsoft Graph 97 Chart and click on the OK button to add a default graph and a Datasheet window. When you do this, you will see a new set of menus appear for your work with the chart. In the cells of the data sheet that appears over the graph, you can type the values that you want to use for the graph. Figure 10-9 shows the graph and the Datasheet window in a document.

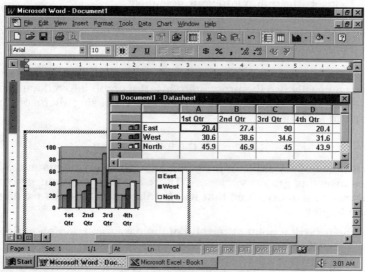

Figure 10-9: A graph and Datasheet window in a Word document.

2. Enter the desired numeric data into the cells of the Datasheet window. You can change the names of the headings in the cells, and the new names will be used for the categories of the chart. When done, close the Datasheet window by double-clicking the icon in its upper-left corner.

3. Choose Chart⇨Chart Type to select the type of chart that you want. In the Chart Type dialog box that appears, choose the desired chart type and click OK.

4. Right-click on any desired part of the chart to display a shortcut menu that allows you to add any desired titles, legends, gridlines, or other items to the chart.

5. When you are finished making the desired refinements to the chart, click anywhere outside the chart. The chart then appears inside your document, and the menus and toolbars revert back to those of Word for Windows.

If you are using Microsoft Excel, Microsoft Works, or another Windows program that conforms to the Windows design standards, you can use the Copy and Paste commands with the Clipboard to copy graphs from those programs into your Word documents. In Excel or in Works, display the graph in a window. Then select the graph and choose Edit⇨Copy. Exit the program and switch to Word in the usual manner. Place the insertion point at the desired location and choose Edit⇨Paste to insert the graph into your document.

Hot Stuff You can use the Clipboard techniques to copy information from any Windows software into a Word document.

Because Microsoft Graph shows a simple bar graph by default whenever it is started, you can easily use the program to insert a graph into a document. For practice, perform the following steps as an exercise in using Microsoft Graph to place a graph in a document:

1. Open a new document and enter the following text:

This is a test of my skills in inserting a graph in my document. Word makes inserting graphs very easy. There are many options provided for the formatting of my chart that will be discussed more as we move along in the chapter.

2. Place the insertion point at the end of the paragraph and press Enter to begin a new line.

3. Choose Insert⇨Object and then choose Microsoft Graph from the dialog box that appears. Click on the OK button to open the Microsoft Graph 5.0 window. A default bar graph appears in the document.

4. Click on the cell that contains East. Enter the name Johnathan and then press Enter. For the cell that contains West, enter Dirk; and for the cell containing North, enter Kevin. Change a few of the numbers using the same methods. After you click anywhere outside the graph, the graph will appear in the sample document, as shown in Figure 10-10.

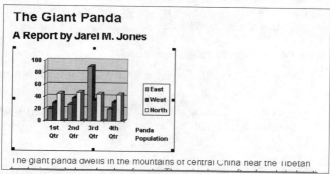

Figure 10-10: The sample document with a bar graph inserted from Microsoft Graph.

If you later want to make more changes to the graph's design, you can double-click on the graph to switch back to the menus and toolbar of Microsoft Graph. For now, leave the document open on-screen because you will use it in an upcoming exercise involving frames.

Working with Text Boxes

As you work with text in Word, you will find times when you want to place text into a freestanding container. One common use for this technique is to draw attention to a specific section of text. You can also manipulate the text using some of the same steps you would if it were a framed object. The text inside a from becomes an absolutely *positioned paragraph*: these are paragraphs that must occupy a specific place in a document. When the text box is placed, you then can reposition the text outside the text outside the text box so that it wraps around your text box. This will give your document a more refined look.

You can insert a text box around an existing section of text by performing the following steps:

1. Select the section of text you wish to create a box for using your favorite method of selection.

2. Choose Insert⇨Text Box. Word then inserts a text box around the text you selected.

Inserting an empty text box into a document

At times you may want to insert an empty text box into a document. This can serve as a placeholder for future text you will be entering. Wrapping will apply in the text box, so you will not need to press return at the end of your lines. To insert an empty text box, perform the following steps:

1. Be sure that no text or objects are selected.

2. Choose Insert⇨Text Box from the Insert menu. The cursor then turns into crosshairs.

3. Click and drag to draw the text box to the size you wish. (If you are not sure of the size that you want, you can always resize the text box at a later time.)

Formatting text boxes

After you have placed the frames in your document, you may want to change the lines used by Word and the wrapping of text that Word uses as defaults. You will have the option to change many of the aspects of the text box, such as its location. You can also change whether adjacent text should be permitted to wrap around the text box. Mouse users can accomplish most of these tasks with relative ease. If you are in a position where you don't have a mouse, just select the text box and choose Format⇨Text Box. This will then open the Format Text Box dialog box, shown in Figure 10-11.

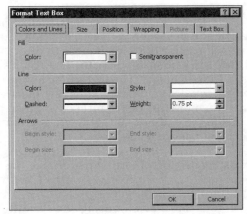

Figure 10-11: Format Text Box dialog box.

The Format Text box dialog box has six tabs. Each of these tabs will aid in the formatting of the text box that you have inserted in your document. You can use the Colors and Lines tab to change the color and lines size of the text box you have inserted. Clicking on the tab shows you the different types of lines available for the text box. Clicking on the corresponding arrow next to the choices gives you a drop-down list containing various choices that you can use to change the appearance of the text box.

The Size tab can manipulate the size of the text box. You can change the height and width of the box. This tab even allows you to rotate the box if you wish. Scaling is also an option in this tab. This allows you change the size of the scale of the text box.

The Position tab can control the position of the text box on the page of your document. Clicking on the arrows next to the Horizontal and Vertical settings changes the position of the text box on the page.

When a text box containing a picture is active, the Picture tab can control the cropping, brightness, and contrast of the image.

The Wrapping tab of the Format Text Box dialog box can control the wrapping of the text around the text box you have inserted. The preview box allows you to see want the wrapping will look like.

The Text Box tab can control the internal margins of the text box. This will allow you to do formatting within the text box so the text appears as you desire. A button on this tab also allows you to convert the text box to a frame, which is useful for more experienced Word users who are more accustomed to working with frames than text boxes.

Moving text boxes

After you have inserted a text box, you can easily move it to any location in a document. (Mouse users will find this easiest to do.) Mouse users can move a text box by performing the following steps:

1. Choose View⇨Page Layout to turn on Page Layout View.

2. Place the insertion point on the border of the frame. The mouse pointer will change to a four-headed arrow.

3. Click and drag the text box to the new location. As you drag the text box, a dotted line will indicate its position. The contents of the text box will move to the new location after you release the mouse button.

Keyboard users can move a text box using the following steps:

1. Turn on Page Layout view by choosing View⇨Page Layout.

2. Using the arrow keys, position the insertion point inside the frame that you want to move.

3. Choose Format ⇨ Textbox from the shortcut menu.

4. In the Format Text box dialog box, enter the horizontal location that you want for the frame in the Horizontal Position box on the Position Tab. (Use the From list box to choose whether the measurement that you enter is relative to the margin, the page, or a column.)

5. Enter the vertical location that you want for the frame in the Vertical Position box on the Position Tab. (Use the From list box to choose whether the measurement that you enter is relative to the margin, the page, or a paragraph.)

6. Click on the OK button (or press Enter).

Sizing text boxes

You can resize text boxes by using the mouse or the keyboard. Mouse users can select the text box and drag one of the sizing handles to resize the text box. Keyboard users can select the text box, use the Format Text Box command, and then enter the desired height and width in the Size tab of the Format Text Box dialog box.

To resize a text box using the mouse, perform the following steps:

1. Turn on Page Layout View by choosing View⇨Page Layout.

2. Click anywhere in the text box that you want to resize. Eight black sizing handles appear on the edges of the text box.

3. Point to one of the sizing handles, and the mouse pointer changes shape into a two-headed arrow.

4. Drag the handle to resize the text box.

Keyboard users can resize a text box by performing these steps:

1. Turn on Page Layout View by choosing View⇨Page Layout.

2. Using the arrow keys, position the insertion point inside the text box that you want to resize.

3. Choose Format⇨Text Box.

4. Click the Size tab of the Format Text Box dialog box and enter the height and width you wish to apply to the text box.

5. Click on the OK button or press Enter.

Wrapping text around text boxes

By default Word wraps adjacent text around text boxes. You can turn this trait on or off for a particular text box with the Text tab of the Format Text Box dialog box. To turn on (or off) text wrapping around text boxes, perform the following steps:

1. Choose View⇨Page Layout to turn on Page Layout view.

2. Using the mouse or the arrow keys, place the insertion pointer inside the text box.

3. Choose Format⇨Text Box to open the Format text box Dialog box.

4. At the Wrapping Tab of the dialog box, choose one of the options listed. Diagrams will give you an idea of what the text will look like when it is wrapped around the text box.

5. You can also make adjustments to the distance the text appears from the text box. After you have made your choices, click on OK or press enter.

Figure 10-12 shows the difference between text wrapping that is on and text wrapping that is off. On the left, the text box containing the graph has been placed in the center of the paragraph, and the surrounding type of wrapping was chosen. Notice how the text wraps around the text box in this figure. On the right, the text box is at the same location, but the text wrapping option has been set to None. As a result, the text does not wrap around the text box that contains the graph. Note that the option applies to the *selected* text box.

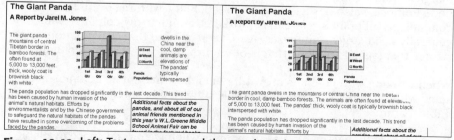

Figure 10-12: Left: Text wraps around the graph. Right: Text wrapping has been turned off.

Using the Organizational Tools of Desktop Publishing

When you need to create a document with a professionally published appearance, you can use different organizational tools and techniques that Word provides. The combination of these techniques and the use of graphics turns an ordinary document into a professional one. These organizational tools include such things as columns, gutter margins, headlines and subheads, headers and footers, and the integration of graphics. Later in this chapter you will learn how to use the Newsletter Wizard to create newsletters, another form of desktop publishing.

Before you attempt to apply desktop publishing techniques to any document, you should first sketch out, on paper, exactly how you want the document to look. It is much easier to pattern a document in Word after one that you've already outlined on paper. This step also helps you avoid mistakes that may detract from the appearance of the finished document. Mistakes in overall layout are often apparent from a paper-based sketch.

Columns and margins

With many documents, the way in which you lay out your columns comprises a significant part of desktop publishing design. One- and two-column layouts are the most popular, although you can have many more than two columns. With text, there is a "visual" limit to keep in mind. As the number of columns increases, you reach a point where readability suffers. Readers don't read individual words; they read phrases, or groups of words. Therefore, column width has a direct impact on readability. Overly wide columns make it difficult for the reader to follow phrases from line to line. Overly narrow columns can also be hard to read because the eyes must often jump lines before absorbing a complete phrase. Page margins, number of columns, and the width between columns all have an impact here. Point size also has an impact on readability, with regard to the number of columns. Small point sizes tend to work better in narrow columns; wide columns generally need larger point sizes. Also, keep in mind that hyphenation helps reduce that jagged-text look that is often prevalent with narrow columns.

When working with columns in Word, remember that not all columns need be the same width if you set up the columns as side-by-side paragraphs by using Word's Table feature.

Keep in mind the effects that page margins will have on the space available for your columns and on the overall design of your document. Larger margins result in a "lighter" document; smaller margins result in a "denser" appearance to the document.

Headlines and subheads

Headlines are vital in calling attention to your message. For this reason, they are commonly used throughout newsletters, magazines, advertisements, and brochures. You can differentiate your headlines from your body text by setting the headlines in different point sizes or type styles. You can also block headlines with borders or shading, or you can separate them from the normal text by means of white space or with rules (vertical or horizontal lines drawn with Format⇨Borders and Shading or the Borders toolbar). You should avoid headlines that are all uppercase letters or ones that contain more than three lines (both tend to be hard to read).

You can use subheads to add clarification to a headline. You may also want to use subheads within your text as a way of breaking up large expanses of text into smaller groups. The smaller groups tend to be visually easier to follow. Figure 10-13 shows an example.

Laser Printers: The Latest and Greatest
PCWorld Tests 20 Laser Printers All Priced Under $1,000

Figure 10-13: A headline with a subheadline.

Hot Stuff Avoid a common blunder with your subheads: make sure that the subheads are visually tied to the text that follows the subhead. To position the subhead accurately, use Format⇨Paragraph and click on the Indents and Spacing tab of the Paragraph dialog box. In the Spacing area, set the value of the Before measurement to one that is greater than the value in the After measurement. This adjustment results in more space above the subhead than below the subhead. If you don't set the measurements in this way, the subhead may be too close to the prior text and not close enough to the text that follows it. In such cases, the subhead appears disconnected from the text that follows.

Graphic images

Word's capability to place graphics into frames means that you have a great deal of flexibility when you integrate graphics into the text. Remember that you can also place a graphic image into a cell of a table and then use the formatting commands that apply to tables to control the location of the graphic. There is no "correct" method to place graphics; use whichever method feels the most comfortable and achieves the desired results.

You can use the sizing (scaling) and cropping techniques covered earlier in the chapter to add visual interest to many graphics. In some cases, you may be able to add interest to an illustration by purposely stretching it out of proportion. For example, you can use a stretched image of a dollar bill to convey an increase in buying power.

With graphics, the possibilities are endless. Remember that professionally published documents are often a source of inspiration for effective graphics. You can obtain ideas about graphic design by examining publications with abundant informational graphics, such as *USA Today, Time,* and *Newsweek.*

Graphs and tables

With Microsoft Graph, you can design business graphs that can be inserted into Word documents. With Word's Table feature, you can design tables of data. Use graphs when you want the reader to see a visual representation of the underlying data. Use tables when you want the reader to see the underlying data itself, rather than a visual representation. With tables that display business figures, you should visually set off any headings or column titles within the table from the remaining contents of the table. You can set the headings apart by formatting the headings or titles or by adding borders or shading.

Informational graphics (such as pie and bar charts) can go a long way in getting business information across to an audience of readers. You may want to consider combining clip art or drawings that are done in Paint with business graphs that are done in a spreadsheet like Excel or in Microsoft Graph.

Using the Newsletter Wizard

Creating newsletters is a common task in many organizations. And because of the complexity of newsletters, they have often presented design challenges. Word includes a powerful tool for creating newsletters, a tool that greatly reduces the tedium involved. The Newsletter Wizard is a very useful aid in creating a document that you send out on a regular basis. It also has perfect examples for how to use headings, columns, and graphics in a document.

To create a newsletter, choose File⇨New and click on the Publications tab in the New dialog box. Then double-click on the Newsletter Wizard to launch the Newsletter Wizard.

The first Newsletter Wizard dialog box lets you choose between two style options: Classic and Modern. After choosing the style that you want for your newsletter, click on the Next button.

The next Newsletter Wizard dialog box asks you to enter the number of columns that you want for your document. You have a choice of one to four columns. Keep in mind that the formats that you set out in the wizard are not set in stone. If you later want to add another column to the document, you can do so by using Format⇨Columns.

The third dialog box asks you to enter a name for your newsletter. If you can't think of one, you don't have to enter one at this time. You can enter the name later, when you complete the setup of the newsletter.

The fourth Newsletter Wizard dialog box asks you how many pages you want in your newsletter. At the top of each of the newsletter pages, you will find the page number and the title of your newsletter in a shaded bar, which gives the document a professional look.

Use the fifth and final Newsletter Wizard dialog box to choose the elements that you want to include in your newsletter. You can choose none, some, or all of the following options: Table of contents, Fancy first letters, Date, and Volume and issue.

You can turn on or off each of these options by clicking on their check boxes. This flexibility gives you the freedom to include some of the elements from the wizard and exclude some of them. After you are finished selecting the desired options, click on the Finish button, and Word will open the newsletter. You can add the desired text, and then you can save and print the document in the usual manner.

Keep in mind that you can change the formats that you specify in the Newsletter Wizard dialog boxes after you create your document. In many cases, you will find it essential to change them and include or exclude some things. Use the normal formatting techniques in Word to make these changes and customize the newsletter to your own needs.

Summary

This chapter has provided an overall look at how you can combine the various tools of Word to perform desktop publishing tasks. The chapter included the following points:

✦ Use Format⇨Columns to place columns in a document.

✦ You can quickly add attractive formatting to a document by using Word's AutoFormat command (from the Format menu).

✦ In Word, you can import graphic images of various types into a document.

✦ You can add business graphs to Word documents by pasting them in from other programs or by using Word's Object command from the Insert menu. You can insert a Microsoft Graph object and change Word's menus and toolbars to those of Microsoft Graph.

✦ You can add frames to your documents, and these frames can contain text or graphics. You can size frames, and you can drag them to any desired location on a page.

The next chapter will outline a number of step-by-step exercises that you can follow to quickly create typical business documents in Word for Windows.

Where to go next...

✦ Much of what you do in desktop publishing involves the complex use of Word's different formatting tools. You can find out more about these tools in Chapter 3.

✦ If you desktop publish documents on a regular basis, you'll want to make use of Word's styles and templates. Chapter 8 has the dirt.

✦   ✦   ✦

Word and the Web

Word 97 differs significantly from its predecessors in that it comes enabled with many features for working with the Internet and with intranets. Using Word 97, you can attach *hyperlinks* to other Office 97 documents or to web sites. These hyperlinks let you easily jump to locations in other Office 97 documents. You can easily export Word documents in HTML format ready for inclusion on your web pages, and you can take advantage of a Web Publishing Wizard, to produce professional web pages. Figure 11-1 shows a Word document published as a web page on a corporate intranet and viewed using Netscape Navigator, a popular web browser.

You can also place hyperlink fields in portions of documents, and you can use these cells to display links in other web pages on an intranet or on the Internet. When you need to retrieve or publish document data across the net, Word 97 can be a powerful tool for accomplishing such a task.

To accomplish most of the tasks described in this chapter, obviously you'll need to be connected to a network. This can be a dial-up connection to the Internet by means of a commercial Internet service provider such as AT&T WorldNet, MCINet, MindSpring, NetCom, or a host of others. Your connection can also be a direct connection through your organization's local area network. You may be connected directly to a corporate intranet, in which case you'll be able to retrieve or publish data to your company's private network. This chapter won't go into specifics on making a net connection, as that topic is an entire book in itself. If you need help in this area, you can take a look at *Creating Cool Interactive Web Sites* and *Creating Cool FrontPage Web Sites*, both by Paul and Mary Summitt.

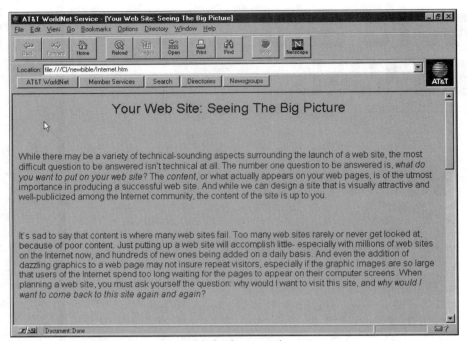

Figure 11-1: A Word document published as a web page.

This chapter also assumes a familiarity with the basics of Word. If you are familiar with the Web or with intranets but you haven't yet learned to work with Word, you should consider Chapters 2 through 4 before proceeding with this chapter.

What's Possible with Word 97 and the Web?

Using Word 97, you can perform a number of net-related tasks as you work with documents. You can insert hyperlinks at any desired location in a document to link to other Office 97 documents or to web sites. When users of the documents click on these hyperlinks, they can jump directly to that location in the other file or to a specified web site. You can also save documents as HTML (HyperText Markup Language), the publishing lingua franca of the World Wide Web. These topics will be covered in further detail throughout this chapter.

About the Web and the Internet

Because intranets and the Internet are newer concepts to many readers than are spreadsheets, a few explanations of terms may be in order. (If you're intimately familiar with the Internet, intranets, and the World Wide Web, you may want to skip this section and the next, and dive right into working with Word and the Web.) First, the *Internet* is a global collection of computers, linked together by means of telephone and microwave lines and accessible to the public by means of various connections in offices and in homes. The Internet grew out of a research project that came into common knowledge in the 1970s, which originally linked university and government computers in the Unites States. Since its inception, the Internet has grown to encompass thousands of computers spread throughout dozens of nations. Any PC user with an Internet connection (either by means of a phone line or a direct hookup) can connect to the Internet and gain access to the volumes of information located there.

One major component of the Internet is the *World Wide Web*. There are other parts of the Internet, but the World Wide Web is the most well-known part. The World Wide Web is that part of the Internet that makes use of graphical software known as web browsers, and of files stored as HTML. The computers on the Internet that store the HTML files are also known as *web servers*. When PCs connect to the Internet to retrieve this data, they use web browser software, which converts the incoming information (encoded in HTML) to graphical pages displayed as a combination of text, graphics, and in some cases audio and video. Commonly used web browsers include Microsoft Internet Explorer, Netscape Navigator, and the custom web browsers built into the software provided by America Online and CompuServe.

Each site on the Internet has a unique address, commonly known as the Internet address (and less commonly known by the official name of *URL*, or *Uniform Resource Locator*). When you establish an Internet connection, open a web browser, and enter an Internet address such as *http://www.whitehouse.gov*, you are entering the address for the web server that provides the home page for the President's office in the Unites States. Web addresses like these can be stored in Word documents and displayed as hyperlinks.

About Intranets

Many net-related uses of Office 97 involve making data available on *intranets*. An intranet is a private network of computers that is available only to the members of a specific organization. Intranets make use of World Wide Web technology— web servers, network connections, and web browser software— to allow members of an organization to share information. Intranets are very popular with corporations, as intranets let employees share work-related information in a confidential manner.

About HTML

As mentioned earlier, HTML is the language used for publishing information to the World Wide Web and to intranets that use World Wide Web technology. HTML is a text-based language that makes use of special codes called *tags*. These tags are included in the text of the HTML documents, and they provide instructions to the web browser software that determine how the data appears when it is viewed by the end user. Although you don't need to know the nuts and bolts of HTML coding to work with Word and the Web, it's a good idea to at least be familiar with the concept of saving your data in HTML file format. In order to publish Word data on the Internet or on an intranet, you'll need to save that data in HTML format and upload it to your web server. If you are dealing with a corporate intranet, your company's webmaster can tell you how to upload the HTML files that Word produces to your company's web server. If you are managing a web site on the Internet or on an intranet, you already know how to do this; much of the rest of this chapter will deal with getting that Word data ready for uploading to your server.

About the Web Toolbar

Like all the major Office 97 applications, Word provides the Web toolbar, a toolbar that helps you browse through the resources on an intranet or on the Web. Using the Web toolbar, you can quickly open, search, and browse through any document or through a web page. You can jump between documents, and you can add favorite sites you find on the web to the Favorites folder, allowing you to quickly go back to those sites at a later time.

In Word, you can display the Web toolbar by choosing View⭢Toolbars and then selecting Web from the submenu that appears, or by clicking the Web toolbar button in the Standard toolbar. Figure 11-2 shows the Web toolbar.

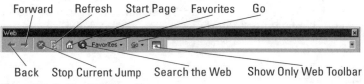

Figure 11-2: The Web toolbar.

You'll find the Web toolbar to be handy when you happen to be in Word and you have a need to go to the Web (or to your company's intranet) for information. For example, you can click the Search the Web button to launch your default web browser and search the web, or you can click the Favorites button to open a list of your favorite web sites. Table 11-1 shows the purpose of the buttons on the Web toolbar.

Table 11-1 The Web Toolbar	
Button	**Purpose**
Back	Moves backward among previously viewed web pages
Forward	Moves forward among previously viewed web pages
Stop Current Jump	Halts the current loading of a web page
Refresh	Refreshes (reloads) the current web page
Start Page	Jumps to the designated start page
Search the Web	Jumps to Microsoft's Search page on the World Wide Web
Favorites	Displays list of favorite sites
Go	Opens the Go menu, which can be used in place of the navigation buttons
Show Only Web Toolbar	Turns off all toolbars except the Web toolbar

Using Word to Open Web Documents

You can open web pages in Word, effectively using Word as a web browser. (A word of caution here: as a browser, Word can be rather slow. If you want to do serious web surfing of the Net, dedicated web browsers like Microsoft's Internet Explorer and Netscape Navigator make better browsers, but if you just want to pull up a web page without leaving Word, you can do so.)

To open a web page in Word, choose File⇨Open. In the Open dialog box that appears, click in the File name text box, enter a web address, and then click Open. Word will connect with the Net via your default Internet or intranet connection, and it will load the web page. Figure 11-3 shows an example of a web page loaded using Word; in this case, the web page is from Yahoo!, the popular Internet search directory.

Once you open and navigate among web pages in Word, the Forward, Back, Stop, and Refresh buttons of the Web toolbar become active. You can use the buttons to navigate forward and backward among web pages you have viewed. Also, note that the Address list box in the Web toolbar keeps a list of the sites you've visited during any web session with Word. To revisit a site, you can open the list, and choose the address you want.

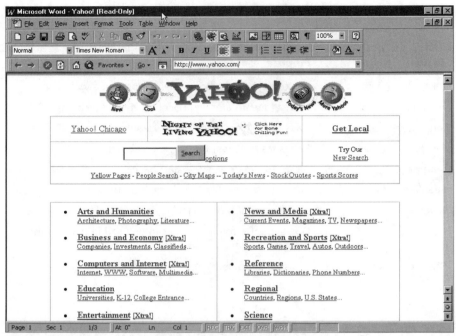

Figure 11-3: Yahoo! Web page loaded in Word.

You can add your favorite sites that you find on the web to the Favorites list of the Web toolbar, so you can quickly go back to them later. While you are at any web site, click Favorites on the Web toolbar, and choose Add to Favorites to add that web site to the Favorites list.

Creating Hyperlinks in Documents

A significant feature of Word 97 is its ability to use *hyperlinks* in documents. You can create hyperlinks to jump to other Office documents stored on your PC, on your company's network, on a company intranet, or on the Internet.

Linking to office documents with copy and paste

If you want to create a hyperlink to a location in Word, or in an Excel worksheet or PowerPoint presentation, the easiest way to do this is to use the Copy and Paste Hyperlink commands of the Edit menu. In a nutshell, you do this by first selecting a location in the Word document, Excel worksheet, or PowerPoint presentation that you want the hyperlink to lead to. You then choose Copy from the Edit menu. Finally, you go back to Word where you want the hyperlink to appear, and you choose Paste as Hyperlink from the Edit menu. In more detail, here are the steps you can use to create a hyperlink from another Office document:

1. Open the document containing the location you want to link to. (If it is in Word, it can be in the same document, or in a different document that's open. If the location is in an Excel or a PowerPoint file, it can be in any area of the worksheet or presentation.)

2. Select the portion of the document you want to link to.

3. Choose Edit⇨Copy.

4. In Word, place the insertion pointer at the location where you want to insert the hyperlink.

5. Choose Edit⇨Paste as Hyperlink.

When you perform these steps, Word inserts a hyperlink back to the original document at the selected location. You can then click on the hyperlink at any time to jump to the linked document.

Hot Stuff
If you want to create a hyperlink to a portion of a Word document, another way to do this is by selecting the data to be linked and then using the right mouse button to click and drag the information to the location that is to serve as the hyperlink. When you release the right mouse button, choose Create Hyperlink Here from the Shortcut menu which appears.

Linking to web sites or files with Insert Hyperlink

If you need to establish a hyperlink to a web site on an intranet or on the Internet, you can use the following steps to do so. (Technically, you can use these same steps to link to another Office document, but it's easier to use the copy and paste methods described earlier.)

1. Select the text in the document that will serve as the hyperlink.

2. Click the Insert Hyperlink button in the Standard toolbar, or choose Insert⇨ Hyperlink. When you do this, the Insert Hyperlink dialog box appears, as shown in Figure 11-4.

3. In the Link to File or URL text box, enter the web address (or the path for the file) of the destination for the link.

4. If you are establishing a link to a file and you want to jump to a specific location, enter that location in the Named Location in File text box. (This can be a cell reference or named range in an Excel worksheet, a Word bookmark, or the name of a PowerPoint slide.) If you link to a file and leave this entry blank, the hyperlink jumps to the beginning of the file.

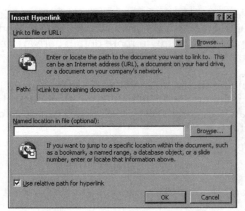

Figure 11-4: The Insert Hyperlink dialog box.

5. If you want a hyperlink to a shared network directory to find the linked file based on a path that's relative to the location where your current document is stored, turn on the Use Relative Path for Hyperlink check box. If you want a hyperlink to a shared network directory to use the same address regardless of where the current document is stored, turn off the Use Relative Path for Hyperlink check box.

6. Click OK to establish the hyperlink.

Saving Word Documents to the Internet

You can save Word documents directly to Internet FTP sites. (In order to do this, you must have permission to save files to the desired FTP site.) You can use the following steps to save documents to the Internet:

1. Choose File⇨Save As.

2. In the Save In box of the dialog box which appears, click Internet Locations (FTP).

3. In the list of FTP sites, double-click the site you want (see the note below if the desired site does not appear).

4. Double-click the location you want within the site.

5. Enter a name for the document in the File name box.

6. Click Save.

Note If the FTP site you want to save your document to doesn't appear in the list of FTP sites, you'll need to add it to the list. Choose File⇨Open, and in the Look in box, click Add/Modify FTP locations. This causes an Add/Modify FTP Locations dialog box to appear, and you can fill in the site name, login, and password information. When done, click OK to add the site to the list.

Publishing Word Documents on the Web

Word 97 allows you to create documents and save them as HTML files. This is a very simple matter in word. You can take an existing Word document and save it as an HTML file for web publication. Before we go on, a word of caution about saving word documents as HTML files. Many of the formatting features of Word are not supported upon conversion to HTML format. The following table gives you an idea of the formats that are retained after conversion to HTML.

Saving existing Word documents as HTML

You can use the Save as HTML option of the File menu to convert existing documents into HTML files. Once converted, you can then upload the documents to your Internet or intranet web server, using the procedures applicable to your server.

To save an existing document in HTML format, choose File⇨Save as HTML. When you do this, the normal Save As dialog box opens, with the only difference being that the dialog box is titled Save As HTML, and HTML is automatically selected as a file type. Enter a desired file name and click OK, and Word will save the existing document in HTML format. When saving existing documents as HTML, keep in mind the limitations of HTML documents, as emphasized in Table 11-2.

Table 11-2 **Limitations of Word Conversions to HTML**		
Word Formatting	*Supported by HTML?*	*Comments*
Font sizes	See Comments	Fonts are converted to the closest HTML font size.
Comments	See Comments	Comments don't appear in the document after web publication.

(continued)

Table 11-2 (*continued*)		
Word Formatting	**Supported by HTML?**	**Comments**
Emboss, shadow, engrave, caps, small caps, strikethrough, and outline text features	No	These formatting options are lost after conversion to HTML format.
Fields	See Comments	The information in a field is retained but the field will not continue to update; the field is converted to text.
Tabs	Yes	Tabs are converted to an HTML tab character. These appear as spaces in some browsers. As an alternate use indents or a table.
Tables of contents or authorities and indexes	See Comments	The information in the tables is converted, but these will not be converted because they are based on field codes. The page numbers are displayed as asterisks that are hyperlinks that readers can click to navigate the web page. You can replace the asterisks with the text that you want to have displayed.
Drop caps	No	These are removed, however, you can increase the size of the letter by increasing the font size and then clicking it in the web page environment.
Table widths	See comments	The tables are converted to a fixed width.
Tables	Yes	Tables are converted but the settings that colored and width borders are not retained.
Highlights	No	Highlights are lost.
Page numbering	No	An HTML document is considered a single web page, therefore web page numbers are lost.
Margins	No	Controlling layout of a page is done via tables.
Page borders	No	There are no HTML equivalents.

Word Formatting	Supported by HTML?	Comments
Headers and Footers	No	There are no HTML equivalents.
Footnotes	No	There are no HTML equivalents.
Newspaper columns	No	For multicolumn effects use tables.
Styles	No	User-defined styles are converted to direct formatting if it is supported by HTML.

Using the Web Page Wizard to create web pages

You can also create web pages using Word's Web Page Wizard, which also produce HTML files. You can use the following steps to produce web-ready files based on your Word documents:

1. Choose File⇨New and click on the Web Pages tab.

2. Next select the Web page Wizard. The Web Page Wizard is then activated. Figure 11-5 shows the First Window of the Web Page Wizard.

Figure 11-5: The first dialog box of the Web Page Wizard.

3. In the first dialog box of the Web Page Wizard, choose the type of web page. As you scroll through the web page types, they appear in the Word window to give you an idea as to what kind of page you wish to create. When done selecting your options, click next.

4. The second dialog box allows you to choose a visual layout for your web page. Again you can see the visual layouts in the Word window. After selecting a visual layout, click next. Figure 11-6 shows the Visual Layout window of the Web Page Wizard.

Figure 11-6: The Visual Layout
dialog box of the Web Page Wizard.

5. Now that you have selected the visual layout for your web page, you can go
on to create the actual web page. To do so, click on finish.

The web page that you created then shows up preformatted. Once this happens,
you can add the text you wish to appear on your web page.

When creating HTML files based on Word documents, keep in mind that Word has
a much wider range of formatting than is possible with HTML. HyperText Markup
Language is a fairly simple formatting language, and if you use some of Word's
more unusual features, they may be lost in the translation, or translated in ways
you didn't expect. For example, if you place text in text boxes within a Word
document and then save the document as HTML, the text stored in the text boxes
does not appear in the HTML file. If you place a graphic in a document and save it
as HTML, Word does write the graphic to a .GIF file and includes a reference in the
HTML code for the graphic. However, the graphic often does not appear (in
relation to the paragraph placement) at the same place it was originally stored in
the Word document.

Summary

This chapter has covered the details behind sharing your Word data with
Internet/intranet users. Points covered in this chapter included the following:

✦ Hyperlinks can be added to the text of a document, and you can store web
addresses or jump locations to other Office documents in Word documents.

✦ Word 97 can open files that are stored on the Internet, and you can save files
to Internet FTP sites.

✦ You can use the Save as HTML option of the File menu to save existing Word documents as HTML files, for publishing on the Internet or on an intranet.

✦ You can use the Web Page Wizard to quickly create web pages that use various styles and formats.

In the next chapter, you learn how to further extend the power of Word by using Visual Basic for Applications.

Where to go next...

✦ Word is just one component of the web publishing capabilities provided by Office 97. Excel, PowerPoint, and Access also offer web publishing and web interaction features. For specifics on Excel and the Web, see Chapter 23; for PowerPoint and the Web, Chapter 32; and for Access and the Web, Chapter 44.

✦   ✦   ✦

Word and Visual Basic for Applications

This chapter details the use of Visual Basic for Applications (VBA), the programming language that is the basis for Word macros. VBA is heavily based on Microsoft's Visual Basic programming language. Because Word macros are based on VBA, you can use VBA to automate common tasks in Word.

VBA can take you much farther than simply duplicating keystrokes. VBA gives you full access to all of Word's commands. You can modify Word's own menus by adding your own commands and options, you can create custom dialog boxes to present messages and query users for information, and you can even construct complete applications that users with a limited knowledge of Word can use. To accomplish these kinds of tasks, you need more than a familiarity with the recording and playing of macros — you need a basic understanding of VBA.

Using Macros to Learn Visual Basic for Applications

Chapter 9 detailed the basics of using macros, which are sequences of instructions that cause Word to perform a particular task. As that chapter demonstrates, macros can be very handy to use in your work because they greatly reduce the time that you spend performing routine, repetitive tasks. Macros are also an excellent starting point for understanding how VBA works and what you can do with the language. As Word's Macro Recorder stores all the actions that you perform or the commands that you choose, it interprets these actions or commands into *statements*, or lines of code, by using VBA. These statements are automatically placed in a *procedure*, which is a block of VBA code. Procedures are stored in *modules*, which you can think of as containers for all VBA code.

To get an idea of how all Word macros use VBA, you should practice on an example. This chapter will familiarize you with Visual Basic code by examining the procedure that results when you record this sample macro. The following steps produce two printed copies of a document, with the document summary sheet included in the printout. Because you can't print multiple copies of a document with nonstandard options (like the document summaries) using just the Print icon in the toolbar, this represents a typical task that can be automated by creating a macro.

Follow these steps to create the worksheet and the sample macro:

1. Open an existing document.

2. Choose Tools⇨Macro⇨Record New Macro.

3. In the Record New Macro dialog box, enter the name **PrintTwo** and then click on the OK button. The Stop Recording toolbar, which you can use to stop recording the macro, appears in the document.

4. Choose File⇨Print. The Print dialog box appears, as shown in Figure 12-1.

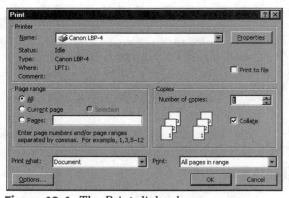

Figure 12-1: The Print dialog box.

5. In the Copies portion of the dialog box, change the number of copies to **2**.

6. Click the Options button.

7. In the dialog box that appears, turn on the Document Properties check box, and click OK.

8. Click OK to close the Print dialog box and begin printing.

9. Click on the Stop Recording button to stop the recording of the macro.

You can verify the effects of the macro by opening any document, choosing Tools⇨Macro⇨Macros, clicking on PrintTwo to select it, and clicking on the Run button. Word prints two copies of the current document, along with document summary sheets for each copy.

How similar is Visual Basic for Applications to Visual Basic?

If you've already worked with Microsoft's Visual Basic as a development language, you'll find Visual Basic for Applications to be a familiar friend; in fact, *sibling* is more accurate. VBA is solidly based on Microsoft's Visual Basic programming language. The whole idea in developing VBA was to replace the old macro-based languages, such as Word Basic and Excel 4.0's macro language, with a common development language so that developers who are familiar with applications development in Word could easily develop applications in Excel or in Access, and vice versa.

Microsoft uses Visual Basic as the base language, and it has added extensions to the language as implemented in the other Office applications. The commands, functions, methods, procedures, and program structures used in Visual Basic can all be used in VBA for Word, Excel, PowerPoint, and Access. So if you are a Visual Basic programmer, you're on very familiar ground.

Understanding VBA Code

Of course, the purpose of the exercise that you just completed is not to demonstrate how to create a macro but to show how VBA code works as the basis of any macro. Choose Tools⇨Macro⇨Macros to open the Macro dialog box, select the PrintTwo macro, and click Edit. This opens the Visual Basic Editor, shown in Figure 12-2. As shown in the figure, the VBA code behind the macro appears in the Module window at the right.

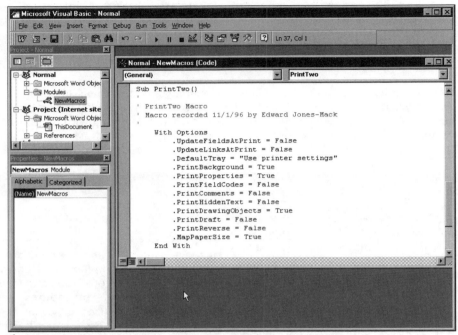

Figure 12-2: An example of macro code within the Visual Basic Editor.

The code looks like this:

```
Sub PrintTwo()
'
' PrintTwo Macro
' Macro recorded 11/1/96 by Edward Jones
'
    With Options
        .UpdateFieldsAtPrint = False
        .UpdateLinksAtPrint = False
        .DefaultTray = "Use printer settings"
        .PrintBackground = True
        .PrintProperties = True
        .PrintFieldCodes = False
        .PrintComments = False
        .PrintHiddenText = False
        .PrintDrawingObjects = True
        .PrintDraft = False
        .PrintReverse = False
        .MapPaperSize = True
```

```
        End With
        With ActiveDocument
            .PrintPostScriptOverText = False
            .PrintFormsData = False
        End With
        Application.PrintOut FileName:="",
            Range:=wdPrintAllDocument, Item:= _
            wdPrintDocumentContent, Copies:=2, Pages:="",
          PageType:=wdPrintAllPages, _
              Collate:=True, Background:=True, PrintToFile:=False
    End Sub
```

Each of the steps that you took during the recording of this procedure resulted in
the addition of one or more lines of Visual Basic code in the module. The code
appears in color: comments are displayed in green, key words of the Visual Basic
language appear in blue, and all other code appears in black. When you run this
(or any) macro, you are in effect running the Visual Basic for Applications code
that is contained in the module that was recorded by the Macro Recorder. As the
module runs, each line of Visual Basic code executes in turn, and Word performs
an appropriate action as a result.

About comments

You can include *comments* (lines that aren't acted upon by Word when the code
runs) by preceding the text with a single quotation mark. In the sample procedure,
you can see that the second and third lines are comments:

```
' PrintTwo Macro
' Macro recorded 11/1/96 by Edward Jones
```

In this case, Word added the comments based on the entries in the Macro Name
and Description text boxes of the Record Macro dialog box, but you can place
comments wherever you desire in your Visual Basic code by typing a single quote
mark followed by the text of the comment. Comments can be quite helpful in your
more complex procedures because they can help you remember what's going on
at a specific point in the procedure. Comments can occupy an entire line, or you
can put them at the end of a valid line of code by starting the comment with a
single quotation mark. When the procedure runs, everything that follows the
single quotation mark is ignored until Word finds a new line of code.

About headers and footers

If you look just above the comments, you see that the first line of the procedure
reads

```
Sub PrintTwo()
```

The matching last line reads

```
End sub
```

Think of these lines as the header and footer for the procedure. Every VBA procedure starts with a header that begins with `Sub` or `Function` and ends with a footer that says `End Sub` or `End Function`. VBA allows two types of procedures: *function procedures* and *sub procedures*. Function procedures accept a value(s), act on the data, and return a value(s). Sub procedures do not return a value (although you can pass values from within a sub procedure through the use of statements inside the procedure). Any arguments used by a function procedure are placed inside the parentheses of the header. The footer tells Word that it has reached the end of the procedure. When Word reaches the footer in the module, it passes program control back to any other VBA procedure that called this one. If the procedure was not called by another procedure, Word returns control from the procedure to Word itself.

About VBA Code

The code between the Sub and the End Sub lines makes up the actual procedure that does all of the work. In this example, many of the lines are *assignment statements*; these assign a value to a property in Word. For example, the line of code which reads:

```
.PrintProperties = True
```

tells Word to include the Document Properties with the printout.

Also included in the VBA code are statements that perform direct actions within Word. For example, the statement that begins with the words `Application.Printout Filename:=` is the statement that tells Word to print the document.

About displaying dialog boxes

One of the reasons that you may actually want to do some Visual Basic programming yourself (rather than using only the Macro Recorder) is that you can do some custom programming — such as displaying dialog boxes — that you cannot do with recorded macros. To display a dialog box on-screen that contains a message with custom text, you can use VBA's `MsgBox` function. The syntax of the statement is simple: you add a line of code that reads `MsgBox("your custom text")` where you put your desired text between the double quotation marks.

If you duplicated the example earlier in the chapter, go to the end of the line prior to the last line of the procedure (the End Sub line) and press Enter to add a new, blank line. With the insertion point at the start of the blank line, enter the following:

MsgBox("Now printing two copies with summaries.")

Choose File⇨Close to exit the Visual Basic Editor. Once you are back in the document, choose Tools⇨Macro⇨Macros. In the Macro dialog box, select the PrintTwo macro and click on the Run button. When the macro completes this time, you see the dialog box shown in Figure 12-3. Dialog boxes such as this one can serve to inform users, providing needed guidance about tasks the user needs to perform.

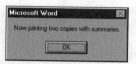

Figure 12-3: The dialog box presented by the MsgBox function.

Editing VBA Code

When you open a module, you can enter program code just like you type text in any word processor. You don't have to know the mechanics of entering text and correcting mistakes, suffice it to say that you can use the same text entry and editing techniques (including cutting and pasting) that you can use in any Windows word processor.

While you are in the Visual Basic Editor, you can also insert text from another file into your existing program code. If you want to insert text into the program code, place the insertion point at the location in the module where you want to insert the code and choose Insert⇨File. In the File dialog box, select the file that contains the text that you want to insert and click on the OK button to read the text into the file.

Printing Visual Basic Code

You can print the code that is contained in your Visual Basic modules. To print the code, open the module that contains the desired code by choosing Tools⇨Macro⇨Macros, selecting the desired macro, and clicking the Edit button. Then choose the Print command from the File menu.

About the Visual Basic Toolbar

If you do much work in VBA programming, you'll find the Visual Basic toolbar (Figure 12-4) to be useful. You can activate the Visual Basic toolbar by right-clicking on the toolbar area and choosing Visual Basic from the shortcut menu. Table 12-1 provides an explanation for the different buttons on the Visual Basic toolbar.

Record Macro

Run Macro   **Visual Basic Editor**

Visual Basic ⊠

— **Design Mode**

— **Control Toolbox**

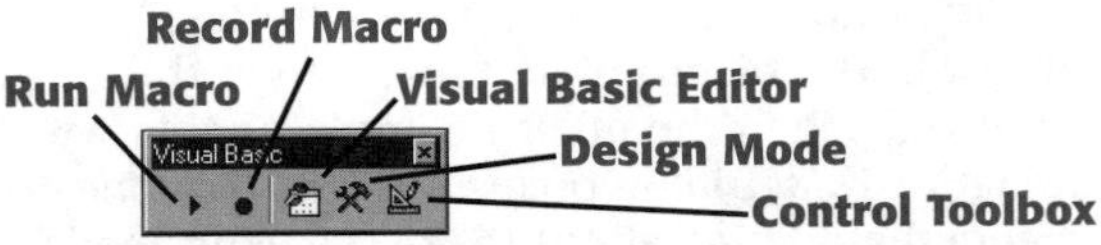

Figure 12-4: The Visual Basic toolbar.

Table 12-1
Buttons on the Visual Basic toolbar

Name	Function
Run Macro	Opens the Run Macro dialog box where you can run, delete, or modify a selected macro.
Record Macro	Open the Record Macro dialog box where you can fill in the desired options used to begin recording a macro.
Visual Basic Editor	Opens the Visual Basic Editor where you can create, edit, and step through macros using Visual Basic.
Control Toolbox	Displays the Toolbox used for adding controls to a worksheet.
Design Mode	Switches in and out of Design mode.
Toggle Breakpoint	Removes or inserts a breakpoint in a line of code.

Just a Beginning...

Make no mistake about it, using VBA falls well into the realm of programming. (If you're completely new to programming, you should be congratulated for pressing this deeply into what, for many readers, is a subject of mystifying complexity.) You've not only learned how VBA lies at the heart of everything that you do with macros, but you've also learned how you can extend the power of your macros by adding your own Visual Basic code to provide items like dialog boxes and customized prompts. Still, you've only scratched the surface of what you can do with this language. VBA is a full-featured programming language that you can use to automate or customize virtually any conceivable task that can be done with Word. If the challenges of programming catch your fancy, you should look into additional resources for learning about Visual Basic programming. It's a subject about which entire books have been written.

Summary

This chapter has provided an introduction to programming by using Visual Basic for Applications, the underlying language behind Word macros. The chapter covered the following points:

✦ Every Word macro exists as a series of Visual Basic program statements.

✦ The Visual Basic statements are stored in procedures, and one or more procedures are placed in modules.

✦ Visual Basic procedures can be function procedures or sub procedures. Function procedures accept a value(s), act on the data, and return a value(s). Sub procedures do not return a value (although you can pass values from within a sub procedure through the use of statements inside the procedure).

✦ You can modify the Visual Basic code that Word's Macro Recorder creates to add special features like dialog boxes and custom prompts.

The next chapter will show how you can put Word to work, by demonstrating how you can create and use various documents for common business tasks.

Where to go next . . .

✦ Because Visual Basic for Applications lies at the heart of macros that you create in Word, you should also be intimately familiar with the use of macros before getting deeply involved with Visual Basic for Applications. See Chapter 9.

✦   ✦   ✦

Word for Windows at Work

CHAPTER

✦ ✦ ✦ ✦

In This Chapter

Designing a fax
cover sheet

Writing an interoffice
memo

✦ ✦ ✦ ✦

I n this chapter, you'll find two of step-by-step exercises
that you can follow to quickly put Word for Windows to
work. These exercises are designed to use some of Word's
wizards to make short work of producing professional-
looking documents.

Designing a Fax Cover Sheet

Figure 13-1 shows an example of a fax cover sheet that you
can quickly create by using Word's Fax Wizard.

To create a fax cover sheet, perform the following steps:

1. Choose File⇨New. The New dialog box appears.

2. Click on the Letters and Faxes tab and then double-click
   on Fax Wizard. In a moment, the first Fax Wizard dialog
   box appears (Figure 13-2).

3. As the dialog box notes, this Fax Wizard helps you
   create a cover sheet and fax a document from within
   Word. Click Next in the dialog box to proceed. In a
   moment, the second Fax Wizard dialog box appears
   (Figure 13-3).

4. Click the Just a cover sheet with note option, then click
   Next. (If you had another document open
   simultaneously, you could choose to send it along with
   the cover sheet by choosing it in the list box.) After you
   click Next, the third Fax Wizard dialog box appears
   (Figure 13-4).

5. If you have a modem and wish to send the fax cover
   sheet, click Microsoft Fax; otherwise, click the I want to
   print my document so I can send it from a separate fax
   machine option. Then click Next.

6. Assuming you choose to fax the cover page, the next dialog box you see is shown in Figure 13-5. This dialog box asks for the recipient's name and the fax number. Enter the desired name and number and click Next.

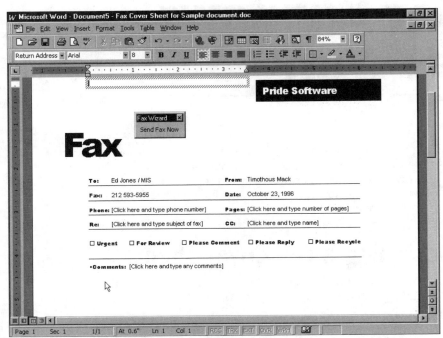

Figure 13-1: An example of a fax cover sheet.

Figure 13-2: The first Fax Wizard dialog box.

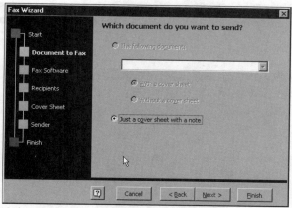

Figure 13-3: The second Fax Wizard dialog box.

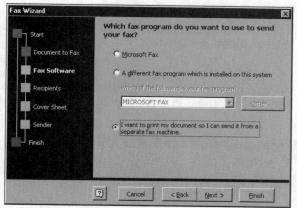

Figure 13-4: The third Fax Wizard dialog box.

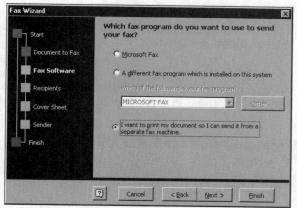

Figure 13-5: The fourth Fax Wizard dialog box.

7. The next dialog box (Figure 13-6) gives you a choice of three styles: professional, contemporary, and elegant. Choose a desired style and click Next.

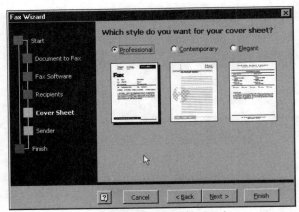

Figure 13-6: The fifth Fax Wizard dialog box.

8. The next dialog box that appears (Figure 13-7) asks for the name of the sender. Enter the desired information and click Next.

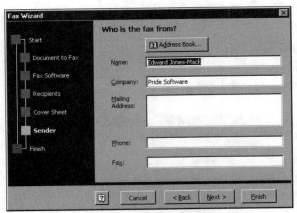

Figure 13-7: The sixth Fax Wizard dialog box.

9. The last dialog box indicates that the process of building the fax cover sheet is complete, and it displays a Finish button. You can click Finish to produce the cover letter and send it using Microsoft Fax.

Writing an Interoffice Memo

Figure 13-8 shows an example of an interoffice memo. You can easily produce a memo like this with Word's Memo Wizard.

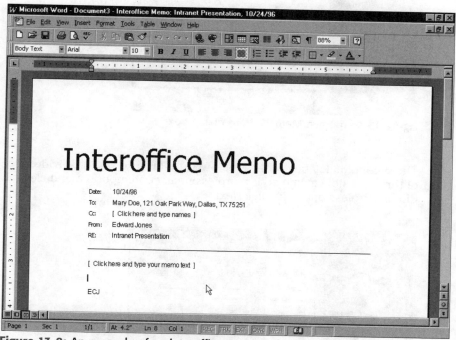

Figure 13-8: An example of an interoffice memo.

To create an interoffice memo, perform the following steps:

1. Choose File⇨New. The New dialog box appears.

2. In the New dialog box, click on the Memos tab and then double-click on Memo Wizard.

3. In the first Memo Wizard dialog box that appears (Figure 13-9), click on the Next button.

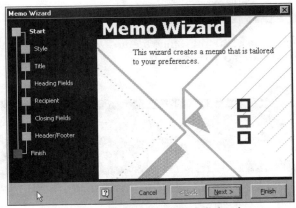

Figure 13-9: The first Memo Wizard dialog box.

4. The second dialog box of the Memo Wizard (Figure 13-10) provides a choice of three possible memo styles: professional, contemporary, and elegant. Choose Professional and click Next.

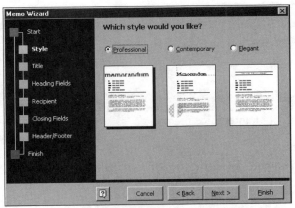

Figure 13-10: The second Memo Wizard dialog box.

5. The next dialog box of the Memo Wizard that appears (Figure 13-11) asks for a desired title. For this exercise, you can accept the default title of Interoffice Memo and click Next.

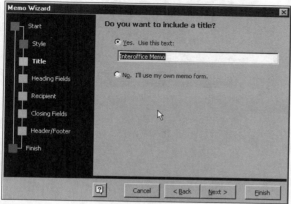

Figure 13-11: The third Memo Wizard dialog box.

6. The next dialog box of the Memo Wizard that appears (Figure 13-12) asks which header items should be included in your memo. Leave the defaults selected and enter a subject if desired and click Next.

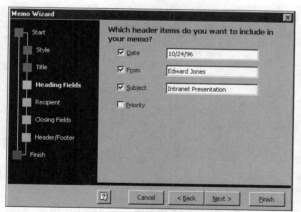

Figure 13-12: The fourth Memo Wizard dialog box.

7. The next dialog box of the Memo Wizard that appears (Figure 13-13) asks for recipients of the memo. Enter a desired addressee name in the To box and click Next.

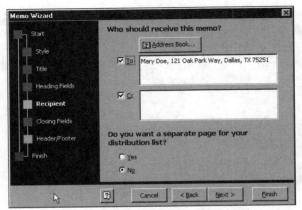

Figure 13-13: The fifth Memo Wizard dialog box.

8. The next dialog box of the Memo Wizard that appears (Figure 13-14) asks which closing items you want in the memo. These fields are all optional, and you can turn on any desired options that are not checked. In this case leave the default options selected and click Next to proceed.

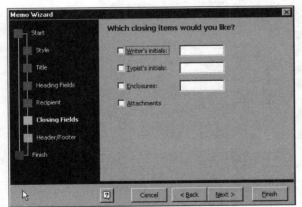

Figure 13-14: The sixth Memo Wizard dialog box.

9. The next dialog box of the Memo Wizard that appears (Figure 13-15) asks which items you desire in the header and the footer. In the header, you can choose the options of Date, Topic (which you fill in), and Page Number. For the footer, you can choose the options of Date, Confidential, and Page Number. In this case, leave the default options selected and click Next.

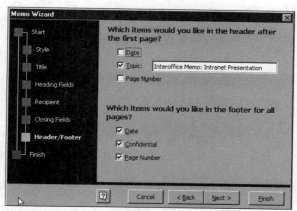

Figure 13-15: The seventh Memo Wizard dialog box.

10. The last dialog box to appear tells you the process is complete. Click Finish to produce the interoffice memo.

Summary

This chapter has provided a step-by-step look at what's involved in using Word for Windows to create typical business documents. You can use the different templates and wizards to ease the drudgery of creating many common types of documents.

- ✦ Use the Fax Wizard to create a fax cover sheet.

- ✦ Use the Memo Wizard to create an attractive memo form, complete with sender, date, recipient(s), and subject, into which you can type your message.

The next chapter answers common questions that arise when you use Word for Windows.

Where to go next...

- ✦ Many of the examples demonstrated in this chapter use the templates that come with Word. Chapter 8 tells the whole story about working with templates.

✦   ✦   ✦

The Word Top Ten

This chapter answers ten common Word for Windows questions. These questions are based on inquiries to Microsoft Technical Support and the Microsoft forums on CompuServe.

1. I have a document that was created with another word processing program. Can I work on this file in Word?

For the most part, Word converts files that have been created in other programs when you open them. There are, however, some things you should keep in mind. In cases where the file extension differs from the default Word .DOC file extension, you should select All Files (*.*) from the List Files of Type list box to see the files.

Note, too, that Word uses file converters when it opens files created by other programs. If you did a complete installation of Word, all the converters were installed. If not, you may need to add the converters by running the Word Setup program. Perform these steps to add converters:

1. From the Windows 95 Start menu, choose Programs, and then choose Microsoft Office Shortcut Bar.

2. When the Office Shortcut Bar appears, right-click on its header (the top of the bar if it is arranged vertically, the left side of the bar if it is arranged horizontally) and choose Add/Remove Office Programs from the shortcut menu that appears.

3. The Office Setup and Uninstall dialog box appears. Choose Microsoft Office, and click on OK.

4. You next see the Office Setup dialog box. The Add/Remove button enables you to choose different components to add or remove from the Office installation.

5. Click on the line that reads Microsoft Word to select it, and click on the Change Options button in the dialog box. The Word Setup dialog box displays the items that are currently installed for Microsoft Word, including the converters. By clicking on the check boxes, you can select and deselect the items that you want to add or remove from the setup.

Word comes with these converters:

✦ WordPerfect for DOS 5.*x*

✦ WordPerfect for Windows 5.*x*

✦ Microsoft Excel BIFF 2.*x*, 3.0, 4.0, and 5.0 (This can be used only to open files, not to save them.)

✦ Microsoft Word for Windows 1.*x* and 2.*x*

✦ Microsoft Word for Windows 6.0/95

✦ Word for Macintosh 4.*x* and 5.*x*

✦ Write for Windows

✦ Lotus 1-2-3

✦ Text with layout

✦ WordStar for DOS and Windows

✦ WordPerfect versions 6.0, 6.1, 5.0, 5.1, and 5.2

✦ Word for Windows 2.0

✦ Word for DOS 3.0 to 6.0

✦ Word for the Macintosh 4.0–5.1

✦ Microsoft Excel

✦ Works for Windows 3.0 and 4.0

✦ RFT-DCA (IBM DisplayWriter)

2. Why do addresses print on envelopes in the wrong position?

The addresses may print on your envelopes in the wrong position for several reasons. The printer bin may be set incorrectly. In this case, you may need to refer to your printer manual to see what the correct setting is for printing envelopes. You may also have other printer options set incorrectly. One good example is the size of the envelope. Business envelopes and personal letter envelopes are different sizes; therefore, you need to check your printer options to see whether they have been set to the correct size.

If you want to print an envelope, follow these steps:

1. Choose Tools⇨Envelopes and Labels. The Envelopes and Labels dialog box appears, as shown in Figure 14-1. In the Envelopes tab, you will see the Delivery address text box and the Return Address text box. The Return address text box contains the name that you entered during setup as the user.

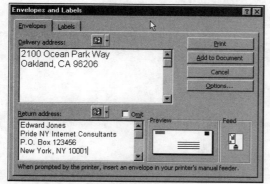

Figure 14-1: The Envelopes and Labels dialog box.

2. To change the envelope size, click in the Preview area to open the Envelope Options tab of the Envelopes Options dialog box. Here you can change the size of the envelope and the position of the delivery and return addresses.

3. To change the type of feed from vertical to horizontal or vice versa, click on the Printing Options Tab of the Envelopes Options dialog box and choose the appropriate feed method.

4. On the Envelopes tab of the Envelopes and Labels dialog box, you will notice an Add to Document button. Clicking on this button produces a dialog box that enables you to add an envelope to the beginning of a document. Then, when you print, you can print the envelope followed by the letter (a convenient feature for writing letters).

5. To print the envelope, click on the Print button.

3. How can I prevent page breaks from appearing in my document where I don't want them?

Unwanted page breaks can occur for any number of reasons. For example, you may have applied paragraph formats, such as Page break before, Keep with next, or Keep lines together. These formats can produce unwanted page breaks. To remove these formats, highlight the paragraph immediately following the page break and then choose Format⇨Paragraph. In the Line and Page Breaks tab of the Paragraph dialog box (Figure 14-2), uncheck the offending format option so that you will not have a page break.

Figure 14-2: The Paragraph dialog box.

Sometimes only a few lines of a paragraph are moved over to the following page in a document. If you want to keep all the lines of the paragraph together on one page, switch to Print Preview and try to adjust the margins to bring the lines back onto the same page. If changing the margins is not effective, choose Format⇨Paragraph and turn on the Keep lines together option. In cases where you are trying to move only a small amount of text to the preceding page, try clicking on the Shrink to Fit button on the Print Preview toolbar.

Also, you may have a section break in your document. If you don't want the section break, you can remove it by placing the cursor in the section immediately after the section break. (If you need to see where the section break is, click on the Show/Hide Paragraph button on the Standard toolbar.) Then choose Insert⇨Break. In the Section Breaks area of the Break dialog box, click on the Continuous option. Finally, delete the unwanted Next Page section break.

You may also have a table in Word that is divided in the middle of a cell. If the entire table does not have to be on the same page, your solution is simple. Place your insertion point anywhere on the row that is being split. Choose Table⇨Cell Height and Width. In the dialog box, click on the Row tab and clear the Allow Row to Break Across Pages check box. (If the table does have to all be on one page, you have no choice but to rearrange adjoining text to allow the table to fit.)

4. Why doesn't Word print the gridlines in my table?

A table's gridlines appear only on-screen. If you want to add lines to your table printouts, you need to apply borders to the table. The Table⇨Table AutoFormat command sets up predefined borders and shading. You select the design that you want from the dialog box that appears. Figure 14-3 shows the Table AutoFormat dialog box.

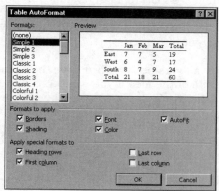

Figure 14-3: The Table AutoFormat dialog box.

If you want to make a custom border, however, choose the Borders and Shading command from the Format menu to bring up the Table Borders and Shading dialog box, as shown in Figure 14-4. In this dialog box, you can apply formatting to the table gridlines or to the text paragraph within a cell. If you want to apply formatting to the gridlines, be sure that you select the end-of-cell mark in the table.

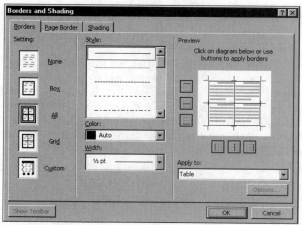

Figure 14-4: The Table Borders and Shading dialog box.

5. Can I run Word for Windows 97 and an earlier version of Word on the same computer, or do I need to remove my earlier version in order to run Word for Windows 97?

You can run both versions of Word on your computer at the same time. However, you need to do two things to keep the versions separate. First, install Word for Windows 97 in a different directory from the earlier version of Word. You may want to install Word for Windows 97 in a directory called Winword97 and allow the earlier version of Word to remain in its current directory.

Next, because the main application files for all versions of Word have the same name (Winword.exe) you should rename one of the files if you want to run the two versions on the same computer without name conflicts. To rename the program file, start either My Computer or Explorer (double-click on the My Computer or the Explorer icon under Windows 95), find the folder for the earlier version of Word, find the applications file Winword.exe, and rename the file. After renaming the Word program file for the earlier version of Word, you will need an easy way to start the program. You can handle this need with the following steps:

1. In My Computer or in Explorer, right-click on the renamed program file.

2. From the shortcut menu that appears, choose Create Shortcut.

3. When the new shortcut icon appears in My Computer or Explorer, click on it and drag it onto the Windows desktop.

You can now start the older version of Word by double-clicking on the shortcut icon on the desktop.

6. Can I delete Word documents without leaving Word?

Yes, and it's ridiculously easy to do. The method is just not intuitively obvious. You have to use the Open command from the File menu, which is not where most people think of going to delete a file. In the Open dialog box, locate the unwanted file, click on it to select it, and press the Delete key. A dialog box appears that asks whether you want to move the file to the Windows Recycle Bin. Click on Yes to move the file to the Recycle Bin. To delete the file permanently from your hard disk, open the Recycle Bin and empty it.

7. Why can't a computer that runs Word 6.0 or Word 2.0 read files from a computer that runs Word for Windows 97?

Word 6.0, Word 2.0, and Word 97 use different file formats. For a computer that runs Word 6.0 or Word 2.0 to read Word 97 files, the files must be saved in Word 6.0 or 2.0 format. Word 97 comes with a converter that lets you save files in Word 6.0 and Word 2.0 format. To save a Word for Windows 97 document in the Word 6.0 or Word 2.0 format, follow these steps:

1. Open the document in Word 97 that you want to save in the earlier Word format.

2. Choose File➪Save As to open the Save As dialog box.

3. Select Word for Windows 6.0 or Word for Windows 2.0 as is appropriate from the Save File as Type list box. Enter a name for the file and specify the directory in which you want to store the file, then click on the OK button in the dialog box.

8. Why aren't all my changes saved in a document, even with AutoSave turned on?

The AutoSave feature doesn't work the way most people think it does. This feature periodically makes a copy of your document and adds the .ASD extension to it. As time passes between the saves, you may have added a substantial amount to your document, but the changes are not in the .ASD document. These files are temporary and are erased when your document is saved: they are deleted when you close the file. AutoSave is designed to recover work in the case of a power outage or system crash. You should always save your document by using the Save command when you exit Word.

If you want to turn on the AutoSave feature or just change the time intervals on the saves, choose Tools➪Options and select the Save tab. Enter the time interval that you want in the Automatic Save Every box, as shown in Figure 14-5.

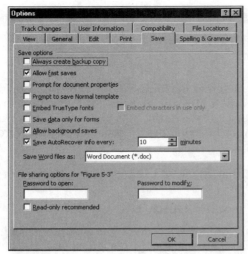

Figure 14-5: The Save Tab of the Options dialog box.

Don't put more faith in AutoSave than it deserves. Often it may save you significant amounts of time and work, but power outages, in particular, are difficult situations for Word (or any word processing program) to handle. We wrote much of the first edition of this book while on assignment in the Caribbean, where power outages are a way of life. After power failures, Word demonstrated an annoying habit of making open files unrecoverable. We quickly learned that the best defense is to back up important work to another media source (like your floppy drive) regularly.

9. How can I set a different font (or font size or style) as the default?

You may want to use a font different from the default font Word uses in the Normal.dot template. Fortunately, changing that font is a piece of cake. Open the Font dialog box by choosing Format⇨Font. In the dialog box, select the desired font, font style, and font size. Then click on the Default button. Word displays a dialog box asking you to confirm the change to the default font; click on OK in this dialog box to put the change into effect.

10. How can I create a bulleted or numbered list?

Word offers an easy way to create a bulleted or numbered list, add the bullets or numbers quickly, and apply a hanging indent to each of the paragraphs. To add bullets or numbers to a list, select all the paragraphs in the list and click on either the Numbering button in the Formatting toolbar (to add numbers), or the Bullets button (to add bullets). If the Formatting toolbar isn't visible, choose View⇨Toolbars and turn on the Formatting option in the dialog box that appears.

Note Word's AutoFormat technology helps you automatically create bulleted and numbered lists. If you begin typing using a number, asterisk, or another form of bullet, Word will keep that format after the second bullet or number is entered. From then on, Word will automatically add the number or bullet followed by the space with which you began the first two lines of text. When you are done typing bulleted or numbered paragraphs, start a new paragraph and use the Backspace key to delete the bullet, and Word stops adding the bullets or numbers to successive paragraphs.

Summary

This chapter has provided coverage of the top ten Word for Windows questions and their answers. The chapter also concludes the Word for Windows section of this book. The section which follows deals with Microsoft Excel, the spreadsheet package provided with Office 97.

Where to go next...

✦ Printing is a task that you will find yourself doing on a regular basis. For more information on the particulars of printing in Word, see Chapter 4.

✦ Formatting question are also common in Word. For answers to your formatting questions, see Chapter 3.

✦   ✦   ✦

Excel

◆   ◆   ◆   ◆

In This Part

◆   ◆   ◆   ◆

Making the Most of Workbooks

This chapter covers topics related to working with Excel workbooks, which are collections of worksheet pages that are saved to the same disk file. Before you can effectively work with Excel, you need to become familiar with the workbook concept.

Understanding Excel Workbooks

For some time, many popular Windows spreadsheets have used the workbook concept, which places multiple pages, each containing a worksheet, inside of a "notebook" of sorts (called *workbook* in Excel lingo). The workbook concept is a case of a computer model imitating real life because Excel's designers assumed that most people who use spreadsheets have different but related groups of number-based data that would best occupy different pages. If, for example, you lived generations before the advent of the computer and you worked with numbers to earn a living, you would have different pieces of paper on your desk, each with related number-based information about a particular project. At the day's end, all the pages would go back into a file folder that was stored in your desk. In Excel, each of these pages becomes a separate worksheet, and the worksheets are identified by tabs at the bottom. All the worksheet pages make up a workbook (the file folder in the analogy).

The workbook concept makes your spreadsheet-related work manageable. Before spreadsheet designers implemented the workbook concept, spreadsheets first accommodated a user's desire for more power by providing larger and larger spreadsheets in the form of a single page. But finding information became quite a challenge as spreadsheet pages approached the physical size of small houses. The next step in spreadsheet design was to give users the ability to base formulas in one spreadsheet on cells of another. This capability partially solved the organizational problem, but you had to remember to open all the spreadsheet files that you needed. The workbook concept overcomes the limitations of earlier spreadsheet designs, however, by placing all your information in an easily accessible notebook.

With the workbook concept, you can easily find information by navigating among the multiple pages of the workbook. And you can name the tabs that indicate each page (worksheet) of the workbook so that they better indicate what is stored in each worksheet. Figure 15-1 shows a typical workbook in Excel, with the House Sales worksheet page of the workbook currently active. (If you would like to work with the actual data in this worksheet, you can find it at the IDG Books web site at www.idgbooks.com.)

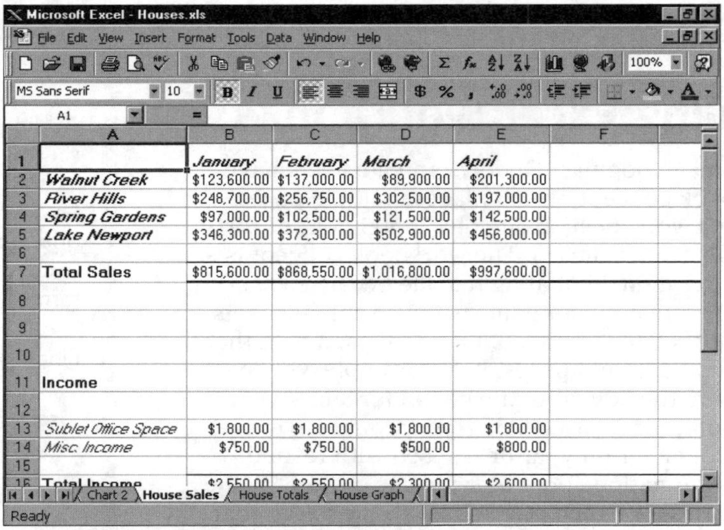

Figure 15-1: A typical Excel workbook.

In Excel, each workbook can contain up to 255 separate worksheet pages. Each worksheet measures 16,384 rows by 256 columns — realistically, more than you should ever need on a single page. Each intersection of a row and column comprises a *cell,* and cells are identified by their row-and-column coordinates (for example, A1 is the cell in the upper-left corner of the worksheet). In addition to containing worksheet pages, an Excel workbook can also contain chart sheets (used to store charts), modules (collections of program code written in Visual Basic for Applications, the programming language used by Excel), Excel 4.0 macro sheets, and dialog box sheets from earlier versions of Excel.

Opening a new workbook

When you start Excel, it opens a new workbook, and you can begin entering your information. If you want to create a new workbook at any time, click on the New Workbook button on the Standard toolbar, or choose File⇨New.

Opening an existing workbook

To open an existing workbook, choose File⇨Open to bring up the Open dialog box, as shown in Figure 15-2. Select the desired file and then click on the Open button to open the file. If the file is in a different folder, you may need to move to that folder by finding the folder in the dialog box and double-clicking on it. You can navigate upward in your PC's folder structure by clicking on the Up One Level button in the dialog box.

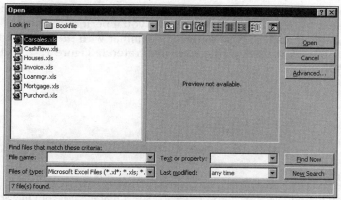

Figure 15-2: The Open dialog box.

If you want to open a workbook that you have recently worked with, open the File menu and choose the file from the bottom of the menu. Excel remembers the last four files that you have worked with and lists them at the bottom of the File menu. If the list of recently used workbooks is not displayed in your File menu, the option for displaying them has been turned off. To turn it back on, choose Tools⇨Options. Next, click on the General tab in the Options dialog box and turn on the Recently Used File List check box to activate the option. Then, click on the OK button.

Hot Stuff If you cannot find the file that you are looking for, enter the name of the file in the File name box, along with an entry in the Text or property area to perform a simple search. The process of searching is explained in more detail later in this chapter.

The more workbooks, the merrier . . .

In Excel, you can have more than one workbook file open at a time. Each workbook that you open is in its own document window. As you need to work with a specific workbook, you bring it to the front by pressing Ctrl+F6 until you see the workbook or by choosing the workbook from the Window menu. You can move and size the windows containing your workbooks by using standard Windows moving and sizing techniques. If you size the windows so that they don't take up the entire screen, you can then navigate between multiple windows by using the mouse to make any desired window the active window.

Working with Worksheets

As you work with Excel worksheets, you'll use various techniques to move around in the sheet and to select areas of the sheet in which you'll perform common operations. First, though, it makes sense to become familiar with the parts of a worksheet. The parts of a worksheet window are illustrated in Figure 15-3, and Table 15-1 describes them.

Table 15-1	
Parts of a worksheet	

Worksheet part	Purpose
Scrollbars	Use these to view sections of the worksheet that are not currently visible by clicking on the arrows, or by moving the scroll box.
Split bars	Use these to split the worksheet window into two panes to enable you to view different portions of the worksheet. To use the split bars, move the pointer to an area between columns or cells and click and drag to size.
Row headers	Identifies each row and can be used to select rows (by clicking on the headers).
Column headers	Identifies each column and can be used to select columns (by clicking on the headers).
Cursor	Indicates the currently selected (or active) cell.

Worksheet part	Purpose
Tabs	Select each worksheet in the workbook.
Standard toolbar	Provides buttons to access common operations, such as opening and saving files, and cutting, copying, and pasting data.
Formatting toolbar	Provides buttons to access common formatting tasks, such as changing the fonts and alignments used to display data.
Formula bar	Displays the contents of the active cell.
Status bar	Displays various messages as you use Excel.
Scroll buttons	Scrolls among the worksheet tabs in a workbook.

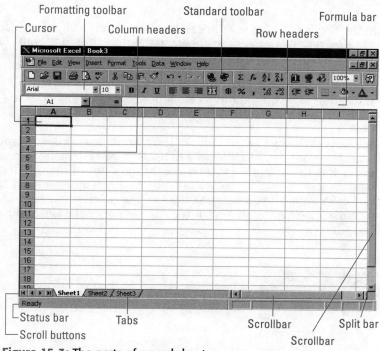

Figure 15-3: The parts of a worksheet.

Navigating within your worksheet

The primary means of navigating within the worksheet is with the mouse. As you move the mouse pointer around the worksheet, the pointer changes shape depending on its location. In most areas of the worksheet, the pointer resembles a plus sign. In most areas outside of the worksheet or over the scrollbars, the pointer changes shape to resemble an arrow. You can scroll the worksheet one row or one column at a time by pointing to the arrows at the ends of the scrollbars and clicking on them with the mouse button.

You can also point to a scroll box, one of the two solid grey blocks within the scrollbars, and use the mouse to drag the block to another position on the scrollbar. Dragging a scroll box causes the worksheet to scroll several rows or columns when you release the mouse button. When you use this technique, notice that the row or column reference that appears on-screen in the upper-left corner changes to indicate your position within the worksheet.

The Tab and Return keys, used alone or in combination with the Shift key, also move the cursor. Pressing Tab moves the cursor to the right; pressing Shift+Tab moves the cursor to the left. Pressing Return moves the cursor down; pressing Shift+Return moves the cursor up.

Hot Stuff If you've lost the cursor and you want to locate it quickly, press Ctrl+Backspace. This action causes the window to scroll as needed to reveal the active cell.

You can also use the Go To key (F5) to move quickly within a worksheet if you know the cell that you want to go to. Press F5 to open the Go To dialog box, as shown in Figure 15-4. In the Reference text box, enter the name of the cell that you want to go to and click on the OK button or press Enter. Excel automatically takes you to that cell. For example, if you enter **AZ400** into the Reference text box and press Enter, the cursor moves to cell AZ400. You can also open the Go To dialog box by choosing Edit⇨Go To.

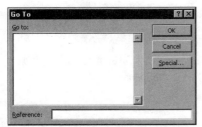

Figure 15-4: The Go To dialog box.

More Info If you're curious, you can use the Go To list box to select a *named range* to go to in a worksheet. Chapter 16 provides details about working with named ranges.

You can also navigate within your worksheet by using arrow keys. As you reach the right side or the bottom row of the worksheet, pressing the same cursor key once more causes the worksheet to scroll, which brings an additional row or column into view.

Keep in mind that the part of the worksheet that you can see is just a small part of the entire sheet. Table 15-2 shows various other key combinations that you will find useful when moving around in an Excel worksheet.

| Table 15-2 | |
| **Useful keys for worksheet navigation** | |
Key	**Function**
Arrow keys	Move the cursor in direction of the arrow
Ctrl+↑ or Ctrl+↓	Moves the cursor to the top or bottom of a region of data
Ctrl+← or Ctrl+→	Moves the cursor to the leftmost or rightmost region of data
PgUp or PgDn	Moves the cursor up or down one screen
Ctrl+PgUp or Ctrl+PgDn	Moves the cursor to the preceding or the following worksheet
Home	Moves the cursor to the first cell in a row
Ctrl+Home	Moves the cursor to the upper-left corner of the worksheet
End	Moves the cursor to the last cell in a row
Ctrl+End	Moves the cursor to the first cell of the last row in a worksheet
End+← or End+→	Moves the cursor to the next blank cell in the direction of the arrow when the active cell is blank
End+Enter	Moves the cursor to the last column in a row

Moving among worksheets

With any spreadsheet that uses the workbook concept, you need a fast, easy way to move among the individual worksheets of the workbook. In Excel, you activate a worksheet by clicking on its tab at the bottom of the worksheet. At the lower-left corner of the worksheet (refer to Figure 15-1) are scroll buttons that enable you to scroll among the different worksheet tabs. If a tab that you want to select is not visible, you can click on the buttons to scroll the tab into view. Clicking on the left- or right-arrow button scrolls you by one tab to the left or right. Clicking on the left-end or right-end button (the one with the line to the left or right of the arrow) scrolls you to the first or last tab in the worksheet. By default, new workbooks in Excel have 16 worksheets, but you can add more (up to the limit of 255 worksheets per workbook) by inserting new worksheets, a topic covered later in this chapter.

Hot Stuff   Remember that you can use the Ctrl+PgUp and Ctrl+PgDn keys to move between worksheets. Ctrl+PgUp moves to the prior worksheet, and Ctrl+PgDn moves to the next worksheet.

Scrolling among the tabs works well if your workbook contains relatively few worksheets, but if your workbook is fairly large (for example, four years worth of projected budgets stored on 48 worksheets), there's an easier way to get around the worksheets: You can use the Go To key (F5). When the Go To dialog box appears, you enter the name of the tab followed by an exclamation point and the cell that you want to go to. Follow these steps to use the Go To key:

1. Press F5 to open the Go To dialog box.

2. In the Reference text box, enter the tab name, an exclamation point, and the cell reference. Then click on the OK button.

   For example, to jump to the first cell in the sixth worksheet, you would press F5 and enter **Sheet6!A1** in the Reference text box.

Unfortunately, this technique doesn't work when you have given your tabs names that include spaces, such as House Sales. With these names, Excel interprets the first word that you type in the Reference text box as a *named range*, and when Excel can't find a range by that name, it displays an error message. The only way around this problem (if you want to be able to jump across pages with the Go To key) is to rename the tab with a name that doesn't include spaces or to create named ranges in the other worksheets so that Excel can find the named range.

Renaming the worksheet tabs

As you work with different worksheets of the workbook, you may find it helpful to rename the tabs to something meaningful. Face it, Sheet4 means a lot less to most people than May 97 Slush Fund. You can easily rename the tabs to whatever you want by right-clicking on the desired tab and choosing Rename from the shortcut menu. When you do this, the existing name appears highlighted within the tab, and you can type a replacement name. While Excel doesn't limit what you can call your tabs, you should keep the names short so that you can view more tabs at one time at the bottom of the workbook.

Selecting multiple worksheets

For many common operations (such as inserting or deleting sheets or applying formatting), you need a way to select more than one worksheet at a time. You can select multiple sheets that are *adjacent* (directly beside one another) by performing these steps:

1. Use the scroll buttons to bring the first tab that you want to select into view and click on the tab to select that worksheet.

2. Use the scroll buttons (if needed) to bring the last tab of the group that you want to select into view. Hold down the Shift key and click on the last tab.

To select multiple sheets that are not adjacent to each other, you can perform the following steps:

1. Use the scroll buttons to bring the first tab that you want to select into view and click on the tab to select that worksheet.

2. Use the scroll buttons (if needed) to bring the next tab that you want to select into view. Hold down the Ctrl key and click on the desired tab.

3. Repeat Steps 1 and 2 for each additional tab that you want to select.

Selecting a range of cells

For many operations, you will need to select large areas of cells, or *ranges* of cells. To select all cells from A1 to F6, for example, you would click in cell A1, hold down the mouse button, and drag down to cell F6 (see Figure 15-5). As you select the A1:F6 cell range, the first cell does not appear in reverse video, as the others do; nevertheless, it is one of the selected cells. By placing the cursor at any cell and clicking and dragging the mouse, you can select any range of cells.

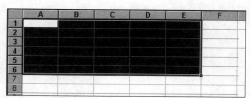

Figure 15-5: Selecting a range of cells in an Excel worksheet.

A similar technique for selecting a range of cells is to use the mouse and the Shift key. Simply click in the first cell of the range and then hold down the Shift key while you click in the last cell of the range. The entire range is then selected, and the active cell is the first cell that you selected. For example, if you click in cell B2, hold down the Shift key, and click in cell E15, the entire range from B2 to E15 is selected, and the active cell becomes cell B2.

If you need to select a very large range of cells, use the Go To key to make your selection process faster. Follow these steps:

1. Select the first cell in the range that you want to select.
2. Press F5 to open the Go To dialog box.
3. In the Reference text box, enter the cell reference for the last cell in the range.
4. Hold down the Shift key while you click on the OK button.

You can also use other methods to select a range of cells. You can select an entire row by clicking on the row header at the left edge of the worksheet, and you can select an entire column by clicking on the column header at the top of the column. To select more than one complete row or column of a worksheet, click on and drag across a series of column headers or down a series of row headers. For example, if you want to select all cells in rows 4, 5, and 6, you click on the row 4 header and drag across rows 5 and 6.

With Excel, you can also select *discontiguous ranges*, or nonadjacent areas. For example, you can select B2:C10 and then select D12:E16. To make this selection, select the first range in the usual manner. Then hold down the Ctrl key and select the second range by clicking and dragging. Excel selects the second area without deselecting the first. Figure 15-6 shows the result of selecting these two ranges.

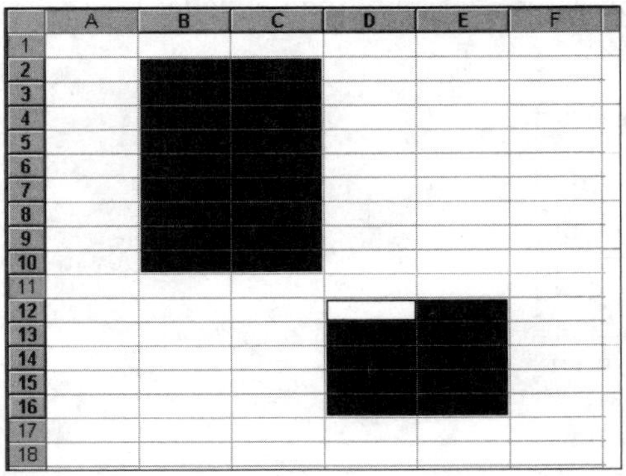

Figure 15-6: Selecting discontiguous ranges of cells.

More Info You may find it helpful to select multiple ranges, such as both rows and columns, as one unit so that you can apply the same formatting to them. (Chapter 17 goes into more detail about formatting your worksheets.) To select rows and columns at the same time, select the first row or column that you want and then hold down the Ctrl key as you select the other rows or columns. Figure 15-7 shows the results of selecting rows 1 and 2 and columns A and B with this technique.

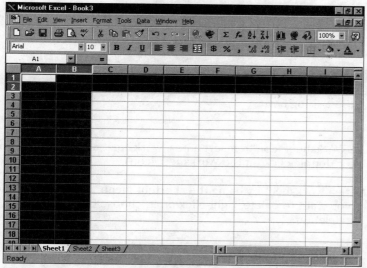

Figure 15-7: The result of selecting rows and columns as one unit.

Adding and deleting worksheets

As you work in an Excel workbook, you may have to rearrange the worksheets in it. Right-clicking on one of the worksheet tabs causes a shortcut menu to open. You can use this shortcut menu to add, delete, and move your worksheets.

Follow these steps to add a worksheet to a workbook:

1. Right-click on the tab of the worksheet that will appear after the worksheet you want to add.

2. Choose Insert from the shortcut menu to open the Insert dialog box with the General tab displayed, as shown in Figure 15-8.

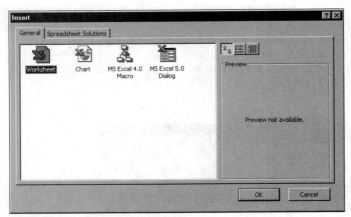

Figure 15-8: The Insert dialog box.

3. Click on the Worksheet icon to insert a new worksheet and then click on the OK button (or double-click on the Worksheet icon).

You can also delete a worksheet by using the shortcut menu. Simply select the tab of the sheet that you want to delete, right-click on it, choose Delete, and click on OK to confirm the deletion.

Moving and copying information in worksheets

You can move or copy information in worksheets and in workbooks in a variety of ways. To copy information from one place to another on a worksheet or to another worksheet, perform the following steps:

1. Select the information that you want to copy.

2. Click on the Copy button in the Standard toolbar or choose Edit➪Copy.

3. Move to the cell in the worksheet in which you want to begin the insertion of the information.

4. Press Enter to place the information in the worksheet.

You can move information in the same worksheet or to another worksheet by following these steps:

1. Select the information that you want to move.

2. Click on the Cut button in the Standard toolbar or choose Edit➪Cut.

3. Move to the cell in the worksheet in which you want to begin entering the information. Be sure that the areas are of the same size so that the move will work without overwriting existing information that you may need.

4. Click on the Paste button in the Standard toolbar or choose Edit⇨Paste to insert the information.

Moving and copying information from one workbook to another is almost as easy as moving and copying information in worksheets of the same workbook. To copy information from one workbook to another, follow these steps:

1. Select the cells that you want to copy.

2. Right-click on the tab of the sheet and choose Move or Copy from the shortcut menu to open the Move or Copy dialog box. In the Move Selected Sheets to Book list box, you can select the (new book) option or the last book that was opened. If you choose the (new book) option, the entire sheet is copied to a new workbook; therefore, if you want to copy only a few cells, use the Copy and Paste buttons on the Standard toolbar.

You can also copy information from one workbook to another by using the Copy and Paste buttons on the Standard toolbar. First select the information that you want to copy. Click on the Copy button on the Standard toolbar. Open the workbook in which you want to copy the information, place your cursor in the cell of the appropriate sheet, and click on the Paste button on the Standard toolbar to insert the information.

To move information from one workbook to another, follow these steps:

1. Select the information that you want to move to another workbook.

2. Click on the Cut button on the Standard toolbar.

3. Open the workbook in which you want to move the information. Or if the workbook is already open, press Ctrl+F6 to move to the other workbook.

4. Place the cursor at the desired location for the data and then click on the Paste button on the Standard toolbar to insert the information.

Splitting the worksheet window

With large worksheets, you may find it helpful to view entirely different parts of the worksheet at the same time by splitting the worksheet window into different panes (see Figure 15-9). To split a worksheet window, drag one of the split bars. You can also place the cursor where you want the window to split and choose Window⇨Split.

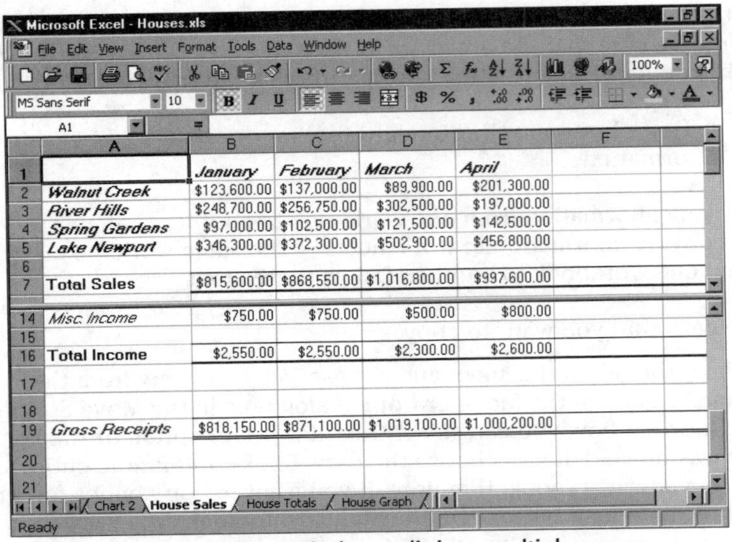

Figure 15-9: A worksheet window split into multiple panes.

You can drag the split bar at the right side of the window to create a horizontal split, and you can drag the split bar at the bottom of the window to create a vertical split. You can then switch between panes by clicking in the pane where you want to work. When you are finished using multiple panes, you can close one pane by dragging the split bar back to the right or bottom of the window, or you can choose Window➪Remove Split.

While a window is split, you can keep the top or left pane from scrolling by choosing Window➪Freeze Panes. This menu option freezes the window panes above and to the left of the split.

Working with Excels Toolbars

Like the other Microsoft Office applications, Excel provides several toolbars that you can use to accomplish common tasks. By default, Excel displays the Standard and the Formatting toolbars, shown earlier in Figure 15-3, but Excel has several other toolbars that you may find useful as you work in Excel. Figure 15-10 shows an Excel worksheet with several toolbars turned on. (Obviously, these toolbars use up a lot of screen real estate.)

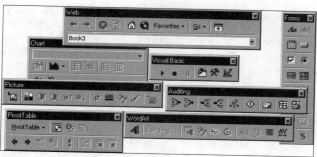

Figure 15-10: Several Excel toolbars.

If you never use the toolbars, you can turn them off to make more space available for viewing your worksheet, and if you want to bring other toolbars into view, you can do so by turning them on. To turn the display of a toolbar on or off, choose View⇨Toolbars then choose Customize to open the Toolbars tab of the Toolbars dialog box (see Figure 15-11). In the dialog box, click the Toolbars tab, and turn on any toolbar that you want to display, or turn off any toolbar that should not be displayed. (A check mark in the check box indicates that the toolbar will be displayed.)

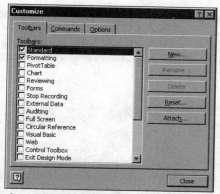

Figure 15-11: The Toolbars tab of the Toolbars dialog box.

The options that are visible if you click the Options tab (Figure 15-12) enable you to choose the way the menus appear, whether menus animations are enabled, whether large buttons should be used, and whether Tooltips (those helpful explanations that appear when you hold the mouse pointer over a toolbar button) should be turned on. When you are finished selecting the desired options, click on the OK button.

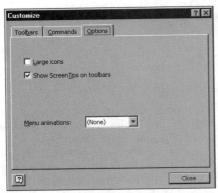

Figure 15-12: The Options tab of the Toolbars dialog box.

Hot Stuff Displaying several toolbars at once does use up memory and resources in Excel (OK, not a great deal of memory, but on some machines, every little bit helps). Even if your machine is the latest and greatest with oodles of memory, turning off toolbars that you are not using gives you more room to see what you're doing.

What's that button do, anyway?

We could have provided a table that would list every toolbar button in Excel, but because there are nearly 300 of them, you would grow tired of seeing the table long before it ended. A better way to find the purpose of any toolbar button is to make use of the Tooltips feature. When you hold the mouse pointer over any toolbar button for more than one second, a Tooltip appears that gives the name of the button. If you want a really detailed explanation of any toolbar button, press Shift+F1 (or choose What's This from the Help menu) and click on the toolbar button that you want more information about.

Toolbars: Have it your way

If you don't like the toolbars that Excel offers, you can create your own. From the View menu, choose Toolbars then choose Customize to open the Toolbars dialog box. Click the Toolbars tab, and click New. In the Toolbar Name text box, enter your own name for a toolbar, and click OK. Excel creates a blank floating toolbar. You can drag any of the buttons from any visible toolbar onto your toolbar. (You can bring a toolbar that's not turned on into view by double-clicking its name in the Toolbars tab of the Customize dialog box.) When you are finished creating your own toolbar, click on the Close button.

After you turn on a toolbar, you can position it anywhere you want in the window. Toolbars can be *floating* (like most of those shown in Figure 15-11), or they can be *docked* to the sides, top, or bottom of the window. The Standard and Formatting toolbars are usually docked to the top of the screen. You use these steps to move a toolbar:

1. Place the mouse pointer over any blank area of the toolbar.

2. Hold down the mouse button and drag the toolbar to the desired area.

If you want to dock the toolbar, you can dock it to any one of four possible areas: the sides of the window, the bottom of the window above the status bar, and the top of the window between the menu bar and the formula bar. Toolbars that contain drop-down lists cannot be docked to the sides of the window.

Hot Stuff You can quickly dock a floating toolbar to the top of the window by double-clicking on the title bar of the toolbar.

Saving and Closing a Workbook

You can save a workbook by clicking on the Save button on the Standard toolbar, entering a name for the workbook in the Save dialog box, and clicking on the OK button. If the workbook had been saved earlier, you can save it again under the same file name that you gave it earlier.

You can also protect the workbook with a password if you want. To protect the workbook, choose File⇨Save As. In the Save As dialog box, click on the Options button, as shown in Figure 15-13. The Save Options dialog box appears, as shown in Figure 15-14. In this dialog box, you can add a protection password to the workbook (which you need to open the workbook), or you can add a modify password (which you need to change the document). You can also make the workbook a read-only workbook, which means that no edits can be added to the document. This is done by turning on the Read-Only Recommended check box. Turning on the Always Create Backup option tells Excel to save the preceding version of the worksheet to a backup file each time that you save the latest version.

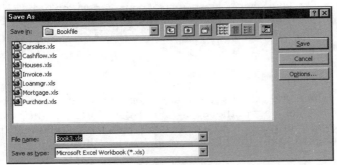

Figure 15-13: The Save As dialog box.

Figure 15-14: The Save Options dialog box.

Adding summary information to your workbook

As part of the information that is saved with your workbook, Excel lets you include specifics about the workbook such as a title, author name, key words, and comments about the workbook. You can view and edit this information by choosing File⇨Properties. In the Properties dialog box, click on the Summary tab (see Figure 15-15). Here you can add any information that you want. The information that you add to the various text boxes can then aid in the file search process. Therefore, give real consideration to entering something in this dialog box that may help you find the workbook at some time in the future.

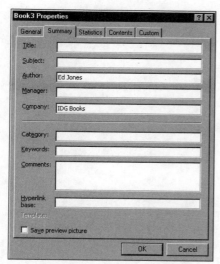

Figure 15-15: The Summary tab of the Properties dialog box.

Using the AutoSave feature

Excel, like other Microsoft products, includes an AutoSave option. This often protects you from losing significant amounts of work in the event of a power failure or system crash (but note that it is *not* infallible).

To enable AutoSave, choose Tools⇨AutoSave. (If you don't see this menu option, read the next paragraph.) In the AutoSave dialog box, turn on the Automatic Save Every check box and enter the time interval that you want Excel to use for the AutoSave. Then choose whether you want to save only the active workbook or all open workbooks with the AutoSave feature and decide whether you want Excel to prompt you before each AutoSave.

If you don't see the AutoSave option on the Tools menu, choose Tools⇨Add-Ins to bring up the Add-Ins dialog box, as shown in Figure 15-16. This dialog box contains different options that you can activate for Excel. After you put a check mark by the AutoSave option, the option becomes available on the Tools menu. Follow the steps in the preceding paragraph to turn on the AutoSave option.

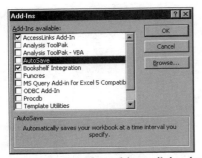

Figure 15-16: The Add-Ins dialog box.

If you still do not see the AutoSave option in the Add-Ins dialog box, you need to install this component of Office 97. To install AutoSave, perform the following steps:

1. Close all other Windows applications.

2. Right-click on the title bar of the Office Shortcut Bar. Figure 15-17 shows the resulting shortcut menu.

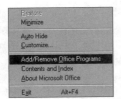

Figure 15-17: The Office Shortcut Bar shortcut menu.

3. From the shortcut menu, choose Add/Remove Office Programs.

4. You are then moved to Office 97 Setup, and you see a Setup dialog box for Office 97.

5. Before you are allowed to proceed, you have to close the Office Shortcut Bar by right-clicking on the title bar and choosing Exit from the shortcut menu.

6. Click on the Add/Remove button in the Setup dialog box. You will then see the Microsoft Office 97 Maintenance window.

7. Select Excel from the list, and click on the Change Options button to the right of the window. The next window you see contains the different installation options for Excel.

8. Choose Add-Ins from the list and click on the Change Options button. You will then see the Microsoft Office 97 - Add-Ins dialog box, as shown in Figure 15-18.

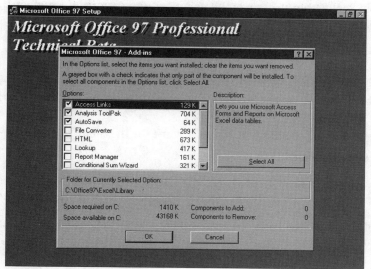

Figure 15-18: The Microsoft Office 97 - Add-Ins dialog box.

9. Click on the check box next to AutoSave to include it as part of the Excel installation. A description is given for each of the options at the right of the dialog box. This description can help you decide whether to include a particular component as part of your setup.

10. Now click on the OK button on the bottom of the dialog box until you see the Continue button on the bottom of the window. When you see the Continue button, place the Office 97 disk in the drive and click on the Continue button. The new components that you chose are then added to your current setup of Office.

Another way to protect your work from being lost in the event of a crash or power failure is to create a backup file for each "parent file" that you are working with. The backup file again minimizes the chances of losing your work in the event of a power outage or other accident.

If you want to take advantage of this option, choose File⇨Save As. In the Save As dialog box, choose the Options button. In the Save Options dialog box, check the Always Create Backup check box. After you activate this option, Excel creates a file with the .BAK extension for the workbook with each save.

Saving in other file formats

Often you may need to save files in formats other than that used by the current version of Excel. Other users may be using earlier versions of Excel, or they may be using other spreadsheets, and you need to provide them with spreadsheet data that they can work with. Saving files in other formats is relatively simple if you follow these steps:

1. Choose File⇨Save As to open the Save As dialog box.

2. In the Save as type list box, you can select the format in which you want to save the file.

3. After selecting the file type, enter a name for the file (or accept the default).

4. Click on the Save button to save the file.

Danger Zone If you save files in a format that is not the native Excel format, some features of the worksheet may be lost if they are not supported by the other program's file format. For example, if you save a file in an Excel 3.0 format, only the current page of the workbook will be saved to a worksheet file because that version of Excel did not support the concept of workbooks with multiple sheets.

Saving Excel data as HTML

One feature added to this version of Excel is the capability to create HTML files. (HTML, or HyperText Markup Language, is the language used to store information on the World Wide Web.) The HTML files that you create using Excel can be uploaded to a web server for availability on the web, or to a corporate intranet.

When you choose File⇨Save As HTML, Excel launches the Internet Assistant Wizard. You can then use this wizard to create web pages based on worksheet data, or on charts. See Chapter 23 for additional details on saving worksheet and chart data as HTML, and on publishing Excel data on the web.

Saving a workspace file

If you work with more than one workbook at the same time on a regular basis, you may grow tired of having to open the same workbooks day in and day out. Excel has a nice feature that allows you to avoid this monotony: the *workspace file*. You can use this file to save the workbooks that you are working on, the order that they are in, and the sheets that are open at the time. The next time that you need to work with these same workbooks, you can open the workspace file, and all the workbooks are in the same position that they were in when you created the workspace file. Follow these steps to create a workspace file:

1. Open the workbooks that you want to include in the workspace file and arrange them in the way that you want them to be when you open the workspace file.

2. Choose File⇨Save Workspace to open the Save Workspace dialog box, as shown in Figure 15-19.

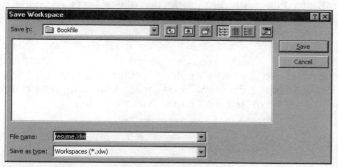

Figure 15-19: The Save Workspace dialog box.

3. Enter a name for the workspace file and click on the OK button.

Danger Zone Remember that the workspace file keeps track of the arrangement of your work area, but it doesn't save changes to your workbook files. If you make changes to the workbooks, you will need to save them before closing them or exiting Excel.

Closing a workbook and exiting Excel

To close a workbook, choose File⇨Close or click on the icon at the left edge of the menu bar. If you made any changes to the workbook that were not saved, Excel asks whether you want to save the changes. (This safeguard is provided to avoid your exiting Excel without saving your work.)

Exiting Excel is about as straightforward as exiting any Windows program. Choose File⇨Exit. If you have any unsaved work, Excel asks whether you want to save the changes before you are returned to the Windows environment.

Opening a workspace file when you start Excel

If you want to open the workspace file when you start Excel, you will need to move the workspace file to the Startup folder (normally \Excel\Xlstart). You have to transfer only the workspace file, not the workbook files themselves.

Finding Workbooks

Finding files in Excel has been made easier with the most recent versions. Finding files is done via File⇨Open. In the Open dialog box, you can perform searches based on name, location, author, and other summary information. This is why it is important to enter information in the Summary tab of the Properties dialog box. The information that you enter in the Properties dialog box can be instrumental in helping you find a file that you have forgotten the name of or that you have not worked with in a long time.

You can also do a search for files based on specific text that appears in the workbook. The specific text may be a name of a column, a key number, or anything that may specify the file for which you are searching. The criteria for the searches can be as narrow or as broad as you want it to be.

Using the Open dialog box

Unlike earlier versions of Windows products, you will find the Open dialog box used with Windows 95 and above very different. This dialog box is especially user-friendly. You will find that working with this dialog box is different from your earlier boxes but in many ways easier to use, so don't let the new box give you reservations.

This box allows you to execute simple searches, perform document maintenance, and create more complex searches. The following section will help familiarize you with the dialog box and make it a little easier to use.

By default, the Open dialog box is in List mode (see Figure 15-20), but you can change the mode of the dialog box by clicking on the buttons on the Open toolbar. Table 15-3 gives the names of the buttons on the Open toolbar and their functions.

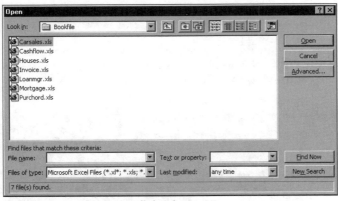

Figure 15-20: The Open dialog box.

Table 15-3
The Open toolbar buttons and their functions

Button	Function
Up One Level	Moves up one folder
Look in Favorites	Looks in the Favorites folder
Add to Favorites	Adds a file to the Favorites folder
List	Places the window in List view
Details	Places the window in Detail view, which lists the size, type, and last modified date
Properties	Lists the author's comments that were entered in the Summary tab of the Properties dialog box
Preview	Previews the files selected in the left half of the window
Commands and Settings	Controls the commands and settings for the Open dialog box (Here you can print, open a file as read-only, sort files, and search subfolders by choosing the corresponding choice from the menu.)

The Open dialog box lets you preview the files when you press the Preview button. This feature can help you remember a file by enabling you to see part of it in a preview. When you press the Preview button, the single window that you see splits into two windows (see Figure 15-21) with the Preview window on the right.

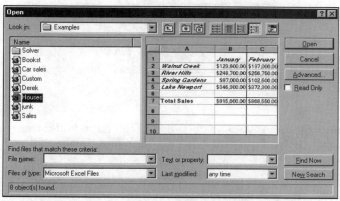

Figure 15-21: The Open dialog box in Preview mode.

You can easily forget where you have stored a file if you have not worked with it for a while; therefore, the features of the Open dialog box come in handy for helping you find a file. By default, you will see all the folders that are contained in the Excel directory when you activate the Open dialog box. Clicking on the folders shows their contents. Remember that, by default, Excel shows only the Excel file types. If you want to see other file types, you must change the file type in the Files of Type list box at the bottom of the Open dialog box.

At the bottom of the Open dialog box are four list boxes that enable you to enter criteria for a search. If you know the name of the file, you can enter it in the File Name list box. Remember that, by default, the program searches in the Excel folder for the file name. If the file is not there, it will not be found. You can use *.*file extension* (such as Sales.xls, Houses.xls, and so forth), as you did in earlier versions of Excel, if you are not sure what the file's name is.

If you want Excel to look for your file in the subfolders, also, click on the Commands and Settings button on the Open toolbar and then select Search Subfolders. Figure 15-22 shows the Commands and Settings menu.

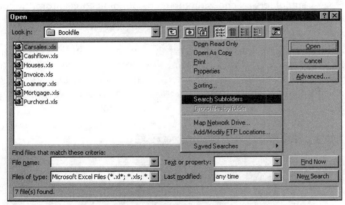

Figure 15-22: The Commands and Settings menu.

After you have set the criteria for your search and specified the folder that you want to look in, you can click on the Find Now button to find the file that you are looking for.

Performing advanced searches

You can also perform advanced searches for files in Excel. Click on the Advanced button in the Open dialog box to open the Advanced Find dialog box shown in Figure 15-23. This dialog box enables you to set up the criteria for your search.

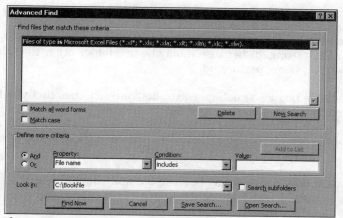

Figure 15-23: The Advanced Find dialog box.

To do an advanced search, follow these steps:

1. Clear any existing searches by clicking on the New Search button.

2. If you want parameters for your search, you can activate the Match All Word Forms option and/or the Match Case option to find the words that are similar to what you are looking for or just the exact word you are looking for.

3. In the Define More Criteria area, you can begin to define your search. Specify a search criterion (which could be a file name if you are just having a problem finding the file but know the name) in the Property list box to tell Excel what to look for. The Property list box enables you to perform searches based on the different sections of the Summary tab of the Properties dialog box. This is the information — file name, author name, or other elements of the document — that you enter when you save a file for the first time.

4. In the Condition list box, choose from Includes, Begins with, or Ends With to look for a search that begins with, includes, or ends with your Value list box entries.

5. Make an entry in the Value text box to work with your property and condition choices. For example, if you choose Ends with in the Conditions list box, enter the ending value in this field.

6. To begin the search, click on the Find Now button.

Note   Don't forget that you may need to look in subfolders, also, so be sure that you check the Search Subfolders check box, located just below the Define More Criteria dialog box and to the right. If you do not check this option, you may not find the file that you are looking for because it may be in a folder other than the one in which the search is being performed.

The Advanced Find dialog box also enables you to activate searches that you have previously performed by clicking on the Open Search button. The Open Search dialog box appears, which contains a list of the searches that you have performed. Click on the name of the search that you want to activate and click on the Open button.

As time goes on, your saved searches may become old and you may want to get rid of them. To remove an old search, select the name of the search and click on the Delete button in the Open Search dialog box. The searches can also be renamed by simply clicking on the Rename button. When you do so, the Rename dialog box opens. Now you can use the Backspace key and rename the search.

Organizing your files

The way you organize your files is very important. An organized file management system helps you keep up with your files and helps you find them when you want them. Grouping related files in the same folder is definitely one way to keep your files organized and prevent the loss of a file. For example, you may want to keep all workbook files related to small-business accounting in one folder. Then you can keep all workbook files related to your personal finances in another folder. When you are looking for a workbook file related to your personal finances, you know that you need look only in the folder that you set aside for your own finances.

Summary

This chapter covered topics related to making good use of workbooks. You learned many different techniques that you can use for working with workbooks. This chapter covered the following topics:

✦ Excel uses the workbook concept, where each file contains a workbook of multiple worksheets occupying different tabbed pages. You can store related information in the different worksheets of the workbook, and they are saved to a single file name.

✦ You can open one or more workbooks, and in each workbook, you can move among the worksheets by using the worksheet tabs.

✦ Excel provides a variety of methods for navigating throughout a worksheet and for moving among worksheets.

✦ You can add and delete sheets in a workbook, and you can move sheets from one location to another in a workbook.

✦ You can save files to Excel format or to a variety of other file formats.

✦ Excel has a Find feature that lets you search for a specific workbook based on certain search parameters that you can enter in a dialog box.

The next chapter will cover data entry and editing specifics.

Where to go next...

✦ Now that you have become familiar with workbooks, an obvious next step is to learn the best ways to handle data entry and editing. See Chapter 16 for more information on entering data.

✦ If you work with a large number of workbooks and other Microsoft Office documents to produce complex projects, you'll want to become familiar with the Binder. See Chapter 49.

✦　　✦　　✦

Getting Information into Excel

This chapter tells you how to put data into your worksheets, how to insert cells, and how to add and delete selected ranges, columns, and rows. It also describes great features like AutoSum, which sums a row or column of numbers at the click of a button; AutoFill, which can fill a range with successive numbers or dates; and the Function Wizard, which quickly helps you find a needed function. The chapter wraps up by telling you how to use formulas and named ranges in your worksheets.

Entering Data

You won't go anywhere working on a spreadsheet without first taking the time to enter data. You can enter either a value or a formula in any cell of an Excel worksheet.

Values are exactly that: constant amounts or sets of characters, dates, or times; for example, 234.78, 5/23/95, 9:35 PM, or John Doe. Formulas are combinations of values, cell references, and operators that Excel uses to calculate a result. For more information about formulas, see "Working with Formulas" later in this chapter.

When you place the cursor in a given cell and begin typing, your entry appears in the Formula bar at the top of the window, as shown in Figure 16-1. In the Formula bar, the insertion pointer (the flashing vertical bar) indicates where the characters that you type will appear. As you type an entry, a Check button and an X (Cancel) button appear enabled in the Formula bar. You can click the Check button when you finish typing the entry to accept it, or you can just press Enter. If you decide that you don't want to use an entry, you can either click the X button in the Formula bar or press the Esc key.

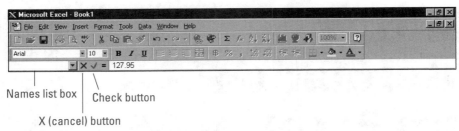

Figure 16-1: Data entered into Excel's Formula bar.

You may notice a Names list box (to the left of the X button). The Names list box displays the name or cell reference of the currently active cell. Use the arrow next to the Names list box to drop a list of named ranges for the current workbook. See "Working with Named Ranges" and "Using the Function Wizard" later in this chapter for more information.

You can also enter data directly into the cells of a worksheet by turning on Excel's Edit Directly in Cell option. To do this:

1. Choose Tools⇨Options. In the Options dialog box that appears, select the Edit tab (shown in Figure 16-2).

2. Turn on the Edit Directly in Cell check box.

3. Select OK.

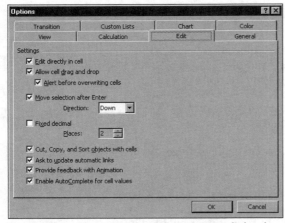

Figure 16-2: The Edit tab of the Options dialog box.

When the Edit Directly in Cell option has been turned on, you can double-click on the cell where you want to enter the data and then begin typing. To abort an entry, press the Esc key.

As many as 255 characters can be entered in one cell at a time. All of them will not be displayed unless you widen the column, which you can do by dragging its right-hand border.

Entering numbers

You can enter numbers into your spreadsheet in several ways. A wonderful feature is that when a number is entered, Excel tries to figure out how the number will be used. This prevents your having to format each cell for each number you want to enter. The worksheet in Figure 16-3 shows some of the ways that you can enter numbers in Excel.

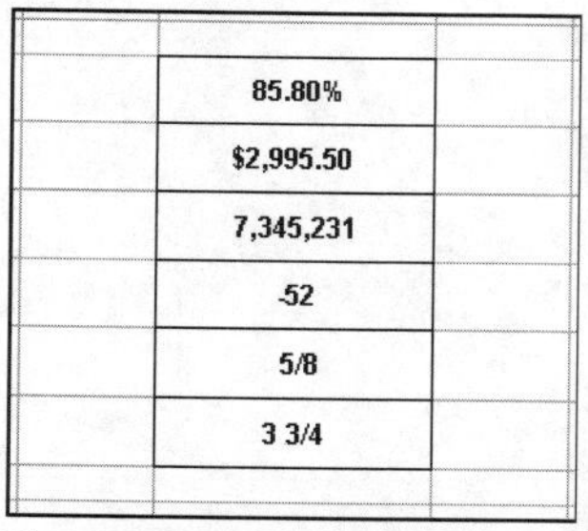

85.80%
$2,995.50
7,345,231
-52
5/8
3 3/4

Figure 16-3: Cells with numbers entered in various formats.

What the heck is ######? Where did my data go?

If you're new to Excel, you're likely to be unpleasantly surprised at some point by the dramatic appearance of the dreaded ####### in one or more of your cells. Don't panic; Excel has not suddenly absorbed all of your data into some mystical black hole. What this means is that the cell is *too narrow* to display your data or your formula's results. You can change the width of the column to see the value; just click and drag the right edge of the column's header. If you don't like the idea of changing the column's width, you can try reducing the size of the font used to display the data. Select the cells containing the data, right-click the selection, and choose Format Cells from the shortcut menu that appears. When the Format Cells dialog box appears, click the Font tab, and choose a smaller font size.

To enter a number, select the cell and then type the number; when finished, press Enter. You can enter numbers as integers, (226), as integer fractions (1/8 or 13/5), as decimal fractions (987.326 or 43.65), or in scientific notation (2.5849E+8).

Table 16-1 shows some number entries and how Excel chooses to format them.

Table 16-1
How Excel formats number entries

Number entered	Format chosen by Excel
97.9%	Number, percentage format
9705 Becker Ct.	Text, left aligned
$200.00	Number, currency format
7862	Number, general
144,000	Number, thousands format
-27	Negative number
(27)	Negative number
0%	Fraction
2%	Fraction

Danger Zone As you can see, even in cases where the numbers are mixed with text, Excel detects what needs to be stored as text. This feature makes a big difference when you're entering database information such as street addresses.

One thing you must remember is that you need to enter an integer in order to enter a fraction. If, as in the next-to-last example in Table 16-1, you need only the fractional part of a number, you must enter a zero and a space before that fraction; otherwise, the number is interpreted as a date, and you can't use it in calculations.

Entering text

Your text entries can be any combination of letters, numbers, or other special characters. To enter text, select the desired cell and start typing. When done with the entry, press Enter or click the Check button in the Formula bar. (A single cell can hold a maximum of 255 characters, so don't get carried away.) By default, Excel aligns text at the left side of the cell. You can change the alignment used for text by selecting the cell and clicking the Center or Align Right buttons in the Formatting toolbar, or you can refer to other formatting techniques covered in Chapter 17.

To format, or not to format?

Because Excel automatically formats a cell upon data entry — when you provide clues by means of how you enter the data — do you always want to use such clues in the data entry process? Maybe, but maybe not, depending on how much data you have to enter. For example, typing a dollar sign in front of an amount does tell Excel to format the entry as currency, but if you're faced with typing in 200 entries, putting a dollar sign in front of each currency amount is a lot of added work. It's easier just to enter all the numbers, letting Excel accept them as a general format, and then go back after data entry to select all the entries and apply a formatting change to the entire range of cells to format them as currency. (Chapter 17 gives details on formatting a range of cells in your worksheet.)

Hot Stuff Sometimes, you may need to enter a number and have Excel accept it as text rather than as a numeric value. You can do so by preceding the value with an apostrophe (') character. For example, if you enter **'2758** in a cell of a worksheet, Excel will store the entry as a text string made up of the characters 2758, and not as a numeric value.

Entering dates and times

You can also store dates and times within an Excel worksheet (see an example in Figure 16-4). This can be useful for recording chronological data, such as employee dates of hire or the time spent on billable tasks.

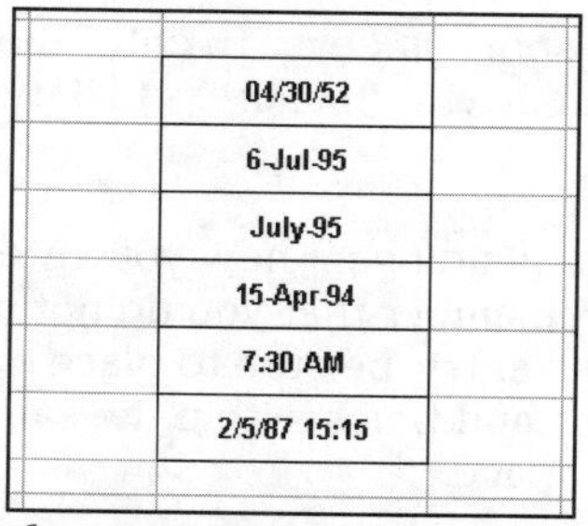

04/30/52
6-Jul-95
July-95
15-Apr-94
7:30 AM
2/5/87 15:15

Figure 16-4: Cells with dates and times entered in various formats.

Dates and times entered in acceptable date and time formats are recognized by Excel as valid date or time values. The times and dates that you enter are converted into serial numbers, with dates being the number of days from the beginning of the century until the date value you entered. Excel sees a time entry as a decimal fraction of a 24-hour day. If Excel recognizes the entry as a valid date or time, it properly displays the date or time on the screen. If you look in the Formula bar for any cell that contains a date you entered, you'll see that all dates appear in the *m/dd/yyyy* form, regardless of how you entered them. Time entries all appear in the Formula bar in AM/PM format with seconds displayed, regardless of how you enter them.

The following examples show ways that Excel can accept valid date entries. You can use a slash, a hyphen, or a space to separate the different parts of the entry:

> 7/6/97
>
> 6/Jul/97
>
> 6/Jul (the current system year is used)
>
> Jul/97
>
> 07/06/1997

Time values can be entered in forms like the examples shown here:

> 7:50
>
> 7:50 AM
>
> 15:23
>
> 15:23:22
>
> 3:23 PM
>
> 3:23:22 PM
>
> 11/13/97 15:23

Hot Stuff You can enter both the current date and time using shortcut keys. To enter the current date, press Ctrl+; (semicolon). To insert the current time, press Ctrl+: (colon).

You can display time using a 12- or 24-hour clock, depending on how you enter your times. If you decide to use a 24-hour format, remember that you do not need to use AM or PM. If you decide to use a 12-hour time entry, be sure to place a space before AM or PM. If you choose to store dates and times within the same cell, the dates and times should be separated by a space.

Excel's capability to handle dates and times as real values is a significant benefit in some applications because you can use Excel's computational capabilities to perform math on dates and times. For example, Excel can subtract one date from another to provide the number of days between the two dates.

Oops? Whadaya mean, oops?

As you enter data into Excel, keep in mind how useful Edit⇨Undo is. Undo can get you out of just about anything you can do to a worksheet. (Note that there are some actions, like saving files, that can't be undone.) You can either open the Edit menu and choose Undo or click the Undo button on the Standard Toolbar, and if you undo something in haste, you can use Edit⇨Redo to correct that, too!

Displayed values versus underlying values

Excel displays values according to precise rules; *which* rules depends on what formats you've applied to the cells in a worksheet.

Here's an example: in a blank worksheet, with no formatting applied, try entering the following data exactly as shown in the cells listed.

In this cell	Enter this
A1	1234567890.1234
A2	$100.5575
A3	2.14159E10

The results appear as displayed values, as shown in the worksheet in Figure 16-5.

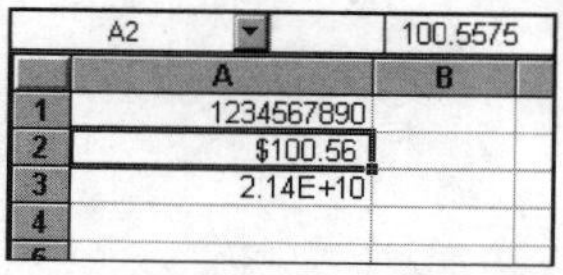

Figure 16-5: A worksheet with displayed values.

If you move the cursor between the cells containing the data and note the contents of each cell in the Formula bar, one fact quickly becomes apparent: Excel may display data differently than it is actually stored.

Excel stores the data as you enter it, but it displays the data according to the formatting rules you established (or according to the rules of the *General* format if you applied no formatting). Because the entries in cells A2 and A3 of the example included symbols, Excel formatted those cells and displayed the contents according to those formats. (You can also select formats by using menu commands; Chapter 17 covers this topic in more detail.) In the case of cell A1, because the value is so large, Excel displayed the whole numbers only.

In each case, what appears in the cell is the *displayed value*. What appears in the Formula bar is the *underlying value*. Excel always uses the underlying value when calculating your formulas, unless you tell it otherwise. So be aware of the possible differences between underlying values and displayed values.

Adding Comments to Cells

Excel offers the capability to add *comments* to any cell of a worksheet. Think of comments as being like the little yellow sticky notes that you probably have cluttering your work area — except that comments in Excel are much neater. Comments replace Notes that were available in earlier versions of Excel. If you used Excel 7.0, be aware that Sound Notes, which provided the capability to add sounds to notes, are no longer available in Excel.

A cell with a comment attached includes a small rectangle in the upper-right corner, but that's the only visible indication of the comment. To attach a comment, place the cursor in the desired cell and then choose Insert⇨Comment. A comment for the cell opens, as shown in Figure 16-6. You can enter the desired text directly into the comment.

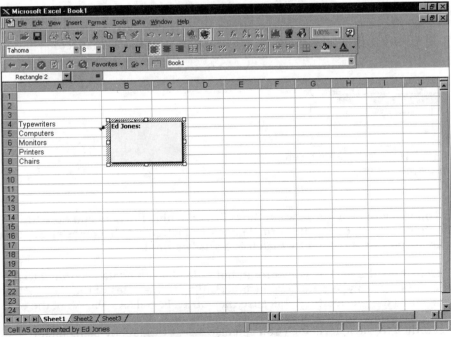

Figure 16-6: A comment added to a cell.

After you've added a comment, you can read the comment's contents by moving the mouse pointer over the cell containing the comment. When you do this, a window like the one in Figure 16-7 appears with the text of the comment.

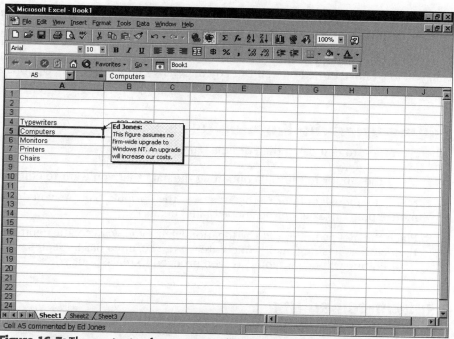

Figure 16-7: The contents of a comment displayed within a worksheet.

If you want to edit an existing comment, you might be tempted to look for an "Edit Comment" option on the Edit menu. While that's the way that *we* would have done it, Microsoft chose otherwise. The Edit Comment option appears on the Insert menu whenever the active cell contains a comment. So, to edit a comment, place the cursor at the desired cell, and choose Insert⇨Edit Comment.

You can review all the comments in a workbook. To do this, choose View⇨Comment. All comments are made visible, a toolbar containing Previous Comment and Next Comment buttons will appear, and you can use the buttons to move between comments. Choosing View⇨Comment again hides the comments.

Editing Data

Excel gives you two ways to make changes to cells. One way is to edit the entry within the Formula bar; the other is to perform editing within the cell itself.

If you're a spreadsheet user from way back, you'll probably prefer to type the entry into the Formula bar because this is how many spreadsheets have operated for years. But if you have a worksheet that's set up like a database of sorts, with a large amount of data to edit, you may prefer to use the *edit-in-cell* method. (To edit in the cell, you must have turned on Edit Directly in Cell by choosing Tools⇨Options and turning on the option in the Edit tab.) Instructions for both methods follow.

Editing using the Formula bar

When you want to edit using the Formula bar:

1. Move the cursor to the cell containing the data that you want to edit.

2. Move the mouse pointer to the area over the Formula bar. (As you do so, the mouse pointer takes on the shape of an I-beam.)

3. Place the mouse pointer at the location where you want to start editing and then click. A flashing insertion pointer in the Formula bar indicates where your editing will occur; you can then proceed to make your edits.

Using in-cell editing

If you want to edit using in-cell editing:

1. Double-click the desired cell, or move the cursor to the cell and press F2. When you do this, an insertion pointer appears within the cell itself.

2. Use the arrow keys to place the insertion pointer where you want it.

3. Make your edits and then press Enter.

Clearing Data from Cells

Excel provides different ways to clear, or erase, the contents of existing cells. The most obvious way is to select the cell or range of cells and then press the Delete key. This does indeed clear the cell of its contents — that is, any values or formulas entered into the cell — but there are ways to clear a cell of formatting and comments, as well.

To clear the contents of a cell and remove more than just the data entered, first select the cell or range of cells that you want to clear. Then open the Edit menu, choose Clear, and select the appropriate choice from the submenu. Table 16-2 lists this menu's suboptions.

<table>
<tr><td colspan="2" align="center">Table 16-2
Edit⇨Clear submenu options</td></tr>
<tr><td>*Option*</td><td>*What it does*</td></tr>
<tr><td>All</td><td>Clears everything from the selected cells, including formatting, the contents of the cell, and any notes attached to the cell. Formatting for the cell returns to the General format.</td></tr>
<tr><td>Formats</td><td>Clears formatting only. Formatting for the cell returns to the General format.</td></tr>
<tr><td>Contents</td><td>Clears the formulas or values entered in the cell but leaves formatting and notes untouched. (This is the functional equivalent of making a selection and pressing the Delete key.)</td></tr>
<tr><td>Comments</td><td>Clears any comments that were attached to the cell but does not change the cell's contents or its formatting.</td></tr>
<tr><td>Hyperlinks</td><td>Clears any hyperlinks to other files or web sites stored in the cell.</td></tr>
</table>

Hot Stuff Excel's Edit menu contains two commands that remove the contents of cells: the Clear command and the Delete command. If you want to clear what's in cells, stick with Edit⇨Clear; the Edit⇨Delete command does more than just clear cells. (For specifics, see the sidebar "Edit⇨Clear and Edit⇨Delete: Understanding the Difference," later in this chapter.)

Copying and Moving Cells

As your work with Excel becomes more complex, you'll find yourself regularly needing to move and copy entire portions of worksheets from one area to another. (How often does the boss make a request like, "Oh, could we also see last quarter's sales, too?" after you've spent hours getting your worksheet just right?)

Sometimes, you can make the changes you need by inserting or deleting entire blank rows and columns, but in many cases, you'll want to leave the overall structure of a worksheet alone and copy or move selected areas of the worksheet around.

Excel lets you copy or move data from place to place using either of two methods. You can use the Cut, Copy, and Paste commands (or their equivalent buttons on the Standard toolbar), or you can use drag-and-drop techniques to move and copy data. The two methods work equally well. Generally, keyboard fans prefer the use of the Cut, Copy, and Paste commands, whereas mouse fans usually lean toward the drag-and-drop techniques.

Hot Stuff

You can use any of the techniques detailed in the following paragraphs to copy data across worksheets, as well as within the same worksheet. When you want to copy across worksheets, first select the desired data, as detailed in the steps below. Then go to the worksheet where you want to place the copy and continue with the steps outlined below.

Copying and moving data with Cut, Copy, and Paste

To copy cells using the Copy and Paste method, perform these steps:

1. Select the cell or cells that you want to copy and either choose Edit⇨Copy or right-click the selection and then choose Copy (alternatively, you can also use the Copy button in the Standard toolbar). The cells to be copied will be marked with a dotted-line border, as shown in Figure 16-8.

5		
6	Widgets	387
7	Gadgets	402
8	Whoosits	565
9	Whatsist	118
10		

Figure 16-8: Cells in a worksheet marked for copying.

2. Move to the cell or cells in which you want to begin your copying. (You can move to cells in a different worksheet, if you wish.)

3. Choose Edit⇨Paste or right-click in the destination cell or selection and choose Paste from the shortcut menu. (Alternatively, you can also use the Paste button in the Standard toolbar.) Either method places the copied information into the chosen cell or cells.

While the highlight is still visible around the source cells, you can copy the cells again if you wish by repeating steps 2 and 3, or you can press the Esc key to remove the highlight.

Moving information with Cut and Paste is done in much the same fashion as copying. Use the following steps to move data from one area to another:

1. Select the cells you want to move.

2. Choose Edit⇨Cut or right-click the selection and choose Cut from the shortcut menu. (Alternatively, you can also use the Cut button in the Standard toolbar.) With either method, the selected cells are marked by a moving border.

3. Select the destination cells for the data. (The destination can be either in the same worksheet or in a different one.)

4. Choose Edit⇨Paste or right-click the destination cell and choose Paste from the shortcut menu. (Alternatively, you can also use the Paste button in the Standard toolbar.) If you choose one cell as the destination cell and you selected more than one cell as the source for the information, the selected destination cell becomes the upper-left corner of the paste area.

Copying and moving data with drag-and-drop

Mouse fans can use drag-and-drop techniques to move and copy data between cells or ranges. Here's how:

1. Select the cell or group of cells that you wish to move.

2. Click and drag on the border of the selected cells.

3. Drag the border to the new location. As you drag, an outline of the selected area appears, as shown in Figure 16-9.

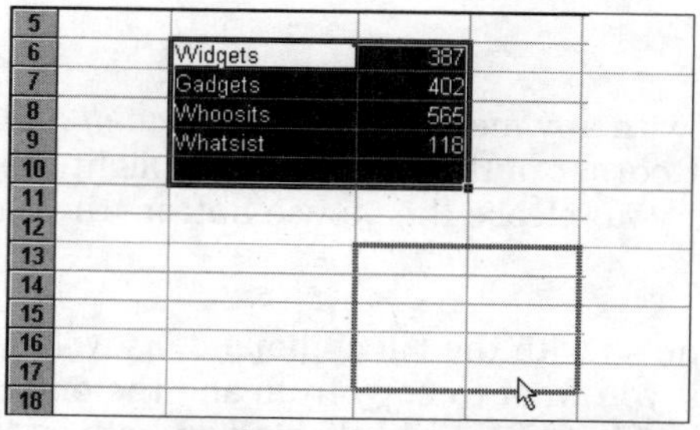

Figure 16-9: The outline of selected cells that appears when moving data using drag-and-drop.

4. Release the mouse button. (Don't forget that if you move cells over others that contain information, those others will be overwritten.)

The same steps can be used to copy a cell or a range of cells. The one difference is that when you want to copy the selection instead of just moving it, you will need to hold down the Ctrl key as you drag and drop.

Copying data with Fill and AutoFill

Excel offers two features that help you quickly fill cells with data: *Fill* and *AutoFill*. The Fill feature fills a range of cells that you select with the data in the original cell. The AutoFill feature fills in a range of cells intelligently, incrementing each successive cell. (For example, if you enter **January** in a cell and then use AutoFill to fill 11 cells to the right of the first cell, Excel fills in the names of the successive months.)

You can copy any existing data from a cell into adjacent cells using the Fill feature. To do so, perform the following steps:

1. Move the cursor into the cell that you want to copy to the adjacent cells.

2. Place the mouse pointer over the selected cell and then click and drag over all the cells that should get a copy of the original cell.

3. Choose Edit⇨Fill. From the submenu that appears, choose the appropriate direction. (Depending on the direction toward which your selection extends, menu choices of Up, Down, Left, or Right may be enabled.) When you make the submenu selection, the data will be copied into the adjacent cells, as in the example shown in Figure 16-10.

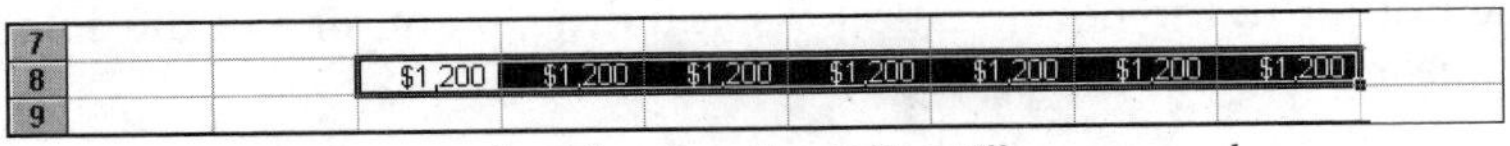

Figure 16-10: The results of using the Edit⇨Fill command.

You can also use Fill without bothering with any menus. Just drag the *Fill handle* (it's the tiny rectangle at the lower-right corner of the cursor) to highlight the cells where you want to copy the data. When you release the mouse button, the data is copied into the cells.

It's possible to copy data across worksheets with the Fill command, as well. To do this, first select both the worksheet that you want to copy from and the one that you want to copy to by holding down the Shift key while clicking on both worksheet tabs. Next, select the cells to be copied, choose Edit⇨Fill, and choose Across Worksheets from the submenu. In the dialog box that appears, choose what you want to copy (All, Contents, or Formats) and then click OK.

If you want intelligent copying, use the AutoFill feature. By default, AutoFill fills in days of the week and months of the year, but you can also add your own custom lists to AutoFill, so it can handle other requirements that you have on a regular basis.

To use AutoFill to fill in dates, type the desired day of the week or month of the year into a cell. Next, drag the Fill handle (the tiny rectangle at the lower-right corner of the cursor) to highlight the cells where you want AutoFill to add the data. When you release the mouse button, the successive days of the week or months of the year appear. Figure 16-11 shows the results of AutoFill when January is entered into a cell and the Fill Handle is dragged across the next eight cells.

Figure 16-11: The results of using AutoFill.

If you regularly fill in any sort of list of your own, you can add it to the possible lists that AutoFill can generate. To do this, choose Tools➪Options. In the dialog box that appears, click the Custom Lists tab. In the tab that appears (shown in Figure 16-12), click New List at the left side of the dialog box and then type your own list in the List Entries box, separating each entry with a comma and a space. (In the figure, a custom list of classrooms in a high school has been entered in the List Entries box.) When done, click Add to add the list and then click OK. From then on, you can type any entry in your list into a cell and use AutoFill to fill in the successive entries based on your own list.

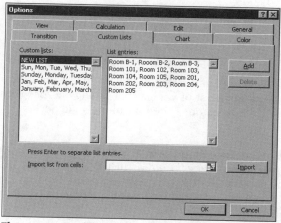

Figure 16-12: The Custom Lists tab of the Options dialog box.

If you choose more cells than the length of the list used by AutoFill, Excel will start the list over until it reaches the end of the selected cells to be filled. To prevent the list from repeating, you may want to count the number of entries that are there and avoid selecting a range that's larger than your possible number of entries.

Making changes to the custom lists used by AutoFill is a simple matter. If you wish to edit one of your custom lists, do the following:

1. Choose Tools⇨Options.

2. From the Custom Lists area of the Custom Lists tab, select the custom list that you want to edit.

3. Click in the List Entries box and make the necessary changes to the list.

4. Click OK.

If you want to delete a custom list that you've created:

1. Choose the name of the custom list from the Custom Lists box of the Custom Lists tab.

2. Click the Delete button to delete the list from the Custom Lists.

When making your list, remember:

✦ Error values and formulas are ignored.

✦ Each list entry can contain up to 80 characters.

✦ Lists cannot start with a number. (If you want an increasing or decreasing series of numbers, use the Series command, as described in the following section.)

✦ A custom list can contain a maximum of 2,000 characters.

Building series

While AutoFill does wonders with simple and straightforward lists, sometimes you may need more flexibility in generating a list of values that change across some kind of series. For those occasions, you can use the Edit menu's Fill Series command.

Excel can work with four types of series: *linear* (as in 1, 2, 3, 4, 5, 6, and so on), *growth* (as in 5, 10, 15, 20, 25, and so on), *date-based* (as in 1995, 1996, 1997, 1998, and so on), and *AutoFill* (which is based on the lists entered in the Custom List tab of the Options dialog box). Create a series of values in a range of cells by doing the following:

1. Enter a value in a cell. (The value that you enter will serve as the starting or ending value in the series.)

2. Starting with the cell containing your value, select the cells you want to extend the series into.

3. Choose Edit⇨Fill⇨Series. The Series dialog box, shown in Figure 16-13, appears.

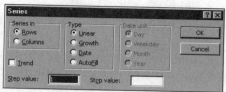

Figure 16-13: The Series dialog box.

4. In the Series in field of the dialog box, make sure that the Rows or Columns selection matches the type of range that you want to fill.

5. If you want the selected values to be replaced by values for a linear or exponential best fit, turn on the Trend check box. (If you do this, your options in Step 6 will be limited to Linear and Growth.)

6. In the Type field of the dialog box, choose the appropriate Type option.

   • **Linear** — This option adds the step value to the number that preceded the current cell in the series. When you select Trend, the trend values become a linear trend.

   • **Growth** — This option multiplies the step value by the number that preceded the current cell in the series.

   • **Date** — This option is used with date values; it lets you set the Date Unit options to Day, Week, Month, or Year choices.

   • **AutoFill** — This option creates a series automatically, based on entries in the Custom List tab of the Options dialog box (choose Tools⇨Options to get there).

   If you choose AutoFill, Excel will fill the selected range based on the entries in the Custom List tab of the Options dialog box.

   If you choose Linear or Growth, continue with the following steps up to Step 9 to finish generating your series. (If you chose Date, go to step 10.)

7. Enter a step value (the number by which the entries change from cell to cell).

8. If you don't want the entries to exceed a certain number, you can enter a Stop value. (If you leave this blank, Excel will continue until it fills the selected range.)

9. Click OK.

Excel stops either at the Stop Value or when it reaches the end of the selected cells. Remember that if the step value is negative and you enter a stop value, it will need to be less than your starting value. Dates and times can be entered in any date or time format Excel understands.

If you chose to enter a series of dates by choosing date in step 6, continue with these steps.

10. Choose Day, Weekday, Month, or Year from the Date Unit field of the Series dialog box. This will apply the step value to the chosen entry type in the Date Unit area.

11. Enter the step value to specify an increment. (For example, if you chose month as the date unit, the entries will increase in the month amount by the step value.) Again a stop value may be entered if you think you have chosen too many cells.

12. Choose OK.

Using Paste Special

Sometimes, after copying cells, you may want to invoke special options when you paste the cells. You can do this using the Paste Special command.

To see what these options are, choose any cell in a worksheet, click the copy button on the Standard toolbar, move the cursor to another cell, and choose Edit⇨Paste Special. When you do this, you see the Paste Special dialog box, as shown in Figure 16-14.

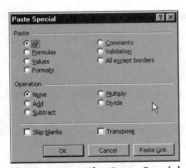

Figure 16-14: The Paste Special dialog box.

You can choose any of the bullets in the Paste portion of the Paste Special dialog box to select the information to be pasted. For example, if you wish to copy only a cell's format, you would choose the Formats option. This copies only the cell's format. This keeps you from having to format the new cell.

You can also combine the contents of the copy and paste areas. Do this by first selecting Formulas or Values in the Paste portion of the Paste Special dialog box. Next, under the Operation portion of the dialog box, select the operation you want. This will combine the copy and paste areas by performing the chosen operation. For example, if cell A:6 contains the formula =SUM(A1:A5) and you want to add this formula to the contents of cell D:6, first select cell A:6 and choose the Copy command. Next, choose Edit⇨Paste Special, choose Formulas in the Paste portion of the Paste Special dialog box, and choose Add under the Operation portion of the same dialog box. The result is that the formula is copied in the new cell with the new cell references. (Formulas are discussed in the section "Working with Formulas," later in this chapter.)

The Paste Special dialog box also allows you to transpose copied rows and columns by selecting the Transpose option. This is used to transfer information entered in rows to columns, and vice-versa.

The Skip Blanks option prevents the copying of blank cells from the copy area to the paste area; a blank cell cannot delete existing cell data in the paste area.

The Paste Link button is also a useful option for pasting, establishing a link with the source of the data pasted into the selected cells. (The source has to be a single cell or a range.) In cases where the source is more than one cell, an *array* — a collection of cells that takes on a single value in relation to a formula — is posted. When the paste area is a single cell, the cell becomes the upper-left corner of the paste area with the rest of the range filled in accordingly.

Inserting and Deleting Cells, Rows, and Columns

Another important aspect of manipulating existing data in worksheets is inserting and deleting cells and adding or deleting entire rows and columns. The first three options that Excel provides on the Insert menu let you insert cells, rows, or columns into an existing worksheet.

Danger Zone: Before you perform major insertions, be warned that inserting cells in the midst of existing data causes cells in the area of the insertion to be pushed either down or to the right. If your worksheet contains formulas that rely on the location of cells and you move those cells by inserting new cells, you will create errors in your worksheet's calculations.

Inserting cells, rows, and columns

Insert cells, rows, or columns this way:

1. Select the cell or range of cells where the new cells must be inserted, or select any cells in the rows or columns where the new rows or columns are to be inserted.

   With rows and columns, note that a new row or column is inserted for each row or column cell you select. If you drag across three columns and then choose to insert columns, you insert three new columns.

2. Choose Insert⇨Cells, or right-click the selection and then choose Insert from the shortcut menu, to reveal the Insert dialog box (Figure 16-15).

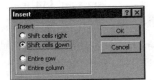

Figure 16-15: The Insert dialog box.

3. If you're inserting cells, choose either Shift Cells Right or Shift Cells Down to move existing cells in the direction you want. If you want to insert entire rows or columns, choose Entire Row or Entire Column.

4. Click OK.

Hot Stuff To insert only rows or columns, just select the number of rows or columns to insert at the point of insertion. For example, say you want to insert two columns ahead of column D. Click and drag across the headers for columns D and E, open the Insert menu, and then choose either Rows or Columns.

Deleting cells, rows, and columns

To delete cells, rows, or columns, follow these steps:

1. Select the cell or range of cells where the cells must be deleted, or select any cells in the rows or columns where the rows or columns are to be deleted.

   Note that a row or column will be deleted for each row or column cell that you select; hence, if you drag across three columns and then choose to delete columns, you will delete three columns.

2. Choose Edit⇨Delete, or right-click the selection and choose Delete from the shortcut menu to reveal the Delete dialog box, shown in Figure 16-16. (Note that if you select an entire row or column, you won't see this dialog box; Excel assumes that you want to delete the entire row or the entire column, and it does so. If the deletion of a row or column was *not* what you had in mind, choose Edit⇨Undo.)

Edit⇨Clear and Edit⇨Delete: Understanding the Difference

Excel users should understand that there's a fundamental difference between the way Edit⇨Clear and Edit⇨Delete work. The two commands may appear to do the same thing when applied to a range of blank cells with no adjacent data nearby, but in reality they behave very differently.

Edit⇨Clear clears the selected cells of the information in them but does not move cells out of the worksheet. Edit⇨Delete, on the other hand, removes the cells completely; other cells must take the place of the removed cells, even if the new cells are blank.

Compare the results of Edit⇨Delete to pulling out toy blocks from a wall made of those blocks; other blocks must be moved into the empty spaces, or the wall becomes unstable. Likewise, understanding how Edit⇨Delete works ensures the stability of the remaining areas of your worksheet.

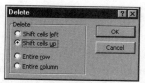

Figure 16-16: The Delete dialog box.

3. If you're deleting cells, choose either Shift Cells Left or Shift Cells Up; this moves existing cells to fill in the space left by the deletion. If you want to delete entire rows or columns, choose Entire Row or Entire Column.

4. Click OK.

Hot Stuff If you want to delete entire rows or columns, here's the fastest way. First, select the rows or columns by dragging across the row or column headers (rather than selecting cells in the rows or columns). Next, open the Edit menu and choose Delete. Excel annihilates your selections, no questions asked.

Working with Named Ranges

You can refer to a cell or group of cells by a name rather than a cell reference, and you can use these names within your formulas. Many spreadsheet users find it easier to remember the logic behind formulas that are composed of names relating to the type of information stored. For example, you could name row 1 of a worksheet *Income,* and you could name row 3 *Expenses.* A formula in row 5 that computes net profits could then read =Income-Expenses rather than =B1-B3. (Formulas are discussed in "Working with Formulas," later in this chapter.)

To assign a name to a cell or group of cells:

1. Select the range of cells that you want to name. (You can select an entire row or an entire column by clicking the row or column header.)

2. Choose Insert⇨Name⇨Define. The Define Name dialog box appears, as shown in Figure 16-17.

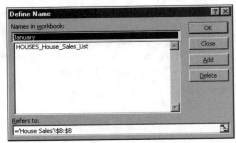

Figure 16-17: The Define Name dialog box.

3. In the text box at the top of the dialog box, either type a name for the range or accept any default. (You can't use spaces in a range name; see the Note at the end of this section.)

When Excel sees a heading at the top of a row or at the left of a column of cells that you've selected, it uses the text of that heading as a default range name.

4. Click the Add button to add the new name to the list and then click Close.

Figure 16-18 shows an example of named ranges in a worksheet. In this worksheet, columns B, C, D, and E have been assigned the names of the months, at the top of the respective columns, as named ranges. As shown in the Formula bar, column F uses formulas like =January+February+March+April to calculate the totals.

| F2 | = =January+February+March+April | | | | |
A	B	C	D	E	F
1	January	February	March	April	Totals
2 Walnut Creek	$123,600.00	$137,000.00	$89,900.00	$201,300.00	$551,800.00
3 River Hills	$248,700.00	$256,750.00	$302,500.00	$197,000.00	$1,004,950.00
4 Spring Gardens	$97,000.00	$102,500.00	$121,500.00	$142,500.00	$463,500.00
5 Lake Newport	$346,300.00	$372,300.00	$502,900.00	$456,800.00	$1,678,300.00
6					$0.00
7 Total Sales	$815,600.00	$868,550.00	$1,016,800.00	$997,600.00	$3,698,550.00

Figure 16-18: An example of named ranges in a worksheet.

Once you've performed the preceding steps, you can refer to the range in your formulas by typing its name rather than using its cells' addresses.

Note The names that you use for ranges can be up to 255 characters in length, and they can include letters, numbers, periods, or underscores, but *cannot* include spaces.

Working with Formulas

In addition to entering values, you will use *formulas* throughout your worksheets. Excel uses the formulas that you enter to perform calculations based on the values in other cells of your worksheets. Formulas let you perform common math operations (addition, subtraction, multiplication, and division) using the values in the worksheet cells.

For example, say you want to add the values in cells B1 and B2 and then display the sum in cell B5. You could do so by placing the cursor in cell B5 and entering the simple formula, =B1+B2.

With Excel, you build a formula by indicating which values should be used and which calculations should apply to these values. Remember that in Excel, formulas *always* begin with an equal symbol.

Figure 16-19 shows examples of various formulas within a typical worksheet.

	A	B	C	D	E	F	G
1		January	February	March	April	1st Quarter	
2	*Walnut Creek*	$123,600.00	$137,000.00	$89,900.00	$201,300.00	$551,800.00	
3	*River Hills*	$248,700.00	$256,750.00	$302,500.00	$197,000.00	$1,004,950.00	
4	*Spring Gardens*	$97,000.00	$102,500.00	$121,500.00	$142,500.00	$463,500.00	
5	*Lake Newport*	$346,300.00	$372,300.00	$502,900.00	$456,800.00	$1,678,300.00	
6							
7	*Total Sales*	$815,600.00	$868,550.00	$1,016,800.00	$997,600.00	$3,698,550.00	
8							
9				=SUM(B2:E2) is the			
10				formula contained in			
11				this cell.			
12						=SUM(F2:F6) is the	
13		=B7-B20 is the formula				formula contained in	
14		contained in this cell.				this cell.	
15	*Income*						
16							
17	*Sublet Office Space*	$1,800.00	$1,800.00	$1,800.00	$1,800.00	$7,200.00	
18	*Misc. Income*	$750.00	$750.00	$500.00	$800.00	$2,800.00	
19							
20	*Total Income*	$2,550.00	$2,550.00	$2,300.00	$2,600.00	$10,000.00	
21							
22							
23	*Gross Receipts*	$813,050.00	$866,000.00	$1,014,500.00	$995,000.00	$3,688,550.00	

House Sales B / Functions / Examples / Named Ranges / Sheet5 /

Figure 16-19: Examples of formulas within a worksheet.

Creating formulas in the Formula bar or with Edit Directly in Cell

If you place the cursor in any cell and then type an equal symbol, the symbol and a flashing cursor appear in the Formula bar. As you enter the formula, it appears within the Formula bar. When you press Enter, Excel performs the calculation based upon the formula and then displays, in the cell, the results of the calculation. If you've turned on Edit Directly in Cell as described earlier in the chapter, you can double-click the cell and type the formula directly into the cell.

Creating formulas by pointing

One handy way to enter the cell references that make up a major part of formulas is to point at the cells. Typing the entire formula manually invites mistakes that you can avoid by entering the cell references this way:

1. Place the cursor in the cell where you want to enter the formula.
2. Start the formula by typing an equal sign (=).
3. Point to the cell that you want as the first cell reference and then click. (Alternatively, you can move the cursor there with the arrow keys.)
4. Type an operator (such as a plus or minus symbol) or other character to continue the desired formula.
5. Point to the next cell that you want to use as a cell reference and then click (or move the cursor there with the arrow keys).
6. Repeat steps 4 and 5 as needed to complete the formula.

Hot Stuff
While using the pointing technique to create formulas, you can enter cell ranges as references. Just click and drag from the starting cell in the range to the ending cell (or hold down the Shift key as you move the cursor from the starting cell to the ending cell).

Allowed elements

Formulas are used to calculate a value based on a combination of other values. These other values can be numbers, cell references, operators (+, -, *, /), or other formulas. Formulas can also include names of other areas in the worksheet, as well as cell references in other worksheets. Individual cells are referred to by their coordinates (such as *B5*), and ranges of cells are referred to by the starting cell reference, followed by a colon, followed by the ending cell reference (such as *D10:D18*). Cells in other worksheets are referred to by the name of the worksheet, followed by an exclamation point, followed by the cell reference (such as *Sheet2!E5*).

You use math operators within your formulas to produce numeric results. Table 16-3 lists them.

Table 16-3 Arithmetic operators	
Operator	**Function**
+	Addition
-	Subtraction
*	Multiplication
/	Division
^	Exponentiation (for example 3^2 is 3-squared, or 9)
%	Percentage

In addition to the math operators, Excel accepts an ampersand (&) as a text operator for strings of text. The ampersand is used to combine text strings (this is known as *concatenation*). For example, if cell B12 contains John followed by a space and cell B13 contains Smith, the formula B12 & B13 would yield the result, John Smith.

Comparison operators are used to compare values and provide a logical value (true or false) based on the comparison. Table 16-4 describes them.

Table 16-4 Comparison operators	
Operator	**Function**
<	less than
>	greater than
=	equal to
<>	not equal to
<=	less than or equal to
>=	greater than or equal to

In a cell, the simple comparison = 6 < 7 would result in a value of True because 6 is less than 7. The result of = 6 < Number depends on the value of *Number*.

Typically, you use comparison operators with cell references to determine whether a desired result is true or false. For example, consider the worksheet shown in Figure 16-20. In this example, the formulas in cells C2 through C5 are based on a comparison. Cell C2 contains the formula, =B2>48000. Cells C3, C4, and C5 contain similar formulas. The comparison translates to this: If the value in B2 is greater than 48,000, then display a value of True in C2; otherwise, display a value of False in C2.

	A	B	C	D
1				
2		54,050	TRUE	
3		47,999.95	FALSE	
4		48,000.01	TRUE	
5		37	FALSE	
6				

Figure 16-20: Use of comparison operators in formulas of a worksheet.

Excel has the following precise order of precedence in building formulas:

1. - (unary minus or negation)

2. % (percent)

3. ^ (exponentiation)

4. * or / (multiplication or division)

5. + or - (addition or subtraction)

6. & (text operator)

7. < > = (comparison operators)

Depending on how you structure your formulas, you may wish to alter the preceding order of precedence. For example, if you want to add the contents of cells B2 and B3 and divide the resulting total by 5, you cannot use the simple formula =B2 + B3 / 5 because Excel performs division before addition in its order of precedence. If you used this formula, the value in B3 would be divided by 5, and that value would be added to the value of B2, producing an erroneous result. To change the order of precedence, insert parentheses around calculations that are to be performed first. Calculations surrounded by parentheses are always performed first, no matter where they fall in the order of precedence. In our example then, the formula =(B2 + B3) / 5 yields the desired result. Excel would calculate the expression within the parentheses first and then divide that figure by the constant (in this example, 5).

Displaying and editing formulas

By default, Excel shows the results of the formulas that you enter in cells and not the actual formulas. (Of course, you can examine any formula by moving the cursor to the cell that contains it and then looking in the Formula bar.) There is a way to see all the formulas in your worksheet, however. Choose Tools⇨Options. When the Options dialog box appears, click the View tab; under Window Options, turn on the Formulas check box and then click OK. The worksheet will show all your formulas in the cells (and Excel will automatically widen the columns to provide room to view the formulas).

You can edit formulas just as you'd edit any other contents of a cell. Select the desired cell, click in the Formula bar, and do your editing there; or double-click the cell and edit the formula within the cell itself.

Changing the recalculation options

By default, Excel recalculates all dependent formulas in your worksheet each time that you make a change to a cell. In a very large worksheet, this can adversely affect performance, as Excel has to do a lot of calculating every time you change an entry in a cell. You may prefer to turn off Excel's automatic recalculation and let the worksheet recalculate only when you tell it to.

What, me make a mistake?

One of the most frustrating aspects of building complex worksheets is the possibility of errors in your formulas. Watching out for common causes of formula errors can help.

Watch out for these in particular:

attempts to divide by zero

references to blank cells

leaving out commas between arguments

deleting cells that are being used by formulas elsewhere in the worksheet

The codes that Excel displays in the cell when an error occurs give you a clue as to what's wrong. #DIV/0! says your formula is trying to divide by zero. #N/A! means that data needed to perform the calculation is not available, and #NAME? means that Excel thinks you're referring to a name that doesn't exist. #NUM says Excel has a problem with a numeric argument you've supplied, #REF says that a cell reference is incorrect, and #VALUE! indicates that a value supplied isn't the type of value that the formula's argument expected.

You can change the recalculation options used by Excel through the Calculation tab of the (yes, you guessed it) Tools⇨Options command. Open the Tools menu and choose Options, click the Calculation tab, and choose Manual in the dialog box that appears. From then on, you can force Excel to recalculate your worksheet at any time by pressing the Calc Now key (F9).

Note   Try to remember when you turn off automatic recalculation; otherwise, you may become easily confused by what appear to be errors in a worksheet but which are really changes that were made when automatic recalculation was turned off and left off. Some operations (including opening and printing a worksheet) will force a recalculation, even if automatic recalculation has been turned off.

Using Functions

Typing each cell reference is fine when you're adding a short column of numbers, but doing this with larger columns can be time consuming. Fortunately, Excel offers *functions* that can be used in your formulas.

You can think of functions as ready-to-run tools that take a group of values and perform some specialized sort of calculation on those values. For example, the commonly used SUM function adds a range of values. So, instead of having to enter a formula like =B2+B3+B4+B5+B6+B7+B8, you could enter the much simpler formula of =SUM(B2:B8).

References: relative versus absolute

In Excel, you can have *relative* or *absolute* cell references. An absolute cell reference does not change when the cell containing the formula is copied to another location. A relative cell reference changes when the cell containing the formula is copied to another location.

You determine whether a cell reference will be relative or absolute by placing a dollar sign in front of the row or column reference. The presence of a dollar sign tells Excel not to muck around with your cell reference, no matter what. For example, perhaps cell B5 of a worksheet contains the formula =B3+B4. If you copy that cell's contents to cell D5, Excel adjusts the references, and the formula in cell D5 reads =D3+D4.

In most cases, you want Excel to adjust references when you copy formulas elsewhere, but in some cases, you don't. You can make cell references absolute by adding the dollar sign in front of the letter and number that make up the cell address. With the preceding example of a formula in cell B5, if the formula were entered as =$B$3+$B$4, the formula could be copied anywhere in the worksheet — and it would still refer back to cells B3 and B4.

Besides making for less typing, functions can perform specialized calculations that would take some digging on your part if you needed to duplicate the calculations manually. For example, you can use Excel's PMT function to calculate the monthly principal and interest on a mortgage. (Not many of us carry the logic for that sort of calculation around in our heads.) Excel's functions can make use of range references (like A2:A10), named ranges (like January Sales), or actual numeric values. Figure 16-21 shows examples of the use of functions in a worksheet.

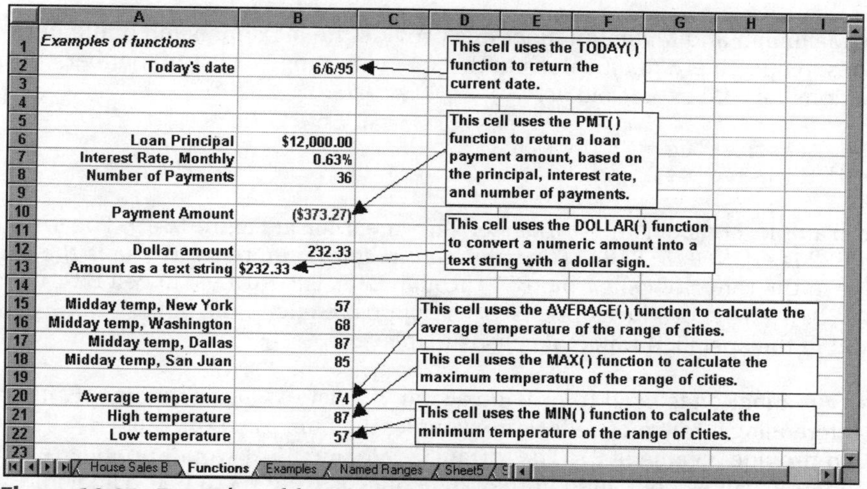

Figure 16-21: Examples of functions used in a worksheet.

Every function consists of two parts:

- ✦ **The function name** — such as SUM, PMT, or AVERAGE, which indicates what the function does.

- ✦ **The argument** — such as B2:B12, which tells Excel what cell addresses to apply to the function. (Note that in this example, the argument is a range of cells, but arguments may be references to single cells, to a group of single cells, or actual values.)

You can enter functions just as you enter values: by typing them directly into the Formula bar or into the cell. You can also use the AutoSum tool and Paste Function (both discussed shortly) to find help with the entry of your functions.

Excel has many different functions for tasks that range from calculating the square root of a number to finding the future value of an investment. You should know about some statistical functions that are commonly used in spreadsheet work: the Average, Maximum, Minimum, and Sum functions.

Average, Maximum, Minimum, and Sum

The Average function calculates the average of a series of values. This function may be expressed as:

```
=Average(1st value, 2nd value, 3rd value...last value)
```

As an example, the expression =Average(6,12,15,18) yields 12.75. Similarly, the expression =Average(B10:B15) averages the values from cells B10 through B15.

The Maximum and Minimum functions provide the maximum and minimum values, respectively, of all values in the specified range or list of numbers. These functions may be expressed as:

```
=MAX(1st value, 2nd value, 3rd value...last value)
=MIN(1st value, 2nd value, 3rd value...last value)
```

For example, consider the worksheet shown earlier in Figure 16-19. The formula in cell B22 is =MIN(B15:B18). The value that results from this formula is the smallest value in the range of cells from B15 through B18. The formula in cell B21, which is =MAX(B15:B18), produces precisely the opposite effect: the largest value of those found in the specified range of cells is displayed.

The Sum function is used to provide a sum of a list of values, commonly indicated by referencing a range of cells. For example, the Sum function =SUM(5,10,12) would provide a value of 27. The formula =SUM(B5:B60) would provide the sum of all numeric values contained in the range of cells from B5 to B60. The Sum function is an easy way to add a column of numbers; you can most easily use it when using AutoSum, too.

Using AutoSum

Because the Sum function is the most commonly used function in Excel, a toolbar button is dedicated to the Sum function's use: the AutoSum tool. Using AutoSum is simple:

1. Place the cursor in the cell below or to the right of the column or row that you want to sum.

2. Click the AutoSum button in the Standard toolbar (it's the one containing the Greek letter Σ).

When you do this, Excel makes its best guess about what you would like summed, based on the current cell's location relative to the row or column. (If Excel guesses wrong, you can always edit the formula to your liking.) When you click the AutoSum button, Excel outlines the area that it thinks you want summed, and it places the appropriate formula using the Sum function in the current cell, as shown in Figure 16-22. If you don't like the range that Excel selected, you can click and drag to a different range, and Excel will change the formula accordingly. When you're happy with the formula, press Enter to accept it.

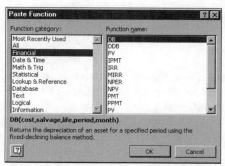

	A	B
1		
2		
3		January
4	Walnut Creek	$123,600.00
5	River Hills	$248,700.00
6	Spring Gardens	$97,000.00
7	Lake Newport	$346,300.00
8		
9	Total Sales	=SUM(B4:B8)
10		
11		

B4 · X ✓ *fx* =SUM(B4:B8)

Figure 16-22: What happens when you use the AutoSum button.

Using the Function Wizard

One of Excel's most useful features is Paste Function. With the help of Paste Function, serious Excel users no longer need to keep a reference dictionary of functions handy or to be constantly looking in the help screens to see how particular functions should be used.

Paste Function steps you through the process of inserting a function into the formula you're building. To use Paste Function:

1. Move the insertion pointer into the cell where you want to insert the function. (If you want to insert the function into an existing formula, you can click in the Formula bar at the point where the function should go; this will place the pointer there.)

2. Click the Paste Function button on the Standard toolbar (the one containing the letters *fx*) or choose Insert⇨Function. The Paste Function dialog box appears, as shown in Figure 16-23.

Paste Function   ? ☒

Function *category*:   Function *name*:

Most Recently Used	DB
All	DDB
Financial	FV
Date & Time	IPMT
Math & Trig	IRR
Statistical	MIRR
Lookup & Reference	NPER
Database	NPV
Text	PMT
Logical	PPMT
Information	PV

DB(cost,salvage,life,period,month)

Returns the depreciation of an asset for a specified period using the fixed-declining balance method.

[?]   OK   Cancel

Figure 16-23: Paste Function dialog box.

3. In the Function Category list box at the left, choose the category of functions that you want. When you choose a category, the functions in that category appear in the Function Name list box at the right. (You can leave the category set to All to see all the functions, but doing that can make it difficult to find your desired function in the Function Name list because Excel has hundreds of functions.)

4. From the Function Name list box, select the function that you want to insert into your formula and then click OK.

5. Depending on which function you choose, you will see another dialog box asking for values appropriate to that function. Enter the necessary values or cell ranges for the arguments needed by the function in the dialog box, and click OK in the dialog box to add the function to your formula.

Using Find and Replace

Some useful features that Excel has borrowed from the word processing world are Edit⇨Find and Edit⇨Replace. Like their counterparts in Word for Windows, these commands search for data and, optionally, replace that data with other data. The data that you search for can be stored as values, as part or all of a formula, or as a cell note.

Finding data

To search for data in a worksheet using Edit⇨Find:

1. Select the cells you wish to search. If you want to search the entire worksheet, select any single cell.

2. Choose Edit⇨Find. You'll see the Find dialog box, as shown in Figure 16-24.

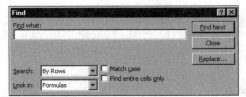

Figure 16-24: The Find dialog box.

3. In the Find what text box, enter your search term. You can include wildcards: the asterisk (*) can indicate any combination of characters, and the question mark can indicate any single character.

4. In the Search list box, choose By Rows if you want to search across rows starting with the current cell, or choose By Columns if you want to search across columns starting at the current cell.

5. In the Look In list box, choose Formulas to search through formulas, Values to search through values stored in cells, or Comments to search all comments that are attached to cells.

6. If you want your search to be case-sensitive, turn on the Match Case check box.

7. Turn on the Find entire cells only check box if you want the entire cell's contents to match your search term. If you leave this option turned off, Excel will find matches where either part or all of the cell's contents matches the search term.

8. Click the Find Next button to find the next occurrence of the search term. (Alternatively, hold down the Shift key and click the Find Next button.) When done searching, click Close.

Once you have entered the parameters for a search in the Find dialog box, you can repeatedly press F4 to continue searching for the same data.

Finding and replacing data

Use the Replace command of the Edit menu to search for data in a worksheet and replace it with other data. The process is similar to using Edit⇨Find (in fact, the dialog box you see is nearly identical). Here are the steps:

1. Select the cells you wish to search. If you want to search the entire worksheet, select any single cell.

2. Choose Edit⇨Replace. The Replace dialog box (Figure 16-25) appears.

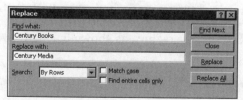

Figure 16-25: The Replace dialog box.

3. In the Find What text box, enter your search term. You can include wildcards: the asterisk (*) can indicate any combination of characters, and the question mark can indicate any single character.

4. In the Replace with text box, type the replacement text.

5. In the Search list box, choose By Rows if you want to search across rows starting with the current cell, or choose By Columns if you want to search across columns starting at the current cell.

6. If you want your search to be case-sensitive, turn on the Match case check box.

7. Turn on the Find entire cells only check box if you want the entire cell's contents to match your search term. If you leave this option turned off, Excel will replace data where either part or all of the cell's contents matches the search term.

8. Click the Replace All button if you want to find and replace all occurrences of the search term with your new term. Alternatively, click Find Next to find the next match in the worksheet and, after examining it, click the Replace button to replace just that match. When done making your replacements, click Close.

Note

Edit⇨Undo rolls back the effects of a replace operation.

Checking Spelling

Another feature that Excel takes from the word processing realm is its built-in spell checker. You can save yourself from possibly embarrassing blunders in your worksheet's text by checking its spelling *before* you pass out those copies at the annual board meeting. You can check any part of a selection (even a single word), or you can check the entire worksheet, including any embedded charts that are in the worksheet. You can also add words to custom dictionaries in order to handle specialized words that you use often (like medical and legal terms).

You spell check a worksheet this way:

1. Select the cells you wish to spell check. If you want to check the spelling of the entire worksheet, select any single cell.

2. Choose Tools⇨Spelling, or click the Spelling button on the Standard toolbar. Excel checks the spelling in the worksheet. If it finds what it thinks is a misspelled word, you'll see the Spelling dialog box, as shown in Figure 16-26.

Figure 16-26: The Spelling dialog box.

When Excel finds a misspelling, it tries to provide several options for a correct spelling of the word. If the Always suggest check box is on, Word suggests proper spellings whenever it can. In the Change to text box, you enter the correct spelling, or you can click one of the suggested spellings in the Suggestions list box, which adds that spelling to the Change to box.

If the Always suggest check box is off, click the Suggest button to see a list of possible spellings in the Suggestions list box. If one of the suggestions is the spelling that you want, select it in the list box and then click Change. The Ignore button lets you leave a word as is, while the Cancel button cancels the entire spell checking operation. Clicking Ignore All tells Excel to ignore all suspected misspellings of the same term; Change All tells Excel to change all misspellings to the entry that you accept in the Change to box. The Add button lets you add a word to the selected custom dictionary (Custom.dic by default), and the Ignore UPPERCASE check box, when turned on, tells Excel to skip all words that are all uppercase letters.

During the spell checking process, it takes a bit of extra time for Excel to suggest corrections to misspelled words. You can speed the process slightly by turning off the Always suggest check box and using the Suggest button to ask for help when you need it.

Adding a custom dictionary

If you make regular use of specialized terms (such as medical or legal terms) in your worksheets, the spell checking capability will be pretty useless unless it can work with those terms as part Excel's dictionaries. You can add words to Excel's default custom dictionary, but another option is to create additional custom dictionaries this way:

1. Place the cursor in any worksheet containing some of your custom terms; this way, the spell check operation will find them.

2. Choose Tools⇨Spelling. When Excel stops at what it thinks is the first misspelled word, the Spelling dialog box appears, as shown earlier in Figure 16-26.

3. Click in the Add Words To list box and then type the name of the new dictionary that you want to create.

4. Click the Add button, to add the current word to the dictionary. Excel will display a dialog box asking if you want to create a new dictionary.

5. Click Yes to create the dictionary. From this point on, you can use the dictionary by choosing it by name in the Add words to list box.

Summary

This chapter has examined the many different ways in which you can put data into an Excel worksheet, and manipulate that data. The chapter covered the following points:

✦ You can enter values or formulas into cells of a worksheet. Values can be numbers, text, dates, or times.

✦ You can attach notes to cells by using the Note command of the Insert menu.

✦ You can move and copy data from place to place on a worksheet or between worksheets.

✦ Excel's Fill, AutoFill, and Series features can fill ranges of cells with data.

✦ You can insert and delete ranges of cells, as well as entire rows and columns.

✦ Formulas manage the calculations within your worksheets.

✦ Excel provides hundreds of *functions*, which you can think of as tools for performing specific types of calculations.

✦ Excel's Function Wizard can help you quickly find and properly enter the correct function for a specific task.

✦ You can use the Edit⇨Find and Edit⇨Replace commands to search for data and to replace data with other data.

✦ You can use the Tools⇨Spelling command to correct the spelling of text in a worksheet.

The next chapter tells you how to format your worksheets so they look good.

Where to go next...

You'll soon want to print what you've created. You'll find the complete scoop on printing in Chapter 20.

✦   ✦   ✦

Excel Formatting

Most spreadsheet users know all too well that a spreadsheet is usually more than just a collection of raw numbers. Since the days of the first spreadsheets, users have resorted to formatting tricks to enhance the appearance of the numbers presented. (How many seasoned spreadsheet pros can remember filling rows of cells with characters like asterisks or hyphens to enclose information within crude borders?) Excel offers many ways to format your worksheets so that you can give them the most visual impact possible. You can change the fonts, sizes, styles, and colors used by the characters in your worksheets. You can also control the alignment of text within cells, both vertically and horizontally. You can change row heights and column widths, you can add borders to selected cells, and you can use Excel's powerful AutoFormat feature to enhance the appearance of part or all of a worksheet quickly, without the need to use any formatting commands.

Using the AutoFormat Feature

A significant feature of recent versions of Excel is that it lets you apply automatic formatting to your worksheet data with the AutoFormat feature. You activate the AutoFormat feature by choosing Format⇨AutoFormat. In the AutoFormat dialog box, you can use the sample formats to create a presentation-quality worksheet quickly, even if you know little or nothing about other formatting options. Figures 17-1, 17-2, and 17-3 show some of the different formats that are possible when you use the AutoFormat feature.

In Figure 17-1, the Classic 1 style of AutoFormat uses traditional accounting-style fonts and simple border lines to separate the data visually.

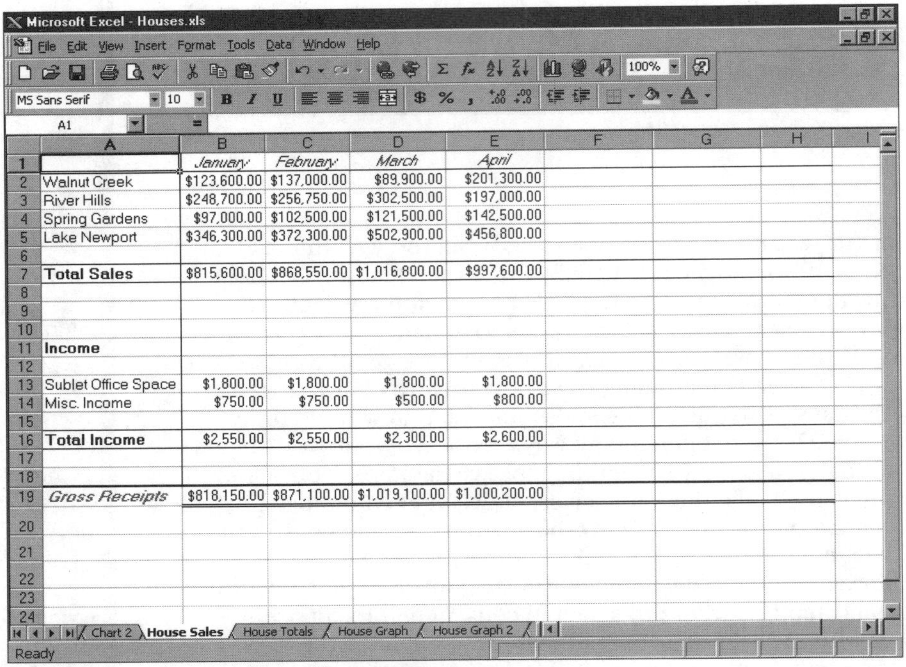

Figure 17-1: The Classic 1 style AutoFormat.

In Figure 17-2, the Colorful 1 style of AutoFormat makes extensive use of various background choices to highlight the worksheet data.

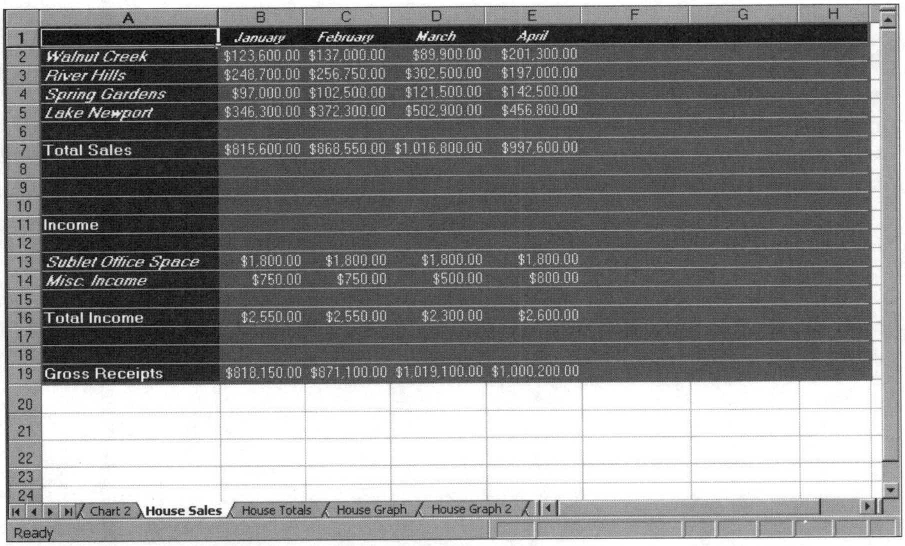

Figure 17-2: The Colorful 1 style AutoFormat.

In Figure 17-3, the List 1 style of AutoFormat uses shading in alternate rows of the worksheet.

	A	B	C	D	E	F	G	H
1		January	February	March	April			
2	Walnut Creek	$123,600.00	$137,000.00	$89,900.00	$201,300.00			
3	River Hills	$248,700.00	$256,750.00	$302,500.00	$197,000.00			
4	Spring Gardens	$97,000.00	$102,500.00	$121,500.00	$142,500.00			
5	Lake Newport	$346,300.00	$372,300.00	$502,900.00	$456,800.00			
6								
7	Total Sales	$815,600.00	$868,550.00	$1,016,800.00	$997,600.00			
8								
9								
10								
11	*Income*							
12								
13	Sublet Office Space	$1,800.00	$1,800.00	$1,800.00	$1,800.00			
14	Misc. Income	$750.00	$750.00	$500.00	$800.00			
15								
16	Total Income	$2,550.00	$2,550.00	$2,300.00	$2,600.00			
17								
18								
19	Gross Receipts	$818,150.00	$871,100.00	$1,019,100.00	$1,000,200.00			
20								
21								
22								
23								
24								

Chart 2 \ **House Sales** / House Totals / House Graph / House Graph 2 /

Ready

Figure 17-3: The List 1 style AutoFormat.

Excel examines the current range to determine levels of summary and detail. Excel also looks for text, values, and formulas, and then applies formats accordingly. AutoFormats are combinations of several different elements: number, alignment, font, border, pattern, column, and row formats. Perform the following steps to apply AutoFormat to your worksheet:

1. Select the range of cells to which you want to apply the format. If you want to select the entire worksheet, click on the row and column header intersection at the upper-left corner of the worksheet.

2. Choose Format⇨AutoFormat to open the AutoFormat dialog box, as shown in Figure 17-4.

AutoFormat

Table format:

Simple
Classic 1
Classic 2
Classic 3
Accounting 1
Accounting 2
Accounting 3
Accounting 4
Colorful 1
Colorful 2
Colorful 3
List 1

Sample

	Jan	Feb	Mar	Total
East	7	7	5	19
West	6	4	7	17
South	8	7	9	24
Total	21	18	21	60

OK

Cancel

Options >>

Figure 17-4: The AutoFormat dialog box.

3. From the Table Format list, choose the desired format. When you click on a format, you can see a preview of it in the Sample window.

4. Click on the Options button if you want to choose which formats to apply. Clicking on the Options button expands the dialog box to reveal check boxes for Number, Border, Font, Patterns, Alignment, and Width/Height (see Figure 17-5). By default, all the boxes are turned on.

5. Click on the OK button to apply the formatting to the selection.

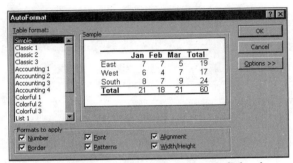

Figure 17-5: The expanded AutoFormat dialog box.

If you don't like the effects of the AutoFormat command, choose Edit⇨Undo. Or, if you have performed too many other tasks since applying the AutoFormat to the selection, don't worry. You can simply select the range, choose Format⇨Auto-Format, and select None from the list box of possible styles.

Remember that you don't have to settle for Excel's default formatting selections in its AutoFormats. The Options button in the AutoFormat dialog box lets you accept or reject certain parts of the formatting that Excel would normally apply. For example, you may have spent a great deal of time formatting different ranges of numeric values with different fonts, and you would rather not have Excel's AutoFormat feature mess around with the fonts. Turn off the Font check box in the Formats to Apply area of the AutoFormat dialog box. Then, when you apply an AutoFormat to the selection, Excel won't override the fonts that you have already applied.

You can turn off only one formatting option or several formatting options, depending on the selection and the formatting that you want applied. After turning off the desired options, you can choose the format that you want in the Table Format list box and click on the OK button to apply it to your selection. Note that any options that you turn off in this manner *aren't* carried over to the next time that you use the AutoFormat feature. You'll need to turn off any options that you don't want each time that you use AutoFormat.

When to stay away from AutoFormat

As helpful a feature as AutoFormat is, it has its limits. Excel has to make some judgment calls when it applies an AutoFormat to your worksheet. For example, Excel tries to figure out what parts of the selection may contain column headings so that it can apply a pleasing format to those headings. In particular, AutoFormat is designed to work well with worksheets that follow a traditional row-and-column format. If your worksheet doesn't follow tradition — perhaps it contains a large number of scientific formulas laid out more like a flowchart — AutoFormat may not give you the results that you'd like. In these cases, you are probably better off applying your desired formats manually by using the formatting techniques covered later in this chapter.

Changing Column Widths and Row Heights

You can adjust column width and row height in Excel as needed. Excel adjusts row height automatically, however, to accommodate wrapped text and large fonts. So, in many cases, you may not need to adjust row height.

Column widths

When you select a new sheet, you can adjust the standard width setting of the columns, or you can change only a few columns. You can choose from two methods to adjust column width. The first method, clicking and dragging the column to size it, is easier to use but is less accurate than the second method. To use the mouse to adjust the size of the columns, follow these steps:

1. Move the mouse pointer to the heading of the column.
2. Double-click on the right edge of the column to size it to the width of the widest entry, or drag the column heading border to size it manually to a width that you want.

The second method is much more accurate but requires the use of commands and dialog boxes. If you know the exact column width that you want, or you are one who likes accuracy, you can choose Format⇨Column and then choose the appropriate command from the submenu that appears. If, for example, you choose the Width command from the submenu, you can enter a numeric value for the width of the column in the Width dialog box. Or, if you choose the Standard Width command, you can accept the standard width or height (8.43 points being the default value) that appears in the Standard Width dialog box. You can also choose the AutoFit Selection command from the submenu, which automatically sizes a column to accommodate the largest entry.

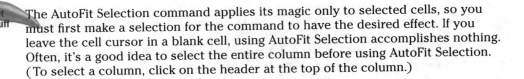

The AutoFit Selection command applies its magic only to selected cells, so you must first make a selection for the command to have the desired effect. If you leave the cell cursor in a blank cell, using AutoFit Selection accomplishes nothing. Often, it's a good idea to select the entire column before using AutoFit Selection. (To select a column, click on the header at the top of the column.)

Row heights

Excel also lets you adjust row height. Again, you have two methods to choose between: the click-and-drag method and the Format menu options. To use the click-and-drag method, perform the following steps:

1. Place the pointer over the bottom border of the row heading.

2. Drag the bottom border of the row heading until the row reaches the desired size.

You can also AutoSize a row's height by double-clicking on the bottom border of a row header. This action adjusts the row to fit the tallest entry. If you want to AutoSize a number of rows, first select the desired row and then double-click on the bottom border of any of the selected rows.

As with columns, you can accurately adjust row height by choosing Format⇨Row and then choosing the appropriate command from the submenu. To set the row height, for example, choose the Height command from the submenu and enter a value for the height in the Row Height dialog box (see Figure 17-6). Or you can choose the AutoFit command to adjust the row height to the largest entry in the row.

Figure 17-6: The Row Height dialog box.

Oh, those shortcut menus

You can easily access many of the format choices that you may want to apply to rows and from Excel's shortcut menus. If you right-click on a column heading (at the top of the column), you select the entire column and open a shortcut menu with choices that include Column Width, Hide, and Unhide. If you right-click on a row heading (at the far left edge of the row), you select the entire row and open a shortcut menu with choices that include Row Height, Hide, and Unhide.

Hiding and Unhiding Columns, Rows, and Gridlines

You can hide selected columns or rows from view, and you can reveal rows or columns that have been previously hidden. You may want to hide rows or columns so that they don't appear in printed copies of the worksheets, or you may want to hide rows or columns so that a viewer's attention is focused on important parts of the worksheet. For example, you may need to compare the data in columns B and D. With column C between B and D, the data is difficult to analyze. If you hide column C, however, the data now lies side-by-side and is easy to compare.

Hiding columns

To hide a column, select it and choose Format⇨Column⇨Hide. If you want to bring the column back, choose Edit⇨Go To (F5), enter the address of any cell in that column in the Reference text box, and click on the OK button. Then, you choose Format⇨Column⇨Unhide. (Alternatively, you can select the two columns surrounding the hidden column, and choose Format⇨Column⇨Unhide.)

Hiding rows

Hiding rows is similar to hiding columns. Select the desired row and choose Format⇨Row⇨Hide. If you want to bring the row back, choose Edit⇨Go To (F5), enter the address of any cell in that row in the Reference text box, and click on the OK button. Then, choose Format⇨Row⇨Unhide. (Alternatively, you can select the two rows surrounding the hidden row, and choose Format⇨Row⇨Unhide.)

Hiding gridlines

With some worksheets, you may not want the gridlines that are normally displayed to appear. To hide the gridlines, you first activate the worksheet page and choose Tools⇨Options. In the Options dialog box, click on the View tab, turn off the Gridlines option, and click on the OK button. As a result, the gridlines disappear from the current worksheet.

The Gridlines option affects only the current worksheet page in a workbook. If you want to turn off gridlines for a different worksheet page, you have to go through all the steps again. If you want to turn off the gridlines for a large number of worksheets, select the worksheets first and then follow the steps to turn off the option. To select several worksheets, hold down the Shift key while you click on each worksheet tab that you want included in the selection.

Changing Alignments

In your quest to give your worksheet a more professional and refined look, you may need to change the alignment of data in your cells. By default, the following alignment applies to cells: right-aligned for numbers, left-aligned for text, and centered for logical and error values. Changing the alignment of text in a cell is especially important because what works with text in one area of your worksheet may not look attractive in another area. You may want to enhance the appearance of certain parts of your worksheet by right-aligning or centering text, for example.

To change the alignment of the cells, first select the range of cells to which you want to apply the new alignment. Then you can choose between two methods to change the alignment. You can use the buttons on the Formatting toolbar, or you can choose Format➪Cells. In the Format Cells dialog box, you then click on the Alignment tab to bring up the options that you need to change. (You can also open the Format Cells dialog box by right-clicking on the selection and choosing Format Cells from the shortcut menu.) Figure 17-7 shows the Alignment tab of the Format Cells dialog box.

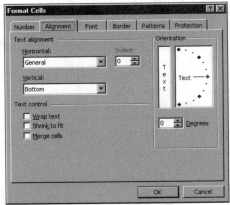

Figure 17-7: The Alignment tab of the Format Cells dialog box.

In the Horizontal list box, you can choose the Left, Center, or Right alignment options. (You can also use the Wrap Text and Justify options with text that occupies multiple lines of a cell, as covered in the next section.) If you've changed the row height of a cell so that the cell is much taller than the text entry, the options in the Vertical list box of the dialog box become equally useful. You can align the text to the top, bottom, or center of the cell, and you can vertically justify it. You can also use the Orientation portion of the dialog box to change the alignment of the entry within the cell.

In the Text Control portion of the dialog box, turning on Wrap text allows a long entry (usually sentences of text) to wrap within a cell. The Shrink to fit option, when turned on, reduces the font of an entry as needed to fit within a cell. You can use the Merge cells option to merge any selection of cells within a row or column into a single cell.

To change the alignment of data in cells by using the Formatting toolbar buttons, follow these steps:

1. Select the cells in which you want to change the alignment.
2. Click on the Align Left button to left-align the selection, the Center button to center entries in the selection, and the Align Right button to right-align the selection.

The disadvantage of using the Formatting toolbar is that it does not offer you the range of options that you get by using the Format Cells dialog box. You can't vertically align text from the toolbar, and you can't use the wrap and justify options, but you can center text across columns, as detailed in the next section.

Centering, Wrapping, and Justifying Text

As you build worksheets with lots of text headings, you'll discover that you need to center headings across a series of multiple cells. Spreadsheet pros from way back routinely center titles across multiple columns through trial and error — they enter the text into a cell where it "looks good" and re-enter the text elsewhere if the results aren't as expected. Excel sends this technique back to the Stone Age, where it belongs, with the Merge and Center button on the Formatting toolbar and the corresponding Center Across Selection option on the Alignment tab of the Format Cells dialog box. Figure 17-8 shows the Projected Sales title before and after it was centered across the selected range of cells.

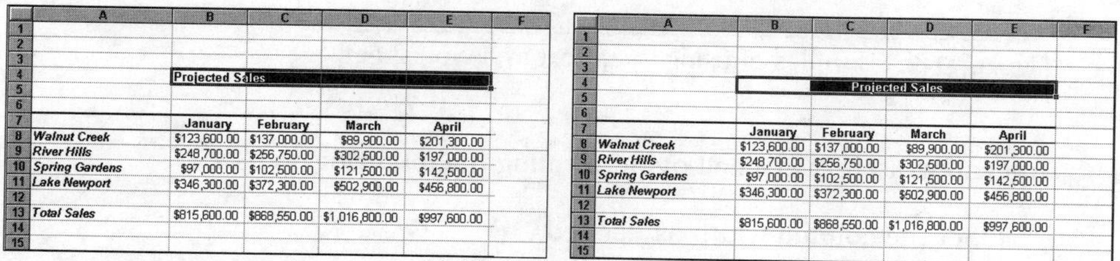

Figure 17-8: Left: A title before centering across a range of cells. Right: The title after centering across a range of cells.

Centering text

You can center the contents of a cell across a selection of blank cells by performing the following steps:

1. Make your selection of cells containing the text that is to be centered across the selection. (For proper results, the leftmost cell in the selection should contain the text that you want centered across the range of cells.)

2. Click on the Merge and Center button in the Formatting toolbar.

Alternatively, you can make the selection, right-click on it, and choose Format Cells from the shortcut menu that appears. In the Alignment tab of the Format Cells dialog box, choose Center Across Selection from the Horizontal list box. But unless you've turned off the display of the Formatting toolbar, it's generally easier to use the toolbar button.

Wrapping text

When you make lengthy text entries within cells, you can force Excel to wrap the text so that it fits into an attractive paragraph inside the cell. When you wrap the text, Excel automatically adjusts the row height so that the entry fits within the width of the cell. Figure 17-9 shows the before-and-after effects of using the wrap text option. In the figure, both cells containing text contain the same information. In the upper cell that contains text, the Wrap text option has not been turned on; in the lower cell that contains text, the Wrap text option has been turned on.

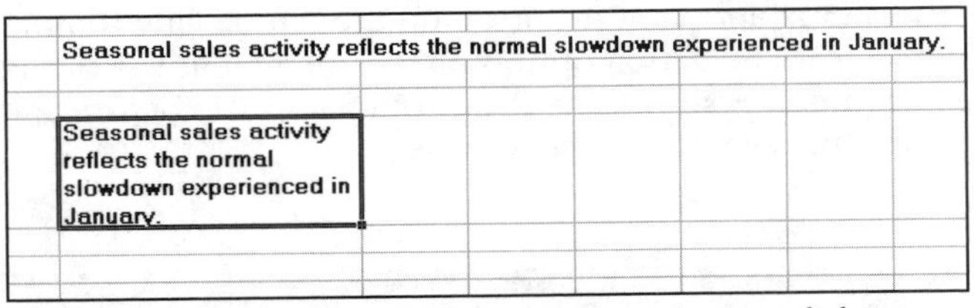

Figure 17-9: Examples of using Wrap text in a worksheet.

You can wrap text in a cell by performing the following steps:

1. Set the column width as desired.

2. Select the cells containing the text that you want to wrap.

3. Choose Format⇨Cells.

4. In the Text control portion of the dialog box, turn on the Wrap text check box.

Justifying text

After you use the Wrap text option to wrap text, you may also want to justify the text so that every line of the paragraph (except the last, if it is too short to fill a line) is aligned on both sides. (A cell has to contain at least two lines of text for justification to have any effect.) Figure 17-10 shows the before-and-after effects of using text alignment in a worksheet. In the figure, the text in cell D4 is not justified; in cell D7, the Justify option has been applied to the text.

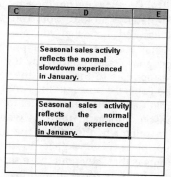

Figure 17-10: Top: Left-justified, right-ragged text. Bottom: Left- and right-justified text.

You can perform the following steps to justify entries in selected cells:

1. Select the text that you want to justify.

2. Choose Format⇨Cells.

3. Click in the Horizontal list box, and choose Justify. The text is automatically justified (assuming it contains two or more lines).

Applying Fonts and Style Formats

Just as in Word, you can apply different fonts to your entries in Excel. Applying fonts in Excel is as simple as it is in Word. You select the cells that you want to change, and you choose the font that you want to apply to the selection from the Font list box on the Formatting toolbar. You can also choose a font size from the toolbar, and you can use the Bold, Italic, and Underline buttons to apply these types of formatting to the characters in the selected cells. Alternatively, you can select the cells, right-click on the selection, choose Format Cells from the shortcut menu, and click on the Font tab to display your possible font choices. Figure 17-11 shows the possible font choices in the Font tab of the Format Cells dialog box.

About TrueType fonts and your other fonts

When you work with different fonts in your Excel worksheet, you should understand the difference between TrueType fonts and non-TrueType fonts. Ever since the introduction of Windows 3.1, Windows has included TrueType technology as part of the operating system. TrueType is a technology that enables Windows to use the same fonts that you see on-screen to print documents. Before TrueType, Windows made use of one set of fonts to display data on-screen and another set to print. Windows would try to pick a screen font that closely resembled the printer font, but it wasn't always successful (especially with some of the more unusual printer fonts). Therefore, what you saw on-screen would not always be what you got from your printer. TrueType was designed to solve this problem by providing the same set of fonts for on-screen viewing as for printing. Windows includes a number of different TrueType fonts, and you can purchase more

TrueType fonts from software vendors or download them from the software libraries of online services, such as America Online and CompuServe.

The point of all this? If you select a TrueType font when you choose a font from the Format Cells dialog box or from the Font list on the Formatting toolbar, you can be reasonably assured that what you see on-screen is what you get from your printer. You can recognize TrueType fonts by the TT symbol that appears to the left of the font name in the Fonts list box or in the Font tab of the Format Cells dialog box. Printer fonts, by comparison, appear in the lists with a picture of a printer to the left of the font name. The minor disadvantage to using TrueType fonts is that they print more slowly than printer fonts because they must be *rasterized* (converted to a printable character representation) by Windows as it downloads information to the printer.

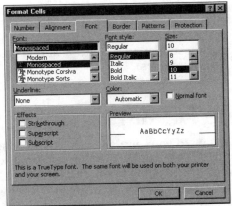

Figure 17-11: The Font tab of the Format Cells dialog box.

On the Font tab, you can use the options in the Font and Font Style list boxes to choose a desired font and font style, and you can choose a point size in the Size list box. You can select a type of underlining (Single, Double, Single Accounting, or Double Accounting) in the Underline list box, and you can select a color for the text in the Color list box. In the Effects area of the tab, you can turn on one of the special effects (Strikethrough, Superscript, or Subscript).

Hot Stuff You can also apply styles or fonts to only *some of the characters* that are in a cell (yes, we said only *some* of the characters). To accomplish this little known trick, place the cursor in the cell that contains the text that you want to change so that the text appears in the formula bar. In the formula bar, click on and drag to select only the text that you want to change. Next, choose Format⇨Cells. When you make this selection, you see the Format Cells dialog box displaying only the Font tab. Here you can choose the Font that you want to use on the characters, along with the character size and style. Make the desired selections and click on the OK button to apply them.

Applying Borders, Patterns, and Colors

Excel makes lots of border types available. All the border types have different widths, patterns, and even colors. You can use these choices to make your worksheets more attractive and much easier to read. You can apply a border to a selection by performing the following steps:

1. Select the cells to which you want to add the border.

2. Click on the down arrow to the right of the Borders button on the Formatting toolbar.

3. Select the border type that you want from the menu that opens (see Figure 17-12). The border you choose is applied to the selected cells.

Border Types

Figure 17-12: Available border types.

You can also choose Format⇨Cells to open the Format Cells dialog box. Then click on the Border tab, as shown in Figure 17-13. You can use the options within this tab of the Format Cells dialog box to apply a border to a selected cell or cells. You can also select the style or color of the border and whether you want the border to appear on all sides or selected sides of the cell.

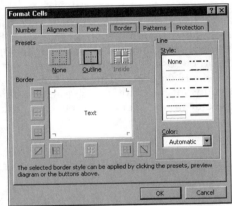

Figure 17-13: The Border tab of the Format Cells dialog box.

You can also add colors and patterns to the cells that you have selected. To apply a color or a pattern, select the desired cells, right-click on the selection, and choose Format Cells from the shortcut menu. When the Format Cells dialog box appears, click on the Patterns tab to bring it to the front, as shown in Figure 17-14.

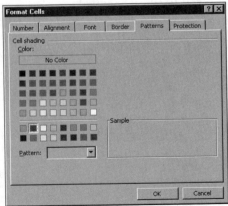

Figure 17-14: The Patterns tab of the Format Cells dialog box.

In the Cell shading area of the dialog box, you can click on any desired color to apply it. The list of colors also includes some of the grays that are used in shading. Then click on the down arrow in the Pattern list box to reveal a box showing the available background patterns and the remainder of the shading choices that you have. Choose a desired pattern from the list. After you make your desired color and pattern selections, click on the OK button in the Format Cells dialog box to apply them.

You can also apply colors to a selection by clicking on the down arrow to the right of the Fill Color and Font Color buttons on the Formatting toolbar and choosing a desired color from the box of colors that appears.

Hot Stuff When applied, some patterns can make cell entries very difficult to read. Remember to use Edit⇨Undo if you don't like the looks of a selection that you've chosen.

Sometimes, you may want to apply a color to the characters that you enter rather than to the background of the cell. Applying color to the characters can make a specific number or title stand out. To make the total earnings for the year stand out, for example, you can apply red formatting to the characters in that cell if the earnings were less than the previous year.

To apply a color to the characters in your worksheet, select the characters to which you want to apply the color and then click on the down arrow to the right of the Font Color button on the Formatting toolbar to open a color selection box. Choose a desired color to apply to the characters.

Hot Stuff With both the Font Color and the regular (cell) Color buttons, you can apply the color that was last chosen to another selection by simply clicking on the button. This is a great shortcut feature.

Working with Number Formats

By default, Excel applies the General format to numbers in a cell. This format displays up to 11 digits if the entry exceeds the cell's width. All the numbers entered in the General format are displayed as integers (such as 21,947 or 12,382), decimal numbers (such as 21.57 or 3.14159), or in scientific notation (such as 9.43E+7 or 21.212E-5).

When you enter a numeric value in a cell, Excel tries to find the number format that is most appropriate for your entry number and assigns that format to the number. If you enter nothing but numbers, and they aren't excessively large or small, Excel is pretty much clueless as to how you want them formatted. In these cases, Excel settles for the General format for the cell.

You can, however, give Excel clues as to how you want it to format an entry by including symbols with your numeric entries. For example, if you enter a dollar amount and precede it with a dollar sign, Excel automatically formats the entry as a currency value. If you want the entry formatted as a percent, you can follow the entry with a percent sign. You can enter scientific notation directly into the cell. For example, if you enter 17.409E+10 in a cell, Excel stores the value of 174,090,000,000,000 in the cell and displays 1.74E+14 in the cell.

If you've already entered the values and you want to go back and change them, using the Formatting toolbar is the simplest way to apply the most commonly used number formats. After selecting the entry that you want to change, click on one of the number formatting buttons to apply the format. Table 17-1 lists the number formatting buttons and their functions.

Table 17-1
Number formatting buttons on the Formatting toolbar

Button	Function
Currency Style	Changes the cell to a currency format
Percent Style	Changes the cell to a percent format
Comma Style	Changes the cell to a comma format
Increase Decimal	Increases the decimal place of the number
Decrease Decimal	Decreases the decimal place of the number

You can also apply number formats via the Number tab of the Format Cells dialog box. To activate the Format Cells dialog box, choose Format⇨Cells (or right-click on the selection and choose Format Cells from the shortcut menu). Click on the Number tab to display the Format Cells dialog box shown in Figure 17-15.

To apply number formats by using the Number tab of the Format Cells dialog box, perform the following steps:

1. Select your desired cells.

2. Choose Format⇨Cells or right-click on the selection and choose Format Cells from the shortcut menu.

3. Click on the Number tab.

4. In the Category list box, select the category that you want to reformat.

5. If a Type list box appears in the center of the dialog box, choose the way you want the number to appear from the list box. (Some categories, such as Text and Accounting, don't offer a list box of types.)

6. Click on the OK button to apply the formatting.

Remember, occasions may arise when you want to format numbers as text. You can do so while you enter the value in a cell of the worksheet by entering an apostrophe before the number. You can also make a selection, choose the cells command from the Format menu, click on the Number tab in the Format Cells dialog box, and choose the Text option from the Category list box.

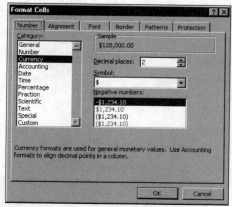

Figure 17-15: The Number tab of the Format Cells dialog box.

Working with Date and Time Formats

More Info If you enter data in an acceptable date or time format, Excel stores the value as a date or time value. For example, if you type 4/30/52 into a cell, Excel stores the entry as a date value of April 30, 1952. Excel also recognizes a value like 22-Jan-95 as a valid date. Similarly, with an entry of 9:45 PM, Excel stores a time value representing that time. (Chapter 16 provides additional specifics on the entry of dates and times in a worksheet.)

You can change the format that Excel uses to display dates and times by performing the following steps:

1. Select the range of cells containing the date or time values.

2. Choose Format⇨Cells, or right-click on the selection and choose Format Cells from the shortcut menu.

3. Click on the Number tab.

4. In the Category list, choose Date or Time as desired. Figure 17-16 shows the Date category selected.

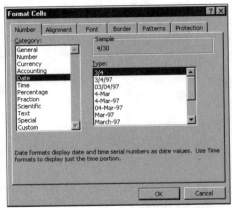

Figure 17-16: Choosing the Date category in the Number tab.

5. In the Type list, choose the desired date or time format and then click on the OK button.

When you enter a date or time in a format that Excel recognizes, Excel displays the value at the right side of the cell by default. If a value appears at the left side of the cell, Excel has not recognized it as an acceptable date or time value and has formatted the entry as text instead. You should re-enter the value in an acceptable format to get the correct date or time into the cell.

Using Custom Number Formats

Besides using the variety of standard formats built into Excel, you also have the power to design your own custom formats. Custom formats are useful for specialized financial or scientific displays of values or for handling such information as phone numbers, part numbers, or other data that has to appear in a specific format. Figure 17-17 shows some examples of custom formats in columns A, B, and, C.

A	B	C
data entered	custom format used	how data appears
1505.99596	0.0000	1505.9960
23562.7678	$#,##0.0000	$23,562.7678
0.15852	0.0000%	15.8520%
3/15/95 14:40	d-mmm-yy h:mm:ss AM/PM	15-Mar-95 2:40 00 PM
2125551212	"(000) 000-0000	(212) 555-1212
1274542	"Part number " ### ####	Part number 127-4542

Figure 17-17: Examples of custom formats.

In working with custom formats, it helps to understand the number format codes that Excel uses. These number formats are available in all the worksheets when you open the workbook. These formats are automatically stored in the correct number format category. Whenever you want to access them, open the Format Cells dialog box and choose Custom from the Category list in the Number tab. Table 17-2 explains the function of the most common symbols that you use to make custom formats.

Table 17-2
Symbols used in custom formats

Symbol	Function
?	Acts as a placeholder for digits in much the same way as zeros. Zeros that are not important are removed and spaces are inserted to keep alignment together.
/	Denotes that the slash symbol is to be used after the integer portion with fractional custom formats. This causes the number to appear as a fractional value, such as 5 2/3.
0	Acts as a placeholder. You can use this number to display a zero when no number is entered. Also note that decimal fractions are rounded up to the number of zeros that appear to the right of the decimal.
#	Acts as a placeholder for digits, as the zero does. The difference between # and zero as a placeholder is that if a number is not entered, no number is displayed. Decimal fractions are rounded up to the number of #s that appear to the right of the value.
General	Denotes the default format for cells that are not formatted.
, (comma)	Marks the thousands position. (Only one comma is needed to specify the use of commas.)
. (decimal)	Marks the decimal point position. For a leading zero, enter a zero to the left of the decimal.

(continued)

Table 17-2 (continued)

Symbol	Function
_ (underscore, followed by character of your choice)	Inserts a space the size of the character that follows the underscore before the character itself appears. As an example, if you enter _) to end a positive format, a blank space is inserted the size of the parenthesis. This lets you align a positive number with a negative one that's surrounded by parentheses.
:$ _ +()	These characters are displayed in the same positions in which they are entered in the number code.
E_E+e_e+	Displays a number in scientific notation. The zeroes or values to the right of the e denotes the power of the exponent.
%	The entry is multiplied by 100 and displayed as a percentage.
@	Takes the role of a format code to indicate where text typed by the user appears in a custom format.
*character	Fills the remainder of the column width with the character that follows the asterisk.
"text"	Displays the text between the quotation marks.
[color]	Indicates that the cell is formatted with the specified color.
\ (backslash)	When this precedes an entry, it indicates a single character or symbol.

Format codes include three sections for numbers and one for text. The sections are separated by semicolons. The first section is the format for positive numbers, the second is the format for negative numbers, the third is the format for zeros, and the fourth is the format for text.

The section you include in your custom format determines the format for positive numbers, negative numbers, zeros, and text, in that order. If you include only two sections, the first section is used for positive numbers and zeros, and the second section is used for negative numbers. If you include only one number section, all the numbers use that format.

The text format section, if it is there, is always last. If you have text that you always want to include, enter it in double quotation marks. If your format has no text section, the text you enter in the cell is not affected by the formatting.

To create your own custom format, perform the following steps:

1. Make a selection and choose Format➪Cells, or right-click the selection and choose Format Cells from the shortcut menu.

2. In the Format Cells dialog box, choose the Number tab.

3. Choose Custom from the Category box. From the Type list box (see Figure 17-18), choose a custom format that is closest to the one that you want. You can then modify the chosen format to meet your needs.

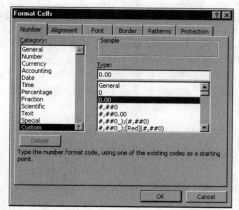

Figure 17-18: The Type list box with the Custom entries.

4. Make the desired changes to the format by editing the entry in the Type text box.

5. Click on the OK button to save the new number format.

Keep the following points in mind when you create custom formats:

✦ Excel uses zeros and number signs as digit placeholders. If you use a zero, the digit is always displayed, and the number sign suppresses the non-significant zeros.

✦ If you follow an underscore by a character, Excel creates a space that is the width of the character. If you follow an underscore with a right parenthesis, for example, you can then be assured that positive numbers will line up correctly with negative numbers that are enclosed in parentheses.

✦ If you want to set a color for a section of the format, type the name of the color in square brackets in the section.

✦ Add commas to your format so that the displayed numbers will appear in multiples of 1,000. (The commas that are not surrounded by digit placeholders can be used to scale the numbers by thousands.)

Copying Formats with the Format Painter

If you've already spent time and effort creating formats in certain areas of a worksheet, and you want to use them elsewhere, you can easily do so with Excel's Format Painter. As its name implies, the Format Painter lets you take an existing format and literally "paint" that format across any other cells in a worksheet. When you use the Format Painter, you copy all formatting — including text, number, and alignment formats; and cell shading, color, and borders — from the currently active cell to the range of cells that you paint. The Format Painter, the button with the picture of a paintbrush, is accessible on the Formatting toolbar.

Use the Format Painter to copy the formatting information from one cell to a range of cells or from a range of cells to another range of cells. To copy formatting from one cell to a range of cells, follow these steps:

1. Select the cell that contains the formatting that you want to copy.

2. Click on the Format Painter button on the Formatting toolbar. A paintbrush now appears beside the mouse pointer.

3. Click on and drag across the range of cells that should receive the format. When you release the mouse button, the format of the original cell is applied to the selected range.

To copy formatting from a range of cells to another range of cells, use these steps:

1. Select the entire range of cells that contains the formatting you want to copy.

2. Click on the Format Painter button on the Formatting toolbar. A paintbrush now appears beside the usual mouse pointer.

3. Click on the upper-left cell in the range of cells that should receive the format. When you release the mouse button, the format of the original range of cells is applied to a range of cells of the same size as the original range.

Creating Your Own Styles

As this chapter emphasizes, Excel's formatting options give you the power to apply formatting in just about every conceivable manner to your worksheets. If you find yourself applying the same formatting choices repeatedly to different parts of a worksheet, it makes sense to save your formatting choices as a style so that you can easily apply the style over and over again to a selection of cells. In Excel, a *style* is a collection of formatting options that you apply to a cell or a range of cells. The nice thing about styles is that once you apply them to your worksheet and you decide to change some aspect of the style later, all the parts of your worksheet that make use of that style will automatically change accordingly. For example, if you create a style, use it in half a dozen worksheets, and later change the font used by that style; the font will automatically change in those worksheets. (If you are accustomed to working with styles in Word for Windows, you will find the concept of Excel styles to be quite similar.)

You can easily define your own styles by choosing Format⇨Style. To define the style, perform these steps:

1. Choose Format⇨Style. The Style dialog box appears, as shown in Figure 17-19.

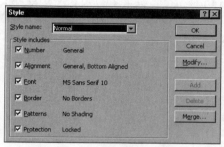

Figure 17-19: The Style dialog box.

2. In the Style Name list box, enter a name for your new style and then click on the Add button to add the new style to the list.

3. Turn off the check boxes for any of the attributes that you don't want included in the style.

4. If you want to change any of the attributes for the format settings shown in the list, click on the Modify button to bring up the Format Cells dialog box.

5. Click on any of the tabs in the Format Cells dialog box and change the settings for the formats.

6. When you are finished setting the formats in the Format Cells dialog box, click on the OK button to go back to the Style dialog box.

7. Click on the OK button to save the new style.

After your custom style exists, using it is a simple matter. Just select the range of cells to which you want to apply the style and choose Format⇨Style. In the Style dialog box, click on the down arrow to the right of the Style Name list box, choose the name of your custom style from the list, and click on the OK button to apply the style to the selected range of cells.

Protecting Your Formatting Changes

You can apply protection to the cells of a worksheet so that the formats and other data cannot be changed. (By default, the cells of a worksheet have protection turned on, but the protection does not take effect until you choose Tools⇨Protection and then choose Protect Workbook from the resulting dialog box.) To make sure that the cells of a worksheet will be protected when you turn on overall protection for the workbook, perform these steps:

1. Choose any range of cells that should *not* be protected. Because the default setting for the cells is to be protected, you will want to turn off protection for any cells that you want to retain the ability to change.

2. Choose Format⇨Cells.

3. Click on the Protection tab of the Format Cells dialog box (see Figure 17-20).

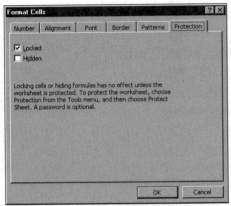

Figure 17-20: The Protection tab of the Format Cells dialog box.

4. Turn off the Locked check box if you want the selected cells to remain unprotected. You can also turn on the Hidden check box to specify that the selected cells' contents do not appear in the formula bar.

5. Click on the OK button and repeat Steps 1 through 4 for every range of cells that should remain unprotected.

6. Choose Tools⇨Protection⇨Protect Workbook.

7. In the Protect Workbook dialog box, enter a password, if one is desired. If you omit the password, you can still protect the workbook, but others can remove the protection without the use of a password. Also, turn on the Windows check box if you want to protect the windows in the workbook from being moved or resized.

8. Click on the OK button to implement the protection.

Note Passwords that you enter to protect a workbook are case-sensitive.

After you have protected the contents of a workbook, you can remove the protection by choosing Tools⇨Protection and then choosing Unprotect Workbook from the submenu. If you entered a password during the protection process, you are asked for the password before Excel unprotects the document.

Fair warning...

If you protect a workbook with a password, *do not, do not, do not* (did we repeat that enough?) forget the password! If you forget the password, you may as well start re-creating the workbook from scratch. Even the technical support people at Microsoft cannot help you get into a workbook that is password-protected when you don't have the password.

Summary

This chapter covered topics related to formatting in Excel. You learned how to use formatting to give a worksheet a more appealing look and to enhance its appearance. We covered the following topics:

✦ By selecting a worksheet range, choosing Format⇨AutoFormat, and selecting the desired options in the dialog box that appears you can quickly give a worksheet a professional look.

✦ In Excel, you can easily change row heights and column widths to accommodate your entries by clicking and dragging the column or row edges, or by choosing the Column or Row commands (as appropriate) from the Format menu.

✦ You can apply specific fonts, font sizes and styles, borders, patterns, and colors to a group of cells or to characters within a cell by choosing Format⇨Cells and using the options in various tabs of the Format Cells dialog box.

✦ In addition to the variety of standard formats provided with Excel, you can create custom formats for the values that you enter in your worksheets.

In the next chapter, you will learn how you can add graphic objects to your worksheets and your charts.

Where to go next...

✦ After you've formatted your worksheet, you may want to pop in a graphic. Chapter 18 tells you how.

✦ You can make charts out of the data in your worksheet. Chapter 19 has the details.

✦   ✦   ✦

Adding Graphics to Worksheets

In Excel, worksheets can be far more than just tables of numbers with a chart added here and there. You can emphasize the points expressed by those numbers, add visual information, and (by means of macro buttons) literally make your worksheets easier for others to use. You can do all these things by adding graphics to worksheets. You can draw lines, circles, rectangles, and squares; and you can add text boxes with as little as a short title or as much as multiple paragraphs of text. You can also make use of clip art or professionally drawn artwork from other Windows programs in your Excel worksheets. If you have an artistic personality (or if your worksheets are facing a demanding audience and you need all the help you can get), you can really get carried away with Excel's graphics.

Why Bother with Graphics in Excel?

Many spreadsheet users don't think of Excel and graphics together. Because Excel is a spreadsheet package, many Excel users crunch numbers with it and leave graphics entirely to a drawing program like CorelDRAW!. If you don't use Excel's graphic capabilities, however, you miss out on all of Excel's power. From its humble origins years ago as a Macintosh product, Excel provided spreadsheet capability with built-in flexible graphics. Microsoft has expanded Excel's capabilities over the years with each release of the product. Excel is now a spreadsheet with the power to add visual oomph to your work. As an example, consider Figure 18-1.

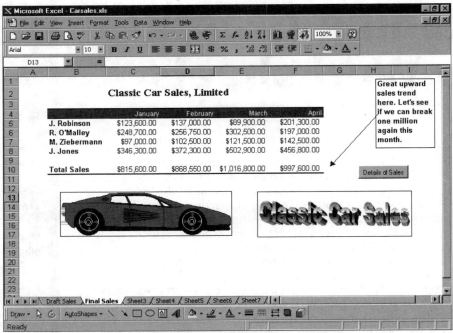

Figure 18-1: A worksheet that makes extensive use of graphics.

In this worksheet, the gridlines have been turned off, and a text box with an arrow has been added to describe points that the numbers in the worksheet are attempting to get across. Clip art has been added to the worksheet, and a button that runs a macro (to display another worksheet) has been added. You can add all these effects and more by using Excel's graphics features.

Inserting Graphics Files into a Worksheet

When you want to insert graphic files into an Excel worksheet, you can use the Picture command from the Insert menu. This command lets you pull graphic pictures from files created in other programs. To insert graphics with the Picture command, do the following:

1. Place the insertion point in the cell where you want the upper-left corner of the picture to appear.

2. Choose Insert⇨Picture⇨From File. The Insert Picture dialog box appears, as shown in Figure 18-2.

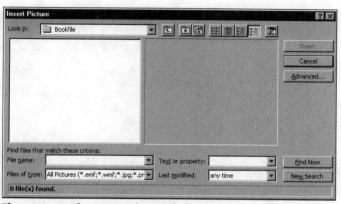

Figure 18-2: The Insert Picture dialog box.

3. In the dialog box, choose the clip art or graphics file that you want to insert into your worksheet.

4. Click on the OK button to insert the graphic into the worksheet.

Another way to insert graphics is to open the graphic in the other Windows program and then use the Copy and Paste commands to copy the graphic into the Excel worksheet. Here's how:

1. Activate the program from which you want to insert the picture. Open the piece of art and select it by using the appropriate Windows selection technique for the program that you are using.

2. Choose Edit⇨Copy.

3. Activate Excel, if it is not already running, and select the cell or the object where you want the upper-left corner of the graphic to appear.

4. Choose Edit⇨Paste. The graphic appears in the worksheet. Remember that you can use your normal sizing and moving methods to change the size or location of the graphic.

Hot Stuff As long as the program from which you inserted the graphic supports OLE, double-clicking on the object activates the menus of that program. This technique lets you perform edits to the graphic without leaving Excel and switching to the other program.

What kinds of graphic files can I import?

Excel's graphic filters let you import graphic files in several file formats, including:

File type	Filename extension
PC Paintbrush	.PCX
Tagged Image File Format	.TIF
Windows Metafile	.WMF
Encapsulated PostScript	.EPS
WordPerfect Graphics	.WPG
CompuServe GIF	.GIF
JPEG Filter	.JPG
Windows Bitmap	.BMP
Portable Network Graphics	.PNG
Macintosh Picture	.PCT

Working with Graphic Objects

You can use the Drawing toolbar (see Figure 18-3) to create graphic objects right in Excel. If the Drawing toolbar is not displayed, choose View➪Toolbars and select Drawing from the dialog box that appears. You can also right-click on a toolbar to display a shortcut menu and then choose Drawing from the shortcut menu. After the Drawing toolbar is displayed, you can move it as you would move any toolbar, by clicking on any blank area of the toolbar and dragging it to a desired location.

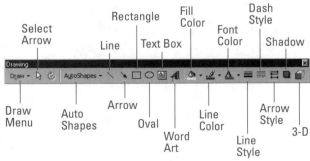

Figure 18-3: The Drawing toolbar.

The Excel Drawing toolbar has a variety of drawing tools that help you enhance your worksheets. This toolbar contains several drawing tools that enable you to create items from lines to polygons. Table 18-1 gives the name of each tool and its function.

Table 18-1
The Drawing toolbar's tools

Tool name	Function
Draw Menu	Opens a menu of additional commands for drawing-related tasks
Select Arrow	Selection pointer used to select objects
Free Rotate	Rotates a selected object to any degree
AutoShapes	Opens a menu used to add AutoShape graphic objects
Line	Draws straight lines
Arrow	Creates a line with an arrowhead
Rectangle	Draws rectangles or squares
Oval	Draws ovals or circles
Text Box	Creates a text box for word-wrapped text
WordArt	Creates a WordArt object
Fill Color	Changes the fill color for an object
Line Color	Changes the line color for an object
Font Color	Changes the font color for an object
Line Style	Used to change the style of the selected solid line
Dash Style	Used to change the style of the selected dashed line
Arrow Style	Used to change the style of the selected arrow
Shadow	Adds a variety of shadow effects to the selected object
3-D	Adds a variety of three-dimensional effects to the selected object

Hot Stuff For a real time-saver, use the shortcut menus while you are working with objects. The shortcut menu that is displayed when you right-click on an object is shown in Figure 18-4. These shortcut menus make available the Cut, Copy, and Paste commands as well as other commands related to formatting the object.

Figure 18-4: An object shortcut menu.

Inserting AutoShapes

One of Excel 97's additions is the capability to add AutoShapes as graphics to your spreadsheets. AutoShapes are groups of ready-made shapes which include lines, rectangles, ovals, circles, arrows, flowchart symbols, and callouts. (If you're curious as to where the freeform and freehand tools of earlier Excel versions have vanished, you can now find these as part of the AutoShape collection of graphics.) The worksheet shown in Figure 18-5 contains several graphics created with the AutoShapes menu in the Graphics toolbar.

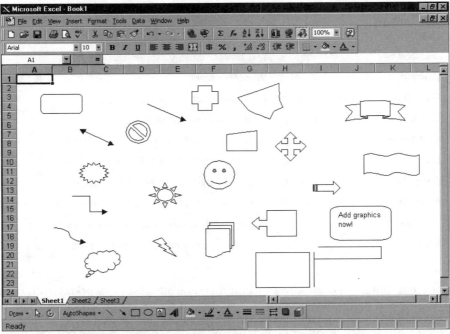

Figure 18-5: Examples of AutoShapes in an Excel worksheet.

You can add any AutoShape graphic to a chart by performing the following steps:

1. If the Drawing Toolbar isn't visible, choose <u>V</u>iew⇨<u>T</u>oolbars⇨Drawing to display the toolbar.

Note

By the way, we didn't forget the hotkey for "Drawing." For whatever reasons, Microsoft didn't add hotkeys for any of the last menu options.

2. On the Drawing toolbar, click AutoShapes, select the desired category of shapes, and click on the desired shape.

3. If you are adding a shape with a preset size, click in the worksheet or chart where you want to add the shape. If you are adding a shape that can vary in size, click and drag the shape to the desired size.

Hot Stuff

You can align a shape with the gridlines of cells by holding the Alt key while dragging the shape. You can set the shape in perfect proportion by holding the Shift key while dragging the shape.

When you open the AutoShapes menu, you are presented with seven options: lines, connectors, basic shapes, block arrows, flowcharts, stars and banners, and callouts. Figure 18-6 shows the shapes that are available under each of these menu choices.

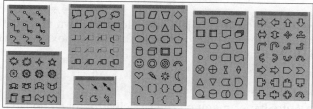

Figure 18-6: Available AutoShapes.

Hot Stuff

Given that well over 100 shapes are provided, to describe how to place each shape in detail would take more text than you'd likely care to read. But you can easily view a help screen that's specific to the use of any AutoShape tool. Press Shift+F1, open the AutoShapes menu, and choose the desired shape. A help screen appears, explaining how to draw or manipulate the chosen shape.

Drawing lines, arcs, ellipses, and rectangles

The Drawing toolbar lets you create lines, arcs, ellipses, and rectangles easily. These are all basic drawing elements, and you can combine these elements to create more complex shapes. You draw an object by first clicking on the desired tool and then clicking on and dragging in the worksheet to place the item.

While drawing lines, ellipses, and arcs, hold down the Shift key while you drag to keep the lines vertical, at a 45° angle, or horizontal. You can also hold down the Alt key to align the corners of the object with a cell's gridlines.

Lines

To draw a line, click on the Line tool, click on the beginning location for the line, and then drag to the ending location. To draw a line with an arrowhead, click on the Arrow tool, click on the point where the line should begin, and drag to the point where the arrowhead should appear.

Squares and rectangles

To draw a square or a rectangle, click on the Rectangle tool, click on a corner of the rectangle, and drag to size the rectangle as desired. To draw a square, hold down the Shift key while you drag to size the square.

Circles and ellipses

To draw an ellipse, click on the Ellipse tool, click on an edge of the ellipse, and drag to size the ellipse as desired. To draw a circle, hold down the Shift key while you drag to size the circle.

Filled objects

To create filled objects, select the desired object and click the down arrow to the right of the Fill Color button in the Drawing toolbar. In the dialog box of colors which appears, choose a desired fill color.

Arcs

To draw an arc, open the AutoShapes menu on the Drawing toolbar, choose Basic Shapes, and select the arc tool. Next, click on and drag to create the arc where you want it on the worksheet.

Don't let others mess with your graphics

If you want to keep others from changing your graphics in your worksheets, you can protect them just as you can protect cells in a worksheet. Right-click on the graphic, choose Format AutoShape from the shortcut menu, click on the Protection tab, and make sure that the Locked option is turned on.

Then, open the Tools menu, choose Protection/Protect Sheet, enter a password (if desired) in the dialog box that appears, and click on the OK button. If you leave the password text box blank, the worksheet will be protected from changes, but you won't need a password to turn off the protection.

Selecting and grouping objects

In Excel, most of the items that you add while drawing are considered *objects*. This includes text boxes, graphics brought in from other sources, and the shapes that you draw. You can have as many objects as you want in a worksheet.

To select the object that you want to work with, click on it. You can then change its orientation, shape, color, or pattern by right-clicking on the object, or by clicking on the object and using the Color, Style, Shadow, and 3-D options of the Drawing toolbar. From the shortcut menu that appears, choose Format AutoShape and select the desired choices in the tabs of the dialog box that appears. You can also select multiple objects by holding down the Shift key while you select the objects. To unselect an object, hold down the Shift key and click on the object again.

You can also group objects together. Grouping objects is useful when you want to change the colors for a group of objects or move or align them as a group. All the objects that you include in the group act as one object; therefore, if you perform an action on one of the items, the action affects all the items in the group. You can group objects by performing the following steps:

1. Select the objects that you want to group. Remember to hold down the Shift key while you select each object.

2. Right-click on any one of the selected objects and choose Grouping⇨Group from the shortcut menu that appears.

Using the Bring To Front and Send To Back tools

As you draw and position multiple objects, you may need to place one object on top of another object (for example, a company logo that consists of a circle on top of a rectangle). If the wrong object appears on top, you can adjust the placement by using the Bring To Front or Send To Back options, available from the shortcut menu for the object. Right-click the desired object, and choose Order⇨Bring to Front to make the object appear on top of another object. You can also right-click the object and choose Order⇨Send to Back to make the selected object appear underneath the other object. You can use the Bring Forward and Send Backward options on the same menu to move a selected object one step closer to the top or to the bottom of a stack of selected objects. Figure 18-7 shows the effects of using the Bring To Front and Send To Back tools.

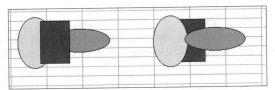

Figure 18-7: Left: Bring To Front brings the rectangle to the front. Right: Send To Back sends the rectangle to the back.

Moving and copying objects

As you work with objects in your worksheet, you may need to move or copy the objects. You have two options to move or copy the objects: you can use the Cut and Copy commands or the click-on-and-drag method. To move or copy objects with the Cut and Copy commands, perform the following steps.

1. Select the object(s) that you want to move or copy.

2. Choose Edit⇨Cut or click on the Cut button on the Standard toolbar to remove the object and place it in the Clipboard. Choose Edit⇨Copy instead to leave the existing object intact and place a copy of it in the Clipboard to copy it to a new location.

3. Move the cursor to the location where you want to place the object.

4. Choose Edit⇨Paste or click on the Paste button on the Standard toolbar to place the Clipboard information in the worksheet. The cell that contains the insertion point becomes the upper-left corner of the entry.

The click-on-and-drag method for moving objects is equally simple. Simply click on the object and hold down the mouse button, and drag to the area where you want to place the object. Release the mouse button to place the object. To remove an object, select it and press the Delete key or choose Edit⇨Clear. You can copy an object by holding the Ctrl key as you click and drag the object.

Resizing objects

You resize objects in Excel in the same way that you resize objects in other Windows programs. First, select the object that you want to resize. You will see small black squares, called *sizing handles,* appear around the object. To resize the object's width, drag one of the side handles to the desired width. To change the height of the object, drag a top or a bottom handle. If you want to resize the length and width of the object simultaneously, drag a corner handle.

Formatting objects

You can apply a variety of formatting options to the object that you have selected with the Color, Style, Shadow, and 3-D options of the Drawing toolbar. You can accomplish the same thing by right-clicking the object, choosing Format ⇨AutoShape, and using the various options shown on the Colors and Lines tabs of the dialog box.

Formatting Colors

To change the color of an object, click the object to select it and click the down arrow to the right of the Fill Color button in the Drawing toolbar. When you do so, a Colors dialog box appears (Figure 18-8), and you can choose the desired color.

Figure 18-8: The Colors dialog box.

If you want to change the patterns or the effects for the color, click on Fill Effects at the bottom of the dialog box to open the Fill Effects dialog box (Figure 18-9).

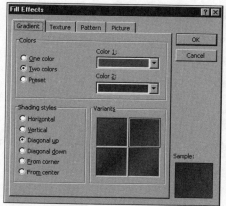

Figure 18-9: The Fill Effects dialog box.

Using the tabs of this dialog box, you can change the colors and shading used for the gradient, the texture of the colors, a desired pattern, and whether a picture should be used as a fill. Under the Gradient tab, you can select the number of colors (one or two), the shading style, and which of the variants for shading that you want. Using the Texture tab, you can select one of 24 possible pre-set textures, or you can click the Other Texture button and choose an image file in the dialog box which appears for use as a texture. Using the Pattern tab, you can choose from one of 48 possible patterns. And the Picture tab lets you choose an image file that will serve as a picture contained within the object. Once you make the desired selections in the Fill Effects dialog box and click OK, the changes are applied to the object.

Formatting Lines

You can change the style, thickness, and colors of lines using either of two methods. You can select the object and use the Line Color, Line Style, Dash Style, and Arrow Style buttons of the Drawing toolbar. Each button opens a menu of possible colors or styles, and you can select the desired option.

You can also right-click on the desired object and choose Format⇨AutoShape from the menu. In the Format AutoShape dialog box which appears, click Colors and Lines. Figure 18-10 shows what the Colors and Lines tab looks like when an arrow is selected.

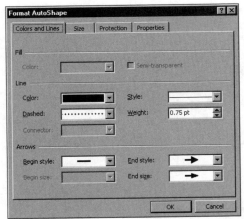

Figure 18-10: The Colors and Lines tab of the Format AutoShape dialog box when you select an arrow.

Hiding objects for better spreadsheet performance

If you have a lot of graphic objects in your worksheet, Excel is forced to redraw the graphics as you scroll within the worksheet. This extra effort can really drag down your system's speed, especially on hardware that meets only the minimum configuration for Windows 95. You can speed up the display of the worksheets by hiding the graphic objects from view or by displaying them as graphic placeholders. Choose Tools ⇨

Options and click on the View tab. In the Objects area of the dialog box, turn on the Show Placeholders option to show the graphic objects as placeholders (empty white rectangles) or turn on the Hide All option to hide the graphic objects. When you need to see the objects again, you can go back into this dialog box and turn on the Show All option.

In the Fill Area of the dialog box, you can choose a fill color for enclosed objects such as rectangles and ovals. However, note that the Fill Color toolbar button (discussed earlier) offers more options, such as the capability to change patterns and gradients.

In the Line area of the dialog box, you can change line colors, styles, weight (the thickness of the line), and whether the line should be dashed or solid. In the Arrows portion of the dialog box, you can choose styles and sizes for the arrowheads. Once you make the desired selections within the dialog box, click OK to apply them to the arrow.

Adding Shadows and 3-D Effects

You can use the Shadow and 3-D Effects buttons of the Drawing toolbar to add shadows or three-dimensional effects to graphic objects. To do so, click the desired object to select it, and click the Shadow button or the 3-D button in the Drawing toolbar to display a submenu of available shadows or special effects. Select the desired effect from the submenu to apply it to the object.

Adding Text Boxes

Excel lets you place text boxes in your worksheets. You can edit and format text in these boxes using typical word processing techniques.

Text boxes make excellent titles for worksheets because they float in a layer over the worksheet. You can position a title of any size without affecting worksheet row or column positions. You can add a text box to your worksheet by performing the following steps:

1. In the Drawing toolbar, click on the Text Box button. Notice that the mouse pointer changes into a thin arrow.

2. Click and drag to form the box in which you will enter the text. If you want a square text box, hold down the Shift key while you drag. If you want a box aligned with the grid, hold down the Alt key while you drag.

3. After sizing the text box, release the mouse button. The insertion point now appears inside the text box (see Figure 18-11), which permits you to begin entering text. You can continue typing until the end of the text box. As you type, the text scrolls up so that part of it is hidden. To make all the text visible, select the text box and drag a handle to make the box larger to accommodate the extra text.

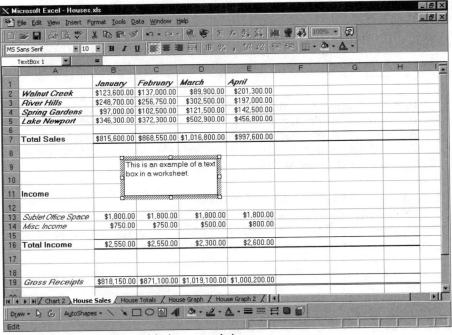

Figure 18-11: A text box added to a worksheet.

Editing text

If you need to edit text in a text box, use the normal Windows navigation methods to do so. To move the cursor, use Ctrl+right arrow or Ctrl+left arrow or use the arrow keys and the mouse. Use the Delete and Backspace keys to delete any unwanted entry and then retype the new entry.

Formatting text

You can also format the text boxes that you add. Select the text box, right-click on it, and choose Format Text Box from the shortcut menu. The dialog box that appears contains one tab, called Font. Using the options shown on this tab, you can change the fonts used by the text. Figure 18-12 shows the Font tab that appears when you select a text box. You can choose a desired font, font style, and point size, and you can turn on special effects, such as underlining, bold, italics, strikethrough, superscript, or subscript. Use the Color list box to change the font's color. Keep in mind that you can change background patterns for the text box by selecting it and using the options of the Fill Color button on the Drawing toolbar.

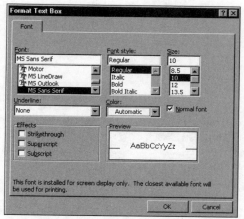

Figure 18-12: The Font tab of the Format Text Box dialog box when you select a text box.

Rotating text

Excel also lets you rotate text within a text box. Figure 18-13 shows some of the different ways that text in a text box can appear in Excel.

To rotate text in a text box, perform the following steps:

1. After creating the text box and entering the text, select the text box and right-click on the edge of the box (not the text within the box).

2. From the shortcut menu that appears, choose Format Text Box to open the Format Text Box dialog box.

3. Choose the Alignment tab (see Figure 18-14). The Text Alignment area lets you control both the horizontal and vertical alignment of the text that you enter in the text box.

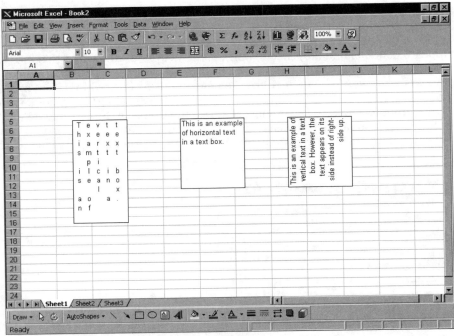

Figure 18-13: Examples of rotated text in boxes.

4. In the Orientation area, choose the desired orientation for the box.

You can use the Automatic Size option in the Alignment tab to size your entries automatically.

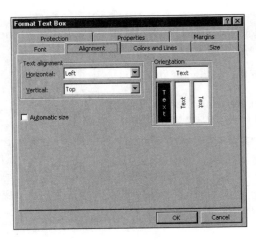

Figure 18-14: The appearance of the Alignment tab when you select a text box.

WordArt

Microsoft WordArt is an applet (think of it as a *mini-application*) that lets you create special effects using text to enhance the appearance of your documents. You can bend and stretch text strings, fit text into a variety of different shapes, add three-dimensional effects, and then insert this twisted text as graphics into your document. Figure 18-15 shows an example of what you can do with WordArt.

Figure 18-15: An example of WordArt in Excel.

To add WordArt to a worksheet, first make the Drawing toolbar visible (if it isn't already) by choosing View➪Toolbars➪Drawing. In the Drawing toolbar, click the WordArt button. You'll see the WordArt Gallery dialog box, as shown in Figure 18-16.

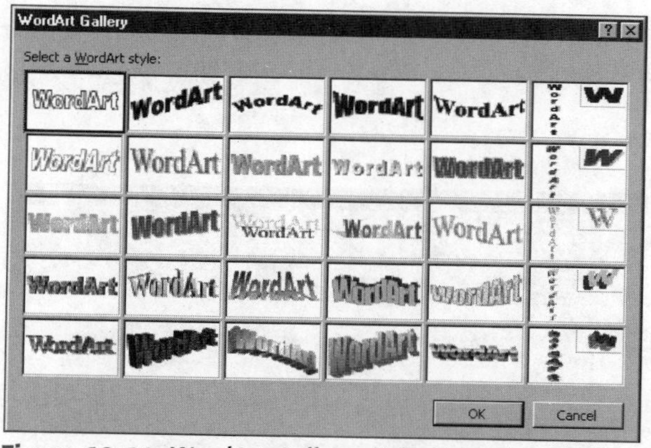

Figure 18-16: WordArt Gallery dialog box shows the available styles of WordArt.

Click a desired style to select it, and click OK. Next, you'll see the Edit WordArt Text dialog box, as shown in Figure 18-17.

You can replace the default text with the text of your choosing. You can also select a desired font and font size using the list boxes at the top of the dialog box, and you can use the Bold and Italic buttons to apply bold or italics to the text.

Figure 18-17: The Edit WordArt Text dialog box displays the WordArt text.

Note Changes you make to the selected font will override the chosen selection in the WordArt Gallery dialog box, but you can always reopen the dialog box by clicking the Gallery button on the WordArt toolbar.

Once you click OK in the Edit WordArt Text dialog box, the completed WordArt appears in the worksheet, and the WordArt toolbar appears, similar to the example shown in Figure 18-18.

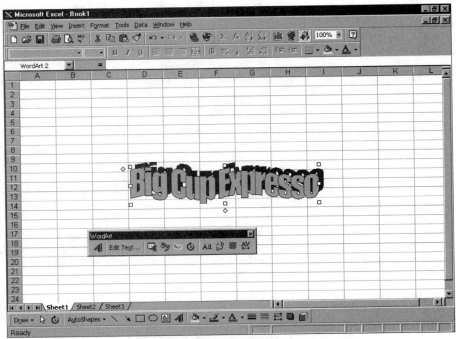

Figure 18-18: WordArt added to an existing worksheet.

As with other graphic objects, you can move and size WordArt using standard Windows click-and-drag techniques.

The WordArt toolbar lets you change the appearance of a WordArt object in several ways. (Users of earlier versions of Excel should note that this toolbar has changed significantly in Excel 97.) Figure 18-19 shows the parts of the WordArt toolbar, and Table 18-2 gives the name of each tool and its function.

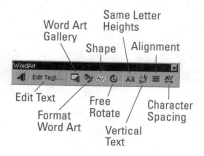

Figure 18-19: The parts of the WordArt toolbar.

Table 18-2
The WordArt toolbar's tools

Tool name	Function
Edit Text	Displays the Edit WordArt Text dialog box
WordArt Gallery	Displays the WordArt Gallery dialog box
Format WordArt	Displays the Format WordArt dialog box
Shape	Opens a dialog box of available WordArt shapes
Free Rotate	Rotates the selected WordArt object to any degree
Same Letter Heights	Sets all letters in WordArt to the same height
Vertical Text	Stacks text in the WordArt object vertically
Alignment	Aligns the text left, center, or right within the dimensions of the WordArt object
Character Spacing	Applies a variety of character spacings to the text of the WordArt object

In addition to displaying the Edit WordArt Text and WordArt Gallery dialog boxes, you can use the WordArt toolbar for many WordArt tasks. You can change the shape and rotation, modify the character spacing, and display the text vertically.

Changing colors and sizes

If you click the Format WordArt button, you see the Format WordArt dialog box, as shown in Figure 18-20. Here you can change the text colors and modify the size and rotation of the object.

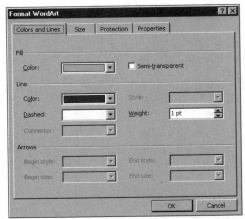

Figure 18-20: The Format WordArt dialog box with the Colors and Lines tab visible.

The Fill color affects the color of the letters, whereas the Line color affects the color of the letter shading. You can click on the Size tab to change the size and rotation of the object. Note, however, that it is easier to change the size and rotation by selecting and dragging the object (to change its size) or by using the WordArt toolbar's Free Rotate button (to change the rotation).

Changing shapes

You can change the overall shape of a WordArt object. To do so, click the WordArt Shape button in the WordArt toolbar. When you do this, a window of shapes appears, as shown in Figure 18-21.

Figure 18-21: Dialog box containing the available WordArt shapes.

The different shapes that you see here represent the way the WordArt text will appear in the worksheet. As you make a selection, the effect is immediately applied to the text.

Rotating objects

Finally, one WordArt toolbar tool whose use may not be intuitively obvious is the Free Rotate tool. You can use this tool to rotate a selected object to any degree. Select the desired WordArt object, click the Free Rotate button in the WordArt toolbar, and click and drag a corner of the WordArt object in the direction you want it to rotate.

Summary

In this chapter, you learned about using Excel's graphics capabilities to add pictures and other graphic objects to a worksheet. The following points were covered:

✦ You can insert graphics in a worksheet with Insert menu's Picture command.

✦ Excel's Drawing toolbar contains a variety of tools that you can use to draw different shapes in a worksheet.

✦ You can select multiple objects to manipulate them as a group and to apply formatting, color, or other design choices.

✦ You can add text boxes to worksheets by using the Text Box tool on the Drawing toolbar.

✦ In the next chapter, you'll learn how to work with charts in Excel.

Where to go next...

✦ For adding visual oomph to your worksheet-based presentations, graphics and charts often go hand in hand. You'll find full details in Chapter 19.

✦ If Excel's graphics are not powerful enough for you, you can add graphics from other drawing programs that support OLE. Chapter 50 has the specifics on adding OLE data to a worksheet.

✦   ✦   ✦

Working with Excel Charts

This chapter details the powerful capabilities that Excel has for displaying and printing charts. In Excel, you can create charts that emphasize numeric trends, support data analysis, and help supply presentation-quality reports. Excel provides you with a rich assortment of formatting features and options for changing and enhancing the appearance of your charts.

What Is a Chart?

Charts graphically represent worksheet data. A collection of values from worksheet cells that you select are illustrated in charts as columns, lines, bars, pie slices, or other types of markers. Figure 19-1 shows some examples of typical charts. The appearance of the markers that are used to represent the data varies, depending on the type of marker that you choose. In a bar or column chart, the markers appear as columns; in a line chart, the markers appear as lines composed of small symbols. The markers in a pie chart appear as wedges of the pie.

Most charts (with the exception of pie charts) have two axes: a horizontal axis called the *category axis* and a vertical axis called the *value axis*. Three-dimensional charts add a third axis (called the *series axis*). Figure 19-2 shows an example of a three-dimensional chart.

Charts also contain *gridlines,* which provide a frame of reference for the values displayed on the value axis. You can add descriptive text to a chart, such as a title, and you can place the text in different locations. Your charts can also contain legends, which indicate which data is represented by the markers of the chart.

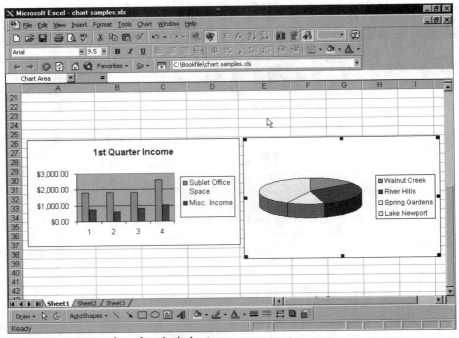

Figure 19-1: Examples of typical charts.

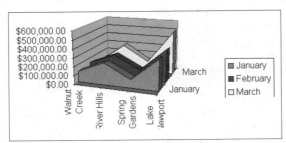

Figure 19-2: An example of a 3-D chart.

Excel makes adding charts a simple matter by providing a Chart Wizard that automatically appears when you add a new chart to a worksheet. Like all Office wizards, the Chart Wizard produces the desired results by asking a series of questions and producing a desired chart in response to the answers that you provide. During each step of the wizard process, the dialog box displays a sample of the chart so that you can see how your choices in the dialog box will affect the final result.

About Embedded Charts and Chart Sheets

You can add charts to Excel worksheets in one of two ways: as embedded charts or as chart sheets. *Embedded charts* are inserted into an existing worksheet page; hence, the page can show worksheet data with the chart. Figure 19-3 shows an embedded chart.

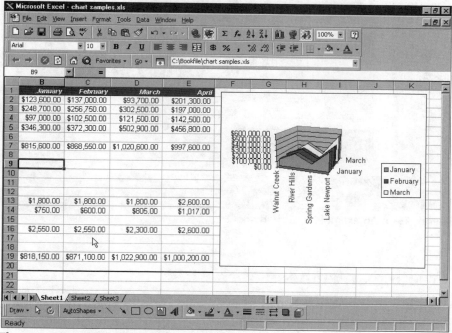

Figure 19-3: An embedded chart.

Chart sheets, on the other hand, are charts that are placed on separate sheets of a workbook, apart from any worksheet data. Figure 19-4 shows a chart added as a chart sheet.

Embedded charts work best when you need to display or print the chart along with worksheet data; chart sheets work best when all you want to show is the chart. Whether you use embedded charts or chart sheets, the data used to produce the chart is always linked to the worksheet. Therefore, as you change the data in the underlying worksheet, the chart changes to reflect the new data.

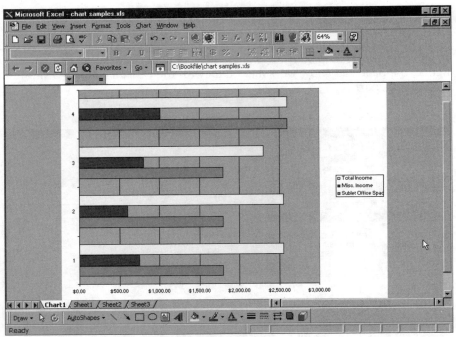

Figure 19-4: An example of a chart sheet.

Creating an embedded chart

You can add an embedded chart to an existing worksheet page by performing these steps:

1. In the worksheet, select the data that you want to chart. Include any labels that should be used as legends in the chart.

2. Click on the Chart Wizard button on the Standard toolbar. When you do this, the first Chart Wizard dialog box appears, showing the available chart types.

3. Choose a desired chart type, click on the Next button, and follow the directions in the successive Chart Wizard dialog boxes to specify the data range, the chart's format, and the desired options for category labels and for the legend text. (The Chart Wizard dialog boxes are described in detail in a later section of this chapter.)

Alternatively, you can add an embedded chart to a worksheet by selecting the data to chart and choosing Insert⇨Chart⇨On This Sheet. Performing these steps displays the first Chart Wizard dialog box, where you can fill in the desired options to produce the chart.

Creating a chart sheet

You can create a chart that resides separately on a chart sheet by performing the following steps:

1. In the worksheet, select the data that you want to chart. Include any labels that should be used as legends in the chart.

2. Choose Insert⇨Chart. The first Chart Wizard dialog box appears.

3. Choose the desired type of chart, then click on the Next button and follow the directions in the next two Chart Wizard dialog boxes to accept the desired data range, and the desired options for category labels, axis and gridlines, and for the legend text.

4. In the last Chart Wizard dialog box (labeled Step 4 of 4), choose As New Sheet to place the chart on a separate worksheet, then click Finish.

With either method of adding a chart, the Chart Wizard displays a series of dialog boxes that help you define precisely how the chart will appear. The first Chart Wizard dialog box appears, as shown in Figure 19-5.

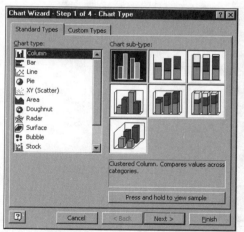

Figure 19-5: The first Chart Wizard dialog box.

In this dialog box, you can select the chart type that you want from one of the 14 available chart types. For each chart type selected in the Chart Type list box (at the left side of the dialog box), you can choose any of the available sub-types at the right side of the dialog box. The Press and Hold to View sample button at the lower right corner of the dialog box can be used to preview an image of any selected chart type. And if none of the dozens of standard type and subtype combinations suit your taste, you can click the Custom Types tab and choose from one of 20 available custom chart types. (For more specifics on the available chart types, see "Working with Chart Types" later in the chapter.) Once you've selected the desired chart type and sub-type, click Next to proceed.

After you click the Next button, the dialog box shown in Figure 19-6 appears. You can use this dialog box to define the range of cells within the worksheet that is used as the underlying data for the chart. When you select a range in the worksheet and then use the Chart Wizard, the range automatically appears in the dialog box, as shown in Figure 19-6. If for any reason you want to change the range, you can do so by typing in a different range.

You can use the Series in option to determine whether the data series appears as rows or columns in the chart, and you can click the Series tab to add or remove a data series from the chart. (For more specifics on how you can use data series in charts, see "Understanding How Excel Plots a Chart" later in the chapter.) When done choosing the desired data range and series options, click Next to proceed.

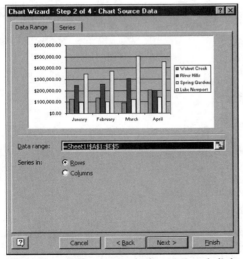

Figure 19-6: The second Chart Wizard dialog box asks for the range of cells to be plotted.

When you click Next, the third Chart Wizard dialog box appears, as shown in Figure 19-7. In this dialog box, you can turn on or off a variety of options for the chart you've selected. The dialog box is divided into six tabs: Titles, Axes, Gridlines, Legend, Data Labels, and Data Table. (If the terminology used throughout this dialog box is unfamiliar, you'll learn more about these terms throughout the remainder of this chapter.) You can use the Titles tab to specify titles for the chart, for the category axis, and for the value axis of the chart. On the Axis tab, you can turn on or off the display of the category axis and the value axis. On the Gridlines tab, you can specify whether gridlines are added to each axis of the chart. The Legend tab lets you show and position the chart's legend. The Data Labels tab lets you add labels to the data points plotted by the chart, and the Data Table tab lets you add an optional data table below the chart. As you change these various settings, you can look at the preview of the chart that is visible in the dialog box, to make sure that you obtain the desired look for the chart. When done selecting the desired chart options, click Next to proceed.

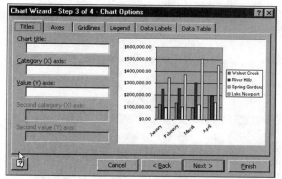

Figure 19-7: The third Chart Wizard dialog box provides various formatting options for the chart.

When you click Next, the fourth Chart Wizard dialog box appears, as shown in Figure 19-8. You can use this dialog box to specify whether the chart should be inserted as an embedded chart in the existing worksheet or placed into a separate chart sheet. If you click the As New Sheet button, you can enter a name for the new sheet or accept the default name (Chart1, Chart2, and so on). If you click the As Object In button, you can then choose the desired sheet by name where the chart should be placed; the default is the same worksheet where you selected the chart data. Click Finish, and your desired chart appears in the chosen location. Remember that, if you embed the chart in an existing worksheet, you can select the entire chart and drag it to any desired location in that worksheet.

Figure 19-8: The fourth Chart Wizard dialog box asks where the chart should be placed.

After a chart exists and is active, you can run the Chart Wizard on this chart at any time by clicking on the Chart Wizard button on the Chart toolbar.

Creating a Sample Chart

The examples shown throughout this chapter make use of the Houses.xls workbook, which you can find at the IDG Books web site on the Internet (www.idgbooks.com). You can use the House Totals page to generate the charts shown throughout this chapter, and you can duplicate the examples by opening the House Sales workbook in Excel. Figure 19-9 shows the House Totals page of the Houses.xls workbook.

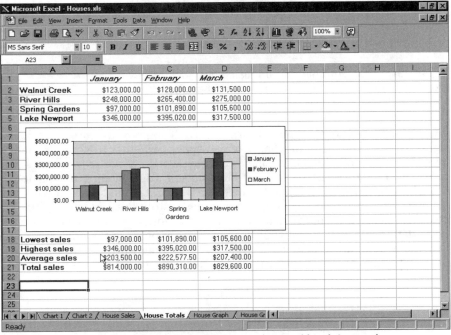

Figure 19-9: The House Totals page of House Sales workbook in Excel.

After you open the workbook and move to the House Totals page, you can perform the following steps to get an idea of how you can easily create charts within Excel:

1. Click in cell A1 and drag to cell E5 to select the range that contains the house sales for all four developments for January, February, March, and April.

2. Choose Insert➪Chart. (In this case, you'll insert a chart as a separate sheet; you can just as easily insert the chart onto the existing worksheet page.) The first Chart Wizard dialog box appears (shown earlier, in Figure 19-5).

3. This dialog box asks for a desired format for the chart. Leave Column selected as the desired chart type, choose the first sub-type shown in the dialog box and then click on the Next button. In a moment, the second Chart Wizard dialog box appears (shown earlier, in Figure 19-6).

4. Because the range matches the cells that you selected in the worksheet, click on the Next button in the dialog box to display the third Chart Wizard dialog box (shown earlier in Figure 19-7). Click Next to accept all the default options for the chart.

5. In the last dialog box (shown earlier in Figure 19-8), click As New Sheet, enter House Chart in the text box, and then click on the Finish button to create the chart and add it to the workbook. Your sample chart should resemble the one shown in Figure 19-10.

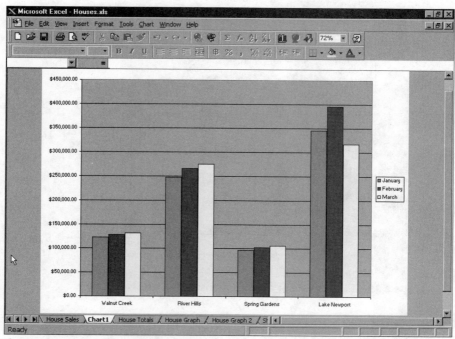

Figure 19-10: The House Sales chart.

Saving and Printing Charts

Because charts are stored with worksheet pages, the tasks of saving and printing charts are no different from saving and printing worksheets. When you save the worksheet by choosing File⇨Save, the chart is saved along with the worksheet. You can print the chart by activating the page that contains the chart and choosing File⇨Print. The Print dialog box that appears contains the same options that you use for printing worksheets.

To print pie charts in the proper proportion to fit a single sheet of paper, first choose File⇨Page Setup, and click the Chart tab of the dialog box that appears. Then turn on the Scale to Fit Page option.

Understanding the Parts of a Chart

Before you explore the options that Excel offers for creating charts, you should know the parts of a chart and the terminology used to describe these parts. Figure 19-11 shows the parts of a two-dimensional chart.

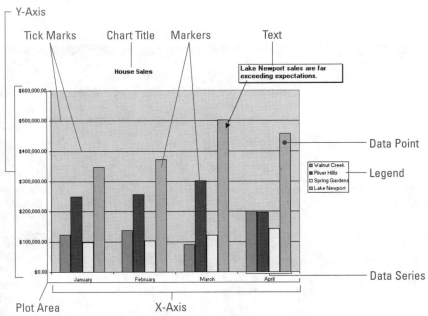

Figure 19-11: The parts of a two-dimensional chart.

Three-dimensional charts have an additional axis that two-dimensional charts do not have. Three-dimensional charts also have a wall, a floor, and corners. The additional parts of a three-dimensional chart are shown in Figure 19-12.

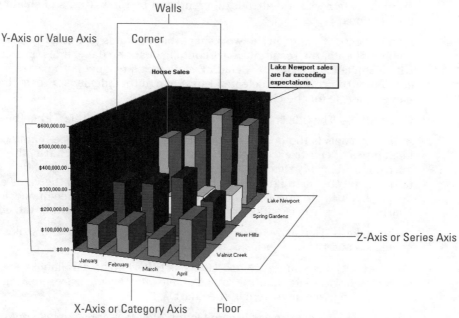

Figure 19-12: The parts of a three-dimensional chart.

The following parts can be found on two- and three-dimensional charts:

✦ **Chart** — The chart is the entire area contained within the chart sheet (on charts placed in separate sheets) or in the chart frame in an embedded chart.

✦ **Plot area** — The plot area contains the chart's essential data: the value axis, the category axis, and all the markers that indicate the relative values of your data.

✦ **Markers** — Markers are the bars, lines, points, or pie wedges that represent the actual data in the chart. The form of the markers depends on the type of chart that you choose. In a pie chart, the markers are wedges, or slices, of the pie. In a line chart, the markers are solid lines, although at some sharp angles, the lines may appear jagged or broken due to the limitations of screen resolution. In a column chart, such as the one shown in Figure 19-10, the markers appear as columns.

Note

Each set of markers in the chart represents a set of values within the worksheet. The set of values represented by the markers is referred to as a *data series*. If a chart displays data from more than one data series, each data series will be represented by a different pattern or symbol. In Figure 19-10, for example, the January data is one data series, and the February data is another. Data series are further differentiated by the patterns of shadings of the columns.

If you selected a range in the worksheet that contains just one row or column of data, the resulting chart contains just one data series. In a chart with a single data series, by default Excel takes any label in the extreme left column or top row of the selected range and automatically suggests that name as a title for the chart.

✦ **Chart title** — The title is a text label that Excel places as a title within the chart.

✦ **Axis** — An axis is the horizontal or vertical frame of reference that appears in all types of charts except pie charts. In two-dimensional charts, the horizontal x-axis is called the category axis because categories of data are normally plotted along this line. The vertical y-axis is called the value axis because values are normally shown along this line. With three-dimensional charts, a series axis is added to show multiple data series within the chart.

✦ **Tick marks** — Tick marks are reference marks that separate the scales of the value axis and the categories of the category axis.

✦ **Text** — Excel lets you create text labels as titles and as data labels (associated with data points). You can have *unattached,* or free-floating text, that you can place anywhere in the chart.

✦ **Data series** — A data series is a collection of data points, such as one month's sales for a housing development.

✦ **Data point** — A data point is a single piece of information inside any data series. In the example shown earlier in Figure 19-10, one month's sales for a specific housing development is a single data point.

✦ **Series name** — You can assign a series name to each series of data contained within a chart. Excel automatically assigns default series names based on headings entered within your worksheets.

✦ **Gridlines** — Gridlines are reference lines that extend the tick marks across the entire area of the graph.

✦ **Legends** — A legend defines the patterns or shadings that are used by the chart markers. A legend consists of a sample of the pattern followed by the series name (or the category name, if the chart displays only one data series). If you include labels as series names in the top row or the left column of the selected worksheet range, Excel can use these names in the legend.

✦ **Arrows** — These are lines with arrowheads that can be moved and sized as desired.

Working with Charts

Excel charts follow the object-oriented nature of Windows 95 in general. This means that when you need to change the appearance of an object within a chart, the easiest way to do so is to right-click the object and choose the desired options from the dialog box or menu that appears. Users of Excel for Windows 95 and Excel 5.0 should notice a significant change in the ways in which you make modifications to charts. In those versions of Excel, you would double-click the chart, and Excel's menus would change to reflect specialized chart options. Now, you can work directly with the charts' formatting options without having to double-click the chart first, and there are no separate chart menus. You can now find your chart options under the Chart menu in Excel.

Selecting parts of a chart

Before applying menu selections to the parts of a chart, you must first select the desired part. For example, if you want to change the way that text in a legend is displayed, you first must select the legend. You can then right-click on the legend and choose Format Legend from the shortcut menu. In the Format Legend dialog box, you can change options for formatting the legend.

You can select objects with the mouse by clicking on them. You can also use the arrow keys to select objects within a chart. The left-arrow and right-arrow keys first move you among items in the same class of objects (such as markers) and then from class to class (such as from the markers to the legend to the axis and so on). When you select an object, it is marked with squares. While the object is selected, the name of the object also appears on the left side of the formula bar. Figure 19-13 shows a set of markers selected in a chart — note that the marker name appears in the formula bar.

Hot Stuff You can also modify the display properties for objects in charts by double-clicking on the object. When you double-click on an object in a chart, a dialog box for that object opens where you can change settings appropriate to the object.

Working with the Chart toolbar

You can make use of the Chart toolbar to add new charts or to change existing charts. Figure 19-14 shows the Chart toolbar. If the Chart toolbar is not visible, you can bring it into view by choosing View⇨Toolbars and selecting Chart from the submenu that appears. Table 19-1 describes this toolbar's buttons.

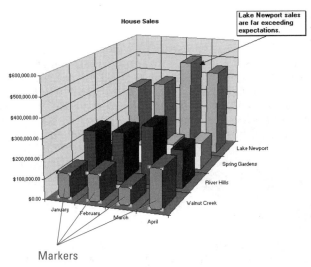

Figure 19-13: A set of markers selected in a chart.

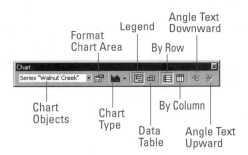

Figure 19-14: The Chart toolbar.

Table 19-1
Chart toolbar buttons

Button	Function
Chart Objects	Lets you select any part of the chart by choosing it from the list box.
Format Chart Area	Displays the Format Chart Area dialog box, which lets you apply formatting to the selected chart area.
Chart Type	Selects a chart type for the chart.

Button	Function
Legend	Adds or removes the legend from the chart.
Data Table	Adds a data table to the chart.
By Row	Arranges the series data by row.
By Column	Arranges the series data by column.
Angle Text Downward	Arranges selected text object downward.
Angle Text Upward	Arranges selected text object upward.

Adding titles

Text boxes containing titles are typically used with charts to help describe the purpose of the chart or to clarify the purpose of the various chart axes. You can add titles to a chart by performing the following steps:

1. Select the chart.

2. Choose Insert⇨Chart⇨Options, and click the Titles tab. The Titles tab of the Chart Options dialog box is shown in Figure 19-15.

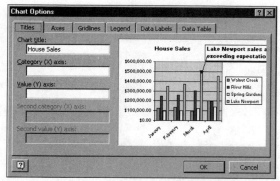

Figure 19-15: The Titles tab of the Chart Options dialog box.

3. In the dialog box, enter the desired titles in the text boxes and then click on the OK button. Excel inserts text boxes for each title that you added, and you can format the text by using the steps under the "Formatting text" section.

Adding unattached text

At times, you may want to add text that is not attached to a title or to a specific axis. Such text is referred to as *unattached text*. You can add unattached text to a chart by displaying the Drawing toolbar, clicking on the Text Box button, and then clicking and dragging in the chart to place a text box of the desired size. When you release the mouse, an insertion point appears in the text box, and you can then type the desired text.

Formatting text

With all the text that you can have in text boxes, you may want to change the formatting properties — the fonts and styles used — to something other than the default text formats. You can format the text in your charts by performing the following steps:

1. Right-click on the text that you want to format and choose Format Chart Title (for titles), Format Legend (for legends), or Format Text Box (for unattached text) from the shortcut menu.

2. In the dialog box that appears, click on the Font tab to reveal the options shown in Figure 19-16.

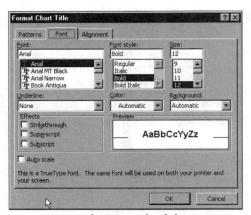

Figure 19-16: The Font tab of the Format Chart Title dialog box.

Choose the desired font, font style, and font size by selecting the options in the dialog box. You can also choose underlining, color, and background; and you can select special effects, such as strikethrough, superscript, and subscript. When you are finished selecting the desired options, click on the OK button to place them into effect.

Formatting chart axes

Excel lets you enhance the appearance of the various axes that you use in your charts. You can change the font, and you can modify the scale. You change the format of any chart axis by right-clicking on the axis that you want to format and choosing Format Axis from the shortcut menu. The Format Axis dialog box appears, as shown in Figure 19-17.

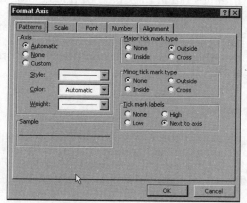

Figure 19-17: The Patterns tab of the Format Axis dialog box.

The dialog box contains five tabs, which you can use to change various formatting aspects of the axis. Use the options in the Patterns tab to change the patterns that you use for the axis, the tick mark labels, and the types of tick marks that you want. The Scale tab options enable you to change the values that you use to create the axis scale. The Font tab contains the options that you use to modify the font of the axis. The Number tab contains list boxes that you can use to choose the desired formatting for numbers along an axis, and the Alignment tab lets you choose an orientation for the text.

Adding legends

If a chart does not have a legend by default, you can add one at any time by selecting the chart, choosing Chart⇨Chart Options, clicking the Legend tab, and turning on the Show Legend check box. After you add a legend to the chart, you can change its appearance by double-clicking on the legend or by right-clicking on it and choosing Format Legend from the shortcut menu. Either method brings up the Format Legend dialog box, which contains tabs for Patterns, Font, and Placement of the legend. Use the options on the Patterns tab to change the patterns used by the legend to identify the markers in the chart. The Font tab contains the options you use to modify the fonts used by the legend. The

Placement tab contains options that specify where in the chart the legend should appear (top, bottom, left, right, center, or corner). Remember that, because the legend is just another object in a chart, you can also move the legend by clicking and dragging it to any desired location within the chart.

Adding gridlines

To add gridlines to an existing chart, select the chart to make it active, choose Chart⇨Chart Options, and click the Gridlines tab in the Chart Options dialog box that appears. The Gridlines dialog box appears. In this dialog box, you can choose between major or minor gridlines along either the category axis or the value axis. Major gridlines are heavier lines, widely spaced. Minor gridlines are fine lines, closely spaced. After you make the desired options and click on the OK button, the gridlines appear within the selected chart.

Customizing a charts area

You can add a lot in terms of visual pizazz to a chart by customizing the default settings for the chart's area. You can change the background colors, the borders, and the fonts used throughout the chart. After the chart is active, click in any blank area of the chart to make handles appear around the entire chart. Then from the Format menu, choose Selected Chart Area or right-click in any blank area of the chart and choose Format Chart Area from the shortcut menu. The Format Chart Area dialog box appears, as shown in Figure 19-18. The dialog box has multiple tabs from which you can choose all sorts of options. (If the chart is embedded, you will see three tabs labeled Patterns, Font, and Properties. If the chart is on a separate sheet, you will see two tabs labeled Patterns and Font.)

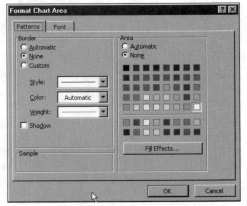

Figure 19-18: The Patterns tab of the Format Chart Area dialog box.

In the Patterns tab of the Format Chart Area dialog box, you can click on the Custom button to choose your own style, color, and weight for the border. Turning on the Shadow option adds a shadow to the border. In the Area section of the Patterns tab, you can choose a background color. Selecting Automatic sets the color to the Windows default (white, unless you changed it in the Windows Control Panel). Selecting None establishes no background color. In addition to the Automatic and None options, you can click on one of the Color boxes to set a desired color, and you can use the Pattern list box to choose a desired pattern.

On the Font tab, you will find various options that you can use to set the fonts used in the entire chart. Choose the desired font, font style, and font size by selecting the options displayed under the tab. You can also select underlining, color, and background; and you can select special effects, such as strikethrough, superscript, and subscript.

On the Properties tab (which appears if the chart is an embedded chart), you can select various options that determine whether the chart will move and resize with the underlying cells, whether the chart should print when the worksheet prints, and whether the chart should be locked (protected against changes) if the worksheet is locked.

After you finish selecting the desired options, click on the OK button so that the chart takes on the chosen effects.

Working with Chart Types

Excel offers several different chart types. Each of these chart types has sub-types that you can also select when you are choosing the type of chart that you want to create. The following list describes the types of charts, and how they can best be used.

 Area charts show the significance of change during a given time period. The top line of the chart totals the individual series, so area charts make it visually apparent how each individual series contributes to the overall picture. Area charts emphasize the magnitude of change as opposed to the rate of change. (If you want to emphasize the rate of change, use line charts instead.)

 Bar charts use horizontal bars to show distinct figures at a specified time. Each horizontal bar in the chart shows a specific amount of change from the base value used in the chart. Bar charts visually emphasize different values, arranged vertically.

 Column charts are very much like bar charts, using columns to show distinct figures over a time period. The difference is that the markers in column charts are oriented along a *horizontal* plane, with the columns running vertically up or down from a base value used in the chart.

Line charts are perfect for showing trends in data over a period of time. Like area charts, line charts show the significance of change, but line charts emphasize the rate instead of the magnitude of change.

 Pie charts show relationships between the pieces of a picture. They also can show a relationship between a piece of the picture and the entire picture. A pie chart can display only one series of data at a time because each piece of a pie chart represents part of a total series. If you have a large number of series to plot, however, you are probably better off with a column chart because a pie crowded with slices is hard to interpret.

 Doughnut charts show relationships between pieces of a picture, as do pie charts. The difference is that the doughnut chart has a hollow center.

 Radar charts show the changes or frequencies of a data series in relation to a central point and to each other. (Every category has an axis value that radiates from a center point. Lines connect all data in the same series.) Radar charts can be difficult to interpret, unless you're accustomed to working with them.

 Scatter charts show relationships between different points of data, to compare trends across uneven time periods, or to show patterns as a set of x and y coordinates. These charts are commonly used to plot scientific data.

 Surface charts show trends in values across two dimensions in a continuous curve.

 Bubble charts compare sets of three values. In appearance, these are similar to scatter charts, with the third value interpreted by the size of the bubbles.

 Stock charts are also known as open-hi-lo-close charts. They are used to display the day-to-day values of stocks, commodities, or other financial market data. Stock charts require series containing four values to plot the four points (open, high, low, and close).

 Cylinder charts are column charts with the columns appearing as cylindrical shapes.

 Cone charts are column charts with the columns appearing as cone shapes.

 Pyramid charts are column charts with the columns appearing as pyramid shapes.

An important decision for you to make is which type of chart will work best to get the desired point across. Excel offers 20 different chart types. All of the available chart types can be two-dimensional, and nine of the available chart types can be three-dimensional. When you create a chart by using the Chart Wizard, Excel asks you which chart type you want to use.

You also may want to change the chart type of an existing chart. You can do so with Chart⇨Chart Type. Follow these steps when you want to change the type of an existing chart:

1. If the chart is on a chart sheet, click on the sheet's tab to make the chart active. If the chart is embedded in a worksheet, click on the chart to select it.

2. Choose Chart⇨Chart Type. (Alternatively, you can right-click in an empty space on the chart and choose Chart Type from the shortcut menu.) The Chart Type dialog box appears, as shown in Figure 19-19.

3. In the Chart Type list box, choose the desired chart type.

4. In the Chart Sub-type area of the dialog box, choose a desired subtype and then click on the OK button.

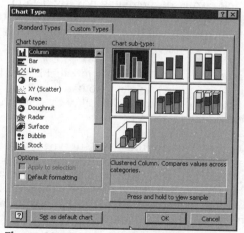

Figure 19-19: The Standard Types tab of the Chart Type dialog box.

The exact appearance of the Sub-type tab will vary, depending on which type you select. Figure 19-20 shows the available sub-types that appear when you choose a Pie chart.

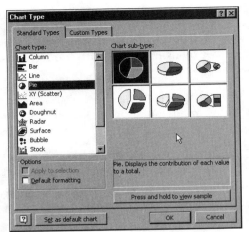

Figure 19-20: The available sub-types for a pie chart.

In the Chart Type dialog box shown in Figure 19-20, note the presence of the Apply to Selection option in the lower-left corner of the dialog box. By default, the chart type you've selected applies to the entire chart. If you select a single data series before using the Chart Type command, you will have the option of applying the chart type to the selected data series as opposed to the entire chart.

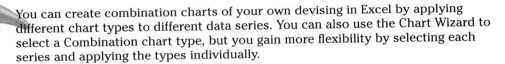

You can create combination charts of your own devising in Excel by applying different chart types to different data series. You can also use the Chart Wizard to select a Combination chart type, but you gain more flexibility by selecting each series and applying the types individually.

If you need to change the type of chart but not the chart subtype, you can also use the Chart toolbar. To display the Chart toolbar, choose View➪Toolbars then select Chart from the submenu which appears. Click on the Chart Type arrow button to drop down a list of chart types. Select a chart type from the list. If you select an individual data series before using the Chart Type list box in the Chart toolbar, your selection gets applied to the individual data series.

Understanding How Excel Plots a Chart

When you select a group of cells and create a new chart, Excel follows specific steps to plot the chart. It first organizes the values contained within the selected range into a data series, based on the responses that you gave in the Chart Wizard dialog boxes. It then plots the data series in the chart.

As an example, consider the chart shown in Figure 19-21. In this chart, the light markers are based on one series of data, the sales for January. The dark markers are based on another series of data, the sales for February. In the same chart, dollar amounts are plotted along the value axis, and subdivision names are plotted along the category axis. The chart values appear as dollars because the worksheet values are formatted in dollars. Excel obtains the category axis labels from cells A2 through A5 of the worksheet shown earlier in Figure 19-9, which contains the names of the subdivisions.

At this point, the column chart that you created earlier (similar to the one shown in Figure 19-10) may still be open on your screen. If it isn't, plot the chart again by selecting cells A1 through D5 in the House Sales worksheet. Then choose Insert⇨Chart. Click on the Finish button in the first Chart Wizard dialog box to accept the default options.

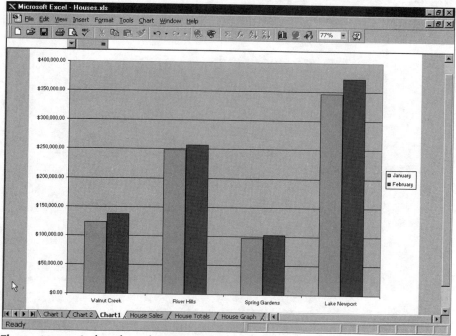

Figure 19-21: A chart based on two data series.

The exact points that Excel uses to graph the data are contained in a *series formula* that Excel builds for you. A series formula is similar to other formulas in that you can it edit from within the formula bar. To see the formula, you must first select the chart marker by clicking on the desired group of markers or by pressing the left- or right-arrow key repeatedly until the desired group of markers is selected. When you select a group of markers, Excel places small rectangles inside them.

As an exercise, you can select the markers representing the Lake Newport home sales by clicking on any of the markers for Lake Newport. When the markers are selected, the series formula appears in the formula bar, as shown in Figure 19-22.

Excel uses a special function called the *series function* to build the data series for each set of markers in the chart. If you click on the second set of markers in the chart, the series formula in the formula bar changes to reflect the points that Excel uses for the second data series.

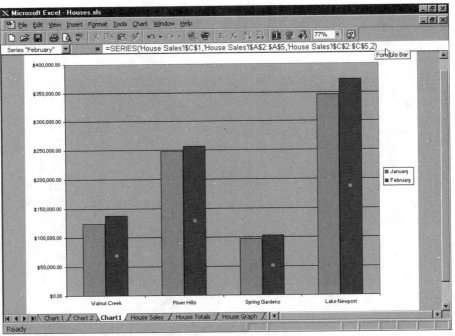

Figure 19-22: The series formula for Lake Newport sales.

Excel can use named ranges from a worksheet rather than absolute cell references so that you can make use of named ranges in your worksheets. If you create a chart that uses absolute references and you later insert rows or columns in the worksheet so that the data referred to by the chart is no longer in the same location, the chart will be unable to plot the data. The result will be a chart with zero values, or even worse, a chart with incorrect data. If you use named ranges in the series formula for the chart, Excel can find the data, even if you insert rows or columns in the worksheet.

It is important to understand how Excel builds a chart automatically because, in some cases, Excel's assumptions may not be what you want, and you can make changes to adjust for those assumptions. For example, when you tell Excel to create a chart and you accept the default entries regarding the data series in the Chart Wizard dialog boxes, Excel plots the data based on certain default assumptions. One significant decision that Excel makes is whether a data series should be based on the contents of rows or columns. Excel assumes that a chart should contain fewer data series than data points within each series. When you tell Excel to create the chart, Excel examines your selected range of cells. If the selected range is wider than it is tall, Excel organizes the data series based on the contents of rows. On the other hand, if the selected range is taller than it is wide, Excel organizes the data series based on the contents of the columns.

To illustrate this operation, consider the worksheet shown in Figure 19-23. In this example, the selected range of cells to be plotted is wider than it is tall. With this type of selection, Excel uses any text found in the leftmost columns as series names. Text labels in the top row are used as categories, and each row becomes a data series in the chart.

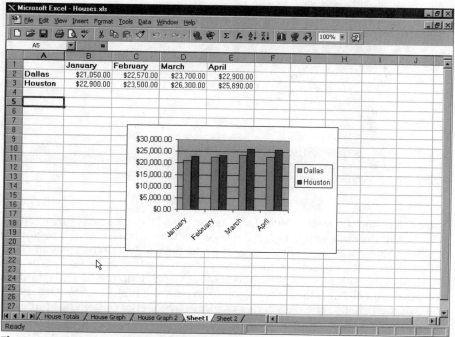

Figure 19-23: A chart oriented by rows.

If the data to be plotted is square (the number of rows is equal to the number of columns) and you accept the default options in the Chart Source Data dialog box of the Chart Wizard (the second dialog box), Excel handles the orientation of the chart in the same manner. On the other hand, if the selected range is taller than it is wide and you accept the default Chart Wizard options, Excel orients the chart differently. In such cases, the text in the top row is used as the series names, text entries appearing in the left columns are used as categories, and each column becomes a data series. This type of worksheet, and the chart resulting from it, are shown in Figure 19-24.

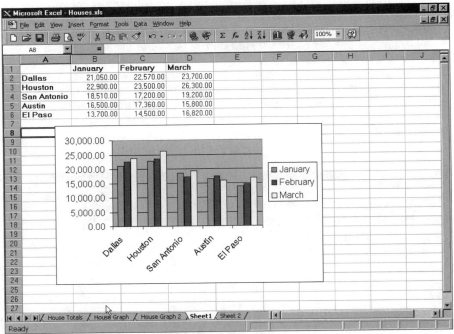

Figure 19-24: A chart oriented by columns.

You can change the method that Excel uses to plot the data series by changing the selection in the Data Range tab of the second Chart Wizard dialog box. With an existing chart, make the chart active (if it's an embedded chart, you can click on it; with a chart that's on a sheet, make that sheet the active worksheet). Then click on the Chart Wizard button on the Chart toolbar to bring up the Chart Wizard dialog box. After you click on the Next button to bypass the first Chart Wizard dialog box, you can then change the data series used by Excel in the Data Range tab of the dialog box that appears, by choosing Series in Rows or Series in Columns.

Summary

In this chapter, you learned how to create charts, how to change the appearance and the basis for the charts, and how to add such items as titles, legends, and text to your charts. The following points were covered:

✦ You can add a chart as an embedded chart (included in an existing worksheet page) or as a chart sheet (included on its own worksheet page).

✦ You can easily add charts to a worksheet by selecting the range of data, clicking on the Chart Wizard button on the Standard toolbar, and following the instructions in the wizard dialog boxes.

✦ You can modify most aspects of a chart by right-clicking on a specific area or object in the chart and the appropriate Format command from the shortcut menu that appears.

In the next chapter, you will learn about the various printing options in Excel, which provide you with different ways to produce your work.

Where to go next...

✦ Many times you'll find yourself creating your chart in Excel — and then later find you need to use the chart in a Word document. You can do this with Object Linking and Embedding (OLE). See Chapter 50 for the story.

✦ Often times you may need to embellish your charts by adding graphics, such as clip art or callouts. For tips on working with graphics, see Chapter 18.

✦   ✦   ✦

Printing with Excel

With Excel, you can print in several ways with typeset-quality results from most laser printers. You have full control over different aspects of printing that affect the appearance of a worksheet, such as margins, page orientation, horizontal and vertical alignment, and the use of headers and footers. You can also do much more than just print pages from a single workbook. You have the flexibility to print entire workbooks, sheets from a workbook, or a section of a sheet. You can access these options via the Print button on the Standard toolbar or by choosing File⇔Print. If you've used Excel under previous versions of Windows, you will also find that printing is considerably faster with Excel 97. (This speed is due more to the faster Print Manager in Windows 95 or Windows NT than to Excel itself.)

The Basics of Printing

Because Excel makes several assumptions about how you want information printed when you choose File⇔Print or when you click on the Print button on the Standard toolbar, you can perform basic printing with just a few steps. These steps are as follows (you'll learn about each step as you work through this chapter):

1. Select the area that you want to print. (If you don't select an area, Excel prints all the data in the worksheet.)

2. Choose File⇔Print to open the Print dialog box, as shown in Figure 20-1.

3. Use the options in the dialog box to decide what you want to print (the current selection, selected sheets, or the entire workbook), a range of pages (the default is All), and the number of copies.

4. Click on the OK button to begin the printing process.

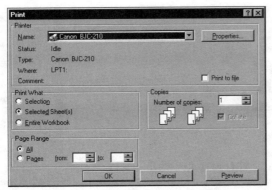

Figure 20-1: The Print dialog box.

If you are sure that you can live with the default options that normally appear in the Print dialog box, you can make the process of printing even faster. Just select the tab of the worksheet that you want printed and click on the Print button on the Standard toolbar.

If you have multiple sheets that you want to print one after the other in a workbook by clicking on the Print button only once, you can easily do so. Click on the tab of the first worksheet that you want to print and then hold down the Ctrl key while you click on each additional worksheet tab that you want to print. When you have selected all the desired tabs, click on the Print button on the Standard toolbar.

About the Print dialog box

After you choose File⇨Print, you see the Print dialog box, which provides many useful options. In the Printer list box, you can choose any printer that you have installed under Windows. In the Print What area, you can choose Selection to print a selected area of a worksheet, Active Sheet(s) to print all the selected worksheets in a workbook or Entire Workbook to print all the data stored in all pages of the workbook.

In the Page Range area of the dialog box, the All option (the default) prints all pages. If you select the Page(s) option instead, enter a range of pages in the from and to boxes. This option works well when you know precisely which pages you want to print. For example, if you know that a worksheet produces a 12-page print run in its entirety and you know that you need only pages 4 through 8 of that print run, you can turn on the Page(s) option and enter **4** in the from box and **8** in the to box.

In the Copies area, you can enter the number of copies that you want, and you can turn on the Collate option if you want the multiple copies to print in collated order.

About the Page Setup dialog box

You can use Excel's Page Setup dialog box to change a variety of settings that will affect your printing of worksheets. After you choose File⇨Page Setup, the Page Setup dialog box appears, as shown in Figure 20-2. This dialog box contains four tabs that affect four different areas of Excel printing: Page, Margins, Header/Footer, and Sheet. In addition to the tabs, the dialog box contains Print and Print Preview buttons. After making the desired changes to the settings, you can click on the Print button to begin printing, or you can click on the Print Preview button to see the worksheet in Print Preview mode.

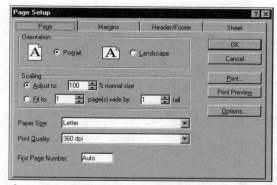

Figure 20-2: The Page tab of the Page Setup dialog box.

The Page tab options

You can use the Page tab's options to control print-related settings that affect all the pages of a print job, such as page orientation and paper size. The Page tab options include:

✦ **Orientation** — In the Orientation area, choose whether to print in *portrait* (default) or *landscape* orientation. Think of a photograph: a portrait is taller than it is wide, whereas a picture of a beautiful mountain scene is wider than it is tall. So it goes with printing: portrait orientation prints lengthwise (like the pages of this book), whereas landscape orientation prints sideways on the paper.

✦ **Scaling** — Use the options in the Scaling area to reduce or enlarge your worksheets. These options are useful for making a worksheet that is slightly too big for a page fit on a single page. You can choose a percentage in the Adjust to list box, or you can use the Fit to option to fit the printed worksheet to a specific number of pages wide by a specific number of pages tall by entering the dimensions in the boxes to the right of the option.

✦ **Paper Size** — Use the Paper Size option to set the paper size. By default, the paper size is Letter (8.5 × 11 inches).

✦ **Print Quality** — Use the Print Quality option to set the level of print quality. The higher the setting, the nicer the appearance; however, in many cases, your printer takes longer to print documents at higher settings.

✦ **First Page Number** — Use the First Page Number setting to start printing at a page other than page 1. The Auto default assumes that you want to start at page 1, but you can replace this entry by typing any number that you want into the box.

The Margins tab options

When you click on the Margins tab of the Page Setup dialog box, you see the options shown in Figure 20-3. You can use the Margins tab's options to control the settings that affect each page's margins, such as the size of the margins and whether printing is centered horizontally or vertically between margins.

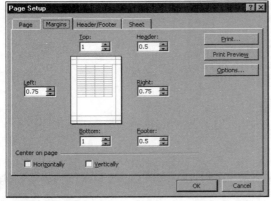

Figure 20-3: The Margins tab of the Page Setup dialog box.

The Margins tab options include the following:

✦ **Top, Bottom, Left, and Right** — Use the Top, Bottom, Left, and Right options to specify a distance from the edge of the paper for the margins. Note that many laser printers will not print closer than 0.5 inch from the edge of the paper.

✦ **Header and Footer** — Use the settings in the Header and Footer areas to indicate how far headers or footers should print from the top or bottom edges.

✦ **Center on Page** — The Center on Page options determine whether printing should be centered horizontally (between the left and right margins) and vertically (between the top and bottom margins) on the page.

The Header/Footer tab options

If you click on the Header/Footer tab of the Page Setup dialog box, you see the options shown in Figure 20-4. You can use the Header/Footer tab's options to control the appearance and placement of headers and footers printed with your worksheet pages.

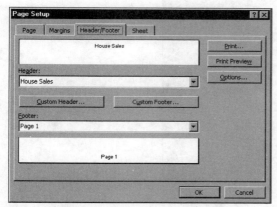

Figure 20-4: The Header/Footer tab of the Page Setup dialog box.

The Header/Footer tab options include the following:

✦ **Header and Footer** — Use the Header and Footer text boxes to specify a header (for example, a title that appears at the top of every page) or a footer (for example, a page number or the current date that appears at the bottom of every page). If you have placed a title in your worksheet, it will appear in the list box as one of your choices for a header or footer.

✦ **Custom Header and Custom Footer** — Use the Custom Header and Custom Footer buttons to open dialog boxes that enable you to design a customized header or footer.

The Sheet tab options

If you click on the Sheet tab of the Page Setup dialog box, you see the options shown in Figure 20-5. You can use the Sheet tab's options to control different print-related settings that affect individual worksheets.

The Sheet tab options include the following:

✦ **Print Area** — In the Print Area text box, you can enter a range of cells that you want to print, or you can enter the name of a named range. If you leave the entry blank, Excel prints all cells that contain data in the worksheet or workbook.

✦ **Print Titles** — In the Print Titles area, you can specify rows or columns that you would like to see repeated on every page.

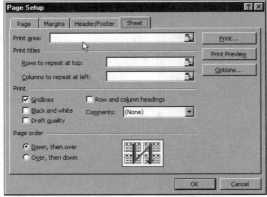

Figure 20-5: The Sheet tab of the Page Setup dialog box.

✦ **Print** — Use the options in the Print area to tell Excel how to handle the printing of certain aspects of a worksheet or workbook. You can determine whether gridlines and notes should be included in the printing; whether the printer should use a faster draft-quality printing; whether color printers should print data only in black and white, even if the cells are formatted as colors; whether row and column headings should be included, and whether the comments for the sheet will be printed, and if so, where.

✦ **Page Order** — In the Page Order area, you can specify whether printing of multiple-page worksheets should occur from top to bottom and then from left to right, or from left to right and then from top to bottom.

Setting the Print Range

When you tell Excel to print a worksheet, it prints the entire worksheet unless you tell it otherwise. When you want to print a specific portion of a worksheet, you first need to tell Excel what area of the worksheet you want printed. You can specify the portion of the worksheet by choosing File ⇨ Page Setup and using the Print Area option of the Sheet tab. To define a print range, use these steps:

1. Choose File⇨Page Setup. In the Page Setup dialog box that appears, click on the Sheet tab.

2. Click in the Print Area text box to place the insertion point there.

3. In the worksheet, select the range of cells that you want to print. (The dialog box will minimize to let you see the selections that you are making.) As you select the range, a dotted line appears around it, and the coordinates for the range appear in the Print Area text box of the Page Setup dialog box.

4. If you want to change any other options, click on the OK button to close the Page Setup dialog box, or if you want to begin printing with the other options as they are, click on the Print button in the Page Setup dialog box.

If you want to cancel the effects of the selection and go back to printing the complete worksheet, choose File⇨Page Setup and click on the Sheet tab. In the Print Area text box, delete the coordinates of the selected range and click on the OK button.

Specifying multiple print ranges

Excel lets you select several ranges of pages to print. Each range is printed on its own sheet, and can be printed with titles. You can tell Excel to print multiple worksheet page ranges by performing the following steps:

1. Choose File⇨Page Setup.

2. Select the Sheet tab of the Page Setup dialog box (see Figure 20-5).

3. Click in the Print Area box to place the insertion point there. (In the figure, the mouse pointer points to this text box.)

4. Click and drag to select the first range that you want to print.

5. Enter a colon in the Print Area text box.

6. Select the next area that you want to print.

7. Repeat Steps 5 and 6 until you select all the areas that you want to print. The areas are printed in the order that you selected them, and they are printed on separate pages.

Another method to do the same thing is to select the ranges that you want to print by using the Ctrl key to move to additional ranges. Then choose File ⇨ Print. In the Print dialog box, click on the Selection option in the Print What area and then click on the OK button to print your selection.

Previewing Print Jobs

Previewing your work before you print it is very useful because you can find mistakes in the layout of your document before you print it, so you can avoid wasting paper. You can also use the Zoom feature that allows you to take a closer look at the document and its contents.

To preview a worksheet, click on the Print Preview button on the Standard toolbar or choose File➪Print Preview to put Excel in Print Preview mode, as shown in Figure 20-6. In Print Preview mode, you can make modifications to the worksheet to further improve its appearance by clicking on the Setup button at the top of the screen to activate the Page Setup dialog box.

You can also modify the margins of your document in Print Preview by clicking on the Margins button at the top of the screen. Clicking on the Margins button activates the "margin grid" (see Figure 20-7). You can move the margin lines by using the mouse. The margin grid feature is very helpful because it lets you see the document as it is being adjusted, and you can also get an idea as to whether the document will fit on a single page. If you intend to set margins in Print Preview, you may want to use the Zoom feature by clicking on the Zoom button at the top of the Print Preview window. The Zoom feature helps you get a better look at what the margins will look like.

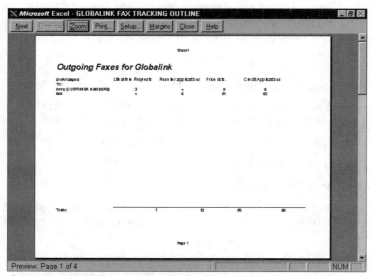

Figure 20-6: Excel's Print Preview mode.

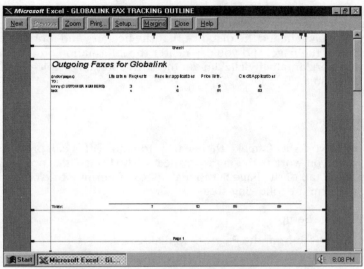

Figure 20-7: The margin grid in Print Preview mode.

Controlling Aspects of Printing

As you learned in the description of the Page Setup dialog box, many different settings are available to control margins, add titles to your worksheets, and insert headers and footers. You can also control page breaks and specify whether gridlines are included in your printed worksheets.

Before you print, you should specify the margins for the selected item that you want to print because spreadsheets have many columns and rows that often exceed the screen. Also, remember many laser and inkjet printers cannot print to the edge of the paper; therefore, you should not set margins less than 0. 5 inch. Also keep in mind that if you have headers or footers, they will automatically print 0.5 inch from the bottom or top of the page unless you change that distance when you add them.

To change the margins for your document, perform the following steps:

1. Choose File⇨Page Setup.

2. Choose the Margins tab of the Page Setup dialog box (see Figure 20-3).

3. Enter the measurements that you want in the Top, Bottom, Left, and Right text boxes. Remember to keep in mind the header, footer, and printer limitations. You can change the distance that the headers and footers appear from the edge of the page, and you can center the information on the page vertically and horizontally by clicking on the corresponding choice in the Center on Page area.

Printing titles

Printing titles on the worksheets make them easier to read. Titles can prove to be very beneficial when you work with long worksheets. The Print Titles options are available on the Sheet tab of the Page Setup dialog box. To print a title on each page of a sheet, perform the following steps:

1. Choose File⇨Page Setup.

2. Choose the Sheet tab from the Page Setup dialog box.

3. Place the insertion point in the Rows to Repeat at Top text box or the Columns to Repeat at Left text box.

4. With the mouse, select the rows or columns that you want to repeat. Move the dialog box, if necessary. (Remember that multiple rows and columns must be adjacent.)

5. Click on the OK button.

If you change your mind and you want to delete the entries that you have made as titles, simply return to the Sheet tab of the Page Setup dialog box and delete the entries that you made in the Rows to Repeat at Top and Columns to Repeat at Left text boxes.

Controlling page breaks

Sometimes automatic page breaks — which are based on paper size, margins, and other settings in the Page Setup dialog box — come at inconvenient places, especially in larger worksheets. When a page breaks at a bad location, you can fix the break by inserting a manual page break instead. Manual page breaks are especially useful when you want to print one section per page. To insert manual page breaks, perform the following steps:

1. Place the insertion point below and to the right of the place where you want to insert the page break.

2. Choose Insert⇨Page Break. The page break appears on-screen and is indicated by lines with dashes.

The page breaks that you insert remain in the same location until you remove them. The automatic page breaks are also repositioned after the insertion of a manual page break. If you want to remove a page break that you inserted, choose Insert⇨Remove Page Break. This option is available only when you return to the cell in which you entered the page break. Selecting the entire document and choosing Insert⇨Remove Page Break removes all the manual page breaks in the worksheet.

You can also set page breaks horizontally and vertically. To do so, select the column or row at which you want the page break to appear and click in its header. Next choose Insert⇨Page Break. The page break is set horizontally or vertically as you specified.

Turning the gridlines on and off

When printing a worksheet, you may need to insert manual page breaks. Sometimes these page breaks are difficult to see because of the gridlines on an Excel worksheet. To turn off the gridlines so that you can see the manual page breaks, choose Tools⇨Options. Click on the View tab and then turn off the Gridlines check box. Click on the OK button to remove the gridlines.

Printing nonconsecutive sheets

You may often have to print nonconsecutive worksheets. This is a task that Excel can easily handle in a few simple steps. Select the tab of the first sheet that you want to print, press the Ctrl key while you select the tabs of all the other worksheets that you want to print, choose File⇨Print, and select the number of copies that you want to print.

Inserting headers and footers

When you use the Page Setup dialog box, Excel lets you enter headers and footers into a worksheet or workbook that you print. Adding headers and footers is relatively simple and painless. They can be very effective in giving a document a more refined and professional look.

To add a header or footer to a worksheet, perform the following steps:

1. Choose File⇨Page Setup.
2. Choose the Header/Footer tab from the Page Setup dialog box (see Figure 20-8).

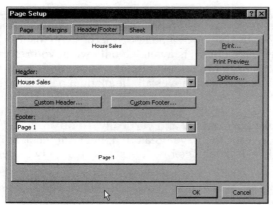

Figure 20-8: The Header/Footer tab of the Page Setup dialog box.

3. Decide whether you want to add a header or a footer to your worksheet.

4. Click on the corresponding Custom button: click the Custom Header button for headers, or click the Custom Footers button for footers. Once you click either button, another dialog box opens (similar to Figure 20-9 and titled "Header" or "Footer" depending on your choice), where you can enter your header or footer text.

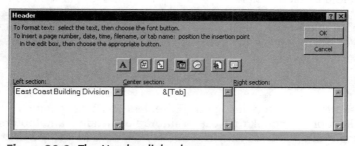

Figure 20-9: The Header dialog box.

5. In the Left Section, Center Section, or Right Section portion of the dialog box, enter the desired text of your header or footer. Use the buttons in the dialog box to add items, page numbers, insert the system date or time, or change the fonts used.

6. Click OK.

Table 20-1 explains the custom header and footer buttons that appear in the dialog box after you click on either the Custom Header or Custom Footer button on the Header/Footer tab.

Table 20-1	
Header/Footer buttons and their functions	
Button	**Function**
Font	Opens the Font dialog box from which you can change the header or footer's font.
Page Number	Inserts the page number.
Total Pages	Inserts the total number of pages in the active worksheet.
Date	Inserts the system date.
Time	Inserts the system time.
Filename	Inserts the active workbook's filename.
Sheet Name	Inserts the active worksheet's name.

Changing the Printer Properties

Selecting a printer is a simple matter in Excel, thanks to the Properties menu that now exists in Excel and other Windows 95 products. To change the printer that you use in Excel, choose File⇨Print and select the printer that you want to use from the list of printers at the top of the dialog box. If you do not see the printer that you want to use, you will need to install it. To install the printer, open the Printers folder under Windows 95 and click on the Add Printer icon to activate the Add Printer Wizard. The wizard guides you through the steps that you need to perform to add the new printer.

You can also change the options that are in effect for your printer by choosing File⇨Print. In the Print dialog box, click on the Properties button to open the Printer Properties dialog box, as shown in Figure 20-10. For many popular printers, this dialog box has four tabs. Use the Paper tab to select the paper size, the orientation, and the source of the paper. Again, keep in mind that these options vary based on the printer that you have installed.

Figure 20-10: The Paper tab of the Printer Properties dialog box.

Use the Graphics tab (see Figure 20-11) to change the intensity of the graphics that you print by adjusting the shading bar to control how dark the shadows will be when an item is printed. Making this adjustment also affects the speed with which the item is printed: the darker the shading, the slower the printing. You also use this tab when you want to speed up printing with graphics. To print graphics faster, decrease the resolution in the Resolution list box. Use the Dithering area to control the amount of space that appears between the dots in a printed item. With printers that support dithering, you can make adjustments in this area to smooth the otherwise jagged appearance of printed characters.

With many popular laser printers, the Fonts tab lets you control how your TrueType fonts are printed, as shown in Figure 20-12. To speed up the printing process, select the Download TrueType fonts as bitmap soft fonts option. In cases where the document contains graphics and some text not repeating frequently on a page, you should use the Print TrueType as graphics option instead. This option is useful in cases where you want to print graphics over text so that only the exposed part of the characters are printed (that is, the graphics partially cover the characters).

With most popular color inkjet printers, the Setting tab of the Properties dialog box (see Figure 20-13) allows you to enable or disable the Setup Analyzer, which makes sure that the settings you have in your printer driver will give you the best output. This tab includes a toggle button for the Color Advisor, a program that allows you to add custom colors to different sections with a theme, and the capability to turn on and off the Cartridge Detection, which will not allow you to print a document with color if you have a black ink cartridge in the printer. This tab also allows for the loading of the factory driver settings and the creation of custom driver settings, which you may prefer.

Figure 20-11: The Graphics tab of the Printer Properties dialog box.

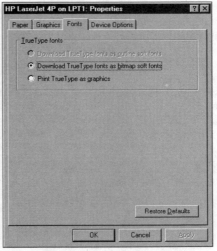

Figure 20-12: The Fonts tab of the Printer Properties dialog box.

Figure 20-13: The Setting tab of the Printer Properties dialog box.

With many popular laser printers, you can choose the Device Options tab to control printer memory tracking (see Figure 20-14). When a document is printed, the printer driver compares the amount of memory that will be used in the printing of the document and the memory that is available in the printer. Then, the printer driver decides whether there is sufficient memory to print a complex document. The nearer the tracking bar marker is to the Conservative side, the less likely it is that the printer driver will overcommit the printer and exceed its memory. In most cases, you should keep the marker in the middle. If your printer starts giving you errors when you print more complex documents, try moving the marker toward the Conservative side.

Finally, the Control tab of the Printer Properties window (shown in Figure 20-15) allows you to run printer tests, clean the printer cartridge, and turn power on and off without doing so from the printer. Keep in mind that your tabs may differ slightly, depending on what printer you are using.

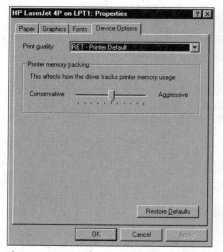

Figure 20-14: The Device Options tab of the Printer Properties dialog box.

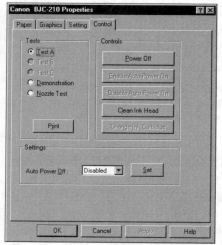

Figure 20-15: The Control tab of the Printer Properties dialog box.

Sending a File on a Network

You can also produce your workbook with the various options found under File⇨Send To. With this command, you can send the workbook to another person on a network to which your computer is attached or to another person on an online service. This option makes use of your network mail server or Microsoft Outlook (Chapter 48 details the complete use of Microsoft Outlook.)

You can send a workbook over the network by using the following steps:

1. Open the workbook that you want to send.

2. If the workbook doesn't have a routing slip attached, point to Send To on the File menu, and then click Mail Recipient. Then, address and send the mail message to whomever you want to receive the workbook.

3. If the workbook has a routing slip attached, choose File⇨SendTo, click Next Routing Recipient, and click OK.

Note This process results in the sending of the Excel workbook in an uncompressed format. If your Internet account is not an unlimited access account (or if you are using a cellular modem), the sending of uncompressed files can drive up your transmission costs.

Summary

This chapter has detailed the different features that Excel offers to help you get your facts and figures on paper. The chapter covered the following points:

✦ You can print a selected area of the current worksheet, selected sheets, or the entire workbook by choosing File⇨Print.

✦ By choosing File⇨Page Setup, you reveal the Page Setup dialog box, which lets you change various settings for printing, such as orientation, paper size, margins, headers, and footers.

✦ Excel's Print Preview feature can be very useful in helping you find errors in a document's layout before printing occurs.

✦ You can change printer properties by choosing File⇨Print and clicking the Properties button in the dialog box that appears.

✦ You can use the File⇨Send command to send a workbook to another person on a local area network.

The next chapter will explain how you can create and work with databases in Excel.

Where to go next...

✦ If you find yourself doing a lot of repetitive printing on a regular basis, you'll want to automate your printing by putting the power of macros to work. Chapter 22 tells you how.

✦ Your document's printed appearance is greatly affected by how you format that document. Formatting specifics are covered in Chapter 17.

✦ If you are in the office and need to send a sheet to another person there, take advantage of Microsoft Outlook. Chapter 48 will show you how.

✦   ✦   ✦

Working with Excel Databases

CHAPTER 21

In This Chapter

Creating a database

Adding, editing, and deleting records from the database

Finding data

Sorting data

Using the AutoFilter command to filter data

Using complex criteria with the AutoFilter command

Designing databases

This chapter details the use of databases (also called *lists*) that are stored in Excel worksheets. Whether you are aware of it or not, you have probably used databases on numerous occasions. Any time you reference a list of business contacts or a Rolodex file or something as familiar as the Yellow Pages, you are working with a database. You can use Excel to manage data in a database, and this chapter will show you how.

What Is a Database?

Although the term *database* is often used in reference to computers, it also applies to any system in which information is cataloged, stored, and used. A database is a collection of related information that is grouped as a single item. Figure 21-1 shows an example of a simple database. Metal filing cabinets containing customer records, a card file of names and phone numbers, and a notebook filled with a handwritten list of store inventory are all databases. The physical container — the filing cabinet or the notebook, for example — is not the database. The database is the contents of the container and the way the information is organized. Objects, such as cabinets and notebooks, are only tools for organizing information. Excel is one such tool for storing information.

Information in a database is usually organized and stored in a table by rows and columns. Figure 21-1, for example, is a mailing list in database form. Each row contains a name, a street address, a city, state, and a zip code. Because the mailing list is a collection of information arranged in a specific order — a column of names, a column of addresses, a column of cities, and so on — it is a database.

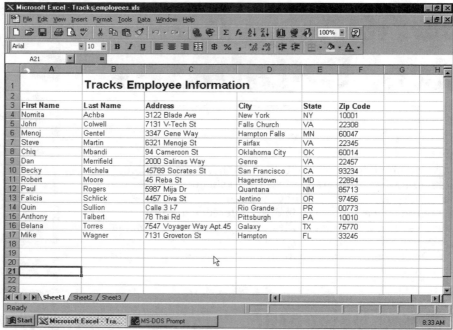

Figure 21-1: A typical database in Excel.

Rows in a database file are called *records*, and columns are called *fields*. Figure 21-2 illustrates this idea by showing an address filing system kept on file cards. Each card in the box is a single record, and each category of information on that card is a field. Fields can contain any type of information that can be categorized. In the card box, each record contains five fields: name, address, city, state, and zip code. Because every card in the box contains the same type of information, the information in the card box is a database.

In Excel, you design a database by following this row-and-column analogy, where each column of the spreadsheet contains a different field, and each row contains an additional record. You keep your data organized by devoting a specific column to each specific category (field) of data. You must enter each specific chunk of data in a separate cell of the worksheet. For example, in the worksheet shown earlier in Figure 21-1, a person's first name goes into a cell of the First Name column, the person's last name goes into a cell of the Last Name column, and so on. You can begin the design of any database by placing the cursor at the top of the worksheet and entering labels for the names of your fields in successive columns.

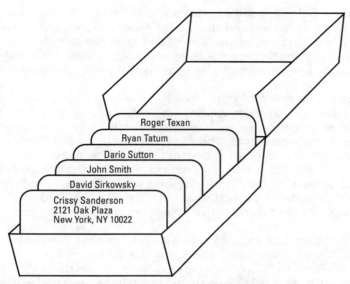

Figure 21-2: A card file shows the logical design of a database.

Creating a Database

You can create a database in an Excel worksheet by performing these steps:

1. In a blank row of the worksheet, enter the desired names of the fields.

2. In each cell of a row directly underneath the field names, type the desired entries for that field into the cell. Don't leave an empty row between the field names and the data because Excel will have problems recognizing where your database begins.

3. To add entries consisting of numbers that really should be stored as text (such as zip codes), begin the entry with an apostrophe.

When you finish adding records to your database, you'll have an organized collection of row-and-column data in a format somewhat like our example shown earlier in Figure 21-1.

Hot Stuff If you need to enter a large number of entries that comprise numbers that should be stored as text (such as zip codes or phone numbers), first format that column containing that field as text. Select the entire column (click on this column header), right-click on the column, and choose Format Cells from the shortcut menu that appears. Click on the Number tab of the Format Cells dialog box. Next, click on the Text option in the Category list box and click on the Number tab of the Format cells on the OK button. If you don't use this trick or if you begin each entry with an apostrophe instead, zip codes that begin with zeroes (such as in 00742) will appear without the zeroes, which is probably not how you want the data to appear.

Your database work will be easier for you to handle if you have only one database per worksheet. To store more than one database in a single worksheet, you would need to define database ranges for each database, a topic that adds an unnecessary layer of complexity. Because each Excel worksheet can contain up to 255 tabs, you can conveniently manage your multiple databases by placing each database on a different worksheet tab. You'll also avoid long-term organizational problems if you don't put other data below your database in the same worksheet. As the database grows, new rows will be added to the bottom of the list. If other spreadsheet data exists below the list, you'll run the risk of overwriting the existing data.

As you work with databases in Excel, keep in mind these points regarding the names of the fields. The database must have its row of field names at the top of the list, and you can't have any blank lines between the row containing the field names and the data. Also, each field name should be unique (for example, having two fields named Date would be confusing). You can have other rows above the list if you want, but only the row immediately above the data is recognized by Excel as the row containing field names. Field names can include up to 255 characters, although for readability reasons you'll probably want to keep your field names relatively short.

Avoid putting other important data (such as formulas) to the left or to the right of your database. If you later use Excel's AutoFilter capability to filter the data in the database, the other data may be hidden.

Creating databases was a lot harder in my old version of Excel...

If you've upgraded from Excel 4.0 and you have worked with databases in the older version, you'll recall things being considerably more complicated. In Excel 4.0 and earlier versions, you had to define a specific range for your data to occupy (called a database range). When you wanted to retrieve specific data, you had to tell Excel what data you wanted by setting up a criteria range and an extract range. You can still use these old methods in the current version of Excel, but the new approach is much easier to use. Excel now makes intelligent guesses regarding your database range (the size of the database) and provides a data form and an AutoFilter capability that you can use to enter criteria and retrieve desired data.

Working with Database Records

You can add and edit records by typing the desired data directly into the cells, and you can delete rows from your database by selecting the unwanted row and choosing Edit⇨Delete. However, most users find basic data entry and editing easier when they use a *data form*, a convenient form that Excel provides for you to enter and display data. To display a data form on-screen, place the cursor in any cell of your database and choose Data⇨Form. A data form that contains the fields of your database appears, such as the one in Figure 21-3.

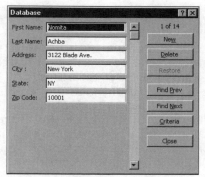

Figure 21-3: A sample data form for a database.

Adding new records

To add a record, click on the New button in the data form. When you do so, the entries in the fields of the form appear blank, and you can type the desired data into each field. Repeat this process for each record that you want to add to the database.

Hot Stuff
If you're adding new records to an existing database, don't be concerned about the order of the records in the database. You can always sort the database to put the records in any order that you want (see "Sorting a Database" later in the chapter).

Editing records

To edit a record by using the data form, first use the Find Next or Find Prev(ious) buttons to locate the desired record, or you can use the scrollbars or the up- and down-arrow keys to find the appropriate record. In a large database, you can also use the Criteria button to perform a search. When the desired record appears, click in the appropriate fields and make the desired edits.

Deleting records

To delete a record by using the data form, first use the Find Next or Find Prev(ious) buttons to locate the desired record. When the record appears, click on the Delete button in the data form.

Hot Stuff If you have a large number of records to delete, it may be faster *not* to use a data form. Instead, you can use Excel's AutoFilter capability (discussed later in this chapter) to display all the records that you want to delete. Then, you drag across the row headers to select the records. With all the desired rows selected, choose the Delete command from the Edit menu.

Finding data by using criteria

Another way to locate data in a database is to specify *criteria* in a data form. The criteria identifies the specific data that you want to find. For example, in a large database of names and addresses, you may want to locate all records in a particular city. Excel also lets you make use of *computed criteria* to find records that pass certain tests based on the contents of a formula. By using computed criteria with a database of expenses, for example, you can find all expenses that exceed $500 by entering >**500**. When you specify computed criteria in a data form, you make use of Excel's *comparison operators* (the same ones that you can use as part of formulas in the cells of a worksheet). Table 21-1 lists the comparison operators that you can use.

Table 21-1 Comparison operators	
Operator	**Function**
<	Less than
>	Greater than
=	Equal to
<>	Not equal to
<=	Less than or equal to
>=	Greater than or equal to

Follow these steps to find individual records in a database by using criteria:

1. Place the cursor anywhere in the database
2. Choose Data⇨Form to bring up a data form on-screen.

3. Click on the Criteria button in the data form. When you do this, the data form changes in appearance to resemble the one shown in Figure 21-4. The data form now says Criteria in the upper-right corner, and the Criteria button on the data form changes into the Form button.

4. Enter the desired criteria in the appropriate fields. You need to fill in only the fields on which you want to base the search. For example, if you want to search for all San Francisco records, you would enter **San Francisco** in the City field of the form.

Figure 21-4: The Criteria mode of the data form.

5. Press Enter or click on the Form button to return to the original data form.

6. Use the Find Next and Find Prev(ious) buttons in the data form to locate the records that match the desired criteria.

7. When you are finished examining the records, click on the Close button.

You can also use *wildcards* to represent characters in your criteria. You can use the question mark to represent a single character, and you can use the asterisk (*) to represent multiple characters. As an example, the criteria **H?ll** in a Name field would locate names such as *Hall*, *Hill*, and *Hull*. The criteria entry ***der** would locate all strings of text ending with the letters *der* such as *chowder* and *loader*.

Hot Stuff If you're familiar with databases in general, you may be wondering how you can perform searches based on multiple criteria, where you find records based on more than a single argument. In some cases, you'll want to find records by using *and-based criteria*, where one condition *and* another condition meet certain requirements. You can easily search on multiple criteria by entering multiple conditions in the different fields of the data form while in Criteria mode. For example, in a table of names and addresses, you may want to find a record that contains the last name Rogers and the city Quantana. Figure 21-5 shows a data form that is set up to search on these criteria.

This data form business is nice, but how do I get a report?

How can you get a printed copy of all records that meet a certain criteria? You can't use the data form to isolate and print a group of records, but you can filter the data in a database by using Excel's AutoFilter command. After you filter the records to show the ones that you want, you can just print the worksheet to produce a report. For details, see "Using the AutoFilter Command" later in this chapter.

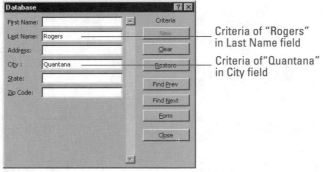

Criteria of "Rogers" in Last Name field

Criteria of "Quantana" in City field

Figure 21-5: The data form set up in Criteria mode to search for multiple criteria.

When you use *or-based criteria*, things become a little more complex. Or-based criteria describe those cases where the contents of a field meets one criteria *or* another criteria. For example, you may want to find records where the City field contains San Francisco *or* San Diego. Unfortunately, you can't do searches with or-based criteria by using a data form, but you can use Excel's AutoFilter command.

Using the AutoFormat Command on Your Database

You can quickly improve the appearance of your database by using Excel's AutoFormat command. As detailed in Chapter 17, AutoFormat applies automatic formatting to parts or all of your worksheet to give the worksheet a presentation-quality appearance quickly.

To apply automatic formatting to a database, place the cursor anywhere within the database and then choose Format⇨AutoFormat. In the AutoFormat dialog box, choose one of the available formats in the list box and then click on the OK button to apply the formatting. If you don't like the effects of the formatting, you can always choose the Undo AutoFormat command from the Edit menu to reverse the effects.

Sorting a Database

After you compile a database, you may need to arrange it in various ways. You can arrange a database by sorting, which changes the order of the records. When Excel sorts a database, it rearranges all records in the database according to a specified new order. If you sorted a database of names alphabetically, the sorted database would contain all the records that were in the old database, but the names would be arranged in alphabetic order.

Danger Zone When you sort fields that contain dates or times, Excel sorts correctly if the data is in an acceptable date or time format. If you use some format of your own devising that Excel doesn't recognize to store dates or times, Excel will sort the data as text, and you probably won't get the results that you want.

When Excel sorts a database in ascending order, it sorts by numbers first, followed by text, and then the logical values True or False. Excel is not case-sensitive: it ignores both case and accent marks while sorting. Blank cells appear at the end of the sort, whether you are sorting in ascending or descending order. You must choose a field, called the *key field*, on which to sort. In some cases, you may need to sort a database on more than one field. For example, if you sort a database alphabetically by using Last Name as the key field, you get groups of records with the last names arranged alphabetically but with the first names in random order. In such a case, you can sort the database by using Last Name as the first key field and First Name as the second key field. To sort a database, use Data⇨Sort.

You can sort your database by performing these steps:

1. If you just want to sort a specific number of rows in your database, select those rows by dragging across the row headers. If you want to sort the entire database, place the cursor anywhere within the database.

2. Choose Data⇨Sort to open the Sort dialog box, as shown in Figure 21-6.

Figure 21-6: The Sort dialog box.

3. In the Sort By area of the dialog box, choose a desired field to sort on from the list and select the Ascending or Descending option to specify the direction of the sort.

4. If you want to use additional fields as the basis for the sort, fill in the Then By area of the dialog box as indicated in Step 3. When you sort on multiple fields, the Sort By list box takes first priority in the sort followed by the first Then By list box and then the second Then By list box.

5. If you did not select a range of rows to sort, make sure that the Header Row option at the bottom of the dialog box remains selected. This option tells Excel not to include the header row, which contains the field names, in the sort.

6. Click on the OK button to perform the sort.

Figure 21-7 shows the effects of sorting. At top, you see a database that contains records entered in random order. At bottom, you see the same database that has been sorted by State and, where State values are equal, by City fields.

Excel users have been known to get less than desirable results from a sort because sorting involves a major rearrangement of data, and there's always a possibility that you'll make a selection that causes Excel to sort your data in a way that you didn't expect. If you have any doubts about how a sort will turn out, it may be a wise idea to save the workbook under a different name. (Choose File⇨Save As and enter a different name for the workbook file in the Save As dialog box.) If you later perform a sort that produces undesirable results, and you're unable to undo the sort, you can always load the original file to get your unchanged data back.

You can quickly sort a database on any single field in ascending or descending order by placing the cursor in any desired field and clicking on the Sort Ascending or Sort Descending button on the Standard toolbar.

	A	B	C	D	E	F	G
1			Tracks Employee Information				
2							
3	First Name	Last Name	Address	City	State	Zip Code	
4	Nomita	Achba	3122 Blade Ave	New York	NY	10001	
5	John	Colwell	7131 V-Tech St	Falls Church	VA	22308	
6	Menoj	Gentel	3347 Gene Way	Hampton Falls	MN	60047	
7	Steve	Martin	6321 Menoje St	Fairfax	VA	22345	
8	Chiq	Mbandi	94 Cameroon St	Oklahoma City	OK	60014	
9	Dan	Merrifield	2000 Salinas Way	Genre	VA	22457	
10	Becky	Michela	45789 Socrates St	San Francisco	CA	93234	
11	Robert	Moore	45 Reba St	Hagerstown	MD	22894	
12	Paul	Rogers	5987 Mija Dr	Quantana	NM	85713	
13	Falicia	Schlick	4457 Diva St	Jentino	OR	97456	
14	Quin	Sullion	Calle 3 l-7	Rio Grande	PR	00773	
15	Anthony	Talbert	78 Thai Rd	Pittsburgh	PA	10010	
16	Belana	Torres	7547 Voyager Way Apt.45	Galaxy	TX	75770	
17	Mike	Wagner	7131 Groveton St	Hampton	FL	33245	
18							
19							
20							
21							
22							
23							

Sheet1 / Sheet2 / Sheet3

	A	B	C	D	E	F	G
1			Tracks Employee Information				
2							
3	First Name	Last Name	Address	City	State	Zip Code	
4	Becky	Michela	45789 Socrates St	San Francisco	CA	93234	
5	Mike	Wagner	7131 Groveton St	Hampton	FL	33245	
6	Robert	Moore	45 Reba St	Hagerstown	MD	22894	
7	Menoj	Gentel	3347 Gene Way	Hampton Falls	MN	60047	
8	Paul	Rogers	5987 Mija Dr	Quantana	NM	85713	
9	Nomita	Achba	3122 Blade Ave	New York	NY	10001	
10	Chiq	Mbandi	94 Cameroon St	Oklahoma City	OK	60014	
11	Falicia	Schlick	4457 Diva St	Jentino	OR	97456	
12	Anthony	Talbert	78 Thai Rd	Pittsburgh	PA	10010	
13	Quin	Sullion	Calle 3 l-7	Rio Grande	PR	00773	
14	Belana	Torres	7547 Voyager Way Apt.45	Galaxy	TX	75770	
15	Steve	Martin	6321 Menoje St	Fairfax	VA	22345	
16	John	Colwell	7131 V-Tech St	Falls Church	VA	22308	
17	Dan	Merrifield	2000 Salinas Way	Genre	VA	22457	
18							
19							
20							
21							
22							
23							

Sheet1 / Sheet2 / Sheet3

Figure 21-7: Top: A database containing records in random order.
Bottom: The same database containing records sorted by State and City fields.

If you make a selection before sorting (as opposed to sorting the entire list by just placing the cursor anywhere within the list), make sure that you select all the data that you want sorted. If you select most columns and leave some adjacent columns containing data unselected, the sort will affect only the data in the selected columns. The result will be a seriously garbled database. When selecting data for sorting purposes, the safest method is to drag across row headings. In this way, you're assured of selecting all data in the rows.

Occasionally you may need to sort a database on more than three fields. Suppose that you have a large mailing list in Excel, and you want to sort the database by State, then by City within each state, then by Last Name within each city, and then by First Name within each group of last names. Because Excel provides only three fields from which to select in the Sort dialog box, this type of sort appears to be impossible. In fact, Excel can handle such a task if you break down the job into multiple sorts. Begin with the least important group of sorts and progress toward the most important group of sorts. Put the most important field first within each group of sorts. In the example, you would first sort by using the Last Name field as the first field and the First Name field as the second field. Then you would perform another sort by using the State field as the first field, the City field as the second field, and the Last Name field as the third field.

Sorting bizarre numbers

Many years ago, one of the authors worked as a service technician for a copier manufacturer, and that company used part numbers made up of alphanumeric combinations of varying widths. A list of such part numbers contained entries like the following:

1R9

4R32

12P182

67S2024

109P182

If you have a database that contains alphanumeric records like this one and you do a sort based on the value, you get results that aren't what you really want. Using the preceding list, Excel puts 12P182 above 1R9, even though in the company's grand scheme of things, 1R9 is a lower part number than 12P182. This is because, in this case, the part numbers actually consist of three component parts: a number of one or more digits, followed by a letter, followed by another multi-digit number. In such a list, all parts beginning with the number 1 would appear first in the sorted list, followed by all parts beginning with the number 2, all parts beginning with the number 3, and so on.

You can correctly sort this type of a list by breaking the codes into their component parts and using a separate cell for each part. Storing each of these components in a separate cell and sorting based on all three cells would solve the problem.

Can you undo the effects of a sort? Maybe

If you sort a database and then go on to do other things with the data, you cannot later undo the effects of the sort. (The Undo command works only if you perform it as the first action after the sort.) If you want to retain your database in the manner in which the records were originally entered, you have two options. You can save the database elsewhere (under another worksheet tab or under another file name) and recall that worksheet if you want to see how the database was originally organized. This approach has problems, however, because it is difficult to keep two databases containing the same data updated. A better approach is to add a column of record numbers to the database. The first record entered becomes record 1, the second record entered becomes record 2, and so on. If you ever want to reorganize the database in the order that the records were originally entered, simply sort on the field that contains the record numbers. You can choose Edit ➪ Fill ➪ Series to fill a column with sequential numbers, as detailed in Chapter 16.

Using the AutoFilter Command

For setting more complex retrieval criteria than is possible with the data form (and for printing reports based on selected data), you can make use of Excel's AutoFilter capability. The AutoFilter command lets you define criteria to filter your database so that only records meeting the specified criteria appear.

The AutoFilter command is a *toggle*, which means that after you turn it on, it's on until you turn it off. If you see a drop-down list box next to each field name or if you see a check mark next to the AutoFilter command after you choose Data ➪ Filter, you know that the AutoFilter command is still on. Turn the option off to clear the previous filters and then turn it on again to use AutoFilter on your database.

You can put an AutoFilter into effect on a database by performing these steps:

1. Place the cursor anywhere in the database.

2. Choose Data➪Filter➪AutoFilter.

3. A drop-down list box appears next to each field name in the database (see Figure 21-8). You can use these list boxes to filter out rows of the database that don't match specified criteria.

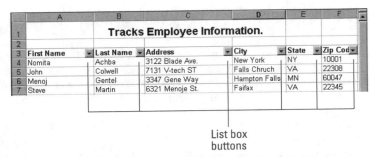

List box
buttons

Figure 21-8: List boxes made visible by using the AutoFilter command.

4. Click on the drop-down list box for the field that you want to filter and choose the entry that you want to use as the filter. You can also select the Custom option from the drop-down list box to create more complex criteria, as described later in this section.

As you make your desired selections from the drop-down list boxes, Excel filters the records according to your selections. You can create and-based criteria by choosing filters from more than one field. For example, in Figure 21-9, a VA filter is used in the State field, and a Genre filter is used in the City field. In this case, choosing VA in the State field is not enough because records would appear from all cities in Virginia. If you choose multiple conditions, records must meet all of the conditions before they will be visible in the database after the AutoFilter is in effect.

First Name	Last Name	Address	City	State	Zip Cod
		Tracks Employee Information.			
Dan	Merrifield	2000 Salinas Way	Genre	VA	22457

Figure 21-9: An example of AutoFilter used on two fields of a database.

Keeping a filtered copy of data handy

You may find it useful to keep a copy of data that you filter from a database. For example, perhaps you'll want to refer often during the week to a listing of records that meet a certain condition. First use AutoFilter to filter the desired records and then select all the records and choose Edit⟹Copy. Move to another worksheet where you want to place a copy of the data and choose Edit⟹Paste to place a copy of the filtered data there.

Printing a report based on specific data

The AutoFilter capability makes it easy to get a report of records from your database that meet a specified condition. After you have filtered your database using the AutoFilter command and the records are visible, you can print them by choosing File⇨Print or by clicking on the Print button on the Standard toolbar. The printout contains the filtered records. Before the addition of Excel's AutoFilter command, you would have had to use some of Excel's advanced database features to declare a criteria range and an extract range to manage the same sort of task. Because that process is no longer necessary (except in very specialized cases), we won't bore you with the sordid details here. If you're curious, you can find specifics in the Excel Help files.

Using complex criteria with AutoFilter

You can also make use of complex criteria (such as records falling within a certain range, records that use computed criteria, or records meeting or-based conditions) with AutoFilter. You can use complex criteria by clicking on the Custom option that appears in the drop-down list boxes in the filtered database. After clicking on the Custom option, the Custom AutoFilter dialog box appears, as shown in Figure 21-10.

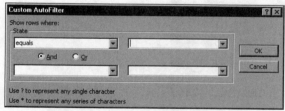

Figure 21-10: The Custom AutoFilter dialog box.

You can use the options in this dialog box to specify ranges of acceptable data and to specify or-based criteria (such as all records with a State value of CA or TX). Choose a desired comparison operator from the first drop-down list box and then enter a desired value in the text box to its right. To add a second comparison, click on the And or the Or button as desired, and use the second drop-down list box and the second text box for the other desired value.

You can see examples of the use of complex criteria by examining the dialog boxes shown in Figure 21-11. At right, the expressions >=M and <=Zz are used to retrieve all last names that start with M through Z. Note the addition of the second z. If this z were omitted, the criteria would actually find all names beginning with M through the letter Z alone, but the criteria would find no names of more than one character beginning with Z. In the middle dialog box, the expression >=40 retrieves all records with a value equal to or over 40 in the Amount field of an Expenses database. At left, the expressions =San Francisco or =San Diego retrieve all entries with either of these city names.

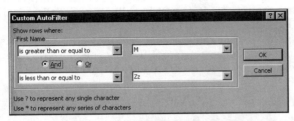

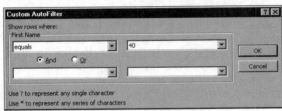

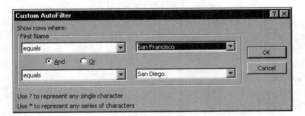

Figure 21-11: Top Complex criteria for retrieving all records with last names starting with letters from M through Z. Middle: Complex criteria for retrieving all records with a value over 40 in the Amount field. Bottom: Complex criteria for retrieving all records with San Francisco or San Diego in the City field.

Keep in mind that you can use the Custom option in more than one field. By specifying Custom options in multiple fields, you can filter data based on complex criteria. To clear the effects of a Custom option, choose the All option from the drop-down list.

Turning off the effects of AutoFilter

When you're finished working with a filtered subset of records, remember to turn off the AutoFilter command by choosing Data⇨Filter⇨AutoFilter. Alternatively, you can also open the drop-down list boxes for any filters that you have set and choose the All option from each of the lists.

When is Excel's database power not enough?

Years ago, computer pundits would occasionally make light of the fact that the world's most popular database manager, Lotus 1-2-3, wasn't a database management software package at all. In today's Windows-dominated world, Excel may reign as the most popular spreadsheet, but one fact hasn't changed: thousands of spreadsheet users still get by with spreadsheet packages as their preferred database managers. A thought worth considering is at what point do your database needs outgrow Excel? If you cross that point and you stick with Excel as a database manager, you're making unnecessary work for yourself. As an obvious example, take this simple list of sales data for a small mail-order operation:

Date	Name	Phone	Item	Cost
6/15/95	Smith, R.	723-1020	calendar	18.00
6/15/95	Williams, E.	853-6723	calendar	18.00
6/16/95	Smith, R.	723-1020	padfolio	21.00
6/16/95	Smith, R.	723-1020	organizer	16.50

What may look like a simple, effective list is in reality (to a professional database developer's eye) the beginnings of a logistical nightmare. This kind of data cries out for normalization, or the separation of data into individual tables, with relationships established between the tables. This is something that isn't possible with Excel but falls right in line with the power of a relational database manager, such as Microsoft Access. If you find yourself regularly entering any kind of data entry in your Excel databases — the same employee names, customer names, item numbers, or descriptions — over and over, trust us. You're using the wrong product for your database management needs.

Another qualification is if your database grows into thousands of records. Such a massive amount of data puts unusual demands on the database power of a spreadsheet. If you need to use a relational database manager, Microsoft Access is an excellent choice: Access is designed to work well with the other Microsoft Office applications. You can move your existing Excel data directly into a table of an Access database. You can then split the table into two or more tables and establish relationships between the tables (that pesky normalization process again). As a database developer for over a decade, I can tell you that Access is one outstanding product (and no, Microsoft isn't paying me to say this).

Performing a Mail Merge with Excel Data

More Info If you have names and addresses stored in an Excel database, you can combine the power of Excel and Word to create a mail merge document that you can use to generate form letters and envelopes. Much of what you do to handle this task is specific to Word, so we give it much more detail in the Word section of this book (see Chapter 6). However, in a nutshell, you use the following steps to generate form letters by using a mailing list stored in Excel:

1. Use Excel's AutoFilter command, if necessary, to show only those records for which you want to print form letters.

2. Select the entire range of data that contains the records.

3. Choose Edit➪Copy.

4. Use the usual Windows technique to switch to Word for Windows and open a new document.

5. Choose Edit➪Paste. When you do this, the data from Excel appears in a table in the Word document.

6. Save the Word document under any desired file name.

7. Open the document that is the basis for the mail merge (or create a new document with the desired text).

8. Choose Tools➪Mail Merge to display the Mail Merge Helper dialog box.

9. Follow the instructions that appear in the dialog box. When you are asked for a data source, choose the Word document that contains the data from Excel.

Designing Databases

Planning is vital to effective database management. Many users create a database and store data in that database only to discover later that the database doesn't provide all the necessary information. Correcting mistakes that you make during the design of a database can become a tedious job. To avoid such time-consuming mistakes, you should give some thought to how you design your database within Excel.

Database design requires that you think about how the data should be stored and about how you and others will ask for data from the database file. During this design process, your business needs (which Excel's database capabilities can help solve) should be outlined on paper. Just as you would not haphazardly toss a bunch of files into a filing cabinet without designing some type of filing system, you should not place information into a database without first designing the database. As you do so, you must define the kinds of information that should be stored in the database.

About data and attributes

Data and attributes are two important terms in database design. *Data* is the information that goes into your database. *Attributes* are the types of data that make up the database. For example, an individual's last name is data. An attribute, on the other hand, is another name for a field, so an entire group of last names is considered to be an attribute. Names, phone numbers, customer numbers, descriptions, locations, and stock numbers are all common examples of attributes that your database file may contain.

In addition to thinking about what kinds of information should go into the database, you must give careful consideration to the ways in which Excel will retrieve information from the database. Information comes from a database in the form of reports. A report is a summary of information. Whether Excel displays a single row of data through a data form or dozens of rows by means of the AutoFilter capability, Excel is providing a report based on the data contained within the database file.

Steps in database design

Designing a database in Excel, regardless of its purpose, involves two major parts:

✦ Data definition (analyzing existing data)

✦ Data refinement (refining necessary data)

During the first phase, data definition, you should list on paper all the important attributes that are involved in your application. To do this, you must examine your needs in detail to determine exactly what kind of information must be stored in the database. You should list all possible attributes of your database even though they may not actually be needed by your particular application. You can eliminate unnecessary attributes during the data refinement stage.

During data refinement, you refine the list of attributes on your initial list so that the attributes form an accurate description of the types of data that you will need in the database. At this stage, it is vital to include suggestions from as many other users of the database as possible. The people who use the database are likely to know what kinds of information they will need from the database. What kinds of reports do they need? What kinds of queries will employees ask of the database? By continually asking these types of questions, you begin to think in terms of your database, and this thought process should help you determine what is important and what is not important.

Keep in mind that even after the database design phases, you can make changes to the design. If you follow the systematic approach of database design for your specific application, however, the chances are better that you won't create a database that fails to provide much of the information you need, and you will avoid extensive redesign.

By inserting rows and columns as needed, you can change the design of a database at any time, but such changes are often inconvenient to make after the database is designed. For example, if you created a database to handle a customer mailing list, you might include fields for names, addresses, cities, states, and zip codes. At first glance, these fields may seem sufficient. Then you begin entering customer information into the database and gradually build a sizable mailing list, but if your company later decides to begin telemarketing by using the same mailing list, you suddenly realize that you have not included a field for telephone numbers. Although you can easily change the design to include a field for telephone numbers by inserting a new column, you would still face the formidable task of going back and adding a telephone number for every name currently in the mailing list. If this information had been entered as you developed the mailing list, you would not face the inconvenience of having to enter the phone numbers as a separate operation. Careful planning during the database design process can help avoid such pitfalls.

Summary

In this chapter, you learned how to work with databases stored within Excel worksheets. The chapter covered the following topics:

✦ In Excel, a database is a list of data that is organized into columns of data directly underneath a row of field names.

✦ You can add data to a database by typing it directly into the cells below the field names or by using a data form.

✦ In addition to adding data, you can use data forms to find specific records and to edit or delete records.

✦ Data⇨Sort lets you sort the data in a database.

✦ You can use Excel's AutoFilter command to filter a database so that only records meeting certain criteria appear. You can then copy these records to a different area of the worksheet or to a different worksheet, or you can print the records.

In the next chapter, you'll learn how you can put macros to work to automate many routine tasks within Excel.

Where to go next...

✦ A major part of setting up and maintaining a database is the tedious but necessary task of *data entry*. You'll find some tips and techniques that you can use to make data entry easier in Chapter 16.

✦ When you've entered data into your database, you'll want to make the most of Excel's printing capabilities to generate reports. Chapter 20 has the story.

✦   ✦   ✦

Working with Excel Macros

Macros are combinations of keystrokes that automate many of the tasks you normally perform with a program. Macros enable you to record a sequence of characters that you can then assign to a keystroke combination, a graphic object, a button on a toolbar, or a button on the screen. Later, you can play back the character sequence by entering the keystroke, clicking on the button, or selecting the menu option assigned to the macro. When you run the macro, Excel performs the steps as if you had just typed the characters, made the menu choices, or done whatever actions that you recorded for that macro. If you must produce daily reports or perform similar repetitive tasks, you can save many keystrokes with macros.

Excel's macros can also be very complex programs that make decisions based on user input. The macros can also call other programs outside Excel. For example, you can open the Windows Calculator with a macro attached to a command button in an Excel worksheet.

Even though you may have no interest in becoming a programmer, you can still use macros. Unlike some older DOS-based spreadsheets that forced you to create macros by typing obscure codes into cells, Excel provides a Macro Recorder feature. You can turn on the Macro Recorder and perform the same steps in your worksheet as you normally do manually. When you are finished with the task, you can simply turn off the Macro Recorder, and you have a complete macro that performs those steps for you.

Understanding the Types of Macros

Excel provides two types of macros: command macros and function macros.

Command macros carry out a series of commands. For example, you can create a command macro that marks a specific range of worksheet and chooses File⇨Print to begin printing. You can also create a macro that applies a preferred format to an entire worksheet. Command macros can range from the very simple to the extremely complex.

Function macros are very similar to Excel's functions in that they act upon values by performing calculations and returning a value. For example, you can create a macro that takes the dimensions of an area in feet and returns the area in square yards.

You can remember the difference between the two types of macros if you keep in mind these points: command macros are similar to commands because they perform tasks. Function macros are similar to functions because they are stored in formulas and accept and return a value. You can create command macros by using the Macro Recorder. To create function macros, you must write Visual Basic for Applications code (see Chapter 24).

Creating a Macro

When you decide that you want to create a macro, you must first do everything that you do not want to include in the macro — such as opening a worksheet or moving to a specific location in the worksheet — because you don't want any unnecessary steps to be included in the macro. Remember that after you begin recording the macro, everything that you do will be included in it.

But when do I really need macros?

The kinds of macros that you can record with Excel's Macro Recorder are best at eliminating any kind of redundant work that you perform regularly. The following list contains the kinds of tasks for which you can create macros to save yourself time and effort:

• Selecting several ranges on one or more sheets of a workbook and printing those selected ranges

• Opening a new workbook, entering titles, formatting different ranges in the worksheet, and adjusting row heights and column widths

• Opening a database, sorting it in a desired order, applying a filter to the data, and printing the result

To begin creating a macro, choose Tools⇨Macro⇨Record New Macro. The Record Macro dialog box prompts you for the name and description of your new macro (see Figure 22-1).

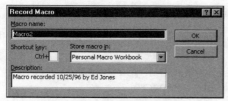

Figure 22-1: The Record Macro dialog box.

In the Description area, you can enter a description of the macro. A description of the macro can be important if you plan on keeping the macro for some time because you may not remember what it does. If you want to assign the macro to a keystroke combination, you type the combination in the Shortcut Key box. By default, you use the Ctrl key as part of the keystroke combination.

The Store macro in area gives you the opportunity to specify the place where you want to store the new macro. The Personal Macro Workbook option makes the macro available to all open worksheets by attaching the macro to a hidden notebook that is opened each time you start Excel. If you need to see the macro sheet, choose Window⇨Unhide. The This Workbook option places the macro in a module sheet that appears at the end of the workbook. Finally, the New Workbook option opens a new workbook and attaches the new module sheet to it.

You can also use another method to record macros in Excel: the Visual Basic toolbar. You can activate the Visual Basic toolbar by right-clicking in the toolbar area and then choosing the Visual Basic option from the shortcut menu. You can then click on the Record button on the Visual Basic toolbar to begin recording a macro. For everyday use of macros outside the world of programming, only two buttons on the Visual Basic toolbar will be of any interest to you: the Record Macro Button and the Run Macro button. For an explanation of the remaining buttons, see Chapter 24, which provides details on programming in Visual Basic for Applications.

Stopping the Macro Recorder

Stopping the Macro Recorder isn't too difficult: you click on the Stop Recording button. This button appears on-screen when you begin to record a macro. Alternately, you can choose Tools⇨Macro⇨Stop Recording.

Now that you have had a general look at creating macros, you need to see how the specifics work. The following steps show you how to create a macro that selects a range in one of your worksheets and prints that range:

1. Open the worksheet to which you want to apply the macro.

2. Choose Tools⇨Macro⇨Record New Macro.

3. In the Record New Macro dialog box, enter **Reportit** in the Macro Name text box.

4. Click under Shortcut Key and enter any key that you want to use (when combined with the Ctrl key) to activate the macro.

5. After you click on the OK button, you are ready to make the choices that you need to print the range.

6. Select a range of data from your worksheet and then choose File⇨Print to open the Print dialog box, as shown in Figure 22-2.

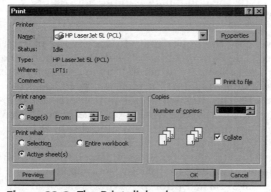

Figure 22-2: The Print dialog box.

7. In the Print What area, choose Selection.

8. Click on the OK button. This prints the selected part of your worksheet.

9. Click on the Stop Recording button to stop recording.

From this point on you can repeatedly select and print the same range of worksheets just by running the macro. To see how this process works, press the keystroke combination that you assigned to the macro or choose Tools⇨Macro⇨Macros. In the Macro dialog box, click on the Reportit macro name and then click on the Run button. With either method, the macro runs, and the worksheet range is again printed. That's the beauty of macros: you can automate any task that you perform regularly, such as printing a worksheet range.

The macros that you create will differ because you will have different tasks that you need to automate with a macro.

Assigning Macros to Buttons

Another method that you can use to place a macro is to assign it to a button on a worksheet. This technique lets you access the macro by clicking on its button. A good example of why you would want to do this is if you have set up a macro to open another worksheet page from the current worksheet page. This is useful when there are two worksheets, and while a user looks at one, you want to provide an easy way for the user to look at the other.

Macro buttons are an easy way to perform repeated tasks, such as printing a range. You can use the Button tool on the Forms toolbar to place a button in your spreadsheet and attach a macro to it. You activate the macro by pressing the button.

You can add a macro button to a worksheet by performing the following steps:

1. Turn on the Forms toolbar by choosing <u>V</u>iew⇨<u>T</u>oolbars and selecting Forms from the submenu that appears.

2. Click the Button tool in the Forms toolbar.

3. In the worksheet, click and drag to create a button.

4. After you create the button, the Assign Macro dialog box appears, as shown in Figure 22-3.

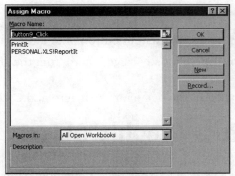

Figure 22-3: The Assign Macro dialog box.

5. From the Macro Name list box, choose the macro that you want to assign to the button.

6. After you click on the OK button, the macro is assigned to the button.

If you want to record a macro to assign to your button, click on the Record button in the Assign Macro dialog box. In the Record New Macro dialog box, enter a name for the macro that you are recording and click on the OK button.

Excel also lets you assign a macro to a completed button or change the macro that you have assigned to the button. You can do these tasks by performing the following steps:

1. Hold down the Ctrl key as you select the button.

2. Right-click on the button and choose Assign Macro from the shortcut menu. In a moment, you will see the Assign Macro dialog box.

3. If you want to assign an existing macro, choose the name from the Macro Name/Reference text box and click on the OK button.

4. If you want to record a macro, type the name of the macro in the Macro Name text box and click on the Record button. Then use the standard macro recording procedures detailed earlier in the chapter.

Macros can also be assigned to buttons on the toolbar. This can prove very useful if you perform certain tasks on a regular basis. The macro button that the macro is assigned to is usually a custom button, but you also have the option of assigning the macro to an existing button on the toolbar, which will cancel the previous function. To assign a macro to a toolbar button, perform these steps:

1. Choose Tools⇨Customize.

2. If the toolbar that contains the desired button isn't visible, click the Toolbars tab of the dialog box and turn on the check box beside the toolbar name.

3. If you want to run the macro from a button that is not on a toolbar, click the Commands tab and then click Macros in the Categories list. In the Commands list that appears, drag the Custom button onto a toolbar.

4. Right-click the toolbar button and choose Assign Macro from the shortcut menu.

5. In the Macro Name text box, enter the name for the macro and click OK.

Assigning a Macro to a Graphic Object

Assigning a macro to a graphic object is also something that you may need to do from time to time in order to make your macro easier to remember. If you use many macros, this technique may not be a bad idea because pictures often help you remember things. The procedure for adding a macro to a graphic object is much the same as the procedure for adding a macro to a toolbar button.

The old way versus the new way

If you've upgraded to this version of Excel from version 4.0 and you've made extensive use of macros and the Excel macro language in Excel 4.0, you'll discover that many things have changed. In Excel 4.0 (and in earlier versions), you recorded macros in Excel's macro language, a language with some similarities to (and a lot of differences from) Visual Basic for Applications.

Programs were known as macros, and they were recorded on macro sheets. In this version of Excel, each individual program (written in Visual Basic for Applications) is a *procedure*, and procedures are stored in *modules*. Each workbook can have an unlimited number of modules and procedures. And there are differences in the languages. For example, Visual Basic for Applications brings object-oriented techniques into the picture, something that just didn't exist in the old Excel 4.0 macro language.

Keep in mind that you don't have to throw away all those macros that you wrote in Excel 4.0 just because you upgraded. You can run an Excel 4.0 macro from the current version of Excel by using the following Visual Basic for Applications statement in the Module tab of the macro:

```
RUN("macrosheetname!macroname")
```

In this statement, `macrosheetname` is the name of the Excel 4.0 macro sheet, and `macroname` is the name of the macro that you want to run. For more specifics on using Visual Basic for Applications code in your macros, refer to Chapter 24.

For example, consider Figure 22-4. In the figure, a macro that prints a report is attached to a picture of a car. To print the report, the user clicks on the car.

Follow these steps to assign a macro to a graphic object:

1. Add the graphic object to your worksheet by using the steps outlined in Chapter 18. If the object currently has another macro assigned to it, hold down the Ctrl key and then select the object to avoid running the currently assigned macro.

2. Click the graphic object so that selection handles appear on its borders.

3. Right-click a selection handle for the button or graphic control and then click Assign Macro on the Shortcut menu. In a moment, the Assign Macro dialog box appears.

4. If you want to assign a macro that you have already created to the object, type or select the name of the macro in the Macro Name list box and then click on the OK button.

5. You also have the option of assigning a new macro to the graphic object by clicking on the Record button and then following the steps for recording a macro.

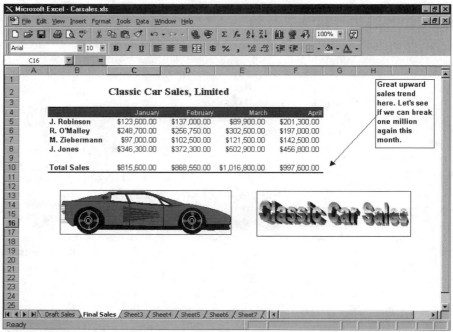

Figure 22-4: A macro attached to a graphic object in a worksheet.

Running the Macro

After you create a macro, you will discover that you can run it in different ways. After reading this section, you can decide for yourself which method is best for your needs.

One obvious way to run a macro is choose Tools⇔Macro⇔Macros. In the Macro dialog box, you click on the name of the macro that you want and then click on the Run button.

Another method for running macros is to use the keyboard combination that you assigned to the macro in the Record New Macro dialog box.

Changing Your Macro Options

After recording a macro, you may have to change some of the options, including the description of the macro, the keyboard combination that runs the macro, or the name of the macro as it appears on the Tools menu. In addition, you can assign the macro to a topic in a Help file.

Perform these steps to change the options for an existing macro:

1. Choose Tools⇨Macro⇨Macros to open the Macro dialog box.

2. In the Macro Name list box, select the name of the macro with the options that you want to change.

3. Click on the Options button to open the Macro Options dialog box, as shown in Figure 22-5.

4. Make the changes that you want for the different options and click on the OK button.

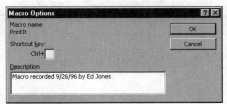

Figure 20-5: The Macro Options dialog box.

Making Macros Available to All Worksheets

You can store macros in many different places, which will directly affect the availability of the macro. You can store a macro in the Personal Macro Workbook, in the active workbook, or in a new workbook.

If you need to make a macro available at all times, you should store it in the Personal Macro Workbook, which is an invisible workbook that is always open, unless you specify otherwise. The Personal Macro Workbook is like the depository for workbooks that you use in a variety of areas throughout Excel. Because this workbook is always open, the macros are all always available, which lets you use them with all the worksheets that you have open.

To control where you store your macro, choose Tools⇨Macro⇨Record New Macro. In the Store macro in list box, choose the Personal Macro Workbook option to store this and all successive macros in that workbook. This option remains in effect for all macros until you change it. In addition to placing the macros in the Personal Macro Workbook, you can also put them in the current workbook or in a new workbook.

The Personal Macro Workbook is similar to other workbooks with the exception that it begins with one worksheet where all the macros that you specify are stored. For those who are into Visual Basic, you may want to add other Visual Basic modules items to the Personal Macro Workbook.

To display the Personal Macro Workbook, choose the Unhide command from the Window Menu and choose Personal.XLS from the dialog box that appears. Figure 22-6 shows what the code stored in the Personal Macro Workbook looks like when the Visual Basic for Applications Editor is opened, using the VBA Toolbar. (For more specifics on VBA, see Chapter 24.) Remember that the Unhide menu option is visible only if a worksheet has been hidden (as the Personal Macro Workbook normally is).

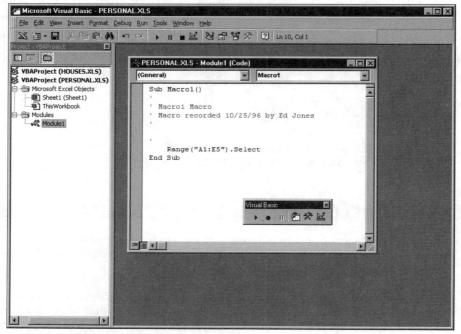

Figure 22-6: The Personal Macro Workbook.

Summary

This chapter covered different topics related to macros. Now you have the tools that you need to record macros efficiently and to put them in use for yourself. We covered the following areas related to macros:

✦ You learned about the different types of macros.

✦ You can create macros with Excel's Macro Recorder.

✦ You can run macros by choosing the Macro command from the Tools menu and selecting the desired macro in the dialog box that appears.

✦ You can attach macros to keyboard combinations, menu options, toolbar buttons, custom buttons, and graphic images.

✦ Macros are recorded in Visual Basic for Applications (VBA) code, the underlying programming language of Excel.

The next chapter will discuss the use of various analysis tools that you can use within Excel.

Where to go next...

✦ Macros can take much of the repetitive drudgery out of formatting and printing tasks. For an explanation of the kinds of formatting tasks that you can consider automating, see Chapter 17. For specifics on printing in Excel, you can refer to Chapter 20.

✦ Excel macros are the key to learning Visual Basic for Applications. Chapter 24 delves more deeply into Visual Basic for Applications programming.

✦　　✦　　✦

Excel and the Web

A major difference between Excel 97 and prior versions of Excel is the addition of numerous options for working with the Internet, and with intranets. Excel 97 lets you attach hyperlinks to other Office 97 documents or to web sites, and the table-like structure of a spreadsheet lends itself to the publishing of web pages in table form. You can easily export worksheets or charts in HTML format, ready for inclusion on your web pages. Figure 23-1 shows data in an Excel worksheet, published as a web page on a corporate intranet and viewed using Netscape Navigator, a popular web browser.

You can also place hyperlink fields in the cells of a worksheets, and you can use these cells to display links in other web pages on an intranet or on the Internet. If you need to retrieve or publish worksheet data across the net, Excel 97 can be a powerful tool for accomplishing such a task.

To accomplish most of the tasks described in this chapter, obviously you'll need to be connected to a net. This can be a dial-up connection to the Internet, by means of a commercial Internet service provider such as AT&T WorldNet, MCINet, MindSpring, NetCom, or a host of others. Your connection can also be a direct connection through your organization's local area network, and you may be connected directly to a corporate *intranet*, in which case you'll be able to retrieve or publish data to your company's private network. This chapter won't go into specifics on making a net connection, as that topic is an entire book in itself. If you need help in this area, you can take a look at IDG's *Creating Cool Interactive Web Sites* or *Creating Cool FrontPage Web Sites* by Paul and Mary Summitt.

This chapter also assumes a familiarity with the basics of Excel. If you are familiar with the Web or with intranets but you haven't yet learned to work with Excel, you should consider chapters 15 through 20 before proceeding with this chapter.

Figure 23-1: An Excel worksheet published as a web page.

What's Possible with Excel 97 and the Web?

Using Excel 97, you can perform a number of net-related tasks as you work with worksheets and charts. You can format text or objects stored in Excel worksheet cells as hyperlinks to link to other Office 97 documents or to web sites. When users of the worksheets click in these cells, they can jump directly to that location in the other file or to a specified web site. You can open workbooks that are stored on the Internet, you can save workbooks directly to Internet FTP sites, and you can save worksheet data as HTML (HyperText Markup Language), the publishing lingua franca of the World Wide Web. These topics will be covered in further detail throughout this chapter.

About the Web and the Internet

Because intranets and the Internet are newer concepts to many readers than are spreadsheets, a few explanations of terms may be in order. (If you're intimately familiar with the Internet, intranets, and the World Wide Web; you may want to skip this section and the next and dive right into working with Excel and the web.) First, the *Internet* is a global collection of computers linked together by means of telephone and microwave lines and accessible to the public by means of various connections in offices and in homes. The Internet grew out of a research project that came into common knowledge in the 1970s, which originally linked university and government computers in the United States. Since its inception, the Internet has grown to encompass thousands of computers spread throughout dozens of nations. Any PC user with an Internet connection (either by means of a phone line or a direct hookup) can connect to the Internet and gain access to the volumes of information located there.

One major component of the Internet is the *World Wide Web*. There are other parts of the Internet, but the World Wide Web is the most well-known part. The World Wide Web is that part of the Internet that makes use of graphical software known as web browsers, and of files stored as HTML. The computers on the Internet that store the HTML files are also known as *web servers*. When PCs connect to the Internet to retrieve this data, they use web browser software, which converts the incoming information (encoded in HTML) to graphical pages displayed as a combination of text, graphics, and in some cases audio and video. Commonly used web browsers include Microsoft Explorer and Netscape Navigator and the custom web browsers built into the software provided by America Online and CompuServe.

Each site on the Internet has a unique address, commonly known as the Internet address (and less commonly known by the official name of URL, or Uniform Resource Locator). When you establish an Internet connection, open a web browser, and enter an Internet address such as *http://www.whitehouse.gov*, you are entering the address for the web server that provides the home page for the President's office in the United States. Web addresses like these can be stored in Excel worksheets, and displayed as hyperlinks.

About Intranets

Many net-related uses of Office 97 involve making data available on *intranets*. An intranet is a private network of computers that is available only to the members of a specific organization. Intranets make use of World Wide Web technology – web servers, network connections, and web browser software – to allow members of an organization to share information. Intranets are very popular with corporations, as intranets let employees share work-related information in a confidential manner.

About HTML

As mentioned earlier, HTML is the language used for publishing information to the World Wide Web and to intranets that use World Wide Web technology. HTML is a text-based language that makes use of special codes called *tags*. These tags are included in the text of the HTML documents, and they provide instructions to the web browser software that determine how the data appears when it is viewed by the end-user. You don't need to know the nuts and bolts of HTML coding to work with Excel and the web, but it's a good idea to at least be familiar with the concept of saving your data in HTML file format. In order to publish Excel data on the Internet or on an intranet, you'll need to save that data in HTML format and upload it to your web server. If you are dealing with a corporate intranet, your company's webmaster can tell you how to upload the HTML files that Excel produces to your company's web server. If you are managing a web site on the Internet or on an intranet, you already know how to do this; much of the rest of this chapter will deal with getting that Excel data ready for uploading to your server.

About the Web Toolbar

Like all the major Office 97 applications, Excel provides the Web toolbar, a toolbar that helps you browse through the resources on an intranet or on the Web. Using the Web toolbar, you can quickly open, search, and browse through any document or through a web page. You can jump between documents, and you can add favorite sites you find on the web to the Favorites folder, allowing you to go back to those sites at a later time.

In Excel, you can display the Web toolbar by choosing <u>V</u>iew⟹<u>T</u>oolbars and then selecting Web from the submenu that appears, or by clicking the Web toolbar button in the Standard toolbar. Figure 23-2 shows the Web toolbar.

Figure 23-2: The Web toolbar.

You'll find the Web toolbar to be handy when you happen to be in Excel and you have a need to go to the Web (or to your company's intranet) for information. For example, you can click the Search the Web button to launch your default web browser and search the web, or you can click the Favorites button to open a list of your favorite web sites. For more specifics on the Web toolbar, see Chapter 11. That chapter provides a description of how you can use the web toolbar and how Word 97 can serve as a web browser if you aren't using Microsoft Internet Explorer or Netscape Navigator.

Creating Hyperlinks in Worksheets

A significant feature of Excel 97 is its capability to use *hyperlinks* in worksheets. You can create hyperlinks to jump to other Office documents stored on your PC, on your company's network, on a company intranet, or on the Internet. You can use text in a cell or a graphic as a hyperlink.

Linking to office documents with Copy and Paste

If you want to create a hyperlink to a location in Excel, in a Word document, or in PowerPoint presentation, the easiest way to do this is to use the Copy and Paste Hyperlink commands of the Edit menu. In a nutshell, you do this by first selecting a location in the Excel worksheet, Word document, or PowerPoint presentation that you want the hyperlink to lead to. You then choose Copy from the Edit menu. And finally, you go back to the Excel cell where you want the hyperlink to appear, and you choose Paste as Hyperlink from the Edit menu. In more detail, here are the steps you can use to create a hyperlink from another Office document.

1. Open the document containing the location you want to link to. (If it is in Excel, it can be in the same workbook, or in a different workbook that's open. If the location is in a Word or PowerPoint file, it can be in any area of the document or presentation.)

2. Select the portion of the document you want to link to.

3. Choose Edit⇨Copy.

4. In Excel, place the cell pointer at the cell where you want to insert the hyperlink. If you want any explanatory text in the cell, enter that text in the cell now.

5. Choose Edit⇨Paste as Hyperlink.

When you perform these steps, Excel inserts a hyperlink back to the original document in the selected cell or cells. You can then click on the hyperlink at any time to jump to the linked document.

Hot Stuff If you want to create a hyperlink to a portion of an Excel worksheet, you can do this by selecting the data to be linked and then using the right mouse button to click and drag the information to the cell that is to serve as the hyperlink. When you release the right mouse button, choose Create Hyperlink Here from the Shortcut menu which appears.

Linking to web sites or files with Insert Hyperlink

If you need to establish a hyperlink to a web site on an intranet or on the Internet, you can use the following steps to do so. (Technically, you can use these same steps to link to another Office document, but it's easier to use the copy and paste methods described earlier.)

1. Select the cell or cells that will serve as the hyperlink.

2. Click the Insert Hyperlink button in the Standard toolbar, or choose Insert⇨Hyperlink. When you do this, the Insert Hyperlink dialog box appears, as shown in Figure 23-3.

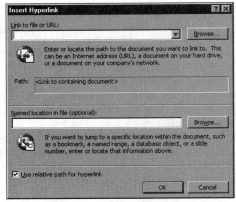

Figure 23-3: The Insert Hyperlink dialog box.

3. In the Link to File or URL text box, enter the web address (or the path for the file) of the destination for the link.

4. If you are establishing a link to a file and you want to jump to a specific location, enter that location in the Named Location in File text box. (This can be a cell reference or named range, a Word bookmark, or the name of a PowerPoint slide.) If you link to a file and leave this entry blank, the hyperlink jumps to the beginning of the file.

5. If you want a hyperlink to a shared network directory to find the linked file based on a path that's relative to the location where your current workbook is stored, turn on the Use Relative Path for Hyperlink check box. If you want a hyperlink to a shared network directory to use the same address regardless of where the current workbook is stored, turn off the Use Relative Path for Hyperlink check box.

6. Click OK to establish the hyperlink.

Opening Workbooks on an Intranet or the Internet

With Excel 97, you can open workbooks that are stored on your company's intranet, or on the World Wide Web. Here are the steps you'll need to do this:

1. Choose File⇨Open.

2. In the File name box, enter the web address for the workbook that you want to open. (As an example, you might enter *http://www.johndoe.com/finances/january.xls* to open a workbook stored on the World Wide Web.)

3. Click OK. Excel will retrieve the workbook, using your default dial-up or network connection to the web.

Saving Workbooks to the Internet

You can save Excel workbooks directly to Internet FTP sites. (In order to do this, you must have permission to save files to the desired FTP site.) You can use the following steps to save workbook files to the Internet:

1. Choose File⇨Save As.

2. In the Save In box of the dialog box which appears, click Internet Locations (FTP).

3. In the list of FTP sites, double-click the site you want (see the note below if the desired site does not appear).

4. Double-click the location you want within the site.

5. Enter a name for the workbook in the File name box.

6. Click Save.

Note   If the FTP site you want to save your workbook to doesn't appear in the list of FTP sites, you'll need to add it to the list. Choose File⇨Open, and in the Look in box, click Add/Modify FTP locations. This causes an Add/Modify FTP Locations dialog box to appear, and you can fill in the site name, login, and password information. When done, click OK to add the site to the list.

Publishing Excel Worksheets and Charts on the Web

Excel 97 includes an Internet Assistant Wizard, a wizard that lets you convert worksheet ranges or Excel charts to HTML format, so you can publish the data on the Internet or on an intranet. The Internet Assistant lets you produce static web pages; these appear on web sites as fixed, unchanging data. Note that as of this writing, you cannot directly show live Excel data on a web page, but you can indirectly accomplish this by linking an Access table to the Excel data and creating a live web page based on the Access data, as detailed in Chapter 44.

You can launch this wizard through the use of the Save as HTML command on the File menu. Use the following steps to produce web-ready files based on your worksheets or charts in Excel:

1. Choose File⇨Save as HTML. In a moment, the first Internet Assistant Wizard dialog box appears, as shown in Figure 23-4.

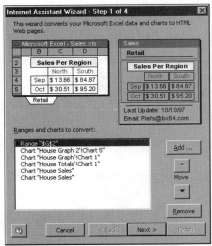

Figure 23-4: The first Internet Assistant Wizard dialog box

2. In the dialog box, add any desired ranges that don't appear in the list box by clicking the Add button and entering the cell range in the next dialog box which appears. Remove any cell ranges or charts you don't want converted by selecting them in the list and clicking Remove. The cell ranges and charts will appear in the HTML document in the same order as they appear in the list. If you want to change this order, click a desired range or chart and use the up and down arrows to move it up or down as desired in the list. When done choosing the ranges and charts you want to convert to HTML, click Next. In a moment, the second Internet Assistant Wizard dialog box appears, as shown in Figure 23-5.

3. Here, you can choose whether to create a new HTML file or whether to insert the converted data into an existing HTML file. Make your desired selection and click Next.

4. The next dialog box to appear (Figure 23-6) lets you enter an optional header and footer and specify horizontal lines if desired before and after the converted data. Select the desired options and click Next.

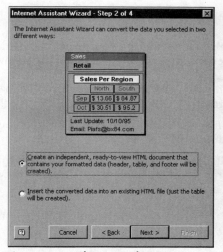

Figure 23-5: The second Internet Assistant Wizard dialog box

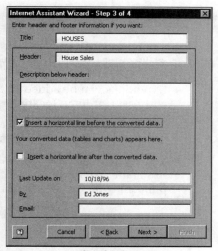

Figure 23-6: The third Internet Assistant Wizard dialog box

5. The final dialog box to appear (Figure 23-7) asks which multinational style of coding you desire and whether the result should be saved as an HTML file or added to a web page you are designing using Microsoft FrontPage. You can also enter the desired filename and path for the file. Enter or choose the desired options and click Finish to produce the HTML files.

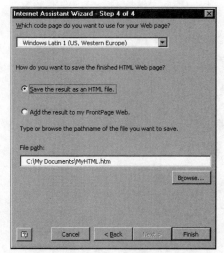

Figure 23-7: The final Internet Assistant Wizard dialog box

Summary

This chapter has covered the details behind sharing your Excel data with Internet/Intranet users. Points covered in this chapter included the following:

✦ Hyperlinks can be added to the cells of a worksheet, and you can store web addresses or jump locations to other Office documents in those fields.

✦ Excel 97 can open workbook files that are stored on the Internet, and you can save workbook files to Internet FTP sites.

✦ You can use the Save as HTML option of the File menu to launch the Internet Assistant Wizard, to convert ranges of worksheets or charts to HTML files for publishing on the Internet or on an intranet.

In the next chapter, you learn how to further extend the power of Excel by using Visual Basic for Applications.

Where to go next...

✦ Excel is just one component of the web publishing capabilities provided by Office 97. Word, PowerPoint, and Access also offer web publishing and web interaction features. For specifics on Word and the web, see Chapter 11; for PowerPoint and the web, Chapter 32; and for Access and the web, Chapter 44.

✦   ✦   ✦

Excel and Visual Basic for Applications

This chapter details the use of Visual Basic for Applications (VBA), the programming language that is the basis for Excel macros. VBA is heavily based on Microsoft's Visual Basic programming language. Because Excel macros are based on VBA, you can use VBA to automate common tasks in Excel.

VBA can take you much further than simply duplicating keystrokes. VBA gives you full access to all of Excel's commands. You can modify Excel's own menus by adding your own commands and options, you can create custom dialog boxes to present messages and query users for information, and you can even construct complete applications for users with a limited knowledge of Excel. To accomplish these kinds of tasks, you need more than a familiarity with the recording and playing of macros: you need a basic understanding of VBA.

Using Macros to Learn Visual Basic for Applications

More Info Chapter 22 detailed the basics of using macros, which are sequences of instructions that cause Excel to perform a particular task. As that chapter demonstrates, macros can be very handy to use in your work because they greatly reduce the time that you spend performing routine, repetitive tasks. Macros are also an excellent starting point for understanding how VBA works and what you can do with the language. As Excel's Macro Recorder stores all the actions that you perform or the commands that you choose, it interprets these actions or commands into *statements*, or lines of code, by using VBA. These statements are automatically placed in a *procedure*, which is a block of VBA code. Procedures are stored in *modules*, which you can think of as containers for all VBA code.

To give you an idea of how all Excel macros use VBA, you should practice on an example. This chapter will familiarize you with Visual Basic code by examining the procedure that results when you record this sample macro. The following steps create the simple time sheet shown in Figure 24-1. Because time sheets are typically created weekly, it represents a typical task that can be automated by creating a macro.

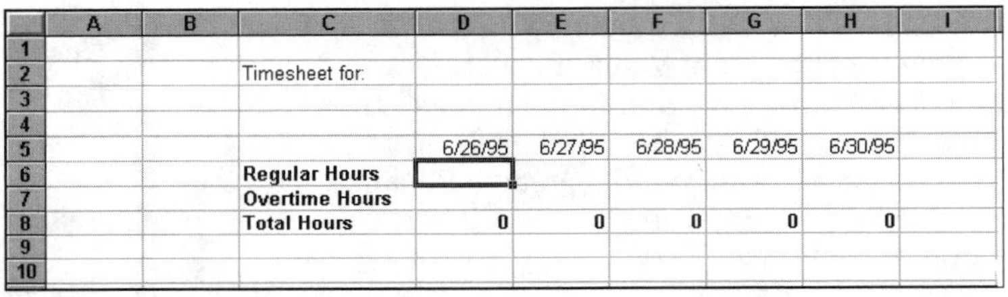

Figure 24-1: A time sheet that results from creating the sample macro.

Follow these steps to create the worksheet and the sample macro:

1. Open a new workbook.
2. Choose Tools⇨Macro⇨Record New Macro.
3. In the Record New Macro dialog box, enter the name **TimeEntry** and click on the OK button. The Stop Macro button, which you can use to stop recording the macro, appears in the worksheet.
4. Click in cell C2 and enter **Timesheet for:** in the cell.
5. Click in cell D5 and enter =**Today( )** in the cell.
6. Click and drag from cell D5 to H5 to select D5 and the next four cells to the right.
7. Choose Edit⇨Fill⇨Series.
8. In the Series dialog box, click on the OK button to accept the default options.
9. Click in cell C6 and enter **Regular Hours** in the cell.
10. Click in cell C7 and enter **Overtime Hours** in the cell.

11. Click in cell C8 and enter **Total Hours** in the cell.

12. Select the range of cells from C6 to C8 and press Ctrl+B to add bold formatting.

13. Click on the border between cells C and D and drag to widen column C until it is wide enough to display the longest text in the column.

14. Click in cell D8 and enter the formula **=D6+D7** in the cell.

15. Click and drag from cells D8 to H8 to select cell D8 and the four cells to the right of it.

16. Choose Edit⇨Fill⇨Right.

17. Press Ctrl+B to apply bold formatting to the selected cells.

18. Click in cell D6 (this repositions the cursor to prepare the worksheet for data entry).

19. Click on the Stop Macro button to stop the recording of the macro.

You can verify the effects of the macro by moving to a blank worksheet, choosing Tools⇨Macro⇨Macros, clicking on TimeEntry to select it, and clicking on the Run button. The time sheet is duplicated in the blank worksheet.

How similar is Visual Basic for Applications to Visual Basic?

If you've already worked with Microsoft's Visual Basic as a development language, you'll find Visual Basic for Applications to be a familiar friend; in fact, *sibling* is more accurate. Visual Basic for Applications is solidly based on Microsoft's Visual Basic programming language. The whole idea in developing Visual Basic for Applications was to replace the old macro-based languages, such as Excel 4.0's macro language and Access Basic, with a common development language so that developers who are familiar with applications development in Excel could easily develop applications in Access or in Word, and vice versa.

Microsoft uses Visual Basic as the base language, and it has added extensions to the language as implemented in the other Office applications. The commands, functions, methods, procedures, and program structures used in Visual Basic can all be used in Visual Basic for Applications for Word, Excel, PowerPoint, and Access. So if you're a Visual Basic programmer, you're on very familiar ground.

Understanding Visual Basic for Applications Code

Of course, the purpose of the exercise that you just completed is not to demonstrate how to create a macro but to show how Visual Basic for Applications code works as the basis of any macro. Choose Tools⇨Macro⇨Macros to open the Macro dialog box. Select the TimeEntry macro, and click Edit. This opens the Visual Basic Editor, shown in Figure 24-2. As shown in the figure, the VBA code behind the macro appears in the Module window at the right.

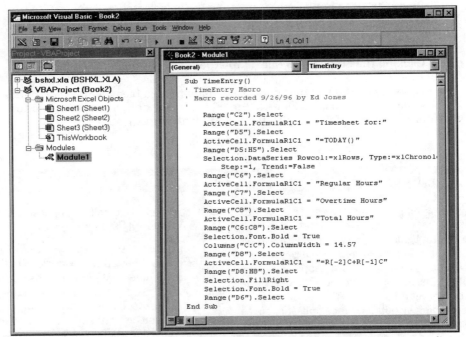

Figure 24-2: An example of macro code within the Visual Basic Editor.

The code looks like this:

```
' TimeEntry Macro
' Macro recorded 9/20/96 by Ed Jones
Sub TimeEntry()
    Range("C2").Select
    ActiveCell.FormulaR1C1 = "Timesheet for:"
```

```
        Range("D5").Select
        ActiveCell.FormulaR1C1 = "=TODAY()"
        Range("D5:H5").Select
        Selection.DataSeries Rowcol:=xlRows, Type:=xlChronological,
           Date _
              :=xlDay, Step:=1, Trend:=False
        Range("C6").Select
        ActiveCell.FormulaR1C1 = "Regular Hours"
        Range("C7").Select
        ActiveCell.FormulaR1C1 = "Overtime Hours"
        Range("C8").Select
        ActiveCell.FormulaR1C1 = "Total Hours"
        Range("C6:C8").Select
        Selection.Font.Bold = True
        Columns("C:C").ColumnWidth = 13.71
        Range("D8").Select
        ActiveCell.FormulaR1C1 = "=R[-2]C+R[-1]C"
        Range("D8:H8").Select
        Selection.FillRight
        Selection.Font.Bold = True
        Range("D6").Select
    End Sub
```

Each of the steps that you took during the recording of this procedure resulted in the addition of one or more lines of Visual Basic code in the module. The code appears in color: comments are displayed in green; key words of the Visual Basic language appear in blue; and all other code appears in black. When you run this (or any) macro, you are in effect running the Visual Basic for Applications code that is contained in the module that was recorded by the Macro Recorder. As the module runs, each line of Visual Basic code is executed in turn, and Excel performs an appropriate action as a result.

About comments

You can include *comments* (lines that aren't acted upon by Excel when the code runs) by preceding the text with a single quotation mark. In the sample procedure, you can see that the first two lines are comments:

```
' TimeEntry Macro
' Macro recorded 6/20/95 by Ed Jones
```

In this case, Excel added the comments based on the entries in the Macro Name and Description text boxes of the Record Macro dialog box. You can place comments wherever you desire in your Visual Basic code by typing a single quote mark followed by the text of the comment. Comments can be quite helpful in your more complex procedures because they can help you remember what's going on at a specific point in the procedure. Comments can occupy an entire line, or you can put them at the end of a valid line of code by starting the comment with a single quotation mark. When the procedure runs, everything that follows the single quotation mark is ignored until Excel finds a new line of code.

About headers and footers

Following the comments, the next line of the procedure reads

```
Sub TimeEntry()
```

The matching last line reads

```
End sub
```

Think of these lines as the header and footer for the procedure. Every VBA procedure starts with a header that begins with Sub or Function and ends with a footer that says End Sub or End Function. VBA allows two types of procedures: *function procedures* and *sub procedures*. Function procedures are like Excel's built-in functions. They accept a value(s), act on the data, and return a value(s). Sub procedures do not return a value (although you can pass values from within a sub procedure through the use of statements inside the procedure). Any arguments used by a function procedure are placed inside the parentheses of the header. The footer tells Excel that it has reached the end of the procedure. When Excel reaches the footer in the module, it passes program control back to any other VBA procedure that called this one. If the procedure was not called by another procedure, Excel returns control from the procedure to Excel itself.

About selecting and entering data

Following the header statement are two lines of code that select cell C2 and insert a text entry into that cell. The Visual Basic code for these two lines is

```
Range("C2").Select
ActiveCell.FormulaR1C1 = "Timesheet for:"
```

The Range statement tells Excel to select a range. Because only one cell's address is given (cell C2), Excel selects only that cell. The next statement tells Excel to enter a text value (in this case, the words "Timesheet for:") in the active cell of the worksheet, which is now cell C2.

About control statements

Besides containing lines of code that cause cursor movement and data entry in the worksheet, various lines of code within the program control certain characteristics of the worksheet in Excel. For example, when you press Ctrl+B to apply bold formatting to a selection, the following code results

```
Selection.Font.Bold = True
```

This line of code, when executed, takes the current selection and turns on bold character formatting. The following lines of code result from opening the Series dialog box (after choosing Edit⇨Fill⇨Series) and accepting the default options in the dialog box:

```
Selection.DataSeries Rowcol:=xlRows, Type:=xlChronological, _
     Date _ :=xlDay, Step:=1, Trend:=False
```

While examining this line, you should also notice the presence of the *continuation character* used in VBA. The underscore at the end of the first line is the continuation character, and it denotes that a line of program code is to be continued onto the line that follows. (Without this character, VBA considers any single line to be a complete program statement.)

As you grow accustomed to working in VBA, you'll find that you can accomplish a great deal of useful work by means of the various cell selection and control statements that can be used in the language.

About displaying dialog boxes

One of the reasons that you may actually want to do some Visual Basic programming yourself (rather than using only the Macro Recorder) is that you can do some custom programming — such as displaying dialog boxes — that you cannot do with recorded macros. To display a dialog box on-screen that contains a message with custom text, you can use VBA's `MsgBox` function. The syntax of the statement is simple — you add a line of code that reads `MsgBox("your custom text")`, where you put your desired text between the double quotation marks.

If you duplicated the example earlier in the chapter, go to the end of the line prior to the end of the last line of the procedure (the `End Sub` line) and press Enter to add a new, blank line. With the insertion point at the start of the blank line, enter the following:

```
MsgBox("Enter your week's time and save under a new name.")
```

Choose File⇨Close to exit the Visual Basic Editor. Go to a blank worksheet page and choose Tools⇨Macro⇨Macros. In the Macro dialog box, select the TimeEntry macro and click on the Run button. When the macro completes this time, you see the dialog box shown in Figure 24-3. Dialog boxes such as this one can serve to inform users, providing needed guidance about tasks the user needs to perform.

Figure 24-3: The dialog box presented by the MsgBox function.

About user input

Another useful task that you can handle by adding your own Visual Basic code is prompting users for information and acting on a user's response. The InputBox function acts in a manner similar to the MsgBox function, but with InputBox, a text box appears within the dialog box. The value that the user enters in the text box is returned by the function.

You can try using the InputBox function by getting back into the module that you created as part of this exercise. Choose Tools⇨Macro⇨Macros to open the Macro dialog box. Click on the TimeEntry macro, and click Edit to open the Visual Basic Editor. Find the following line:

```
ActiveCell.FormulaR1C1 = "Timesheet for:"
```

Place the cursor at the end of the line, and press Enter to add a new line underneath this one. Enter the following two lines as new code in the procedure:

```
Range("D2").Select
ActiveCell.FormulaR1C1 = InputBox("Employee Name:")
```

Choose File⇨Close to exit the Visual Basic Editor. Move to a blank worksheet and run the macro again. (Choose Tools⇨Macro⇨Macros. In the Macro dialog box, select the TimeEntry macro and click on the Run button.) When the macro runs, a dialog box like the one shown in Figure 24-4 appears, asking for an employee name. After you enter a name, the macro will store that name in cell D2 of the worksheet.

Learn by example

If you plan to get involved in VBA programming, one of the best ways to become familiar with what can be done with the language is to examine other tested, working applications and macros that range from the simple to the complex. If you installed the example worksheets when you installed the Excel portion of Office, you'll find some code samples in the Examples folder that is stored in the Excel folder. You will also find complete Excel applications (written in Visual Basic for Applications) available at the IDG Books web site (www.idgbooks.com).

Figure 24-4: The dialog box presented by the InputBox function.

Editing Visual Basic for Applications Code

When you click on a module tab, you can enter program code just like you type text in any word processor. You don't have to know the mechanics of entering text and correcting mistakes; suffice it to say that you can use the same text entry and editing techniques — including cutting and pasting — that you can use in any Windows word processor.

While you are in the Visual Basic Editor, you can also insert text from another file into your existing program code. If you want to insert text into the program code, place the insertion point at the location in the module where you want to insert the code and choose Insert➪File. In the File dialog box, select the file that contains the text that you want to insert and click on the OK button to read the text into the file.

Printing Visual Basic Code

You can print the code that is contained in your Visual Basic modules. To print the code, open the module that contains the desired code by choosing Tools➪Macro➪Macros, selecting the desired macro, and clicking the Edit button. Then, choose the Print command from the File menu.

About the Visual Basic Toolbar

If you do much work in Visual Basic for Applications programming, you'll find the Visual Basic toolbar (Figure 24-5) useful. You can activate the Visual Basic toolbar by right-clicking on the toolbar area and choosing Visual Basic from the shortcut menu. Table 24-1 provides an explanation for the different buttons on the Visual Basic toolbar.

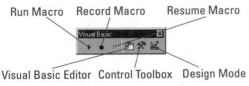

Run Macro   Record Macro   Resume Macro

Visual Basic Editor   Control Toolbox   Design Mode

Figure 24-5: The Visual Basic toolbar.

Table 24-1 **Buttons on the Visual Basic toolbar**	
Name	*Function*
Run Macro	Opens the Run Macro dialog box, where you can run, delete, or modify a selected macro.
Record Macro	Open the Record Macro dialog box, where you can fill in the desired options used to begin recording a macro.
Resume Macro	Resumes playing a macro that you have paused.
Visual Basic Editor	Opens the Visual Basic Editor, where you can create, edit, and step through macros using Visual Basic.
Control Toolbox	Displays the Toolbox used for adding controls to a worksheet.
Design Mode	Switch in and out of Design mode.

Just a Beginning...

Make no mistake about it, using Visual Basic for Applications falls well into the realm of programming. (If you're completely new to programming, you should be congratulated for pressing this deeply into what, for many readers, is a subject of mystifying complexity.) You've not only learned how VBA lies at the heart of everything that you do with macros, but you've also learned how you can extend the power of your macros by adding your own Visual Basic code to provide items like dialog boxes and customized prompts. Still, you've only scratched the surface of what you can do with this language. VBA is a full-featured programming language that you can use to automate or customize virtually any conceivable task that can be done with Excel. If you're encouraged (dare we even say excited?) by the challenges of programming, you should look into additional resources for learning about Visual Basic programming. It's a subject about which entire books have been written. A good place to start is Wallace Wang's great book *Visual Basic 4 for Windows for Dummies* (IDG Books, 1995).

Summary

This chapter has provided an introduction to programming by using Visual Basic for Applications, the underlying language behind Excel macros. The chapter covered the following points:

✦ Every Excel macro exists as a series of Visual Basic program statements.

✦ The Visual Basic statements are stored in procedures, and one or more procedures are placed in modules. Each module occupies a module sheet in a workbook.

✦ Visual Basic procedures can be sub procedures or function procedures. Function procedures are like Excel's built-in functions because they accept a value(s), act on the data, and return a value(s). Sub procedures do not return a value (although you can pass values from within a sub procedure through the use of statements inside the procedure).

✦ You can modify the Visual Basic code that Excel's Macro Recorder creates to add special features like dialog boxes and custom prompts.

The next chapter will show how you can put Excel to work by demonstrating how you can create and use worksheets for common business tasks.

Where to go next...

✦ Because Visual Basic for Applications lies at the heart of macros that you create in Excel, you should also be intimately familiar with the use of macros before getting deeply involved with Visual Basic for Applications. See Chapter 22.

✦   ✦   ✦

Excel at Work

This chapter gets you started on your own applications by providing some examples and step-by-step instructions that you can use to build models of worksheets for various tasks.

Cash-Flow Management

Managing cash flow, or your accounts receivable and accounts payable, is a basic job that faces virtually every modern business. The following cash-flow worksheet is relatively simple to set up, yet it keeps a clear "picture" of available funds. The worksheet is patterned after the common single-entry debits and credits bookkeeping system. You enter a starting balance into cell H4. Use column A to record the dates of each transaction, whether a credit or a debit. Use columns B, C, and D to record credits by listing the creditor, the description, and the amount. Use columns E, F, and G to record debits by listing to whom the amount is paid, the description, and the amount. Column H contains the formulas that you use to keep a running total of the cash on hand. You compute the total by taking the preceding entry's running balance, adding the credits, and subtracting the debits. You can maintain this type of system by creating a separate worksheet for each month. At the end of the year, you can consolidate the totals into another worksheet to show yearly figures for cash flow. The worksheet is shown in Figure 25-1.

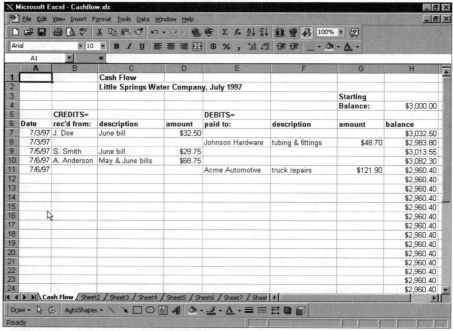

Figure 25-1: A cash flow worksheet.

To build the worksheet, enter the following labels and formulas into the cells as shown:

Cell	Entry
A6	Date
B5	CREDITS=
B6	rec'd from:
C1	Cash Flow
C6	description
D6	amount
E5	DEBITS=
E6	paid to:
F6	description

Cell	Entry
G3	Starting
G4	Balance:
G6	amount
H6	balance
H7	=H4+D7-G7
H8	=H7+D8-G8

In the area below cell C1, you may want to add the name of your company or organization. In the example, we used "Little Springs Water Company."

To copy the formula into successive cells in column H, select the range of cells from H8 to H40. Choose Edit⇨Fill⇨Down. To format the cells in Column H, select the range of cells from H4 to H40. Then choose Format⇨Cells to open the Format Cells dialog box, and then click on the Number tab. Click the Currency option in the list box, and then click OK. Using the same steps, choose the same currency format for the cells from D7 to D40 and from G7 to G40. To format a range of cells to display dates, select the range of cells from A7 to A40, choose Format⇨Cells to open the Format Cells dialog box, click the Number tab, click the Date option in the list box, and select the *d-mmm-yy* format.

At this point, the worksheet is ready to use. Although you may want to use your own figures, Figure 25-1 shows part of the cash-flow worksheet that has been filled in with figures from a typical small business.

Break-Even Analysis

A common what-if scenario for almost any firm is the break-even analysis, which determines how many units of a given product must be sold before the producer shows a profit. A break-even analysis requires the juggling of two groups of figures: fixed costs and variable costs. *Fixed costs* do not directly increase with each unit sold. Such costs include the rental of the manufacturing plant, utilities to power the production line, and advertising expenses. Variable costs directly increase with each unit sold. Such costs include the cost of the materials to assemble each unit, labor costs per unit, packaging costs, and shipping costs.

A typical break-even analysis performs a one-time deduction of the fixed costs and then calculates the per-unit costs for each unit produced. These negative amounts are balanced against the net profits (the net sales cost times the number of units sold). As the number of units sold increases, a break-even point is reached where the total profit equals the negative fixed and variable costs. An example of a break-even analysis worksheet illustrates the break-even point for a child's bicycle (see Figure 25-2).

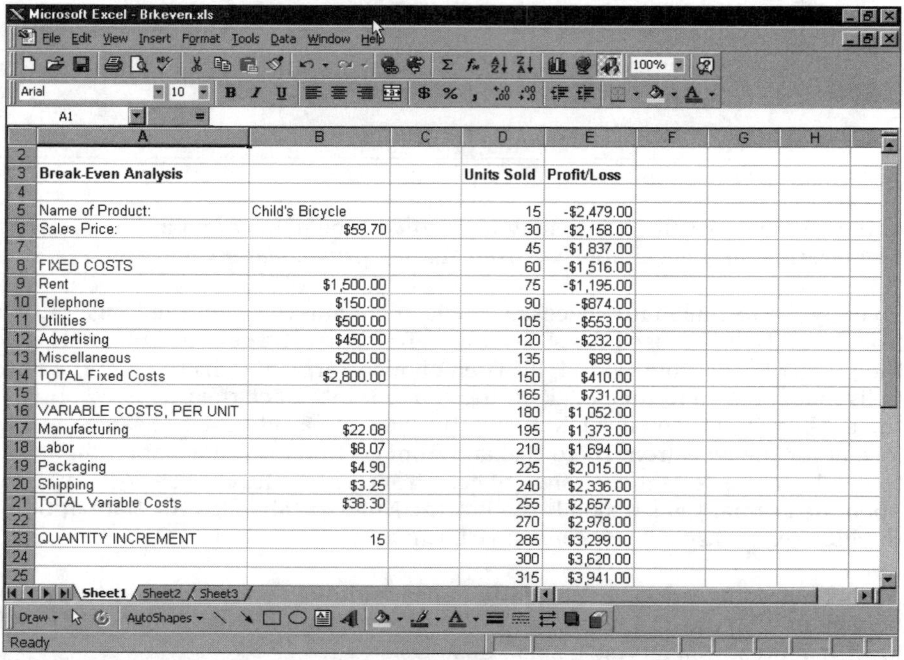

Figure 25-2: A break-even analysis worksheet.

To build the model, open a new worksheet. Widen column A to roughly three times its default width and widen column B to roughly twice its default width. The other columns can remain at the default widths. Enter the following formulas into the cells shown:

Cell	Entry
A3	**Break-Even Analysis**
A5	**Name of Product:**
A6	**Sales Price:**
A8	**FIXED COSTS**
A9	**Rent**

Cell	Entry
A10	**Telephone**
A11	**Utilities**
A12	**Advertising**
A13	**Miscellaneous**
A14	**TOTAL Fixed Costs**
A16	**VARIABLE COSTS, PER UNIT**
A17	**Manufacturing**
A18	**Labor**
A19	**Packaging**
A20	**Shipping**
A21	**TOTAL Variable Costs**
A23	**QUANTITY INCREMENT**
B5	**Child's Bicycle**
B6	**59.7**
B9	**1500**
B10	**150**
B11	**500**
B12	**450**
B13	**200**
B14	**=SUM(B9:B13)**
B17	**22.08**
B18	**8.07**
B19	**4.9**
B20	**3.25**
B21	**=SUM(B17:B20)**
B23	**15**
D3	**Units Sold**
D5	**=B23**
D6	**=D5+$B$23**

You can create the remaining formulas in column D quickly by selecting the range from D6 to D41. Then choose Edit⇨Fill⇨Down.

Cell	Entry
D7	=D6+$B$23
D8	=D7+$B$23
D9	=D8+$B$23
D10	=D9+$B$23
D11	=D10+$B$23
D12	=D11+$B$23
D13	=D12+$B$23
D14	=D13+$B$23
D15	=D14+$B$23
D16	=D15+$B$23
D17	=D16+$B$23
D18	=D17+$B$23
D19	=D18+$B$23
D20	=D19+$B$23
D21	=D20+$B$23
D22	=D21+$B$23
D23	=D22+$B$23
D24	=D23+$B$23
D25	=D24+$B$23
D26	=D25+$B$23
D27	=D26+$B$23
D28	=D27+$B$23
D29	=D28+$B$23
D30	=D29+$B$23
D31	=D30+$B$23
D32	=D31+$B$23
D33	=D32+$B$23
D34	=D33+$B$23
D35	=D34+$B$23

Cell	Entry
D36	=D35+$B$23
D37	=D36+$B$23
D38	=D37+$B$23
D39	=D38+$B$23
D40	=D39+$B$23
D41	=D40+$B$23

In column E, enter the following values and formulas:

Cell	Entry
E3	Profit/Loss
E5	=D5*$B$6-($B$14+($B$21*D5))

You can create the remaining formulas in column E quickly by selecting the range from E5 to E41. Then choose Edit⇨Fill⇨Down.

Cell	Entry
E6	=D6*$B$6-($B$14+($B$21*D6))
E7	=D7*$B$6-($B$14+($B$21*D7))
E8	=D8*$B$6-($B$14+($B$21*D8))
E9	=D9*$B$6-($B$14+($B$21*D9))
E10	=D10*$B$6-($B$14+($B$21*D10))
E11	=D11*$B$6-($B$14+($B$21*D11))
E12	=D12*$B$6-($B$14+($B$21*D12))
E13	=D13*$B$6-($B$14+($B$21*D13))
E14	=D14*$B$6-($B$14+($B$21*D14))
E15	=D15*$B$6-($B$14+($B$21*D15))
E16	=D16*$B$6-($B$14+($B$21*D16))
E17	=D17*$B$6-($B$14+($B$21*D17))
E18	=D18*$B$6-($B$14+($B$21*D18))

(continued)

(continued)

Cell	Entry
E19	=D19*$B$6-($B$14+($B$21*D19))
E20	=D20*$B$6-($B$14+($B$21*D20))
E21	=D21*$B$6-($B$14+($B$21*D21))
E22	=D22*$B$6-($B$14+($B$21*D22))
E23	=D23*$B$6-($B$14+($B$21*D23))
E24	=D24*$B$6-($B$14+($B$21*D24))
E25	=D25*$B$6-($B$14+($B$21*D25))
E26	=D26*$B$6-($B$14+($B$21*D26))
E27	=D27*$B$6-($B$14+($B$21*D27))
E28	=D28*$B$6-($B$14+($B$21*D28))
E29	=D29*$B$6-($B$14+($B$21*D29))
E30	=D30*$B$6-($B$14+($B$21*D30))
E31	=D31*$B$6-($B$14+($B$21*D31))
E32	=D32*$B$6-($B$14+($B$21*D32))
E33	=D33*$B$6-($B$14+($B$21*D33))
E34	=D34*$B$6-($B$14+($B$21*D34))
E35	=D35*$B$6-($B$14+($B$21*D35))
E36	=D36*$B$6-($B$14+($B$21*D36))
E37	=D37*$B$6-($B$14+($B$21*D37))
E38	=D38*$B$6-($B$14+($B$21*D38))
E39	=D39*$B$6-($B$14+($B$21*D39))
E40	=D40*$B$6-($B$14+($B$21*D40))
E41	=D41*$B$6-($B$14+($B$21*D41))

Use Format⇨Cells to format the ranges from B6 to B21 and from E5 to E41 with the currency format (click the Number tab, choose Currency in the list box, and then click OK). To use the worksheet, enter your respective fixed and variable costs in the cells provided. In the quantity increment cell, enter the quantity that you want to use as a scale for the break-even analysis. For example, to see how many hundreds of units it will take to break even, enter 100 for a quantity increment. For a more detailed analysis, enter a smaller increment. You can extend the analysis to cover even more units by simply copying the respective formulas down the column past row 41. However, if you're not breaking even by row 41 of the worksheet, the analysis is trying to tell you that your pricing or manufacturing strategy has a serious flaw!

IRA Calculator

An IRA calculator is a straightforward financial tool that is designed to plot the increasing value of an IRA (Individual Retirement Account). Four columns within the worksheet contain a beginning balance in the account, a yearly contribution, an interest rate, and an ending balance. A less complex worksheet would assume a standard interest rate and yearly contribution, but in real life, your yearly contribution may vary, and it is virtually impossible to plan for a standard interest rate. Keeping separate columns for these values for each year gives you the ability to insert each year's interest rate and the amount of the IRA contribution.

In column C, you enter the beginning balance (starting with zero in the first row). Column D contains the yearly contribution, which for purposes of example, is $1,700 the first year, $1,850 the second, $1,900 the third, and assumed to be $2,000 per year afterwards. Column E contains the interest rate, assumed to be 8.5 percent the first year, 7.25 percent the second year, 6.75 percent the third year, and 6.5 percent per year afterwards. Column F contains the formula that calculates the effect of the accumulating interest and the added yearly investment. The formula calculates on the basis of simple interest by adding the current balance to the yearly contribution and adding the result multiplied by the yearly interest rate to provide the new balance. Each year's new balance is then carried to the successive balance column. The worksheet is shown in Figure 25-3.

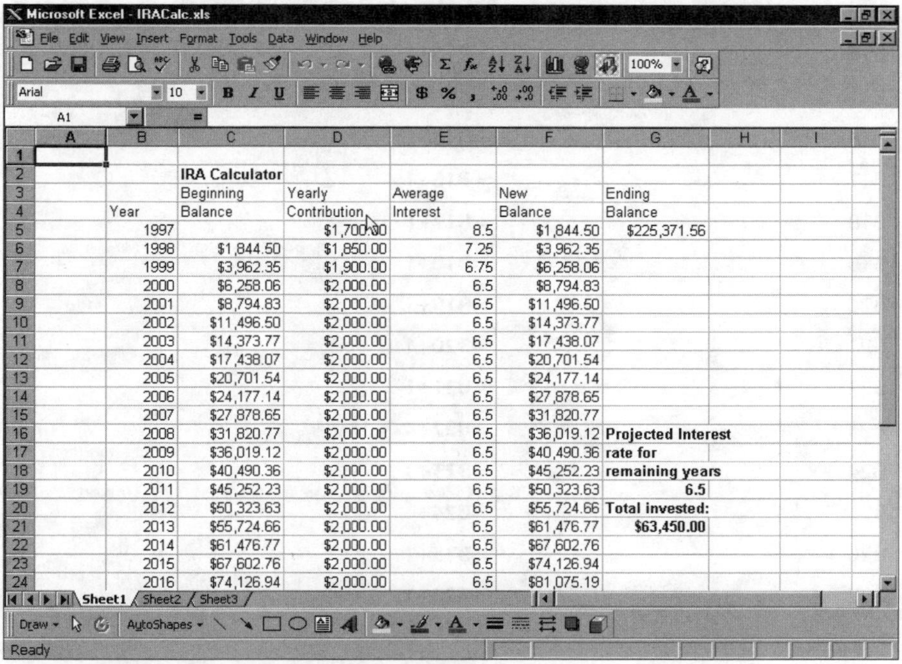

	A	B	C	D	E	F	G
1							
2			IRA Calculator				
3			Beginning	Yearly	Average	New	Ending
4		Year	Balance	Contribution	Interest	Balance	Balance
5		1997		$1,700.00	8.5	$1,844.50	$225,371.56
6		1998	$1,844.50	$1,850.00	7.25	$3,962.35	
7		1999	$3,962.35	$1,900.00	6.75	$6,258.06	
8		2000	$6,258.06	$2,000.00	6.5	$8,794.83	
9		2001	$8,794.83	$2,000.00	6.5	$11,496.50	
10		2002	$11,496.50	$2,000.00	6.5	$14,373.77	
11		2003	$14,373.77	$2,000.00	6.5	$17,438.07	
12		2004	$17,438.07	$2,000.00	6.5	$20,701.54	
13		2005	$20,701.54	$2,000.00	6.5	$24,177.14	
14		2006	$24,177.14	$2,000.00	6.5	$27,878.65	
15		2007	$27,878.65	$2,000.00	6.5	$31,820.77	
16		2008	$31,820.77	$2,000.00	6.5	$36,019.12	Projected Interest
17		2009	$36,019.12	$2,000.00	6.5	$40,490.36	rate for
18		2010	$40,490.36	$2,000.00	6.5	$45,252.23	remaining years
19		2011	$45,252.23	$2,000.00	6.5	$50,323.63	6.5
20		2012	$50,323.63	$2,000.00	6.5	$55,724.66	Total invested:
21		2013	$55,724.66	$2,000.00	6.5	$61,476.77	$63,450.00
22		2014	$61,476.77	$2,000.00	6.5	$67,602.76	
23		2015	$67,602.76	$2,000.00	6.5	$74,126.94	
24		2016	$74,126.94	$2,000.00	6.5	$81,075.19	

Figure 25-3: An IRA calculator worksheet.

To build the worksheet, enter the following formulas into the cells shown:

Cell	Entry
B4	Year
B5	1997
B6	=B5+1

To create the following formulas, select the range from B6 to B37. Then choose Edit⇨Fill⇨Down.

Cell	Entry
B7	=B6+1
B8	=B7+1
B9	=B8+1
B10	=B9+1
B11	=B10+1
B12	=B11+1
B13	=B12+1
B14	=B13+1
B15	=B14+1
B16	=B15+1
B17	=B16+1
B18	=B17+1
B19	=B18+1
B20	=B19+1
B21	=B20+1
B22	=B21+1
B23	=B22+1
B24	=B23+1
B25	=B24+1
B26	=B25+1
B27	=B26+1

Cell	Entry
B28	=B27+1
B29	=B28+1
B30	=B29+1
B31	=B30+1
B32	=B31+1
B33	=B32+1
B34	=B33+1
B35	=B34+1
B36	=B35+1
B37	=B36+1

In column C of the worksheet, enter the following values and formulas:

Cell	Entry
C2	**IRA Calculator**
C3	**Beginning**
C4	**Balance**
C6	=F5

To create the following formulas, select the range from C6 to C37. Then choose Edit⇨Fill⇨Down.

Cell	Entry
C7	=F6
C8	=F7
C9	=F8
C10	=F9
C11	=F10
C12	=F11
C13	=F12

(continued)

(continued)

Cell	Entry
C14	=F13
C15	=F14
C16	=F15
C17	=F16
C18	=F17
C19	=F18
C20	=F19
C21	=F20
C22	=F21
C23	=F22
C24	=F23
C25	=F24
C26	=F25
C27	=F26
C28	=F27
C29	=F28
C30	=F29
C31	=F30
C32	=F31
C33	=F32
C34	=F33
C35	=F34
C36	=F35
C37	=F36

In column D of the worksheet, enter the following values:

Cell	Entry
D3	Yearly
D4	Contribution
D5	1700

Cell	Entry
D6	1850
D7	1900
D8	2000

To create the following entries, select the range from D8 to D37. Then choose Edit⇨Fill⇨Down.

Cell	Entry
D9	2000
D10	2000
D11	2000
D12	2000
D13	2000
D14	2000
D15	2000
D16	2000
D17	2000
D18	2000
D19	2000
D20	2000
D21	2000
D22	2000
D23	2000
D24	2000
D25	2000
D26	2000
D27	2000
D28	2000
D29	2000
D30	2000
D31	2000

(continued)

(continued)

Cell	Entry
D32	2000
D33	2000
D34	2000
D35	2000
D36	2000
D37	2000

In column E of the worksheet, enter the following values and formulas:

Cell	Entry
E3	Average
E4	Interest
E5	8.5
E6	7.25
E7	6.75
E8	=$G$19

To create the following formulas, select the range from E8 to E37. Then choose Edit⇨Fill⇨Down.

Cell	Entry
E9	=$G$19
E10	=$G$19
E11	=$G$19
E12	=$G$19
E13	=$G$19
E14	=$G$19
E15	=$G$19
E16	=$G$19
E17	=$G$19

Cell	Entry
E18	=$G$19
E19	=$G$19
E20	=$G$19
E21	=$G$19
E22	=$G$19
E23	=$G$19
E24	=$G$19
E25	=$G$19
E26	=$G$19
E27	=$G$19
E28	=$G$19
E29	=$G$19
E30	=$G$19
E31	=$G$19
E32	=$G$19
E33	=$G$19
E34	=$G$19
E35	=$G$19
E36	=$G$19
E37	=$G$19

In column F of the worksheet, enter the following:

Cell	Entry
F3	New
F4	Balance
F5	=((C5+D5)*E5/100)+C5+D5

Select the range of cells from F5 to F37. Then choose Edit⇨Fill⇨Down to copy the formula into the successive cells.

In column G of the worksheet, enter the following values and formulas:

Cell	Entry
G3	Ending
G4	Balance
G5	=F37
G16	Projected interest
G17	rate for
G18	remaining years
G19	6.5
G20	Total invested:
G21	=SUM(D4:D36)

Using Format⇨Cells, format the ranges from C6 to C37, D5 to D37, and F5 to F37 in the dollars-and-cents format. Also format cells G5 and G21 for the same type of display.

After you have entered the formulas, the worksheet displays the interest accumulation and yearly balances, as shown in Figure 25-3. You can change the interest rates and investment amounts to correspond to your desired investment rates.

Mortgage Analysis and Amortization Schedule

The mortgage analysis worksheet has a straightforward design. It uses the PMT (payment) function to calculate the payments on a loan and displays an amortization schedule for the term of the loan. Figure 25-4 shows the worksheet.

Cells D5, D6, and D7 of the worksheet contain the principal loan amount, interest rate, and term of the loan in years. In cell D9, the following formula supplies the rate, number of periods, and present value:

=PMT((D6/12),(D7*12),-D5)

The rate and the number of periods are converted to months, and the present value is shown as a negative value representing cash paid out.

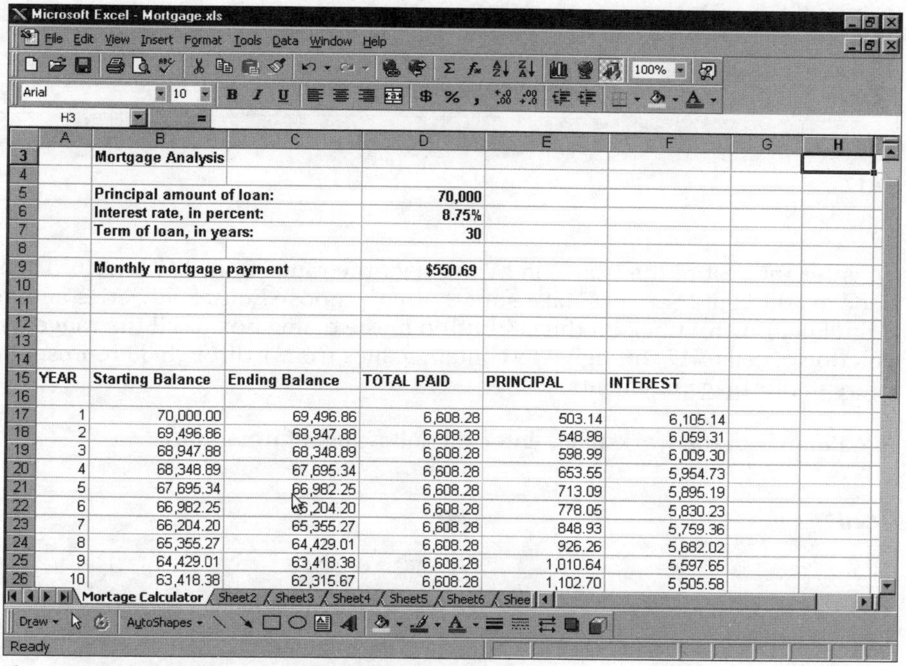

Figure 25-4: A mortgage analysis worksheet.

Year one of the amortization schedule begins in row 17. The starting balance is de-rived from the amount entered in cell D5. To arrive at the ending balance in column C for the first year, use a formula containing the following variation of Excel's PV (Present Value) function:

=PV(($D$6/12),(12*($D$7-A17)),-$D$9)

It is now a simple matter to calculate the remaining forms in the row. The total paid (column D of the amortization schedule) is the monthly payment (cell D9) multiplied by 12 to compute a yearly amount. The principal in column E is calculated by subtracting column C of the schedule (the ending balance) from column B (the starting balance).

You calculate the interest (column F) by subtracting the difference between the starting and ending balance from the total paid. As the formulas are duplicated down the worksheet, relative references are adjusted upwards for each successive row location.

Choose Format⇨Column⇨Width to change the width of column A to 5 spaces and the width of columns B, C, D, E, and F to 15 spaces.

To build the worksheet, enter the following formulas in the cells shown:

Cell	Entry
A15	YEAR
A17	1

To enter the rest of the year numbers, select the range from A17 to A46. Then choose Edit⇨Fill⇨Series. (Make sure that you choose Edit⇨Fill⇨Series and *not* Edit⇨Fill⇨Down.) Click on the OK button in the dialog box to fill the range. When you do so, cells A17 through A46 contain values from 1 through 30 representing 30 years of mortgage payments.

In column B of the worksheet, enter the following information:

Cell	Entry
B3	Mortgage Analysis
B5	Principal amount of loan:
B6	Interest rate, in percent:
B7	Term of loan, in years:
B9	Monthly mortgage payment
B15	Starting balance
B17	=D5
B18	=C17

In column C of the worksheet, enter the following information and formulas:

Cell	Entry
C15	Ending balance
C17	=PV(($D$6/12),(12*($D$7-A17)),-$D$9)
C18	=PV(($D$6/12),(12*($D$7-A18)),-$D$9)

In column D of the worksheet, enter the following values and formulas:

Cell	Entry
D5	70000
D6	8.75%
D7	30
D9	=PMT((D6/12),(D7*12),-D5)
D15	TOTAL PAID
D17	=$D$9*12
D18	=$D$9*12

In column E of the worksheet, enter the following information and formulas:

Cell	Entry
E15	PRINCIPAL
E17	=B17-C17
E18	=B18-C18

In column F of the worksheet, enter the following information and formulas:

Cell	Entry
F15	INTEREST
F17	=D17-(B17-C17)
F18	=D18-(B18-C18)

When you have entered these formulas, select the range of cells from B18 to F46. Choose Edit⇨Fill⇨Down to fill the successive formulas into the selected rows. To apply formatting to a range, select the range from B17 to F46. Choose Format⇨ Cells and click on the Number tab in the Format Cells dialog box. Click Currency in the list box and then click OK. At this point, your worksheet should resemble the example in Figure 25-4.

The range in this example assumes a 30-year loan. If you enter a period of 15 years but leave the formulas intact for 30 years, however, you will get the interesting benefit of a nest egg that has been calculated as an increasing negative balance when the mortgage ends and the amortization schedule shows mortgage payments still being added. To avoid this situation, just adjust the range when you fill down as needed to match the number of years for the mortgage. If you want to get really fancy, you can record a macro that clears the range, gets the number of years from cell D7, selects a new range equivalent to that number of years, and performs a Fill Down command.

Summary

This chapter provided you with a step-by-step look at what is involved in creating various models that are typical of the types that you may find useful in Excel.

✦ You created a worksheet to handle mortgage loan calculation and amortization.

✦ You created a worksheet to handle break-even analysis.

✦ You created a worksheet to handle cash-flow management.

✦ You created a worksheet to handle IRA calculations.

The next chapter answers common questions that arise when you use Excel.

Where to go next...

As these examples demonstrate, much of the basic work behind creating and using spreadsheets involves routine data and formula entry and simple to moderately complex formatting. For many spreadsheet users, these tasks are 90 percent of what they do in Excel.

✦ You can find tips and techniques that help ease the tedium of basic data and formula entry in Chapter 14.

✦ For the complete scoop on how you can format your Excel worksheets, see Chapter 15.

✦   ✦   ✦

The Excel Top Ten

As a whole, Excel users routinely find the same questions arising as they gain proficiency with the program. To save you time and effort, we've compiled the top ten Excel questions and their answers, based on inquiries to Microsoft Technical Support and the Microsoft forums on CompuServe.

1. Can I set up a workbook so that it opens each time I start Microsoft Excel?

You can open a workbook each time you start Excel by placing the workbook in the Xlstart folder. This folder is located in the same folder as the Excel program itself. All the workbooks placed in this directory will be opened at the start of Microsoft Excel. These workbooks can include worksheets, chart sheets, visual basic modules, Excel 5.0/7.0 dialog sheets, and Excel 4.0 macro sheets.

If a template is placed in the Xlstart folder, it appears as an option when you choose File⇨New. The template also appears as an option in the Insert dialog box that appears when you choose the Insert command from the sheet tab shortcut menu. (This shortcut menu appears after you right-click on a sheet tab.)

2. How do I change the default working directory or the standard font in Microsoft Excel?

Changing the working directory and the standard font are simple tasks in Excel 97. To set these options for all workbooks, use the General tab of the Options dialog box, which appears after you choose Tools⇨Options. Follow these steps to change the default working directory:

1. Choose Tools⇨Options and click on the General tab in the Options dialog box.

2. In the Default File Location text box, enter the full path of the directory that you want to use for your Excel work directory.

3. Click OK.

To change the default font for all new workbooks, follow these steps:

1. Choose Tools⇨Options and click on the General tab in the Options dialog box.

2. In the Standard Font list box and in the Size list box, select the font and size that you want to use.

3. Click on the OK button to make the changes.

3. How can I display more than one workbook at a time?

By default, each time that you open a workbook, it occupies the entire window. You can display multiple workbooks simultaneously with these steps:

1. Use the File⇨Open command to open as many workbooks as you want to view.

2. Choose Window⇨Arrange.

3. In the Arrange Windows dialog box that appears, choose tiled, horizontal, vertical, or cascade as desired, and then click on OK to display the workbooks simultaneously.

4. I'm an accomplished Lotus 1-2-3 user, and I'm having trouble getting used to the menu structure of Excel 97. Does Excel 97 offer any help for Lotus users?

You can enable customized help for Lotus 1-2-3 users. This help displays the Excel menu equivalents for any Lotus 1-2-3 keystroke combination that you enter in the Help dialog box.

1. Choose Tools⇨Options and click on the Transition tab in the Options dialog box.

2. Turn on the Lotus 1-2-3 Help option and click OK.

5. How can I prevent a slash (/) or a hyphen (-) from being formatted as a date when it is entered?

Excel automatically applies built-in number formats to values entered in an unformatted cell. Normally the appearance of the value is not altered because the format is a general number format. However, if the entry contains a slash or a hyphen that separates values, Excel may have trouble interpreting the value because it may think it is a date. If the entry contains a colon, Excel may think that the value represents a time value (hours, minutes, seconds, and so on). If you want to display the value exactly as it was entered — with slashes, hyphens, or colons — and you don't want Excel to confuse the value with a date or time, you must format the value as a text value. To create a text value, simply precede the entry with a single quotation mark (') or follow these steps:

1. Select the cells in which you want to enter data.

2. Choose Format⇨Cells and select the Number tab from the dialog box that appears.

3. In the Category list box, select the Text option.

4. Click on the OK button.

When you enter values in the selected cells, the values are displayed as you typed them. Remember that the cells must be formatted as text prior to entering your data.

6. What are some shortcuts for selecting cells and ranges?

Along with the normal clicking and dragging technique, you can use the Name list box on the left side of the formula bar to select cells and ranges on the active sheet and on other sheets within a workbook. The Name list box displays the cell reference or the cell name of the currently selected cell, and it provides a list of all the defined names in your workbook when you click on the arrow to the right of the list box. When you select a name or enter a cell reference in this list box, Excel selects the specified cell or range. You can also use the Name list box to define a name and insert the name into a formula. If you want to define a name for a cell or cell range so that you can select it later or use it in a formula, select the cell or range, click on the Name list box, enter a new name, and press the Enter key. Table 26-1 contains a list of shortcuts for selecting cells and ranges.

To select	Do the following

Table 26-1
Shortcuts for selecting cells and ranges

To select	Do the following
A named cell or range on the active or another worksheet	In the Name list box, type or select the name.
An unnamed cell	In the Name list box, enter the cell reference and press Enter.
An unnamed range	With your mouse, select the first cell in the range. If the last cell in your range is a named cell, hold down the Shift key and select the name from the Name list box or enter a cell reference and press Shift+Enter.
Nonadjacent named and unnamed cells	With your mouse, select the first cell or range. To make subsequent selections, hold down the Ctrl key while you select a name from the Name list box or enter a cell reference in the Name list box and press Crtl+Enter.

7. How do I format characters in a cell that I want to be superscript, subscript, or in a different font?

In Excel, you can add such character formatting as superscript, subscript, different fonts, styles, size, underlining, color, and so on to individual characters in a single cell. Table 26-2 contains a few examples of different kinds of formatting that you can add to the characters in a cell.

Table 26-2
Formatting that you can add to characters in a cell

Formatting	Example
Italics	*4th Quarter*
Superscript	2^3
Subscript	10_2
Different font	$\Phi(R\text{-}S)=\Phi\text{-}1(S)$

Note The Φ character is a capital F in the Symbol font. (Use the Font list box in the toolbars to change to the Symbol font, and type **F**.) You can select individual text in a cell by clicking on the formula bar and then dragging to select the text. If you are using the in-cell editing feature, you must double-click in the cell and drag to select the text that you want to format. If you are in a text box, double-click in the text box and drag to make the selection that you want. When the text is highlighted, choose Format⇨Cells and select the Font tab from the Format Cells dialog box. Then choose the options that you want. The multiple-character formatting applies only to text.

To enter superscript and subscript, you must enter the values as text by preceding the value with a single quotation mark ('). For example 2^3 and 10_2 would be displayed as 23 and 102 if they are not entered as text. A second option is to format the cell with the text number format before the value is entered.

8. How can I combine the contents of two cells into one cell?

If you have information in two separate cells that you want to combine into one cell, or if you want to combine text with a formula in a cell, use the CONCATENATE( ) function, which takes up to 30 arguments and can consist of cell references, text, and formulas. Note that the text arguments must be enclosed in quotation marks.

Say that someone's first name is stored in cell C1 and the last name is stored in cell D1. If you want to combine the text in those cells, enter the following formula in cell E1:

=CONCATENATE(C1, "",D1)

The second argument in the formula is a space enclosed in quotation marks. If you wanted to combine the text *Amount Payable: $* with the sum of cells A1:B1, you could enter the following formula in cell E1:

=CONCATENATE("Amount Payable: $",SUM(A1:B1))

9. How can I define an area on my worksheet for printing?

To define a print area, choose File⇨Page Setup and click on the Sheet tab of the Page Setup dialog box. Place the insertion point in the Print Area text box and, on your worksheet, select the range or ranges that you want to print. You can also enter references or names for the print area yourself. To make this task easy to do, you may want to add the Set Print Area button to a toolbar.

You also can simply select a range and print it. To do so, select the range or ranges that you want to print, choose File⇨Print, and then choose the Selection option in the Print What area of the Print dialog box.

10. How can I make my titles print on each page?

If you want to print titles on each page, choose the Page Setup command from the File menu and click on the Sheet tab. Place your insertion point in the Rows to Repeat at Top box or the Columns to Repeat at Left box and then, on your worksheet, select the rows or columns that you want to print on each page. You may also enter references or names for the rows or columns in these boxes yourself.

Summary

This chapter covered the top ten Excel questions and their answers. The chapter also concludes the Excel section of this book. The section that follows describes Microsoft PowerPoint, the presentation graphics package provided with Office 97.

Where to go next...

✦ If you have questions regarding formatting that aren't covered here, you can find answers in Chapter 17.

✦ You can get help with your printing questions in Chapter 20.

✦   ✦   ✦

PowerPoint

Working in PowerPoint

CHAPTER
27

This chapter provides methods that you will find useful as you use PowerPoint. You will learn about the uses of the PowerPoint presentation window. You will learn how to move your toolbars, save presentations, and align objects. Objects become more important in PowerPoint as you experiment with different layouts. You will learn how to perform different tasks with the objects that you add to your presentation. You will also learn methods that you can use to rearrange a slide show and to make changes to the slide layout itself.

Learning About the Presentation Window

PowerPoint's *presentation window* is where you create slides and arrange them in your presentation — this is the bulk of the work you'll do in PowerPoint. Familiarizing yourself with the PowerPoint window (Figure 27-1) is very important in helping you function easily in PowerPoint.

At the lower-left corner of the presentation window, you will notice the view buttons, which enable you to switch among different views in the PowerPoint presentation window. The view buttons include the following: Slide view, Outline View, Slide Sorter View, Notes Pages View, and Slide Show. You can also change views by choosing the appropriate commands from the View menu.

Click on the Slide view button when you want only one slide to appear on-screen. Slide view enables you to do different maintenance on the slide, such as editing. Figure 27-1 shows Slide view.

Click on the Outline View button to show the slide in outline form so that you can move headings and other information by clicking and dragging (see Figure 27-2). Outline view enables you to see the title and body text of all your slides at the same time.

◆ ◆ ◆ ◆

In This Chapter

Understanding the presentation window

Working with shortcut menus and buttons

Using the toolbar

Using PowerPoint's default presentations

Opening and saving presentations

Working with text

Inserting, deleting, copying, rearranging, laying out, and moving between slides

Selecting, grouping, moving, copying, cropping, aligning, and stacking objects

Drawing, modifying, and manipulating shapes

◆ ◆ ◆ ◆

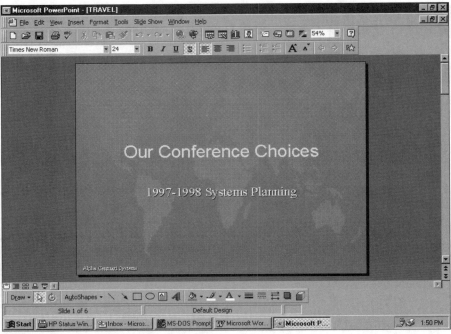

Figure 27-1: The PowerPoint window.

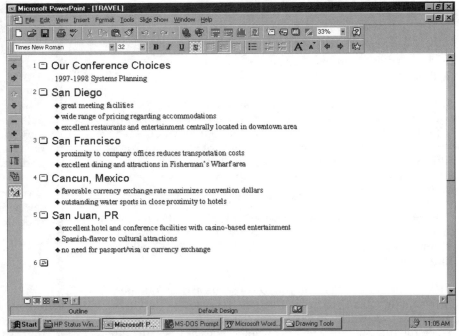

Figure 27-2: Outline view.

Click on the Slide Sorter View button to give you a view of all the slides in a presentation so that you can quickly see their layout and sequence (see Figure 27-3).

Click on the Notes Page View button to enter any notes that you may want to attach to the slide or to display any notes that you may have already written (see Figure 27-4).

Click on the Slide Show button to run the slide show after you have completed the slides. Notice how the slide now fills the screen (see Figure 27-5). You can also view your slides as a timed presentation.

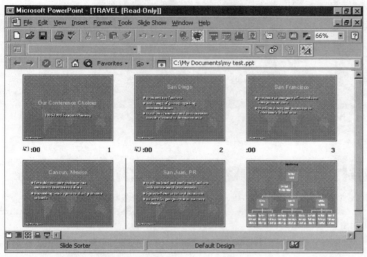

Figure 27-3: Slide Sorter view.

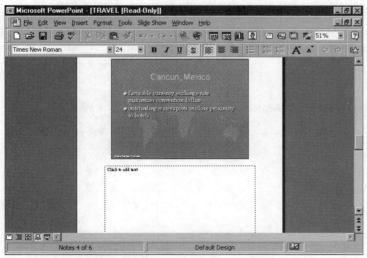

Figure 27-4: Notes Page view.

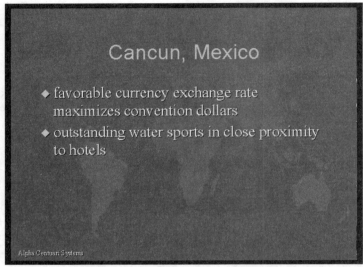

Figure 27-5: Slide Show view.

Working with Shortcuts and Toolbars

Just as with other Microsoft programs, PowerPoint offers shortcut menus, shortcut buttons, and toolbars to make it as easy as possible for you to create your presentations.

Using shortcut menus

PowerPoint provides shortcut menus so that you can perform different commands without having to use the pull-down menus. Shortcut menus can save lots of time. To activate any of the shortcut menus, move the pointer to the object that you want the command to act on and right-click with the mouse. Figure 27-6 shows a shortcut menu in PowerPoint.

Figure 27-6: A shortcut menu in the PowerPoint window.

Using shortcut buttons

PowerPoint also offers three shortcut buttons that are located at the right side of the toolbar. These buttons include the New Slide, Layout, and Apply Design buttons. The New Slide button inserts a new slide into your presentation following the current one. The Slide Layout button displays the Slide Layout dialog box (see Figure 27-7). From here, you can choose a layout for the slide by clicking on the desired layout in the dialog box. The Apply Design button applies a new design to the presentation.

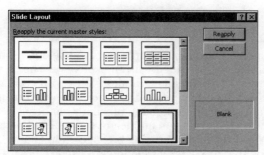

Figure 27-7: The Slide Layout dialog box.

Using the toolbars

When you open the PowerPoint window and enter Slide View, you see three toolbars. Use the Standard toolbar to open presentations, to save, to print, or to insert objects and charts. Use the Formatting toolbar to perform tasks related to formatting, such as applying different fonts and styles and changing the indentation of the presentation. Use the Drawing toolbar, located at the bottom of the screen, to perform tasks related to controlling the appearance of shapes. You can draw shapes, rotate them, and control different aspects of their appearance on-screen. You can activate the other toolbars that are available in PowerPoint by choosing the Toolbars command from the View menu and then selecting the toolbars from the list in the Toolbars drop-down menu (see Figure 27-8). Or you can right-click on the toolbar area of the screen and then select the toolbars that you want from the shortcut menu that appears.

While you are in Slide View, you can use the AutoShapes portion of the Drawing toolbar to insert trapezoids, diamonds, or other shapes into your presentation and to size them. Use the Animation Effects toolbar to add different animation effects to your presentation. With the different effects, you can have words appear from left to right across a slide, or the words can appear as if they were being typed. You can also have words appear in a camera-like style.

Figure 27-8: The Toolbars drop-down menu.

Using PowerPoint's Default Presentations

By far, the easiest way to create a presentation in PowerPoint is to use one of the many default presentation formats that are provided with the software. The advantage of using a default format is that it already contains slides with content guidelines that you can follow to quickly build a presentation for a typical business need. PowerPoint provides one blank presentation, many presentation designs, and complete presentations. The following list gives you an idea of the types of default presentations you will see in the New Presentation dialog box shown in Figure 27-9. Keep in mind that the presentations that are listed as Online are used to create presentations that can be saved as HTML files for viewing on the Internet :

✦ **Company Meeting** creates a presentation for a company meeting.

✦ **Corporate Financial Overview** creates a presentation that allows you to give a financial overview of your company.

✦ **Marketing Plan** creates a presentation that allows you to show a marketing plan for a company.

✦ **Project Status (Online)** shows the progress of a company project. This is one of the online presentations which means that it will be saved as an HTML file.

✦ **Recommending a Strategy** offers a slide layout that is useful for determining a strategy.

✦ **General** creates a blank presentation — you have to provide all of the formatting, layout, and content.

The last default presentation format is the Blank option, which enables you to create your own layout. You need to be an experienced PowerPoint user to feel comfortable using this option.

To create a presentation by using a default presentation format, follow these steps:

1. Start a new presentation by choosing New from the File menu. The New Presentation dialog box appears, as shown in Figure 27-9.

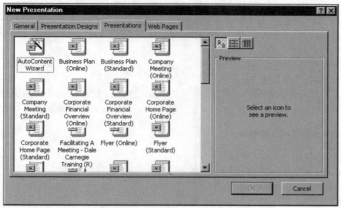

Figure 27-9: The New Presentation dialog box.

2. Click on the Presentations tab, if it is not already open, to show the default presentation formats.

3. Click on the desired presentation format and then click on the OK button (or double-click on the desired presentation format). PowerPoint loads the presentation format, and the first slide of the presentation appears. Figure 27-10 shows the first slide of the Project Status presentation format.

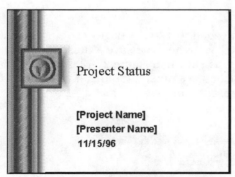

Figure 27-10: The first slide of the Project Status presentation.

After you use these steps to create a presentation, you can modify the text in the slides by clicking on the text to select each item that you see (titles, subtitles, or text within the presentation) and typing your desired text. You can use the Page Up and Page Down keys or the Previous Slide and Next Slide buttons at the lower-right side of the window to move among the various slides of your presentation.

Each slide contains text in the form of suggestions that you can modify. For example, Figure 27-11 shows the second of nine available slides in the Project Status presentation. You can click on the existing text and edit it as desired while in Slide view.

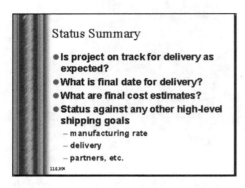

Figure 27-11: The second slide of the Project Status presentation.

If you don't want one of the default slides in your presentation, just move to the unwanted slide and choose Edit⇨Delete Slide. If you want to add a new slide to the presentation, move to the slide that you want the new slide to follow and choose Insert⇨New Slide. The New Slide dialog box appears. Now choose the slide layout you want. Then you can click in the boxes and type the desired text for the slide. (You'll learn more about adding slides and about adding items to slides later in this chapter.)

After you've finished adding the needed text to the pages of your presentation, you can save it by choosing File⇨Save. When you save a presentation for the first time, the Save dialog box appears, as shown in Figure 27-12. Enter a name for the file in the File name text box and choose a different folder, if you want. Then click on the Save button to save the presentation.

Figure 27-12: The Save dialog box.

More Info You can print your finished presentation by choosing File⇨Print to open the Print dialog box. Choose All if you want to print all the slides in the presentation or choose Current Slide if you just want to print the slide that's currently visible in the PowerPoint window. After you make your selection, click on the OK button to begin printing. You can print information in PowerPoint in several ways. You'll find a full description of printing and of the other options in the Print dialog box in Chapter 30.

When you're finished with the presentation, choose File⇨Close if you want to do other work in PowerPoint or choose File⇨Exit to get completely out of PowerPoint.

Working with Presentations

The information that you have read so far can easily get you started with creating effective business presentations. However, you can do a lot more with PowerPoint, and the rest of this chapter will fill you in on the basics. For example, PowerPoint does not differ from other Microsoft applications in how you open and save a file — in this case, a presentation. Choosing File⇨Open opens a presentation; choosing File⇨Save saves the current presentation.

Opening a new presentation

When you want to open a new presentation, choose File⇨New to open the New Presentation dialog box (see Figure 27-9, a few pages back). The dialog box contains four tabs: General, Presentation Designs, Presentations, and Web Pages. By default, the General tab is open, from which you can choose a default presentation format (see "Using PowerPoint's Default Presentations" earlier in the chapter).

The Presentation Designs tab contains a host of designs that you can use for your slide backgrounds (see Figure 27-13). Use the Preview window to view a design after you click on the icon of your choice.

After you click on the General tab, you will see the icon for a Blank Presentation (see Figure 27-14). Choose the Blank Presentation to create a default blank presentation.

After you have chosen the template that you want for your presentation, click on the OK button to begin filling out the template.

You can also create a presentation based on another presentation. Find the presentation you want to use as a base, and save it as a template (use File ⇨ Save As and choose PowerPoint Templates in the Save as type area). Then choose Format⇨Apply Template and choose the presentation you just saved as a template.

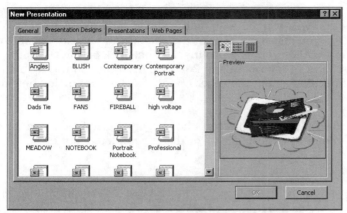

Figure 27-13: The Presentation Designs tab of the New Presentation dialog box.

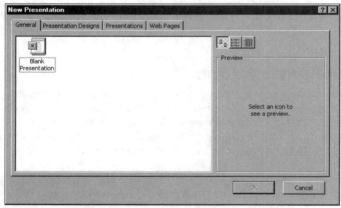

Figure 27-14: The General tab of the New Presentation dialog box.

Several presentations can be opened at the same time in PowerPoint. Use File⇨Open. Hold down the Ctrl key as you click on the presentations in the Open dialog box. The current presentation that you are working on appears on the top window. All the presentations that are open can be displayed using Ctrl+F6.

Saving a presentation

You save a presentation in PowerPoint the same way that you save a file in other Microsoft programs: you choose File⇨Save. If you have not saved the presentation before, the Save As dialog box opens, where you are prompted to enter a name for the presentation. If you have already given the presentation a name, it is saved under that name.

You can also perform other tasks in the Save As dialog box. You can change the name of a presentation by entering a new name in the File name text box. You can save files as metafiles or outlines by selecting the new file type from the Save as type list box and then clicking on the OK button to save the file. Keep in mind that you can also save a presentation as a PowerPoint 4.0 file for use with PowerPoint 4.0.

When you have completed your work in PowerPoint and you want to exit, choose File⇨Close.

Entering summary information

You can include summary information with the presentations that you save. You enter summary information — which includes a title, subject, and other key information to help you keep track of the presentations — in the Summary Information dialog box. To enter summary information for your presentation, perform the following steps:

1. Choose File⇨Properties. The Properties dialog box appears, with the Summary tab open, as shown in Figure 27-15.

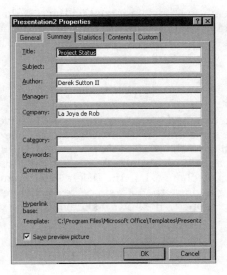

Figure 27-15: The Summary tab of the Properties dialog box.

2. Enter the information that you want in each of the following text boxes:

- **Title** — Enter a name for the presentation.

- **Subject** — Enter a brief description of the contents of the presentation.

- **Author** — Enter the name of the author. The default name is the name that you entered when you installed Microsoft Office.

- **Manager** — Enter a manager name, if you wish.

- **Company** — Enter a company name, if you wish.

- **Category** — Enter a category for the presentation if you wish to categorize it.

- **Keywords** — Enter keywords that you associate with the presentation. These words can help you in a Find File search, if you need to use this command from the File menu. You can use the Copy and Paste commands from the Edit menu to insert the titles of your slides in the Keywords list box.

- **Comments** — Enter any comments that you feel are needed.

3. When you have finished entering the information, click on the OK button to store the information.

4. The summary information can be viewed by choosing File⇨Properties. This displays the properties for the presentation. Then choose the Summary tab to display the summary info.

Working with Text

After you have opened a new presentation, it will not contain the text that you want to use, so you will have to add and edit your own text. The following section will teach you the basics of editing text in Outline and Slide views. Later in the chapter, you'll learn how to add objects to your presentation.

Editing in Outline view

Outline view is excellent for editing text, and it enables you to see the overall content of your presentation at the same time. You can switch to Outline view by choosing View⇨Outline or by clicking on the Outline View button in the status bar. After you are in Outline view, you can edit text by simply clicking on it and moving the cursor to the area that you want to change. Use the Delete key to remove characters to the right of the cursor and use the Backspace key to delete characters to the left of the cursor. Figure 27-16 shows a slide in Outline view ready for editing.

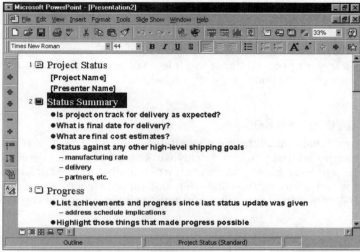

Figure 27-16: A slide in Outline view.

When you select text in PowerPoint, the program selects whole words. If you want to select individual characters, choose Tools➪Options. In the Options dialog box, choose the Edit tab. Next, uncheck the Automatic Word Selection option and click on the OK button to turn it off.

Editing in Slide view

Slide view also provides an easy way to edit text, and you get a good opportunity to see the appearance of an individual slide. You can switch to Slide view by choosing View➪Slide or by clicking on the Slide view button in the status bar. As Figure 27-17 demonstrates, you can edit text or an object by clicking on the text or the object to select it and then clicking in the space where you want the cursor to appear and making the changes.

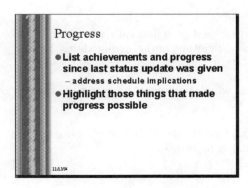

Figure 27-17: A slide in Slide view.

Working with Slides

You use slide view to do most of your work with slides. Slide view lets you see each slide pretty much as it will appear in your presentation. It also lets you move between the slides in your presentations, and it lets you click and drag to move the slide within your presentation.

Moving between slides

When you have more than one slide in a presentation, you must be able to move easily among the slides so that you can quickly work on all of them. (Remember that in all views except Slide Show you can perform edits by double-clicking on the slide.) How you move among the slides depends on the view that you are in at the time. Table 27-1 shows how you can move among slides in each of the views.

Table 27-1	
Moving among slides in different views	
View	*How to move among slides*
Outline	Use the scrollbar to move to the slide, click on the slide icon to the left of the slide's title, or click inside the text to perform the changes.
Slide Sorter	Click on the slide that you want to see. A border appears around the slide. If you then double-click on the slide, you are switched to Slide view where you can make changes to your slide.
Slide	Drag the scrollbox until the slide that you want appears or press the Page Up key.
Notes Pages	Drag the scrollbox until the slide that you want appears or press the Page Down key.

Inserting slides

As you build your presentations in PowerPoint, you naturally will need to make changes to the presentation by inserting, deleting, and copying slides. Follow these steps to add a slide to a presentation:

1. In any view, choose the slide after which you want the new slide to appear.

2. Choose Insert⇨New Slide.

3. The New Slide dialog box appears. Choose the slide layout you want and click the OK button to choose that slide layout.

If you want to change the new slide's layout (or create a slide layout), follow these steps:

1. In Slide View, right-click on the slide and choose Slide Layout from the shortcut menu. The Slide Layout dialog box appears.

2. Choose the layout that you want and click on the Reapply button. (If you are creating a slide layout, the button is Apply.)

The layout is then applied to the slide.

Hot Stuff Another way to add a new slide is by clicking on the New Slide button on the Standard toolbar.

You can also add slides from a previous presentation to your current presentation. This shortcut is useful because it prevents you from taking the time to create an entirely new presentation when you already have slides that you can use from an old presentation. First, you must open the presentation to which you want to add the slide and choose the place where you want to insert the slide. The new slide will appear after the chosen slide. Then choose Insert⇨Slides from Files. The Slide Finder dialog box appears, as shown in Figure 27-18.

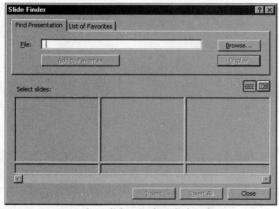

Figure 27-18: The Slide Finder dialog box.

Click Browse, and choose the drive and the folder that contains the presentation from which you want to insert the slides. To see the slides before you insert them, switch to Preview mode by clicking on the Preview button located at the top of the dialog box. Finally, double-click on the desired filename, and all the slides contained in that presentation will be inserted into the new presentation. Note that the inserted slides take on the look of the presentation in which they are inserted. This prevents you from having to make any changes to the look of the imported slides.

This then returns you to the Slide Finder dialog box. Click on the display button to show the slides of the presentation in the Slide Finder dialog box. If you just want to insert one slide, click on the Insert button. If you want to insert the entire presentation, choose the insert all button.

Deleting slides

Deleting a slide is relatively simple and can be performed in any view except Slide Show. Navigate to the slide, and choose Edit➪Delete Slide to remove the slide. If you delete a slide by accident, choose Edit➪Undo or click on the Undo button on the Standard toolbar to bring back the slide.

Copying and moving slides

You copy slides in PowerPoint just like you copy items in other Windows programs by using the Copy and Paste commands from the Edit menu. You can copy a slide by performing the following steps:

1. Switch to Slide Sorter view.
2. Choose the slide(s) that you want to copy. To select more than one slide, hold down the Shift key while you select the slides.
3. Choose Edit➪Copy.
4. Move to the slide after which you want to place the copied slide.
5. Choose Edit➪Paste.

You use the same method to move a slide, except that you use the Cut command rather than the Copy command.

Rearranging slides

From time to time you will need to change the order in which the slides appear in your presentation. PowerPoint provides for this need in Slide Sorter or Outline views. In these views you can use the drag-and-drop technique to move slides around.

Follow these steps to rearrange the order of your slides in Outline view:

1. Click on the icon for the slide that you want to move.
2. Drag the icon up or down in the outline.

You can also select just one piece of information on a slide and move it to another slide by clicking and dragging it to the desired place.

In Slide Sorter view, perform the following steps to rearrange slides:

1. Select the slide that you want to move to a new location.

2. Drag the slide to its new location. As you drag the slide, a vertical line will mark the place where it will appear.

3. Release the mouse button to insert the slide in its new location.

Changing the slide layout

You can also change the slide layout after you have created a slide. To change a slide layout, follow these steps:

1. In Slide Sorter view, move to the side that you want to change.

2. Choose Format ⇨ Slide Layout.

3. In the Slide Layout dialog box, choose the layout that you want to apply to the slide and click on the Reapply button (see Figure 27-19).

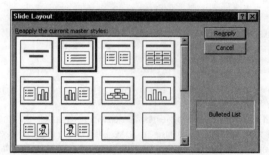

Figure 27-19: The Slide Layout dialog box.

Working with Objects

In PowerPoint, the basic component that you use to create a slide is an *object*. An object can be the box where you enter text, a picture brought in from another source, or the shape that you draw. You can have as many objects as you want on a slide.

Selecting and grouping objects

To select the object that you want to work with, click on it. Then you can add text to it and change its orientation, shape, color, or pattern. You can also select multiple objects by holding down the Shift key as you select the objects. To deselect an object, simply hold down the Shift key and click on the object again.

You can also group objects together, which is useful when you want to change the colors for a group of objects or align them horizontally. All the objects that you include in the group will act as one object. Therefore, if you perform an action on one of the objects, the action will affect all the objects in the group. When you group objects, you can flip, resize, or rotate them. If you want to change the grouping, you can do so by choosing Draw ⇨ Regroup after the objects have been grouped and ungrouped. Remember that the Regroup command will affect only the objects that were included in the original group.

You can also select and deselect noncontiguous objects in PowerPoint by clicking on the objects while you hold down the Shift key.

Moving and copying objects

As you work out a presentation, you may often have to move your objects around. PowerPoint provides for this need nicely with two options: the cut-and-copy method or the click-and-drag method.

To use the cut-and-copy method to move objects, follow these steps:

1. Switch to Slide view and select the object(s) that you want to move or copy.
2. Choose Edit⇨Cut to move the object to a new location via the Clipboard; choose Edit⇨Copy to copy it.
3. Move to the slide on which you want to place the information.
4. Choose Edit⇨Paste to place the Clipboard information onto the slide.

Using the click-and-drag method to move objects is equally simple. To use this method, click on the object and hold down the mouse button. Then move to the area where you want to place the object. Release the mouse button to place the object.

Sometimes you may find that you need to remove an object from a slide. To remove an object, select it and press the Delete key or choose Edit⇨Clear.

Cropping objects

In your quest to give your presentation a refined look, you may find it necessary to crop the objects, both pictures and graphic insertions, that you add to your presentation. *Cropping* is the trimming of an object to remove elements that you don't want from the picture. Follow these steps to crop an object:

1. After you add an object to a slide and the Picture toolbar appears, click on the Crop button.

2. Place the mouse pointer over a selection handle. If you want to crop two sides at once, you will need to use a corner handle. If you want to crop only one side, use a top or bottom handle. Figure 27-20 shows a cropped image. Click and drag to do the cropping.

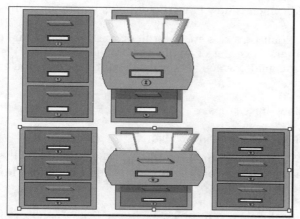

Figure 27-20: An image cropped in PowerPoint.

Aligning objects

When you create presentations, it is important that the objects have the same sort of alignment. Figure 27-21 shows a before and after shot of some objects on a slide in PowerPoint. As you can see, the slide with aligned objects has a better appearance than the one in which the objects are not aligned. Aligned objects make your objects appear more organized than those that aren't aligned.

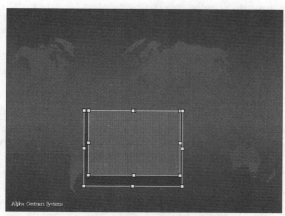

Figure 27-21: Objects aligned on a slide.

The Align command enables you to choose the method of alignment that you want to use. You can select objects and then align them, or you can use the rulers available in the PowerPoint window. PowerPoint is equipped with a reference system for aligning objects on slides. The system uses a grid and guides. The invisible grid covers the slide with twelve gridlines per inch and five lines per centimeter. When the objects are drawn, their corners align on the nearest intersection of the grid, which is how PowerPoint helps you to align objects.

The guides that PowerPoint provides are two rulers: one horizontal and one vertical. When the corners or center of an object (whichever is closer) is close to the guide, it snaps to the guide, which is how you align the object. You can even align a group of objects.

To align an object, follow these steps:

1. Select the object(s) that you want to align.

2. Choose Draw⇨Align or Distribute from the Drawing toolbar and then choose the alignment that you want from the submenu. You can choose from Lefts, Centers, Rights, Tops, Middles, or Bottoms.

If you want to automatically align your objects, choose Draw⇨Snap⇨To Grid from the Drawing toolbar. If the grid is on, you will see a check mark beside the choice on the menu. The Draw⇨Nudge choice allows you to align objects by moving the image in the direction you choose, a little at a time.

Hot
Stuff
You can use a number of toolbar buttons in the Customize dialog box that you'll find helpful in aligning objects. Choosing Tools⇨Customize opens the Customize dialog box with the Toolbars tab chosen. Choose the Commands Tab and you will see other toolbar buttons appear that you may find very useful in your work in PowerPoint. To add each of these buttons to your toolbar, click on the name of the button you wish to add from the Commands box. Next, drag the name up to the toolbar. You will notice the outline of a button appears. When you add the buttons to the top of the screen, you will notice that a toolbar is created for the button. Each of the alignment buttons that you wish to add will be added to that toolbar. If you are not sure of what each of the buttons do, the box at the bottom of the tab gives a description for each of the buttons as it is selected.

Stacking objects

When you are working with different objects, you will see that sometimes you have to overlap the objects to give them the correct effect. You may even want to change their order. You can also stack groups of objects in PowerPoint by moving a group of objects forward or backward. You can use the Tab key to navigate through the stacked objects.

Objects in a stack can be moved up or down one level at a time, or you can send an object all the way to the back or to the front at once. This feature prevents you from having to keep track of the objects as you draw them: in other words, you don't have to draw the bottom object first or the top object last and so on.

To bring an object to the front or to the back of a stack, right-click the object that you want to move and choose Order either Bring Forward, Send Backward, Send Back, or Bring. You can also choose Draw⇨Order⇨Bring Forward, Send Backward, Send Back or Bring Front from the Drawing toolbar. Figure 27-22 shows the original positions of objects on a slide, and how Bring Forward can change their positions.

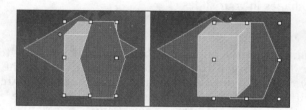

Figure 27-22: Left: The original positions of objects on a slide. Right: Changing the position of the objects with the Bring Forward command.

Working with Shapes

Sometimes when you work with PowerPoint, you will want to add your own shapes or art to the presentation. (Remember that these shapes are still considered objects by PowerPoint.) You can draw lines, arcs, rectangles, and ovals by using the Drawing toolbar. Figure 27-23 shows some examples of shapes that you can create in PowerPoint.

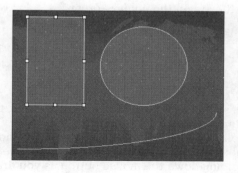

Figure 27-23: Examples of shapes that you can create in PowerPoint.

You can also add different attributes to the lines and shapes that you create. For example, you can insert dotted lines, color the lines, fill in the shapes, and add arrowheads to lines. Remember that you can't add text to your shapes except by grouping.

Drawing shapes

There are many tools you can use to perform your drawing tasks. On the Drawing toolbar you can use the Rectangle tool to draw rectangles, and the Line tool to draw lines. You can also use the Oval and Arc tools to create shapes.

Follow these steps to draw shapes in your slides:

1. Switch to Slide view, if you are not already there.

2. On the Drawing toolbar, click on the button for the object that you want to draw. Click on the Line Tool button if you want to draw a line; click on the Ellipse Tool button if you want to draw an oval or a circle; click on the Arc Tool button if you want to draw an arc; and so on. You can also click the AutoShapes Button on the Drawing toolbar, and select any of a variety of shapes.

3. Click on the place where you want the shape to begin and drag to the place where you want the shape to end.

4. Release the mouse button.

Constraint keys are used to create shapes that are difficult to create freehand. These constraint keys are available:

✦ Hold down the Shift key to draw a quarter of a circle.

✦ Hold down the Ctrl key to center the arc on the point of origin.

✦ Hold down Shift+Ctrl to draw a quarter of a circle centered on its starting point.

Drawing freeform shapes

You may want to add a freeform shape, such as a flower or an ice-cream cone, to a slide. You can create any kind of drawing that you want by clicking the AutoShapes button on the Drawing Toolbar, choosing Lines from the menu, and selecting the freeform button in the submenu that appears. Then you draw the shape that you want by clicking and holding down the mouse button as you draw. Double-click to stop drawing.

You can also use the Freeform tool to draw a *polygon*, a series of points joined by lines. After you click on the Freeform Tool button, you click on the point where you want the first vertex of the polygon to appear and release the mouse button.

Then you click on the point where you want the second point to appear and release the mouse button. Continue to click on the desired points and release the mouse button until you create the polygon shape that you want.

Changing the color and style of shapes

You can change the color or style of the lines in a shape and you can apply a fill color to a shape, as well. To change the color or style of a line in a shape, follow these steps:

1. Select the shape that you want to change.

2. Choose Format➪Colors and Lines to open the Colors and Lines dialog box, as shown in Figure 27-24. In the Line area, you can choose to change the color or style of the line in any shape. You also can add dashed lines and an arrowhead, if you want.

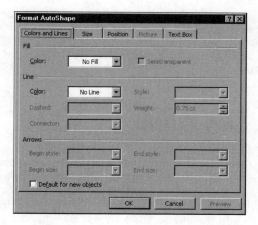

Figure 27-24: The Colors and Lines tab of the Format AutoShape dialog box.

3. Clicking on the Preview button applies the selected options to the slide, so that you can see what they look like before making the changes. You may need to drag the dialog box out of the way to see the results, because the box appears on top of the slide.

You may also want to add a fill color to a shape. Simply select the shape that you want to fill in with color and then choose Format➪Colors and Lines. In the Colors and Lines dialog box, select a color in the Fill list box and then click on the OK button.

Rotating and sizing shapes

Rotating and changing the size of a shape is also a simple matter with PowerPoint. To rotate a shape on its center point, first select the shape. Then click on the Free Rotate Tool button on the Drawing toolbar. Now drag a handle of the shape to rotate it. Figure 27-25 shows the difference with one arc rotated.

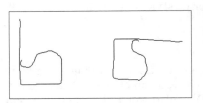

Figure 27-25: Left: A freeform object. Right: The same object, rotated.

To change the size of a shape, select the shape. You will see small black squares, called handles, appear around the shape. To resize the width of the shape, drag one of the side handles to the desired width. To change the height of the shape, drag a top or bottom handle. If you want to resize the shape proportionally, drag a corner handle. A shape can also be resized from its center by holding down the Ctrl key and dragging the handles.

Using AutoShapes and Clip Art

PowerPoint has many standard shapes and pieces of clip art available. To activate the Drawing toolbar, switch to Slide View and choose View➪Toolbars and click on Drawing. Click the AutoShapes button in the toolbar and choose the type of shape that you want to add to your presentation and you will see a submenu for each of them. Make your choice from the submenu. Next, move to the area of the presentation where you want to add the shape. Click to add the shape and then size it by using the resizing techniques. Remember that you can also add color to the shapes by choosing Format ➪ Colors and Lines opening the Colors and Lines dialog box.

PowerPoint comes with a whole bunch of clip art — invaluable in creating your presentations. The clip art comes in many different categories. To access the ClipArt Gallery, perform the following steps:

1. Click on the Insert Clip Art button on the Standard toolbar.

2. The Microsoft ClipArt Gallery dialog box appears, as shown in Figure 27-26.

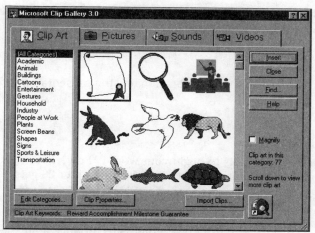

Figure 27-26: The Microsoft ClipArt Gallery dialog box.

3. Choose the category of clip art that you want.

4. Select the clip art that you want and click Insert. PowerPoint inserts it at the insertion point.

Summary

This chapter described many techniques that you can use in the everyday use of PowerPoint. With these skills you can build presentations, enter the text that you want, and choose the correct slide layout. This chapter covered the following areas:

✦ You learned how to use the convenient shortcut menus. This makes life easy for you, providing you with quick access to the commands that you may need in Power Point.

✦ We also discussed different methods to lay out new slides and edit text. This ranged from slides with place holders for clip art and the other available slide layouts.

✦ You learned how to insert objects into your presentations and edit them. The use of the objects will help you make nicer presentations.

✦ You learned how to use the built-in templates and prefabricated presentations to make creating a presentation less time consuming.

✦ You learned how to save your presentations and how to enter summary information that will help you find the presentations if you tend to forget where they are. This is quite useful for those of you who create many presentations.

The next chapter covers ways that you can enhance the presentations you create in PowerPoint.

Where to go next...

✦ Now that you have the tools to begin your work in PowerPoint, you can begin refining the presentations that you create. Chapter 28 gets you started.

✦ Chapter 30 provides you with step-by-step details on how you can create some presentations you may need in the office.

✦ The obvious goal when you use PowerPoint is to produce a finished presentation from the slides you created with the software. Chapter 30 tells you how.

✦   ✦   ✦

Enhancing a Presentation

PowerPoint gives you lots of tools you can use to give your presentation a more professional look. To help you along, PowerPoint provides several wizards, most notably the AutoContent Wizard, which provides simple ways to help you make your presentations look better. Creating columns and bulleted lists also helps you set up the information in a way that grabs the attention of your audience. Using different fonts and colors is another technique that can help your presentation take on a different look. This chapter covers these methods and a few others that enhance the appearance of your presentation.

Using the AutoContent Wizard

PowerPoint includes the AutoContent Wizard to help you define your presentation's look — *and contents.* To use the AutoContent wizard, perform the following steps:

1. Choose AutoContent from the dialog box that appears after you activate PowerPoint. If you have already activated PowerPoint, choose File⇨New. From the New Presentation dialog box that appears, choose the Presentations tab. From the Presentations tab choose the AutoContent Wizard. This activates the AutoContent Wizard (Figure 28-1), and you can click Next to proceed.

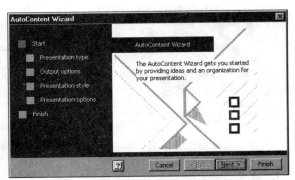

Figure 28-1: The first AutoContent Wizard dialog box.

2. The second dialog box asks you to choose the type of presentation you want to give. You have choices divided into several categories. Clicking on the button corresponding to the category makes all the choices for that category appear. The default is Aֵll, which shows all the listings from all the categories. Figure 28-2 shows the second dialog box of the AutoContent Wizard.

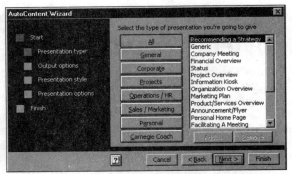

Figure 28-2: The second AutoContent Wizard dialog box.

3. After you choose the type of presentation you want to create, click on the Next button. You see the third AutoContent Wizard dialog box, as shown in Figure 28-3. In this dialog box, you can select the manner in which your presentation will be used. Your choices are Presentations, informal meetings, handouts or Internet, kiosk. After you choose an option, click on the Next button to move to the fourth dialog box.

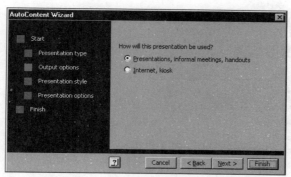

Figure 28-3: Third box of the Auto Content Wizard.

4. The fourth dialog box (Figure 28-4) is used to choose the presentation output options. Under the type of output section, you will want to select the way you will be presenting your slides. You can choose from On-screen presentations, Black and white overheads, Color overheads, or 35 mm slides. Also, you can tell the wizard whether you will be printing out the slides. After you have made your selections, click Next to go to the fifth window of the AutoContent Wizard. When you are finished click on next to move to the fifth dialog box. If you choose Internet, kiosk, you will not see the Presentation Style dialog box. For more information on PowerPoint presentations and the Web, see Chapter 32.

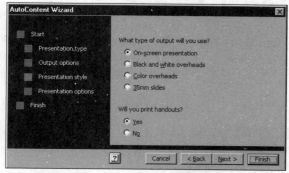

Figure 28-4: The Fourth AutoContent Wizard dialog box.

5. This Fifth dialog box to the AutoContent wizard (Figure 28-5) is used to set up your title slide. Here, see your system profile information entered in the boxes. If you wish to change the information, click and change the information. The wizard also allows space for any additional information that you wish to add to the title slide of the presentation. After you have finished making your desired entries, click Next to go to the final window of the AutoContent Wizard.

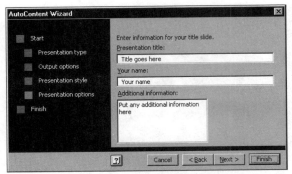

Figure 28-5: The Fifth AutoContent Wizard dialog box.

6. In the final AutoContent Wizard dialog box, you can change any of the choices you made if you wish. To do so, click on the Back button to return to the box you used to make the choice and make the necessary changes.

7. After you have made your final choices on all your settings, click on the Finish button. PowerPoint then creates the presentation using the settings you chose. Keep in mind that if you wish to change the layout of the slides at a later time, you can do so by simply choosing the Apply Design command from the Format menu.

Using the AutoLayout feature

The AutoLayout feature provides a series of slide layouts that you can use to speed up the process of laying out a slide. The layouts vary greatly. They may include the use of a graph, a piece of clip art, or just text. Figure 28-6 shows the Slide Layout dialog box. This is very useful when creating a presentation or adding slides to an existing one.

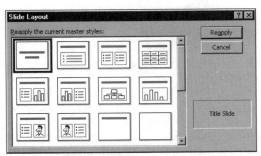

Figure 28-6: The Slide Layout dialog box.

To use the AutoLayout feature, follow these steps:

1. After opening a presentation, switch to Slide view by clicking on the Slide View button at the lower-right corner of the PowerPoint window and move to the slide you wish to change.

2. Next choose Format⇨Slide Layout or click on the Slide Layout button on the Standard Toolbar.

3. In the Slide Layout dialog box, select the layout that you want to use on the slide.

4. After selecting the layout, click on the Apply button to apply the layout to the slide.

Using the Slide Master

You can use the Slide Master to control the overall appearance and layout of each slide in a presentation. Editing with the Slide Master is very useful because you can change all the slides in your presentation, not just one slide. You can even add graphics or other layouts to the Slide Master, and they will automatically show up in all the slides in that presentation. Make all the changes that you want on the Slide Master, and these new formats are applied to all the slides in your presentation.

The Slide Master contains two important elements: a title area and an object area. The formatting in the title area is specific to the title of each slide in your presentation. The title area tells PowerPoint the font size, style, and color to use for the text. The object area contains the formatting for the remaining text on the slide. The object area also sets up specifications for bulleted lists, which include the indents for each of the lists, the font styles, and size of the fonts. Figure 28-7 shows the Slide Master.

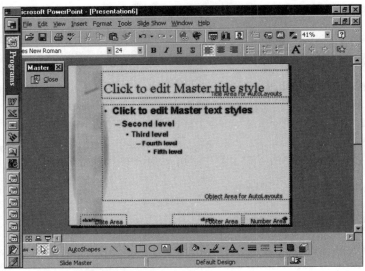

Figure 28-7: The Slide Master.

Along with the usual text formats and object setups, you can use the Slide Master to include borders, page numbers, logos, clip art, and many other elements on the slides of your presentation. Perform the following steps to view the Slide Master:

1. Open a presentation and choose View➪Master➪Slide Master. The Slide Master appears as shown in Figure 28-7.

2. You now can make any adjustment that you want to the Slide Master. To bring up a shortcut menu of available formatting options, right-click on the area beside the slide. You can change the Master Layout dialog box (Figure 28-8), the Background dialog box (Figure 28-9), or the Color Scheme dialog box (Figure 28-10) options.

Figure 28-8: The Master Layout dialog box.

Figure 28-9: The Custom Background dialog box.

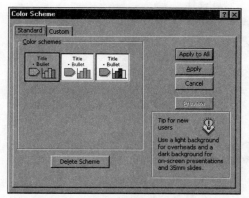

Figure 28-10: The Color Scheme dialog box.

3. When you have finished making the adjustments to Slide Master, you can return to your regular slide by choosing the Slides command from the View menu or by clicking on the Slide View button at the lower-left corner of the PowerPoint window.

You can create a custom color scheme for your slides by clicking on the Custom tab in the Color Scheme dialog box (Figure 28-11). In the Scheme Colors area, click on the box whose color you want to change and then click on the Change Color button. A color dialog box appears appropriate to the box you selected. For example, if you selected a Fill box, the dialog box is titled Fill Color, whereas if you selected an Accent box, the dialog box is titled Accent Color, as shown in Figure 28-12. After creating the color scheme that you want, you can add it to the standard color schemes available by clicking the Add as Standard Scheme button.

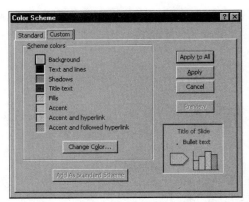

Figure 28-11: The Custom tab of the Color Scheme dialog box.

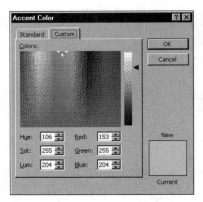

Figure 28-12: The Custom tab of the Accent Color dialog box.

After you apply the editing in the Slide Master to all your slides, you can still edit and change individual slides in whatever way you want. You can even change the headings or the formatting that you have added with the Slide Master. If you don't like the editing that you have done to a slide, however, and you want to return it to its Slide Master state, you can simply reapply the Slide Master formatting. Follow these steps:

1. Move to the slide to which you want to reapply the Slide Master formatting.

2. Choose Format⇨Slide Layout. The Slide Layout dialog box appears with the current layout selected.

3. Click the Reapply button to reapply the format. The slide now contains the formatting of the Slide Master.

Working with Lists and Columns

When creating your presentations, columns and bulleted lists become important parts of your slides because you use them often. Putting columns and bulleted lists into your slides is easy with PowerPoint. This is another layout feature you will find useful when creating slides.

Creating bulleted lists

In PowerPoint, you use indents to create bulleted lists. You can use this technique for objects (shapes you can add) too. Figure 28-13 shows a bulleted list in PowerPoint.

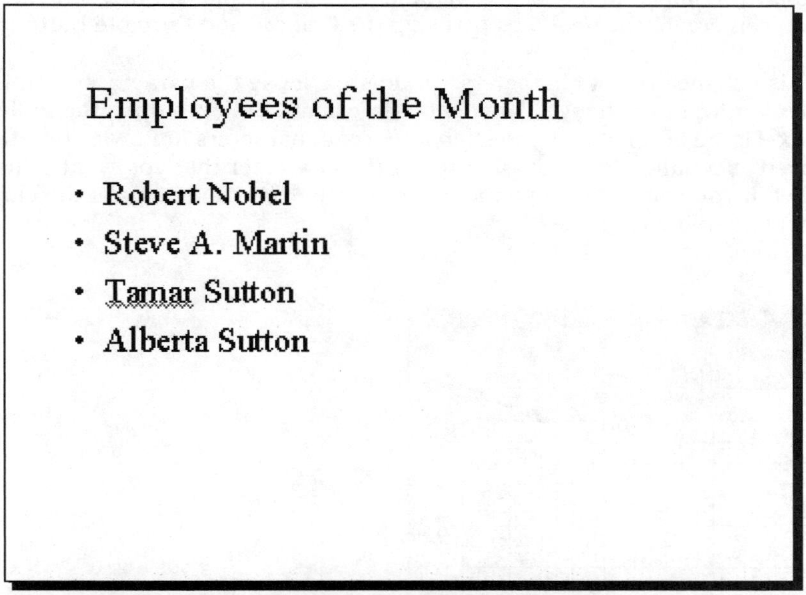

Employees of the Month

- Robert Nobel
- Steve A. Martin
- Tamar Sutton
- Alberta Sutton

Figure 28-13: A bulleted list of text in PowerPoint.

Perform the following steps to create a bulleted list:

1. After opening a presentation, switch to Slide View and select the New Slide button in the toolbar. Then choose the Bulleted List layout from the AutoLayout dialog box.

2. Choose View⇨Ruler so that the PowerPoint ruler is displayed on-screen.

3. Now enter the following names so you can get an idea of how the indent markers affect the text that you have entered on the bulleted list:

> **Robert Nobel**
>
> **Steven A. Martin**
>
> **Tamar Sutton**
>
> **Alberta Sutton**

4. Now drag the bottom indent marker in the ruler to the right. You will notice that the bottom marker moves the text from the bullets, and the top marker moves the bullets. You can use this to set indentations.

In a text box, you can create up to five indent levels. To add an indent level, select the item to indent and click on the Demote (Indent more) button on the Formatting toolbar. You may find it easier to handle your indents in Outline View, in which you can create the headings by using the Demote and Promote buttons.

You can also change bullet characters. To do so, choose the paragraph with the bullet that you want to change. Then choose Format⇨Bullet to open the Bullet dialog box. Figure 28-14 shows the many different characters in PowerPoint that can be used as a bullet. From the list, select the character that you want to use as your bullet. If you want to change the color or size of the bullet, make the changes in the corresponding list boxes.

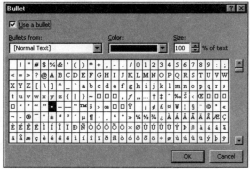

Figure 28-14: The Bullet dialog box.

In the Bullets From list box, choose the font from which you want to select the bullet; remember that each font has a set of bullet characters that go with it. Along with a bullet type you can select a color and size for the bullet also by making your choices from the desired boxes.

Creating columns

Columns are also a useful thing you can create in PowerPoint. (See Figure 28-15.) Most people have an easier time reading shorter lines of text, and columns are a good way to make them narrower. This is why newspapers contain multiple columns. If you have a large amount of textual information to get across in your presentation, you can take advantage of columns to make the information easier to comprehend.

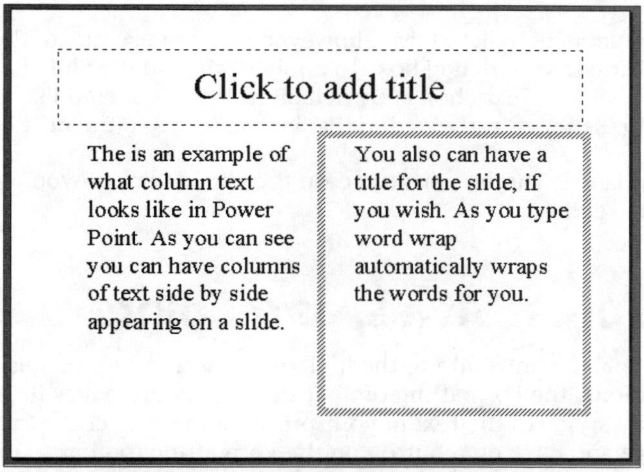

Figure 28-15: Columns displayed on a PowerPoint slide.

To add columns to a slide, perform the following steps:

1. Select the text in which you want to set the tabs.

2. Choose View⇨Ruler.

3. Click on the Tab button in the upper-left corner of the presentation window (to the left of the ruler). Keep clicking on the button until you get the type of tab that you want.

4. Click on the place on the ruler that you want that particular tab type. Do this for each of the tab stops that you want.

5. If you want to change the position of a tab, click on it and drag it to the desired position. To remove a tab, click on it and drag it off the ruler.

So you can see that columns can be set up the old-fashioned way, by setting the tabs the way you want and then entering the text you wish and tab to create your text columns. This method is still useful if you have a specific columnar layout in mind. If you wish to use a preset column, you can perform the following steps.

1. Before entering the text, choose the Slide Layout button and select 2 Column Text as the layout for the slide.

2. Next, right-click on the bullet in the column text box. From the shortcut menu that appears, choose Bullet.

3. When the Bullet dialog box appears, choose the box at the upper left, which contains nothing. This removes the bullet and lets you enter columnar text.

If you want to create columns of bulleted lists, however, you can use one of the slide layouts from the Slide Layout dialog box. To apply it, choose the Slide Layout button and select the 2 Column Text choice. By default, this is a bulleted list. Enter the text you want and press Enter at the end of the lines to move to the next bullet.

Remember that these changes can be performed on the Slide Master if you want them to apply to all your slides.

Working with Fonts, Styles, and Colors

Fonts, styles, and colors also contribute to the look of a presentation. Just as with most Windows applications, the Formatting toolbar in PowerPoint makes it easy to change the font or apply styles to the text in your presentation. Select the text that you want to change and click on a button on the Formatting toolbar to change the font or the point size or to apply bold, italic, underlining, shadow, or color. The two font-sizing buttons enable you to change the font of the selected text painlessly by just clicking on them. If you click on a formatting button before you begin to type, the formatting is applied to all the text that you type until you click on the button again.

Applying shadowing and embossing

Shadowing and embossing are techniques that you can use to add emphasis to text in a presentation. These techniques are extremely effective in making certain words or phrases stand out. They also add a more refined look to a presentation when you use them correctly.

Shadowing adds a drop shadow behind your text to emphasize it. This effect is useful in headings. To add shadowing to your presentation, select the text and click on the Shadow button on the Formatting toolbar.

Embossing is similar to shadowing, but it adds a highlight rather than a shadow to words. This effect gives the text the appearance of being slightly raised. To add embossing to your presentation, select the text and choose Format⇨Font. In the Font dialog box, click on the Emboss check box in the Effects area (see Figure 28-16) and click on OK.

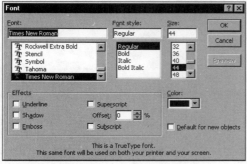

Figure 28-16: The Font dialog box.

Applying superscript and subscript

You can also apply superscript and subscript to text in your slides. Choose Format⇨ Font. In the Effects area of the font dialog box, you will see the two check boxes for these options. After you click on one of the options, enter a percentage by which to offset the text in the Offset box and click on OK. Superscript looks like ^this^; subscript looks like ~this~.

Creating Special Effects with WordArt

You can also enhance a presentation by using WordArt, a program in Office that lets you make text take on a variety of shapes. The following steps will show you how to use WordArt to give your text some of the available appearances:

1. Highlight the text where you wish to apply WordArt. Choose ⇨Insert⇨Picture and WordArt from the submenu.

2. Scroll down the Object Type list in the Insert Object dialog box until you come to the Microsoft WordArt choice. Microsoft WordArt produces the dialog box shown in Figure 28-17.

3. From the list, choose the form you wish your text to take on.

4. Click on OK at the Edit WordArt window.

5. The text is then inserted into the slide. You can make any other changes to WordArt with the WordArt toolbar that appears at the bottom of the slide window.

Figure 28-17: The WordArt dialog box.

If you use WordArt a lot, you may want to set it as one of your active toolbars. You can do this by choosing Tools⇨Customize. On the Toolbars tab, click in the check box for Word Art. This will activate the WordArt toolbar and it will then become a toolbar that is active each time you start PowerPoint. Now simply dock the toolbar where desired on the screen, and it will be there for your use during each of your PowerPoint sessions.

After your toolbar is active, click on the leftmost button of the WordArt toolbar to open the WordArt Gallery and see the effects that WordArt offers. Next choose a layout for your WordArt. To do so, click on the WordArt Shape button on the WordArt toolbar. See Figure 28-18. This will open a layout listbox with Layout options for your WordArt. From there, you can make your desired selection.

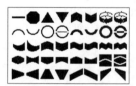

Figure 28-18: The WordArt Layout options list.

Table 28-1 explains the menu options available on the WordArt Toolbar.

Table 28-1
WordArt Toolbar options

Button	Function
WordArt Character Spacing	Opens the Spacing Between Characters shortcut menu shown in Figure 28-19, which lets you adjust the spacing between the characters.
WordArt Alignment	Allows you to choose an alignment for the WordArt you have inserted in your slide.
WordArt Vertical Text	Changes the WordArt text to a vertical appearance.
WordArt Same Letter Heights	Changes all the WordArt letters to the same height.
Free Rotate	Rotates the WordArt object to any degree.
WordArt Shape	Gives the text the shape you select from The Layout options box.
Format WordArt	Allows you to change the color and fill for the WordArt. See Figure 28-20.
WordArt Gallery	This allows you to choose a style for the WordArt you are inserting. If you want to change the WordArt text after you have inserted it into the slide, double-click on the text to activate the text box and to make changes to it. Figure 28-21 shows an example of text that has been formatted with WordArt.

Figure 28-19: The Spacing Between Characters shortcut menu.

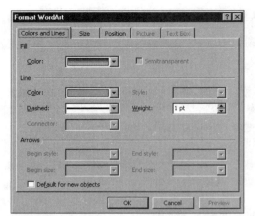

Figure 28-20: The Format WordArt dialog box.

Figure 28-21: Examples of what you can do with WordArt.

Adding Excel Worksheets and Word Tables

Working Together Another strong feature of PowerPoint is that it lets you embed Excel worksheets and Word tables in the slides. This feature saves a lot of time because you don't have to retype the information. You can use the information that already exists.

It is important to explain the difference between the two methods that can be used to insert information into PowerPoint. One method uses Edit⇨Copy and Edit⇨Paste. The other method uses Insert⇨Object. Although the two methods accomplish the same goal, they do work differently. If you want to insert a workbook, you will need to use Insert⇨Object. If you wish to insert more than one worksheet, you will need to use copy and paste. (To select the worksheets, shift-click on the worksheets you wish to insert. Then use File⇨Copy to copy the worksheets, move to where you want to paste the worksheets, and choose File⇨Paste to place them there.)

More Info You may find that you may not want to insert an entire worksheet because it may be too hard to see on a slide. It is often better to just paste in the table that you created in Excel. See Chapter 15 for information.

Double-clicking on the sheet after it is inserted activates the Excel menus. Now you can also perform maintenance on the workbook or worksheet. These tasks would normally have to be performed in Excel. Remember that the embedding principles that are explained here apply to all applications that support OLE2.

Inserting Excel worksheets into PowerPoint

Follow these steps to insert an Excel worksheet into a PowerPoint slide by using Edit⇨Copy and Edit⇨Paste:

1. From Excel, choose the worksheet that you want to insert into your presentation.

2. Select the information by using the standard selection methods. Remember that you need to select just the area of the worksheet you wish to paste on the slide. This will let you size your insertion to fit the slide. If you don't do this, the worksheet will appear to flow off the slide.

3. Click on the Copy button on the Standard toolbar or choose Edit⇨Copy.

4. Switch to PowerPoint and the slide in which you want to place the information.

5. Click on the Paste button on the Standard toolbar or choose Edit⇨Paste.

6. Size the worksheet as you please.

Figure 28-22 shows an Excel worksheet on a PowerPoint slide.

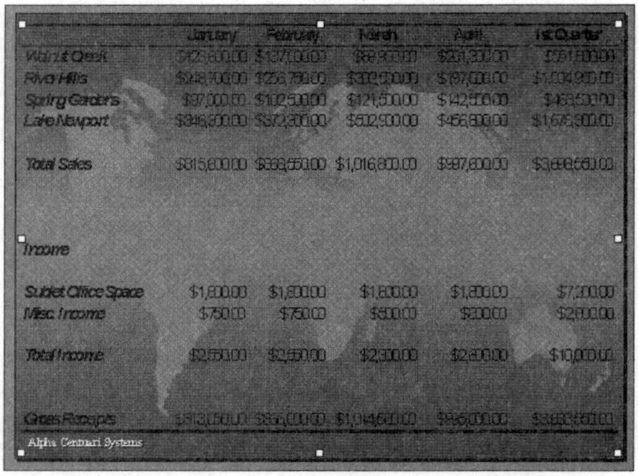

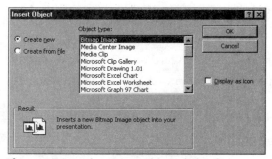

Figure 28-22: A PowerPoint slide with an Excel worksheet.

To add an Excel worksheet to a PowerPoint presentation with Insert⇨Object, follow these steps:

1. From PowerPoint choose Insert⇨Object to bring up the Insert Object dialog box shown in Figure 28-23.

Figure 28-23: The Insert Object dialog box.

2. Now choose the Microsoft Excel Worksheet. An Excel worksheet is then inserted onto the slide. The default addition to PowerPoint is a workbook that contains one sheet. To add a sheet, select the workbook and choose Microsoft Excel Worksheet from the Insert menu.

3. After inserting the worksheet onto the slide, you may want to insert an object or create a new object from another application to insert into the Excel worksheet. To do this, choose Insert⇨Object again, click on the Create New tab to create a new object, and select the application you wish to use. If

you want to create an object from an existing file, click the Create from File tab. If you wish to create a new worksheet, click on OK. If you want to use a preexisting worksheet, click on the browse button to help you find the file that you want to insert. Click on OK.

Inserting Word tables into PowerPoint

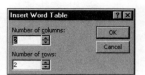

Word tables can also be inserted into PowerPoint slides. Because Word tables are the easiest way to insert tabular information, many prefer to use Word tables when they need to insert table information onto a slide in PowerPoint. The following steps will help you insert a Word table into a PowerPoint slide.

1. Choose Insert⇨Picture⇨Microsoft Word Table to bring up the Insert Word Table dialog box (see Figure 28-24).

Figure 28-24: The Insert Word Table dialog box.

2. Enter the number of columns and rows that you want for the table. A Word table is then inserted onto the slide (see Figure 28-25). If you open the Insert menu you will notice that the Word menu options are now active.

3. Enter the desired text in the table. When done, click anywhere outside of the table.

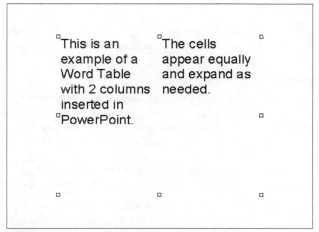

This is an example of a Word Table with 2 columns inserted in PowerPoint.

The cells appear equally and expand as needed.

Figure 28-25: A Word table inserted into PowerPoint.

Adding Sound to Presentations

When it comes to enhancing a presentation, sound can also be an effective tool. If you have sound files (.WAV or .MID files) stored on your computer, you can place sound in your presentation. Remember that you will need a sound card in order to play the sound files. To add sound to your presentation, perform these steps:

1. Move to the slide to which you want to add sound.

2. Choose Insert⇨Movies and Sounds and select Sound From File from the submenu. Figure 28-26 shows the Insert Sound dialog box that appears.

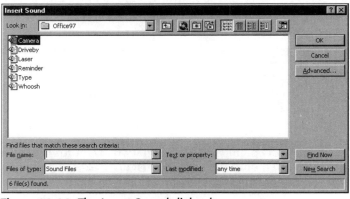

Figure 28-26: The Insert Sound dialog box.

3. After finding the desired sound file, click on OK. A small icon then appears in the center of the slide.

You can use the usual selection techniques to drag the icon to a desired location on the slide. When you run the presentation, clicking on the icon plays the sound.

Adding narrations to a presentation

PowerPoint also offers you the capability to add narrations for the slides in your presentation. This is very useful as a back up for presentation in case of absence, loss of voice, or other events that seem to occur when you don't need them to. To record a narration for a slide, first move the slide in Slide View and do the following:

1. Choose Record Narration from the Slide Show menu and click on OK. PowerPoint changes to Slide Show view, and you can begin recording.

2. After recording, right-click on the screen and choose end show. You are then asked if you want to save times for the slides or review time settings in Slide sorter View.

3. Answer these questions as desired and continue for subsequent slides in the presentation.

Slide animation

As you progress in setting up your slide show, you'll work with techniques where you can make truly professional slide shows. Along with the transition effects and timing settings that you can set using the Slide Transition dialog box, you can add animation to your presentation and function buttons to your presentation.

Animation effects can especially help hold the attention of your audience. PowerPoint offers some interesting animation effects that you can add to a slide show. First you will need to activate the Animation toolbar. To do so, choose Toolbars from the View menu and turn on the Animation toolbar.

To animate the text of a slide perform the following steps:

1. Move to the slide in which you want to animate the title in Slide View.
2. Click on the Animate Title button on the Animation toolbar.
3. Choose from one of the following for the effect you want to apply to the title animation:
   - **Drive-in effect** will cause the title to come in from the right side.
   - **Flying effect** will cause the title to come in from the left side.
   - **Camera** will cause the title to appear with the click of a camera.
   - **Flash Once effect** will cause the title to flash on the slide once.
   - **Laser Text effect** will cause the letters of the title to appear one by one with the sound of a laser.
   - **Typewriter effect** will cause the text to appear as if being typed with the sound of a typewriter.
   - **Drop-in effect** will cause the title to fall from the top of the slide.

Adding action buttons to a slide

Action buttons are another way of enhancing a presentation. PowerPoint now offers you the capability to use a button to perform an action that you specify. This can include sounds, links to web pages, links to other slides in the presentation, or links to other files of any kind. One good use for this is if you need to show a worksheet in Excel that you may not be able to show on a slide so readily. Another is linking your presentation to a web site of a page that you can then view with your default web browser.

To add an action button to your presentation, perform the following steps:

1. Move to the slide in which you want to place the button.
2. Choose Action Buttons from the AutoShapes menu of the Drawing toolbar.
3. Select the kind of button you wish to represent your action.
4. You are next prompted to save your work if you have not done so already.
5. The Action settings dialog box is then activated.
6. Choose either the Mouse click tab or the Mouse Over tab, depending on the mouse action you want to activate the hyperlink.
7. Click on the Hyperlink To: radio button.
8. Specify the type of hyperlink you want to create, be it to another slide, a web page, or another choice from the list box.
9. If you wish it to run a program, choose the Run Program radio button.
10. To run a macro, choose the Run Macro radio button.
11. If you want to open, edit, or play an object, select the action in the object action list.
12. After you have set up your button action, click on OK.

Now, you are all set. You will want to test the object you have linked to make sure that it works properly. Any other adjustments that you wish to make, simply repeat the steps and make the changes.

Summary

This chapter covered the techniques that you can use to enhance the appearance of a presentation. This included the following topics:

✦ The different methods of formatting text

✦ How WordArt can be used to enhance text entries

✦ How the Slide Master can be used to apply universal options to your presentation

✦ How you can use the AutoContent Wizard to create a presentation

Where to go next...

Now that you have learned steps to enhance a presentation, you will want to produce your work. Chapter 30 tells you how.

✦   ✦   ✦

Working with Charts in PowerPoint

Among PowerPoint's strong features is its capability to create charts that you can include in your business presentations. Charts in PowerPoint are based on numeric data that you enter into a spreadsheet-like window called a *datasheet*. The charts are generated by Microsoft Chart, a Windows miniapplication included with many Microsoft applications (including Word and Access).

One improvement in PowerPoint 97 over early versions is that both the program and Microsoft Chart support OLE2. In a nutshell, this means that when you work with a chart, you no longer temporarily leave PowerPoint and go to what was a separate application (Microsoft Chart). You now remain within PowerPoint as you work with a chart, and the menus and toolbars change to reflect choices appropriate to working with charts.

Figure 29-1 shows an example of a typical chart in a PowerPoint presentation. (Note that charts are sometimes referred to as *graphs*; in fact, Microsoft uses the terms interchangeably.) Each chart consists of a series of *markers*, which represent the data that you enter in the datasheet. The appearance of the markers varies according to what type of chart you decide to insert in your presentation. In a bar chart, the markers appear as a series of horizontal bars. In a column chart, they look like a series of vertical columns. Line charts use markers that look like a series of thin lines. In pie charts, they are the wedges of the pie, and doughnut charts use markers that appear as slices of the doughnut.

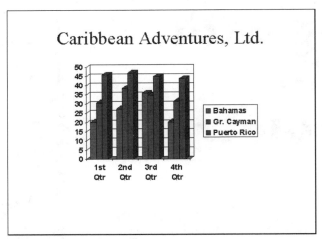

Figure 29-1: A typical chart.

With the exceptions of pie charts and doughnut charts, all charts use at least two axes: a horizontal axis (also known as the *category axis*) and a vertical axis (also known as the *value axis*). With three-dimensional charts, you also have a third axis, called the *series axis*.

In addition to the markers aligned along the axes, charts can also contain titles and *legends* (which serve to identify the categories indicated by the various markers). Microsoft Chart, running from within PowerPoint, lets you customize any of these items in your charts.

Charts in Excel or in PowerPoint?

You can create charts in PowerPoint using Microsoft Chart and the techniques detailed in this chapter, or you can create charts in Excel using the techniques detailed in Chapter 19. Because Excel charts can be selected, copied, and pasted into a PowerPoint presentation, you have *two* ways of creating charts in PowerPoint. So, where should you create your charts?

If you don't mind the added complexities of a spreadsheet (maybe you're already an accomplished Excel user), you're probably better off creating your charts in Excel and then pasting them into PowerPoint. Why?

Because Excel's charting capabilities exceed those of Microsoft Chart, and Excel has Chart Wizards that help you quickly design the precise kind of chart that you need. Also, you can take advantage of Excel's capability to perform calculations on the data that's used as the basis of the chart. In contrast, the Microsoft Chart Datasheet window won't let you add two and two, much less perform any complex calculations.

On the other hand, if you're not an Excel user and have no desire to become one, stick with Microsoft Chart within PowerPoint for producing your charts.

Chart Types

Microsoft Chart, the program used to insert charts in PowerPoint, provides area, bar, column, line, pie, doughnut, radar, XY scatter, surface, bubble, stock, cylinder, cone, and pyramid charts. Each chart type has optional subtypes that can also be chosen. The following descriptions identify the various chart types:

 Area charts show the significance of change during a given time period. The top line of the chart totals the individual series, so area charts make it visually apparent how each individual series contributes to the overall picture. Area charts emphasize the magnitude of change as opposed to the rate of change. (If you want to emphasize the rate of change, use line charts instead.)

 Bar charts use horizontal bars to show distinct figures at a specified time. Each horizontal bar in the chart shows a specific amount of change from the base value used in the chart. Bar charts visually emphasize different values, arranged vertically.

 Column charts are very much like bar charts, using columns to show distinct figures over a time period. The difference is that the markers in column charts are oriented along a horizontal plane, with the columns running vertically up or down from a base value used in the chart.

 Line charts are perfect for showing trends in data over a period of time. Like area charts, line charts show the significance of change, but line charts emphasize the rate instead of the magnitude of change.

 Pie charts show relationships between the pieces of a picture. They also can show a relationship between a piece of the picture and the entire picture. You can use a pie chart to display only one series of data at a time because each piece of a pie chart represents part of a total series. If you have a large number of series to plot, however, you are probably better off with a column chart because a pie crowded with slices is hard to interpret.

 Doughnut charts show relationships between pieces of a picture, as do pie charts. The difference is that the doughnut chart has a hollow center.

 Radar charts show the changes or frequencies of a data series in relation to a central point and to each other. (Every category has an axis value that radiates from a center point. Lines connect all data in the same series.) Radar charts can be difficult to interpret, unless you're accustomed to working with them.

 XY Scatter charts show relationships between different points of data to compare trends across uneven time periods, or to show patterns as a set of x and y coordinates. These charts are commonly used to plot scientific data.

Surface charts show trends in values across two dimensions in a continuous curve.

 Bubble charts compare sets of three values. In appearance, these are similar to scatter charts with the third value interpreted by the size of the bubbles.

 Stock charts are also known as "open-hi-lo-close" charts. They are used to display the day-to-day values of stocks, commodities, or other financial market data. Stock charts require series containing four values to plot the four points (open, high, low, and close).

 Cylinder charts are column charts with the columns appearing as cylindrical shapes.

 Cone charts are column charts with the columns appearing as cone shapes.

 Pyramid charts are column charts with the columns appearing as pyramid shapes.

Inserting Charts

PowerPoint includes a miniapplication, Microsoft Chart, that helps you create charts. Microsoft Chart displays a Datasheet window, where you can enter the numeric data that will serve as the chart's basis. After you enter your data, Microsoft Chart translates it into professional-looking charts.

The nice thing about Microsoft Chart is that, thanks to OLE2, it now lets you create your chart right in PowerPoint. Here's how to insert a chart on a PowerPoint slide:

1. Choose Insert➪Chart or click on the Insert Chart button on the Standard toolbar. A column chart appears in your presentation (this is the default type, but you can easily change it), and a Datasheet window appears atop the chart, as shown in Figure 29-2. Also, note that the menus and toolbar change to reflect the fact that Microsoft Chart is active within PowerPoint.

2. Enter your data directly into the Datasheet window. (You'll find more details on this in "Entering and editing data in the Datasheet window" later in this chapter.)

3. Choose Chart➪Chart Type to select the type of chart that you want. After selecting the chart type you want, click on OK. (You can also right-click the chart and choose Chart Type from the shortcut menu which appears.)

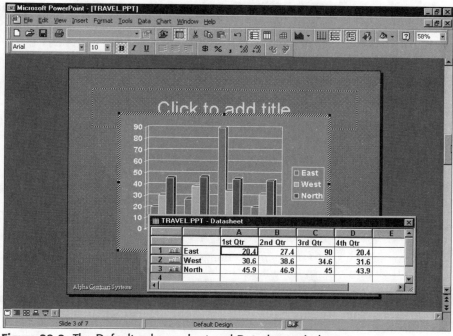

Figure 29-2: The Default column chart and Datasheet window.

4. Open the Chart menu and choose Chart Options to use the various options to add titles, axes, gridlines, legends, data labels, and data tables. The Chart Options dialog box contains the following options (see Figure 29-3):

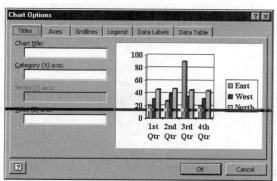

Figure 29-3: The Chart Options dialog box.

Titles — This tab displays chart title fields, which you can use to add titles to the chart or its axes.

Axes — This tab allows you to show or hide axes in the chart.

Gridlines — This tab gives you the option to show or hide major and minor gridlines along any of the chart axes.

Legend — This tab allows you to add legends to your chart.

Data Labels — You can use this tab to add data labels to a data series or to all data points in the chart.

Data Table — This table allows you to show or hide a data table for your chart.

5. When done refining the chart, click anywhere outside it. The chart will appear inside your presentation, and the menus and toolbars will revert back to those of PowerPoint.

If you later want to make more changes to the chart's design, you can double-click on the chart to switch back to the Microsoft Chart menus and toolbar.

Hot
Stuff
You can move and size your completed chart as you would any other object in a presentation — either by dragging it to the desired location or by dragging its size handles.

Entering and editing data in the Datasheet window

To enter data in the Datasheet window, just move to the desired cell and type the data. You'll also want to enter the names for each data series into the leftmost column, and the labels for each category into the top row. (The default data that appears in the Datasheet window gives you a model that you can follow when you enter your own data.) When you enter text in the top row and the leftmost column, Microsoft Chart assigns that text as category names and legend names in the resulting chart.

For example, with the default data provided in the Datasheet window in Figure 29-4, the text labels in the leftmost column of the datasheet — Bahamas, Grand Caymans, and Puerto Rico — are automatically used for the legend that accompanies the chart. The headings that are entered in the top row of the datasheet — 1st, 2nd, 3rd, and 4th Qtr — appear as labels for the markers in the chart.

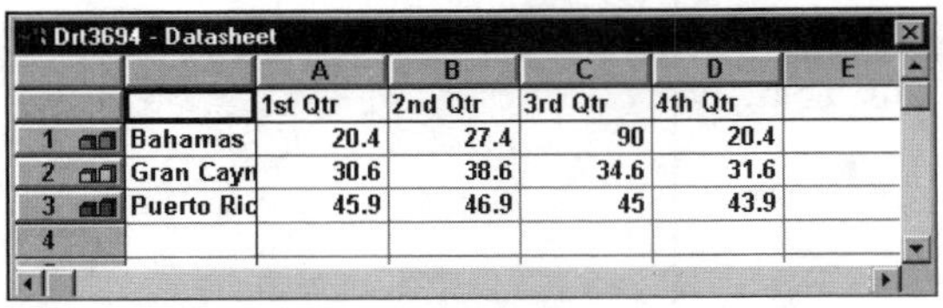

		A	B	C	D	E
		1st Qtr	2nd Qtr	3rd Qtr	4th Qtr	
1	Bahamas	20.4	27.4	90	20.4	
2	Gran Cayn	30.6	38.6	34.6	31.6	
3	Puerto Ric	45.9	46.9	45	43.9	
4						

Drt3694 - Datasheet

Figure 29-4: The Datasheet window.

Navigate within the Datasheet window with either the mouse or the arrow keys. You can widen the columns if they're too narrow to display the numbers that you enter. Do this either by dragging the column's right edge with the mouse or by clicking in any cell in the column that you want to widen, choosing Format➪Column Width, and then entering a width for the column.

When typing numeric data into cells, you can include dollar signs in front of the numbers to cause them to appear as currency values. When you do this, Microsoft Chart automatically includes the dollar sign with the values in the value axis in the chart. To apply a specific format by selecting a cell or group of cells in the datasheet, open the Format menu and choose Number. In the Number Format dialog box that appears, choose a desired number format and then click on OK.

After the chart exists on a slide, you can bring up the Datasheet window at any time by double-clicking on the chart to make it active, and choosing View➪Datasheet.

Editing Charts

Changing circumstances may require the figures used to create a chart to change. When this happens, you'll need to make adjustments to the chart's datasheet. At times you many also want to edit a chart for the sake of altering a presentation.

If you wish to update figures used when you created a chart, choose View➪Datasheet and then make the necessary changes in the datasheet (using the customary methods of editing).

Excel users may prefer Excel charts

If you're familiar with Excel, you may prefer using Excel's worksheet and charting techniques for producing charts to use in your PowerPoint presentations.

To add an existing Excel chart to a PowerPoint presentation, go into Excel, select the chart and choose Edit➪Copy. Switch to PowerPoint, move to the slide where you want to insert the chart, and choose Edit➪Paste. The Excel chart appears in the slide, and you can move and size it to your liking using the usual Windows moving and sizing techniques.

To add a new Excel chart to a PowerPoint presentation, go into PowerPoint and move to the slide where you want to place the chart. Next, choose Insert➪Object and then choose Microsoft Excel Chart from the list of objects to insert. PowerPoint then inserts a default Excel chart on the PowerPoint slide, and Excel menus become active within PowerPoint. You can then use Excel techniques (detailed in the Excel section of this book) to manipulate the data that produces the chart and to change the chart's appearance.

Changing the data series

In some cases, you may want to swap the data series for a chart. For example, you'd want to do this if you had set up a chart to show the total of sales over four years for divisions of a company and you wanted the columns to symbolize each division — but instead, the columns represent years. Swapping the data series would fix that.

You do this by choosing either Data⇨Series in Rows or Data⇨Series in Columns. Alternatively, you can click on the By Row or By Column buttons in the Standard toolbar while the datasheet is active. To see an example of the effects of the selection of data series, take a look at Figure 29-5, which shows a data series arranged by rows.

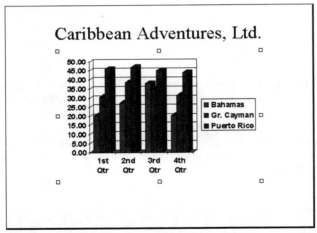

Figure 29-5: A data series arranged by rows.

In contrast, note the same data shown in Figure 29-6. Here the data in the datasheet is arranged by columns in the resulting graph.

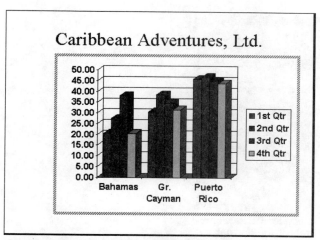

Figure 29-6: A data series arranged by columns.

You can also change the actual display of the information. Do this using the shortcut menu that appears when you right-click on the bars, columns, lines, or pie slices of the chart. This shortcut menu contains commands related to changes in the display of the chart information. The shortcut menu is shown in Figure 29-7 and includes the following commands:

Figure 29-7: The shortcut menu for a data series.

✦ **Format Data Series** — This command lets you add labels or change the color of the data series. When you choose this option, the Format Data Series dialog box appears (Figure 29-8) with the Patterns tab visible. Using the Patterns tab, you can add a border to the data series by setting the options in the Borders portion of the dialog box. You can vary the border's style, color, and thickness by selecting what you want in the Style, Color, and Thickness list boxes.

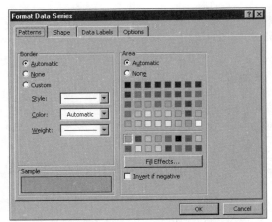

Figure 29-8: The Patterns tab of the Format Data Series dialog box.

In the Area portion of the dialog box, you can change the color of the data series to your liking. You can select a color, or you can turn on the Automatic option, which applies the Windows default. Choosing None makes the marker invisible. Turning on the Invert If Negative option in the dialog box reverses the foreground and background colors for a marker if the value is negative.

The Shape Tab of the dialog box lets you choose the 3-D shape you want to appear in for the selected data series.

The Data Labels tab (Figure 29-9) of this dialog box lets you determine whether labels appear beside the markers to the data series. You can also have a legend appear next to the label; do this by turning on the corresponding check box.

✦ **Chart Type** — This command lets you change the chart type. When you choose this option from the shortcut menu, the Chart Type dialog box (Figure 29-10) appears. The options for this dialog box are discussed in the next section.

✦ **Add Trendline** — This option adds trendlines to area, bar, column, lines and scatter charts.

✦ **Clear** — This command removes a data series, the actual markers related to that series of numbers.

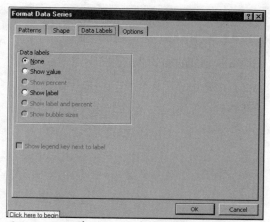

Figure 29-9: The Data Labels tab of the Format Data Series dialog box.

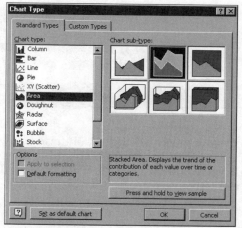

Figure 29-10: The Chart Type dialog box.

Changing the chart type

After creating a chart, you can experiment to be sure you've selected the type that best represents your data. Microsoft Chart provides a range of chart types that can be viewed with a few mouse clicks; Table 29-1 lists them.

Table 29-1 PowerPoint's chart types	
Two-dimensional charts	*Three-dimensional charts*
Column	3-D Column
Bar	3-D Bar
Line	3-D Line
Pie	3-D Pie
Area	3-D Area
Doughnut	3-D Surface
Radar	3-D Bubble
Scatter	3-D Cylinder
Area	3-D Cone
Bubble	3-D Pyramid
Stock	
Cylinder	
Cone	
Pyramid	
Surface	

You can select chart types using different methods. The fastest of these is to click the down arrow at the right of the Chart Type button on the Standard toolbar. This will give you a drop-down list of chart types as shown in Figure 29-11. Select the chart you like and the values will be applied to it.

Figure 29-11: The Chart types available from the Chart Type button on the Standard Toolbar.

The other methods of changing the chart type are to choose Chart Type from the Chart menu or right-click on the chart and choose Chart Type from the shortcut menu. The Chart Type dialog box then appears, as shown in Figure 29-10.

When you select a chart type, you can also click on the Custom Types tab to use built-in custom chart types or user-defined chart types. The Custom Types tab will contain many combinations of formatting such as exploded pie charts, floating bars, and other chart types that can be very useful for specialized chart needs.

Enhancing a Charts Appearance

You can do several things to enhance the appearance of a chart. A few are simple, such as changes to fonts and colors. Others, however, are a little more involved, such as adding text boxes. All can make a difference in the appearance of the presentation.

Changing fonts

You can easily change the fonts used for text anywhere in your chart. This includes fonts used for titles, legends, or axes.

To change the fonts, right-click on the text for what you want to change. For example, if you want to change the fonts used for a legend, right-click on the legend. From the shortcut menu that appears, choose either the Format Axis or Format Legend option. Depending on which you select, you will see either the Format Axis dialog box or the Format Legend dialog box. Both contain the same three tabs (we will discuss the additional ones shortly): Pattern for making pattern changes to the chart, Font for making font changes to the chart, and Placement for controlling the placement of the object. Figure 29-12 shows the Font tab of the Format Axis dialog box.

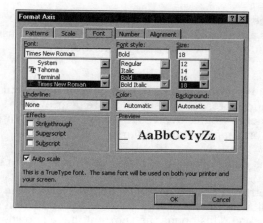

Figure 29-12: The Font tab of the Format Axis dialog box.

Looks aren't everything, but...

As you work with fonts, colors, and other appearance-related aspects of a chart, remember the principles of good design by using fonts and colors wisely. It's easy to get carried away with fonts and colors and produce a chart that is so visually "busy" that it distracts the reader. You should rarely need more than two and never more than three fonts in the same chart. You'll probably need more colors because each set of markers typically uses its own color — but again, be judicious. Stick with complementary colors. PowerPoint does this automatically, but if you customize the colors, avoid clashing combinations like bright pink against lime green. (Some designers argue strongly against using these two colors anywhere, anytime!) Keep colors elsewhere in the chart to a minimum. Before committing the chart to your presentation, step back and give it a critical, overall review for visual clarity and organization. Better charts in your presentations make for better overall presentations.

Under the Font tab, you'll see your options for setting the fonts used by the selected item. Choose a font, font style, and font size using the options displayed. You can also select underlining, color, and background, and you can turn on special effects such as strikethrough, superscript, and subscript. Under the Patterns tab, you can change various options that control the style and color of the background pattern for the object. Under Placement, you can indicate where in the chart the object appears. When done making selections, click on OK to put them into effect.

Changing chart colors

Creating and changing color schemes is another effective way to improve your chart's appearance. Color schemes are sets of colors that are designed to be used as main colors for presentations and to ensure that the presentations have a professional look.

Each presentation that you open in PowerPoint has a default color scheme, but as you work with the program more and more, you'll want to create your own schemes. Chapter 27 discusses in detail what's involved in doing this for an entire presentation. This section focuses on changing chart colors.

Changing the colors of your chart is relatively simple, thanks to shortcut menus:

1. After choosing a chart and setting it up on your slide, double-click on the chart to make it active for edits and then right-click on the bar or section of the chart that you want to change. This opens the shortcut menu shown earlier in Figure 29-7.

2. From the shortcut menu, choose Format Data Series. The Format Data Series dialog box is then opened with the Patterns Tab visible, as shown earlier in Figure 29-8. This dialog box lets you change the Border Settings, selecting from a range of line styles.

3. To change the color of the particular section of the chart that you want to change, move to the Area portion of the Patterns tab and then click on the color that you want. You can also add patterns if you wish by clicking on the Patterns list box and then choosing a pattern from the list. When done, click on OK to accept the changes.

Adding titles

You might find it useful to add titles to your charts. For one thing, titles help an audience understand what a chart means, and they help you quickly find values that you want to point out when giving your presentation.

To add titles to a chart area, right-click on the area to open the shortcut menu. Next, choose the Titles tab of the Chart Options dialog box, shown in Figure 29-12.

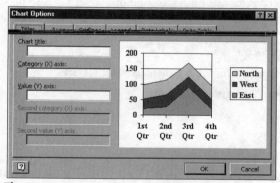

Figure 29-13: Titles tab of the Chart Options dialog box.

The Titles tab lets you add a title either to your entire chart or to just one of the available axes. Turn on the option that you want and then click on OK; the cursor appears in a text box where you insert the title. If you choose more than one area to receive a title, use the mouse and click on the text boxes for each of the titles. To enter the titles, click in the text boxes and type the titles that you want.

You can also format the text on a chart after the text has been entered. To do this, double-click on the text and choose the formats that you want from the Format dialog box.

Changing axes

You can modify the axes used by your charts in order to emphasize the points that you're trying to get across. You can change the line style, the font of the axes' text, the scale used by the numbers, and the alignment.

To change any of these formats, select one of the axes by clicking on it. Next, either choose Format⇨Selected Axis, right-click on the axis and choose Format Axis, or double-click on the selected axis. This opens the Format Axis dialog box, as shown in Figure 29-12. You can now select the options that you want from the various tabs. Table 29-2 tells what you can accomplish with each of these tabs.

Table 29-2 Tabs of the Format Axis dialog box	
Tab	**Purpose**
Patterns	Change axis formatting or choose tick mark types, both major and minor.
Scale	Control the scale settings for axis values. Logarithmic scales can also be set, along with reversing the order of the values and setting the Floor XY Plane (the floor of the chart) at a value other than zero.
Font	Change font settings for the axis.
Number	Control the number formats for the numbers used for the axis.
Alignment	Control the alignment of text used in the axis.

Changing borders

You can also change a chart by changing its borders. To do this, right-click outside the chart's area and choose Format Chart Area from the shortcut menu. The Format Chart Area dialog box appears, as shown in Figure 29-14. This dialog box has two tabs, Patterns and Font. Make the changes that you want and then click on OK.

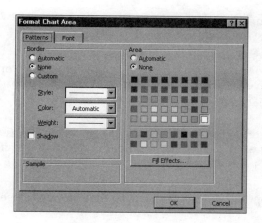

Figure 29-14: The Format Chart Area dialog box.

Changing the Appearance of 3-D Charts

Three-dimensional (3-D) charts are a popular variation of basic charts. Creating 3-D charts is simple in PowerPoint: when you choose Chart⇨Chart Type, the Chart Type dialog box that appears (shown earlier in Figure 29-10) gives you the option of selecting a 2-D or a 3-D chart.

If you use 3-D charts often, it's good to know about the flexibility that Microsoft Chart offers for changing various aspects of appearance of 3-D charts. You can change the elevation, the rotation, and the perspective used for the chart with the following steps:

1. Double-click on the 3-D chart to activate it, and choose Chart⇨3-D View. (Alternatively, you can right-click on the area of the chart and select 3-D View from the shortcut menu that appears.) The 3-D View dialog box (Figure 29-15) appears. As you change the settings in this dialog box, the picture of a chart near the center of the dialog box reflects your changes.

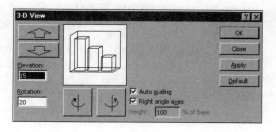

Figure 29-15: The 3-D View dialog box.

2. To change the chart's elevation, either click on the Up Arrow or Down Arrow buttons above Elevation or enter a value in the Elevation text box.

3. To change the chart's rotation, either click on the Left or Right Rotation buttons or enter a value in the Rotation text box.

4. To change the chart's perspective (if Right Angle Axes is not turned on), either click on the Up Arrow or Down Arrow buttons above Perspective or enter a value in the Perspective text box. The Format 3-D View dialog box also contains options for AutoScaling, Right Angle Axes, and Height % of Base.

   * **Right Angle Axes** — This option, when turned on, sets the chart's axes at right angles independent of what you set the rotation or elevation to. (If you want to see the axes in perspective, you must turn off this option.)

   * **Auto Scaling** — If Right Angle Axes is turned on, then this option is enabled. The AutoScaling option scales 3-D charts so that they are closer in size to 2-D charts.

   * **Height % of Base** — This option controls the height of the value axis and walls of the chart, relative to the length of the category axis (the base of the chart). For example, if you enter **300%** in this box, the chart's height becomes three times the length of the base.

You can see how your changes will affect your chart in PowerPoint while leaving the dialog box open; do this by clicking on the Apply button. When done with your changes, click on the OK button. You can use the Default button to undo your changes and return the settings to their defaults.

3-D Charts can lie (or at least, greatly mislead...)

With 3-D charts, it's easy to get carried away with changing the various viewing angles by modifying the chart's elevation and perspective. Get *too* carried away, and you can wind up with a chart that's so hard to interpret, it becomes meaningless. Get even slightly carried away, and you can produce charts that distort the meaning of the underlying numbers.

For example, changing the elevation so that a chart is viewed from a high angle tends to overemphasize growth; presenting the chart as viewed from a low angle tends to minimize growth. (Could that be why many advertisements in business and financial magazines use 3-D charts viewed at high angles?) As an example, the figure on the next page shows a 3-D chart with an elevation of 90, which severely distorts the visual growth represented by the chart.

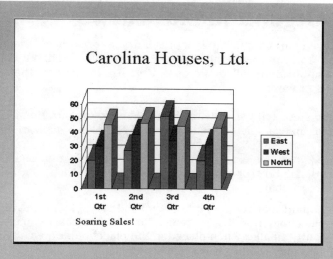

By comparison, this next figure shows the same 3-D chart with a moderate elevation of 10, which avoids the visual distortion produced by the earlier chart.

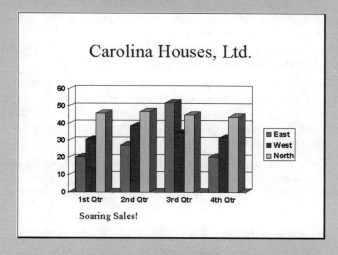

Be aware of the effects that such changes can have on your charts and use them only when you intend to obtain such distorted results.

Creating Organizational Charts

Organizational charts are useful in a presentation for showing the hierarchy of an organization. You can create this type of chart from scratch, but PowerPoint provides an application called Microsoft Organizational Chart that greatly simplifies the process.

The following steps tell you how to create a simple organizational chart. (See Chapter 33 for an example of creating a more complex organizational chart.)

1. Choose Insert⇨Object and then select MS Organization Chart from the Insert Object dialog box (or you can click on the Insert Chart button in the Standard toolbar).

   Keep in mind that you should select a slide layout with the organizational chart placeholder on it. Also remember that the chart you create will be significantly smaller when placed in the placeholder area; if you have a large chart, you may want to use a blank slide.

2. The window then opens with a simple chart layout. You can proceed with this default layout if you wish, adding boxes to the chart as needed. On the toolbar, you'll see buttons for adding boxes for the different levels of an organization. Each of the buttons lets you add boxes for the respective level of the chart. Choose the button that corresponds to the level of organization you want and then click next to the box that you want to add the selection under or next to; the box is then added to the chart.

3. After creating your chart, you may want to edit it. To do that, first click on the box containing the name or entry that you want to change; you can then make the changes. Afterward, be sure to update the presentation within PowerPoint by choosing File⇨Update Presentation. Then if you want to save the changes to the presentation, choose File⇨Save.

4. If you prefer, you can create an organizational chart from scratch. Choosing Style from the menu bar gives you a selection of organizational chart types. As Figure 29-16 shows, you can lay out these charts in several ways .

Figure 29-16: Organizational Chart Style dialog box.

After choosing a chart style, you can add boxes to it using the toolbar. Choose the level of the chart to which you want to add boxes and then click on the box that you want connected.

Once the chart is placed in PowerPoint, you can size it to your liking by selecting the object and clicking on the handles.

Summary

This chapter showed you the different options for using charts in your PowerPoint presentations. The following topics were covered:

✦ You can add a chart to any slide of a presentation either by choosing Insert⇨ Chart or by clicking on the Insert Chart button on the Standard toolbar.

✦ When you add a chart, a Datasheet window appears where you can enter the numeric information that serves as the chart's basis.

✦ After adding a chart to a presentation, you can double-click on the chart and then choose Chart⇨Chart Type to change the chart's type.

✦ You can right-click on any object in a chart and then choose Format from the shortcut menu that appears in order to display a dialog box that lets you change the appearance of the selected object.

✦ In addition to conventional charts, you can create organizational charts in PowerPoint.

Where to go next...

✦ Now that you have completed charts in PowerPoint, you will want to produce your work. Chapter 30 has the story.

✦ If you want to produce more elaborate charts, use Excel's chart making feature. Head straight for Chapter 19.

✦   ✦   ✦

Producing Your Work

After you have created all the slides, you will want to prepare your work for presentation. This chapter covers the methods that you can use to produce your work, including printing presentations, creating slide shows, and creating speaker's notes and audience handouts.

Printing Presentations

PowerPoint lets you print slides, outlines, speaker's notes, and audience handouts. These items all can be printed on overhead transparencies or on paper. Slides can also be saved to a file or shipped to an outside graphics shop to create them. The printing process is pretty much the same, regardless of whether you are printing outlines, notes, or handouts: you open the presentation, identify what you want printed, specify the range of slides to be printed, and choose the number of copies.

Setting up your slides for printing

Before you print your presentation, you need to open it and set it up for printing. Follow these steps:

1. Choose File⇨Page Setup. The Page Setup dialog box appears, as shown in Figure 30-1.

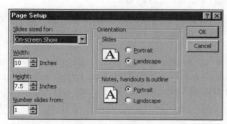

Figure 30-1: The Page Setup dialog box.

2. In this dialog box, select the desired size for the slides. Keep in mind that, by default, PowerPoint is set up to create and print slides in Landscape orientation. Also remember that, by default, the slides are set up to print 10 inches wide by 7.5 inches tall. The Slides Sized for list box is set at Custom, which lets you change these settings to the following:

- **On-screen Show** — This option sets the width at 10 inches and the height at 7.5 inches with Landscape orientation.

- **Letter Paper (8.5 × 11 inches)** — This option sets the width at 10 inches and the height at 7.5 inches with Landscape orientation. These measurements cause the slides to fill the page. Choose this option when you want to print on paper and fill the entire page.

- **A4 Paper (210 × 297 mm)** — This option sets the width at 10.83 inches and the height at 7.5 inches with Landscape orientation. The slides then fill A4 (European size) paper.

- **35mm Slides** — This option sets the width at 11.25 inches and the height at 7.5 inches. These measurements allow the contents to fill the slide area in Landscape orientation, ideal for reduction to a 35mm slide.

- **Overhead** — Use this option when you want to create transparencies. It makes slides fill the transparencies, making them easier to see when they are placed on an overhead projector.

- **Banner** — Use this option to change the layout of your slides to a banner layout. This is both for printing and an on-screen presentation.

- **Custom** — This option lets you set dimensions of your own choosing, either by entering values in the Width and Height boxes or by clicking on the up and down arrows to enter the desired value.

3. In the Orientation portion of the dialog box, choose the desired orientation (Portrait or Landscape). Keep in mind that you can separately set the orientation for your speaker's notes, handouts, and outlines.

4. If you want to use a starting number other than 1 for your slides, enter a desired number in the Number Slides from list box.

5. Click on OK.

Printing parts of your presentation

After your printing dimensions have been set by means of the Page Setup dialog box options, you can choose File⇨Print to reveal the Print dialog box (see Figure 30-2).

In this dialog box, you can choose what parts of the presentation you want to print. In the Print range area, choose All to print all slides, or choose Current Slide to print just the slide that is currently visible. In the Number of copies box, you can enter the number of copies that you want, and you can turn on the Collate option if you want multiple copies to come out in collated order.

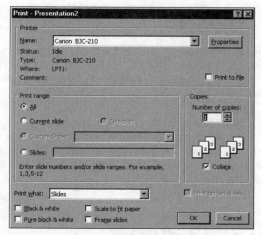

Figure 30-2: The Print dialog box.

Use the Print what list box to tell PowerPoint exactly which parts of your presentation you want to print. The choices that you have from the Print what list box include the following:

✦ **Slides** — This option prints your slides on paper or on overhead transparencies.

✦ **Notes Pages** — This option prints the speaker's notes pages that correspond to the slides that you decide to print.

✦ **Handouts** — You can print audience handouts that contain two, three, or six slides per page. Two slides per page is a good choice for a large image with great detail. Use three slides per page if you want to leave space for the audience to write notes. If you want to provide a presentation outline with the most information on each page of the audience handout, use six slides per page. You have the option to print two, three, or six handouts per slide.

✦ **Outline View** — This option prints the outline that appears on-screen in Outline view.

In the dialog box you can also specify the number of copies that you want to print, along with the range of slides or notes. If any slides in the presentation have been hidden (by choosing Slide Show➪Hide Slide), the Print Hidden Slides check box becomes available in the Print dialog box (choose File➪Print), and you can click on it to tell PowerPoint to include hidden slides in the printout. The Black & White option tells PowerPoint to optimize the printing of color slides when printed on a black and white printer. The Pure Black and White option is used to print the slides in black and white while printing on a color printer; this will change all the shades of gray to either black or white. (This option is useful only if you have a color printer and, for some reason, you don't want the presentation in color.)

The Frame Slides option frames the printouts so that they best fit transparencies when they are reduced, and the Scale to Fit Paper option scales the printout to the paper that you have loaded in the printer. Choose your desired printing options in the dialog box and then click on OK.

Note   If you turn on the Print to file check box after you choose the other desired options and click on OK, a Print to File dialog box appears where you can enter a file name. When you enter a name and click on OK, PowerPoint writes the file as an encapsulated print file that can be used at a later time (you can select the file in Explorer or in My Computer and print it).

Producing On-Screen Slide Shows

Slide shows are another strength of PowerPoint because you can create professional-looking slide shows without a great deal of hassle. You can create a slide show by accepting PowerPoint's defaults and then choosing the Slide Show command from the View menu. The Slide Show will then begin. If you wish to change the default settings, the time settings between each of the slides, and any transition effects you wish to add to the presentation slide, you will first need to go to slide sorter view. In Slide Sorter View, you will need to do the following to change the timing settings to the slide presentation:

1. Select the slide you want to set timings or effects for. Click on the Slide Transitions button on the Slide Sorter tool bar or choose Slide Show then Slide Transitions. This will open the Slide Transitions dialog box shown in Figure 30-3.

2. Choose the effects you want for the slide from the Effect area of the dialog box.

3. Next move on to the Advance section to set your timings or choose the mouse as the signal to move to the next slide.

4. In the Sound area of the dialog box, you can add one of the default sounds as you move to the next slide or open another sound file for moving to the next slide. Keep in mind that all the effects you set are for the slide you currently have selected in Slide Sorter View unless you click on Apply to All.

5. Move through your presentation setting the effects you wish for each of the slides if you wish to vary them for each of the slides.

Getting the results you want

Don't be in a rush to print by clicking on the Print button on the Standard toolbar or by immediately clicking on the OK button in the Print dialog box to accept the defaults, which you do in many Windows applications. Because PowerPoint has so many options for what you can print and how you can print it, you may not get what you want by fast clicking. Think of the Print dialog box and the Slide Setup dialog box as working in combination to give you exactly what you want. Be sure that you set the options correctly before you start printing.

Each of the effects you set in the Slide Transition box can be set using the Slide Sorter toolbar. The toolbar begins with a transition button that opens the Slide Transition dialog box discussed earlier. Next is a Slide Transition Effects list box that allows for the setting of slide transitions. This is followed by a Text Preset Animation listbox that allows you to set the effects for the slide. You next see the hide Slide button used to hide slides in a show. This is followed by the Rehearse Timings button. This button is used to set and rehearse the timings that the entire slide show will run for and how long each of the slides is visible. The Summary slide button is used to create a slide that will give you a summary of your presentation. The Show Formatting button switches between showing the text and graphics for each of the slides and showing just the title. You will find this toolbar to be very useful in quickly assigning settings to each of your slides for a slide show.

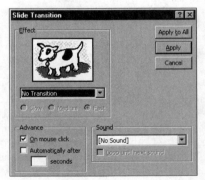

Figure 30-3: The Slide Transition dialog box.

In the Advance area of the dialog box, choose Manual Advance if you want to move from slide to slide manually during the show or choose Use Slide Timings if you want the slides to advance automatically at timed intervals. (You'll learn how to change the intervals later.)

Giving slide shows with polish

Giving a good presentation isn't entirely a matter of mastering PowerPoint technique. Most of what creates a presentation that captivates (rather than enslaves) your audience falls under the more general heading of "tips for better presentations."

Always, always, always, *always* (did we say that enough?) test your presentation on the hardware that you plan to use *before* the audience starts taking their seats. No matter how well things worked back in the home office and at the last 27 on-site presentations you've given, there's no guarantee that the hardware you're using at the 28th site is correctly set up or will behave as well as the rest.

Try not to spend too much time on a single slide. If a slide stays on-screen for five min-

utes or more, rethink your content. Believe it or not, five minutes is a long time when a speaker drones — this has put many an audience to sleep. The audience stays with you if you break up big chunks of information into two or three separate slides.

Add a blank slide (or a slide with nothing more than an attractive background) as the last slide in your presentation. Then when you finish, the audience has an attractive slide to look at, as opposed to being dumped back in Slide view of PowerPoint.

As you verbally emphasize points, you can use the mouse pointer as an on-screen pointer. (A commercial laser pointer is nicer but also costs a lot more than the mouse that's already installed on your computer.)

The Loop Continuously Until 'Esc' check box can be turned on if you want slides that are set for timed intervals to run continuously until the Escape key is pressed (a great option for unattended displays, like those you see running in computer stores).

When you are finished choosing the various options in the dialog box, click on Show to run the presentation.

If you want to set your own timings for the slide show, choose the Rehearse New Timings option, which lets you advance the slides by using the Page Down button or clicking on the mouse. PowerPoint then keeps track of the time that you take to advance from one slide to another. If you forget the timings that you set from one slide to another, switch to Slide Sorter view. Underneath each slide you will see the time that you have allotted for the slide.

Creating progressive slides

Have you ever seen a presentation that included a slide that was nearly blank at first, but as the speaker talked, points seemed to magically appear on it? That savvy speaker used a *progressive disclosure slide* to create that effect. Progressive slides let your audience see your presentation develop and help them remember the last point that you made. You may remember a Progressive slide as a build slide from earlier versions of Power Point because you progressively build the points of your presentation. You can create a progressive slide by performing the following steps:

1. Switch to Slide view and locate the text or the text object that you want to be the first to show up in your progressive slide.

2. Right-click on the text or object and choose Custom Animation from the Shortcut menu. You will then see the Custom Animation dialog box, as shown in Figure 30-4.

3. Click on the Effects tab and choose the type of effects you want for the text or object.

4. Click on OK.

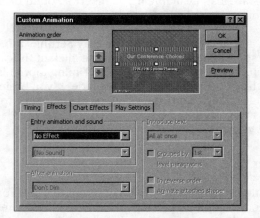

Figure 30-4: The Custom Animation dialog box.

You've just created the first animation in your progressive slide. To continue with your second object, repeat Steps 1–4 and do the following:

1. Click on the Timing tab of the Custom Animation box.

2. In the timing tab, you will see a list of the objects without animation in your slide. From this point on, you can continue with the building of your slide without going back to the slide to select the next object.

3. In the Slide Objects without animation box, select the next object you want to enter your slide by double-clicking on it.

4. Choose the effects from the Effects tab that you want to attach to the object.

5. If you have a chart on your slide, you can use the Chart Tab to add animation to it. First Select the chart and use the choices on the Chart Effects tab to add animation to the chart. You will have much of the same choices as in the other tabs: you can introduce the chart by series category, elements of the series, and elements of the category. As with all of your animation, sound is also available for introduction of your chart. Use the Entry Animation and Sound section to make sound choices.

6. It will then appear as the next item on the Animation order list in the top-left corner of the dialog box.

If you wish to change the order of the text presentation, simply use the arrows beside the Animation order box to change the position of the animation. Keep in mind that the default is for these actions to begin after a click of the mouse. If you want them to start automatically, you will need to do so by clicking on the Automatically button, which allows you to set a time interval for the beginning of the next part of the slide. These options are also available if you insert a sound or a chart into a Power Point presentation.

You can make other changes to the animation order using the Play Settings tab. In this tab, you can play the movie or sound automatically or on the click of the mouse. This would depend on which option you selected in the Timing tab. This would occur before the running of the other animations of the slide. If you prefer to have the options run after the slide's animations have run, clear the check from the check box. Keep in mid that this tab will only be active when the selected object is a movie, sound, or an OLE object.

Hiding and unhiding slides

The capability to hide or unhide slides is another useful PowerPoint feature. You may want to give similar presentations to different groups but modify the content to fit each group. For example, you might want to present revenue data to each department in a company. It might make sense to show detailed financial data to, say, Sales, but more general numbers to production workers. PowerPoint lets you use one presentation for both groups — but you hide slides so that they do not appear for one group and then unhide the slides so that they do appear for the other group. To hide a slide, perform the following steps:

1. Display the slide that you want to hide. In Slide Sorter view, you can select more than one slide by holding down the Shift key while you click on each slide that you want to hide. When you do this, the slide's number is marked with a line through it.

2. Choose Slide Show⇨Hide Slide. (If you are in Slide Sorter view, you can also click on the Hide Slide button in the Slide Sorter toolbar.) During the slide show, the slide will not appear, but you will know that you have a hidden slide because a hidden slide icon appears in the lower-right corner of the preceding slide.

The menu option is a toggle, so you can unhide a hidden slide by selecting it in Slide Sorter view and choosing Slide Show⇨Hide Slide or you can simply click on the Hide Slide button again.

During a slide show, you can display a hidden slide. Simply click on the hidden slide icon that appears on the preceding slide in the lower-right corner of the screen.

You can also "unhide" slides before you give a presentation. To do this, right-click on the slide in Slide Sorter view and choose Hide Slide from the shortcut menu.

Adding Speaker's Notes and Audience Handouts to a Presentation

In PowerPoint, you can add two items to your presentation that help improve the presentation: speaker's notes and audience handouts. Each of the slides has a companion notes page that includes a small version of the slide and room for typed notes. You can print the notes and use them to recall the points that you want to make for each slide. You can also print audience handouts. Audience handouts make it easy for the audience to follow your presentation and give the audience members something to take with them after the presentation is over. The handouts can contain two, three, or six slides per page.

To create speaker's notes for a presentation, perform the following steps:

1. Select the slide to which you want to add a notes page. Choose View⇨Notes Pages. The notes page appears, as shown in Figure 30-5.

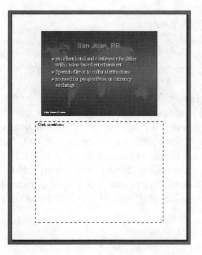

Figure 30-5: A typical notes page.

2. At this size, you will have difficulty reading the notes that you add to the notes page. Use the Zoom Control on the Standard toolbar to increase the size of the notes page to 75 percent (see Figure 30-6).

3. To enter the notes, click on the box provided for notes and type your entry. After you have added speaker's notes to a presentation, you can print the notes by using the steps outlined under "Printing parts of your presentation" earlier in this chapter.

Hot Stuff It's generally easier to see the text that you type in the notes box if you change the default magnification. From the Zoom Control list box on the Standard toolbar, choose a magnification of 75 percent or larger.

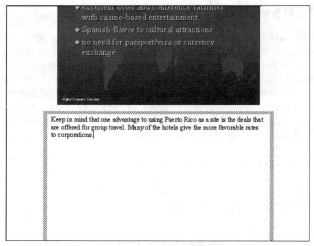

Figure 30-6: The notes page magnified by 75 percent.

You can create audience handouts by performing the following steps:

1. Choose View⇨Master⇨Handout Master. Your screen takes on the appearance shown in Figure 30-7. In the figure, the areas outlined by means of dotted lines represent where your slides will appear, depending on whether you've selected two, three, or six slides per page. Two slides appear in the two large dotted-line boxes, three slides appear in the three smaller boxes at the left side of the page, and six slides appear in the six smaller boxes that occupy the full page. To select the number of slides you want to appear per page, choose File⇨Print and specify the number in the Print what list box of the Print dialog box.

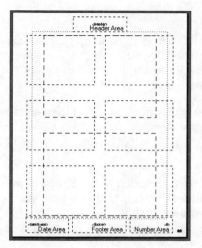

Figure 30-7: The Handout Master screen.

2. Choose <u>I</u>nsert⇨Te<u>x</u>t Box and click and drag the desired text box to the desired size. You can then type the desired text.

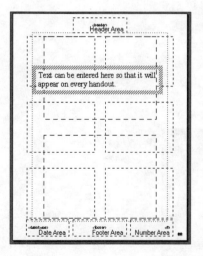

Figure 30-8: Adding a text box and text to the Handout Master.

Hot Stuff   You can add the date and time or page numbers to text boxes in your handouts. To do so, place the insertion point where you want the text inside the text box, open the Insert menu, and choose the Date and Time or Page Number command. Then select the format that you want in the dialog box that appears.

Custom Shows

PowerPoint 97 offers you the flexibility of custom slide shows. These are basically variations of the same presentation. Beneficially, you can give the same presentation to different sections of a company, for example. You can create custom shows by performing the following steps:

1. From the Slide Show menu, choose Custom Shows. You then see the Custom Shows dialog box as shown in Figure 30-9.

2. Choose the New button. This activates the Define Custom Show dialog box shown in Figure 30-10.

3. You want to select the slides you want included in the Slides in presentation area of the dialog box and click Add. (Remember that if you wish to select multiple slides, hold the Ctrl key while clicking.)

4. Using the Arrows beside the Slides in custom show box, move the slides to appear in the order that you want.

5. Give the slide show a name and save it.

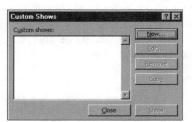

Figure 30-9: The Custom Shows dialog box.

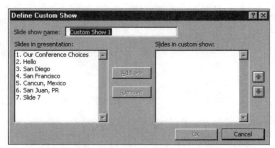

Figure 30-10: The Define Custom Show dialog box.

This feature can really come in handy when making on-the-fly adjustments to a presentation, something that many presentation givers do. It also provides you with a way to make a presentation more adaptable to the circumstances. In addition, what was at one time three presentations on the same topic directed at different audiences with some slides in common can now become one presentation with several ways of running the presentation.

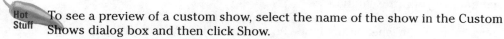

Hot Stuff To see a preview of a custom show, select the name of the show in the Custom Shows dialog box and then click Show.

Just before you run your slide show, you will want to Select Slide Show then Set Up Show. This will allow you to make some final adjustments to the slide show. Figure 30-11 shows the Set Up Show dialog box. This dialog box offers you the option to select a type of show you want to give, be it of a browsing nature, where the presentation shows up in a window, or the typical slide show in full screen. You are also able to show the presentation in a looping manner or without the animation. You can make these choices by clicking on the corresponding check box.

You can also specify which slides you wish to show in that particular session or whether you want to use one of your previously created custom shows. Pen color and Slide Advancing options are also included here.

Figure 30-11: The Set Up Show dialog box.

Using the PowerPoint Viewer

Your Microsoft Office package includes the PowerPoint Viewer, a separate program that is useful when you want to view a presentation with another computer that does not have PowerPoint installed. The PowerPoint Viewer provides the software needed to load and view any presentation created in PowerPoint. You can also use the Pack and Go Wizard in PowerPoint to package any presentation onto one or more floppy disks (see the next section). Then all you need to give your presentation at a site lacking PowerPoint is the PowerPoint Viewer disk and the disks containing your presentation.

According to the label on the PowerPoint Viewer disk, Microsoft freely gives permission for this disk to be copied and installed on other systems. The Viewer disk does not provide an operational copy of PowerPoint. Let's get real: to do that would be a *major* violation of your software license agreement! The Viewer only lets you view presentations.

Note　If you are traveling and you don't have the PowerPoint Viewer disk handy, you can also download the PowerPoint Viewer from Microsoft's web site at www.microsoft.com.

To install the PowerPoint Viewer, perform these steps:

1. Insert the PowerPoint Viewer disk (it's provided with your software) into the computer's floppy drive.

2. Choose Run from the Start menu.

3. In the Run dialog box, enter **A:\SETUP** (if the disk is in drive A) or **B:\SETUP** (if the disk is in drive B) and then click on OK.

The installation program runs, and a dialog box appears that asks for a folder name, which is where the program should be installed. After the installation is complete, you can run the PowerPoint Viewer on that computer by opening the Start menu, choosing Programs, and then choosing PowerPoint Viewer. The Viewer displays an Open dialog box that asks for the name of the PowerPoint presentation that you want to view. Find the desired presentation in the folder it is stored in, select it, and click on Open to view the presentation.

Notes and handout pages have masters, too

In PowerPoint, both notes pages and handout pages have masters, so you can use them the way you use the Slide Master. When you change the appearance of something in Notes Master, for example, the change is reflected in every notes page of the presentation. Likewise, any change in the Handout Master is reflected in every handout page of a presentation. You can take advantage of this design trait by placing information on the masters that should appear on every notes page or handout page.

Using the Pack and Go Wizard

You can use the Pack and Go command from the File menu to create a packaged presentation on one or more disks. This menu command launches the Pack and Go Wizard, which then steps you through the process of packaging a presentation and saving it to as many floppy disks as are needed. You can then carry the disks from site to site and give the presentation on any computer that has either PowerPoint or the PowerPoint Viewer installed. To package a presentation for use elsewhere, perform the following steps:

1. Choose File⇨Pack and Go to display the first Pack and Go Wizard dialog box. This dialog box explains the purpose of the wizard but in other respects is pretty useless. Click on the Next button.

2. In the next dialog box presented by the wizard, you can choose to package the presentation that is currently open, or you can click on the Other Presentations button and choose another presentation from the dialog box that appears. Make your desired selections and then click on the Next button.

3. The next dialog box asks which floppy disk drive you want to use to store the presentation. (If you have only one floppy drive, you obviously won't be able to choose anything but the default.) Select the desired drive, if necessary, and then click on the Next button.

4. The next dialog box asks whether you want to include any linked files (such as an Excel worksheet that may be pasted into your presentation or hyperlinks you may have added) and any embedded fonts that may be in your presentation. Turn on any desired options and then click on the Next button.

5. The last dialog box asks you if you wish to include the view for a computer that does not have Power Point installed. It also asks if you want to include a viewer for Windows 95 or NT. If you need to show your presentation on a computer that has Windows 3.1, click on the Help Button to activate the Office Assistant. Next, choose Help with this feature and choose Make Viewer Disk for Windows 3.1. Make sure that there is a blank floppy disk in the drive that you selected earlier. If any additional disks are needed, PowerPoint asks you to insert them when it needs one. When the process is complete, you are returned to whatever view of PowerPoint you were in when you started the wizard.

To install the presentation on another machine, insert the first floppy disk created by the wizard into the drive and choose the Run command from the Windows 95 Start menu. In the Run dialog box that appears, browse the floppy drive, find and select the program called PNG Setup, and click on Open to run that program. When you run the program, it displays a Pack and Go Wizard setup dialog box like the one shown in Figure 30-12, which asks you for a destination folder in which to store the presentation. Enter a folder name and then click on OK. (If you enter a new folder name, the program asks you for confirmation before creating the folder.)

All this wizard stuff! Why can't I just copy the presentation file to the other computer?

Actually, you probably can. The Pack and Go Wizard makes life easier if you're not comfortable with moving files around to package a presentation and install it on another system. If you're perfectly comfortable with using Explorer, My Computer, or (horrors!) MS-DOS commands to copy files from place to place, you can always just copy the presentation file onto the other system and open it in PowerPoint or in the PowerPoint Viewer. Keep in mind that if your presentation has any OLE objects in it (such as parts of Word documents or Excel worksheets), it's probably a wise idea to use the Pack and Go Wizard, because it includes any linked files. You, on the other hand, may very well leave them in New York and discover that they are missing when you are in Omaha. Using Pack and Go, however, prevents you from forgetting those needed files for your big presentation.

Figure 30-12: The Pack and Go Wizard dialog box.

If the program created more than one disk, the program asks for the additional disks as it needs them. When the installation is complete, you can view the presentation by opening it in PowerPoint or by using the PowerPoint Viewer (described in the preceding section).

Using the Send Command

One other common option that you have for "producing" your presentation (in a manner of speaking) is the Send To command from the File menu. With this command, you can send the presentation to another person on a network. This command uses Microsoft Exchange, which is provided with Windows 95. (The complete use of Microsoft Exchange is a subject beyond the scope of this book, but you can find details about it in your Windows documentation or in Alan Simpson's *Windows 95 Uncut,* another fine book from IDG Books Worldwide.) To send a presentation by using Microsoft Exchange, choose File⇨Send To⇨Mail Recipient. PowerPoint saves the presentation to a temporary file, launches Microsoft Exchange, and displays the Choose Profile window of Microsoft Exchange with your default server selected, as shown in Figure 30-13. (If you have configured a network mail server to work with Microsoft Exchange, you'll see a new message window for your particular mail service instead.)

Figure 30-13: The Choose Profile window of Microsoft Exchange.

From here, you can use the techniques that apply to Microsoft Exchange to send the presentation to the desired recipient.

Summary

As demonstrated in this chapter, producing your work in PowerPoint is not an incredibly involved process. This chapter showed you how you can print presentations and how you can use different methods to improve your slide presentations. The chapter covered the following points:

✦ You can print presentation slides by choosing File⇨Print, but you should first set up your presentation for the type of printing that you want. First choose File⇨Page Setup and then select the desired options in the Slide Setup dialog box.

✦ You can produce on-screen slide shows by Slide Show menu and selecting the desired options from the Slide Show dialog box.

✦ You can add transitions or builds to each slide to enhance the effects of an on-screen presentation.

✦ You can add speaker's notes or audience handouts to presentations. You can print these items separately for distribution to the speaker or the audience.

✦ You can use File⇨Pack and Go to launch a wizard that lets you package a presentation to run on any computer.

The next chapter will demonstrate how you can use macros within PowerPoint to automate various tasks.

Where to go next...

✦ PowerPoint offers lots of ways to enhance your presentation. It's never too late to make a better presentation! See Chapter 28 for details.

✦ PowerPoint presentations can be used as part of complex documents in Word. Chapter 50 has the scoop on using linking and embedding to share data between applications.

✦   ✦   ✦

Working with PowerPoint Macros

CHAPTER

31

Macros are combinations of keystrokes that automate many of the tasks you normally perform with a program. Macros enable you to record a sequence of characters that you can then assign to text or a graphic on a slide or to a button on a toolbar. Later, you can play back the character sequence by choosing a menu option used for running macros or by clicking on the slide object or toolbar button assigned to the macro. When you run the macro, PowerPoint performs the steps as if you had just typed the characters, made the menu choices, or done whatever actions that you recorded for that macro. If you must perform any repetitive tasks in PowerPoint, you can save many keystrokes and mouse option choices with macros.

Before you record a macro, you might want to sit down and plan the steps for the macro you want to record. This will prevent having to make corrections. Each of the macros you record is stored in a new Visual Basic module and attached to the open presentation. As a final point to keep in mind, you will want to store your macros with your presentation and not with a PowerPoint template because macros that are stored in templates are not attached to the presentation.

Creating a Macro

When you decide that you want to create a macro, you must first do everything that you do not want to include in the macro — such as opening a presentation or moving to a specific location in the presentation — because you don't want any unnecessary steps to be included in the macro. Remember that after you begin recording the macro, everything that you do will be included in it.

To begin creating a macro, open the desired presentation and choose Tools⇨ Macro⇨Record New Macro. The Record Macro dialog box prompts you for the name and description of your new macro and asks where the macro should be stored (see Figure 31-1). By default, macros are stored in the active presentation, but you can also store macros in Visual Basic for Applications programs (called *modules*) that are attached to presentations.

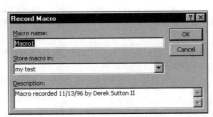

Figure 31-1: The Record Macro dialog box.

In the Description area, you can enter a description of the macro, which can be important if you plan on keeping the macro for some time because you may not remember what it does.

You can also use another method to record macros in PowerPoint: the Visual Basic toolbar. You can activate the Visual Basic toolbar by right-clicking in the toolbar area and then choosing the Visual Basic option from the shortcut menu. You can then click on the Record Macro button on the Visual Basic toolbar to begin recording a macro. For everyday use of macros outside the world of programming, only two buttons on the Visual Basic toolbar will be of any interest to you: the Record Macro Button and the Run Macro button. The remaining buttons delve into the realm of programming in Visual Basic for Applications for PowerPoint, a subject that's beyond the scope of this book.

Stopping the Macro Recorder

Stopping the Macro Recorder isn't too difficult: you click on the Stop Recording button. This button appears on-screen when you begin to record a macro. Alternately, you can choose Tools⇨Macro⇨Stop Recording.

Now that you have had a general look at creating macros, you need to see how the specifics work. The following steps show you how to create a macro that prints two copies of slide handouts for a presentation that's open:

1. Open any presentation in PowerPoint.

2. Choose Tools⇨Macro⇨Record New Macro.

3. In the Record New Macro dialog box, enter **MyHandouts** in the Macro Name text box. After you click on the OK button, the Stop Recording button appears, and you are ready to make the choices that you need to print the handouts.

4. Choose File⇨Print to open the Print dialog box, as shown in Figure 31-2.

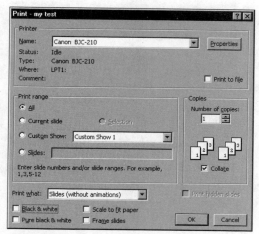

Figure 31-2: The Print dialog box.

5. In the Print What area, choose Handouts (2 slides per page).

6. In the Copies area, change the Number of Slides entry to 2.

7. Click on the OK button. This prints the selected part of your presentation.

8. Click on the Stop Recording button to stop recording.

From this point on, you can repeatedly select and print the same set of handouts just by running the macro. To see how this process works, choose Tools⇨ Macro⇨Macros. In the Macro dialog box, click on the MyHandouts macro name and then click on the Run button. The macro runs, and the presentation handouts are again printed. That's the beauty of macros: you can automate any task that you perform regularly, such as printing a set of handouts.

The macros that you create will differ because you will have different tasks that you need to automate with a macro.

Note If you do something that you didn't want to do while recording a macro, don't bother trying to use the Undo option of the Edit menu to undo the action within the macro: PowerPoint doesn't record the Edit⇨Undo action as part of a recorded macro. You should just stop recording the macro, delete it, and record a new one.

A note about macro viruses

Macro viruses are computer viruses that are stored in macros within PowerPoint presentations. PowerPoint does not have the capability to scan a floppy disk, hard disk, or network drive for a macro virus and remove it. (You can obtain this kind of protection from the use of antivirus software, commonly available from your software retailer.) PowerPoint does warn you about the possibility of macro viruses when you open a presentation that contains macros. The reason for this is that the macros in the presentation may contain harmful macros. At that point you are given the option of opening the presentation with or without the macros.

A good rule of thumb is if the presentation contains useful macros, you may want to open it with the macros, but if you don't know the source (if it is attached to an e-mail for example) of the presentation, you may want to open it without the macros. This will prevent you from running the risk of contamination.

If you want to stop the checking for macro viruses, you can turn off the Always ask before opening presentations with macros check box. If you decide to turn off the option later, choose Options on the Tools menu, click on the General tab, and remove the Macro virus protection check box. If you want more information on macro viruses, you can go to download virus protection information from Microsoft's World Wide Web site.

Setting Up Macros to Run During Slide Shows

Another method that you can use to place a macro is to assign it to an object (such as text or a graphic) that's placed on a slide. This technique lets you access the macro by clicking on the object.

You can attach a macro button to an object on a slide by performing the following steps:

1. In Slide View, select the text or graphic you want to use to run the macro.
2. Choose Slide Show⇨Action Settings. The Action Settings dialog box appears, as shown in Figure 31-3.
3. If you want to run the macro by clicking the selected object during the slide show, click the Mouse Click tab. If you want to run the macro by moving the mouse pointer over the object, click the Mouse Over tab.
4. Click Run Macro and then choose the desired macro in the list box.

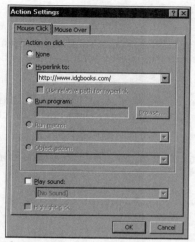

Figure 31-3: The Action Settings dialog box.

5. Choose any other desired options in the dialog box.

6. Click on the OK button, and the object in the slide will take on a highlighted appearance. When you click on the object during a slide show, the macro will run.

Assigning Macros to Toolbar Buttons

You can assign macros to buttons on the toolbar. This can prove very useful if you perform some tasks on a regular basis. The macro button that the macro is assigned to is usually a custom button, but you also have the option of assigning the macro to an existing button on the toolbar. This will cancel the previous function. To assign a macro to a toolbar button, perform these steps:

1. Choose Tools⇨Customize.

2. If the toolbar that you want to add a button to isn't visible, click the Toolbars tab of the dialog box and turn on the check box beside the toolbar name.

3. Click the Commands tab of the Customize dialog box.

4. Scroll down in the Categories list and click Macros to select it.

5. In the right half of the dialog box, click and drag the desired macro onto the desired toolbar. When you release the mouse button, a button appears on the toolbar for the macro.

Running the Macro

After you create a macro, you will discover that you can run it in different ways. After reading this section, you can decide for yourself which method is best for your needs.

One obvious way to run a macro is choose Tools⇨Macro⇨Macros. In the Macro dialog box, you click on the name of the macro that you want and then click on the Run button.

Another method for running macros is to click on an object in a slide that you assigned to the macro.

Hot Stuff You can stop a macro that's running at any time by pressing Ctrl+Break.

Deleting a Macro

After you have created a presentation, you may want to eliminate the macros. This is another task that you can accomplish with relative ease. If you wish to delete a macro, perform the following steps:

1. Choose Tools⇨Macro⇨Macros.
2. In the Macro dialog box shown in Figure 31-4, choose the name of the macro.
3. Click on the delete button.

When you perform these steps, the macro is removed from the presentation. This is also an alternative for those times when you misrecord a macro and wish to start over.

About the Code Behind the Macros

Without a knowledge of Visual Basic for Applications (VBA), you can't easily edit existing macros. If you want to make a change to a macro and you are not a VBA programmer, you're probably better off rerecording the macro from scratch.

If you are familiar with the workings of VBA, you can make changes to an existing macro by editing the VBA code that lies at the heart of the macro. Choose Tools⇨Macro⇨Macros, select the desired macro in the Macro dialog box that appears, and click Edit. When you do this, the VBA code of the macro appears in a VBA Editor window. Figure 31-5 shows the code for the macro created earlier, as an example in this chapter.

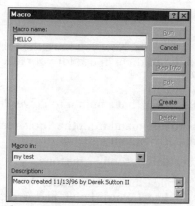

Figure 31-4: The Macro dialog box.

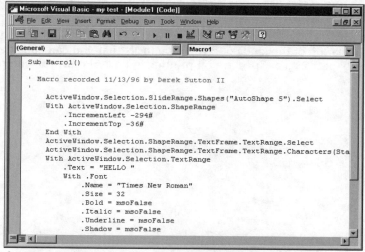

Figure 31-5: The VBA code behind the sample macro.

As mentioned earlier, VBA programming for PowerPoint is a subject that's beyond the scope of this chapter. We bring up the topic here to make the point that those readers who do work with VBA can use the VBA Editor to make changes to existing macros. If you'd like to delve deeply into programming in Visual Basic, you can take a look at a good book on the subject, such as IDG's *Excel for Windows 95 Power Programming with VBA*, 2nd edition, by John Walkenbach.

Summary

This chapter covered different topics related to macros. Now you have the tools that you need to record macros efficiently and to put them in use for yourself. The following areas related to macros were covered:

✦ You can create macros with the Macro Recorder that's built into PowerPoint.

✦ You can run macros by choosing the Macro command from the Tools menu and selecting the desired macro in the dialog box that appears.

✦ You can attach macros to objects on slides and to toolbar buttons.

✦ Macros are recorded in Visual Basic for Applications (VBA) code, the underlying programming language of Word, Excel, PowerPoint, and Access.

The next chapter will discuss the use of the Internet with PowerPoint.

Where to go next...

Macros can take much of the repetitive drudgery out of formatting and printing tasks. For an explanation of the kinds of formatting tasks that you can consider automating, see Chapter 28. For specifics on printing in PowerPoint, you can refer to Chapter 30.

✦   ✦   ✦

PowerPoint and the Web

PowerPoint 97 differs significantly from its predecessors in that it comes enabled with specific features for producing presentation-quality web pages for use with the Internet and with intranets. Using PowerPoint 97, you can attach hyperlinks to other Office 97 documents or to web sites. These hyperlinks let you easily jump to locations in other Office 97 documents. You can easily save PowerPoint slides in HTML format, ready for inclusion on your web pages and you can take advantage of a Web Publishing Wizard to produce professional web pages. Figure 32-1 shows a PowerPoint slide, published as a web page on a corporate intranet and viewed using Netscape Navigator, a popular web browser.

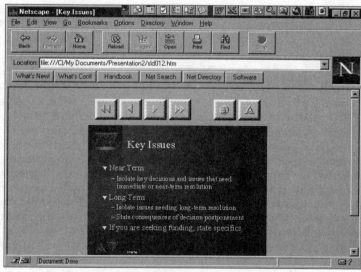

Figure 32-1: A PowerPoint slide published as a web page.

To accomplish most of the tasks described in this chapter, obviously you'll need to be connected to a net. This can be a dial-up connection to the Internet by means of a commercial Internet service provider such as AT&T WorldNet, MCINet, MindSpring, NetCom, or a host of others. Your connection can also be a direct connection through your organization's local area network, and you may be connected directly to a corporate *intranet*, in which case you'll be able to retrieve or publish data to your company's private network. This chapter won't go into specifics on making a net connection, as that topic is an entire book in itself. If you need help in this area, you can take a look at IDG's *Creating Cool Interactive Web Sites* or *Creating Cool FrontPage Web Sites* by Paul and Mary Summitt.

This chapter also assumes a familiarity with the basics of PowerPoint. If you are familiar with the Web or with intranets but you haven't yet learned to work with PowerPoint, you should consider Chapters 27 through 30 before proceeding with this chapter.

What's Possible with PowerPoint 97 and the Web?

Using PowerPoint 97, you can perform a number of Net-related tasks as you work with presentations. You can insert hyperlinks at any desired location in a presentation, to link to other Office 97 documents or to web sites. When you click on these hyperlinks while viewing a presentation, you can jump directly to that location in the other file, or to a specified web site. You can also save PowerPoint slides as HTML (Hypertext Markup Language), the publishing lingua of the World Wide Web. These topics will be covered in further detail throughout this chapter.

About the Web and the Internet

Because intranets and the Internet are newer concepts to many readers than are presentations, a few explanations of terms may be in order. (If you're intimately familiar with the Internet, intranets, and the World Wide Web; you may want to skip this section and the next and dive right into working with PowerPoint and the Web.) First, the *Internet* is a global collection of computers, linked together by means of telephone and microwave lines and accessible to the public by means of various connections in offices and in homes. The Internet grew out of a research project that came into common knowledge in the 1970s, which originally linked university and government computers in the United States. Since its inception, the Internet has grown to encompass thousands of computers spread throughout dozens of nations. Any PC user with an Internet connection can connect to the Internet (either by means of a phone line or a direct hookup), and gain access to the volumes of information located there.

One major component of the Internet is the *World Wide Web*. There are other parts of the Internet, but the World Wide Web is the most well known part. The World Wide Web is that part of the Internet that makes use of graphical software known as web browsers and of files stored as HTML. The computers on the Internet that store the HTML files are also known as *web servers*. When PCs connect to the Internet to retrieve this data, they use web browser software, which converts the incoming information (encoded in HTML) to graphical pages displayed as a combination of text, graphics, and in some cases audio and video. Commonly used web browsers include Microsoft Internet Explorer, Netscape Navigator, and the custom web browsers built into the software provided by America Online and CompuServe.

Each site on the Internet has a unique address, commonly known as the Internet address (and less commonly known by the official name of *URL*, or *Uniform Resource Locator*). When you establish an Internet connection, open a web browser, and enter an Internet address such as *http://www.whitehouse.gov*, you are entering the address for the web server that provides the home page for the President's office in the United States. Web addresses like these can be stored in PowerPoint slides and displayed as hyperlinks.

About Intranets

Many Net-related uses of Office 97 involve making data available on *intranets*. An intranet is a private network of computers that is available only to the members of a specific organization. Intranets make use of World Wide Web technology — web servers, network connections, and web browser software — to allow members of an organization to share information. Intranets are very popular with corporations, as intranets let employees share work-related information in a confidential manner.

About HTML

As mentioned earlier, HTML is the language used for publishing information to the World Wide Web and to intranets that use World Wide Web technology. HTML is a text-based language that makes use of special codes called *tags*. These tags are included in the text of the HTML documents, and they provide instructions to the web browser software that determine how the data appears when it is viewed by the end-user. While you don't need to know the nuts and bolts of HTML coding to work with PowerPoint and the web, it's a good idea to at least be familiar with the concept of saving your data in HTML file format. In order to publish PowerPoint data on the Internet or on an intranet, you'll need to save that data in HTML format and upload it to your web server. If you are dealing with a corporate intranet, your company's webmaster can tell you how to upload the HTML files that PowerPoint produces to your company's web server. If you are managing a web site on the Internet or on an intranet, you already know how to do this; much of the rest of this chapter will deal with getting that PowerPoint data ready for uploading to your server.

About the Web Toolbar

Like all the major Office 97 applications, PowerPoint provides the Web toolbar, a toolbar that helps you browse through the resources on an intranet or on the Web. Using the Web toolbar, you can quickly open, search, and browse through any document or through a web page. You can jump between documents, and you can add favorite sites you find on the web to the Favorites folder, allowing you to quickly go back to those sites at a later time.

In PowerPoint, you can display the Web toolbar by choosing View⇨Toolbars and then selecting Web from the submenu that appears or by clicking the Web toolbar button in the Standard toolbar. Figure 32-2 shows the Web toolbar.

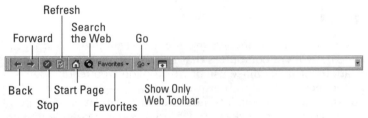

Figure 32-2: The Web toolbar.

You'll find the Web toolbar to be handy when you happen to be in PowerPoint and you have a need to go to the Web (or to your company's intranet) for information. For example, you can click the Search the Web button to launch your default web browser and search the web, or you can click the Favorites button to open a list of your favorite web sites. Refer to Chapter 11 for more specifics on the use of the Web toolbar.

Creating Hyperlinks in Documents

A significant feature of PowerPoint 97 is its Ability to use *hyperlinks* in documents. You can create hyperlinks to jump to other Office documents stored on your PC, on your company's network, a company intranet, or on the Internet.

Linking to office documents with Copy and Paste

If you want to create a hyperlink to a Word document or in an Excel worksheet or another location in the PowerPoint presentation, the easiest way to do this is to use the Copy and Paste Hyperlink commands of the Edit menu. In a nutshell, you do this by first selecting a location in the PowerPoint slide, Excel worksheet, or Word document that you want the hyperlink to lead to. You then choose Copy from the Edit menu. Finally, you go back to PowerPoint where you want the hyperlink to appear, and you choose Paste as Hyperlink from the Edit menu. In more detail, here are the steps you can use to create a hyperlink from another Office document.

1. Open the document containing the location you want to link to. (If it is in PowerPoint, it can be in the same presentation or in a different presentation that's open. If the location is in an Excel or a Word file, it can be in any area of the worksheet or document.)

2. Select the portion of the document you want to link to.

3. Choose Edit⇨Copy.

4. In PowerPoint, go into Slide view or Outline view and place the insertion pointer at the location where you want to insert the hyperlink.

5. Choose Edit⇨Paste as Hyperlink.

When you perform these steps, PowerPoint inserts a hyperlink back to the original document at the selected location. When you view the presentation in Slide view mode, you can click on the hyperlink to jump to the linked document.

Linking to web sites or files with Insert Hyperlink

If you need to establish a hyperlink from a PowerPoint slide to a web site on an intranet or on the Internet, you can use the following steps to do so. (Technically, you can use these same steps to link to another Office document, but it's easier to use the copy and paste methods described earlier.)

1. In Slide view or in Outline view, select the text in the slide that will serve as the hyperlink.

2. Click the Insert Hyperlink button in the Standard toolbar, or choose Insert ⇨ Hyperlink. When you do this, the Insert Hyperlink dialog box appears, as shown in Figure 32-3.

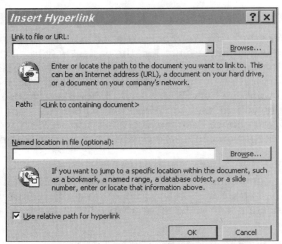

Figure 32-3: The Insert Hyperlink dialog box.

3. In the Link to File or URL text box, enter the web address (or the path for the file) of the destination for the link.

4. If you are establishing a link to a file and you want to jump to a specific location, enter that location in the Named Location in File text box. (This can be a cell reference or named range in an Excel worksheet, a Word bookmark, or the name of another PowerPoint slide.) If you link to a file and leave this entry blank, the hyperlink jumps to the beginning of the file.

5. If you want a hyperlink to a shared network directory to find the linked file based on a path that's relative to the location where your current document is stored, turn on the Use Relative Path for Hyperlink check box. If you want a hyperlink to a shared network directory to use the same address regardless of where the current document is stored, turn off the Use Relative Path for Hyperlink check box.

6. Click OK to establish the hyperlink.

Saving PowerPoint Presentations to the Web

You can save PowerPoint presentations directly to Internet FTP sites. (In order to do this, you must have permission to save files to the desired FTP site.) You can use the following steps to save a presentation to the Internet:

1. Choose File⇨Save As.

2. In the Save In box of the dialog box which appears, click Internet Locations (FTP).

3. In the list of FTP sites, double-click the site you want (see the note below if the desired site does not appear).

4. Double-click the location you want within the site.

5. Enter a name for the document in the File name box.

6. Click Save.

Note   If the FTP site you want to save your document to doesn't appear in the list of FTP sites, you'll need to add it to the list. Choose File⇨Open, and in the Look in box, click Add/Modify FTP locations. This causes an Add/Modify FTP Locations dialog box to appear, and you can fill in the site name, login, and password information. When done, click OK to add the site to the list.

Opening PowerPoint Presentations Stored on the Web

Because you can save PowerPoint presentations to web sites, it makes sense that you can open them from web sites as well. Opening a PowerPoint presentation that's stored at a web site is intuitively simple. Just choose File⇨Open and enter the web address in the File Name box of the Open dialog box. When you click Open, Power-Point will connect to the web using your default Windows Internet connection, and it will download the presentation from the web site. (If you are using Windows 95 Dial-Up Networking, a Connect To dialog box will appear, and you'll need to click the Connect button to connect to your Internet Service Provider.)

Keep in mind that PowerPoint presentations can be fairly large in terms of disk space, and the Internet is (as of this writing) not one of the fastest ways to transfer large amounts of data. Hence, it may take some time to open a presentation that's stored on the Web.

Publishing PowerPoint Slides on the Web

The Save as HTML option of the File menu allows you to save existing presenta-tions as HTML files for web publication. You can use the Save as HTML option of the File menu to convert existing PowerPoint slides into HTML files. Once converted, you can then upload the HTML files to your Internet or intranet web server, using the procedures applicable to your server. Choosing File⇨Save as HTML starts the Save as HTML Wizard, which displays a series of dialog boxes that let you control the content and format of the resulting web pages.

To save an existing presentation in HTML format, choose File➪Save as HTML. When you do this, the Save as HTML Wizard is then launched. Figure 32-4 shows the first dialog box of the Save as HTML Wizard.

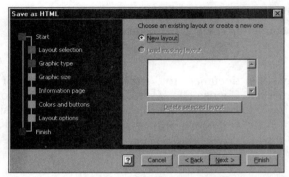

Figure 32-4: The second dialog box of the Save as HTML Wizard.

Click Next to begin preparing to save your presentation as an HTML file. The second dialog box of the wizard (Figure 32-4) allows you to create a new layout or use an existing one for the layout of your web pages. (*Layouts* are saved settings from previous uses of the Save as HTML Wizard. At the end of each session with the wizard, you are given the opportunity of saving that session's dialog box selections as a layout.) If you want to use an existing layout, click Load Existing Layout, select the desired layout in the dialog box, and click Next. Otherwise, leave the New Layout option selected and click Next. Note that if you use an existing layout, the following dialog boxes (with the exception of the last one) will be skipped.

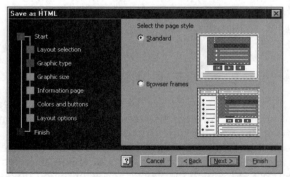

Figure 32-5: The Layout Selection dialog box of the Save as HTML File Wizard.

If you haven't chosen an existing layout, you will next see the dialog box shown in Figure 32-5. This dialog box allows you to choose a standard page style for the design of the web pages or a page style that makes use of browser frames, a popular feature of web pages.

Note   Before choosing browser frames, keep in mind that most but not all web browsers support the use of frames. If the general public will be viewing your presentation on the Internet, you may want to use the standard page style option instead.

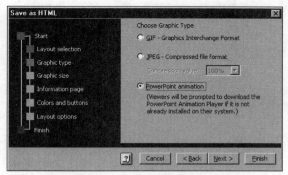

Figure 32-6: The Graphics Type dialog box.

After clicking on Next, you will see the Graphics Type dialog box (Figure 32-6). Here, you will need to select the type of graphics you want to use to produce images and backgrounds on your web pages. You can select .GIF or .JPEG files as your format. You also have the option of using PowerPoint animation as your graphics type. If you use the PowerPoint animation as the graphics type, viewers of your presentation will be prompted to download a PowerPoint animation viewer if they do not have one.

In deciding which graphics file formats to use, keep in mind that either of these commonly used formats, GIF and JPEG, have advantages and disadvantages. GIF files offer good all-around image quality but tend to be larger in size than JPEG files. JPEG files are usually smaller than GIF files, but at a cost of image quality. If you use JPEG, you'll also need to set a Compression Value in the dialog box (the default is 100 percent). The higher the value, the better the image quality. The lower the value, the smaller the image files that are produced.

Clicking Next takes you to the dialog box that lets you choose how the graphics should be sized in comparison to the common monitor resolutions used by PCs (see Figure 32-7). Using the options in the dialog box, select the monitor resolution that you think will work best for the showing of your presentation. (You should avoid resolutions above 800×600, unless you know that your viewing audiences all have monitors that make use of that resolution or better.) You can also set a width for the presentation. Your choices here are the full width of the screen, three-fouths–width of the screen, half-width of the screen, and a quarter-width of the screen. When done choosing the desired options, click Next.

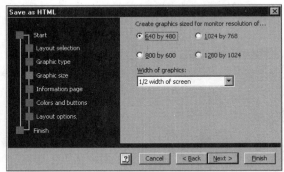

Figure 32-7: The Graphic Size dialog box.

Next you will see the Information Page Options dialog box, as shown in Figure 32-8. Here, you can enter your e-mail address, home page, and other information you may want to add to an information page that's included in the web pages produced by the wizard. You can also include buttons that will allow users to download the original presentation or the latest version of Microsoft Internet Explorer by checking the corresponding check boxes.

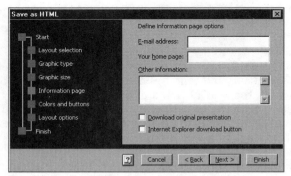

Figure 32-8: The Information Page dialog box.

The Page Colors and Buttons dialog box that appears next (Figure 32-9) allows you to choose a page color and the Text, Background, Link, or Visited Link colors for the presentation. You can leave the Use Browser Colors option selected to use the default browser colors, or you can select the Custom Colors option to use custom colors of your own choosing. For each of the items shown, you can click on the appropriate Change button to open a color palette after choosing the Custom Colors option. You also have the option of using transparent buttons for the presentation.

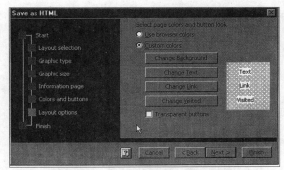

Figure 32-9: The Colors and Buttons dialog box.

Clicking Next takes you to the Button Style dialog box, as shown in Figure 32-10. Here you can select a button style to be used for the navigation buttons in your presentation. Select a desired button style and click Next.

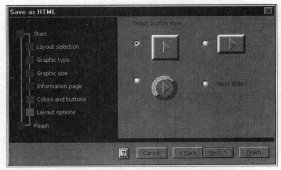

Figure 32-10: The Button Style dialog box.

Clicking Next takes you to the Layout options dialog box, as shown in Figure 32-11. In this dialog box, you choose the layout for the navigation buttons used to move between the web pages of the presentation. You can also choose to include the slide notes page by clicking on the corresponding check box.

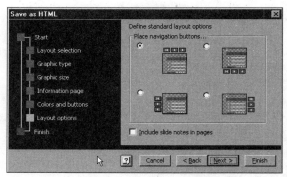

Figure 32-11: The Layout Options dialog box.

Clicking Next takes you to the Folder dialog box of the wizard, shown in Figure 32-12. This dialog box asks you to choose a folder in which to save the HTML file. After choosing the desired folder, click Next, and click Finish.

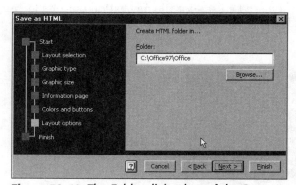

Figure 32-12: The Folder dialog box of the Save as HTML Wizard.

After you click Finish, the dialog box shown in Figure 32-13 appears. This dialog box asks if you want to save the settings you used throughout the wizard as a layout. Any name that you enter here then appears in the list box of available layouts when you initially use the wizard. To save the settings, enter a name for the layout, and click Save. If you don't want to reuse the settings later, click the Don't Save button in the dialog box.

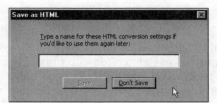

Figure 32-13: The dialog box used for saving layout settings.

Once you respond to the dialog box, PowerPoint will proceed to produce the HTML files needed for the presentation, and it will store them in the folder that you specified earlier. You can then use the procedures appropriate to your web server or your Internet service provider to upload the HTML files to your web site.

Keep in mind that you can also create web pages using PowerPoint's online presentation templates. Many of the presentations that are included with PowerPoint are online presentations. This means they are presentations that are easily prepared for web publication. If you wish to use one of these, simply choose File⇨New, then select the Presentations tab of the New dialog box. This will allow you to see some of the presentations available for easy web publication. Remember, if you don't find one that meets your needs you can always alter the presentation using the techniques described in Chapters 27 and 28.

Summary

This chapter has covered the details behind sharing your PowerPoint data with Internet/intranet users. Points covered in this chapter included the following:

✦ Hyperlinks can be added to PowerPoint slides, and you can store web addresses or jump locations to other Office documents in PowerPoint slides.

✦ PowerPoint 97 can save presentations to Internet FTP sites.

✦ You can use the Save as HTML option of the File menu to save existing PowerPoint slides as HTML files, for publishing on the Internet or on an intranet.

The next chapter will demonstrate how you can put PowerPoint to work in real-world applications.

Where to go next...

✦ PowerPoint is just one component of the web publishing capabilities provided by Office 97. Excel, Word, and Access also offer web publishing and web interaction features. For specifics on Excel and the Web, see Chapter 23; for Word and the Web, Chapter 11; and for Access and the Web, Chapter 44.

✦   ✦   ✦

PowerPoint for Windows at Work

◆ ◆ ◆ ◆

In This Chapter

Creating an
organization chart

Creating a travel
presentation

◆ ◆ ◆ ◆

This chapter shows you a pretty nifty trick: you can create organization charts in PowerPoint. Executive secretaries throughout the corporate world rejoice in this feature, because so many companies regularly play Musical Vice Presidents in these days of downsizing.

This chapter also walks you step-by-step through creating a presentation about choosing a site for a convention. In this case, the presentation's contents are less important than the general ideas you'll learn — you can use them to create *any* kind of presentation.

Creating an Organization Chart

PowerPoint's organization chart feature lets you create company hierarchy diagrams in a hurry. By way of example, here's how to create a chart for the fictitious Trejo Music Corporation (see Figure 33-1).

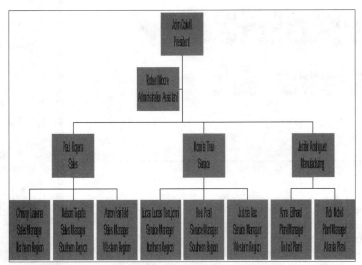

Figure 33-1: The completed organization chart in PowerPoint for the Trejo Music Company.

To create this organization chart, perform the following steps:

1. Create a new presentation in PowerPoint by choosing the Template option from the opening PowerPoint window. You then see the New Presentation dialog box, as shown in Figure 33-2.

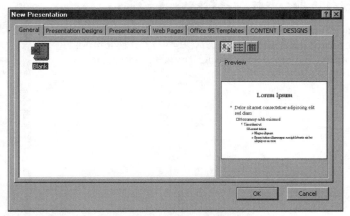

Figure 33-2: The New Presentation dialog box.

The New Presentation dialog box contains four tabs: General, which has a template for a blank presentation; Presentation Designs, which has templates that can be used to create new presentations; Presentations; and Web Pages, which is used to design web pages (see Chapter 32) and which contains templates for presenting presentations for different occasions. These templates are useful in cases when time is an important factor because they simplify the creation of your presentation. The templates also have placeholders that make suggestions on what you can include in the presentation.

2. From the General tab of the New Presentation dialog box, choose Blank Presentation and click on OK.

3. The New Slide dialog box appears. Choose the Organization Chart layout (see Figure 33-3).

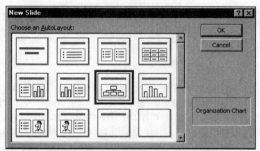

Figure 33-3: Choosing the Organization Chart layout in the New Slide dialog box.

4. Next double-click on the Organization Chart placeholder to activate the Microsoft Organization Chart application and to display a default chart. Organization Chart opens with the default chart shown in Figure 33-4.

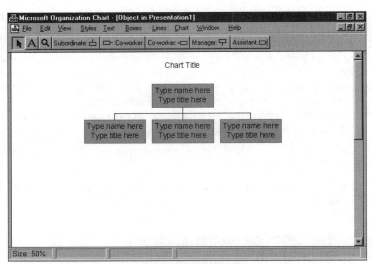

Figure 33-4: The default organization chart.

5. Click in the first box of the chart. In the box, type **John Colwill** for the name and **President** for the title (or enter a name and title of your own choosing). Use the tab or down arrow keys to move from the name to the title. If you wish to add a comment in the chart box, simply move to the comment area and begin entering your information.

6. Next you add the administrative assistant.

7. Click on the Assistant button on the toolbar and move the pointer and click in the President's box. Enter **Robert Moore** for the name and **Administrative Assistant** for the title (or enter a name and title of your own choosing).

8. Enter the following names and titles for the division managers (or names and titles of your own choosing), from left to right in the next level of boxes that appear below Administrative Assistant.

   Paul Rogers, Sales

   Nomita Trevi, Service

   Jenifer Rodriguez, Manufacturing

9. Click on the Styles menu to drop down its Groups styles options. Click the upper left icon shown in Figure 33-5. This creates subordinate levels in the chart levels.

Figure 33-5: The Groups styles menu.

10. Click on the Subordinate button on the Organization Chart toolbar and then click on Paul Rogers's box. Then enter the following names and titles (or use names and titles of your own choosing). Remember that you will need to click on the Subordinate button for each of the subordinate entries that you make:

    Chrissy Laviena, Sales Manager, Northern Region

    Nelson Tejada, Sales Manager, Southern Region

    Aaron Fairfield, Sales Manager, Western Region

11. Using the procedure in Step 10, enter the following names and titles (or use names and titles of your own choosing) underneath Nomita Trevi's box:

    Lucas Derujonni, Service Manager, Northern Region

    Bee Prat, Service Manager, Southern Region

    Jenifer Arroyo, Service Manager, Western Region

12. Using the procedure in Step 10, enter the following names and titles (or use names and titles of your own choosing) underneath the box of Jenifer Rodriguez:

    Anne Edhard, Plant Manager, Detroit Plant

    Rob Nobel, Plant Manager, Atlanta Plant

13. Now choose File⇨Update Presentation to update your presentation and to place the chart on the blank slide.

14. Click on File⇨Exit to return to PowerPoint to see the chart.

15. Choose File⇨Save to save the presentation. Save your presentation as Chart. Your finished chart should look like the one shown in Figure 33-1.

Creating a Travel Presentation

You head the committee to choose the site for your company's annual convention this year. Your first meeting with the committee is right around the corner. It's PowerPoint to the rescue.

Applying a template to the presentation

This example applies a template to the presentation. This gives the presentation's slides a consistent look. PowerPoint comes with many different templates that you can apply to your presentation — choose the one that works best for you.

Perform the following steps to duplicate this example:

1. Choose File⇨New. Click on the Blank Presentation option in the New Presentation dialog box.

2. Choose the Blank slide option from the New Slide dialog box. A slide appears without any formatting.

3. Right-click on the slide and choose Slide Layout from the shortcut menu. You will then see the Slide Layout dialog box. From the Slide Layout dialog box, choose Title Slide as the slide layout and then click on the Apply button.

4. Enter the title Convention Site Option for 1997.

5. Right-click on the PowerPoint window. From the shortcut menu that appears, choose Apply Design to open the Apply Design dialog box, as shown in Figure 33-6. Choose a template design that is to your liking and click on the Apply button.

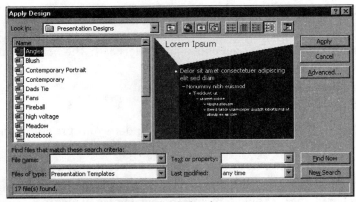

Figure 33-6: The Apply Design dialog box.

6. Click on the Insert New Slide button on the Standard toolbar and select Bulleted List as the slide layout. Enter **San Diego** as the title, and in the bulleted list, enter the following:

Wide range of pricing regarding accommodations

Excellent restaurants and entertainment

Close to Mexico

Beautiful scenery

7. Click on the Insert New Slide button on the Standard toolbar and select Bulleted List as the slide layout. Enter **San Francisco** as the title, and in the bulleted list, enter the following:

Excellent dining and attractions in Fisherman's Wharf area

Proximity to sites of interest reduces transportation costs

8. Click on the Insert New Slide button on the Standard toolbar and select Bulleted List as the slide layout. Enter **Cancun, Mexico** as the title, and in the bulleted list, enter the following:

Favorable currency exchange rate maximizes dollar usage

Outstanding water sports in close proximity to hotels

9. Click on the Insert New Slide button on the Standard toolbar and select Bulleted List as the slide layout. Enter **San Juan, PR** as the title, and in the bulleted list, enter the following:

Excellent hotel and conference facilities with casino-based entertainment

Spanish flavor to cultural attractions

No need for passport/visa or currency exchange

Applying a background to the slides

Now that you have applied the template to the presentation and entered the text, apply a background to all the slides in the presentation by performing the following steps:

1. Switch to Slide Master view by choosing View➪Master➪Slide Master.

2. Choose Format➪Background to open the Background dialog box (see Figure 33-7).

Figure 33-7: The Background dialog box.

3. Choose gray as the background color by clicking the arrow in the background fill area to open the list box. Select gray from the submenu of colors that appears and click on the Apply to All button.

Adding notes and handouts to the presentation

After you have created the presentation and applied a template to it, you can create a set of speaker's notes. Perform the following steps to create these items:

1. The notes page that appears on-screen corresponds to the slide that you are currently working on. Therefore, switch to Slide view and move to the San Diego slide.

2. Choose View ⇨Notes Page.

3. Click inside the notes box to make it active. Note that you may need to use the Zoom Control so that you can see the text better. Click on the Zoom Control button on the Standard toolbar and choose a larger percentage to increase the size of the box.

4. Enter the following notes:

   To Garfinkles/$75 and up a meal/two persons

   Broadway shows at San Diego Theater

   Venture to Tijuana to purchase authentic Mexican arts and crafts

   Genuine Mexican food available (not those so-called imitations)

5. Move to the San Francisco slide and create a notes page by entering the following notes:

   From Hilton/double occupancy/$200 per night

   To La Quinta/double occupancy/$75 per night

   From Fisherman's Wharf/$20-$75 a meal/two persons

Down by the Sea Restaurant rated best in San Francisco, widest selection of seafood

12 other wharf restaurants to choose from

5 different options of transportation with low costs as opposed to cabs

6. Move to the Cancun, Mexico slide and create a notes page by entering the following notes:

5 pesos to a dollar

Outstanding snorkeling and scuba diving

Most hotels offer snorkeling gear on-site and are located on the beach

7. Move to the San Juan, Puerto Rico slide and create a notes page by entering the following notes:

ESJ Hotel facilities perfect for working vacation

Many Puerto Rican art museums

Puerto Rico is a commonwealth of the United States, so you need no special paperwork to visit there.

Adding headers and footers to your presentation

After creating the notes pages, you can add page numbers by choosing View⇨Header and Footer. The Header and Footer dialog box appears, as shown in Figure 33-8.

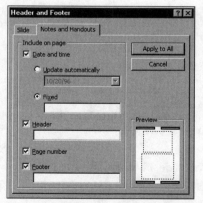

Figure 33-8: The Notes and Handouts tab of the Header and Footer dialog box.

You can use this dialog box to include headers and footers on the slides and slide notes. (You can do this only from the Slide Master.) If you click on the Slide tab, you can add the date, time, and slide numbers to your slides. While you're at it, you can exclude the title slide from getting these additions. You apply these items by clicking the corresponding check boxes on the Slide tab.

You use the Notes and Handouts tab to apply these same elements to the notes pages and handouts that may be included with a presentation. The one additional option you have here is the addition of headers. You may need to add headers to identify your handouts or notes. You can click on the Page Number box to add page numbers to your speaker's notes. The Preview box shows you where the page numbers will appear.

Printing your notes pages

You can print your notes pages by performing these steps:

1. Be sure that your printer is ready (check to see if it is online).
2. Choose File⇨Print.
3. In the Print what list box of the Print dialog box, choose Notes Pages.
4. Click on OK.

Adding transitions to your presentation

Transitions are another feature that you can add to the presentation. Transitions are visual changes between the slides. For example, one kind of transition makes one slide appear to dissolve into another. Transitions can make a presentation more appealing to an audience and can be a good special effect to add to a presentation. Perform the following steps to create a transition between two slides. You must perform these steps for each slide transition.

1. Switch to Slide Sorter view by clicking on its button on the left side of the status bar.
2. Choose the slide transition you want by clicking on the Slide Transition box on the Slide Sorter Toolbar that appears. (see Figure 33-9).

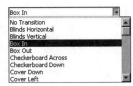

Figure 33-9: The Slide Transition list box.

3. In the Effect list box, choose Box Out for the transition. You can see the effect of this transition in the Preview box.

4. In the Speed area, choose Slow.

5. Click on OK.

You can also insert transitions by using the Transition Effects list box on the Slide Sorter toolbar at the top of your screen. Use the arrow keys to move to the slide that you want to set a transition for. Then click the arrow of the list box and choose the effect that you want to apply to the slide.

The benefit of using the dialog box is that you have a chance to preview the transition before it is applied. However, you can click on the Transition button on the Slide Sorter toolbar to open the Transitions dialog box. Here you can preview the transition by selecting it from the list of transitions.

Finally, save the completed presentation by choosing the Save command from the File menu. When asked for a name, you can call the presentation **Travel 1**. Run the presentation by clicking on the Slide Show button on the left side of the status bar.

Summary

This chapter provided you with a step-by-step look at what is involved in creating an organization chart and walked you through creating a presentation.

✦ You can use the Organization Chart layout in the New Slide dialog box to create organization charts.

✦ To apply a design to a presentation, you right-click on any blank part of the PowerPoint window and choose Apply Design Template from the shortcut menu.

✦ While in Slide View, you can create notes pages that provide speaker's notes to work from while giving your presentation.

✦ While in Slide Sorter view, you can use Tools⇨Slide Transition to add transitions to your slides.

The next chapter answers common questions PowerPoint users have.

Where to go next...

✦ Now that you have created a presentation in PowerPoint, you may want to take some time to make it more visually appealing. Chapter 28 tells you how.

✦ You also may want to produce the presentation that you may have created with this chapter. See Chapter 30.

✦   ✦   ✦

The PowerPoint Top Ten

In this chapter you'll find questions and answers detailing the most common problems encountered by users of PowerPoint. As usual, the answers are based on information we picked up from the Microsoft Technical Support and the Microsoft forums on CompuServe.

1. How can I format the title and text for an entire presentation?

Sometimes you will need to make formatting changes to an entire presentation, whether those changes are for the text or for the layout of your slides. Choose View⇨Master⇨Slide Master. When you make the changes in the Slide Master, they are applied to the entire presentation.

2. How can I group and edit objects as one?

To group objects, select them and click the Draw Group button on the drawing toolbar. This action groups the selected objects as one. If you want to edit the objects, use the editing techniques that you learned in the PowerPoint section of this book.

3. How can I copy the formatting of one object to another?

First, highlight the object that contains the formatting you want to copy. Next, double-click on the Format Painter button on the Standard toolbar. Finally, select the object(s) to which you want to apply the formatting, and the formatting is automatically applied.

4. How can I apply a PowerPoint presentation as a template?

Applying a PowerPoint presentation as a template is, in essence, creating a new template. First, create the presentation exactly the way you want it with all the formatting and objects. Next, choose File⇨Save As Presentation Template. In the Save As dialog box, choose Save As type. In the File Type box, choose Design Template. The file is then saved as a template file that you can later use to create new presentations.

5. How can I change the layout of my slide without losing my existing work?

If you decide to change the layout of your slide while you are working on it, first click on the Layout button on the right side of the status bar to open the Slide Layout dialog box. From this dialog box, choose the desired slide layout. After you click on OK, the layout is applied to the slide.

6. How can I preview all my slide transitions?

To preview all your slide transitions, switch to the Slide Sorter view by clicking on its button on the left of the status bar. After switching to Slide Sorter view, click on the transition icon underneath each slide to see the transition.

7. How can I view my presentations on a business trip without installing PowerPoint?

PowerPoint comes with the PowerPoint Viewer, which lets you view PowerPoint presentations on a computer that does not have PowerPoint installed on it. Install the PowerPoint Viewer on the other computer, open a copy of the presentation in PowerPoint Viewer, and run it. Remember that you must save the presentation on a separate disk. (Choose File⇨Pack & Go to launch a wizard that helps you put a presentation on a floppy disk.). You can also give the presentation and the PowerPoint Viewer to others so that they can view the presentation that you have created — without pressure from you. Microsoft lets you freely copy and distribute the PowerPoint Viewer disk.

8. How can I print slides in reverse order?

To print slides in reverse order, choose File⇨Print to open the Print dialog box. In the Slides text box under the Print Range portion of the dialog box, enter the order of the slides as you want them to print and remember to enter a comma after each slide number. For example, to print slide 3, then slide 2, then slide 1; enter **3,2,1** in the Slides text box.

9. How can I add and erase on-screen annotations in a slide show?

Annotations are useful in a slide show to make different points in your presentation. To add annotations, switch to the Slide Show view and then right-click on any portion of the screen. In the shortcut menu that appears, choose Pen. The pointer then becomes a pen allowing you to make the needed annotations to your slide show. You can also change the color of the marks by using the same shortcut menu. Choose Pointer Options and then Pen Color. From the next menu that appears, choose the color of your choice.

If you want to draw a straight line with the pen cursor in Slide Show view, hold down the Shift key while you draw the line.

After you have made the marks that you need, you can press the E key to remove them. Remember that all annotation marks are temporary. When you advance to the next slide, the marks are automatically erased.

10. How can I create new slides without using the New Slide dialog box?

If you want to create new slides without using the New Slide dialog box, you need to make an adjustment in the Options dialog box. To do so, choose Tools⇨Options to open the Options dialog box. Here, turn off the Show New Slide Dialog check box. With this option turned off, you can add new slides without using the New Slide dialog box each time. PowerPoint adds a slide with a title box and text area each time you ask for a new slide.

Summary

This chapter has covered the top ten PowerPoint questions and their answers. The chapter also concludes the PowerPoint section of this book.

Where to go next...

✦ Many of the common PowerPoint questions have to do with working with presentation formats and layouts. Chapter 28 gives you specifics that will help you change your presentation's appearance.

✦ Producing finished presentations generates a disproportionate number of questions, too. Chapter 30 takes you by the hand and leads you through it.

✦   ✦   ✦

Access

Working with Tables

This chapter explains how to use tables and databases in Access. You can think of tables as one of the four major objects you use in Access. The others are queries, forms, and reports. Simple uses of database software may require only one table, but you'll use more than one table as a part of the same database in applications where you must establish relationships between more than one table.

Working with the Database Window

By design, Access stores everything associated with a database in a single file. This includes your tables, queries, forms, and reports. Before you create any tables, you need to create a database in which to store your tables and other Access objects.

When you first start Access, you see the dialog box shown in Figure 35-1. The main window in Access is the desktop, or the working surface where you manipulate your various Access objects (such as tables). You use the dialog box in the center of the desktop to choose whether you want to work with an existing database or a new database. If you want to start with a new database, you can use one of two methods:

- ✦ Choose the Database Wizard option and click on OK to use this wizard to step you through the process of creating a database containing pre-designed tables.

- ✦ Choose Blank Database and click on OK to create an empty database.

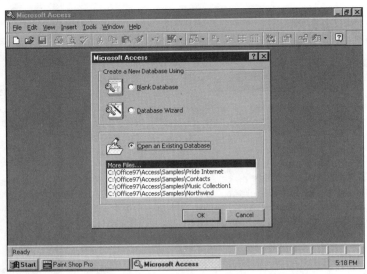

Figure 35-1: The Access main window and the initial dialog box.

If you close the dialog box with the Cancel button, you can still create or open databases. To create a database, choose File⇨New Database or click on the toolbar's New Database button. To open an existing database, choose File⇨Open Database or click on the Open Database button in the toolbar.

Understanding the Database window

After you open an existing database in Access, you see the Database window, shown in Figure 35-2. In this figure, the Database Window shows the objects in the Northwind sample database that's provided with Access. By default, the Tables tab appears selected, and you see a list of all tables in your database. You can click on any of the remaining tabs to see the other objects in an Access database; for example, clicking on the Reports tab displays all reports in the database.

From within any of the tabs, you can work with an existing object by selecting it and clicking on the Open button, or by double-clicking on the object. You can create a new object by clicking on the New button. For example, when you click on the Forms tab and then click on New, you begin the process of creating a new form. You use the Design button to change the design of an existing object from anywhere within the Database window. For example, when you click on the Tables tab, select a table named Employees inside the window, and then click on the Design button; you open that existing table in Design mode.

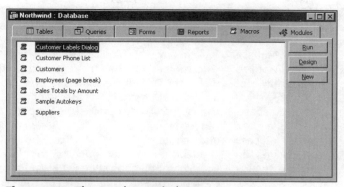

Figure 35-2: The Database window.

Note   While you work in Access, the Database window has an annoying habit of being covered by the other objects you are working with. You can quickly bring the window back into view at any time by clicking on the toolbar's Database window button, or by pressing F11 or Alt+F1.

Using shortcut menus

Since version 2.0, Access has offered *shortcut menus*: menus that appear when you right-click on an object in the Database window. For example, right-clicking on a table opens the menu shown in Figure 35-3.

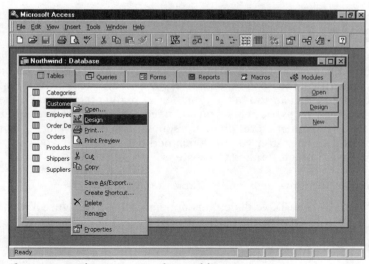

Figure 35-3: Shortcut menu for a table.

Put the Database window to real use!

For many Access users, the Database window serves as little more than a glorified File Manager designed specifically for Access: in other words, just a place where you can see the objects in your database. That's a shame because you can do a lot of work on objects directly from the Database window by selecting or right-clicking on various objects and then using the toolbar buttons and shortcut menus.

For example, you can click on the Tables tab to display all the tables in a database, right-click on any table, and choose Print from the shortcut menu to print the data contained in that table. Or, you can right-click on a report in the Reports tab of the window and choose Preview to preview the report. You can even right-click on any Access object and choose Create Shortcut from the shortcut menu that appears to place a shortcut for that object on your Windows 95 desktop (pretty neat, huh?). You later double-click on the shortcut to launch Access and open the object in one easy step.

You can use the menu choices to open the object, open it in Design mode, print it, view a Print Preview, delete it, or rename it. You can use the cut and copy choices on the menu to cut or copy the object to the Windows Clipboard. (You can then open another database and use the Edit/Paste commands to place the object into the other database.) You can use the Save As/Export choice to save the object under a different name or to export the object to an external file or to another database. The Create Shortcut lets you add the item to the Windows desktop or to any folder as a shortcut.

Creating Tables

Before you create a new table, you should determine precisely what kinds of fields you need. Poor planning is one of the main causes behind problems you encounter while using tables with databases. You need to resolve issues such as how many tables you need for a particular job before you begin creating tables. You'll then need to decide what *attributes*, or fields, you will need in your tables, and what types of data those fields must store (characters, numbers, dollar values, yes/no values, graphics, and so on). After you have mapped out your table, you can create a table in Access by performing these steps:

1. In the Database window, click on the Tables tab.

2. Click on New. The New Table dialog box appears, shown in Figure 35-4.

3. Choose the desired option in the right half of the New Table dialog box, as explained in the following paragraphs.

The New Table dialog box displays five choices in the right window that let you choose how you create the table: Datasheet View, Design View, Table Wizard, Import Table, and Link Table. The descriptions of what these options do appear in the left window of the dialog box when the option is selected.

Figure 35-4: The New Table dialog box.

Datasheet view opens a spreadsheet-like table into which you can enter actual data. The Table Wizard option starts a wizard that gives you a list of common tasks and creates a table based on the task you select. Both the Import Table and Link Table options start a wizard that lets you use a table stored in a different file format as the basis for your table. (For more specifics about the Table Wizard, see "Using the Table Wizard" later in this chapter.) If you want to take complete control of the table design process, choose Design view and click on OK. When you choose Design view and click on OK, a table design window opens, much like the one shown in Figure 35-5.

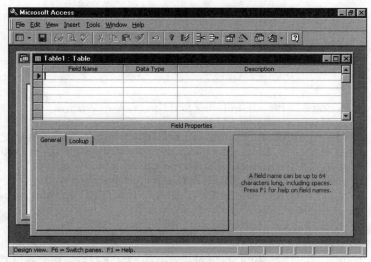

Figure 35-5: The Design window for a new table.

Assigning field names

Three columns appear in the table's design window: Field Name, Data Type, and Description. In the Field Name column, enter the desired name for a field. Field names can be up to 64 characters in length, and you can use letters, numbers, spaces, or punctuation marks in them.

Note   Although the flexibility of Access means that you can create more descriptive field names than with some older database products rooted in the DOS world, keeping field names short is a good idea. Access uses your field names as default field labels in forms and as default column headings in reports. If you give your fields long names, your report design in particular may become a bit of a nightmare because Access creates overly wide columns to accommodate the field names.

Selecting data types

After you've entered the field name, press Tab to move the insertion point into the Data Type column. Here, you select a type for the data that will be stored in the field. Access defaults to a text data type. To change the data type, click on the arrow at the right side of the Data Type column to open a drop-down list box of data types, as shown in Figure 35-6.

Figure 35-6: Drop-down list box of available data types.

Access offers you a choice of nine data types and the Lookup Wizard.

✦ **Text** — Stores any combination of characters, which can include letters, numbers, punctuation marks, blank spaces, or special symbols. Text fields can contain up to 255 characters, and Access defaults to a length of 50 characters. (To change this length, click in the Field Size box in the General tab at the bottom of the window and change the default to the value you want.)

✦ **Memo** — Stores large amounts of text (such as entire paragraphs). Memo fields can store up to 32,000 characters. Typical uses for memo fields include employee evaluations, descriptions of sales products, portions of legal briefs, or medical transcripts. (If you plan to store the text of entire word processing documents, consider the use of an OLE field instead; see the sidebar "Should I use a memo field or an OLE Object field?" later in this section.)

✦ **Number** — Stores numeric values other than currency. You can enter fractional values with decimals, and you can enter negative values by preceding the value with a minus sign, or by enclosing it in parentheses. Number fields are typically used for any noncurrency values that must be calculated. If you won't need to perform calculations on the number (as with postal codes or phone numbers), store it in a text field instead.

✦ **Date/Time** — Stores dates or times. Although you can store dates and times in a text field, using the date/time type has advantages. Validation of proper dates and times is automatic (you can't get away with storing a date such as 13/42/95 or a time such as 25:47 PM), and you can perform calculations based on the entries in date/time fields for tasks such as adding a number of days to a date already stored in the field.

✦ **Currency** — Stores numeric amounts used specifically for currency. Access automatically adds a fixed number of digits to the right of the decimal point to prevent rounding errors that may occur if you use number fields for this task.

✦ **AutoNumber** — Automatically increments a numeric value in the field for each record that you add. Hence, the first record receives a value of 1, the next record receives a value of 2, and so on. (In earlier versions of Access, these were called *counter fields*.) AutoNumber fields are useful for data such as customer ID numbers, where you want to add a means of identification to each record in a table. Keep in mind that after records are added, the values stored in AutoNumber fields cannot be changed.

✦ **Yes/No** — Stores logical (yes or no) values. During data entry, the fields can contain true or false, yes or no, on or off, or some other logical value (such as 0 for no, or –1 for yes).

✦ **OLE Object** — Contains OLE data. OLE data is data that is stored in other Windows applications that support OLE (object linking and embedding). OLE data may include sound clips, video clips, or parts or all of a spreadsheet or word processing document.

✦ **Hyperlink** — Stores a combination of text and numbers that serves as a *hyperlink address*, or a path to an object, document, or web page. A hyperlink address can be a URL (an address to an Internet or intranet web site) or an address to a file on a local area network.

✦ **Lookup Wizard** — Lets you restrict a field type so that it can only accept data from a list of acceptable values or from a field in another table. For example, if you want to add a field to your current table to store the names of states, you can create another table that has a State field and enter the two-letter code for every acceptable state. Then, if you use the Lookup Wizard to create a field in the current table based on a lookup of the State field in the other table, users of your table are only able to enter values that match the two-letter codes in the other table.

Using description fields

After you've selected the desired field type, press Tab again to move the insertion point into the Description column. Here, you can enter an optional description for the column.

At first glance, descriptions may appear to be a useless item. However, when you use forms to view and edit data, any entry that you make in a field's Description column appears in the status bar when the cursor is in that field. Descriptions can provide a kind of help for novice users of your database if you enter short explanations or other helpful comments in the description field.

After entering the description, press Tab again to move the insertion point to the next line (record). You continue to enter the needed field names, data types, and any desired descriptions for the remaining fields. Figure 35-7 shows the fields of a sample table after they have been entered.

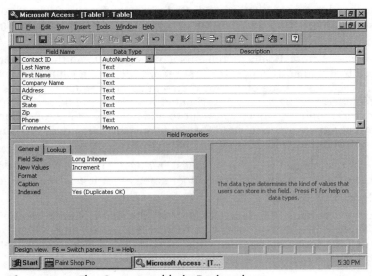

Figure 35-7: The Contacts table in Design view.

Using field properties

In the lower half of the Design window, you see an area of the dialog box called Field Properties. You can specify the properties for each field of a table in this half of the Design window. Ignoring this area of the window during the table design process is easy because Access doesn't require you to make any changes to this area, but assigning field properties can significantly aid you in controlling data entry after you create the table.

Should I use a memo field or an OLE Object field?

If you're thinking of using a memo field to store the entire text of word processing documents, you may want to consider whether you should use an OLE Object field instead. Memo fields tend to work well when you have several sentences of text, perhaps comprising a few paragraphs. OLE Object fields usually work well when you have large amounts of text, such as multiple-page documents, stored in a Windows word processor. If your Windows word processor supports OLE (and most do), you can use Edit ⇨ Copy in your word processor and Edit ⇨ Paste in Access to insert documents into table records that are in OLE data form. Remember that if you *embed* the data rather than *link* it, your Access database can quickly consume monstrous proportions of disk space as you add records. For additional details on the use of OLE, see Chapter 50.

For example, in text fields you can change the field size from the default of 50 characters and define other specifics, such as the format that the field's data follows or validation rules that apply to the data. The exact properties you see vary, depending on the data type chosen for the current field. Table 35-1 lists the field properties and their different uses.

Table 35-1
Field properties and their uses

Field property	Use
Field Size	Specifies the maximum length of a field for text fields. With number fields, limits the allowable values.
New Values	Used only with AutoNumber fields. Specifies whether new values should be generated on an incremental basis or randomly.
Format	Determines how data will be displayed. You can select from a choice of predefined formats, or you can enter a format you create.
Input Mask	Specifies a pattern that data entered in the field must follow.
Decimal Places	Specifies the number of places that appear to the right of the decimal point.
Caption	Specifies a default label (other than the name of the field) that appears as a default label in forms and reports.
Default Value	Specifies a default value that appears in the field automatically when new records are added.

(continued)

Table 35-1 (continued)	
Field property	**Use**
Validation Rule	Specifies data entry rules that data must follow before it can be accepted in the field.
Validation Text	Specifies the message that appears in the status bar if data entry fails the validation rule.
Required	Specifies whether an entry in the field is required for any record added to the table.
Allow Zero Length	Specifies whether zero-length (empty) strings are allowed.
Indexed	Names a single-field index to be added for the field. Indexes are useful in speeding searches.

You can set any of the field properties by performing these steps:

1. While in Design view for the table, click anywhere in a field whose properties you want to set.

2. In the Field Properties dialog box, click on General tab and click on the desired property.

3. If an arrow appears to the right of the property, click on the arrow to open a list box and choose an option; otherwise, enter the desired setting. If you are unsure about what to enter in the box, press F1 to see a help screen dealing with that particular property.

Hot Stuff With text fields, you may be tempted to reduce the Field Size property below the default of 50 characters to save disk space. You won't hurt your table this way, but in Access this process isn't really necessary. Access uses a format called *variable-length fields* to store text data so that in text fields, each field only uses the amount of space necessary to contain the entered data. This design differs from the design of earlier database products, which used the entire specified length of a field to store text data, even when no data was entered in the record. If you want to enter more data than the 50-character default allows, you need to increase the value of the Field Size property.

Among the most powerful (and commonly used) properties for a table are the *format properties* and the *validation rules*. You can use the Format property of a field to control how data appears in the field of a table. (You cannot use the Format property with the OLE Object field types, but you can apply it to every other field type.) After you click anywhere in a field's row to select it, you can click in the Format property and choose a standard format, or you can enter a format of your own design. Access provides a choice of standard formats for number fields, date/time fields, and yes/no fields. For text fields and memo fields, you can use any of the symbols shown in Table 35-2.

Table 35-2
Symbols for text and memo field formats

Symbol	Meaning
@	Text character or a space is required
&	Text character not required
<	Forces characters into lowercases (only one symbol is needed to force the entire entry into lowercase)
>	Forces characters into uppercase (only one symbol is needed to force the entire entry into uppercase)

For number and currency fields, you can use any of the symbols shown in Table 35-3 for custom formats.

Table 35-3
Symbols for number and currency field formats

Symbol	Meaning
. (period)	Decimal separator
, (comma)	Thousands separator
0	Digit placeholder (displays a digit or zero)
#	Digit placeholder (displays a digit or nothing)
$	Displays the dollar symbol ($)
%	Multiplies the value by 100 and adds a percent symbol
E+ or e+	Displays as scientific notation, with a plus symbol beside a positive exponent (such as with 0.00E+00 or ##E+###)
E- or e-	Displays as scientific notation, with a minus symbol beside a negative exponent (such as with 0.00E-00 or ##E-###)

With *validation rules*, you control precisely how data can be entered into the fields of your table. These rules (which you specify) govern whether or not data will be accepted or rejected during the data entry process. To enter a validation rule, first click anywhere in the row of the desired field in the Design window, and then, in the Validation Rule box in the Field Properties dialog box of the Design window, enter the desired rule. In the Validation Text box, you can enter the text of a message that appears when the data entered doesn't meet the validation rule you've specified.

Validation rules are entered as *expressions*. Expressions define what can and can't be entered in terms of data. Expressions can include standard math symbols, and any dates entered in expressions must be enclosed with # symbols. Table 35-4 shows some examples of common expressions used with validation rules.

Validation rules can include expressions which base the rules on other fields in the same table. For example, if you have a table with currency fields labeled Regular Salary and Overtime Salary and you want to limit the entries in the Overtime Salary field to not exceed twice the amount in the Regular Salary field, you can use a validation rule such as this one:

```
< = [Regular Salary] * 2
```

As you discover in Chapter 37, you can also design validation rules into forms. However, the advantage of designing validation rules into the table is that the rules are always active for the table. If you design your validation rules into a form, they only apply when you add and edit data using the form.

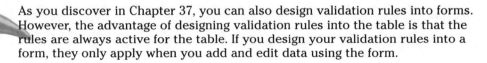

Table 35-4
Examples of expressions used in validation rules

Expression used	Meaning
"NY" or "NJ" or "PA"	Entry must contain "NY" or "NJ" or "PA"
Between #4/15/95# and #12/31/95#	Must be a valid date between 4/15/95 and 12/31/95
< = #12/15/95#	Must be a date earlier than 12/15/95
Like 112M####	Entry must contain eight characters, starting with "112M"
> = 4.50 and < = 12.00	Entry must be between 4.50 and 12.00

Adding a primary key

While you are designing a table, Access lets you specify one or more fields to serve as a *primary key*. Primary keys are unique fields in records that provide Access with a method of identifying every record in a table. Primary keys are quite useful (so useful that if you try to save a table without specifying a primary key, Access displays a dialog box suggesting that you add one). Primary keys speed performance and also make the addition of default relationships possible (a topic that is covered later in this chapter).

By default, Access displays table data with the primary key listed first. You always want to use data that can never be duplicated in more than one record for a primary key. Common choices for primary keys include customer numbers, social security numbers, account numbers, stock numbers, or invoice numbers. It's inappropriate to use a single field like Last Name as a primary key because you would not be able to add two records with the same last name.

Also, keep in mind that sometimes it makes sense to use a combination of fields as the primary key. For example, in a table that tracks data from weekly timesheets submitted by employees, a combination of an employee ID field and a week ending field may be an appropriate primary key because no one employee would submit two timesheets for the same workweek. You establish a primary key using these steps:

1. While in Design view for the table, choose the field or fields that you want to use as the primary key. To choose one field, click on the row selector for that field (at the far left). To choose more than one field, select the first desired field, hold down the Ctrl key, and click on the row selector for each additional field that you want to use.

2. Choose Edit⇨Primary Key, or click on the Primary Key button in the toolbar (it's the one containing a picture of a key). Access displays a Primary Key icon within the row selector for the chosen field or fields, as shown in Figure 35-8.

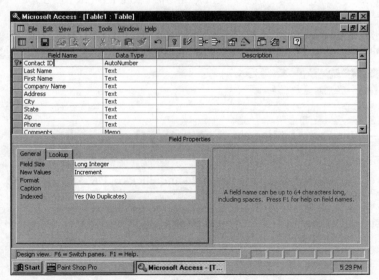

Figure 35-8: Example of a table containing a primary key.

Note   Because, by default, Access displays the table's data with the primary key listed first, you may want to designate one (if possible) for fields that you want to appear in a certain order (assuming that the fields contain data that's unique for each record) even when you don't need a primary key for your table.

Rearranging and deleting fields from a table's design

If you decide to change the structure of a table's design, you can easily make changes. To change a field's name, type, or description, just click within the desired field and make the desired change. To delete a field, first click on the row selector (at the far left edge of the field) to select the entire row and choose Edit⇨Delete Row or press Delete.

To insert a new field between two existing fields, place the insertion point anywhere in the row where you want the new field to appear and choose Insert⇨Row or press Insert. (The new row appears above the existing row.)

To move a field to a new location, first click on the row selector (at the far left edge of the field) to select the entire row, then click on the row selector again, and while holding down the mouse button drag the row to the desired location within the table.

Saving the table

When you've made all the desired additions or changes to the table, you can save it by following these steps:

1. Choose File⇨Close or double-click on the Table icon at the upper-left corner of the table. (You can also press Ctrl+F4.)

2. A dialog box appears asking whether you want to save the changes to the table. Click on Yes and the Save As dialog box appears, shown in Figure 35-9.

Figure 35-9: The Save As dialog box.

3. Enter the desired name for the table and click on OK.

Note   For your table names, you can use a name up to 64 characters long. You can include spaces in the name, but you cannot include periods, exclamation points, brackets, or leading blanks.

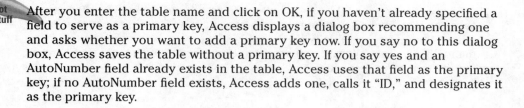

After you enter the table name and click on OK, if you haven't already specified a field to serve as a primary key, Access displays a dialog box recommending one and asks whether you want to add a primary key now. If you say no to this dialog box, Access saves the table without a primary key. If you say yes and an AutoNumber field already exists in the table, Access uses that field as the primary key; if no AutoNumber field exists, Access adds one, calls it "ID," and designates it as the primary key.

Using the Table Wizard

When you create a table manually, you have to decide what field names and field types to use, and you have to type in all of the information that defines the table's structure. Even for experienced database pros, defining tables is no small amount of work. Access does provide you with an alternative to the manual drudgery of defining tables, though. You can use the Table Wizard to create many different types of tables quickly.

Like all Microsoft Office wizards, the Table Wizard asks you questions in a series of dialog boxes and uses your answers to accomplish the desired task (in this case, the creation of a table). You start the Table Wizard with the following steps:

1. Click on the Tables tab in the Database window.

2. Click on the New button.

3. Choose Table Wizard in the New Table dialog box that appears, and click on OK.

After you complete this process, the first Table Wizard dialog box appears.

At the left side of the dialog box in the Sample Tables list box, you can choose the type of table. For example, if you click on the Business button, business-related table types appear; some of the tables in the business category include Mailing List, Employees, Products, Orders, Contacts, Suppliers, Parts, Payments, Invoices, Assets, and so on. If you click on the Personal button, home and personal-related table types appear; the tables in the personal category include Exercise Log, Wine List, Photographs, Recording Artists, Addresses, and more.

After you select a table type, the available fields for that table appear in the center of the Table Wizard dialog box in the Sample Fields list box. You can select the fields you want in the table by clicking on the field and then clicking on the right-arrow key or by double-clicking on the desired field. The chosen field is added to the Fields in the new table list box displayed on the right side of the dialog box.

After you've chosen the fields that you want to include in the table, you can click on Next to proceed to the next dialog box presented by the Table Wizard. This dialog box and additional dialog boxes presented by the wizard help you choose a primary key for your table, give the table a name, and decide whether you want to save the table or begin adding records immediately. The entire process is easy to follow, thanks to the Table Wizard. Even if you prefer to create your tables manually, the Table Wizard can save you time by creating a table that you can modify to meet your needs.

Creating a Database with the Database Wizard

If you're creating tables for a common task (such as basic product inventory, a mailing list, tracking of employees and tasks, or a video collection), Access provides the Database Wizard. The Database Wizard creates the tables needed for a common database management task and automatically defines the default relationships required between the tables.

To create a database with the aid of the Database Wizard, start Access in the usual manner and choose File⇨New Database. When the New dialog box appears, click on the Databases tab (shown in Figure 35-10).

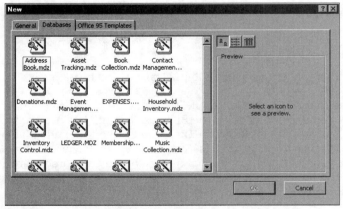

Figure 35-10: The Databases tab of the New dialog box.

In this tab of the dialog box, you see icons for each of the Database Wizards. You can select any of these wizards by clicking on the desired wizard (you can scroll down in the list box, if necessary, to see all of the available wizards). After you select the desired wizard, you can click on OK in the dialog box to start that wizard (alternatively, you can just double-click on the desired wizard in the list box to start it). Available Database Wizards include:

✦ Asset Tracking

✦ Address Book

✦ Book Collection

✦ Contact Management

✦ Donations

✦ Event Management

✦ Expenses

✦ Household Inventory

✦ Inventory Control

✦ Ledger

✦ Membership

✦ Music Collection

✦ Order Entry

✦ Picture Library

✦ Recipes

✦ Resource Scheduling

✦ Service Call Management

✦ Students and Classes

✦ Time and Billing

✦ Video Collection

✦ Wine List

✦ Workout

After you start the wizard, Access displays a File New Database dialog box (Figure 35-11), asking for the name for your new database and where you want to save it.

In the File name portion of the dialog box, you enter a name for your database or accept the default name. You can use the Save in list box and the Up One Level button, if desired, to change the folder location where the database will be stored. When you're finished choosing a name and location for the new database, click on the Create button to proceed.

The wizard displays a series of dialog boxes that step you through the process of creating the database. These dialog boxes vary depending on which database you decided to create. In every case, however, the wizard clearly explains your options every step of the way. For example, Figure 35-12 shows the first dialog box presented by the Database Wizard when you choose to create a Music Collection database.

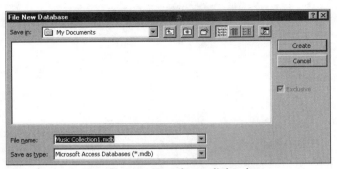

Figure 35-11: The File New Database dialog box.

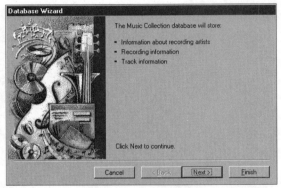

Figure 35-12: The first Music Collection Database Wizard dialog box.

After you click on Next, the Database Wizard presents another dialog box asking whether you want to add any optional fields to the tables that the Wizard creates for the database. Figure 35-13 shows this dialog box for the Music Collection Database Wizard. You can select any of the tables shown in the left half of the dialog box (sometimes only one table appears; other times more than one appear). As you select a table, fields for that table appear in the right half of the dialog box, and the check boxes for the default fields that Access proposes to use are selected. You can check any check boxes for additional fields that you want to include. You also can select the Yes, include sample data check box at the bottom of the dialog box to add sample data to your completed database.

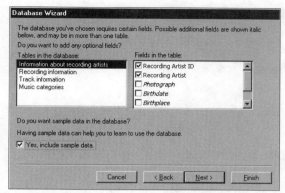

Figure 35-13: The second Music Collection Database
Wizard dialog box.

After you accept the field options, click on Next, and you see a dialog box similar
to the one shown in Figure 35-14. This dialog box provides a choice of styles for
the screen displays (*forms,* in Access lingo) that will be created for your database.
After you select one, a representative sample of that style appears in the left
window of the dialog box. Make your desired selection and click on Next.

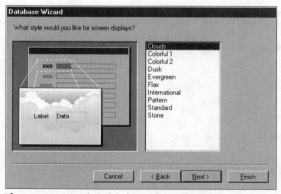

Figure 35-14: The third Music Collection Database
Wizard dialog box.

Next, the Database Wizard presents a dialog box that offers you a choice for the
styles of reports, as shown in Figure 35-15. As with screen display styles, when you
select a report style, a representative sample of that style appears in the left
portion of the dialog box. Make your desired selection and click on Next.

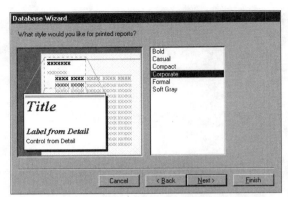

Figure 35-15: The fourth Music Collection Database Wizard dialog box.

The next dialog box that appears (shown in Figure 35-16) asks for a title for the database and whether you want a decorative picture to appear in the main menu window of the database and on reports. You can enter a desired title (or accept the default proposed by Access), select the check box to include the picture, and click on Next.

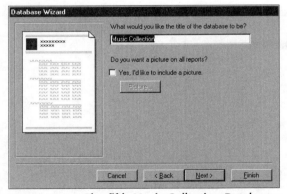

Figure 35-16: The fifth Music Collection Database Wizard dialog box.

The final dialog box presented by the Database Wizard (Figure 35-17) asks whether you want to start the database after the wizard builds it and whether you want to display Help screens on using the database. You can check the desired options and then click on the Finish button to complete the process of creating the database.

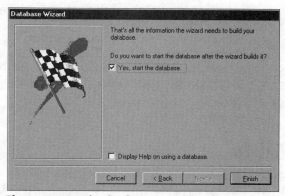

Figure 35-17: The final Music Collection Database Wizard dialog box.

When you click on Finish, Access displays a dialog box that tells you it is creating the database. This process may take a few minutes because Access must create all the needed tables, forms, and reports. Access will also create a *switchboard* (a type of main menu that is common in Access database applications) that makes the database easier to use. If you turned on the option to start the database in the last dialog box, you see the switchboard for the database when the Access loads the database. Figure 35-18 shows the switchboard created for the Music Collection database.

Figure 35-18: The switchboard created for the Music Collection Database.

Note Regardless of which database you create with the Database Wizards, you always see a switchboard similar to this one when you open the database. The switchboard provides buttons for working with the data, printing a report, customizing the switchboard, and exiting from the database. The options you see after choosing one of the switchboard buttons vary depending on which database you created with the wizards, but in every case you see clearly labeled options for working with your new database.

Adding Data to a Table

You can add records to an existing table in *Datasheet view*. To open a table in Datasheet view, double-click on the table you want in the Database window, or click on the table and then click on Open. The selected table opens in Datasheet view, as shown in Figure 35-19.

Contact ID	Last name	First name	Company	Address	City	State
2	Benson	Terry	Swift Technology	2100 Stanford St.	Santa Monica	CA
3	Alvarez	Maria	Image Systems, L	9090 Telstar Drive	El Monte	CA
1	Johnson	Mary	Acme Fibers, Inc.	1700 La Costa Mes:	Hayward	CA
4	O'Malley	Sandy	Corporate Support	1111 Lincoln Ave.	Hayward	CA

Figure 35-19: Datasheet view for a table.

You can use Datasheet view to add or edit data: you just type the new data into the fields of the datasheet. Every Access table always contains one blank record at the bottom of the table; the presence of an asterisk at the far left indicates the blank record, as shown in Figure 35-19. When you start entering data in the blank record, a new blank record appears directly beneath it. You can place the insertion point in any field and enter the data; pressing Tab at the end of each entry moves you to the next field. Pressing Tab at the end of the last field moves you to the next blank record, where you can continue the data entry process.

Adding data to memo fields

You can try to enter data directly into a memo field while you are in Datasheet view, but usually it's impossible to see all data at once. You can easily remedy this problem by pressing Shift+F2 while the insertion point is in a Memo field. This action opens a Zoom box in the Memo field, shown in Figure 35-20 so that you can see the data while you work with it. After making your entries or edits in the Zoom box, click on OK to accept the changes.

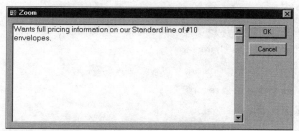

Figure 35-20: The Zoom box in a Memo field.

Adding data to OLE Object fields

As mentioned earlier in the chapter, you can specify OLE Object as a field type in an Access table. OLE Object fields store OLE data, such as word processing documents, spreadsheets, or sound or video clips. When you need to insert OLE data into an OLE Object field, follow these steps:

1. In the Windows application that contains the data you want to insert into the Access field, select the desired data.

2. Choose Edit⇨Copy.

3. Switch to Access, and place the insertion point in the OLE Object field of the desired record.

4. In Access, choose Edit⇨Paste to paste the OLE data into the field.

Editing and Deleting Data

To edit data in Access, you simply place the insertion point in any field of a datasheet and begin typing or making any desired corrections. To replace an existing field's entry with entirely new data, select the existing data and then begin typing. As you edit a record, Access displays a pencil at the left edge of the record's row selector, indicating that the record is being edited. As you move off the row, the changes are stored to the table. Certain navigation keys are available that you can use during the editing process to move around in the datasheet. These keys are listed in Table 35-5.

Table 35-5
Navigation techniques for editing in a datasheet

Key combination	Result
Left-arrow key	Moves left one character
Right-arrow key	Moves right one character
Up-arrow key	Moves to the prior record
Down-arrow key	Moves to the next record
Tab	Moves to the next field
Shift+Tab	Moves to prior field
Ctrl+Home	Moves to the first field of the first record
Ctrl+End	Moves to the last field of the last record
PgUp	Scrolls up one page
PgDn	Scrolls down one page

You cannot edit certain fields in Access:

✦ **AutoNumber fields** — Access automatically increments and stores values in AutoNumber fields. When the record exists, Access does not let you change the value.

✦ **Locked fields** — When a field's Enabled property is set to No or its Locked property is set to Yes, you cannot edit the contents of the field.

✦ **Fields in certain types of queries** — You cannot edit some fields in queries that establish relationships between more than one table, and you cannot edit totals in some queries.

✦ **Calculated fields** — Because calculated fields do not exist as a separate field (but are displayed using a calculation based on one or more fields), you can't edit these fields.

Hot Stuff   Using forms to perform data entry or editing is often more convenient than adding or editing records. Forms usually display a single record at a time; Figure 35-21 shows an example of such a form.

More Info Forms are discussed at length in Chapter 37, but you can quickly create a standard form for any table with the following two steps:

1. In the Database window, select the desired table.

2. Click on the New Object button in the toolbar.

After you perform these steps, Access creates a form based on the selected table's structure, saves it under the same name as the table, and opens the form. With the form open, you can use the navigation buttons at the bottom of the form or press Ctrl+PgUp and Ctrl+PgDn keys to move through the records of the table. You can find a specific record by choosing Edit⇨Find and then entering the desired search criteria in the dialog box which appears. (For more specifics on this dialog box, refer to the "Finding Data" section later in this chapter.)

Figure 35-21: You can quickly create a default form like this one in Access.

To delete a record, follow these steps:

1. Click on the row selector at the left edge of the record or place the insertion point anywhere within the record you want to delete.

2. Choose Edit⇨Select Record.

3. Press Delete or choose Edit⇨Delete Record.

4. Access displays a dialog box, asking if you want to delete the selected record: click on Yes to delete it or No to cancel.

Danger Zone Deletions are permanent in Access. The only way to retrieve a deleted record is to re-enter the record. If you're used to xBASE products (dBASE, FoxPro, and so on) where you can revoke deletions, beware!

Changing the Appearance of a Table

As you work with datasheets, you can rearrange the appearance of the data to suit your preferences. You can widen and narrow columns, move columns to other locations, hide columns, and *freeze* columns (force them to stay visible while you scroll horizontally). Changes that you make to a table's appearance, or *layout*, affect only the appearance of the table on-screen; the underlying order of the data in the table does not change. You can perform any of the following procedures on a table's appearance:

✦ **To change a column's width** — Place the insertion point over the right edge of the column until it changes to the shape of a double-headed arrow and then click on and drag the column to the desired width.

✦ **To change the height of the rows** — Place the insertion point at the far left edge of the table between two record selectors until it changes to the shape of a double-headed vertical arrow and then click on and drag the row to the desired height. (An alternate method is to choose Format⇨Row Height and enter a value in the dialog box that appears.)

✦ **To move a column to another location** — Select the column by clicking on its field selector at the top of the column and then click on and drag the column to the new location. While you are dragging the column, a thick vertical bar indicates its position, as shown in Figure 35-22.

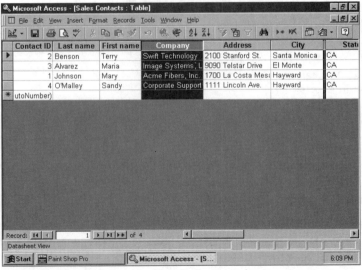

Figure 35-22: A thick vertical bar indicates column movement.

✦ **To hide and show columns** — Click on the Column's field selector (at the top of the column) to select it and choose Format⇨Hide Columns. To show a column that you hid earlier, choose Format ⇨ Unhide Columns and select the column you want to show in the dialog box that appears.

✦ **To freeze and unfreeze columns** — First, select the column or columns to freeze. (You can select more than one column by clicking on the first column's field selector, holding the Shift key, and clicking on the field selector for all additional columns.) With the desired columns selected, choose Format ⇨ Freeze Columns. When you freeze columns, the frozen columns remain in place while the remaining columns in the table scroll horizontally. To unfreeze columns that you froze earlier, choose Format ⇨ Unfreeze All Columns.

✦ **To change the fonts used by the datasheet:** Choose Format⇨Font. When you do so, the Font dialog box appears, shown in Figure 35-23. In the Font dialog box, choose the font, font style, and font size you want. You also can turn on underlining and change the color used to display fonts (and print in color on color printers). When you complete the changes, click on OK.

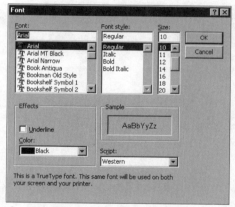

Figure 35-23: The Font dialog box.

After you make changes to a table's layout, the next time that you close the table, Access asks if you want save the layout changes. Click on Yes to make the changes permanent or No to revert the table to its old layout.

Printing a Table

While a table is in Datasheet view, you can print its contents.

A printout from Datasheet view resembles the datasheet's on-screen appearance. If you want anything fancier than this, you'll need to design a report. See Chapter 38 for details.

You can print the contents of a table by following these steps:

1. If you want to print all records, select the table in the Database window. If you want to print a select group of records, you need to open the table in Datasheet view.

2. To print selected records, select the records in the datasheet by clicking on them and dragging along the record selectors at the left edge of the table.

3. Choose File⇨Print, or click on the Print button in the toolbar. If you use the toolbar button, the records are printed. If you choose File⇨Print, the Print dialog box appears, shown in Figure 35-24.

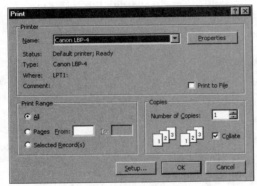

Figure 35-24: The Print dialog box.

4. To print all records, click on OK. To print a select group of records, click on the Selection button and click on OK.

You can take advantage of the capability to change the table's layout of a table when you need to print data. For example, if you want a quick printout of all records in a table but you don't want to see all the columns, you don't have to design a complex query to perform this task. Instead, you can use Format⇨Hide Columns, as described earlier, to hide the columns you don't want in the printout. Then print the table using the preceding steps.

Finding Data

As your table grows, you'll need a way to find specific data. If you just want to find a specific record so that you can edit or delete it, the Edit⇨Find command provides the simplest technique.

More Info If you want to retrieve a subset of records that meet a specified criteria (such as all customers living in Arizona), you can perform this task by using a *query*. See Chapter 35 for details.

Follow these steps to find a record:

1. Open the table you want to retrieve the records from and click anywhere within the field you want to search.

2. Choose Edit⇨Find. The Find dialog box appears, shown in Figure 35-25.

3. In the dialog box, enter the search text in the Find What box.

4. Under the Match box, choose Any Part of Field to search for any part of the string, Whole Field to find a record only if the entire field's contents matches the search string, or Start of Field to start a search from the beginning of the field.

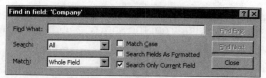

Figure 35-25: The Find dialog box.

5. Leave the Search Only Current Field checkbox selected to search the field that contains the insertion point, or turn off this check box to search all fields (this can slow a search considerably).

The Search list specifies the direction of the search, and the Match Case check box tells Access whether case is significant; when the option is not checked, Access treats upper- and lowercase letters as equals in a search. You can turn on the Search Fields as Formatted check box if you want Access to perform a search based on the display format for the field.

To locate the first occurrence of the search text, click on the Find First button. Use the Find Next button to see the next occurrence of the search text and so on to find all additional occurrences.

In the real world, you'll find some cases where the Edit⇨Find command doesn't bring you close enough to the specific search item you want, usually because of the number of table records and a lack of precise data that you can use in the search. For example, if a customer named Ed Smith calls and doesn't have his customer number, and you have to search a table of customers that has 200 entries with the last name *Smith*, you probably don't want to perform an Edit⇨Find search based on his last name. If you can't perform the search based on entries in a unique field (or at least a field with less common entries, such as phone numbers), you may need to use queries instead to locate the desired data.

If you regularly search for certain fields that are not primary key fields, you can speed your searches by adding indexes for those fields; see the following section for specifics.

Adding Indexes to Tables

In addition to using primary keys, Access lets you add *indexes* to fields of a table. An index is an internal ordering of the records by the chosen field that Access maintains internally to improve performance. Indexes are useful for speeding performance, particularly in searches and reporting tasks. As an example, you may have a table of employees with a primary key based on Social Security number, but perhaps you regularly generate reports based on the order of last names. In such a case, if the table is a sizable one, you could improve performance by adding an index to the Last Name field. If you want to add an index based on a single field, follow these steps:

1. Open the desired table in Design view. (In the Database window, right-click on the desired table and choose Design from the shortcut menu which appears).

2. Click anywhere in the field where you want to add the index.

3. If the General tab isn't already displayed at the bottom of the window, click on the General tab.

4. In the Index Properties box at the bottom of the window, click on the arrow to open the list and choose Yes (Duplicates OK) or No (No Duplicates). If you choose Yes (Duplicates OK), you allow the existence of more than one record with the same data in the field. Choosing No (No Duplicates) prohibits multiple records with the same value in the field.

If you want to add an index based on more than one field, the procedure is a little different. You need to perform these steps:

1. Open the desired table in Design view.

2. Click anywhere in the field where you want to add the index.

3. Click on the Indexes button in the toolbar, or choose View⇨ Indexes to open the Indexes dialog box, shown in Figure 35-26.

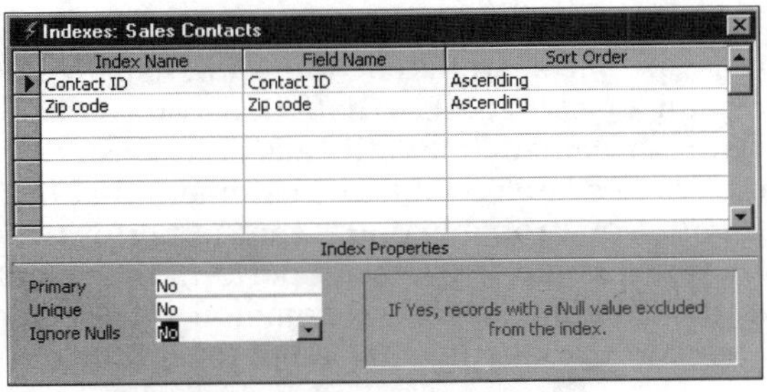

Figure 35-26: The Indexes dialog box.

4. In the Index Name column, enter a name for the index.

5. Click in the Field Name column, choose the first field that you want to use as the basis of the index from the list box, and then choose Ascending or Descending (your choice) in the Sort Order column.

6. In successive rows of the window, repeat Steps 4 and 5 for each additional field on which you want to base the index.

To see an example of a multiple index, look at the dialog box shown in Figure 35-27. In this example, the index is based on a combination of the Social Security field and the Week Ending field.

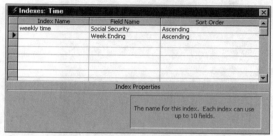

Figure 35-27: An index based on a combination of fields.

In the Index Name Column for the first row of your multiple index, remember to include the index name only alongside the first field name. If you add another name in the next row within the Index Name column, Access treats that row as a separate index.

Establishing Relationships Between Tables

One of the most powerful features of Access is the capability to establish relationships between multiple tables. You can establish relationships in Access with the Tools⇨Relationships command. After you establish relationships in Access, the relationship is automatically used to link fields in the queries, forms, and reports that you create. Although you're not required to establish relationships between tables, this feature saves you time and ensures proper end results when you are designing complex forms and reports.

Note   Another advantage of establishing relationships between tables is that you can use *referential integrity*, which requires relationships between tables to work. Referential integrity is a method Access uses to automatically protect data against certain changes or deletions that would break the links between records in related tables.

You can view the relationships that you establish at the database level in the Relationships window, which you open by choosing Tools⇨Relationships from the Tools menu. Figure 35-28 shows an example of the Relationship window.

You establish relationships at the table level by performing the following steps:

1. With the Tables tab selected in the Database window, choose Tools⇨Relationships (or right-click on the Tables tab of the Database window and choose Relationships from the shortcut menu). The Relationships window appears. If you are establishing the relationship for the first time, the window contains the Show Table dialog box, shown in Figure 35-29.

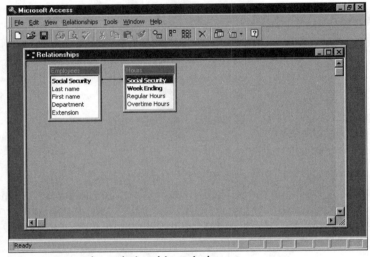

Figure 35-28: The Relationships window.

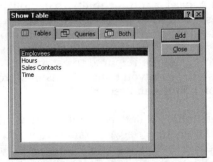

Figure 35-29: The Show Table dialog box.

2. Select the table or query that you want to use as a part of the relationship and click on Add to add the table to the Relationships window.

3. Repeat Step 2 for each table or query you want to add to the window and click on Close.

4. To create the links between tables which form the relationship, drag the field(s) you want to use for the link from the primary table or query to the matching field(s) of the related table or query. (In most relationships, the primary key of the first table is related to a similar field of the second table.) After you drag and drop the field, the Relationships dialog box appears, as shown in Figure 35-30.

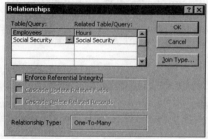

Figure 35-30: The Relationships dialog box.

5. If needed, you can change the field names that Access suggests in the dialog box. (Access usually suggests the best possible relationship, but sometimes its best guess is not what you prefer to use.)

Note

Fields that you use to establish a relationship do not have to have the same name, but they must have the same field type (with the exception of AutoNumber fields, which you can relate to number fields).

6. If you want to use referential integrity, click on the Enforce Referential Integrity check box. When the box is turned on, you can also use the options shown below it, if you want.

When the Cascade Update Related Fields option is on, changes made to the linking field in the first table are automatically updated in the fields of a related table containing the same data. When the Cascade Delete Related Records option is on, the deletion of records in the first table automatically deletes associated records in the linked table.

7. Choose the desired type of relationship (One-to-One or One-to-Many). In most cases, you will use a One-to-Many relationship.

8. Click on the Create button to create the relationship.

9. Repeat Steps 1–8 for every relationship that you want to add between tables. When you're finished, close the Relationships window. When Access asks if you want to save the changes to the relationship, click on Yes.

Note You can edit existing relationships by opening the Relationships window as described earlier and then double-clicking on any line between two tables. This action opens the Relationships dialog box, where you can make design changes. To delete a relationship, click on the line connecting the tables and press Delete.

Getting Data In and Out of Access

One can certainly say that "no PC is an island." Access was designed from the ground up to let you move data between an Access database and other databases, both inside and outside of Access. The sections which follow explain the different ways in which you can move data to and from your Access databases.

Copying tables to other Access databases

Sometimes you need to copy an existing table from one Access database to another; for example, other departments may need to use the same data in different databases within an organization. You can copy the data from an existing database to another by following these steps:

1. Click on the Tables tab in the Database window.

2. Click on the table to select it.

3. Choose Edit⇨Copy.

4. Close the current database, and open the database to which you want to copy the file. (Choose File⇨Open Database and specify the desired database name.)

5. Choose Edit⇨Paste. The Paste Table As dialog box appears, as shown in Figure 35-31. By default, the Structure and Data option is selected, which means that Access copies both the data and the structure (or design) of the table.

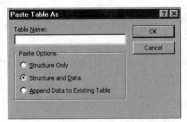

Figure 35-31: The Paste Table As dialog box.

6. Turn on the Structure Only option when you want to copy only an empty table with the same structure and turn on the Append Data to Existing Table option when you want to copy data to a table that already exists in another Access database. When you use this option, Access asks for the name of the table that will receive the data. Enter the name and click on OK.

Importing and linking to other tables

It's pretty common these days to have to deal with data that exists in a wide variety of formats. The data you want may be stored in spreadsheet form or in a file format used by another database manager, such as dBASE or Paradox. Access provides unusual flexibility because not only can it import data from a variety of sources, but it can also *link* to tables in other file formats. This powerful feature enables Access to work with data in its native format. (Microsoft chose the name Access to emphasize the product's flexibility in dealing with different types of data.)

When you want to use Access to use data stored in other file formats, you have two choices. First, you can import the data into an Access database where Access stores it in an Access table in its own format. Or, you can link to the table stored in the different file format and work with the data without changing its file format. (In prior versions of Access, the process of linking to another table was called *attaching*.)

Hot
Stuff
In general, if other applications need to use the data, linking to it is the best option. If you plan to use the data just in Access, it is usually best to import the data because Access works faster with data stored in its own format.

There are some tasks that you cannot perform on linked tables. You cannot make changes to the table's structure, nor can you add primary keys to a linked table. You cannot establish any rules for referential integrity, and you also cannot establish relationships at the table level, although you can get around this limitation by designing relational queries. You *can* import a file into Access by performing these steps:

1. Make sure that the Database window is the active window. To import data, choose File⇨Get External Data⇨Import. To link data, choose File⇨Get External Data⇨Link Tables.

If you chose Import, the Import dialog box appears, as shown in Figure 35-32. If you chose Link, you see a nearly identical dialog box titled "Link" instead of "Import."

2. In the Files of type list box, choose the data source. (Your options include files stored in other Access databases, text files, Excel files, Paradox files, dBASE files, FoxPro files, Lotus 1-2-3 files, and files supported by ODBC drivers, but see the note below.)

3. Use the Look in list box and the Up One Level button in the dialog box to locate the file you want to import and click on the file to select it.

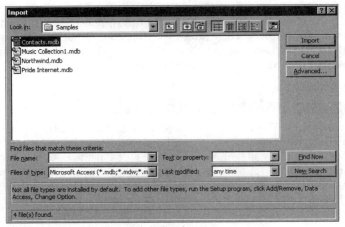

Figure 35-32: The Import dialog box.

4. Click on the Import button (or if you are linking, the Link button) and Access imports the file or establishes a link to the file. When you import files from a spreadsheet file format, a dialog box for the Spreadsheet Wizard appears, and you can follow the directions in the dialog box to determine which rows and columns of the spreadsheet you want to import. (You may want to rename tables imported from DOS-based products with more descriptive names.)

By default, Access only installs import and export file types of other Access versions and for Excel. To add other file types (like Paradox, dBASE, and FoxPro), run the Setup program, click on Add/Remove, click on Data Access, and then click on Change Option. Choose the desired file types in the dialog box that appears.

Exporting table data

Access offers the same kind of flexibility when you want to provide data in a file format other than the Access 95 file format. When you choose File➪Save As/Export, the dialog box that appears lets you export data in the following file formats:

✦ Delimited text (values separated by commas, tabs, or other characters)

✦ Fixed-width text (values arranged in columnar fashion, in which each field has a pre-defined width)

✦ Microsoft Excel versions 3, 4, 5, and Windows 95

✦ Lotus 1-2-3 and 1-2-3 for Windows

✦ Paradox versions 3, 4, and 5

✦ Microsoft FoxPro 2.0, 2.5, 2.6, and 3.0

✦ Microsoft Access 1.0, 1.1, and 2.0

✦ dBASE III, dBASE IV, and dBASE V

✦ RTF (Rich Text Format)

✦ Word for Windows Merge files

✦ Files for use with ODBC databases

Note

You can export data from an Access table or a query by performing the following steps:

1. In the Database window, select the table or query that will provide the desired data.

2. Choose File⇨Save As/Export. A Save As dialog box appears.

3. Leave the To an external File or Database option selected in the dialog box, and click on OK. The Save Table In dialog box appears, shown in Figure 35-33.

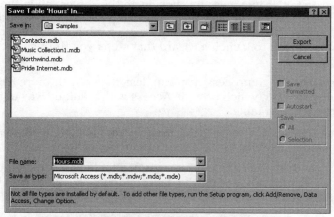

Figure 35-33: Save Table In dialog box for file export.

4. In the Save as type list box, choose the data type you want for the exported file.

5. Use the Save in list box and the Up One Level button of the dialog box to select the folder where the file should be stored.

6. Click on the Export button to export the data.

Note

Before you export data, you may want to consider using a query as a source of the exported data. If you only want to make selected records or fields in the data available to the other program, creating and saving a query first and then basing the export on the query may be the easiest way to accomplish this task. (To perform this task, you select the query in the Database window rather than in the table and then choose File⇨Save As/Export.

Saving tables as HTML

One feature added to this version of Access is the capability to create HTML files. (HTML, or HyperText Markup Language, is the language used to store information on the World Wide Web.) The HTML files that you create using Access can be uploaded to a web server for availability on the web or to a corporate intranet.

When you choose File⇨Save As HTML, Access launches the Publish to the Web Wizard. You can then use this wizard to create static web pages (ones that don't change until you re-create and upload them) or to create dynamic pages that can query a web server database. See Chapter 44 for additional details on saving tables (and other database objects) as HTML and on publishing Access data on the web.

Summary

In this chapter, you learned how to create and use databases and tables in Access.

✦ You can create tables in Access by clicking on the Tables tab in the Database window and clicking on the New button. In the New Table dialog box which appears, you can choose Design view to create a table manually, or you can choose Table Wizard to launch a wizard that steps you through the process of creating a table.

✦ During the table design process, you can designate one or more fields to serve as *primary keys*, which provide Access with a unique way of identifying every record within a table.

✦ You can use Database Wizards in Access to create complete databases containing multiple tables as well as forms and reports.

✦ You can add new records and edit records in a table by opening the table in *Datasheet view*. You can perform this task by double-clicking on any table shown in the Database window.

✦ Access lets you change the appearance of a table. You can widen and narrow columns in the datasheet, you can move columns to different locations, and you can hide columns from view.

✦ You can print the contents of a table by selecting the table in the Database window or opening the table in Datasheet view, and choosing File⇨Print.

✦ You can search for data in a table by opening the table in Datasheet view and choosing Edit⇨Find.

✦ You can add indexes to tables to speed the performance of searches and reporting, and you can establish *relationships* between multiple tables to make creating forms and reports based on those tables an easier task.

✦ You can import data from other file formats into Access tables, and you can also link (or *attach*) to data that is stored in other file formats.

✦ You can export data from Access tables to most common file formats, including as HTML code for publishing on the Internet or on an intranet.

In the next chapter, you learn how to obtain specific data from your Access tables by formulating *queries* that retrieve desired data.

Where to go next...

✦ Queries are an important part of getting what you want from your database — so much so that queries are covered in three different chapters. For the basics of query use, look at Chapter 36. For specifics on queries that deal with more than one table at a time, look at Chapter 39. For the lowdown on specialized query types, see Chapter 40.

✦ After you've stored data in your Access tables, you'll probably want to generate reports based on that data. To get up and running quickly on how you can produce reports, take a look at Chapter 38.

✦   ✦   ✦

Working with Simple Queries

After you put your data into Access tables, you can
perform the next (and very useful) task of database
management: you can ask questions and receive answers
about your data. In Access, you use *queries* to ask questions
about data in tables. This chapter details how you can use
and create simple queries to find answers to questions about
your data.

The Basics of Queries

Access uses *query-by-example*, a common technique for
obtaining data from databases invented by IBM in the 1970s.
Queries provide an easy way for you to obtain specific fields
and records from one or more tables to form a subset of your
overall data. For example, Figure 36-1 shows a query based
on four tables, which retrieves a specified set of data. The
query in this example displays all orders shipped to Spain or
Germany and lists additional information about these orders:
the customer names from the Customers table, the dates of
the orders from the Orders table, and the product name and
quantity from the Products and Order Details table. The
Query window (in the top half of the illustration) partially
covers a datasheet window containing the resulting data from
the query (in the bottom half of the illustration). Every
query's design appears in a Query window as seen in the top
half of the illustration. The Query window always contains
one or more tables or other queries used as a source of data,
along with a query grid where fields can be added. Criteria
can be entered to determine what the results of the query
will be.

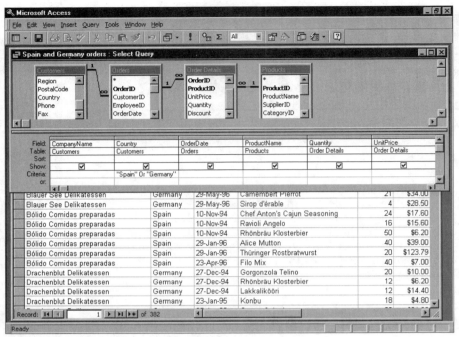

Figure 36-1: A query and the resulting data.

If you use Access to perform advanced tasks, such as developing complete applications, you'll find that queries can be important tools for helping you complete your tasks. Although you can use Visual Basic for Applications to retrieve and manipulate Access data, you can perform the mass majority of data manipulation tasks more easily by using queries.

When you run the typical type of query in Access (known as a *select* query, which simply retrieves desired data), Access displays the results in the form of a *dynaset*. A dynaset looks a great deal like a table's datasheet but is actually a *dynamic* (or *virtual*) set of records based on the query's design. The records in a dynaset don't actually exist, so when you close the dynaset, the records are gone — but, of course, the underlying data remains stored in the original tables. You can save a query, but the data that the query retrieves is not saved along with it. Only the structure, or design, of the query is saved in the form of a *SQL* statement. (How Access uses SQL is further detailed under "A Note about SQL and Your Queries" later in this chapter.)

If you're familiar with older, PC-based databases that use query-by-example, you need to be aware that the dynaset Access displays contains *live* data, not a static imitation of the data in the actual table like some database products display. Therefore, when you modify the data in the records of a query's dynaset, you also are modifying the actual data contained in the underlying tables. Because dynasets and datasheets use the same format for displaying data, you can modify the way that a dynaset displays data the same way you modify the appearance of a datasheet. You can move columns around, change the height of rows and the widths of columns, and hide columns in the dynaset.

Using the Query Design Toolbar and the Query Menu

When you open a query in Design view, the toolbar changes appearance to one that is specific for working with queries, as shown in Figure 36-2. The active buttons in the toolbar, from left to right, are detailed as follows in Table 36-1.

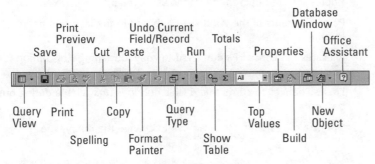

Figure 36-2: The toolbar in Query Design view.

There's more than one way to ask a question

This chapter deals with select queries, the most common query type. Select queries let you select the data you want and receive an answer based on the criteria that you supply to the query.

Access also provides action queries and crosstab queries. Action queries change data in an underlying table according to the criteria specified in the query's design. Action queries are typically used to perform mass updates on data; for example, you could increase every value in a Price field of an Inventory table by 6 percent with an action query.

Crosstab queries let you examine data from Access tables in a spreadsheet-like format, a great deal like the crosstab feature found in many spreadsheets. You can find out more about action queries and crosstab queries in Chapter 40.

	Table 36-1
	Toolbar buttons that appear in Query Design view

Button	Purpose
Query View	Changes between Design view, SQL view, and Datasheet view
Save	Saves current query design
Print	Prints the current document (this option is unavailable during query design)
Print Preview	Opens a Print Preview window for the current document (this option is unavailable during query design)
Spelling	Performs spell checking on the current selection
Cut	Cuts selected data to the Windows Clipboard
Copy	Copies selected data to the Windows Clipboard
Paste	Pastes contents of the Windows Clipboard to the insertion point location
Format Painter	Activates the Format Painter used to copy formatting (this option is unavailable during query design)
Undo Current Field/Record	Erases changes to current field (this option is unavailable during query design)
Query Type	Opens a menu which you can use to change the query type
Run	Runs the query
Show Table	Displays the Show Table dialog box which you can use to add a table to the query's design
Totals	Shows or hides Totals row
Top Values	Quickly shows top set of records only, while the query processes the remainder of the dynaset
Properties	Opens the Properties window for the query
Build	Launches Expression Builder, a dialog box that you can use to construct an expression quickly
Database Window	Makes the Database window the active window
New Object	Opens the New Object menu that you can use to create a new object (form, report, and so on)
Office Assistant	Accesses context-sensitive help

Additionally, as you design a query, the Query menu is available on the menu bar to help you in the design process. Table 36-2 details the Query menu's options.

Table 36-2
Query menu options

Command	Purpose
Run	Runs the query
Show Table	Displays a dialog box that you can use to add a table to the query's design
Remove Table	Removes a table from the query's design
Select Query	Changes query type to a select query
Crosstab Query	Changes query type to a crosstab query
Make Table Query	Changes query type to a make-table query
Update Query	Changes query type to an update query
Append Query	Changes query type to an append query
Delete Query	Changes query type to a delete query
SQL Specific	Displays a submenu to define the SQL type of statement that the query uses
Parameters	Displays the Parameters window that you can use to specify parameters for parameter queries

Creating and Using a Query

Access provides two ways to create a query: manually or with the help of the Query Wizards. The Query Wizards in Access include specialized tools that you use to design queries for fairly complex tasks, such as finding duplicate records or providing a crosstab view of data in tables. (You learn how to use the Query Wizards in Chapter 40.) But for simple, everyday queries that ask basic questions about your data, you can open a query, add the fields that you want, ask any questions that you need to ask about the data (in the form of criteria), and run the query to get the results.

To create a new query manually, follow these steps:

1. Click on the Queries tab in the Database window.

2. Click on New. The New Query dialog box appears.

3. In the New Query dialog box, click on New Query and click on OK. When you do this, a window into a new query's design opens with the Show Table dialog box above it, as shown in Figure 36-3.

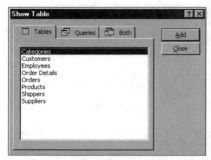

Figure 36-3: The Show Table dialog box.

After you open a design window into a new query, you can perform many different operations as part of the design process. You can add tables to the query, add fields from the tables that you've added to the query, specify the criteria that the query uses, choose a sort order for the query, hide fields, run the query, save the query, and print the query's results. The following sections explain these operations in detail.

Adding tables to a query

After you have opened a Query window, the first step in the design process is to add the table or tables that provide the data you want to search. In the Show Table dialog box, (shown in Figure 36-3 previously) click on the table (or tables) that you want to use as the data source for the query.

Hot Stuff Keep in mind that you are not limited to using tables as a data source. You can base queries on existing queries or on a combination of tables and existing queries.

More Info Queries can be based on a single table or on more than one table. When you base queries on more than one table, you must designate the common field that links the tables by dragging the common field from one table's list box to the other. Queries based on multiple tables are called *relational queries*. (Relational queries are discussed in detail in Chapter 39.)

When you are building a relational query, you select a table or query in the Show Table dialog box and click on the Add button for every table or query that you want to add as a data source. After you have finished adding the desired tables or existing queries to the query's design, you can click on Close to close the Show Table dialog box.

Note If you close the Show Table dialog box and then decide that you want to add another table or existing query to the query's design, you can click on the Show Table button in the toolbar, or choose Query⇨Show Table to redisplay the Show Table dialog box.

After you close the Show Table dialog box, you have a full screen view of the Query Design window containing list boxes for the tables or existing queries that you've added. Figure 36-4 shows an example of this window. (In this example, a single table, Customers, has been added to the query design.)

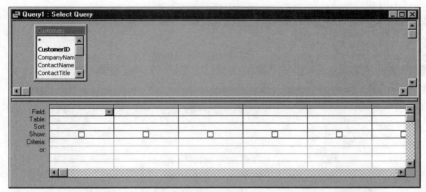

Figure 36-4: The Query Design window with the Customers table added.

The Query Design window is divided into two parts. The upper portion contains the list boxes for all the tables or queries that you have added as the basis of the query. The lower portion contains the *query grid*. The query grid is where you specify the fields that you want to include, the criteria that control which records appear in the query and the sorting order (if any) that you want to use to affect the query's results.

Adding fields to the query

After you provide the data source(s) for the query, you add the desired fields to the different columns of the Field row of the query. To add fields, you can use many different drag-and-drop techniques:

✦ You can drag one field at a time from the list box for a table to the Field row.

✦ You can double-click on any field in the list box to add it to the next available column of the query.

✦ You can select multiple fields and drag them using the Shift or Ctrl keys.

✦ You can drag the asterisk at the top of the list box to add all fields in the table to the query.

Dragging each desired field from the list box to the desired location in the Field row of the query one at a time is the most basic method you can use. For example, if you want to create a query based on the Customers table shown in Figure 36-4, you can drag each of the fields in the Customers list box to the Field row of the query grid. Figure 36-5 illustrates this process.

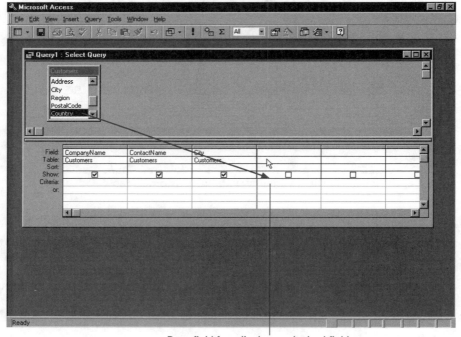

Drag field from list box to desired field row

Figure 36-5: Dragging fields from a table's list box to the query grid.

You can also double-click on any field within a Field list; this action adds the field to the next blank column in the Field row of the query's design.

You can add all fields to a query by selecting them as a group and dragging them to the first empty column of the query grid, or by dragging the asterisk from the top of the Fields list box to the first empty column of the query. To select the fields as a group, click on the first desired field, hold down the Shift key, and click on the last desired field. This action highlights all the fields in the group. You can then click on and drag the selected fields to an empty column in the query grid.

To use the asterisk method to select all the fields, either double-click on the asterisk or drag the asterisk at the top of the list box to the empty column. With either method, the table's (or existing query's) name appears in the column of the query grid, followed by an asterisk, as shown in Figure 36-6. The asterisk indicates that all fields are to be included in the query.

Note   If you use the asterisk method to denote all fields, you cannot specify criteria for any of the fields. If you want to specify criteria, use the individual method of dragging fields to individual columns of the query grid.

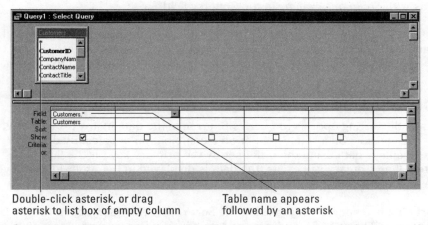

Double-click asterisk, or drag
asterisk to list box of empty column

Table name appears
followed by an asterisk

Figure 36-6: The asterisk adds all fields of a table to a query grid.

Hot Stuff   If you want to add multiple fields that are not adjacent, you click on the first desired field, hold down the Ctrl key, and click on each additional field you want in the Fields list box. Then, with the desired fields selected, click on any of the selected fields and drag them as a group to the first empty column of the Field row of the query grid.

Specifying criteria

After you have added the fields that you want to the query, you can optionally specify any criteria that Access needs to select the desired data. In the criteria rows of the query, you enter *expressions*, which tell Access exactly how to limit the data it retrieves from the underlying tables or queries.

For example, entering **San Diego** in a Criteria row under a City column of a table of addresses tells Access to retrieve all records where the words *San Diego* appear in the City field of the table. Adding > **10.00** in a Criteria row under a Salary column of a table of employee salaries tells Access to retrieve all records with a value greater than 10.00 in the Salary column.

You can specify multiple conditions by entering criteria in more than one column or by including OR statements as part of an expression. For example, in a customers table, entering **Johnson** in the criteria row under the LastName column and entering **San Diego** in the criteria row under the City column tells Access to retrieve all records that contain the terms *Johnson* in the LastName field and *San Diego* in the City field. By contrast, including *San Diego* in the first Criteria row under the City column and including *San Francisco* in the next criteria row under the City column tells Access to retrieve all records with either San Diego or San Francisco in the City field. (The query shown earlier in Figure 36-1 retrieves all records with *Spain* or *Germany* in the Country field.)

To enter the desired criteria, click anywhere in the Criteria row for the desired field and type the expression. You can enter long expressions and see the full text of the expression by pressing Shift+F2 to open a Zoom dialog box into the row.

Choosing a sort order

You can add sorting options to queries to arrange the data in any order that you need. You can sort on a single field or on a combination of fields. By default, Access displays data using the order set by the primary key for the first table selected. If no primary key exists, the data is displayed in the order in which you entered the records.

To sort data in a specific way, click in the Sort row of the query, open the list box that appears (Figure 36-7), and choose Ascending or Descending. Ascending order sorts alphabetic data from A to Z and numeric data from 0 to 9. Descending order sorts alphabetic data from Z to A and numeric data from 9 to 0. You click in the Sort row of the query and choose Ascending or Descending from the list box.

If you want to sort on a combination of fields, the order in which the fields appear in the query grid determines the priority of the fields in the sort. The leftmost field with a checked sort option has the highest priority in a multiple-field sort, and the rightmost field with a checked sort option has the lowest priority. Figure 36-8 shows a sort on a combination of fields.

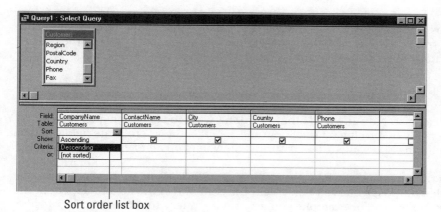

Sort order list box

Figure 36-7: The Sort Order List box.

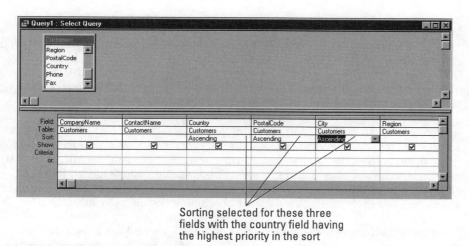

Sorting selected for these three
fields with the country field having
the highest priority in the sort

Figure 36-8: A sort order within a query.

This query displays a dynaset sorted by Country first. In cases where entries in the Country field are the same, the data is sorted by Postal Code; in cases where entries in the Postal Code field are the same, the data is sorted by City.

Note To create this sort order, the Country and Postal Code columns had to be dragged to the left of the City column. You can move any column by clicking in the Field Selector at the top of the column to select it and dragging the column to the desired location within the query grid.

Note You may notice that when you save a query that has fields selected for a sort, Access moves the fields to the leftmost field locations in the Query Design window. When you view the dynaset, the fields are placed back in the order originally specified as part of the query's design.

Hiding fields

You can also hide any fields that you don't want to see in the query's results. You hide fields by turning off the Show check box in the appropriate field's column. By default, the Show check box is turned on when you add a field to the query.

Hot Stuff This option is useful when you need to include fields in queries for criteria or sorting purposes but you don't want the contents of the field to appear in the query's results. For example, you may want a query to retrieve all records for customers in a certain city. You need to include the City field so that you can define the selection criteria, but you do not need to view the City name in the dynaset because the query results contain records with the same city.

Running the query

After you have set up the query and assigned all the options that you want, you can run the query by clicking on the Run button in the toolbar, or by choosing Query⇨Run. The query retrieves the specified data and displays the results in a dynaset containing live data. (For specifics on working with the dynaset, see "Working with the Dynaset" at the end of this chapter.)

Note As you work with queries, you may notice the Datasheet option of the View menu and the corresponding View Datasheet button on the toolbar. Choosing either of these options from the Query Design window appears to run the query, so you may be wondering what difference exists between choosing Query⇨Run and choosing View⇨Datasheet from the menus. For select queries, both methods are identical: they each produce a dynaset containing the query results.

More Info The difference between these methods becomes apparent for action queries, which are discussed in Chapter 40. (Action queries perform some sort of action on the data, such as deleting all records produced by the query.) When you choose View⇨Datasheet or click on the toolbar's View Datasheet button for action queries, the data that will be affected by the action query displays, but the action does not take place. On the other hand, choosing Query⇨Run from the menus (or clicking on the toolbar's Run button) runs the query and makes all the specified changes to the data.

Saving and printing queries

You can save queries for later use with the same techniques you use to save objects elsewhere in Access. While the window containing the query is active, choose File⇨Save (or click on the Save button in the toolbar). If you are saving the query for the first time, a dialog box prompts you for the name of the query. Enter the desired name in the dialog box and click on OK to save it.

To print a query's results, run the query to view the resulting dynaset and choose File⇨Print (or click on the Print button in the toolbar). In the Print dialog box that appears, make your desired selections and click on OK. This method gives you a simple columnar report with a layout resembling the layout of the dynaset. If you want a fancier layout, you'll need to save the query and create a report that uses the query as a data source.

You can also print a query from the Database window by clicking on the desired query to select it and then clicking on the Print button in the toolbar, or by choosing File⇨Print. (This method is faster if the query isn't already open in a window.)

Working with Criteria

Up until now, this chapter has detailed the mechanics of creating a query (such as choosing the underlying tables, naming fields you want to include, and specifying a sort order), but rarely will you want to include every scrap of data in a database in the results of a query. To obtain the specific data that you need, you use *criteria*, or conditions that outline the data you want to retrieve.

The criteria you use in your queries can vary a great deal more than demonstrated in the simple examples earlier in this chapter. You can use a complex range of criteria to work with text, numeric values, dates, or a combination of data types. For example, look at some of the criteria expressions listed in Table 36-3. This table shows query expressions you can use in queries based on different fields in your tables.

Table 36-3
Typical expressions used within queries

Field	Expression	Results
Last Name	O'Malley	Retrieves records containing O'Malley in the Last Name field
Country	Spain	Retrieves records containing Spain in the Country field
Country	Germany or Spain	Retrieves records containing Germany or Spain in the Country field
Country	not Venezuela	Retrieves records containing any country name other than Venezuela in the Country field
Country	Like [A-G]*	Retrieves records with country names that begin with the letters *A* through *G*
Unit Price	>=30.00	Retrieves records containing a value of $30.00 or more in the Unit Price field
Unit Price	between 30.00 and 40.00	Retrieves records containing values between $30.00 and $40.00 in the Unit Price field
Order Date	between 3/1/95 and 12/31/95	Retrieves records containing entries in the Order Date field which fall between 3/1/95 and 12/31/95
Purchase Date	<= Date( ) - 60	Retrieves records containing entries in the Purchase Date field which are 60 days old or more
Phone	(919) 555-????	Retrieves records containing phone numbers with an area code of 919, a prefix of 555, a hyphen, and any four digits

Using text-based criteria

Probably the most common type of criteria you'll include in your queries are *text-based criteria*. When you type a name like **London** as the criterion for a City field, you are using a text-based criterion.

You can see an example of using text-based criteria when you start a new query. (In the Database window, click on the Queries tab, click on New, choose New Query in the list box, and click on OK to start the query.) Use the Show Table dialog box to add the Customers table to the query, double-click on the title bar in the Field List to select all fields, and click on and drag the fields as a group to the first empty Criteria cell of the query grid. Click in the Criteria row under the

Region field and enter **WA** (the abbreviation for Washington state). When you click on the Run button in the Toolbar (or choose Query⇨Run from the menus), you see results like those shown in Figure 36-9.

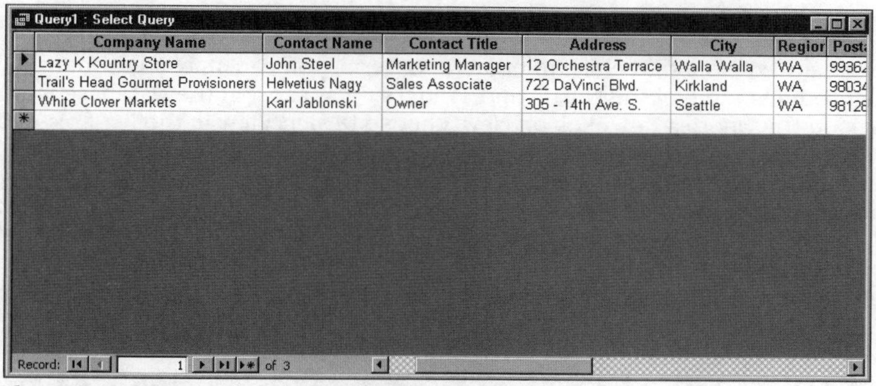

Query1 : Select Query

Company Name	Contact Name	Contact Title	Address	City	Regior	Post
Lazy K Kountry Store	John Steel	Marketing Manager	12 Orchestra Terrace	Walla Walla	WA	99362
Trail's Head Gourmet Provisioners	Helvetius Nagy	Sales Associate	722 DaVinci Blvd.	Kirkland	WA	98034
White Clover Markets	Karl Jablonski	Owner	305 - 14th Ave. S.	Seattle	WA	98128

Record: 1 of 3

Figure 36-9: The results of a text-based query.

When you've finished using the query, you can use Ctrl+F4 to close the Database window and answer No when Access asks you if you want to save the query.

Access is quite flexible in how you enter text-based expressions. You can enter text with or without quotes, precede the text with an equal symbol, or omit the equal symbol. (When you move the insertion point out of the field that contains the text expression, Access automatically adds quotes around the text.) Hence, you can enter any of these expressions into a text field, and Access interprets them all the same way:

London

"London"

=London

="London"

Hot Stuff

You can use the Like operator with text-based criteria along with the asterisk, a wildcard character that represents any number of characters, to find text that is a partial match for your query string. For example, in a Criteria row for a Last name field, you can enter **Like "R*n"** to find last names which include Robinson, Rayson, and Remies-Brighton.

Using numeric criteria

When you have fields that contain number or currency values, you can use math operators in expressions to obtain the desired data. Expressions such as **=20.00** and **between 5 and 12** are typical types of expressions that you can enter as *numeric criteria*.

To see an example of the use of numeric criteria, you can start a new query using the Products table of the Northwind Traders database. (In the Database window, click on the Queries tab, click on New, choose Design View in the list box, and click on OK.) Use the Show Table dialog box to add the Products table to the query, double-click on the title bar in the Fields list box to select all fields, and click on and drag the fields as a group to the first empty Field row of the query grid. Click in the Criteria row under the Unit Price field and enter **>=20.00** in the cell and then run the query by clicking on the Run button in the toolbar. The results resemble those shown in Figure 36-10.

Product Name	Supplier	Category	Quantity Per Unit	Unit Price
Chef Anton's Cajun Seasoning	New Orleans Cajun Delights	Condiments	48 - 6 oz jars	$22.00
Chef Anton's Gumbo Mix	New Orleans Cajun Delights	Condiments	36 boxes	$21.35
Grandma's Boysenberry Spread	Grandma Kelly's Homestead	Condiments	12 - 8 oz jars	$25.00
Uncle Bob's Organic Dried Pears	Grandma Kelly's Homestead	Produce	12 - 1 lb pkgs.	$30.00
Northwoods Cranberry Sauce	Grandma Kelly's Homestead	Condiments	12 - 12 oz jars	$40.00
Mishi Kobe Niku	Tokyo Traders	Meat/Poultry	18 - 500 g pkgs.	$97.00
Ikura	Tokyo Traders	Seafood	12 - 200 ml jars	$31.00
Queso Cabrales	Cooperativa de Quesos 'Las Cabras'	Dairy Products	1 kg pkg.	$21.00
Queso Manchego La Pastora	Cooperativa de Quesos 'Las Cabras'	Dairy Products	10 - 500 g pkgs.	$38.00
Tofu	Mayumi's	Produce	40 - 100 g pkgs.	$23.25
Alice Mutton	Pavlova, Ltd.	Meat/Poultry	20 - 1 kg tins	$39.00
Carnarvon Tigers	Pavlova, Ltd.	Seafood	16 kg pkg.	$62.50
Sir Rodney's Marmalade	Specialty Biscuits, Ltd.	Confections	30 gift boxes	$81.00
Gustaf's Knäckebröd	PB Knäckebröd AB	Grains/Cereals	24 - 500 g pkgs.	$21.00
Gumbär Gummibärchen	Heli Süßwaren GmbH & Co. KG	Confections	100 - 250 g bags	$31.23
Schoggi Schokolade	Heli Süßwaren GmbH & Co. KG	Confections	100 - 100 g pieces	$43.90
Rössle Sauerkraut	Plusspar Lebensmittelgroßmärkte AG	Produce	25 - 825 g cans	$45.60
Thüringer Rostbratwurst	Plusspar Lebensmittelgroßmärkte AG	Meat/Poultry	50 bags x 30 sausg	$123.79
Nord-Ost Matjeshering	d-Ost-Fisch Handelsgesellschaft mbH	Seafood	10 - 200 g glasses	$25.89
Mascarpone Fabioli	Formaggi Fortini s.r.l.	Dairy Products	24 - 200 g pkgs.	$32.00
Gravad lax	Svensk Sjöföda AB	Seafood	12 - 500 g pkgs.	$26.00
Côte de Blaye	Aux joyeux ecclésiastiques	Beverages	12 - 75 cl bottles	$263.50
Ipoh Coffee	Leka Trading	Beverages	16 - 500 g tins	$46.00
Maxilaku	Karkki Oy	Confections	24 - 50 g pkgs.	$20.00
Manjimup Dried Apples	G'day, Mate	Produce	50 - 300 g pkgs.	$53.00

Figure 36-10: The results of a number-based query.

When you're finished using the query, you can use Ctrl+F4 to close the window and answer No when Access asks you if you want to save the query.

Table 36-4 lists the math operators that you can use with numeric queries.

Operator	Meaning
	Table 36-4 **Numeric query operators**
=	Equal to
<	Less than
>	Greater than
< =	Less than or equal to
> =	Greater than or equal to
< >	Not equal to
between	Specifies a range of values, such as **between 4.50 and 12.00**

Using date-based criteria

For fields that contain date values, you can also use math operators to specify date-based criteria in your expressions. You can enter dates in any acceptable date format. Access is also very flexible when it comes to how you enter dates. In Access, any of the following entries are acceptable in a Criteria row of a query grid:

Jun 23 94

#6/23/94#

6/23/94

23-Jun-94

Surrounding dates with the # symbol dates is optional; if you don't add the symbols, Access inserts them automatically when you move the insertion point out of the Criteria row. To see an example of using date-based criteria, you can start a new query using the Orders table of the Northwind Traders database. (In the Database window, click on the Queries tab, click on New, choose Design View in the list box, and click on OK to start a new query.) Use the Show Table dialog box to add the Orders table to the query, double-click on the title bar in the Field List to select all fields, and click on and drag the fields as a group to the first empty Field row of the query grid. Click in the Criteria row under the OrderDate field and enter **between 1/1/96 and 12/31/96**. Now run the query by clicking on the Run button in the toolbar. The results resemble those shown in Figure 36-11.

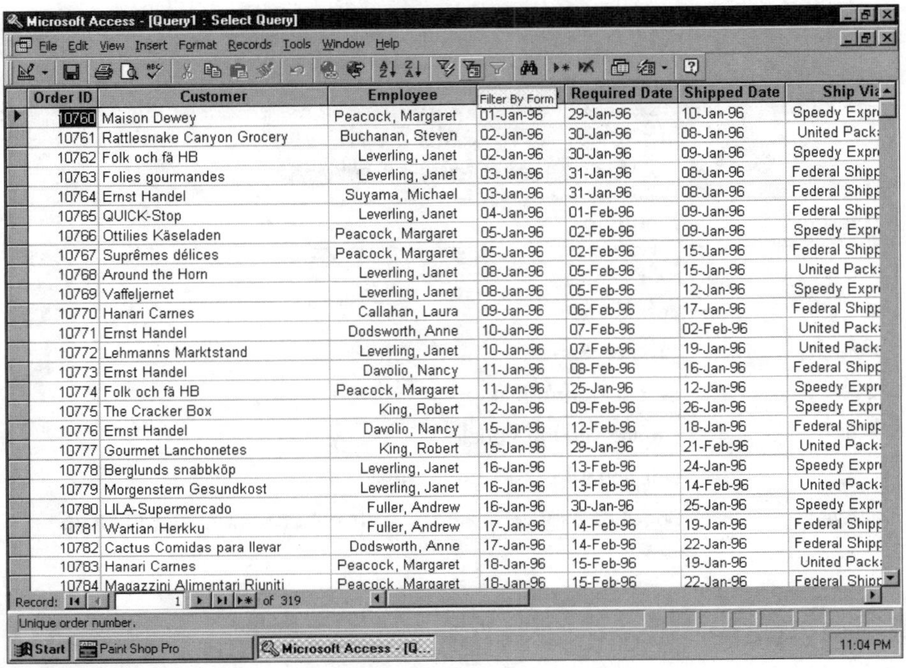

Figure 36-11: The results of a date-based query.

When you're done with the query, you can use Ctrl+F4 to close the window and answer No when Access asks if you want to save the query.

Hot Stuff

You can use the date( ) function of Access to find records which match the current date or fall within a specified time period related to the current date. If you enter the expression **date( )** in a Criteria row for a date field, the selected records must have an entry in the field that matches the current date according to the computer's clock. You can use an expression such as **between 6/15/94 and date( )** to include all records with dates in the field falling between June 15, 1994 and the current date. You also can use an expression like **between date( ) and date( ) + 30** to retrieve all records with a date value falling between the present date and 30 days in the future.

Using AND-based criteria

When you need to retrieve a subset of data based on more than one condition, you can enter the criteria in the desired format in the appropriate fields of the query grid. These queries depend on *AND-based criteria* because one criterion *and* another criterion must be true to retrieve the record. You can enter as many multiple conditions as you need to produce the desired results. For example, consider the query design based on the Customers table, shown in Figure 36-12.

In this example, records must have *Madrid* in the City field and *Spain* in the Country field to be included in the query's results.

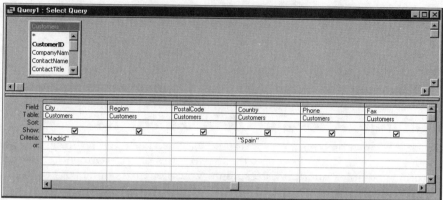

Figure 36-12: This query uses AND-based criteria.

Using OR-based criteria

In many cases, you need a different type of logic in which queries retrieve records that meet any one of a number of conditions. These queries use *OR-based logic* because one criterion *or* another criterion must be true to retrieve the record. To enter multiple conditions using OR-based logic, you can add as many additional rows as you need below the first Criteria row of the query grid. For example, consider the query design shown in Figure 36-13, again based on the Customers table.

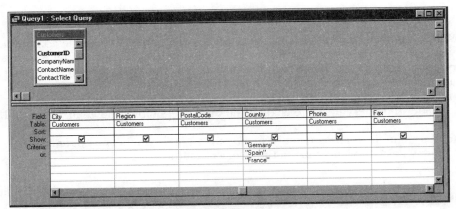

Figure 36-13: This query uses OR-based criteria.

In this query, all records that contain either Germany or Spain or France are retrieved.

Combining AND- and OR-based criteria

You can use any combination of AND- and OR-based criteria in the same query to produce the desired results. Using these two types of criteria together allows you to produce complex queries. For example, consider the complex query that uses of both types of criteria shown in Figure 36-14.

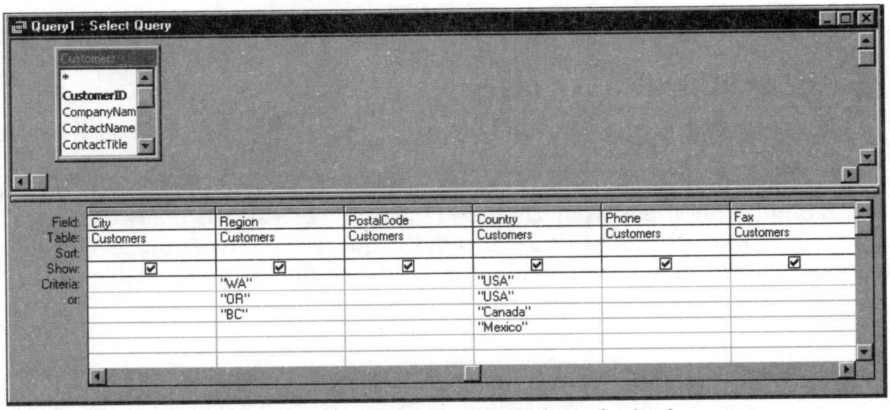

Figure 36-14: This query combines AND- and OR-based criteria.

In this query, records must have *WA* in the Region field and *USA* in the Country field, *OR* in the Region field and *USA* in the Country field, *BC* in the Region field and *Canada* in the Country field, or *Mexico* in the Country field to be included in the query's results.

Working with the Dynaset

As mentioned earlier in this chapter, when you run the query, the results appear in a *dynaset*. A dynaset looks like a table's datasheet, as you can see in the example shown in Figure 36-15.

Note As you add or edit data in the dynaset, remember that the field properties defined at the table level affect the fields of the query. For example, if a text field in a table has a maximum length of 100 characters, you will not be able to enter more than 100 characters in that field of the query's dynaset.

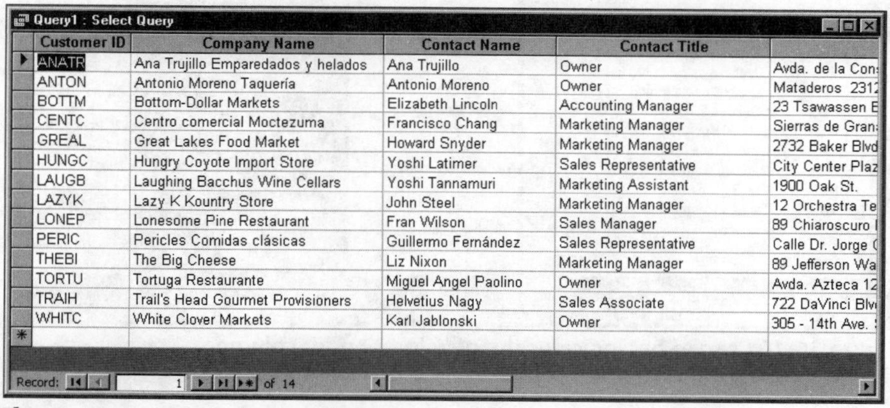

Customer ID	Company Name	Contact Name	Contact Title	
ANATR	Ana Trujillo Emparedados y helados	Ana Trujillo	Owner	Avda. de la Con
ANTON	Antonio Moreno Taquería	Antonio Moreno	Owner	Mataderos 231
BOTTM	Bottom-Dollar Markets	Elizabeth Lincoln	Accounting Manager	23 Tsawassen E
CENTC	Centro comercial Moctezuma	Francisco Chang	Marketing Manager	Sierras de Gran
GREAL	Great Lakes Food Market	Howard Snyder	Marketing Manager	2732 Baker Blvd
HUNGC	Hungry Coyote Import Store	Yoshi Latimer	Sales Representative	City Center Plaz
LAUGB	Laughing Bacchus Wine Cellars	Yoshi Tannamuri	Marketing Assistant	1900 Oak St.
LAZYK	Lazy K Kountry Store	John Steel	Marketing Manager	12 Orchestra Te
LONEP	Lonesome Pine Restaurant	Fran Wilson	Sales Manager	89 Chiaroscuro
PERIC	Pericles Comidas clásicas	Guillermo Fernández	Sales Representative	Calle Dr. Jorge
THEBI	The Big Cheese	Liz Nixon	Marketing Manager	89 Jefferson Wa
TORTU	Tortuga Restaurante	Miguel Angel Paolino	Owner	Avda. Azteca 12
TRAIH	Trail's Head Gourmet Provisioners	Helvetius Nagy	Sales Associate	722 DaVinci Blv
WHITC	White Clover Markets	Karl Jablonski	Owner	305 - 14th Ave.

Figure 36-15: A typical query dynaset.

You may want to work with the fields in your query's dynaset. You can change the order of fields, insert new fields, and delete existing fields. To work with the fields of the dynaset, you select the fields you want by using the Field Selector row, the thin gray row located directly above the Field row. To select a row, place the mouse pointer at the desired column and directly above the Field Selector row until it changes to the shape of a downward-pointing arrow and click on the desired column. To select multiple columns, you can click the desired column in the Field Selector row area for the first column and drag across all the columns you want to select.

Changing the order of fields

You can rearrange the location of fields after they've been placed in the query column using the same techniques that you use with datasheets. Use the following steps to move fields in a query dynaset:

1. Select the field you want to move by clicking on the Field Selector above the field.

2. Click and hold down on the Field Selector again. The Field Icon (a small square) appears as part of the mouse pointer.

3. While holding down the mouse button, drag the column to the desired position. As you drag the column, a solid bar appears indicating where the column will appear, as shown in Figure 36-16.

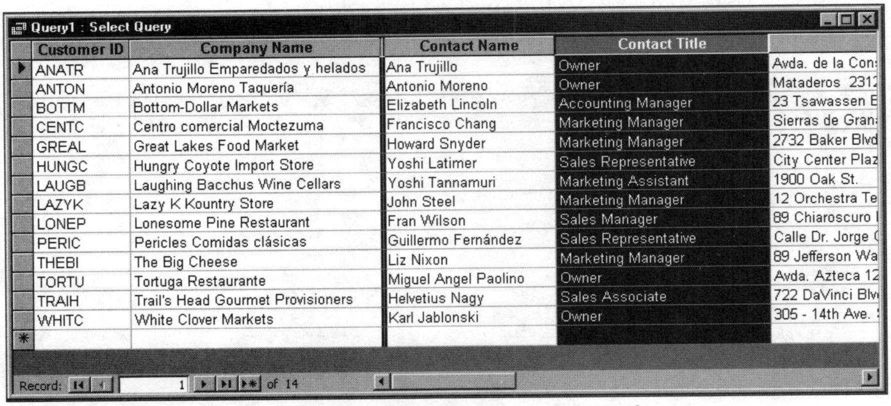

Figure 36-16: A solid bar indicates the new location for column.

Removing fields

You can remove any field from the query grid. To perform this task, select the field or fields you want to delete and press Delete, or choose Edit⇨Clear Grid.

Inserting fields

To insert a field into the query grid, select the desired field or fields in the list boxes at the top of the Query Design window, drag them to the desired column, and release the mouse button. If you drop the field over an existing column, the existing column and all columns to the right move to the right by one column to make room for the inserted field.

A Note about SQL and Your Queries

If you are familiar with the database language *SQL* (Structured Query Language), you may want to know that Access uses SQL as the underlying language for all queries. Although the query is usually designed visually while working in the Design View window, when you save the query Access translates the visual design into a SQL statement that it processes whenever you run the query. For example, consider the query design shown in Figure 36-17. (This relational query uses more than one table; relational queries are detailed further in Chapter 39.)

You can view the SQL statement used by any query by opening the query in Design View, then choosing View⇨SQL View. The query's Design window then displays the underlying SQL statement for the query, such as the one shown in Figure 36-18.

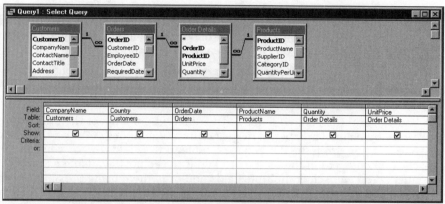

Figure 36-17: The visual design of a relational query.

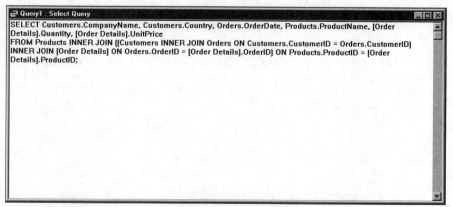

Figure 36-18: The relational query's underlying SQL statement.

Danger Zone Although you can directly edit the language used in the SQL statement, Microsoft doesn't recommend performing this task unless you are intimately familiar with the SQL syntax that Access uses. However, advanced users may find it worthwhile knowing how SQL works behind the scenes in Access because you can use SQL statements directly in the RecordSource properties of forms and reports.

Summary

This chapter detailed the basic use of queries that you can use to obtain desired data from your Access tables. Using queries, you can select the specific records containing the specific fields that you desire. You can also sort the information so that it appears in a specific order, and you can construct queries that retrieve data based on a number of complex conditions. This chapter included the following points:

✦ You can start a new query by clicking on the Queries tab in the Database window and clicking on New. In the dialog box that appears, you click on Design View and click on OK to open a design window into the query.

✦ You can add desired tables to a query's design by selecting one or more tables from the Show Tables dialog box. (If the dialog box isn't visible, you can display it at any time by choosing Query⇨Show Table.)

✦ You can add the desired fields to the different columns of the Field row of the query by using a number of drag-and-drop techniques. You can drag fields one at a time from the list box for a table to the Field row, or you can double-click on any field in the list box to add it to the next available column of the query. You can select multiple fields and drag them using the Shift or Ctrl keys, and you can drag the asterisk at the top of the list box to add all fields in the table to the query.

✦ In the criteria rows of the query, you enter *expressions*, which tell Access what data you want it to retrieve. You can specify multiple conditions by entering criteria in more than one column or by including OR statements as part of an expression.

✦ You can add sorting options to arrange the data in any needed order. To add a sorting option, click in the Sort row of the query and choose Ascending or Descending from the list box. You can sort on a single field or on a combination of fields.

✦ You can hide any fields that you don't wish to see in the query's results by turning off the Show check box in the columns that you want to hide.

✦ You can run a query by clicking on the toolbar's Run button or by opening the Query menu and choosing Run. In Access, running a query produces the dynaset, the row-and-column display that resembles a datasheet and contains live data based on the query.

✦ You can print a query's results by opening the query and choosing File⇨Print. You can also select the query in the Database window and choose File⇨Print, or you can right-click on the query in the Database window and choose Print from the shortcut menu that appears.

In the chapter that follows, you learn how to work with your data in Access by using forms.

Where to go next...

✦ You can use queries to get data from more than one table at a time. For details, see Chapter 39.

✦ You can create queries for specialized tasks, such as making global changes to a table or creating a new table based on an existing table's data. For specifics, see Chapter 40.

✦   ✦   ✦

Working with Forms

Previous chapters showed you how you can use the datasheets that appear when you open a table to view and edit data in an Access database. *Forms* provide an additional way to work with your data.

Forms offer several advantages over using datasheets to view and edit your data. For example, whereas datasheets display the data using a columnar, spreadsheet-like layout, you can design forms to show data in a variety of formats. This chapter details the use of forms in Access and the advantages of using forms to manipulate your data.

Understanding Forms

Access forms resemble paper-based forms, and often they are designed to display a single record of an underlying table or query at a time. In Access, forms can provide much more than fields from a single table with text labels. You can include graphic images in forms, whether they are OLE objects in fields or are part of the form's design. You can include data from related tables in forms. For example, a single form may display a customer in an order entry database, along with details of all orders placed by that customer. You also can design different forms that provide different views of the same data. For example, Figure 37-1 shows two forms based on the same table. The Employees form displays a single record at a time vertically, whereas the other form, Employees2, displays several records horizontally at the same time.

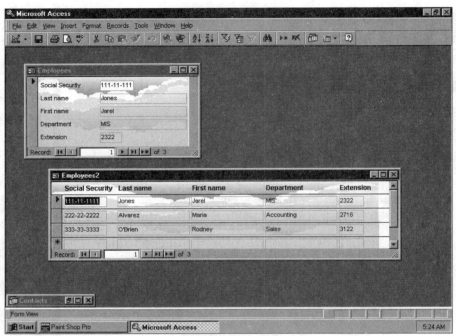

Figure 37-1: Different forms can offer multiple views of a single table.

Using forms for basic data entry and editing has advantages over using datasheets for the same tasks. Viewing all fields of a specific record is frequently difficult or impossible when you use datasheets; however, unless the table has an unusually large number of fields, you can design your forms to display all fields of a table. Forms also let you place fields in the locations you want them, and forms make it easy to see the graphic objects (such as pictures) stored in OLE object fields. Figure 37-2 shows an example of a typical form.

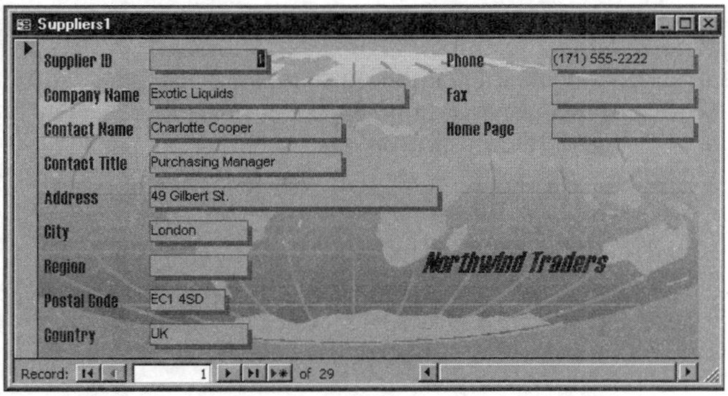

Figure 37-2: A typical form.

Creating Forms

Access lets you quickly create forms using the toolbar's New Object button or the Form Wizards. You also can design forms manually by opening a new form and dragging objects (such as fields, text, and graphics) to the desired locations in the form. You can also design forms using a combination of automated and manual methods. For example, you can use the Form Wizards to provide the basic design for a form, open the form in Design view, and make changes to the form's design.

Creating forms with the New Object button

The fastest way to create a form is by using the AutoForm option of the New Object button in the toolbar. If you select any table in the Database window and then click on the New Object button in the toolbar (or open the menu of the New Object button and choose AutoForm), Access creates a default form for the selected table, using a simple, single-column layout.

In the default format, all fields align at the left side of the form, and the field names are used as default labels for the fields. The first form in Figure 37-1, Employees, shows an example of a form created using the New Object button. The form shown is based on a table of employees containing the five fields shown in the form.

Creating forms with the Form Wizards

If you want more control over the forms creation process but you still want to be able to create a form with little or no design work, you'll like the Form Wizard. Like other Access wizards, the Form Wizard asks you a series of questions about the form you want to create and builds the form based on your responses. Generally, you perform the following steps to build a form using the Form Wizards:

1. In the Database window, click on the Forms tab and click on New. (In the example, we're using the Northwind Traders sample database provided with Access.) The New Form dialog box appears, shown in Figure 37-3.

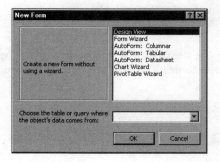

Figure 37-3: The New Form dialog box.

2. In the dialog box, click on Form Wizard, and in the list box at the bottom of the dialog box, choose the table or query on which you want to base the form. (If you want to base the form on more than one table, choose the table that you want to use as the primary source of data for the form.) In the example, we used the Customers table from the Northwind Traders database.

3. Follow the directions that appear in the Wizard dialog boxes. (These directions are detailed later in the chapter.) When you complete the process, the Form Wizard gives you the option to open the form with data in it or in Design view, where you can manually make additional changes to the form.

The New Form dialog box that appears in Step 1 offers several options in addition to the Form Wizard option you clicked. Table 37-1 details these options and their purposes.

Table 37-1
The New Form dialog box options

Option	Purpose
Design View	Creates a blank form that you can design manually
Form Wizard	Launches the Form Wizard, which asks a series of questions and produces the desired form based on your responses
AutoForm: Columnar	Creates a default form using a columnar layout (all fields in a single column align on the left-hand side)
AutoForm: Tabular	Creates a default form with a tabular appearance, with space surrounding each field
AutoForm: Datasheet	Creates a default form with a tabular appearance, with no space around fields (like a datasheet)
Chart Wizard	Launches the Chart Wizard, which builds a form that displays numeric data in the form of a chart
Pivot Table Wizard	Creates a form containing an Excel pivot table

After you select Form Wizard and click on the desired table (or main table, when you want to base the form on more than one table), the first dialog box for the Form Wizard appears, shown in Figure 37-4.

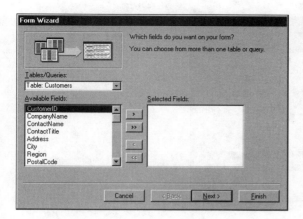

Figure 37-4: The first Form Wizard dialog box.

In this dialog box, you use the Tables/Queries list box to choose the tables or queries you want to use as the form's data source, and you use the Available Fields and Selected Fields boxes to enter the fields that you want in the form. When you select a table in the Tables/Queries list box, all fields of that table or query appear in the Available Fields list box. You can click on a field in this list to select it and click on the Right arrow button to add the field to the Selected Fields list box, or you can double-click on the field in the Available Fields list box to add it to the Selected Fields list box.

Notice that a double-arrow button also appears between the list boxes. Click on this button to add all fields in the Available Fields list box to the Selected Fields list box. If you make a mistake and want to remove a field from the Selected Fields list box, click on the unwanted field in the Selected Fields list box and click on the Left arrow button to remove the field from the list.

When you want to base the form on more than one table and you have added all desired fields for the first table, choose another table in the Tables/Queries list box and add the desired fields for that table. You have the option of using relational queries or multiple tables for forms that are based on more than one table. You can use a relational query, or you can select one table and add fields from that table and then select another table and add fields from that table. When you are done adding the desired fields, click on Next to proceed.

The dialog box that you now see depends on whether you have chosen fields from a single table or fields from more than one table. If you have chosen fields from more than one table, you see the dialog box shown in Figure 37-5.

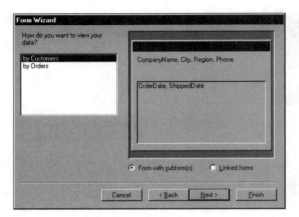

Figure 37-5: The second Form Wizard dialog box (used with multiple tables).

Using the options shown in this dialog box, you can decide which table you should use to view the data. In effect, you are deciding which table will be the *main table*, or table with the highest priority, in a form that shows data from more than one table. Click on the desired table in the list box to select it and choose the Form with subform(s) or Linked Forms option. If you choose the Form with subform(s) option, Access creates a single form that shows one record at a time from the main table and all associated records from the secondary, or *linked*, tables. If you choose the Linked forms option, Access creates two or more forms, with the additional form(s) linked to the first, to display the data from all the tables.

If you originally chose fields from only one table, you see the Form Wizard dialog box shown in Figure 37-6.

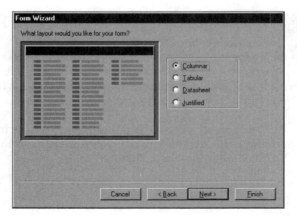

Figure 37-6: The second Form Wizard dialog box (used with a single table).

In this dialog box, you are asked to specify a layout for the form. Your choices are Columnar, Tabular, Datasheet, and Justified. The Columnar option creates a default form with columnar layout, arranging all fields in a single column on the left-hand side of the form. The Tabular option creates a default form with a tabular appearance, with space surrounding each field. The Datasheet option creates a default form that has a tabular appearance (similar to that of a datasheet) but with no space around each field. The Justified option creates a form with the fields in successive order, widened sufficiently to create a justified right margin. Choose one of these options in the dialog box and click on Next to proceed.

The next dialog box presented by the Form Wizard gives you a choice of styles for the form, as shown in Figure 37-7.

Access provides ten different styles, or background designs, for forms created with the Form Wizard. Select a style and click on Next to proceed.

Danger Zone Even though some of these styles are quite colorful, adding varied designs to a form will increase the time Access takes to open and display the form. This effect is particularly noticeable on machines running the minimum requirements for Windows 95.

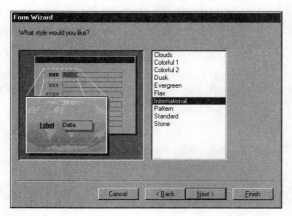

Figure 37-7: The third Form Wizard dialog box.

The final dialog box that appears asks you for a title for the form. If the form is based on multiple tables, it also asks you to provide titles for the subforms that display the data from the secondary tables. Using the options in the dialog box, you can choose to open the form and view or enter information, or to open the form in Design view where you can make additional changes to the form's design.

Designing forms manually

You may prefer to design forms using the manual method, in which you open a blank form and add the desired *design objects* (text, text boxes that display fields, graphics, lines and rectangles, and so on) in the form. You can create a form manually by performing the following steps:

1. In the Database window, click on the Forms tab and click on New. The New Form dialog box appears, as shown earlier in Figure 37-3.

2. From the list, select Design View but don't double click it. Then, in the table/queries list box in the same dialog box, choose or type the name of the table (or query) that you want to serve as the form's basis.

   More Info If the data you want to use is in one table, select that table by name; if the data you want is stored in more than one table, you can choose the primary table needed, or you can select a query that provides fields from all needed tables. See Chapter 36 for details on creating and saving queries.

3. After you type or make the selections, click on OK. Access displays the form in Design View, as shown in Figure 37-8.

4. Place the desired objects (fields, text, and any graphics or other types of controls) in the form. You can use the Toolbox (choose View⇨Toolbox to access it) to place different control types in the form, as discussed later in this chapter.

5. Save the completed form by choosing File⇨Save.

Hot Stuff You can save time by using the Form Wizard to create a rough equivalent of the form you want. After building the form with the Wizard, open it in Design view, and make any changes you want to the form's design.

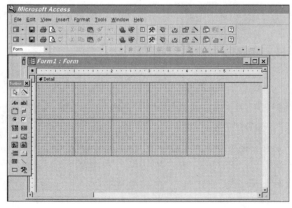

Figure 37-8: A blank form in Design view.

While you are designing a form manually, you work within a window in Design view, as shown earlier in Figure 37-8. Think of this window as "drawing area" where you can lay out the design of your form.

While you are designing a form, notice that the toolbar contains a button menu on the far left for the three different types of form views in Access: Design view, Form view, and Datasheet view. These choices control how you see the form. You can open the menu by clicking on the down arrow to the right of the button menu. See Figure 37-9.

Figure 37-9: This button menu lets you choose how to view your data.

The Design View menu choice places you in Design view, where you can design the form. The Form View menu choice switches you to Form view, where you can add, edit, delete, and print the data in the underlying table or query. The Datasheet View menu choice displays the underlying datasheet of a table (or, in the case of queries, the dynaset).

Changing a Form's Height and Width

You can change the width of a form and increase or decrease the height of the individual sections in the form using these steps:

1. While in Design view, place the mouse pointer over the bottom or right edge of the form, until it changes shape into a double-headed arrow.

2. Drag this arrow up or down to change the form's height, or left or right to change the form's width.

As you drag the edges, the form's dimensions are highlighted in the horizontal or vertical rulers at the top and left sides of the form, providing a visual guide to the form's size. Also, keep in mind that you can change the height and width at the same time by clicking on and dragging the lower-right corner of the form until the form reaches the desired size.

Working with Controls

During the form design process, most objects that you place in the form (such as fields, text, and graphics) are called *controls*. As you manually design forms and reports, you need to know how to add, size, and move controls within the Design view window. You'll be able to carry these same techniques over to report design because Access uses the same techniques with report design that it uses with form design. Even if you use the Form Wizards to build your forms, you'll need these techniques to work with the controls in forms built by the wizards. You can place three types of controls in Access forms and reports: *bound, unbound,* and *calculated.*

✦ **Bound controls** — Bound controls are related, or "tied," to a specific field of a table or query. In Figure 37-2, the fields that display the table's data (Supplier ID, Company Name, Contact Name, and so on) are all bound controls.

✦ **Unbound controls** — Unbound controls are not tied to a table or query in any way. In Figure 37-2, the title "Northwind Traders" at the lower right side of the form is an unbound control. (You can use an unbound control with your data, but to do so, you must use a macro or Visual Basic, the programming language used with Access, to work with your data.)

✦ **Calculated controls** — Calculated controls display the results of a calculation; the calculation is based on a value in the underlying table or query. (If you have experience with other database managers, such as FoxPro, dBASE, or Paradox, you can compare calculated controls with calculated fields used in those products.)

Placing bound controls

Probably the most commonly used controls placed in Access forms are text box controls that are bound to and display data from fields of a table or query. As you move through records in a table or query, the contents of the field appear inside the bound control. Text boxes are the most commonly used type of bound control, but your Access forms can also use toggle buttons, check boxes, and OLE Object frames that are bound to fields.

The easiest way to add bound text box controls is to open the Field List (choose View ➪ Field List from the menus, or click the Field List button in the toolbar) and drag the field you want to the desired location in the form. Figure 37-10 shows a form after three fields (Company Name, Contact Name, and Contact Title) have been dragged from the Field List into the form.

If you need to add more than one field at a time, you can select and add multiple fields to the form using a variety of different methods. If the desired fields are adjacent in the Field List, click on the first field, press and hold down Shift, and then click on the last field in the list. Then click and drag all the fields as a group to the desired location in the form. When you release the mouse button, all fields are added to the form as a group. You can add every field in the list by double-clicking on the Field List's title bar and dragging all the fields as a group to the form.

If you want to add multiple fields that are not adjacent in the list, select the first field you want, press and hold down Ctrl, and then click on additional fields. After you've selected the desired fields, click on and hold down the mouse button on any of the selected fields, and drag the fields as a group to the desired location in the form.

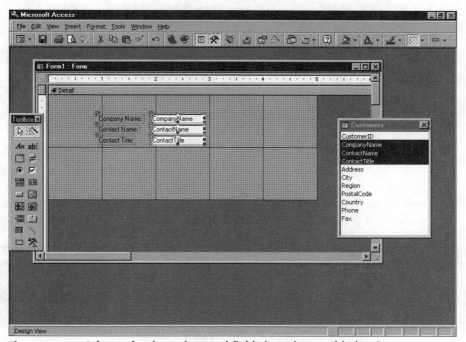

Figure 37-10: A form after bound control fields have been added to it.

Selecting controls

Before you can resize, move, or otherwise work with a control, you have to select it. To select any control, click once anywhere within the control. *Moving handles* and *sizing handles* appear around the control after you select it. For example, you can see these handles around the selected Company Name field in Figure 37-11.

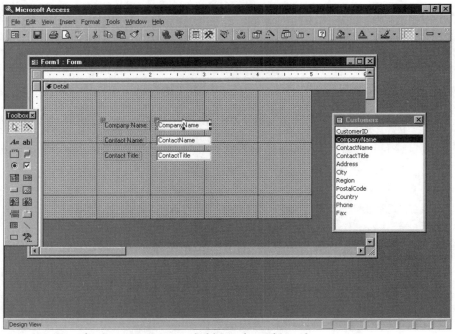

Figure 37-11: The Company Name field is selected in a form.

Additionally, the controls used to display data from fields usually have a label along with the text box. The following list describes how you can select and work with the various controls you use within your forms:

✦ **Selecting adjacent controls** — To select a group of adjacent controls, place the mouse pointer above and to the left of the first control in the group and click on and drag through all the desired controls.

✦ **Selecting nonadjacent or overlapping controls** — To select controls that are not adjacent or controls that overlap, press and hold down Shift and click on each desired control.

✦ **Selecting all controls** — To select every control on a form, choose Edit ➪ Select All.

✦ **Moving and sizing controls** — To move a control, select it as described previously and place the mouse pointer on the border of the control. After the mouse pointer changes to the shape of a hand, click on and drag the control to the desired location.

✦ **Moving controls or labels separately** — You can move a text box control separately from its attached label (or move the label separately from the control) by selecting the control and then placing the mouse pointer on the upper-left corner of the control or label where it changes to the shape of an outstretched finger. Next, click on and drag the control or the label to the desired location.

✦ **Resizing controls** — To resize a control, select the control and click on and drag any of the control's sizing handles (at which point the pointer changes shape to a double-arrow) until the control reaches the desired size.

✦ **Aligning controls** — As you move controls around on a form, you can maintain their alignment by holding down Shift while you move them. (When you hold down Shift, the controls move horizontally or vertically as you drag the mouse but not in both directions at the same time.)

✦ **Deleting controls** — To delete a control, select the control and press Delete (or choose Edit ⇨ Delete). If you only want to delete the label attached to a text box control, make sure that you select the label and not the entire control (click on the upper-left corner of the label).

✦ **Changing labels** — If you want to change the default label assigned to a text box, you can easily do so. Double-click on the label, click on the Format tab in the Properties window that opens, and change the Label property to the desired text.

Using the Toolbox to add controls

So far, this chapter has described techniques commonly used when working with bound controls, the controls attached to a field of a table or a query. Often, you also will want to add *unbound controls* to forms. Examples of unbound controls include titles of forms, graphics (which are not stored in any OLE object fields of a table), and objects like rectangles or lines. You can also add *calculated controls* to forms to display a calculation based on a field of the underlying table or query. To add controls like these, you use the Toolbox, shown in Figure 37-12.

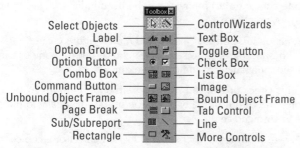

Figure 37-12: The Toolbox lets you add controls to a form.

If the Toolbox was visible the last time you worked in Design view, it appears again when you open another form in Design view. If the Toolbox does not appear when you enter Design view, you can display it by clicking on the Toolbox button in the toolbar, or by choosing View➪Toolbox.

Note   You can move the Toolbox to a location beneath the toolbar by double-clicking on its title bar. To move it back into the Design view window for the form, click at its left edge and drag to the desired location.

To add a control to a form using the Toolbox, first click on the type of control you want in the Toolbox. (To aid you, when you hold the mouse pointer over any of the Toolbox buttons, a Tooltip appears, indicating the purpose of the button.) After you have selected the desired type of control, click within the form where you want the upper-left corner of the control to appear and drag to the lower right corner for the desired control. Table 37-2 summarizes the Toolbox tool functions.

Table 37-2 Toolbox tools	
Tool	**Purpose**
Select Objects	Selects, moves, sizes, or edits objects in the form
Control Wizards	Turns the Control Wizards on or off
Label	Adds labels that are convenient for titles, instructions, or descriptive text
Text Box	Creates text boxes that can display the contents of fields
Option Group	Adds an option group to the form; option groups contain check boxes, option buttons, or toggle buttons for a group
Toggle Button	Adds toggle buttons; can be used with option groups to select one choice out of many or can be used individually to indicate a yes/no choice
Option Button	Adds option buttons (also called *radio buttons*); can be used with option groups to select one choice out of many or can be used individually to indicate a yes/no choice
Check Box	Adds check boxes; can be used with option groups to select one choice out of many or can be used individually to indicate a yes/no choice
Combo Box	Creates combination boxes that let you select one choice from a list of choices or type in a desired value

Tool	Purpose
List Box	Creates list boxes that let you select one choice from a list of choices
Command Button	Adds a command button that you can use in the form to carry out commands
Image	Inserts a frame that displays a static image
Unbound Object Frame	Inserts a frame that contains an OLE object
Bound Object Frame	Inserts a frame that contains the contents of an OLE object field
Page Break	Inserts a page break at a specified location in the form
Tab Control	Adds a tabbed form with multiple pages
Subform / Subreport	Adds an object that contains a subform or a subreport
Line	Draws lines in a form
Rectangle	Draws rectangles or squares in a form
More Controls	Opens a new menu used for adding additional controls (such as Visual Basic VBX controls) to a form

When you are done with the Toolbox, you can close it by choosing View⇨Toolbox again, or by clicking on the Close button in the Toolbox.

Changing control properties

You can change the behavior of controls by changing the *properties* for the control. All controls have assigned, or *default*, properties, but sometimes you will want to change a control's properties. For example, you may want to change the default font or color of a label attached to a text box, or you may want to attach a macro to a command button. To display the properties for any control, right-click on the control and choose Properties from the shortcut menu that appears. The Properties window for the selected control opens, as shown in Figure 37-13.

In the Properties window, click on the tab for the type of property you want (Format, Data, Event, Other, or All). Then, click on the property that you want to change. If a down arrow appears, you can click on the down arrow and choose the desired property from the list box; if no arrow appears, type in an appropriate value for the desired property.

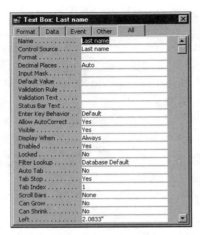

Figure 37-13: A control's Properties window.

Note

You can obtain help on what entries are appropriate for a given property by clicking on the property and then pressing F1 to open a help window.

Keep in mind that controls aren't the only objects that have properties. Access forms also have their own properties that you can change so that the form better meets your needs. You can change a form's properties by performing the following steps:

1. Open the form in Design view.

2. Choose Edit➪Select Form.

3. Click on the Properties button in the toolbar, or choose View➪Properties to display the Properties window for the form.

4. Make any needed changes to the appropriate property.

The following list describes some of the more common properties that you will find useful when you work with forms and the controls in those forms:

✦ **Control Source** — This property tells the control where to obtain the data displayed within the control. When you create text box controls by dragging them from the Field List into the form, the control is created automatically. You can enter expressions in the Control Source property by typing them in directly, or by right-clicking on the property and choosing Build from the shortcut menu to bring up Expression Builder.

✦ **Format** — This property defines any format used to display the data. (The precise types of formats you can use vary, depending on the type of data displayed by the control; for example, with controls that display the contents of number fields, you can use number formats.) You can click on the down arrow that appears at the right side of the selected property to open a list box showing the formats available for the type of field with which you are working.

✦ **Decimal Places** — When working with number or currency fields, you can use this property to display how many decimal places should be used with the numbers displayed.

✦ **Input Mask** — You can use this property to define an *input mask*, or a format that data must follow when you type data into the control. For example, if you set this property to 000-00-0000, hyphens display in the locations shown, and digits display in the other locations. You can see a list of the symbols you can use for input masks, and examples of input masks, by placing the insertion point in the property and pressing F1.

✦ **Default Value** — Use this property to specify a default value for the control. As new records are added to the form, the default value appears in the field used by the control, and users can change it to something else if needed. You can also establish default values during the table design stage, and those default values will always apply regardless of whether you use the form or not.

✦ **Display When** — This property determines when objects or entire sections of a form appear or print. You can set this property to Always, Print Only, or Screen Only. When set to Always, the object appears when you view the form and also when you print the form. Choosing Print Only causes the object to appear when you print the form but hides the object when you view the form in a window. The Screen Only option displays the object when you view the form in a window but omits it when you print the form.

✦ **Enabled and Locked** — You can use these properties to determine whether a control can receive the *focus* (that is, the user can move the insertion point into the control) and whether the user can edit the data in the control. Setting the Enabled property to Yes allows the focus to move into the control, whereas setting it to No prevents the focus from moving into the control. When the Locked property is set to Yes, the property does not permit data to be edited in the control.

✦ **Can Grow and Can Shrink** — These properties are useful for forms that you want to print. They allow the controls to expand and contract as needed to accommodate the data in the control. Setting the Can Grow property to Yes allows the control to increase in size to accommodate the data. Setting the Can Shrink property to Yes allows the control to shrink beyond its default size when the data in the control does not fill the entire control.

✦ **Caption** — This property is one of the form properties, and it contains the caption which appears in the form's title bar. You may discover that if you go into the Database window and rename a form you've created with the Form

Wizards, the name of the form within the title bar does not change. To change the name shown in the title bar, you need to rename the caption in this property.

✦ **Modal** — This property is another form property, and it determines whether the form is a *modal* form. When a form is a modal form, a user cannot work with any other forms or objects in Access until the modal form is closed. You may find this property useful if you want to prevent users from doing anything else until they finish working with the form. Developers of applications also find this property useful to create forms that can be used as dialog boxes within applications.

Entering expressions for controls

When you design complex forms manually, you may need to enter *expressions* to display data that you can't directly retrieve from a table or query. Expressions are the basis of calculated controls that display calculations in text boxes when the displayed data is based on one or more fields of the underlying table or query. You use expressions for calculated controls and other common tasks, both in forms and in reports. When you place an expression in a control for a form, Access evaluates the expression every time you display a new record in the form.

Text boxes are commonly used with expressions, but Access lets you use expressions in any control that has a Control Source property. With text boxes, you can enter an expression in two ways: you can type expressions manually into the text box (starting with an equal symbol), or you can use Expression Builder. To enter the expression directly into the text box, follow these steps:

1. Open the desired form in Design view.

2. Using the Toolbox, add a text box to the form (or select an existing text box).

3. Click once inside the text box and type the expression, starting with an equal symbol.

Note   If you enter expressions manually, remember that you have the option of using the Zoom box. When expressions are too long to see comfortably in the text box, while the insertion point is in the text box you can press Shift+F2 to open the Zoom box where you can see the full text of the expression.

To enter an expression with Expression Builder, you can use these steps:

1. Open the desired form in Design view.

2. Using the Toolbox, add a text box to the form (or select an existing text box).

3. Right-click on the text box and choose Properties from the shortcut menu to open the Properties window for the selected text box.

4. Click on the Data tab in the Properties window.

5. Click on the Build button (the button with three dots) to the right of the Control Source property. The Expression Builder window appears, shown in Figure 37-14. To use Expression Builder, you choose the table and field names, functions, and math or logical symbols that you need to build the expression you want.

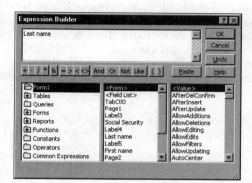

Figure 37-14: The Expression Builder window.

Note

Keep in mind that you can obtain help on using Expression Builder by clicking on the Help button in the Expression Builder dialog box.

6. When you are done building the expression, click on OK, and the expression appears within the text box.

Adding calculated controls to a form

As mentioned earlier, one common use for expressions is creating *calculated controls* that you place in forms. For example, you may want to display a tax that is 6 percent of the amount displayed in a Price field, or you may want to display a date that is 30 days after the current date according to the computer's clock. You add a calculated control to a form by performing these steps:

1. Click on the Text Box button in the Toolbox to select it.

2. Click in the form where you want the upper-left corner of the text box to begin and drag to where the lower-right corner of the text box should appear.

3. Click once inside the text box and type the desired expression, beginning with an equal symbol. For example, if you want the text box to display the contents of a field called "Price" multiplied by 6 percent, you enter **=Price * .06** in the text box. If you want to display a date 30 days in the future, you

enter **=Date( ) + 30** in the text box. Alternatively, you can right-click on the control, choose Properties from the shortcut menu, click on the Data tab, and enter the desired expression into the Control Source box.

Changing colors and effects

You can use an object's Properties window to change the colors and other visual effects for that object. Right-click on the desired object and choose Properties. In the Properties window that opens, click on the Format tab; click on the Fore Color property (to change the foreground), Back Color (to change the background), or Border Color (to change the border) as desired; and click on the Build button to the right of the property to open a Color dialog box, such as the one shown in Figure 37-15. You can click among the colors within the dialog box to change the color for the selected object.

Note   You can also change foreground and background colors by right-clicking the object and choosing Fill/Back Color or Font/Fore Color from the shortcut menu that appears.

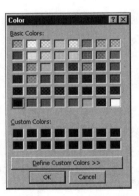

Figure 37-15: The Color dialog box.

Hot Stuff   Often, you can improve the appearance of a basic form by right-clicking in any blank area of the form, opening the Properties window, and changing the Back Color property to something other than the default white. (Soft cyan works well for me, but you may find other colors that are more to your liking.)

To change the fonts and the justification used for objects containing text or data, first select the object you want to change and then use the list boxes and buttons of the toolbar that control the fonts, font size, and justification. You can change the font size and style; select boldface, italics, or underlining; and choose a justification format.

Note If you increase the font size for an object and the text becomes too large to display within the object, you can quickly resize the object by selecting it and choosing Format⇨Size⇨to Fit.

Displaying Yes/No values with check boxes, option buttons, and toggle buttons

You can use check boxes, option buttons, and toggle buttons to display and edit values stored in Yes/No fields. Figure 37-16 shows a form with a check box (at the top), an option button (in the center), and a toggle button (at the bottom). Technically, you can use these controls with other types of fields, but they are the most useful for Yes/No fields. If the box or button is selected, Access stores a value of true in the field; if not selected, Access stores a value of false in the field. With other field types, Access stores a value of 1 if the option is selected, and a value of 0 if it isn't.

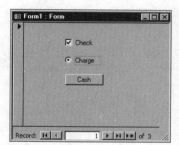

Figure 37-16: A form containing a check box, an option button, and a toggle button.

To create a check box, option button, or toggle button, click on the desired control (check box, option button, or toggle button) in the Toolbox. Then, click on and drag the desired field from the Field List to the form.

Hot Stuff If you use toggle buttons in your forms, you can place bitmaps that contain pictures on the face of the buttons. To do this task, double-click on the button's edge, and choose the Picture property. Then, click on the Build button (the button with the three dots) to the right of the property to open Picture Builder. From within Picture Builder, you can choose one of the available pictures shown, or you can choose a file containing the picture you want and click OK to close the Picture Builder.

Adding list boxes and combo boxes

Additional types of controls that you may want to use in your forms include the *list box* and the *combo box*. List boxes display choices from a predefined list. Combo boxes are similar in design: they let you choose an entry from a predefined list or type in a value. Figure 37-17 shows an example of a form containing a list box.

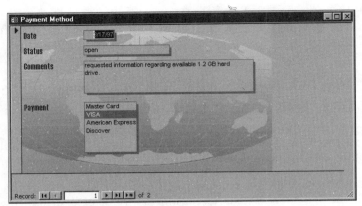

Figure 37-17: A form with a list box.

You can specify the values that the list provides, or you can base the list on data contained in the rows of a table. (You can also use the values retrieved from a SQL SELECT statement or from a Visual Basic function, but techniques for performing these tasks are beyond the scope of this chapter.) Access provides a List Box Wizard and a Combo Box Wizard to make the creation of list boxes and combo boxes a simple matter. To create either a list box or a combo box, you perform these steps:

1. Open the form in Design view and display the Toolbox if it isn't already visible.

2. In the Toolbox, click on the List Box button or the Combo Box button as desired.

3. Click in the form at the location where you want to place the control. The first dialog box for the List Box or the Combo Box Wizard appears.

4. Follow the directions that appear in the dialog boxes of the List Box Wizard or the Combo Box Wizard to place the desired control.

Adding command buttons

Access offers a Command Button Wizard that lets you easily add command buttons to forms. You can use the command buttons to perform common data management operations, such as moving around in the underlying table or printing the current record. For example, Figure 37-18 shows a form containing a number of command buttons.

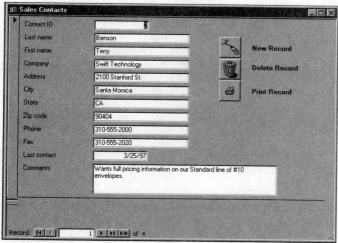

Figure 37-18: A form containing command buttons.

You can create command buttons with the Command Button Wizard by performing the following steps:

1. Open the form in Design view and display the Toolbox if it isn't already visible.

2. In the Toolbox, click on the Command button as desired.

3. In the form, click on the location where you want to place the upper-left corner of the command button.

4. Follow the directions that appear in the dialog boxes of the Command Button Wizard to place the command button.

Adding page breaks

In forms that contain a large number of fields, often you have too much data to fit on a single page. You can add *page breaks* to forms to define how data is broken up for a multipage form. To add page breaks to your form, follow these steps:

1. Open the form in Design view and if the Toolbox isn't already visible, choose View⇨Toolbox to display it.

2. Click on the Page Break button in the Toolbox to select it.

3. Click in the form at the point where you want to place the page break.

Adding pictures and graphics

You can easily insert graphics or pictures from your favorite graphics or photo package (such as CorelDRAW! or Adobe Photoshop) into your forms as design elements. The easiest method of performing this task is to use the Windows Clipboard, as detailed in the numbered steps that follow. When you paste a graphic from the Clipboard into a form, Access automatically adds an unbound object frame containing the graphic to the form. (You can use these same techniques to paste pictures or graphics into reports.)

Alternately, you can add an object frame to a form and change its properties or use the Insert⇨Object command to add OLE objects containing graphics to the form.

You can copy graphics from other Windows packages into an Access form using the following steps:

1. Open the form in Design view.

2. Start the graphics program in the usual manner and then open the document containing the graphic image that you want to insert into the Access form.

3. Using the Windows selection techniques appropriate for the package you are using, select the portion of the graphic that you want to place into the Access form.

4. Choose Edit⇨Copy from your application's menus.

5. Switch back to Access, either with Alt+Tab or with the taskbar.

6. Click on any blank area of the form and choose Edit⇨Paste. The graphic appears within the form.

7. Using the moving and sizing techniques of Access, place the graphic at the desired location in the form. After you've inserted the graphic, you can manipulate it using the original application by double-clicking on the graphic (assuming that the original application supports Windows OLE).

Previewing the Form

At any point during the design process, you can test the form by opening the button menu at the left side of the toolbar and choosing Form view, or by choosing View⇨Form. Using either method, a record appears within the form, and then you can use the PgUp and PgDn keys to view additional records. To return to the design process, open the button menu at the left side of the toolbar and choose Form Design, or choose View⇨Form Design.

Saving a Form

You save a form using the same techniques you used to save other objects in Access: choose File⇨Save, or double-click on the form's Close button and choose Yes in the dialog box that asks if you want to save the changes. If you are saving the form for the first time, Access displays a dialog box that asks for a name for the form; enter the name that you want to give it, and Access saves the form as part of the current database.

Using Forms

To open a previously saved form, double-click on the desired form in the Database window, or click on the form to select it and click on Open. The form opens in a Form view window, where you can work with the data.

When you add records to a database through a form, many of the techniques that you use are the same as the ones you use to add data to a table through a table's datasheet. To add records, you move to the blank record that always exists at the end of any Access table, and you enter the data by choosing Edit⇨Go To⇨New.

Hot Stuff You also can use the navigation buttons that appear at the bottom of the form. Click on the Last Record button and click on the Next Record button to move to the blank record.

As you edit data, you can move between the desired fields by pressing Tab or Shift+Tab. In forms, the up arrow and down arrow keys move you between fields, and PgUp and PgDn move you from record to record. Table 37-3 shows the various navigation keys and key combinations which you can use in a form.

<table>
<tr><td colspan="2" align="center">**Table 37-3**
Navigation keys used in forms</td></tr>
<tr><td>*Key*</td><td>*Purpose*</td></tr>
<tr><td>Home</td><td>Moves to first field in current record.</td></tr>
<tr><td>End</td><td>Moves to last field in current record.</td></tr>
<tr><td>Ctrl+Home</td><td>Moves to first field in first record.</td></tr>
<tr><td>Ctrl+End</td><td>Moves to last field in last record.</td></tr>
<tr><td>Tab, right arrow, or Enter</td><td>Moves to next field (the Enter key may have a different effect if defaults have been changed using View ⇨ Options).</td></tr>
</table>

(continued)

Table 37-3 *(continued)*	
Key	**Purpose**
Shift+Tab	Moves to prior field.
Up arrow	Moves up one line (in text boxes containing multiple lines).
Down arrow	Moves down one line (in text boxes containing multiple lines).
PgUp	Moves up one page, or when at the beginning of a record, moves to top of preceding record.
PgDn	Moves down one page, or when at the end of a record, moves to top of next record.
Ctrl+Tab	In multitable forms, exits a subform and moves to the next field in the main form. In single table forms, moves to the next field.
Ctrl+Shift+Tab	In multitable forms, exits a subform and moves to the preceding field in the main form. In single table forms, moves to the prior field.
Ctrl+Shift+Home	Moves to the first field in the main form.

As you work with forms, you'll find the various options of the View, Edit, and Record menus to be useful. Figure 37-19 shows the Edit menu that appears for an active form. You can use these options to make changes while you are working with the data displayed through the form. Using these options, you can undo previous actions; go to specific records; cut, copy, and paste data between different fields; select records for further action (such as copying and deleting); delete records; find values; search for specific values and replace them with other values; and insert the contents of the Windows Clipboard into fields.

The View menu and its options are shown in Figure 37-20. You can use the options shown in this menu to switch between the three views of forms: Form view, Design view, and Datasheet view. If you are using a multitable form, the Subform Datasheet option is enabled; this option lets you change from Form view in the subform to Datasheet view, if you so desire. The Toolbars option shows or hides the toolbar, or displays a Toolbars dialog box, which you can use to customize the appearance of the toolbars used by Access.

Figure 37-19:
The Edit menu.

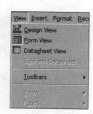

Figure 37-20:
The View menu.

The Records menu offers the options shown in Figure 37-21. You can use these options to apply a filter that restricts the records available in the form to a specific set of records. If a filter was applied previously, the Show All Records option removes the effects of the filter. (Filters are discussed later in this chapter, under the heading "Applying a Filter.") The Save Record option saves the current changes to the underlying table or query (although you can accomplish the same task by moving off the record). The Refresh option is useful on a local area network: it updates the screen with the latest table data, showing any changes that other users have made to the record since you used the form to bring it into view. You use the Data Entry option to switch to data entry mode, which hides all existing records from view while you enter new ones.

Figure 37-21: The Records menu.

Entering data in OLE Object fields

Although you can enter data into OLE Object fields in a form with the same cut-and-paste methods that you use in a datasheet, you can also use Insert⇨Object. Choose Insert⇨Object, and you see the Insert Object dialog box, shown in Figure 37-22.

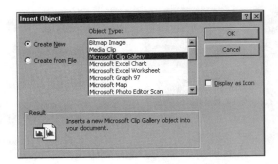

Figure 37-22: The Insert Object dialog box.

To create a new object, select the type of object you want from the list box and click on OK. To add an object based on an existing file, click on the Create from File button, choose the desired file in the dialog box that appears, and click on OK.

If you leave the Create New button selected and click on OK, the application used to create the desired object type opens, and you can create the object. After you've created the object, choose File⇨Exit from the application's menus. A dialog box appears, asking if you want to update the embedded object. Click on Yes, and you return to Access with the embedded object added to the field.

Applying a filter

Access has a new feature called *Filter By Form*, which lets you filter records (or limit the available records a user can view through the form) by using the form to set your selection criteria. For example, if you want to see all records with the word *Spain* in a Country field in a table that contains international addresses, you can use Filter By Form to restrict the records available in the form to only those records that have *Spain* in the Country field. To use this feature, follow these steps:

1. With the form open in Form view, click on the Filter By Form button in the toolbar, or choose Records ⇨ Filter⇨Filter By Form. The form reappears with no data in any of the fields.

2. Type the criteria into the appropriate fields of the form. You can enter multiple criteria by separating the criteria with the word *Or* or *And*; for example, entering **Spain or Mexico** in a country field filters the form to display records that have either Spain or Mexico in the Country field.

3. After you've entered the desired criteria, click on the Apply Filter button in the toolbar, or choose Filter⇨Apply Filter/Sort. The selected records appear in the form.

Until you tell Access otherwise, the filter remains in effect. If you want to cancel the effects of the filter, click on the Remove Filter button in the toolbar, or choose Records⇨Remove Filter/Sort.

Hot Stuff You can save filters as a part of the form. If you apply a filter and then click on the Save button in the toolbar, or choose File⇨Save, Access stores the filter along with the form.

Basing new forms or reports on filters

While a filter is active, you can create another form or report that uses the same filtered data. You use these steps to perform this task:

1. With the filtered records displayed, click on the arrow to the right of the New Object button in the toolbar to open the button menu.

2. To use the AutoForm or AutoReport Wizard, choose AutoForm or AutoReport from the menu. If you want to control all design aspects of the new form or report, choose New Form or New Report.

3. Complete the design or make any other changes you want to the form or report, then save it. Then you can use the form or report, and it uses your filter's design to retrieve data.

Note Another, easy way to filter for specific information while using a form is to right-click in any field you want to filter by and choose Filter For from the next menu which appears. In the text box, enter the value you are searching for.

Printing a Form

If you need a printed copy of a single record, you can print the contents of a form; you can also print every record in the underlying table or query used by the form. To print data in the form layout, perform these steps:

1. Open the form (or in the Database window, select the form).

2. To print just a single record, find the record you want and click on the record selector (at the far left edge of the form), or choose Edit⇨Select Record.

3. Choose File⇨Print to display the Print dialog box, shown in Figure 37-23.

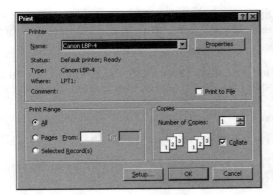

Figure 37-23: The Print dialog box.

4. To print a selected record, click on the Selected <u>R</u>ecord option in the Print Range portion of the dialog box. To print all records, leave the <u>A</u>ll option selected. Make any additional choices in the dialog box, and click on OK to begin printing.

Converting a form into a report

Sometimes, you may need to create a report similar in design to a form you have already created. Rather than design the report from scratch, you can use Access to save the form as a report. To save a form as a report, follow these steps:

1. In the Database window, right-click on the desired form and choose Save As Report from the shortcut menu that appears.

2. A Save Form as Report dialog box appears, asking for a name for the report. Enter a desired name and click on OK to save the report. You can then use the report as you would use any other report. (You'll find more specifics on reports in Chapter 38.)

Creating Multitable Forms Manually

One of the strengths of Access is the ease with which you can create *multitable forms*, or forms that display data from more than one table at a time. Figure 37-24 shows an example of a multitable form; the form displays a single record from a table of employees, along with data from another table containing all the hours worked by the employee.

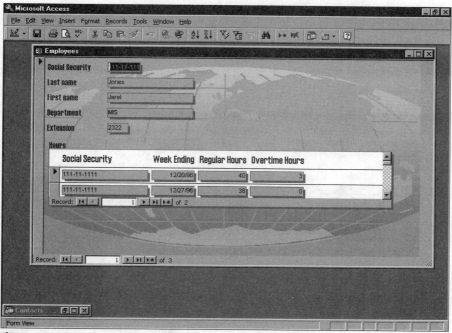

Figure 37-24: A multitable form.

Keep in mind that you can use the Form Wizards to create this type of form. However, if for some reason you want to create a multitable form manually, you can do this task by performing these steps:

1. Open the main form in Design view.

2. Switch to the Database window and click on the Forms tab to display all your stored forms.

3. Drag the form that you want to use as a subform from the Database window to the main form. When you drop the icon onto the main form, a subform control appears, as shown in the lower half of Figure 37-25. You then can place the subform control at the desired location in the main form.

4. Right-click on the subform and choose Properties from the shortcut menu. When the Properties window opens, click on the Data tab.

5. Look in the Link Master Fields property. If an entry already exists, you need to make sure that Access created the link using the fields you want. If Access was unable to establish the link, type the name of the field that should be used as a link to the records within the subform.

You can click on the button with the three periods to the right of the property to bring up the Subform Linker dialog box. In this dialog box, you can choose the fields you want to use as links from the list boxes which appear.

6. Close the form and save it using the methods described earlier for saving forms.

When you bring up a multitable form in Form view, records for the main table appear in the main portion of the form, and all associated records appear within the subform, as illustrated earlier in Figure 37-24.

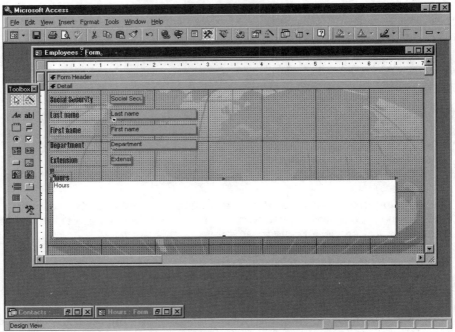

Figure 37-25: The subform control in a main form shown in Design view.

Note   Step 5 deals with the fact that multitable forms you create manually may or may not have a proper relational link between the tables. You need to verify the existence of a working link between the main form and the subform by opening the Properties window.

Access automatically establishes the proper link if a relationship was defined at the table level. Access also establishes an automatic link when fields having the same name and type exist on the main form and the subform, and the main form's matching field is a key field in the underlying table. If Access is unable to establish the proper link, the Link Master Fields property will be blank. When this happens, you need to type in the name of the desired field, or click on the button at the right side of the Link Master Fields property to bring up a Subform Linker dialog box where you can choose the desired fields to establish the link.

Creating Tabbed Forms

One feature that is new to Access 97 is the use of tabbed forms. Tabbed forms contain multiple tabs, and each tab can contain different fields or other design objects. In functionality, tabbed forms are similar to the tabbed dialog boxes used by many Windows 95 products to set various system options. Figure 37-26 shows an example of a tabbed form in Access.

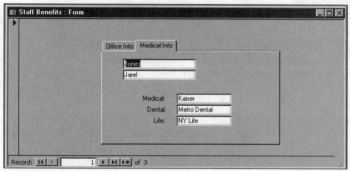

Figure 37-26: Tabbed form displays employee office information on one tab and medical information on another.

To create a tabbed form, you use the Tab Control of the toolbox. You can use the following steps to create a tabbed form:

1. Open the form in Design view.

2. If the Toolbox isn't visible, choose View⇨Toolbox to display it.

3. In the Toolbox, click the Tab Control tool.

4. In the form, click at the upper-left corner where you want to place the control and drag to the lower-right corner to size the control as needed. When you release the mouse button, Access adds a tabbed control containing two tabs, as shown in Figure 37-27.

5. To add controls to the tabs, click the desired tab to select it and add the desired controls by dragging them from the Field List, or by placing them with the Toolbox.

6. To add additional tabs, select the tab which a new tab should follow and choose Edit⇨Copy. Then choose Edit⇨Paste to add the new tab.

7. To change the title of a tab, double-click the desired tab to open a Property window for that tab of the form. Click the Format tab and enter the desired title in the Caption text box.

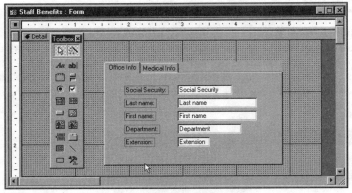

Figure 37-27: A tabbed control shown in Design view.

As you work on the design of a tabbed form, remember that you can test the form at any time by clicking the View button in the Standard toolbar, or by choosing Form⇨View.

Summary

In this chapter, you learned how to create and work with forms in Access. This chapter covered the following points:

✦ You can quickly create a default form for any table or query by selecting the table or query in the Database window and choosing the AutoForm option of the New Object toolbar button.

✦ You can easily create a form while exercising some control over the form's appearance by using the Form Wizards to create your desired forms.

✦ You can design forms manually by starting with a blank form and using the Toolbox and the Fields List to add desired objects (such as text boxes, labels, and graphics) to the form.

✦ You can right-click on any control that you want to add to a form and choose Properties from the menu which appears to change various properties for the control.

✦ You can add controls that contain expressions to perform specialized calculations within your forms.

✦ You can add pictures and graphics as design elements.

✦ You can use a feature of Access called Filter By Form to limit the records that can be viewed through the form.

✦ Access lets you create multitable forms manually or with the aid of the Form Wizards. With multitable forms, you can view data from more than one table at a time.

In the following chapter, you learn how to create and produce reports to provide printed or visual summaries of your data.

Where to go next...

✦ Access is a relational database, and most likely, you will need forms that simultaneously deal with multiple tables. You can find additional coverage of this topic in Chapter 41.

✦ Graphs are a kind of form that let you visually highlight numeric information stored within your tables. For specific details on designing and using graphs, take a look at Chapter 43.

✦   ✦   ✦

Working with Reports

This chapter details the use of reports, which are the desired end result of many of your database management tasks in Access. Using reports, you can display your data in virtually any format with different levels of detail. Although you can structure queries to obtain the specific data you need, you'll want to use reports to produce a visual or printed record of that data. Access reports can be quite visual in nature: you can include lines, boxes, pictures, and graphics in a report.

 **More Info** This chapter focuses on reports that use only one table. *Relational reports*, or reports which make use of more than one table, are covered further in Chapter 41.

Access offers many ways to produce reports, all varying in complexity. You can use the AutoReport menu option of the New Object button to produce, in a single step, a default report based on any table or query in the database. You can use the Report Wizards to design reports that provide a fair level of customization for a given reporting need. (Like their Form Wizards counterparts, the Report Wizards ask a series of questions about the type of report desired, its overall style, and the fields you want to use. After you answer these questions, Access creates the report, and you can use it as-is or further modify it manually.) Finally, you can exercise complete control over a report's design by working with the report in the Report Design window.

The Available Report Types

Nearly all reports that you can create in Access fall into one of three categories:

✦ **Groups/totals reports** — These reports, also known as *tabular reports*, display data in rows, with each field's data occupying a separate column. Figure 38-1 shows an example of a groups/totals report.

✦ **Columnar reports** — These reports, also known as *form-oriented reports*, display all fields in a single column, usually aligned at the left side of the page. Columnar reports often resemble forms, but they are used only to display or print the data, not to enter or edit data. Figure 38-2 shows an example of a columnar report.

✦ **Mailing labels** — These reports display the printed data to appear as mailing labels, like the reports shown in Figure 38-3. Access provides a Report Wizard specifically designed to produce mailing labels that fit a variety of formats, including most Avery label sizes.

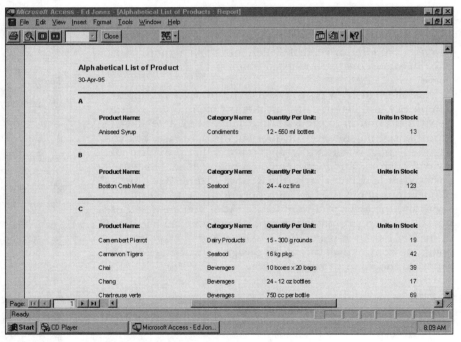

Figure 38-1: A groups/totals report.

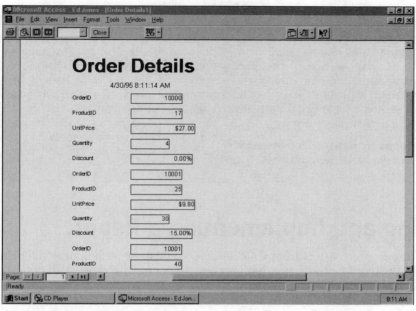

Figure 38-2: A columnar report.

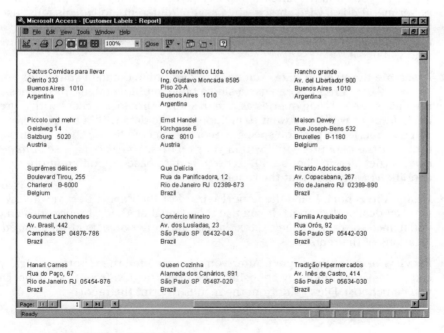

Figure 38-3: Mailing labels.

Forms versus reports

In Access, forms and reports share many control types and design techniques. Because you can print both forms and reports in Access, sometimes you may find it hard to determine what will do a better job of serving a particular need.

Generally, forms are designed for interactive use, whereas you use reports when you need to display or print summaries or details for groups of records. The job of data entry and editing will always be the province of forms; other than data entry and editing, anything that you can do with a form, you can do with a report. Reports also can display or print records in groups, something that you can't do with forms.

Planning and Implementing a Report

To get the desired results from your reports, you'll need to include some planning steps in the overall report creation process. The complete process of creating a report includes the following steps:

1. **Define the report's layout.** Before you start laying out a report, either with the Wizards or manually (by manipulating objects through the Report Design window), you should define the report's layout mentally or on paper. The on-paper method is a wise choice when several different individuals must use the resulting report: passing around a hand-drawn sketch can help refine a report design and ensure that the final product serves the needs of those who will use it.

2. **Assemble the needed data.** You need to determine the data source for your reports. Access reports can use a single table, multiple tables, or queries as the data source. Using queries as a data source provides Access with a great deal of power when you want to include specific data within a report. You can use queries to provide specific records, selected fields, and a given sort order for the data presented within your reports. You also can use *parameter queries* (detailed in Chapter 40) to provide data based on different query conditions each time that the report runs.

3. **Design the report.** Using the Report Wizard or the Report Design window, you can design the report. If you use the manual method of report design, you'll need to place the fields, text labels, and other objects at the desired locations of the report.

4. **Preview or print the report.** After you've completed the report's design, you can preview the report by choosing File⇨Print Preview from the menus. Or, you can choose File⇨Print from the menus to print the report.

Creating a Report with AutoReport

You can use the New Object button on the toolbar to create a default columnar report for any table or query that is selected or active when you choose the AutoReport option from the button's menu. To generate an AutoReport, open the desired table or query, or click on the table or query in the Database window to select it. Click on the down arrow to the right of the New Object button to open the button's menu and choose AutoReport from the menu. After you complete this process, Access creates a default columnar report, such as the one shown in Print Preview mode in Figure 38-4.

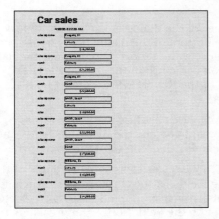

Figure 38-4: A typical report created with AutoReport.

As you can see from the figure, the AutoReport option gives you a columnar style of report with all the fields aligned in a single column at the left side of the page. Field names appear to the left of the fields as labels, and the name of the underlying table or query appears at the top of the first page. If you want any other type of report, you need to use the Report Wizards or use manual report design.

Creating Reports Using the Report Wizards

For ease of use and flexibility, you can't beat the Report Wizards. Like other wizards throughout Access, the Report Wizards ask a series of questions about the report that you are designing, and they produce a report based on your answers to those questions. You can use Report Wizards to create columnar reports, tabular reports with or without groups, mailing labels, or summary reports. You create a report with the Report Wizards by performing the following steps:

1. In the Database window, click on the Reports tab and click on New. After you do these tasks, the New Report dialog box appears, shown in Figure 38-5.

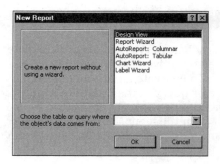

Figure 38-5: The New Report dialog box.

2. In the list box at the upper-right corner of the dialog box, click on Report Wizard. Then, in the list box near the bottom of the dialog box, choose the table or query that will supply the data for the report. (If you want the data to come from more than one table, you can click on the primary table.) Then, click on OK to display the first of the Report Wizard dialog boxes, shown in Figure 38-6.

3. In this dialog box, you use the Tables/Queries list box to choose tables or queries as the report's source of data, and you use the Available Fields and Selected Fields list boxes to place the fields that you want in the report.

   After you select a data source in the Tables/Queries list box, all fields of that table or query appear in the Available Fields list box. You can click on a field to select it and then click on the right-arrow button to add it to the Selected Fields list box, or you can double-click on the field. Notice the presence of the double-arrow button; you can click on this button to add all the fields in the Available Fields list box to the Selected Fields list box. If you make a mistake and want to remove a field from the Selected Fields list box, click on the unwanted field in the Selected Fields list box and click on the left-arrow button to remove the field from the list.

4. If you want to base the report on more than one table and you have added all the fields you want from the first table, choose another table in the Tables/Queries list box and add the desired fields from that table. You're not required to use queries for reports based on more than one table; you can use a query, or you can select one table, add fields from the table, then select another table, and add fields from that table. After you finish adding the fields, click on Next to proceed.

   The dialog box that you now see depends on whether you have chosen fields from a single table or from more than one table. If you have chosen fields from more than one table, you see the dialog box shown in Figure 38-7. (Reports that make use of fields from more than one table are known as *relational reports*. Chapter 41 covers them in detail.)

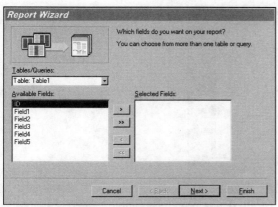

Figure 38-6: The first Report Wizard dialog box.

5. Using the options shown in this dialog box, you choose which table you want to use to group the data shown in your report. Click on the desired table in the list box to select it and click on Next. After you click on Next (or, if you originally chose fields from only one table) you see the Report Wizard dialog box shown in Figure 38-8.

6. If you want to specify the field(s) that Access should use to group the records, you can select each field and click on the right arrow button to add a group band for the field to the report. (Group bands are sections of a report that allow records within the report to be divided into groups.) After choosing the grouping, click on Next.

7. The next dialog box you see asks for a sort order for your records (Figure 38-9). You can sort the records in a report by up to four fields. Choose any desired sort order by selecting the desired fields in the list boxes and click Next, or, if you don't want a sort order within the report, leave the boxes blank and click Next.

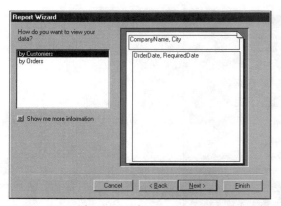

Figure 38-7: The second Report Wizard dialog box (for multiple tables).

If you want to sort the data in the report by more than four fields, don't panic. Just use the query as the data source for the report and sort the fields of the query in the desired order. Leave the sorting options within the report blank. The records shown in the report will appear in the order specified by the query.

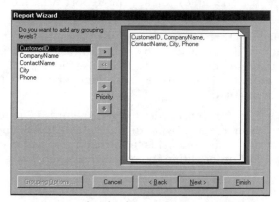

Figure 38-8: The third Report Wizard dialog box.

8. The next dialog box that appears (Figure 38-10) asks you to specify a columnar, tabular, or justified layout for the report, whether you want the report to use portrait or landscape format and whether Access should adjust the field width so that all the fields will fit on a single page. Enter the choices you want and click on Next.

9. The next dialog box that appears (Figure 38-11) lets you choose a report style from a list box. Access offers a number of different report styles, and a representative sample of each style appears in the dialog box as you click on each style name. Select the style you want and click on Next to proceed.

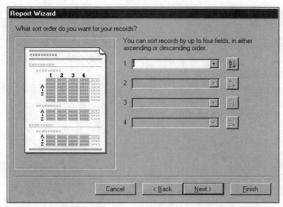

Figure 38-9: The fourth Report Wizard dialog box.

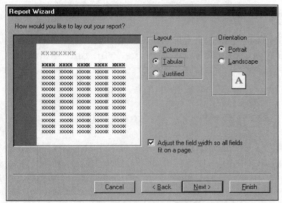

Figure 38-10: The fifth Report Wizard dialog box.

10. The final dialog box to appear asks for a title for the report. Using the options in the dialog box, you can choose to preview the report or open it in Design view where you can make additional changes to the report's design.

When you close a new report that you haven't saved yet, Access asks if you want to save the report. Click on Yes in the dialog box, and Access asks for a name for the report. Enter any name of up to 64 characters, with or without spaces, and click on OK. Access saves the report to the current database.

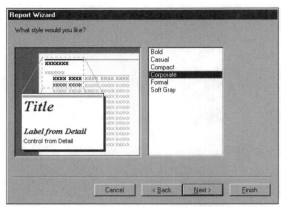

Figure 38-11: The sixth Report Wizard dialog box.

Printing the report

You can print the report by selecting it in the Database window and choosing File⇨Print (or, by selecting the report and clicking on the Print button in the toolbar). For additional details, refer to "Printing Reports" later in this chapter.

Designing Custom Reports

If the reports you can create with the New Object menu or the Report Wizards don't provide the kind of design flexibility that you need, you must resort to using the custom design capabilities of Access to create your report manually. You can open a blank report and then place fields in desired locations, add custom headers and footers, specify grouping, and set formatting attributes. Although the exact procedure varies depending on the type of report that you want to create, the following steps outline the general process of creating a report manually:

On what do I base my reports?

One decision that you have to make early in the report design process is what data source you should use for your report. In the New Report dialog box that appears when you begin designing a report, you can select any table or query in your database as the report's data source. Unless you're sure that the report should include every scrap of data in a table, you'll want to use a query that provides you with the specific data needed by the report. You can find more information on creating and using queries in Chapter 36.

1. In the Database window, click on the Reports tab and click on New. After you do this task, the New Report dialog box appears, as shown earlier in Figure 38-5.

2. Leave Design view selected in the list box, click on the down arrow next to the Choose a Table or Query text box to open the list box, and click on the name of the table (or query) that should provide the data for the report.

More Info

If the data that you need for the report is stored in more than one table, you need to design a relational query and use it as the source of data; for information on designing relational queries, see Chapter 39.

3. Click on OK. Access displays a blank report in the Report Design window, as shown in Figure 38-12.

4. Place fields, text labels, pictures or graphics, and other design objects at the locations where you want them within the report.

5. Add any needed bands to establish sorting or grouping within the report. (You'll find more details about how such bands are used under the heading "Enabling Sorting and Grouping in a Report" later in this chapter.)

6. Choose File⇨Save to save the completed report.

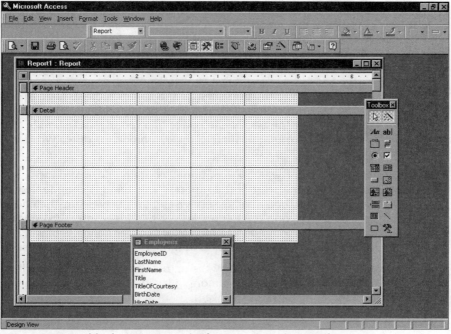

Figure 38-12: A blank report open in the Report Design window.

If you want to modify the design of an existing report, you can bring up that report in a Report Design window by selecting the report in the Reports tab of the Database window and clicking on the Design button, or by right-clicking on the report in the Database window and choosing Design from the shortcut menu that appears.

As you begin the report design process, you work in the Report Design window, shown earlier in Figure 38-12. You can think of this window as a drawing area where you visually create the report's structure by placing and positioning controls, tying controls to fields in the underlying tables or queries, adding lines or graphics, and changing the properties of controls placed in the report.

Hot Stuff   When you're in the Report Design window, the toolbar contains a Preview button at the far left. At any point during the design process, you can click on this button to see what the report will look like, based on actual data. Also, keep in mind that if you make a change or addition to a report that you don't care for later, you can choose Edit⇨Undo command from the menus to undo the effects of the change.

Understanding the Reports Layout

The report's layout is composed of a number of different parts, as Figure 38-13 shows. Access uses the band-oriented style of report design that is commonly used by database management software: with this design style, every report is divided into a series of bands:

✦ **Page Header bands** appear once at the start of each page of a report. Typically, you insert information such as the names of fields that should appear above columns of data in this area. Correspondingly, *Page Footer bands* appear once at the end of each page of a report; these bands are typically used for information such as page numbers or other types of footnotes.

✦ **Report Header bands**, which are optional, contain information which should appear just once at the start of the report. (This band is commonly used for report titles.) *Report Footer bands* serve a similar purpose for the end of the report; any data placed in the Report Footer band is printed just once at the end of the report. (A common use for Report Footer bands is placing summary fields that provide the total of numeric or currency values.)

✦ The **Detail band** is used to identify the actual data that appears within the body of the report. Fields are commonly placed here; you can also include labels identifying the fields if you want.

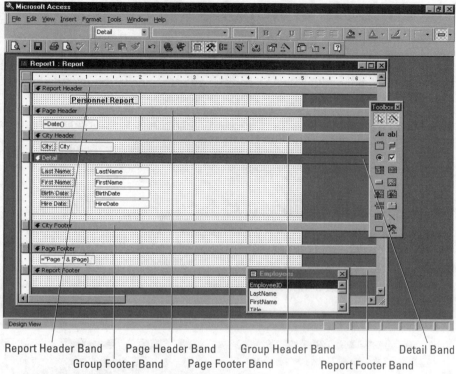

Report Header Band   Page Header Band   Group Header Band   Detail Band

         Group Footer Band   Page Footer Band

                                           Report Footer Band

Figure 38-13: The parts of a report layout.

✦ **Group bands**, which are optional, appear once for each specified group of records; when you add Group bands, you specify how the data in the report is to be grouped. For example, with a report containing dozens of customer records from different cities, you may choose to group the report based on the contents of the City field. The report would be sorted by the City field, and each time that the name of the city changes, a new group begins within the report.

Note   You can easily resize any of the bands by holding the mouse pointer above the band's border (where it changes shape to a double-headed arrow) and dragging the border up or down as desired.

Using Controls in Reports

After you establish the drawing area, you can insert the controls your report needs to accomplish the desired result. You can use the Toolbox (choose View⇨Toolbox from the menus to display it), the Field List (choose View⇨Field List from the menus to display it), and the different menu options to add and remove fields; add text, lines, shapes, or graphics; and change the layout of the report. Note that a great deal of the information that follows is covered in the preceding chapter in greater detail because techniques for working with controls in forms are virtually identical to the techniques used to work with controls in reports. These common techniques are repeated here in condensed form so you don't have to refer back to the chapter on forms.

Adding controls bound to fields

Many controls that you add to reports are *bound controls*, or controls that are tied to the fields of an underlying table or query. You can quickly add bound controls by opening the Field List if it isn't already visible (Choose View⇨Field List), and clicking on and dragging the desired field from the list to the desired location on the report. Figure 38-14 shows the process of dragging a field from the Field List into a report.

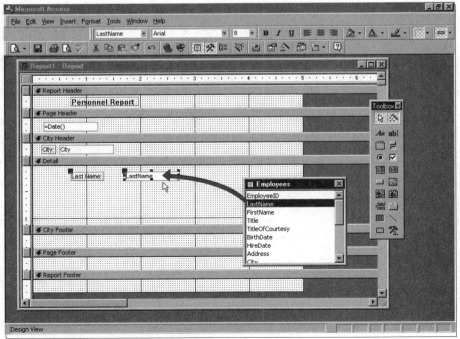

Figure 38-14: Dragging a field into a report.

You can select and place multiple fields simultaneously (with each successive field appearing beneath the previous one) by clicking on the first desired field in the list, pressing and holding down Shift, and clicking on the last desired field to select them as a group. Then, click on any of the selected fields and drag the group to the location where you want it within the report.

Hot Stuff You can quickly select all the fields in the Field List by double-clicking on the title bar of the Field List.

Selecting controls

Before you can resize, move, or otherwise work with a control, you have to select it. To select any control, click once anywhere within the control. *Moving handles* and *sizing handles* appear around the control after you select it. For example, in Figure 38-15, the First Name field appears selected.

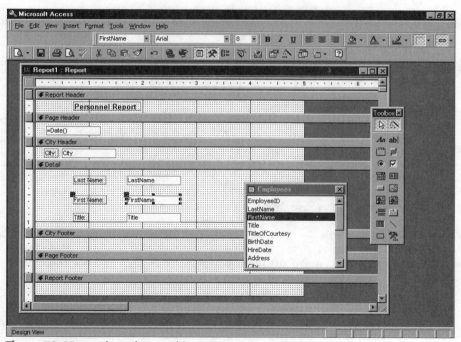

Figure 38-15: A selected control in a report.

Additionally, controls that you use to display data from fields usually have a label that appears along with the text box. The following list describes how you can select and work with the various controls you use in your reports.

✦ **Selecting adjacent controls** — To select a group of adjacent controls, place the mouse pointer above and to the left of the first control in the group, and click on and drag through all the desired controls.

✦ **Selecting nonadjacent or overlapping controls** — To select controls that are nonadjacent (not beside each other) or controls that overlap, press and hold down Shift, and then click on each desired control.

✦ **Selecting all controls** — To select every control on a report, choose Edit⇨Select All.

✦ **Moving controls** — To move a control, select it as described previously and move the mouse pointer to the border of the control. After the pointer changes to the shape of a hand, click on and drag the control to the desired location.

Hot Stuff

You can move a text box control separately from its attached label (or move the label separately from the control) by selecting the control or label and moving the mouse pointer to the upper-left corner of the control or the label, where it changes to the shape of an outstretched finger. Then, click on and drag the control or label to the desired location.

✦ **Sizing controls** — To resize a control, select the control and click on and drag any of the control's sizing handles (where the pointer changes shape to a double-arrow) until the control reaches the size you want.

✦ **Aligning controls** — As you move controls around on a report, you can maintain their alignment by holding down Shift as you move them. (When you press and hold down Shift, the controls move horizontally or vertically as you drag the mouse, but not in both directions at the same time.)

✦ **Deleting controls** — To delete a control, select the control and press Delete (or choose Edit⇨Delete). If you want to delete just the label attached to a text box control, make sure that you select the label and not the entire control (click on the upper-left corner of the label to select it).

✦ **Changing labels** — If you want to change the default label assigned to a text box, you can easily perform this task. Double-click on the label, click on the Format tab in the Properties window that opens, and change the Caption property to the desired text.

As with form design, you can add many types of controls to reports using the Toolbox. (If the Toolbox does not appear by default when you open a report in Design view, you can display it by choosing View⇨Toolbox.) The Toolbox used with reports is shown in Figure 38-16.

Figure 38-16: The Toolbox used with report design.

Hot Stuff You can relocate the Toolbox to the side of the Access window by double-clicking on its title bar. To move it back into the Design view window for the report, double-click on any blank space in the Toolbox. You can also resize the Toolbox by clicking and dragging one of its borders.

To add a control to a report using the Toolbox, first click on the type of control you want in the Toolbox. (If you hold the mouse pointer over any of the Toolbox buttons, a ToolTip appears, indicating the purpose of the button.) After you have selected the type of control you want, click on the report in the location where you want the upper-left corner of the control to appear and drag to where you want the lower-right corner of the control to appear. Table 38-1 summarizes the purposes of the Toolbox tools.

Table 38-1
Toolbox tools

Tool	Purpose
Select Objects	Selects, moves, sizes, or edits objects within the report
Control Wizards	Turns the Control Wizards on or off
Label	Adds labels, which are convenient for titles, instructions, or descriptive text
Text Box	Creates text boxes that can display the contents of fields
Option Group	Adds an option group to the report; option groups contain check boxes, option buttons, or toggle buttons within a group

(continued)

Table 38-1 *(continued)*	
Tool	**Purpose**
Toggle Button	Adds toggle buttons that can be used with option groups to select one choice out of many, or individually to indicate a yes/no choice
Option Button	Adds option buttons (also called *radio buttons*) that can be used with option groups to select one choice out of many or individually to indicate a yes/no choice
Check Box	Adds check boxes, which can be used with option groups to select one choice out of many or individually to indicate a yes/no choice
Combo Box	Creates combination boxes, which display the selection of one choice from a list of choices
List Box	Creates combination boxes, which display the selection of one choice of a list of choices
Command Button	Adds a command button; you can add a command button to a report, but it won't do anything because you cannot interact with reports
Image	Inserts a frame that displays a static image
Unbound Object Frame	Inserts a frame that contains an OLE object
Bound Object Frame	Inserts a frame that contains the contents of an OLE object field
Page Break	Inserts a page break at a specified location in the report
Tab Control	Adds a tabbed form with multiple pages
Subform / Subreport	Adds an object containing a subreport
Line	Draws lines in a report
Rectangle	Draws rectangles or squares in a report
More Controls	Opens a new menu used for adding additional controls to the form

When you are done with the Toolbox, you can close it by choosing View⇨Toolbox again, or by clicking on the Close icon in the Toolbox window.

Working with label controls and text

A major portion of your reports consists of controls containing text and having text labels. Because one secret behind great-looking reports is the proper use of text throughout it, you need to be familiar with the ways in which you can best manipulate the location and appearance of the text presented in your reports.

Creating unattached labels

To create text labels that are not attached to a field or expression, you use the Label tool in the Toolbox. You can create unattached labels by performing the following steps:

1. If the Toolbox is not already visible, choose View⇨Toolbox to display it.

2. Click on the Label tool in the Toolbox.

3. Click on the location where you want the first character of the text to appear.

4. Type the text you want to appear in the text label and click anywhere outside the text box to deselect it.

Note   If you are typing in a large amount of text, keep in mind that you can press Shift+F2 to open a Zoom box where you can see more of the text as you type it. Also, if you want to add multiple lines to the text label, press Ctrl+Enter to add a new line.

Changing the appearance of text in a control

To modify the appearance of the text, first select the control by clicking on its border. Then, use the appropriate toolbar list boxes and buttons to change the desired properties of the text. You can change the font used and the font size by selecting the desired font and font size in the Font and Font Size list boxes. You also can use the Bold and Italic buttons on the toolbar to apply boldface or italic styles to the text. Additionally, you can control the alignment of the text by using the Left, Center, and Right alignment buttons on the toolbar.

Working with text boxes attached to fields and expressions

In reports, you commonly use text box controls to display the contents of the fields in the underlying query or table. (You also can use controls to display the results of *expressions*, which are calculations that use Access functions.)

As mentioned earlier in the chapter, to add text boxes attached to fields, you display the Field List if it isn't already visible (choose View⇨Field List), then drag the desired field from the list box to the desired location on the report.

To add text boxes containing expressions, you add the text box using the text box button on the Toolbox. One easy way to add the expression is to type it directly into the text box, beginning with an equal sign. You can use the following steps:

1. If the Toolbox is not already visible, choose View⇨Toolbox to display it.

2. Click on the Text Box tool in the Toolbox.

3. Click on the location in the report where you want to place the text box.

4. Click within the text box and type an equal sign followed by the desired expression.

The expression that you enter depends on what you want to accomplish. For example, you may choose to display a calculation based on the contents of a Salary field multiplied by 6 percent, by entering an expression like =[Salary] * .06. You may enter an expression such as =Date( ) to display the current date, or =Page to display the current page number of the report. If you are entering a particularly lengthy expression, keep in mind that you can press Shift+F2 to open a Zoom box, where you can see more of the expression.

Hot Stuff With expressions, you can make use of the *concatenation operator* (the ampersand character) to combine text strings. For example, a table may have two fields named First name and Last name. If you want a text box control in a report that combines the contents of these fields into a single text expression containing the person's name, you can use an expression such as the following in a text box control:

=[First name] & " " & [Last name]

You can also use expressions to display the results of calculations, or to show the current date, time, or a combination of both. For more details on how to do this, see "Adding Page Numbers and Page Breaks," "Adding the Current Date or Time," and "Adding Calculated Controls to Reports" later in the chapter.

Changing the control's properties

You can change the variety of properties that apply to the control by opening the Property window for the control. To do this task, you perform the following steps:

1. Right-click on the control.

2. From the shortcut menu that appears, choose Properties.

After the Property window opens, you can click on the desired tab (Format, Data, Event, Other, or All) and change the appropriate property. Notice that most properties that affect the display of the contents of the text box are located in the Format tab. These properties include various font size and style properties; alignment; and border styles, colors, and widths.

Two important properties that you can assign to the text box controls you use to display fields containing large amounts of text are the CanGrow and CanShrink properties. Access gives you these options to enable text box controls to grow or shrink vertically, depending on how much text is in the record being displayed or printed. The CanGrow property, when set to Yes, allows the text box control to grow vertically in size to accommodate additional text if the text in the record cannot fit within the confines of the field. The CanShrink property, when set to Yes, allows the text control to shrink vertically if the text in the record does not fill up the field.

Hot Stuff   The CanGrow property is particularly useful with memo fields to allow the fields in your report to expand as needed to contain the entire text of the memo field.

Previewing the Report

At any point during the report design process, you can preview the report to examine an on-screen representation of what the report will look like when printed. To preview the report, choose File⇨Print Preview, or click on the Preview button on the toolbar. Using either method, the preview of the report appears in a window, as shown in Figure 38-17.

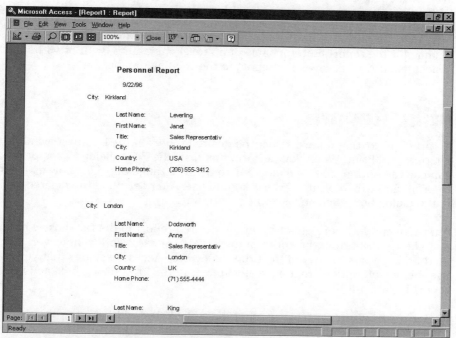

Figure 38-17: An example of a report preview.

You can use the scrollbars or PgUp and PgDn to see more of the current page. You can use the buttons at the lower-left corner of the window to move between pages of the report. The leftmost button moves to the first page, the button beside it moves to the previous page, the rightmost button moves to the last page, and the button beside it moves to the next page.

While in the preview mode, the second and third buttons from the left in the toolbar are the Print and Zoom buttons. You can use the Print button to send the report to the printer. You can click on the Zoom button to alternately zoom in and out of the preview mode. (You can also zoom in and out by placing the mouse pointer over any area of the report in the Preview window and clicking.) When you are done previewing the report, you can click on the Close button in the toolbar to return to the design mode.

Saving Reports

To save a completed report, click on the Save button in the toolbar, or choose File⇨Save. Alternatively, you can just close the Report Design window by clicking on the Close box or pressing Ctrl+F4 and answering Yes to the Save changes prompt that appears. If you're saving the report for the first time, Access asks for a name for the report. Enter a name of up to 64 characters (with or without spaces), and Access saves the report to the existing database.

Printing Reports

To print an existing report, select the desired report in the Database window and choose File⇨Print. When you perform this task, the Print dialog box appears. You can use the options in this dialog box to define a range of pages, how many copies to print, and which printer Access should use. After selecting the desired options in the dialog box, click on OK to begin printing.

Alternatively, you can right-click on the desired report in the Database window and choose Print from the shortcut menu that appears. Notice, however, that this method bypasses the use of the Print dialog box. Access assumes that you want to use the default options that normally appear in the Print dialog box, and the report begins printing.

Hot Stuff   If your reports print with every other page blank, the width of your report is wider than the page width for the type of paper that you are using. If the width of the report exceeds the printable width of the page, Access generates an additional page to contain the added width. Access follows this procedure even when no objects occupy the overflow area, so the result is often a report with a blank page as every other page. The solution to this dilemma is simple: just go back into the report's design and narrow the width of the report by clicking on and dragging the right edge until it measures less than the printable width of your page.

Changing a Reports Data Source

During the initial part of the report design process, you normally indicate the table or queries Access uses as a source of data for the report. When you first create a new report, you choose a table or query name as the data source in the list box of the New Report dialog box. That table or query name is stored to the report's Record Source property. Occasionally, you may need to change the entry in a report's Record Source property. For example, if you create a custom report based on a specific query and you later define and save a new query that you want to use as the same report's data source, you need to change the Record Source property to tell the report to use a different data source. You can change the Record Source property for a report by performing these steps:

1. Open the desired report in Design view.

2. Choose Edit⇨Select Report.

3. If the Properties window isn't already visible, choose View⇨Properties to display it.

4. After the Properties window opens, click on the Data tab.

5. In the Record Source property box, select or type the name of the table or query that should provide the data for the report.

6. Press Alt+F4 to close the Properties window.

7. Save the report in the usual manner.

Note   If you are familiar with the data retrieval language known as SQL, you should note that Access lets you enter SQL statements directly into the Record Source property box. When the report runs, Access then uses the SQL statement as a basis for the record selection.

Enabling Sorting and Grouping in a Report

Often, you'll want the data contained within your reports to appear in a specific order. You can specify a *sort order* as part of a report's design. (If the report is based on a query, you also have the option of specifying a sort order as part of the query's design, to accomplish the same end result.) Additionally, you can also group the records in a report by specific categories, and where the categories are equal, by subcategories.

Sorting and grouping are related because a sort of the data forces the data to appear in groups based on the fields used for the sort. Optionally including group headers and footers is what creates a visual break between the groups of sorted data. For example, Figure 38-18 shows a report with data sorted and grouped by country, and where the data for the country is the same, sorted and grouped by city.

You can base your sorting and grouping on fields or expressions which consist of combinations of fields. (Access lets you include up to ten levels of grouping in a report.) To define sorting and grouping, you use the options in the Sorting And Grouping dialog box. Open the report in Design view, and choose View⇨Sorting And Grouping to reveal the dialog box shown in Figure 38-19.

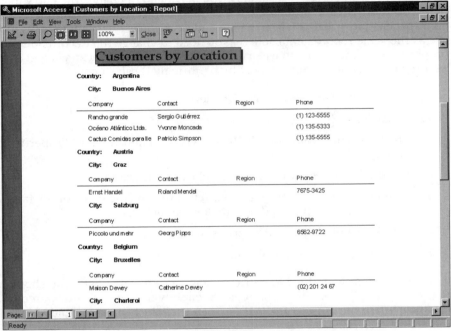

Figure 38-18: An example of sorting and grouping in a report.

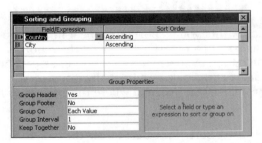

Figure 38-19: The Sorting and Grouping dialog box.

When the Sorting and Grouping dialog box appears, you can specify your sorting and grouping options by performing the following steps:

1. In the first row of the Field/Expression column, open the list box by clicking on the arrow at the right. From the list box, choose the field name on which you want to base the sort. You can type the field name directly into the box or you can type in an expression (such as a combination of field names).

2. In the Sort Order column, if you want a descending sort, click on Descending; otherwise, leave the default of Ascending selected. (Descending sorts from Z to A and from 9 to 0; Ascending sorts from A to Z and from 0 to 9.)

3. If you also want to use the chosen field as a basis for grouping, turn on the Group Header and Group Footer properties shown at the bottom of the dialog box. Changing the Group Header property to Yes creates a group header, whereas changing the Group Footer property to Yes creates a group footer.

4. Repeat steps 1 through 3 for as many levels of sorting and grouping as you want (up to Access' maximum of ten levels). Keep in mind that the priority of the sort occurs from top to bottom in the dialog box; hence, the first row defines the highest level of sorting, followed by the second row, followed by the third row, and so on. For example, the Sorting and Grouping dialog box shown in Figure 38-20 defines three levels of sorting. First, the report is sorted by the Country field; then, where entries in the Country field are the same, by the Region field; and then, where the entries in the Region field are the same, by the City field.

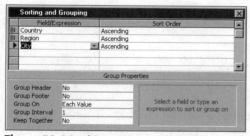

Figure 38-20: This Sorting and Grouping dialog box specifies three levels of sorting.

Adding Page Numbers and Page Breaks

You can include the current page number or the total number of pages in a report by adding the *Page* or *Pages* properties to a text box control. The Page property displays the current page number, whereas the Pages property displays the total number of pages in a report. If you add a text box control to a report and enter the expression =**Page** in the control's Control Source property (or type the expression directly into the text box), the box displays the current page number. Entering an expression such as =**"Page " & Page** produces the page number preceded by the word *Page*, as in *Page 7*. You can use an expression such as =**"Page " & Page & " of " & Pages** to produce text such as *Page 17 of 32* on page 17 of a 32-page report.

To add page breaks to a report, you use the Page Break tool of the Toolbox. Click on the Page Break tool in the toolbar to select it, then click in the section of the report where you want to add the page break. The small dotted line that appears indicates the presence of the page break in the report.

Adding the Current Date or Time

You can use the built-in Access functions of Date( ), Time( ), and Now( ) to add the current date, time, or both to a report. The Date( ) function generates the current date, the Time( ) function generates the current time, and the Now( ) function generates both the date and time. To add any of these features to a report, you perform these steps:

1. Open the report in Design view.
2. Add a text box at the location where you want to display the current date or time.
3. Click inside the text box to place the insertion point there. Enter =**Date( )** to produce the current date enter =**Time( )** to produce the current time, and enter =**Now( )** to produce the current date and time.

You can change the default format used to display the date or time. To do so, right-click on the control you added, choose Properties from the shortcut menu which appears, click on the Format tab in the Properties window, and choose a format from the list box in the Format property.

Adding Calculated Controls to Reports

As with forms, you can add calculated fields to reports to display data based on calculations. You can use any of the valid Access functions within your calculations; in addition to the Date( ) and Time( ) functions mentioned earlier, Access also provides the following functions which may prove useful within calculations:

Function	Purpose
Avg(*value*)	provides an average value in a set of records
Max(*value*)	provides maximum value in a set of records
Min(*value*)	provides minimum value in a set of records
Sum(*value*)	provides a sum (total) of the values

For example, if you want to display a calculation which shows an amount based on the value of a Quantity Ordered field multiplied by the value of a Unit Price field, you can use an expression such as =**[Quantity Ordered] * [Unit Price]** in the text box. You can add a calculated control to a report by performing these steps:

1. Click on the Text Box tool in the Toolbox.

2. Click in the report where you want the upper-left corner of the text box to begin and drag to where you want the lower-right corner.

3. Click once inside the text box and type the desired expression, beginning with an equal symbol. Alternatively, you can right-click on the control and choose Properties from the shortcut menu, click on the Data tab, and enter the desired expression into the Control Source box.

If the calculation that you need in a report is a *running sum* (a sum total of a given field for each page of a report), use the Sum() function, with the field name enclosed in the parentheses of the function. For example, with a field named Order Total, you can use an expression such as =**Sum([Order Total])** in the Page Footer band to display a running total on each page of the report.

Hot Stuff How Access performs the calculation varies depending on the band in which the control is placed. If you want the calculation to apply to a single record, place the calculated field in the Detail band of the report. If the calculation should be based on a group of records, place the field in the appropriate Group band. For calculations that should appear at the bottom of each page, place the field in the Page Footer band. For calculations based on all records in the report, place the field in the Report Footer band.

Adding Pictures and Graphics to a Report

You can include graphics or pictures as design elements in reports. You can insert pictures or graphics from your favorite Windows graphics or drawing package into a report while in Design view. The easiest methods for inserting pictures and graphics work with the Windows Clipboard: when you paste a graphic from the Clipboard into a report, Access automatically adds an unbound object frame containing the graphic to the report. An alternate method is to add an object frame and change its properties, or to choose the Insert⇨Object command to add OLE objects containing graphics to the report. Figure 38-21 shows a graphic inserted into a report, using the techniques outlined in the following list.

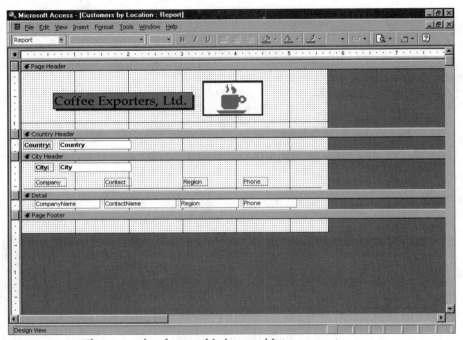

Figure 38-21: The example of a graphic inserted into a report.

Here's how to copy graphics from other Windows packages into an Access report:

1. Open the report in Design view. Start the graphics program in the usual manner, and open the document containing the graphic image that you want to insert into the Access report.

2. Using Windows selection techniques applicable to the package you are using, select the portion of the graphic that you want to place in the Access report. Choose Edit⇨Copy from the application's menus.

3. Use Alt+Tab to switch back to Access. Click on any blank area of the report, and choose Edit⇨Paste. When you perform this task, the graphic appears within the report.

4. Using the moving and sizing techniques of Access, place the graphic at the desired location in the report. After you've inserted the graphic, you can change it using the original application by double-clicking on the graphic (assuming that the original application supports Windows OLE).

You can add graphics fields in tables to your reports in the same manner as you would add any other field: by dragging the field from the Field List to the desired location in the report. After placing the field, you use the sizing techniques described earlier in the chapter to increase the size of the field (as necessary) to show and print the graphics image.

Producing Mailing Labels

One of the common uses of database management programs is handling the mailing needs of businesses. Creating mailing labels is a routine part of this need, and Access makes this job an easy one by providing a Mailing Label Wizard designed specifically for this task.

As with most reports, it's a good idea to first design a query that produces the specific records you need to generate the labels. After the query exists, you can design mailing labels with the following steps:

1. In the Database window, click on the Reports tab and click on New to begin designing a new report. The New Report dialog box appears, as shown earlier in Figure 38-5.

2. Choose Label Wizard in the list box, and choose the desired table or query that contains the fields you want to use for the mailing labels. Click on OK, and the first Label Wizard dialog box appears, shown in Figure 38-22.

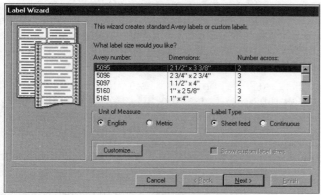

Figure 38-22: The first Label Wizard dialog box.

3. In this dialog box, you choose the desired label size. Scroll down the list to find the label size you want and click on it to select it. Notice that the dialog box contains buttons for English or Metric label sizes. When the default (English) is selected, the label sizes are in inches; if you change this setting to Metric, the list box shows common metric label sizes. You can also select Continuous (used with many dot-matrix printers) or Sheet Feed (used with virtually all laser printers and most inkjet printers) to specify the label type. After you make the desired selections in this dialog box, click on Next.

4. You can use the next dialog box that appears (Figure 38-23) to choose the font, font size, font weight (normal or bold), and text color. Check boxes are also provided to choose Italics or Underlining for the text. Again, you can make the desired selections in the dialog box and click on Next.

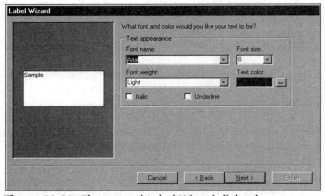

Figure 38-23: The second Label Wizard dialog box.

Note

Using large fonts can cause problems when you need to fit a relatively large amount of information on mailing labels that are relatively small to begin with. Unless you are using large mailing labels, you should avoid using large fonts. The default of 8-point Arial works well with the popular Avery #5160 (three-across) style of labels.

5. The next dialog box (Figure 38-24) provides a list of the fields available from the underlying query or table. You can add fields to your label by clicking on the desired field name in the list box and then the right arrow button. To add punctuation such as spaces or commas, type in the punctuation at the desired location. To move to a new line of a label, just click below the existing line. When you've added the fields and any punctuation to the label, click on Next.

6. The next dialog box to appear (Figure 38-25) asks you to choose a desired sort order for the labels. You can bypass this dialog box by clicking on Next, or you can choose a field or fields as a basis for a sort. (With mailing labels, you want to sort based on a zip code or postal code field because post offices in most nations prefer to receive mail sorted by the zip or postal code.)

For example, to sort on a field named Zip code, you click on the Zip code field and then click on the right arrow button (or alternately, you can double-click on the Zip code field). To sort based on the Country fields and the then City fields, you first click on the Country field and click on the right arrow button to add it to the Sort Order list, you click on the City field, and click on the right arrow button to add it to the Sort Order list. When you've specified a sort order, click on Next.

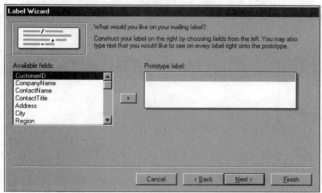

Figure 38-24: The third Label Wizard dialog box.

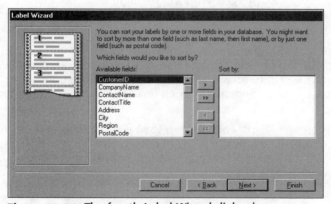

Figure 38-25: The fourth Label Wizard dialog box.

7. The final dialog box that appears tells you that the design of the mailing labels is complete and provides two options: See the labels as they will look printed and Modify the label design. Choosing the first option and clicking on Next displays the labels in preview mode, whereas choosing the second option and clicking on Next opens the report in Design view, where you can perform any additional modifications.

8. Choose File⇨Save to save the report. After you save the report, you can print it at any time as you would print any report by selecting it in the Database window and choosing File⇨Print from the menus.

Danger Zone Before printing mailing labels, make sure that the type of label you are using is the correct type for your printer. Labels designed for use with dot-matrix printers are different in design than labels used with laser printers, and you can damage your printer if you use the wrong type of label.

Using the Word Mail Merge Feature of Access

Working Together Assuming that you are using Word for Windows 97 (after all, it is a major part of your Office software package), you can use the Microsoft Word Mail Merge Wizard to create a mail merge document in Word that links to your data in Access. After you have created the document in Word, you can open and print that document at any time to produce a new set of form letters based on the latest data in your Access tables. Here's how:

1. In the Database window, click on the name of the table or query that contains the data you want to use for the mail merge.

2. Choose Tools⇨OfficeLinks⇨MergeIt With MS Word. In a moment, you see the first dialog box of the Microsoft Word Mail Merge Wizard, shown in Figure 38-26.

3. If you want to use an existing document in Word as the basis for the mail merge, click on the Link your data to an existing Microsoft Word document option and click on OK. Or, to create a new document for the mail merge, click on the Create a new document and then link the data to it option and click on OK.

More Info The wizard launches Microsoft Word, and you can then use the Insert Merge Field option of Word's Merge toolbar to add the fields of the Access table at the desired locations within the Word document. (You can find full details on working with mail merge documents in Word in Chapter 6.)

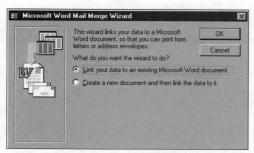

Figure 38-26: The first Microsoft Word Mail Merge Wizard dialog box.

Summary

This chapter detailed the basics of working with reports. The chapter included coverage of the following points:

✦ You can quickly create a default report for any table or query by selecting the table or query in the Database window and choosing the AutoReport option of the New Object toolbar button.

✦ You can easily create a report while exercising some control over the report's appearance by using the Report Wizards to create your reports.

✦ You can design reports manually by starting with a blank report and using the Toolbox and the Fields List to add desired objects, such as text boxes, labels, and graphics, to the report.

✦ You can right-click on any control that you add to a report and choose Properties from the shortcut menu that appears to change various properties for the control.

✦ You can preview a report at any point during the design process by choosing File➪Print Preview, or by clicking the Preview button in the toolbar.

✦ You can print a report by selecting the desired report in the Database window and choosing File➪Print.

✦ You can add a sort order to a report by choosing View➪Sorting and Grouping to open the Sorting and Grouping dialog box while designing the report.

✦ While designing a report, you can also add page numbers or page breaks, the current date or time, calculated controls, or pictures or graphics to a report.

✦ You can use the Mailing Label Wizard to easily produce mailing labels in Access.

Where to go next...

✦ If you need to create reports that contain data from more than one table, see Chapter 41.

✦ Keep in mind that to obtain only the data you want in your reports, you'll want to base your reports on queries. For the complete scoop on designing and using those queries, see Chapter 36, as well as Chapters 39 and 40.

✦   ✦   ✦

Working with Relational Queries

You can use queries to work with data from more than one table at a time. These queries are known as *relational queries*. Chapter 36 touched on the concept of relational queries when it discussed the techniques of adding more than one table to a query and establishing a link between common fields of tables by dragging a field from one table to the other. That chapter emphasized what you can accomplish with simple to moderately complex queries; this chapter details how you can work with your data further with complex relational queries.

Using Relational Queries

You can use relational queries to create a *virtual table*, or a set of data that appears in the form of one table but actually is drawn from several tables. Virtual tables make working with relational data manageable, when compared to working with the tables separately. Figure 39-1 illustrates an example of this process. In this figure, one table contains a list of contact names in a contacts database, and the other contains a list of the phone calls made to each contact. The query shown at the bottom is based on data from both tables and provides a listing of the phone calls made to each contact, along with the contact names.

After you build a relational query, you can create forms or reports and base those forms or reports on your relational queries.

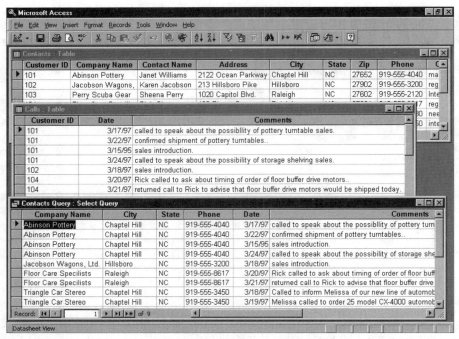

Figure 39-1: A tables and query dynaset from a Contacts Manager database.

Structuring the Relational Query

The overall steps for creating relational queries follow. The sections that follow this list describe these steps further.

1. In the Database window, click on the Queries tab and click on New. The New Query window appears, containing the available query wizards at the right side of the dialog box.

2. Among the available queries, select Design View and click OK. The Query window appears, containing the Show Table dialog box.

3. Add the tables you want by double-clicking on each table in the Show Table dialog box and click on Close to put away the Show Table dialog box.

4. Create the relational joins you need between the tables by dragging the common field or fields from one table to another. After you do this, lines appear connecting the tables. (If default relationships were established between the tables at the database level, Access adds the default relational joins.)

5. Add the desired fields to the query by dragging the field names from the Field Lists to the query columns.

6. Add any criteria, sorting specifications, and calculated fields that you need to the query's design.

7. Save and run the query.

Add multiple tables to the query

The first two steps outlined in the preceding section involve opening the new query and adding multiple tables to it. After you click on the Queries tab in the Database window, click on New, choose Design View, and then click on OK. Access displays an empty Query Design window with the Show Table dialog box placed above it, as shown in Figure 39-2.

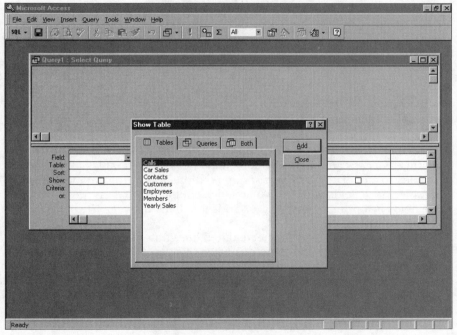

Figure 39-2: The empty Query Design window with the Show Table dialog box placed in front of it.

In the Show Table dialog box, you add each table needed in the query by double-clicking on the table name, or by clicking on the table to select it and clicking on the Add button in the dialog box. After you add each table, a Field List for the added table appears in the Query Design window. (An alternate way to add tables to the Query Design window is to drag them from the Database window and drop them into the upper half of the Query Design window.)

Create relational joins

After you have added multiple tables to a query's design, you must connect the common field(s) of the table with *join lines*. Using join lines, you connect the primary key of one table to the foreign key of another. (In a relationship, a foreign key is a key field or fields providing a match to the primary key.) Figure 39-3 shows a join line between the Contacts table and the Calls table.

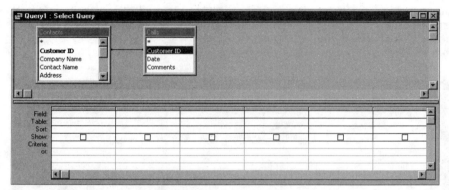

Figure 39-3: A join line between tables.

Sometimes Access automatically adds join lines between tables as you add multiple tables to a query. If you have set up relationships at the database level or if two tables have fields with the same name, compatible data types, and one of these fields is a primary key; Access adds join lines between the fields for you.

When Access does not add the needed join lines automatically, you must use drag-and-drop techniques to add them manually. Click on a field in the Field List for one table and drag it over to the matching field for the other table. After you perform this task, a join line appears in the Query Design window, indicating a relational join between the two tables. You can add as many tables as you need and create an additional join line for each table that you add.

Hot Stuff When you add several tables to a single query, the join lines can cross or overlap, making them look pretty confusing. You can drag the Field Lists around within the Query Design window so that you can see the join lines more clearly, although in some cases it's impossible to avoid having the join lines cross.

After you have established the relational links between the tables, the remaining steps of the relational query design process are the same as the steps for designing nonrelational queries. You add the fields you want to the Field row of the query grid by dragging them from the Field Lists to the appropriate columns in the Query Design window. In the Criteria row, you can specify any desired criteria that select the subset of data that you want. You also can change the sorting options for the query; Chapter 36 covers all of these options individually. Figure 39-4 shows an example of using a relational query on the tables, and Figure 39-5 shows the results of the query after the query runs.

When you create joins by clicking on and dragging a field from one table to the matching field of another, Access creates an *equi-join*, a join in which Access provides records from both tables when the values in their joined fields match. Access also lets you create *outer joins* (in which Access retrieves records from one of the tables whether a matching record is found in the other table or not) and *self-joins* (in which a field in a table is linked to a different field in the same table). (You learn how to change the type of join in "Changing the Default Join Type," later in this chapter.)

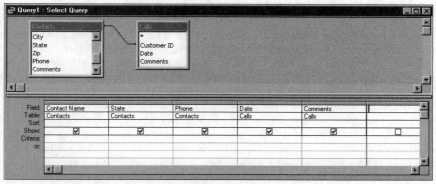

Figure 39-4: An example of a relational query.

Contact Name	State	Phone	Date	Comments
Janet Williams	NC	919-555-4040	3/17/97	called to speak about the possibility of pottery turntable sales.
Janet Williams	NC	919-555-4040	3/22/97	confirmed shipment of pottery turntables..
Janet Williams	NC	919-555-4040	3/15/95	sales introduction.
Janet Williams	NC	919-555-4040	3/24/97	called to speak about the possibility of storage shelving sales.
Karen Jacobson	NC	919-555-3200	3/18/97	sales introduction.
Rick Simpson	NC	919-555-8617	3/20/97	Rick called to ask about timing of order of floor buffer drive motors..
Rick Simpson	NC	919-555-8617	3/21/97	returned call to Rick to advise that floor buffer drive motors would be s
Melissa Jones	NC	919-555-3450	3/18/97	Called to inform Melissa of our new line of automobile CD-players.
Melissa Jones	NC	919-555-3450	3/19/97	Melissa called to order 25 model CX-4000 automobile CD-players..

Record: ◄ ◄ 1 ► ►I ►* of 9

Figure 39-5: The results of a relational query.

Note   Fields that you use to establish a join must have the same data type, with one exception: you can join an AutoNumber field to a Number field whose Field Size property is Long Integer.

Deleting joins and tables

If Access adds a join that isn't exactly the type of relationship you had in mind, you can delete the join. To do this, click on the join line to select it and press Delete. (You can also right-click on the line and choose Delete from the Shortcut menu that appears.) You also can remove the tables that you no longer need from a query's design. Just click anywhere in the table's Field List and press Delete to remove the table from the design.

Limitations of Relational Queries

As you work with relational queries, keep in mind that limitations exist for editing the data in the resulting dynaset. One of the longtime claims to fame of Access is that it lets you edit data in a query or dynaset and reflects the changes in the underlying tables. This feature usually works with relational queries as well, but some limitations apply. You can't edit key fields on one side of the relationship when you've established referential integrity at the database level and included the key field as part of the relationship. (Typically, you can update all fields on the *many* side of the relationship in a one-to-many query.) Also, you can't edit fields when the query includes crosstabs or totals or when the Unique Values Only property is active for the query. (For more specifics on defining referential integrity at the database level, see Chapter 35. For specifics on working with queries that include crosstabs, see Chapter 40.)

Changing the Default Join Type

By default, when you create a join by dragging and dropping a field onto a matching one (or when Access creates a join automatically), Access creates an equi-join type of join. (In database terminology, equi-joins are also known as *inner joins*.) With equi-joins, Access adds records to the resulting dynaset when the linked field for a record in one table matches the linked field in the record of the other table. If the table with the foreign key has *orphan* records, or records that do not match any records in the table with the primary key, those records do not appear in the query's dynaset. The term *orphan record* comes from the fact that the table containing the primary key is sometimes called the *parent table*, and the related table the *child table*. The term *orphan* implies children without parents, or records in the related (child) table having no matches in the primary (parent) table. The presence of orphan records is usually a sign that data has been entered incorrectly at some point.

You don't have to settle for that default Query window!

By default, tables that you add to a query's design appear in the *top pane,* or the area of fixed size at the top of the Query Design window. The query grid appears in the *bottom pane* of the Query Design window. For queries based on multiple tables, you may find it advantageous to resize the top pane so that you can see more of the area containing the query grid. You can resize the panes of the Query Design window by plac-

ing the mouse pointer over the thick line dividing the panes (where the pointer changes shape to a double-headed arrow) and clicking on and dragging the line upward or downward as desired. The figure below is an example of a Query Design window in which the top pane has been expanded to give a better view of the tables involved in the relationship.

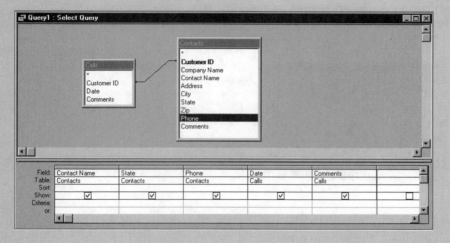

A warning about missing joins

If you omit a join line in an Access table, the resulting dynaset is incorrect and displays erroneously large amounts of data. The reason is that when a join line is left out of a query, Access joins every record in one table with every record in the other table. The result is something called a Cartesian pro-

duct, or a cross product of the two tables. For example, omitting a join for a query containing two tables (each having 200 records) produces a dynaset with 40,000 records, of which 39,800 of the records are absolutely meaningless.

Sometimes the type of join you want is an *outer join*, in which Access includes records from one of the two linked tables whether or not all records in the other table have matching entries. Access lets you change the default join type to *left outer joins* or *right outer joins*. Left outer joins are those joins that include all records in the first table, whether all records in the second table have a match for them or not. Right outer joins are those joins that include all records in the second table, whether all records in the first table have a match for them or not. (The other type of join that Access supports, the *self-join*, is created by adding the same table to a query twice; this type of join is discussed in "Creating Self-Joins," later in the chapter.)

To change the type of join, open the query in Design view and double-click on the join line between the tables (or click on the line to select it, right-click on the line, and choose Join Properties from the shortcut menu that opens). The Join Properties dialog box appears, shown in Figure 39-6.

Figure 39-6: The Join Properties dialog box.

The first option (the default) listed in the Join Properties dialog box produces an equi-join, the second option produces a right outer join, and the third option results in a left outer join. When you click on the desired option and then click on OK, the appearance of the existing join line changes to indicate the new type of join. Left outer joins contain an arrow pointing toward the table on the left side of the relationship, whereas right outer joins contain an arrow pointing toward the table on the right side of the relationship.

For example, look at the Calls and Contacts tables, shown in Figure 39-7. (You can find these tables at the IDG Books web site (www.idgbooks.com), if you want to work with the data and duplicate the examples shown here.)

As you can see by examining the tables, the Contacts table includes a list of people whom the company's sales force have not called yet. The Calls table has two *orphaned* records (108 and 601), calls for which no corresponding Customer ID number exists in the Contacts table. Figure 39-8 shows a query design for obtaining a list of phone calls made to contacts, along with the contact's name, city, state, and phone number.

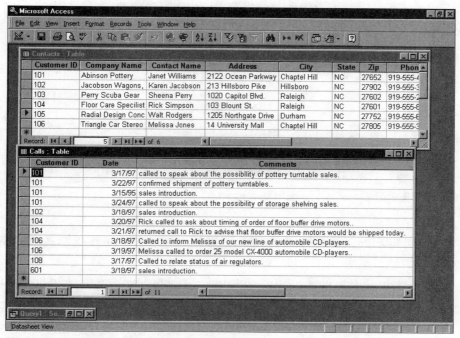

Figure 39-7: The Contacts and Calls tables.

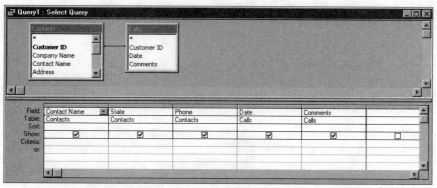

Figure 39-8: A query design that draws data from the Contacts and Calls tables.

If you duplicate this query, double-click on the join line, and then choose the second option; the result is a right outer join with the arrow pointing toward the Calls table. When you run the query, the results resemble those shown in Figure 39-9.

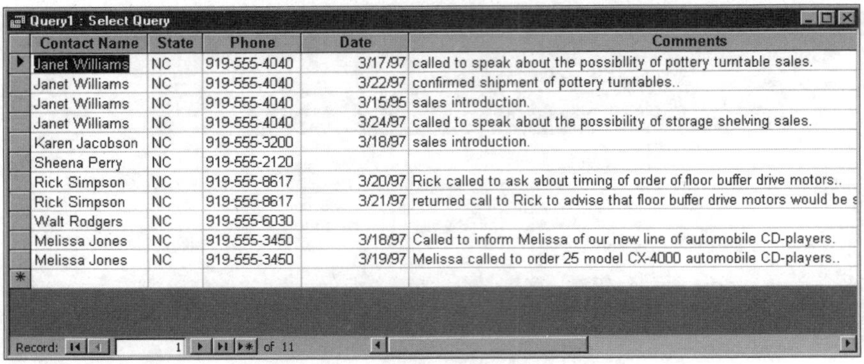

Figure 39-9: The results of a right outer join.

The resulting dynaset lists all contacts, even though two contacts have no record of phone calls made to them.

If you go into Design view for the same query, double-click on the join line and chose the third option; a left outer join results with the arrow pointing toward the Contacts table. When you run the query, the results resemble the results shown in Figure 39-10.

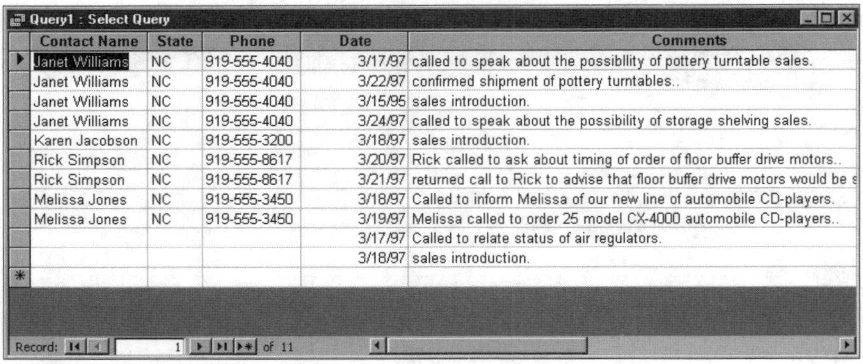

Figure 39-10: The results of a left outer join.

The dynaset includes all dates and comments from the Calls table, even though two of the records do not have matching Customer ID entries in the Contacts table. As shown by the last example, outer joins can prove useful for locating orphan records.

More Info If you establish relational integrity at the database level, you prevent the creation of orphan records in the first place. Chapter 35 provides details on how you can use relational integrity.

Creating Self-Joins

An unusual type of join (but one that you will use occasionally in your Access applications) is the *self-join*. You create a self-join when you bring a table into a query twice and link a field in the table to a different field in the same table. You can see an example of how the self-join works when you open the Northwind Traders database (supplied with your copy of Access), create a new query, and add the Employees table to the query twice. You can create a self-join link by dragging the Reports To field at the bottom of the list box in the first table to the EmployeeID field in the list box for the duplicate table. You can then add the LastName, FirstName, and Title fields from the first list box to the query, and you can add the Last Name and First Name fields from the second list box to the query. At this point, the query's design resembles the one shown in Figure 39-11.

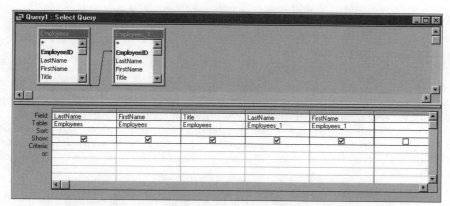

Figure 39-11: An example of a self-join design for a query.

When you run the query, the results show the names of the employees who report to managers in the table, along with the names of their managers, as shown in Figure 39-12.

Because the manager names are stored in the same table as the employee names, the only way that you can obtain this kind of data is by using a self-join. Self-joins can be any of the three join types (equi-joins, left outer joins, or right outer joins).

You change the join type using the same steps as outlined earlier in the chapter: You double-click the join line indicating the self-join and choose the desired type from the Join Properties dialog box that appears.

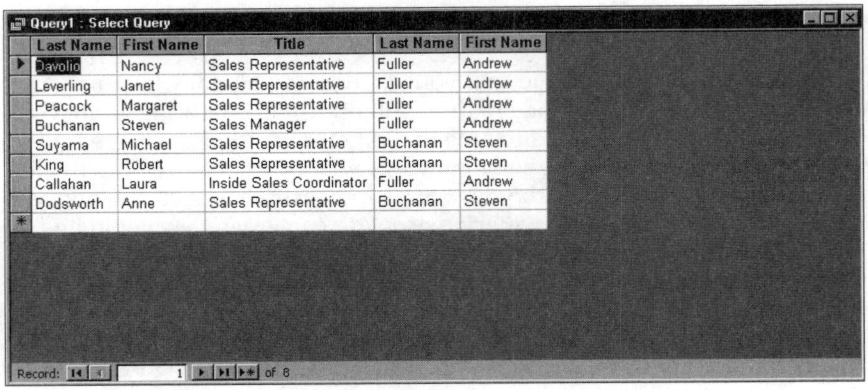

Last Name	First Name	Title	Last Name	First Name
Davolio	Nancy	Sales Representative	Fuller	Andrew
Leverling	Janet	Sales Representative	Fuller	Andrew
Peacock	Margaret	Sales Representative	Fuller	Andrew
Buchanan	Steven	Sales Manager	Fuller	Andrew
Suyama	Michael	Sales Representative	Buchanan	Steven
King	Robert	Sales Representative	Buchanan	Steven
Callahan	Laura	Inside Sales Coordinator	Fuller	Andrew
Dodsworth	Anne	Sales Representative	Buchanan	Steven

Figure 39-12: The results of a self-join query.

Working with Multiple-Field Links

With most relational applications, the database design allows you to use a single field containing unique data as the primary key. Most applications use commonly used ID numbers, such as employee numbers, social security numbers, part numbers, or customer numbers, for this task. Sometimes, however, no single field will work as a primary key, so you must base the primary key on a combination of fields that together uniquely identify every record in the table. For example, look at Figure 39-13.

In this example, the primary key for the tables shown are based on a combination of the Last Name, First Name, and Address fields. As shown in the figure, the two tables are related by three join lines. One join line links the Last Name fields of both tables, another links the First Name fields, and a third join line links the Address fields. This type of database design has its drawbacks in terms of greatly increased data-entry. In this example, users of the database would need to enter the same users and addresses in matching records in both tables. Had a scheme like an ID number been used as a matching field instead, only the ID number would need to be duplicated in records in both tables, but this example illustrates that you can establish relationships between tables by using multiple fields as the primary key.

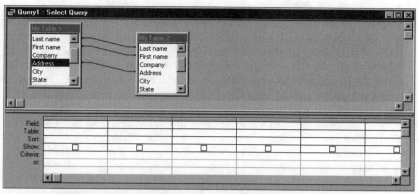

Figure 39-13: A relational link based on multiple fields.

An Analysis of Relationship Types

If you plan on working with related data in Access, you should be familiar with the various types of relationships that you can establish between tables. PC-based database managers support three types of relationships: *one-to-one, one-to-many,* and *many-to-many.* The names represent the number of records in the first, or *parent*, table that are related to the number of records in the second, or *child*, table. For example, when a field in one record (and only one record) of a table relates to a field in one record (and only one record) in another table, you have a *one-to-one* relationship. Figure 39-14 demonstrates this concept.

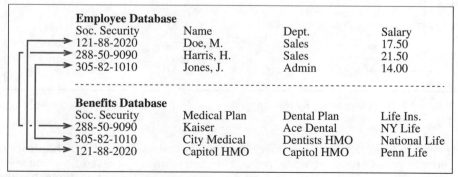

Figure 39-14: A one-to-one relationship.

In this example based on a personnel database, one table contains employee names and addresses, and another table contains health insurance information for every employee. Every employee has one record detailing his or her health insurance information and one record containing the employee's name and address. The tables are linked only by the social security number for the employee. Because only one record in the Insurance table is related to only one record in the Employees table, the relationship is one-to-one.

By comparison, consider the example shown in Figure 39-15, which illustrates a typical one-to-many relationship. In this example, the Customer table contains names and addresses of customers for computer parts. A second table, Sales, contains a listing of all purchases of computer parts made by each customer. Each record in the Customer table can be related to a number of records in the Sales table. The result is a one-to-many relationship between the Customer table and the Sales table. Most relationships are one-to-many.

Finally, a less-common type of relationship (but one that you sometimes need) is the many-to-many relationship. With this relationship, many records in one table can be related to many records in another table. For example, consider the relationship needed to track inventory items and the possible suppliers of those items. Figure 39-16 illustrates this type of relationship.

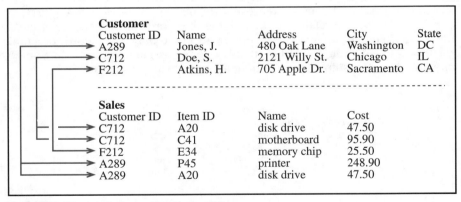

Figure 39-15: A one-to-many relationship.

If you are just starting to work with relational databases, two of the hardest concepts to grasp firmly are when you should use relationships and how you should structure them. No hard and fast rules exist to answer these questions, but thinking about how your data needs to appear in forms and reports supported by your relational queries can be helpful. Typically, an indication of the fact that relationships between tables are needed is evident when you find yourself duplicating data repeatedly. For example, entering the same customer number or part name over and over in a table of records is a good indication that the table's data might better exist within two tables, with a common field used to establish a relationship between the tables.

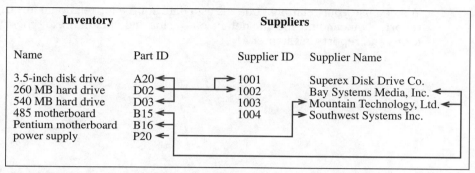

Figure 39-16: A many-to-many relationship.

Summary

This chapter expanded on the basic topics covered in Chapter 36 by detailing how you can work with relational queries. The chapter covered the following points:

✦ You can create a relational query by opening a design window into a new query, adding the desired multiple tables to the window, and creating joins by dragging the matching fields from one table to another. The remaining steps of the query design process are identical to steps for creating queries based on single tables.

✦ You can change the type of join used in a relational query by double-clicking on the join line while in Design view and choosing the desired join type from the Join Properties dialog box that appears.

✦ You can delete an existing join by selecting the join line while in Design view and pressing Delete.

✦ Relationships that you establish between your Access tables can be one-to-one, one-to-many, and many-to-many.

In the next chapter, you learn how to work with specialized queries that can prove useful for working with your databases.

Where to go next...

✦ A solid understanding of the basics of query design is necessary before you can delve into creating and using relational queries. The overall science of query design is covered in exquisite detail in Chapter 36.

✦ You can use your relational queries as a data source for relational forms and reports. You can find specific details on the ins and outs of these types of forms and reports in Chapter 41.

✦   ✦   ✦

Working with Specialized Queries

C H A P T E R

In This Chapter

Working with action queries

Creating specialized queries with the Query Wizards

Using parameter queries

This chapter tells you how to create and work with three specialized types of queries: *action queries*, *crosstab queries*, and *parameter queries*. This chapter also describes how you can use the Query Wizards to create queries that find duplicate and unmatched records. You use action queries to change data in your tables and crosstab queries to get a spreadsheet-like view of numeric data in tables. A parameter query is a special type of query that lets you dynamically change the query criteria when the query runs; these queries provide custom reports that produce different sets of data on demand when you run the reports.

Working with Action Queries

Whereas select queries retrieve and display data in the form of a dynaset, action queries perform some type of action on the data it retrieves. You can think of action queries as select queries that are given a job to do, such as creating another table based on the query's results or deleting every record in the query's dynaset. In Access, action queries are created in the same manner as select queries. In fact, you begin the design process by creating a select query that will get the desired data. You then convert the select query to an action query by clicking on the appropriate toolbar button or by opening the Query menu and choosing the appropriate type of action query.

Action queries are visible in the Queries tab of the Database window, as are all queries. You can visually differentiate action queries from other queries by the exclamation point that appears to the left of the query when you view it in the Database window; Figure 40-1 shows action queries contained in the Database window.

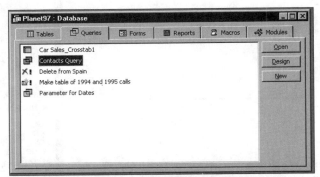

Figure 40-1: The action queries listed in the Database window.

Here are some practical uses for action queries:

✦ **Deleting or archiving records** — A common task when working with large, transaction-based systems (such as inventory control) is deleting groups of records, or moving groups of records to an archive file. You can design action queries to delete groups of records or to copy groups of records to another table and then delete them from the first table.

✦ **Handling batch updates** — If each customer in a customer table is assigned a certain sales representative and then a sales rep leaves the company, you won't want to manually re-enter a sales rep's name for each affected customer record. You can design and run an update query to handle the changes in a single step.

✦ **Handling complex, changing reporting needs** — You may have a half-dozen reports based on a complex query that uses data that changes monthly. Every time you want to run one or more reports, you must run the query first, which can be time-consuming. To save time, you can create a make table query, which runs on a monthly basis, to create a new table that has the specific data that the original query normally produces. You can then base all reports on the new table produced by the make table query.

In Access, you can create four types of action queries: *make table queries*, which create new tables based on the results of the query; *append queries*, which add records to existing tables; *update queries*, which change the data in existing queries; and *delete queries*, which delete the records selected as a result of the query.

Are you *sure* you want to do that?!?

By nature, action queries can be quite destructive. Update queries have the power to make major changes to your table data, and delete queries are designed to delete the retrieved records — a process that you cannot undo.

Before you run an action query, you should first view the query's result in Datasheet view and make sure that the results are the records to which you want the action to apply before you run the action query.

Creating and using make table queries

You use make table queries in Access to create new tables from the results of another query. All records selected by the original query are added to the new table created by the make table query. Make table queries are commonly used for creating backups or archives of data, or for exporting selected data to files in foreign file formats. To create a make table query, you perform these steps:

1. Create the select query that will retrieve the records you want to copy to the new table, using the query design techniques outlined in Chapter 36. You can test the query to ensure that it provides the desired results by clicking on the Datasheet button in the toolbar.

2. With the select query open in Design View, choose Query⇨Make Table Query, or click on the Make Table button on the toolbar. After you perform this task, you see the Make Table dialog box, shown in Figure 40-2.

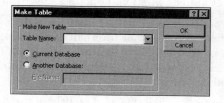

Figure 40-2: The Make Table dialog box for the make table query.

3. In the Table Name text box, type the name for the new table, or click on the down arrow at the right and choose a table name from the list (if you want to overwrite an existing table). To append the data to another table in a different database, click on the Another Database button and enter the filename for the other database in the File Name list box.

4. After you choose the desired options, click on OK. The title of the query changes to Make Table Query, indicating that the query's design has changed from a select query to a make table query.

5. Run the make table query by choosing Query⇨Run, or by clicking on the Run button on the toolbar. Access displays a confirmation dialog box indicating how many records will be added to the new table. Click on OK, and the query runs and adds the records to the new table.

Note When you create a new table using a make table query, Access does not transfer field properties or key field specifications to the new table. You need to recreate any key field designations or custom field properties after the new table has been created.

Creating and using append queries

You can use append queries to append data from an existing table to another table. Append queries can copy data to other tables in the same database or to tables in different databases. (By default, the data is appended to tables in the same database.) The tables do not need identical structures, but the field types between the tables must match. You can create and run an append query by performing the following steps:

More Info
1. Create the select query that will retrieve the records you want to copy to the new table using the query design techniques outlined in Chapter 36. You can test the query to verify that it provides the desired results by clicking on the Datasheet button in the toolbar.

2. With the query still open in Design view, choose Query⇨Append Query, or click on the Append button on the toolbar. You see the Query Properties dialog box, shown earlier in Figure 40-2. (The dialog box is titled Append rather than Make Table in this case, but all other options in the dialog box are identical to the options that appear when you create a make table query.)

3. In the Table Name text box, type the name for the table to which you want to append the data, or click on the down arrow at the right and choose the table name from the list. To append the data to another table in a different database, click on the Another Database button and enter a file name for the other database in the File Name list box.

4. After you choose the desired options, click on OK. The title of the query changes to Append Query, indicating that the query's design has changed from a select query to an append query.

5. Run the query by choosing Query⇨Run, or by clicking on the Run button on the toolbar. Access displays a confirmation dialog box indicating the number of records Access will add to the end of the existing table. Click on OK, and the query runs and adds the records to the new table.

Hot Stuff If you use append queries to add data to another table that contains an AutoNumber field, you can keep the value in the AutoNumber field from the original table, or you can force Access to add new AutoNumber values for all records that it adds to the destination table. To keep the AutoNumber values the same as those stored in the original table, include the AutoNumber field in the query grid when you design the append query. To force Access to add new AutoNumber values, omit the AutoNumber field from the query grid when you design the append query.

Creating and using update queries

Update queries are action queries that update (or make specific changes to) all records that meet the criteria specified by the query. Update queries are very useful when you need to make global, or *batch*, updates to a subset of data. For example, in a table of item prices, you may want to increase all prices of items in a certain category by 5 percent, or you may need to change the area codes of phone numbers for records with a certain city name. You can use the following steps to create an update query:

1. Create the select query that will retrieve the records you want to update in the table using the query design techniques outlined in Chapter 36. You can test the query to confirm that it provides the desired results by clicking on the Datasheet button in the toolbar.

2. With the query still open in Design view, choose Query⇨Update Query, or click on the Update button on the toolbar. After you perform this task, the title of the query changes to Update Query. Also, Access adds a new row to the query called Update To, shown in Figure 40-3.

3. Click in the Update To row underneath the field that you want to update and enter the expression that determines how the data will be updated. For example, if your query contains a Unit Price field with currency amounts and you want to increase every entry in the field by 6 percent, you can enter an expression such as **[Unit Price] * 1.06** to get the desired results.

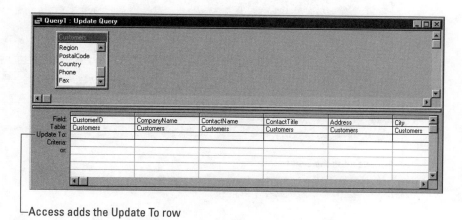

Access adds the Update To row

Figure 40-3: The query grid with the Update To row added.

4. Run the query by choosing Query⇨Run, or by clicking on the Run button on the toolbar. You see a confirmation dialog box telling you how many records the query will update. When you click on OK, Access runs the query and updates the data in the table.

Creating and using delete queries

Delete queries delete all records that meet the criteria specified by the query. One common use for delete queries is with operations that archive records: you routinely run a make table query that copies selected records to another table, and then you run a delete query that deletes the previously copied records from the first table. You can create delete queries by performing the following steps:

1. Create the select query that will retrieve the records you want to delete from the table using the query design techniques outlined in Chapter 36. You can test the query to ensure that it provides the desired results by clicking on the Datasheet button in the toolbar.

2. With the query still open in Design view, choose Query⇨Delete, or click on the Delete button on the toolbar. After you perform this task, the title of the query changes to Delete Query. Also, Access adds a new row to the query called Delete, shown in Figure 40-4.

3. Choose Query⇨Run, or click on the Run button on the toolbar. You see a confirmation dialog box telling you how many records the query will delete.

4. Click on OK in the dialog box to run the query and delete the records.

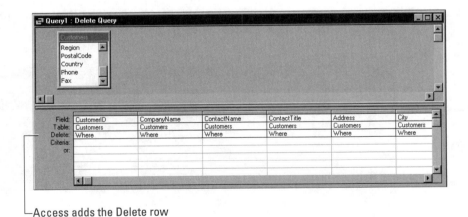

└Access adds the Delete row

Figure 40-4: The query grid with the Delete row added.

Creating Specialized Queries with the Query Wizards

Access provides Query Wizards that you can use to construct a number of specialized queries. These include simple queries, crosstab queries, find duplicates queries, and find unmatched queries. You have the option of choosing any of these specialized query types from the New Query dialog box that appears when you begin to create a new query.

Creating crosstab queries with the Query Wizards

You can use crosstab queries to consolidate numeric or currency data stored in a table into a crosstab-like format. (Crosstabs are typically used to summarize large amounts of data.) For example, Figure 40-5 shows a table containing a set of financial data of automobile sales, along with a crosstab query of the data in the table.

You can use the Query Wizards to create a crosstab query by performing the following steps:

1. In the Database window, click on the Queries tab and click on New.

2. In the New Query dialog box that appears, click on Crosstab Query Wizard in the list box of possible query types and click on OK.

3. Next, you see the first Crosstab Query wizard dialog box, shown in Figure 40-6. This dialog box asks which table or query you want to use as the basis for the crosstab. In the View portion of the dialog box, you can select Tables to show all available tables, Queries to show all available queries, or Both to show both tables and queries. Click on the table or query that you want to use, then click on Next.

4. The next dialog box, shown in Figure 40-7, asks which fields you want to use as row headings in the crosstab. Choose the fields that you want to serve as the row headings, then click on Next.

5. The next dialog box, shown in Figure 40-8, asks which fields you want to use as the basis for the column headings. Select the desired field(s) and then click on the right arrow button to add the fields to the column headings list, then click on Next. As you make your selections, the Sample portions of the Crosstab Query Wizard dialog boxes display field names reflecting your choices, as shown in the figure.

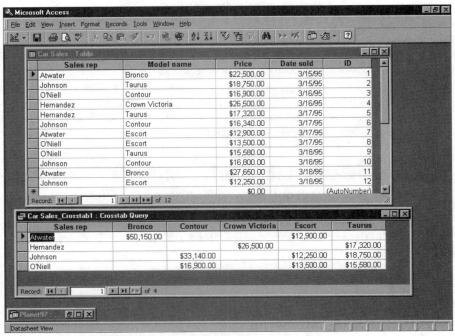

Figure 40-5: The financial data and the resulting crosstab.

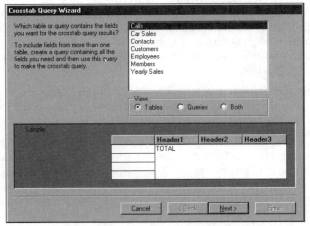

Figure 40-6: The first Crosstab Query Wizard dialog box.

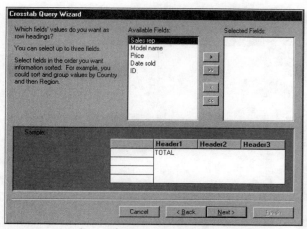

Figure 40-7: The second Crosstab Query Wizard dialog box.

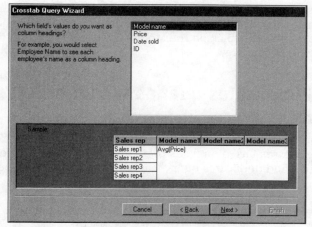

Figure 40-8: The third Crosstab Query Wizard dialog box.

6. The next dialog box, shown in Figure 40-9, asks which fields and what type of calculation you want to use to supply the values that will appear in the crosstab query. After choosing a field, you can choose from the list of math functions to apply the desired calculation to that field. If you turn on the Yes, include row sums option, each row of the crosstab will include a summary. Choose the field type and the type of calculation and click on Next.

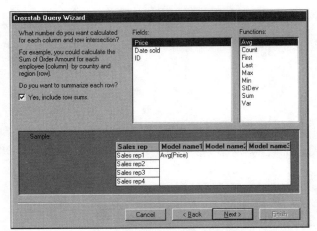

Figure 40-9: The fourth Crosstab Query Wizard dialog box.

7. The last dialog box that appears asks you for a name for the query. Enter a name (or accept the default name proposed by Access). Then you can click on the View the query radio button to run the query and display the results of the dynaset, or you can click on the Modify the design radio button to open the query in Design view.

Creating find duplicates queries with the Query Wizards

You can use find duplicates queries to find duplicate records in a table. You can search for duplicate records based on fields that you choose from a dialog box in the wizard. To create a find duplicates query using the Query Wizards, perform the following steps:

1. In the Database window, click on the Queries tab and click on New.

2. In the New Query dialog box that appears, click on Find Duplicates Query Wizard in the list box of query types and click on OK.

3. The first Find Duplicates Query Wizard dialog box that appears (Figure 40-10) asks which table or query you want to search in for duplicate records. Click on the desired table or query and click on Next.

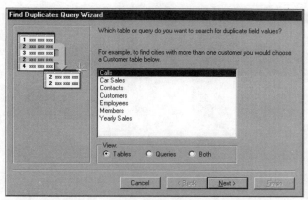

Figure 40-10: The first Find Duplicates Query Wizard dialog box.

4. The next dialog box that appears (Figure 40-11) asks which fields you want to use to search for possible duplicates. Choose the desired fields and click on the right arrow button to add the fields to the Duplicate-value Fields list box and click on Next.

5. The next dialog box that appears (Figure 40-12) asks for any additional fields that you want to include in the query results. Select the desired fields, and then click on the right arrow button after each selection to add the fields to the Additional query fields list box. After you've performed this task, click on Next.

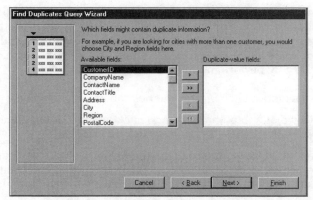

Figure 40-11: The second Find Duplicates Query Wizard dialog box.

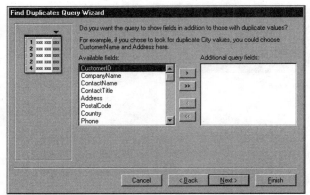

Figure 40-12: The third Find Duplicates Query Wizard dialog box.

6. The final dialog box that appears asks you for a name for the query. Enter a name (or accept the default name proposed by Access). Then you can click on the View the query option to run the query and display the results of the dynaset, or you can click on Modify the design to open the query in Design view. When you run the query, all duplicate records that Access finds with the query appear in the resulting dynaset.

Creating find unmatched queries with the Query Wizards

You can use find unmatched queries to locate records in one table that have no related records in another table. For example, you may have a table of customers and a related table of orders placed by each customer. You can use a find unmatched query to locate all customers that do not have orders. You can create a find unmatched query by performing the following steps:

1. In the Database window, click on the Queries tab and click on New.

2. In the New Query dialog box that appears, click on Find Unmatched Query Wizard in the list box of query types and click on OK.

3. The Find Unmatched Query Wizard dialog box (Figure 40-13) appears. This dialog box asks which table or query contains the records you want to see in the query results. Click on the desired table or query to select it and click on Next.

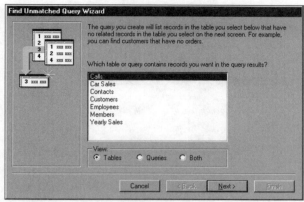

Figure 40-13: The first Find Unmatched Query Wizard dialog box.

4. The next dialog box to appear (Figure 40-14) asks which table or query contains the related records. Click on the desired table or query to select it and click on <u>N</u>ext.

5. The next dialog box to appear (Figure 40-15) asks which fields should be used as the matching field between both tables. Click on the desired field in the first table (at the left side of the dialog box) and click on the matching field in the second table (at the right side of the dialog box) and click on the double arrow button between both lists and click on <u>N</u>ext.

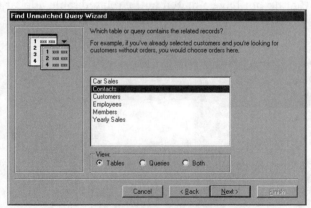

Figure 40-14: The second Find Unmatched Query Wizard dialog box.

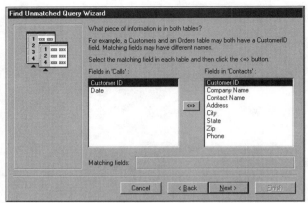

Figure 40-15: The third Find Unmatched Query Wizard dialog box.

6. The next dialog box to appear (Figure 40-16) asks which fields should be included in the query's results. Choose all desired fields, and click on the right arrow button after each field to add the field to the query's results. When you're done with this task, click on Next.

7. The final dialog box to appear asks for a name for the query. Enter a name (or accept the default name proposed by Access). You can then click on the View the query option to run the query and display the results of the dynaset, or you can click on the Modify the design option to open the query in Design view. After you run the query, any records Access finds in the primary table that do not have a match in the related table appear in the results.

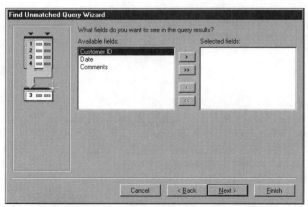

Figure 40-16: The fourth Find Unmatched Query Wizard dialog box.

A note about Archive Queries

If you used the Archive Query Wizard in earlier versions of Access, don't be puzzled when you can't find it: the Archive Query Wizard is no longer available in Access. You can accomplish the same thing by creating a Make-Table query that copies all the records to be archived into a new table. After running the query and creating the new table, change the query type to a Delete query and run it again to delete the records from the original table.

Using Parameter Queries

If you run the same query repeatedly, entering different criteria every time that you run the query, you'll find that *parameter queries* will save you lots of time. A parameter query asks for the needed criteria every time it runs. For example, you can design a query to provide a list of customer orders for a specific period of time. Every time the query runs, Access asks you for a starting and an ending date, and the query uses those dates to establish a range of acceptable records. You can change existing queries into parameter queries by adding parameters to the existing query designs, as outlined in the following steps. You can create parameter queries by performing these steps:

1. Design the select query, using the query design techniques outlined in Chapter 36.

2. In the Criteria cells below the fields that you want to use as parameters, enter the text of the parameter, enclosed within square brackets. For example, if you want a parameter in a Date Ordered field to ask for a date when the query runs, you can enter an expression such as **[Enter the order date:]** in the Order Date column of the Criteria row. If you want a parameter in a Quantity field to ask for a minimum and a maximum amount, you can use an expression such as **between [Enter minimum amount:] and [Enter maximum amount:]** in the Quantity column of the Criteria row.

3. Save the query by choosing File⇨Save or by pressing Ctrl+F4 and answering Yes in the dialog box that appears.

For an example of a parameter query, consider the query design shown in Figure 40-17. The parameter query's design includes a parameter for a range of dates for phone calls. (In the figure, the Date column was widened to show the text of the complete parameter.)

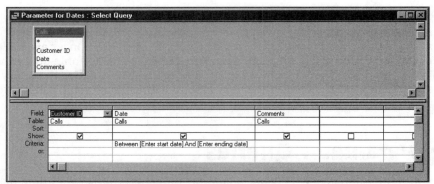

Figure 40-17: A parameter query.

When the query runs, it produces a dialog box like the one shown in Figure 40-18.

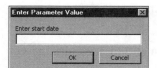

Figure 40-18: The dialog box presented by a parameter query.

After entering a starting date, another dialog box appears, asking for the ending date. After you supply these values, Access uses them as the query criteria to produce the query results.

Okay, but what are parameter queries good for?

Parameter queries are an excellent data source for reports that require different underlying data sets every time that you produce the report. Suppose, for example, that once a month you need a sales report containing sales for the last 30 days. You can create a parameter query that asks for the starting and ending dates for the desired month and retrieves sales records for the range of dates entered for the parameters. You then can create the sales report using the parameter query as the data source for the report. Every time that you print the report, the parameter query runs first and prompts you for the desired starting and ending dates and runs the report, retrieving records that match the requirements of the parameter query.

The various types of queries detailed throughout this chapter are all designed to serve different needs. You can consider them to be specialized power tools that you can add to your arsenal of Access tools to get at the data that you need in Access. As you work with action queries, crosstab queries, and parameter queries, remember that they can all serve as important sources of data for your reports in Access.

Summary

This chapter detailed how you can use specialized query types, including action queries for appending, updating, and deleting data; crosstab queries for viewing data in a consolidated format; and parameter queries for specifying criteria at a report's run time. The chapter detailed the following points:

✦ In Access, you can use *action queries* to create new tables, append records to existing tables to perform global updates, or delete groups of records.

✦ You can create an action query by creating a select query that retrieves the desired records first. You then open the Query menu and choose Make Table, Append, Update, or Delete as the query type to convert the select query into the desired type of action query.

✦ You can use the Query Wizards in Access to create crosstab queries, queries that find duplicate records, or queries that find unmatched records.

✦ You can create *parameter queries* that prompt for specific data when run and retrieve selected records based on the responses to the prompts.

In the next chapter, you learn how to effectively work with relational forms and reports.

Where to go next...

✦ Action queries are routinely used as part of complex applications that also involve macros. Chapter 42 tells you all about macros.

✦ Crosstab and parameter queries can be useful as data sources for specialized custom reports. For the complete story on designing and running custom reports, take a look at Chapter 38.

✦   ✦   ✦

Working with Relational Forms and Reports

This chapter examines the concepts and techniques that you use when working with *relational forms and reports*, which are forms and reports that use more than one table at a time. The chapters on forms (Chapter 37) and reports (Chapter 38) touched on working with multiple tables while designing forms and reports using the wizards. This chapter provides additional details on designing and working with relational forms and reports manually.

Designing Relational Forms and Reports

One way to design relational forms and reports manually is to embed forms within forms and reports within reports. With forms, the embedded form is called the *subform* (or *detail* form), and the form that contains the subform is called the *main* (or *master*) form. A relational form typically displays one record from the one side of a one-to-many relationship in the main form and all associated records from the many side of the relationship in the subform. Figure 41-1 shows an example of a relational form designed around a main form and a subform.

Note   Another way to design relational forms and reports is to build a relational query and base the form or report on the query, but this method is basically the same form or report design method discussed in earlier chapters. You'll find tips on this type of design at the end of this chapter.

Relational reports use the same design techniques as forms. The embedded report is known as the *subreport* (or *detail* report), and the report containing the subreport is known as the *main* (or *master*) report. Like a relational form, a relational report displays one record from the one side of a one-to-many relationship in the main report, and all associated records from the many side of the relationship in the subreport. Figure 41-2 shows a relational report designed around a main report and a subreport.

While in Design view for a form or a report, you can add subforms to main forms and subreports to main reports by using the appropriate Toolbox tool (use the Subform tool when designing forms and the Subreport tool when designing reports). Or, you can add them by dragging the subform or subreport from the Database window to the main form or main report. The drag-and-drop method is easier than the Toolbox method, because with drag-and-drop you don't have to specify the name of the form or report used as the subform or subreport. Access adds the form's or report's name to the Properties window for the subform or subreport.

Note Before you create a form or report that contains a subform or subreport, you first must create and save the subform or subreport using the usual design techniques detailed in Chapters 37 and 38. Keep in mind that you can often avoid the tedious work of creating a subform or a subreport manually. Instead, use the Form Wizards or the Report Wizards to save a form or a report in the style that you want, and then use that form or report as the subform within your main form or main report. You should also note that you'll want to be efficient in terms of size when designing the subform or subreport because it must fit inside of the main form or main report.

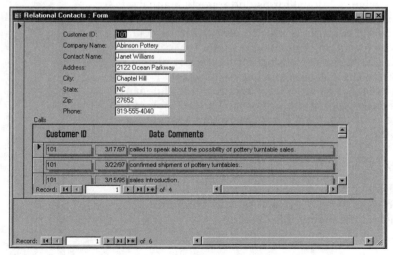

Figure 41-1: A relational form based on a main form and a subform.

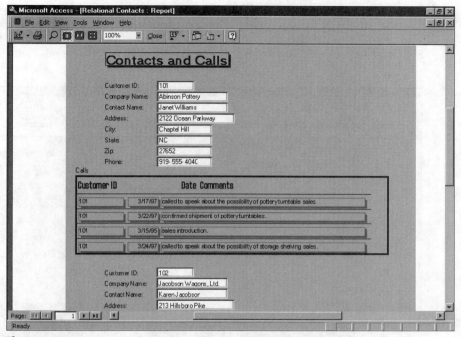

Figure 41-2: A relational report based on a main report and a subreport.

Creating a Relational Form

When you want to create a multitable form manually by embedding the subform within the main form, you can perform this task by using these steps:

1. Open the main form in Design view and lay out the main portion of the form as desired, placing all needed fields and other objects in the form.

2. Switch to the Database window and click on the Forms tab to display all your stored forms.

3. Drag the form that you want to use as a subform from the Database window to the main form. When you drop the subform icon onto the main form, a subform control appears, as shown in Figure 41-3. You can then place the subform control at the desired location in the main form.

4. Right-click on the subform control and choose Properties from the shortcut menu. When the Properties window opens, click on the Data tab.

5. Look in the Link Master Fields property. If an entry already exists, you need to make sure that Access created the link using the fields you want. If Access was unable to establish the proper link, you need to type in the name of the field that Access should use as a link to the records within the subform.

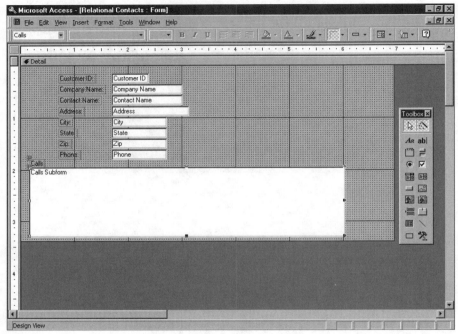

Figure 41-3: The subform control as part of the main form shown in Design view.

Hot Stuff

You can click on the button with the three periods to the right of the property to bring up a Subform Linker dialog box. In this dialog box, you can choose the fields you want to use as links from the list boxes that appear.

6. Close the form. When Access asks if you want to save the form, click on Yes in the dialog box that appears. Then enter a name for the form in the Save As dialog box that appears next.

When you bring up a multitable form in Form view, records for the main table appear in the main portion of the form, and all records associated to these records appear within the subform, as illustrated earlier in Figure 41-1.

Step 5 brings up the fact that the multitable forms you create manually may not have a proper relational link established between the tables. You need to verify that a working link exists between the main form and the subform by opening the

Properties window. Access automatically establishes the proper link if you defined a relationship at the table level, or if matching fields (fields having the same name and the same data type) exist on the main form and the subform, and the matching field on the main form is a primary key in the underlying table. If Access is unable to establish the proper link, the Link Master Fields property will be blank. In this case, you need to type in the name of the desired field, or click on the button at the right side of the Link Master Fields property to bring up a Subform Linker dialog box where you can choose the fields to establish the link.

Creating a Relational Report

You use the same overall techniques to build a relational report: as with forms, you first create and save the report that will act as the subreport, you open the main report in Design view, and you drag the subreport from the Reports tab of the Database window to the main report. The following steps are the steps involved in creating a relational report:

1. Open the main report in Design view and lay out the main portion of the report as desired, placing all needed fields and other objects in the report.

2. Switch to the Database window and click on the Reports tab to display all your stored reports.

3. Drag the report that you want to use as a subreport from the Database window to the main report. When you drop the subreport icon onto the main report, a subreport control appears, as shown in Figure 41-4. You then can place the subreport control at the desired location in the main report.

4. Right-click on the subform and choose Properties from the shortcut menu. When the Properties window opens, click on the Data tab.

5. Look in the Link Master Fields property. If an entry already exists, you need to make sure that Access created the link using the fields you want.

Note   As Figure 41-4 indicates, when you add a subreport to a report's design by using drag-and-drop methods, the subreport control that Access adds is sized automatically to accommodate the existing subreport.

As with relational forms, you should verify that a working link exists between the main report and the subreport by viewing the entries in the Properties window. If Access cannot establish the proper relational link between the tables, the Link Master Fields property will be blank. In this case, you need to type in the name of the field you want, or click on the button at the right side of the Link Master Fields property to bring up a Subform Linker dialog box where you can choose the fields needed to establish the link.

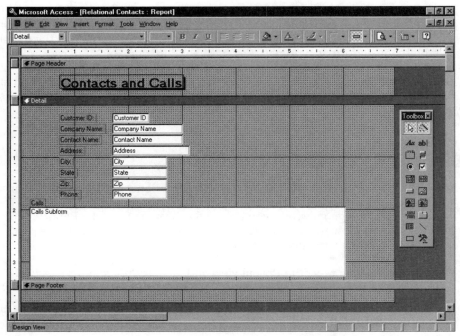

Figure 41-4: The subreport control as part of the main report shown in Design view.

Creating Relational Forms Using Pop-up Forms

A common type of relational form that often comes in handy is the *pop-up* form. A pop-up form is a subform that, by default, Access does not make visible. You make the form appear ("pop up" into view) when you click on a command button on the main form. Figure 41-5 shows an example of a pop-up form.

Creating a pop-up form is a simple task because Access provides a wizard that adds the command button to open a pop-up form. To add a pop-up form and a command button that makes it appear, first create and save the form that you want to use as the main form, as well as the subform that you want to use as the pop-up form. Then, perform these steps to change the subform to a pop-up form and add the command button.

Figure 41-5: A pop-up form.

1. Open the form that you want to use as the pop-up form in Design view, and choose View⇨Properties to open the Properties window (Figure 41-6).

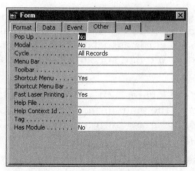

Figure 41-6: The Properties window.

2. Click on the Other tab in the window and change the value of the Pop-Up property to Yes and save the form.

3. Open the form that you want to use as the main form in Design view.

4. If the Toolbox is not already visible, choose View⇨Toolbox to display it.

5. In the Toolbox, turn on the Control Wizards if they are not on already (click on the Control Wizard button at the upper-right corner of the Toolbox).

6. In the Toolbox, click on the Command Button tool. Then, click in the form where you want to place the button. When you perform this task, the first Command Button Wizard dialog box appears, as shown in Figure 41-7.

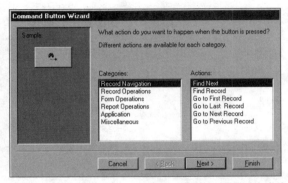

Figure 41-7: The first Command Button Wizard dialog box.

7. Under Categories, click on Form Operations. Then, under Actions, click on Open Form, then click on Next.

8. In the next Command Button Wizard dialog box that appears, select the form that you want to use as the pop-up form, then click on Next.

9. The next dialog box that appears (see Figure 41-8) asks whether you want to display specific information or show all records. Because you usually want the pop-up form to show only those records associated with the record in the main form, choose Open the form and find specific data to display and click on Next.

10. The next dialog box that appears (see Figure 41-9) asks which fields Access should use to link the pop-up form to the main form. Select the appropriate field from each list, click on the double-arrow button between the lists to apply the selection and click on Next.

11. The next dialog box to appear asks whether you want text or a picture on the button. (If you choose Picture, Access adds a default picture for the given task you've assigned to the button.) Make the desired selection and click on Next.

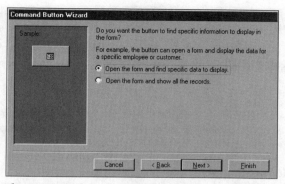

Figure 41-8: The Command Button Wizard dialog box that asks what kinds of records you want to display.

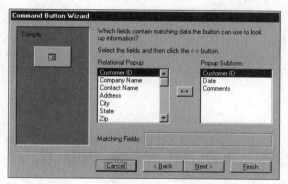

Figure 41-9: The Command Button Wizard dialog box that asks which fields you want to use as links.

12. In the final wizard dialog box that appears, Access asks you for a name for the button. You can enter any name and click on Finish to place the button on the form.

When you run the main form and click on the button you placed using these steps, the pop-up form appears over the main form, as shown earlier in Figure 41-5. Because the value of the Pop Up property is set to Yes in the form, the form remains over the main form, even when you designate the main form as the active form.

Note Pop-up forms are great design choices when you have a detail form (one that shows the "many" side of a one-to-many relationship) that you don't need to see always but that you want to have readily available while you are viewing the main form.

Design tips for relational forms and reports

You should keep in mind some overall design tips when you are designing relational forms and subreports:

Keep in mind the size limitations of the subform or subreport. Because you need to fit a form inside a form or a report within a report, you'll want to be as efficient as possible with the use of space in your subforms and subreports. Include only those fields that are necessary, and consider using Datasheet view for subforms to allow as many fields as possible to fit in the subform.

Don't duplicate main form and report controls in the subform or subreport. Controls that are in the main form or report already generally serve no useful purpose when they appear again in the subform or subreport. Because the subform or subreport repeats the contents of a control

for each record, any control that contains the entries from the common (linking) field should be placed in the main form or report, rather than in the subform or subreport.

Avoid page breaks or page numbers in subreports, and remove unneeded headers and footers. You usually do not want to insert a forced page break inside a subreport, and you usually do not need headers and footers, because typically the main report has its own headers and footers.

Protect referential integrity by locking fields in forms if necessary. If you didn't protect referential integrity at the database level, you should definitely do it now by locking any fields in the subform which, if edited, will break the link between the master record and the detail record.

Creating Relational Forms and Reports with Relational Queries

As mentioned earlier in this chapter, using subforms and subreports inside forms and reports is one approach to creating relational forms and reports. The other approach is to base the form or report on a relational query. First, you must design the relational query, using the techniques outlined in Chapter 39. After you save the query, you then can proceed to create the desired form or report. When Access asks you for a data source for the form or report, you give it the name of the relational query. If you are designing a report, you probably will want to group the data based on the field used to establish the relational link so that a group of associated records appears for each record in the parent table. For example, Figure 41-10 shows a relational query using the tables in the Northwind Traders database provided by Access.

After the relational query exists, you can design a report using a design like the one shown in Figure 41-11 to produce a report like the one shown in Figure 41-12. The report's design includes grouping on the Company Name and Order Date fields, as shown in Figure 41-11. The Sorting and Grouping dialog box in the report's design uses both of these fields to establish grouping in the report. As the query's design indicates, the Customers and Orders tables are linked by the Customer ID field, and the Orders and Order Details tables are linked by the Order ID field.

If you base forms on relational queries that you create, keep in mind the limitations of editing data in a relational query. You can edit nearly all fields, but some exceptions exist. For full details on the fields that you can edit through a relational query, see Chapter 39.

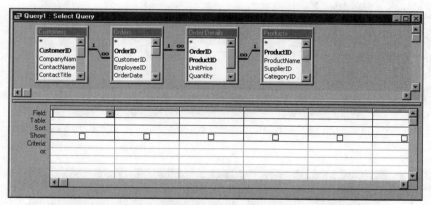

Figure 41-10: A relational query used to support a relational report.

Generally, there are no hard and fast rules as to when you should use relational forms and reports based on subforms and subreports and when you should use relational forms and reports that are based on queries. One point worth noting is that with one-to-many relationships, the subform and subreport approach tends to produce more attractive results, whereas with one-to-one relationships, a form or report based on a relational query tends to produce more attractive results.

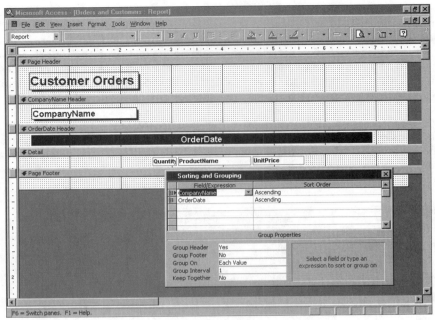

Figure 41-11: The design of this relational report uses a relational query as a data source.

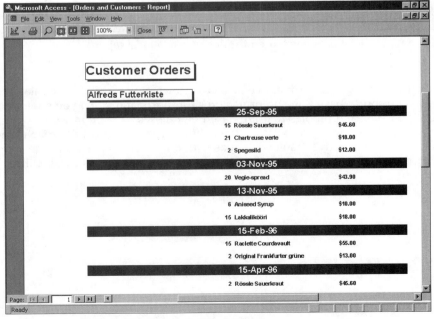

Figure 41-12: The results of the relational report.

Summary

This chapter looked at how you can manually design forms and reports to take advantage of the relational power of Access. The chapter included coverage of the following points:

✦ You can manually create a multitable form or report by first creating a form or report that will serve as the subform or subreport. You then create the main form or main report, and during the design process, you use the Subform or Subreport tool in the Toolbox to add the subform or subreport to the main form or main report.

✦ You can create subforms that act as *pop-up* forms, by changing the value of the Pop Up property in the Properties window for the form to Yes and using the Command Button Wizard to add a button to the main form that "pops up" the subform.

✦ You can use subforms and subreports as a design basis for your relational forms and reports, or you can use relational queries (discussed in more detail in Chapter 39).

In the next chapter, you learn how to use macros to automate tasks in Access.

Where to go next...

✦ For more complete details on designing forms manually, take a look at Chapter 37.

✦ For the lowdown on report design techniques, see Chapter 38.

✦ ✦ ✦

Working with Macros

This chapter details how you can use *macros*, which can significantly help you accomplish routine tasks in Access. As your tasks in Access grow in complexity, you may find yourself working in the same ways with the same tables, forms, and reports. Macros can help you reduce the tediousness of working with common objects in Access.

Understanding Macros

In Access, a macro is a list of actions specified in advance. These actions are stored in a table-like window called a Macro window, and the actions appear in the order that you want the macro to carry them out. When you run the macro, Access carries out the specified actions. For example, you may routinely open the same three tables each day and bring two reports onto the Access desktop. You can design a macro that accomplishes all of these steps in a single operation.

If you are accustomed to dealing with spreadsheets from the earlier generation of DOS-based products, you may be accustomed to *macro recorders,* which record actions that users carry out and then play them back as macros later. Macros are created very differently in Access. Access has no macro recorder. Instead, in the macro sheet where you create macros, you choose desired options from list boxes of available choices. This process may seem more difficult than letting a product "watch" your keyboard and mouse operations and then record them, but the flexibility of macro operations gained by the methods Access uses makes the added effort worthwhile.

Macros also can be a powerful aid in making Access easier for others to use. One particularly useful feature of macros is that you can attach them to command buttons, which can be placed on forms. These command button macros can perform common operations, such as opening dialog boxes to perform searches, changing the sort order of the data, or printing an associated report. Access users can then click on the desired buttons to carry out these tasks without needing to know all the operations that the macros carry out. You can create complete applications with custom menus and dialog boxes using macros, although Access applications development is a topic beyond the scope of this book.

Exploring a Macro Example

To see an example of a macro's usefulness, consider the tables and forms stored in the Planet database (available at the IDG Books web site — www.idgbooks.com). Suppose that you start each day's work by opening the Contacts form, the Calls table, and the Contacts report; you can create a macro to handle all these actions by first opening the database — if it isn't already open — and performing the following steps:

1. In the Database window, click on the Macros tab and click on New to open a new Macro window, shown in Figure 42-1. Move and size the window so that you can see the Macro window and the Database window simultaneously.

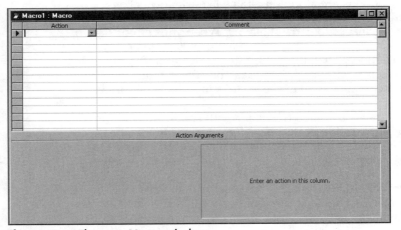

Figure 42-1: The new Macro window.

2. Click on the Forms tab of the Database window to show all forms currently stored in the database.

3. Click on and drag the Contacts form to the first blank row underneath the Action column within the Macro window. After you release the mouse button, OpenForm appears in the Action column, and various arguments

appear in the Action Arguments portion of the dialog box. (These arguments are detailed later in the chapter, in the "Specifying macro actions manually" section.)

4. Click on the Tables tab of the Database window to show all tables stored in the database.

5. Click on and drag the Calls table to the second blank row underneath the Action column in the Macro window. OpenTable appears in the Action column after you release the mouse button.

6. Click on the Reports tab of the Database window to show the reports stored in the database.

7. Click on and drag the Contacts report to the third blank row underneath the Action column in the Macro window. After you release the mouse button, the macro contains three actions (OpenForm, OpenTable, and OpenReport), shown in Figure 42-2.

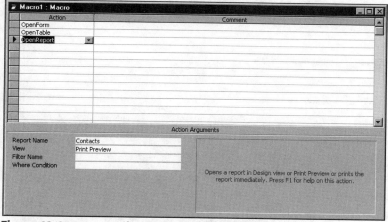

Figure 42-2: An example of a completed macro.

8. Choose File⇨Save. When Access asks for a name for the macro, enter **Sample Macro**, click on OK, and then press Ctrl+F4 to close the Macro window.

After the macro is completed, you can test its effects by clicking on the Macros tab in the Database window, selecting the macro, and clicking on the Run button. When the macro runs, the form and table open in their respective windows, and the Contacts report opens in preview mode, as shown in Figure 42-3.

This example illustrates the usefulness of macros in Access. You can use macros to perform common tasks (such as opening documents) and more complex operations; the remainder of this chapter details how you can create and work with the different features of macros in Access.

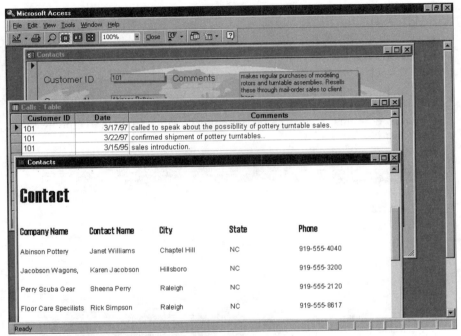

Figure 42-3: The results of the sample macro.

Creating and Running Macros

To create a macro, click on the Macros tab of the Database window and click on New. When you perform this task, a new Macro window opens, as shown earlier in Figure 42-1. (Alternatively, you can choose Insert⇨Macro to create a new macro.)

The Macro window contains two parts: an upper half, which contains *actions* that tell Access what steps to perform and optional *comments* which describe those actions; and a lower half, which contains *action arguments*. In the Action column, you select actions that you want Access to perform (or you create actions by dragging and dropping objects from the Database window, as described in the previous example). In the Comments column, you can type any desired comment that may help you keep track of what tasks the macro performs. (Comments are completely optional.) After you select (or create via drag and drop) a desired action, you can use the action arguments to control the specifics of the action. For example, the action arguments for opening a form let you specify the name of the form and whether the form should be opened in Form view, Design view, Print Preview, or Datasheet view.

Notice that the Action columns and the Comment columns appear by default in a Macro window. Depending on whether your defaults have been changed, however, you may also see a Macro Name column, a Conditions column, or both. If you see these columns, you can ignore them for now; the purpose of these columns is detailed later in the chapter.

While a macro is open in Design view, the toolbar takes on the appearance shown in Figure 42-4. Table 42-1 details the purposes of the toolbar buttons.

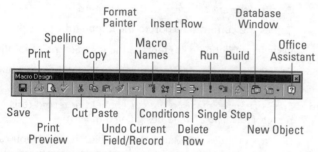

Figure 42-4: The toolbar appearance when a macro is open in Design View.

Why bother with macros?

Macros can automate many tedious, repetitive tasks. Here are some of the common tasks you can accomplish with macros:

Add convenience to the use of forms and reports. If you regularly open a set of forms or reports, you can create macros to handle this task for you. You can add a command button to a form that, when pressed, runs a macro that prints the form's contents or opens another form.

Locate and filter records. If you regularly establish filter conditions for a given form's or table's dataset, you can create a macro to establish the conditions and apply the filter.

Automate data transfers. If you regularly export data to a format other than Access, you can create macros to run the needed queries and export the resulting dynaset in the preferred file format so that you can use the data in another software package.

Perform specialized data validation. You can use macros to handle complex types of data validation that ordinary validation rules cannot handle.

Customize your working environment. You can provide custom menus and dialog boxes to manage a complete application, such as inventory or sales management.

Table 42-1
Macro toolbar buttons

Toolbar button	Purpose
Save	Saves the current macro (equivalent to choosing File⇨Save from the menus)
Print	Prints the selected item (this button is unavailable while designing a macro)
Print Preview	Displays a print preview of the selected item (this button is unavailable while designing a macro)
Spelling	Checks the spelling of the current selection
Cut	Cuts the current selection to the Clipboard
Copy	Copies the current selection to the Clipboard
Paste	Pastes the Clipboard contents at the insertion point location
Format Painter	Copies the appearance of one control to another (this button is unavailable while designing a macro)
Undo Current Field/Record	Erases changes made to the current field or record (this button unavailable while designing a macro)
Macro Names	Displays or hides the Macro Names column, which you can use to store macros as a group in a single Macro window
Conditions	Displays or hides the Conditions column, which you can use to specify conditions that a macro must evaluate before performing the macro actions
Insert Row	Adds a new row above the current one
Delete Row	Deletes selected rows, or if no selection exists, deletes the current row
Run	Runs the current macro
Single Step	Runs the macro a single action at a time
Build	Displays the Expression Builder, which you can use to enter expressions in the Conditions column
Database Window	Makes the Database window the active window
New Object	Creates a new Access object
Office Assistant	Displays the Office Assistant, which you can use to obtain context-sensitive help

Specifying macro actions manually

A great deal of your work in designing Access macros involves specifying the actions that you want the macro to perform, such as opening a form, printing a report, running a query, or exporting a table's contents to a spreadsheet file. In Access, you can specify actions in two ways. The first way is to choose them from a list box at the right of the Action column (or manually type them into the Action column). The second way is to use *drag and drop* to drag objects from the Database window to the Action column of the Macro window, as demonstrated by the example at the beginning of the chapter. This portion of the chapter describes how you can manually choose your macro actions (drag-and-drop techniques are discussed in the "Specifying macro actions with drag and drop" section that follows). You can specify actions in a macro manually by performing these steps:

1. In the Macro window, click on the first empty cell under the Action column. Click on the down arrow at the right of the column (or press Alt+down arrow) to open the list of possible actions, shown in Figure 42-5.

Figure 42-5: The list of possible macro actions.

2. Choose the action you want your macro to perform from the list. (Alternatively, if you know the precise syntax for the action, you can just type it into the column.)

3. Click in the lower half of the window (or press F6 to switch to the lower half) and specify the arguments for the action. (Keep in mind that most, but not *all*, actions require arguments; some actions, such as the Beep action, do not use arguments.)

4. If desired, add any optional comments for the action in the Comment column.

As you choose your macro actions, selecting the needed action arguments is important so that the macro action has the desired effect. For example, when you specify an action to open a report, you use the action arguments to identify the report Access should use and the view in which Access should open it. Table 42-2 details the various macro actions available in Access, along with their uses and arguments.

Table 42-2
Macro actions and arguments

Action	Purpose	Arguments
AddMenu	Adds a drop-down menu to a custom menu bar	Menu Name
ApplyFilter	Applies a filter, query, or SQL WHERE clause to a form or report to filter or sort the records	Filter Name, Where Condition
Beep	Sounds a beep using the PC speaker	None
CancelEvent	Cancels the event that caused Access to run the macro containing the action	None
Close	Closes the specified object, or the active window when no object is specified	Object Type, Object Name
CopyObject	Copies the selected database object to a different database or to the same database under another name	Destination Database, New Name, Source Object Name, Source Object Type
DeleteObject	Deletes the specified object	Object Name, Object Type
Echo	Determines whether Access updates the screen as the macro executes	Echo On, Status Bar Text
FindNext	Finds the next record that meets criteria specified by the last Find Record action or by the entries in the Find dialog box	None
Find Record	Finds the first record that meets criteria specified by the Find Record action, or by the entries in the Find dialog box	Find What, Where, Match Case, Direction, Search as Formatted
GoToControl	Moves the insertion point to the field or control on the active form, datasheet, or query dynaset	Control Name
GoToPage	Moves the insertion point to the specified page of the active form	Page Number, Right, Down
GoToRecord	Moves the insertion point to the specified record	Object Name, Object Type, Record, Offset
Hourglass	Changes the shape of the mouse pointer to an hourglass as the macro runs	Hourglass On, Hourglass Off
Maximize	Maximizes the active window	None

Action	Purpose	Arguments
Minimize	Minimizes the active window	None
MoveSize	Moves or resizes the active window	Right, Down, Width, Height
MsgBox	Displays a message box containing an informational message or a warning	Message, Beep, Type, Title
OpenForm	Opens a form in Form View, Design View, Print Preview, or Datasheet View	Form Name, View, Filter Name, Where Condition
OpenModule	Opens the specified Visual Basic for Applications module	Module Name, Procedure Name
OpenQuery	Opens a select query in Datasheet View, Design View, or Print Preview	Query Name, View, Data Mode
OpenReport	Opens a report in Design View or Print Preview, or prints a report	Report Name, View, Filter Name, Where Condition
OpenTable	Opens a table in Datasheet View, Design View, or Print Preview	Table Name, View, Data Mode
OutputTo	Outputs data to foreign file	Object Type, Object Name, Output Format, Output File, Auto Start
PrintOut	Prints the active object	Print Range, Page From, Page To, Print Quality, Copies, Collate Copies
Quit	Exits Access	Options
Rename	Renames the selected object	New Name, Object Type, Old Name
RepaintObject	Finishes any pending screen updates for the specified object or for the active object if an object is not specified	Object Type, Object Name
Requery	Updates the data in a specified control by requerying the data source	Control Name
Restore	Restores a maximized or minimized window to its previous size	None
RunApp	Runs a Windows or DOS application	Command Line
RunCode	Runs a Visual Basic procedure	Procedure Name

(continued)

Table 42-2 *(continued)*

Action	Purpose	Arguments
RunCommand	Executes a menu command	Menu Bar, Menu Name, Command, Subcommand
RunMacro	Runs another macro	Macro Name, Repeat Count, Repeat Expression
RunSQL	Runs a query using a SQL statement	SQL Statement
Save	Saves the specified object	Object Type, Object Name
SelectObject	Selects the specified object	Object Type, Object Name, In Database Window
SendKeys	Sends keystrokes directly to Access or to an active Windows-based application	Keystrokes, Wait
SendObject	Includes specified object in an e-mail message	Object Type, Object Name, Output Format, To, Cc, Bcc, Subject, Message Text, Edit Message
SetMenuItem	Sets the state of a menu item	Menu Index, Command Index, Subcommand Index, Flag
SetValue	Sets the value of a field, control, or property	Item, Expression **on a form, a datasheet, or a report**
SetWarnings	Turns system messages on or off	Warnings On, Warnings Off
ShowAllRecords	Removes applied filters from the active form	None
ShowToolbar	Displays or hides the toolbar	Toolbar Name, Show
StopAllMacros	Halts all macros that are currently executing	None
StopMacro	Halts the current macro	None
TransferDatabase	Imports or exports data between the current database and another Access database	Transfer Type, Database Type, Database Name, Object Type, Source, Destination, Structure Only

Action	Purpose	Arguments
Transfer-Spreadsheet	Imports or exports data between the current database and a spreadsheet file	Transfer Type, Spreadsheet Type, Table Name, File Name, Has Field Names, Range
TransferText	Imports or exports data between the current database and a text file	Transfer Type, Specification Name, Table Name, File Name, Has Field Names

As you build the macro, you can insert new actions between existing ones by selecting the row where the new action's row should be added and pressing the Insert key or by choosing Insert⇨Row. You can delete existing actions by selecting the row that contains the action and pressing Delete or by choosing Edit⇨Delete Row. You can move existing rows to new locations in the macros (changing the order of actions performed by the macro) by first selecting the row you want to move and clicking on and dragging the row to the new desired location.

Specifying macro actions with drag and drop

As shown in the first example of the chapter, one way to specify common macro actions is to use *drag and drop* to click on and drag objects from the Database window to the Action column of the Macro window. You can use this technique to create macro actions that open any database object (such as a table, form, query, or report). Figure 42-6 illustrates the concept of dragging and dropping to create macro actions.

You specify macro actions with drag and drop by using the following steps:

1. Move and resize the Database window and the Macro window so that you can view both windows at the same time.

2. In the Database window, click on the tab for the object you want the macro to open. (For example, if you want the action to open a form, you click on the Forms tab of the Database window.)

3. Click on and drag the desired object in the Database window to an empty row under the Action column in the Macro window. When you perform this action, the appropriate name of the action appears in the Action column.

4. Change the default Action Arguments as desired.

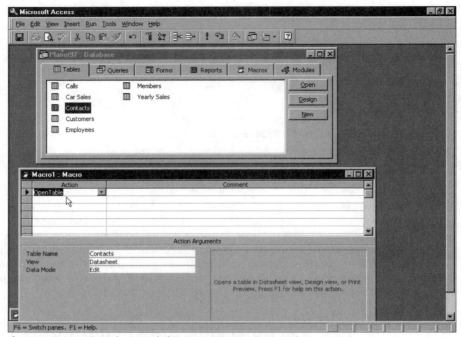

Figure 42-6: Using drag and drop to create macro actions.

You can also use drag and drop to create a macro to run another macro. When you drag an existing macro to the Action column of a Macro window, Access adds an action that runs the existing macro from the current macro.

Saving the macro

To save the macro, choose File⇨Save, or click on the Save button in the toolbar. If the macro is being saved for the first time, Access asks you for a name for the macro. Enter the name in the dialog box, and click on OK to save the macro to the current database.

Running the macro

Access offers a variety of different ways to run a macro. Probably the most obvious way is to select the macro in the Database window and click on Run, or to double-click on the macro in the Database window. Another way is to choose Tools⇨ Macro⇨ Macros and enter the macro name in the Run Macro dialog box that appears. Also, when a macro is open in Design View, you can run it by clicking on the Run button on the toolbar.

Additionally, you can run macros with command buttons that you add to forms. An easy way to create macro commands buttons is to use drag-and-drop techniques, as follows:

1. Open the desired form in Design View and move and size the form so that you can see it and the Database window at the same time.

2. Click on the Macros tab in the Database window to display the macros.

3. Click on and drag the desired macro to a location on the form where you want to place the button. When you drop the macro on the form, a command button appears.

If you press this button while the form is in Form View, the macro runs. You also can set up a macro so that it runs automatically when you start up a database, using the instructions described in the following section.

Creating Macros That Execute Automatically When You Open a Database

You can create and save a macro that automatically runs every time you open a database in Access. When Access opens a database, it looks for a macro in the database named *Autoexec*. If Access finds a macro under that name, Access runs the macro. Hence, you can create a new macro, record opens actions for forms and reports that you want to open automatically, and save the macro. When Access asks you for a name, call the macro Autoexec (case doesn't matter). Autoexec macros typically are used to open forms that a database user commonly works with, or to place a group of commonly used forms and/or reports on the screen.

You can prevent an Autoexec macro from running when you open a database by holding down Shift while you open the database.

Copying Macros

You can copy macros from one database to another, and you can copy them to new macro names in the same database. This can be a time-saving technique when you need to create a number of macros than perform similar tasks; instead of creating each macro from scratch, you can create one macro, copy it to different names, and modify the actions and arguments of the copied macros to fit the desired action. You can copy an existing macro with the following steps:

1. In the Database window, click on the macro to select it.

2. Choose Edit⇨Copy.

3. If you want to copy the macro to a different database, close the current database, open the database to which you want to copy the macro, and click on the Macros tab.

4. Choose Edit⇨Paste.

5. In the dialog box that appears, enter a name for the macro. (If you are copying the macro to the same database as the existing macro, you have to give the copied macro a different name than the original.)

Using Conditions in Macros

As part of a macro's design, you can specify conditional expressions. Conditional expressions control whether or not the macro is carried out: if a specified condition is true, the action is performed; if the condition is false, the action is ignored and the macro does not run. For example, you can attach a macro to a button on a form showing names and addresses in a mailing list. If you use an expression such as **[Country]** = "USA" in a Condition column of the macro, the corresponding action executes only if the Country field of the form contains "USA" as an entry. (The macro assumes that the name applies to a field in the current form, because you placed the button with the macro attached on that form.) You specify conditions in the Condition column of the Macro window. If the Condition column isn't visible when you open a macro in Design View, you can display it by choosing View⇨Conditions, or by clicking on the Conditions button on the toolbar.

Figure 42-7 shows an example of a macro that uses conditions. In this case, the macro is activated from the On Exit property of a Total for Salesperson field in a sales form, and the macro performs a custom validation of the data entered in a field and then takes an appropriate action (such as displaying a congratulatory message).

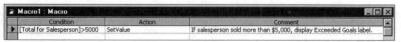

Figure 42-7: A macro that evaluates conditions for a Salary field of a form.

You can enter conditional expressions in macros by performing the following steps:

1. Open the desired macro in Design View.

2. If the Condition column isn't already visible, open the View menu and choose Conditions, or click on the Conditions button in the toolbar.

3. In the desired row and in the Condition column, enter the expression.

4. In the Action column, select the action that you want Access to carry out if the condition is true.

When you run the macro, Access evaluates the condition. If the condition is true, Access executes the action specified in that row, and in each additional row containing an ellipsis (. . .) in the Condition column. If the expression is false, Access skips the action and all subsequent rows that contain an ellipses in the Condition column, and Access moves to the next action row containing a blank Condition column or an expression.

If you need to refer to controls in your forms or reports within your conditions, you must use the correct syntax. For controls in forms, use the syntax `Forms!formname!controlname`, where `formname` is the name of the form, and `controlname` is the name of the form's control. For controls in reports, use the syntax `Reports!reportname!controlname`, where `reportname` is the name of the report, and `controlname` is the name of the report's control.

Handling Errors (or Oops!)

As your macros grow in complexity, you may occasionally run across errors when something goes wrong. Even the most expert programmers spend significant amounts of time debugging programs, and complex macros that you create can be considered as a kind of program because they tell Access what steps to take. Access offers a tool that can help you locate problems in macro design called the Action Failed dialog box. This dialog box appears whenever a macro halts because of a problem; the information in the dialog box can provide clues as to the source of the difficulty. Once you have located the cause of the problem, you can go to the Macro window and correct the actions.

When an error occurs while a macro is running, you'll see an error message indicating the possible cause of the problem. Click on OK in the dialog box of the error message, and you then see the Action Failed dialog box, shown in Figure 42-8.

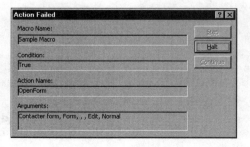

Figure 42-8: The Action Failed dialog box.

The dialog box contains the name of the macro, the name of the action where the problem was detected, the action's arguments, and a condition's logical value. Hopefully, you can use this information to track down and correct the cause of the problem. Common causes of failed macros are missing objects (such as when the macro tries to open a form that doesn't exist), and syntax and punctuation errors.

Summary

This chapter detailed the use of macros and covered topics such as creating macros, assigning macro actions, running macros, and defining conditional macros. The chapter covered the following topics:

✦ In Access, a *macro* is a list of actions stored in a table-like window called a Macro window.

✦ You can create a macro by clicking on the Macros tab in the Database window, clicking on the New button, and filling in the desired actions in the Macro window that appears.

✦ The upper half of the Macro window contains the actions that tell Access what steps to perform as the macro is carried out. The lower half of the Macro window contains arguments that further define each macro action.

✦ You can specify macro actions manually by choosing them in the Action column, or you can use drag and drop, dragging objects from the Database window into the Action column of the Macro window.

✦ You can run macros by selecting them in the Database window, or you can drop macros onto forms to create command buttons that, when clicked on, run the macro.

✦ If a macro is saved with the name Autoexec, that macro runs when the database containing the macro is opened.

✦ You can use the Condition column of a Macro window to specify conditions that must be met before a macro action is carried out.

In the next chapter, you learn how to create graphs within Access to provide a visual representation of your numeric data.

Where to go next...

✦ If you are using macros to perform tasks such as global updates or archiving, you'll want to look into using specialized query types. You can find details about this topic in Chapter 40.

✦ Another common use for macros is to automate repetitive reporting needs. For the complete details on how you can design and implement reports for use with your macros, read Chapter 38.

✦   ✦   ✦

Working with Charts in Access

One unusual feature of Access is its Ability to create charts that can be displayed within a form. These charts are generated by Microsoft Graph, a Windows mini-application included with many Microsoft applications (including Word and PowerPoint). If you read the material in Chapter 29, you'll find that many of the points covered in this chapter are the same because both PowerPoint and Access use Microsoft Graph to produce and edit charts.

Figure 43-1 shows an example of a typical chart in an Access form. (Charts are sometimes referred to as *graphs;* in fact, Microsoft uses the terms interchangeably.)

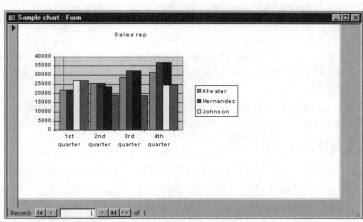

Figure 43-1: A typical chart.

Each chart comprises a series of *markers* that represent the numeric data stored within your table or query. The appearance of the markers varies according to what type of chart you insert into your Access document. In a bar chart, the markers appear as a series of horizontal bars. In a column chart, the markers look like a series of vertical columns. Line charts use markers that look like a series of thin lines. In pie charts, the markers are the wedges of the pie, and doughnut charts use markers that appear as slices of the doughnut.

With the exceptions of pie charts and doughnut charts, all charts have at least two axes: a horizontal axis (also known as the *category axis*) and a vertical axis (also known as the *value axis*). Three-dimensional charts also have a third axis, called the *series axis*.

In addition to the markers aligned along the axes, charts can also contain titles and *legends* that identify the categories that various markers represent. Microsoft Graph lets you customize all of these items in your charts.

Chart Types

Microsoft Graph provides several different chart types. Each chart type has optional subtypes that you can also choose. The following descriptions identify the various chart types:

Area   **Area charts** show the significance of change during a given time period. The top line of the chart totals the individual series, so area charts make it visually apparent how each individual series contributes to the overall picture. Area charts emphasize the magnitude of change as opposed to the rate of change. (If you want to emphasize the rate of change, use line charts instead.)

Bar   **Bar charts** use horizontal bars to show distinct figures at a specified time. Each horizontal bar in the chart shows a specific amount of change from the base value used in the chart. Bar charts visually emphasize different values, arranged vertically.

Column   **Column charts** are very much like bar charts, using columns to show distinct figures over a time period. The difference is that the markers in column charts are oriented along a *horizontal plane,* with the columns running vertically up or down from a base value used in the chart.

Line   **Line charts** are perfect for showing trends in data over a period of time. Like area charts, line charts show the significance of change, but line charts emphasize the rate instead of the magnitude, of change.

Pie   **Pie charts** show relationships between the pieces of a picture. They also can show a relationship between a piece of the picture and the entire picture. A pie chart can display only one series of data at a time, because each piece of a pie chart represents part of a total series. If you have a large number of series to plot, however, you are probably better off with a column chart because a pie crowded with slices is hard to interpret.

Charts in Excel or in Access?

Microsoft Office provides more than one way to create a chart. You can use the techniques in this chapter to create charts in Access, or you can use the techniques outlined in Chapter 19 to create charts in Excel. You can even create a chart in Excel and copy it as an OLE object into an Access form. So, where should you create your charts?

Excel's charting capabilities exceed Microsoft Graph's, and Excel has Chart Wizards that help you quickly and precisely design the chart that you need. The Access Chart Wizard makes a lot of assumptions about how your data should be plotted that you may or may not agree with. Although you can manually edit an Access chart to change assumptions made by its Chart Wizard (this process is discussed later in this chapter), you probably should use Excel if you want to get technical about working with your charts. In Excel, you can easily control the full range of assumptions used to construct charts. (Chapter 19 offers the complete scoop on working with Excel charts.)

The bottom line? If you're not an Excel user and have no desire to become one, you can stick with Microsoft Graph within Access for producing your charts. But if the added complexities of a spreadsheet don't scare you off, you're better off creating your charts in Excel.

 Doughnut charts show relationships between pieces of a picture, as do pie charts. Each section of the doughnut chart represents a part of the total series. The difference between pie charts and doughnut charts is that the doughnut chart has a hollow center

 Radar charts show the changes or frequencies of a data series in relation to a central point and to each other. (Every category has an axis value that radiates from a center point. Lines connect all data in the same series.) Radar charts can be difficult to interpret, unless you're accustomed to working with them. For reasons we don't understand, the Chart Wizard in Access doesn't provide you with the option of using a radar chart, but you can modify any chart that you create in Access and change the chart type to a radar chart.

 XY Scatter charts show relationships between different points of data to compare trends across uneven time periods or to show patterns as a set of *x* and *y* coordinates. These charts are commonly used to plot scientific data.

 Surface Charts are used when you want to display the best combinations between two sets of data.

 Bubble Charts are variations of XY scatter charts. They use bubbles as markers instead of the smaller points of XY scatter charts.

 Stock charts are also known as high-low-close charts and are commonly used to illustrate stock prices or other market data.

Cylinder charts are column charts with the columns appearing as cylindrical shapes.

 Cone charts are column charts with the columns appearing as cone shapes.

 Pyramid charts are column charts with the columns appearing as Pyramid shapes.

Creating Charts

In Access, charts are just another type of form. Like other Access forms, you can create charts manually or with a Chart Wizard. To create a chart manually, you follow these steps:

1. Open a blank form in Design View.

2. Use the Chart tool in the Toolbox to drop a chart onto the form.

3. Double-click on the chart and then modify it using the Microsoft Graph toolbars and menu options.

Unless you have unusual design requirements, using the Chart Wizard to create charts is easier than creating charts manually. You can use a Chart Wizard to create a chart by performing the following steps:

1. Click on the Forms tab in the Database window, and then click on New to open the New Form dialog box, shown in Figure 43-2.

Figure 43-2: The New Form dialog box.

2. In the list box, click on Chart Wizard to select it.

3. In the list box at the bottom of the New Form dialog box, choose the table or query that will provide the data for the chart. After you make a selection and click on OK, the first Chart Wizard dialog box appears, shown in Figure 43-3.

4. The dialog box asks which fields contain the data you want to use for the chart. Make the selections and then click on Next.

5. The second Chart Wizard dialog box (Figure 43-4) asks what type of chart you want. (The various chart types are listed in "Chart Types," earlier in this chapter.) Click on the appropriate chart type and then click on Next.

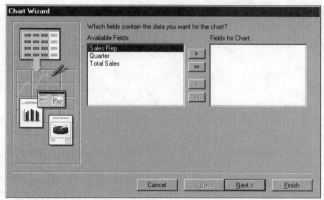

Figure 43-3: The first Chart Wizard dialog box.

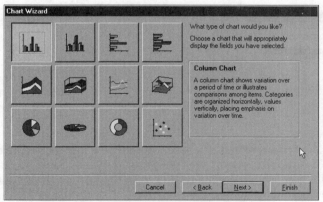

Figure 43-4: The second Chart Wizard dialog box.

6. The third Chart Wizard dialog box (Figure 43-5) asks you to choose how you want to lay out the data in the chart. In this dialog box, you can drag and drop the field buttons at the desired locations on the sample chart to change which field serves as the value axis, which field serves as the category axis, and which field summarizes or groups the data. At any point in this step, you can click on the Preview Chart button to see a representative sample of how your chart will appear.

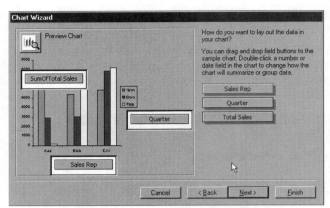

Figure 43-5: The third Chart Wizard dialog box.

7. If you want to change how the chart summarizes or groups data, double-click on any desired number field or date field you've placed in the dialog box. A Summarize dialog box appears, shown in Figure 43-6. You can choose the summary method that the chart will use, and click on OK. After you've finished using the options in the third Chart Wizard dialog box, click on Next to proceed.

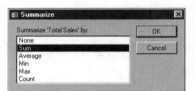

Figure 43-6: The Summarize dialog box.

8. The final Chart Wizard dialog box asks for a title for the chart. The dialog box also provides options for displaying a legend. You can choose to open the form with the graph (chart) displayed or with the form in Design View, where you can modify the design of the form. Make the desired selections in the dialog box, and click on Finish to produce the form containing your chart.

Editing Charts

After your chart appears in an Access form, you may want to alter certain aspects of that chart's appearance. Using the toolbar and menu options of Microsoft Graph, you can change design aspects such as the chart type, the data series used by the chart, and the appearance of the axes, the legends, and any added titles.

You can use that data in Excel, too!

If you prefer using Excel's worksheet and charting techniques for producing charts but feel stuck using Access charts because your numeric data is in Access, listen up: this problem no longer exists. Microsoft has built some automated export features into recent versions of Access. In the Database window, select the table or query containing the data that you want to chart in Excel. Then, choose Tools ⇨ OfficeLinks ⇨ Analyze it With MS Excel. Access launches your copy of Microsoft Excel, and the data from your table or query appear in an Excel worksheet. You can then use Excel charting techniques (see Chapter 19) to create the type of chart you want based on the data.

To edit a chart, open the form that contains the chart in Design View (click on the Forms tab in the Database window, click on the form to select it, and click on the Design button). When the form opens in Design View, double-click anywhere within the chart. In a moment (it may take a long moment because Microsoft Graph must start up behind the scenes), the window containing Microsoft Graph running within Access appears. Figure 43-7 shows the appearance of a chart, the menu bar, and toolbars after starting Microsoft Graph within Access.

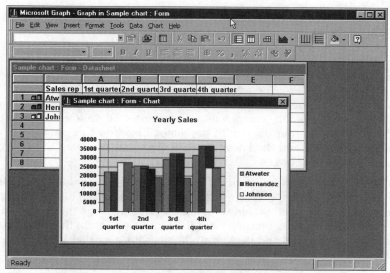

Figure 43-7: The appearance of a chart while it is being edited.

Changing the data series

Sometimes, you may want to swap the data series for an existing chart. For example, suppose that you have a bar chart that shows the total sales over four years for the divisions of a company, and you want the columns to represent each division — but instead, the columns represent years. You can swap the data series used by the chart to fix this problem.

To perform this task, choose either Data⇨Series in Rows or Data⇨Series in Columns. Alternatively, you can click on the By Row or By Column buttons in the Standard toolbar while the datasheet is active to get the same results.

You can also change the actual display of the information. To perform this task, use the shortcut menu that appears when you right-click on the bars, columns, lines, or pie slices of the chart. This shortcut menu contains commands related to changes in the display of the chart information. The shortcut menu is shown in Figure 43-8 and includes the following commands:

Figure 43-8: The shortcut menu for a data series.

✦ **Format Data Series** — This command lets you add labels or change the color of the data series. When you choose this option, the Format Data Series dialog box appears with the Patterns tab visible (shown in Figure 43-9). Using the Patterns tab, you can add a border to the data series by setting the options in the Border portion of the dialog box. You can vary the border's style, color, and thickness by selecting what you want in the Style, Color, and Weight list boxes.

In the Area portion of the dialog box, you can change the color of the data series to your liking. You can select a color or you can turn on the Automatic option, which applies the Windows default. Choosing None makes the marker invisible. Turning on the Invert if Negative option in the dialog box reverses the foreground and background colors for a marker if the value is negative.

The Shape tab (Figure 43-10) of this dialog box lets you choose from six possible shapes for the columns or bars of the chart.

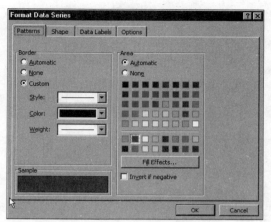

Figure 43-9: The Patterns tab of the Format Data Series dialog box.

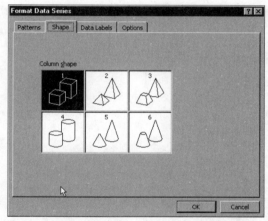

Figure 43-10: The Shape tab of the Format Data Series dialog box.

The Data Labels tab (Figure 43-11) of this dialog box lets you determine whether labels appear beside the markers to the data series. You also can have a legend appear next to the label; you do this by turning on the corresponding check box.

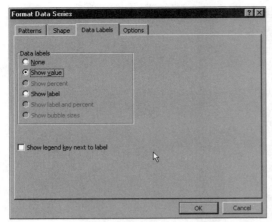

Figure 43-11: The Data Labels tab of the Format
Data Series dialog box.

The Options tab (Figure 43-12) of this dialog box lets you change the gap
depth, gap width, and chart depth for the chart.

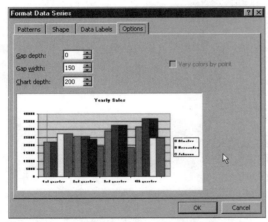

Figure 43-12: The Options tab of the Format
Data Series dialog box.

✦ **Chart Type** — This command lets you change the chart type. When you
choose this option from the shortcut menu, the Chart Type dialog box
(Figure 43-13) appears. The options for this dialog box are discussed in the
next section.

✦ **Add Trendline** — This command adds trendlines to the data series in area, bar, column, line, and XY (scatter) charts.

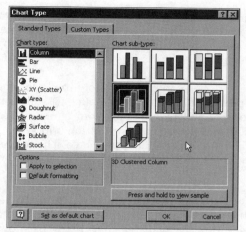

Figure 43-13: The Chart Type dialog box.

✦ **Clear** — This command removes a data series, the actual markers related to that series of numbers.

Changing the chart type

After creating a chart, you can experiment with it to make sure that you've selected the type that best represents your data. Microsoft Graph provides a range of chart types that you can view with a few mouse clicks; Table 43-1 lists them.

Table 43-1	
Access chart types	
Two-dimensional charts	*Three-dimensional charts*
Area	3-D Area
Bar	3-D Bar
Column	3-D Column
Line	3-D Line
Pie	3-D Pie
Doughnut	3-D Surface
Radar	
XY Scatter	

You can select chart types using different methods. One way is to select the chart and then choose C̲hart⇨C̲hart Type. The Chart Type dialog box then appears, as shown in Figure 43-13.

The left side of the dialog box contains a list of the available chart types. As you select a chart type, the right side of the dialog box displays subtypes available for the chart that you selected. Click on the chart type that you want and the sub-type and then click on OK.

While any chart and subtype are selected, you can click and hold the Press and hold to view sample button to see a preview of how any style of chart will look with your data. The Apply to Selection option lets you apply your choices to a specific part of a chart you've selected, and the Default Formatting option removes formatting and returns the chart to its default appearance. The Set As Default Chart button uses the current chart formatting as the default for all new charts created under Access.

You can also change the chart type by using the Chart Type button in the Standard toolbar. Click on the down arrow to the right of the Chart Type button on the Standard toolbar; a list box appears showing the available chart types, as shown in Figure 43-14. Just select one of the chart types from the list box.

Figure 43-14: Chart types available from the Chart Type button on the Standard toolbar.

Enhancing a Chart's Appearance

You can do several things to enhance the appearance of a chart. A few tasks are simple, such as changes to fonts and colors; other tasks, however, are a little more involved, such as adding titles. All can make a difference in the appearance of the chart.

Changing fonts

You can easily change the fonts used for text anywhere in your chart, including fonts used for titles, legends, or axes.

Tips for becoming a graphics-design wizard

As you work with fonts, colors, and other appearance-related aspects of a chart, keep in mind some principles of good overall design. It's easy to get carried away with fonts and colors, and produce a chart that is so visually "busy" as to be distracting to the user.

Never use more than two or three fonts within the same chart. Sans serif fonts, such as the one used for this sidebar, are good for charts.

Stick with complementary colors. The Chart Wizard used by Access chooses complementary colors automatically, but if you customize the colors, avoid clashing combinations such as bright pink and lime green.

Before committing the chart to any sort of public display, give it a critical, overall review for visual clarity and organization.

To change the fonts, right-click on the text for the item you want to change. For example, if you want to change the fonts used for a legend, right-click on the legend. From the shortcut menu that appears, choose the Format option. (If you right-click on a legend, the menu choice is Format Legend; if you right-click on a title, the menu choice is Format Chart Title; and if you right-click on an axis, the menu choice is Format Axis.) In the Format dialog box that opens, click on the Font tab, which in the case of an axis looks like Figure 43-15.

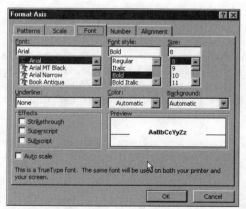

Figure 43-15: The Font tab in the Format Axis dialog box.

Under the Font tab, you see your options for setting the fonts used by the selected item. Choose a font, font style, and font size using the options displayed. You can also select underlining, color, and background, and you can turn on special effects such as strikethrough, superscript, and subscript. If the AutoScale option is turned on, text and numbers attached to the selected object are automatically resized whenever you resize the object. When you are done making selections, click on OK to put them into effect.

Changing chart colors

Creating and changing color schemes is another effective way to improve your chart's appearance. Changing the colors of your chart is relatively simple, thanks to shortcut menus:

1. Open the form containing the chart in Design View, double-click on the chart to make it active for edits, and then right-click on the bar or section of the chart that you want to change. This opens the shortcut menu shown earlier in Figure 43-8.

2. From the shortcut menu, choose Format Data Series. The Format Data Series dialog box opens with the Patterns tab visible, as shown earlier in Figure 43-9. This dialog box lets you change the border settings, selecting from a range of line styles.

3. To change the color of the particular section of the chart, move to the Area portion of the Patterns tab and then click on the color that you want. If you want, you also can add patterns by clicking on the Fill effects list box and then using the various options in the Fill Effects dialog box that appears. When you've made the changes you want, click on OK to accept the changes.

Adding titles

You may find it useful to add titles to your charts. Titles can help others who view your chart to understand what it means. To add titles to a particular chart area, right-click on the area to open the shortcut menu. Next, choose Chart Options, which opens the Chart Options dialog box. Click the Titles tab of this dialog box, as shown in Figure 43-16.

The Titles tab of the Chart Options dialog box lets you add a title either to your entire chart or to just one of the available axes. Turn on the option that you want and then click on OK.

Hot Stuff You also can format the text on a chart after the text has been entered. To do this, double-click on the text and choose the formats that you want from the Format Chart Title dialog box that appears.

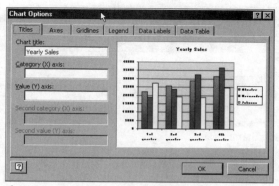

Figure 43-16: The Titles tab of the Chart Options dialog box.

Changing axes

You can modify your chart's axes to emphasize the points that you're trying to get across. You can change the line style, the font of the axes' text, the scale used by the numbers, and the alignment.

To change any of these formats, select one of the axes by clicking on it. Next, either choose Format➪Selected Axis, right-click on the axis and choose Format Axis, or double-click on the selected axis. These actions open the Format Axis dialog box, as shown in Figure 43-17. You can now select the options that you want from the various tabs. Table 43-2 tells what you can accomplish with each of these tabs.

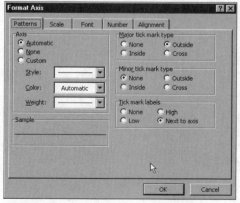

Figure 43-17: The Format Axis dialog box.

Table 43-2
Tabs of the Format Axis dialog box

Tab	Purpose
Patterns	Changes axis formatting or chooses tick mark types, both major and minor.
Scale	Controls the scale settings for axis values. Also sets logarithmic scales, or reverses the order of the values and sets the Floor XY Plane (the floor of the chart) at a value other than zero.
Font	Changes font settings for the axis.
Number	Controls the number formats for the numbers used for the axis.
Alignment	Controls the alignment of text used in the axis.

Changing borders

You can also change a chart by changing its borders. To do this, click outside the chart's object area and choose Format➪Selected Chart Area. The Format Chart Area dialog box appears, as shown in Figure 43-18. This dialog box has two tabs, Patterns and Font. Make the changes that you want in the dialog box and then click on OK.

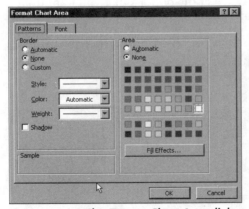

Figure 43-18: The Format Chart Area dialog box with the Patterns tab displayed.

Changing the Appearance of 3-D Charts

Three-dimensional (3-D) charts are a popular variation on basic charts. Creating 3-D charts is simple in Access: when you choose Chart⇨Chart Type, the Chart Type dialog box that appears (shown earlier in Figure 43-13) gives you the option of selecting a 2-D or a 3-D chart.

If you use 3-D charts often, you can take advantage of the flexibility that Microsoft Graph offers for changing the appearance of 3-D charts. You can change the elevation, the rotation, and the perspective used for a 3-D chart with the following steps:

1. Double-click on the 3-D chart to activate it, and choose Chart⇨3-D View. (Alternatively, you can right-click on the chart and select 3-D View from the shortcut menu that appears.) The Format 3-D View dialog box (see Figure 43-19) appears. As you change the settings in this dialog box, the picture of a chart in the center of the dialog box reflects your changes.

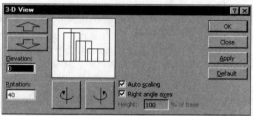

Figure 43-19: The Format 3-D View dialog box.

2. To change the chart's elevation, either click on the Up Arrow or Down Arrow buttons above the Elevation text box or enter a value in the Elevation text box.

3. To change the chart's rotation, either click on the Left or Right Rotation buttons to the right of the Rotation text box or enter a value in the Rotation text box.

4. To change the chart's perspective, either click on the Up Arrow or Down Arrow buttons above Elevation or enter a value in the Elevation text box (if the Right Angle Axes is not checked). The Format 3-D View dialog box also contains options for Auto Scaling, Right Angle Axes, and Height: % of Base.

   • **Right Angle Axes** — This option, when selected, sets the chart's axes at right angles independent of what you set the rotation or elevation to. (If you want to see the axes in relation to the chart's perspective, you must turn off this option.)

- **Auto Scaling** — When Right Angle Axes is selected, this option is enabled. The Auto Scaling option scales 3-D charts so that they are closer in size to 2-D charts.

- **Height: % of Base** — This option controls the height of the value axis and the walls of the chart, relative to the length of the category axis (the base of the chart). For example, if you enter **300%** in this box, the chart's height changes to three times the length of the base.

You can see the effect your changes have on your Access chart while the dialog box is open; you do this by clicking on the Apply button. After you make your changes, click on the OK button. You can use the Default button to undo your changes and return the settings to their defaults.

Summary

This chapter provided details for using charts within Access forms. The following topics were covered in the chapter:

✦ You can create a chart in Access by clicking on the Forms tab in the Database window, clicking on New, and choosing Chart Wizard in the New Form dialog box that appears. After the Chart Wizard starts, you can answer the questions presented by the Wizard to produce the chart.

✦ After adding a chart to a form, you can double-click on the chart and then choose Chart Type from the Format menu to change the chart's type.

✦ You can right-click on any object in a chart and then choose Format from the shortcut menu that appears to display a dialog box that lets you change the appearance of the selected object.

Where to go next...

✦ Charts are one part of forms in Access. You may want to combine charts with other form elements that you can add while manually designing a form. You can find a full range of techniques regarding form design in Chapter 37.

✦ If you want to produce more elaborate charts, use Excel's powerful chart-making feature. Chapter 19 covers the ins and outs of making charts in Excel.

✦   ✦   ✦

Access and the Web

C H A P T E R

44

As far as new features go, Office 97's major claim to fame is its addition of so many options for working with the Internet, and with intranets. Access 97 is no slouch in this area. For the first time, you can dynamically publish Access databases to the Web, and you can produce reports in HTML (Hypertext Markup Language) format, ready for inclusion on your web pages. Figure 44-1 shows data in an Access table, published as a web page on a corporate intranet and viewed using Netscape Navigator, a popular web browser.

You can also place hyperlink fields in tables, and you can use these fields in forms or reports to display links in other web pages on an intranet or on the Internet. If you need to retrieve or publish data across the net, Access 97 is a powerful tool for accomplishing such a task.

More Info To accomplish any of the tasks described in this chapter, obviously you'll need to be connected to a net. This can be a dial-up connection to the Internet, by means of a commercial Internet service provider such as AT&T WorldNet, MCINet, MindSpring, NetCom, or a host of others. Your connection can also be a direct connection through your organization's local area network. You may also be connected directly to a corporate *intranet*, in which case you'll be able to retrieve or publish data to your company's private network. This chapter won't go into specifics on making a net connection, as that topic is an entire book in itself. If you need help in this area, you can take a look at *Creating Cool Interactive Web Sites* and *Creating Cool FrontPage Web Sites* from IDG books.

More Info This chapter also assumes a familiarity with the basics of Access. If you are familiar with the web or with intranets but you haven't yet learned to work with Access, you should consider chapters 35 through 38 before proceeding with this chapter.

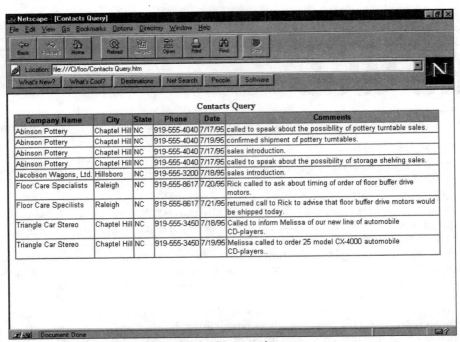

Figure 44-1: An Access table published as a web page.

What's Possible with Access 97 and the Web?

Using Access 97, you can perform a number of net-related tasks in designing and producing your databases. You can include *hyperlinks* as fields in the design of a table. As data is entered in the table, web site addresses can be stored in the hyperlink fields. You can place these same fields in forms and reports; when users of the database click the fields in a form, they can jump directly to that web site. You can save table data as HTML, the publishing lingua of the World Wide Web. And you can produce reports for static or dynamic publishing to the net. Each of these topics will be covered in further detail throughout this chapter.

About the Web and the Internet

Because intranets and the Internet are newer concepts to many readers than are databases, a few explanations of terms may be in order. (If you're intimately familiar with the Internet, intranets, and the World Wide Web, you may want to skip this section and the next and dive right into working with Access and the Web.) First, the *Internet* is a global collection of computers, linked together by means of telephone and microwave lines and accessible to the public by means of various connections in offices and in homes. The Internet grew out of a research project that came into common knowledge in the 1970s, which originally linked university and government computers in the US. Since its inception, the Internet has grown to encompass thousands of computers spread throughout dozens of nations. Any PC user with an Internet connection (either by means of a phone line or a direct hookup) can connect to the Internet and gain access to the volumes of information located there.

One major component of the Internet is the *World Wide Web*. There are other parts of the Internet, but the World Wide Web is the most well-known part. The World Wide Web is that part of the Internet that makes use of graphical software known as web browsers, and of files stored as HTML. The computers on the Internet that store the HTML files are also known as *web servers*. When PCs connect to the Internet to retrieve this data, they use web browser software, which converts the incoming information (encoded in HTML) to graphical pages displayed as a combination of text, graphics, and in some cases audio and video. Commonly used web browsers include Microsoft Explorer and Netscape Navigator, and the custom web browsers built into the software provided by America Online and CompuServe.

Each site on the Internet has a unique address, commonly known as the Internet address (and less commonly known by the official name of URL, or Uniform Resource Locator). When you establish an Internet connection, open a web browser, and enter an Internet address such as *http://www.whitehouse.gov*; you are entering the address for the web server that provides the home page for the President's office in the United States. Web addresses like these can be stored in Access tables and displayed as links in forms and as addresses in reports.

About Intranets

Many net-related uses of Office 97 involve making data available on *intranets*. An intranet is a private network of computers that is available only to the members of a specific organization. Intranets make use of World Wide Web technology — web servers, network connections, and web browser software — to allow members of an organization to share information. Intranets are very popular with corporations, as intranets let employees share work-related information in a confidential manner.

About HTML

As mentioned earlier, HTML, is the language used for publishing information to the World Wide Web and to intranets that use World Wide Web technology. HTML is a text-based language that makes use of special codes called *tags*. These tags are included in the text of the HTML documents, and they provide instructions to the web browser software that determine how the data appears when it is viewed by the end user. While you don't need to know the nuts and bolts of HTML coding to work with Access and the web, it's a good idea to at least be familiar with the concept of saving your data in HTML file format. In order to publish Access data on the Internet or on an intranet, you'll need to save that data in HTML format and upload it to your web server. If you are dealing with a corporate intranet, your company's webmaster can tell you how to upload the HTML files that Access produces to your company's web server. If you are managing a web site on the Internet or on an intranet, you already know how to do this; much of the rest of this chapter will deal with getting that Access data ready for uploading to your server.

About the Web Toolbar

Like all the major Office 97 applications, Access provides the Web toolbar, a toolbar that helps you browse through the resources on an intranet or on the Web. Using the Web toolbar, you can quickly open, search, and browse through any document or through a web page. You can jump between documents, and you can add favorite sites you find on the web to the Favorites folder, allowing you to quickly go back to those sites at a later time.

In Access, you can display the Web toolbar by choosing View⇨Toolbars and then selecting Web from the submenu that appears or by clicking the Web toolbar button in the Standard toolbar. Figure 44-2 shows the Web toolbar. Note that the first three buttons of the toolbar are not active in Access: these buttons are operational in Word 97 because Word 97 can serve as a web browser.

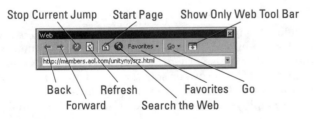

Figure 44-2: The Web toolbar.

The buttons on the Web toolbar don't specifically relate to the use of Access. However, it is helpful to know that the Web toolbar exists, as you'll find it useful when you happen to be in Access and you have a need to go to the Web (or to your company's intranet) for information. For example, you can click the Search the Web button to launch your default web browser and search the web, or you can click the Favorites button to open a list of your favorite web sites. For more specifics on the Web toolbar, see Chapter 11, which provides a description of how you can use the web toolbar and how Word 97 can serve as a web browser if you aren't using Microsoft Internet Explorer or Netscape Navigator.

Including Hyperlinks in a Table Design

As Chapter 35 details, when you create tables in Access, you define your fields with an appropriate data type. In Access 97, one of the available data types is the hyperlink. Hyperlink fields are designed to store Internet addresses, or locations to jump to in other documents. Access recognizes the format of web addresses, and it automatically translates the text you type into the hyperlink field into valid Internet addresses. Hyperlink fields make it easy for persons using your Access database to jump to the web sites stored in the fields as addresses — of course, these users must have Internet or intranet connections to reach the web.

When you begin the process of creating a new table, you see the Table Design window, as detailed in Chapter 35. After entering a name for the field in the Field Name column, click the arrow to the right of the Data Type column, and choose Hyperlink from the list of data types, as shown in Figure 44-3. You can then continue the design process and save the table's structure in the usual manner.

Adding Hyperlink Data to Tables

Once the table exists, you can enter web addresses in the same manner as you enter other textual data in an Access field: by typing it directly into the field of a table's datasheet or into the field of a form that's based on the table. You can also place the insertion pointer in the field and then click the Insert Hyperlink button on the Standard toolbar to open an Insert Hyperlink dialog box where you can type the path for the link.

If you want to edit the entry stored in the hyperlink field, you can't just click in the field and retype it because clicking in a field with an existing entry takes you to the link. Instead, right-click the entry and choose Hyperlink⇨Edit Hyperlink from the shortcut menus. An Edit Hyperlink dialog box appears, and you can change the entry.

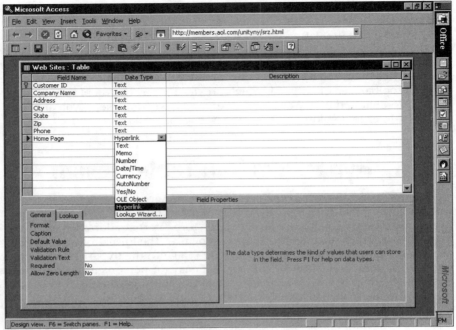

Figure 44-3: Choosing a hyperlink field type during the table's design.

Using Hyperlinks in Forms and Reports

You can use the same design techniques detailed in Chapters 37 and 38 to add hyperlink fields to the design of forms and reports. You can add a hyperlink field to a form or a report by performing the following steps:

1. Open the desired form or report in Design view.

2. If the Field List is not visible, choose View⇨Field List to display it.

3. Drag the desired hyperlink field from the Field List to the desired location in the form or report.

Figure 44-4 shows the process of adding a hyperlink field to a form.

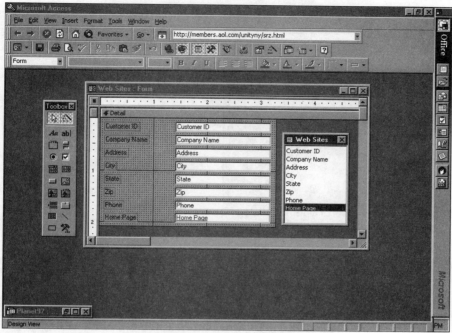

Figure 44-4: A hyperlink field added to the design of a form.

When you view the form, the contents of the hyperlink field changes as you move between records, to reflect the addresses stored in the field for each record in the table. With reports, the addresses stored in each record print out in the reports like all other data.

You can also add a hyperlink to a form that doesn't change with each record (one that always jumps to a specific address). To do this, open the form in Design view and click the Insert Hyperlink button in the toolbar. In the Insert Hyperlink dialog box that appears (Figure 44-5), specify a web address in the Link to File or URL text box (or to link to a file, enter a path for the file in the text box).

When viewing hyperlinks in a form, you can jump directly to the address by clicking once in the hyperlink field. (You'll notice that as you move the mouse pointer over the hyperlink field, its shape changes to an outstretched finger similar to the pointer used by most web browsers.) When you click the field, Windows launches your default web browser and takes you directly to the site.

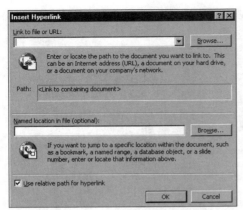

Figure 44-5: The Insert Hyperlink dialog box.

Whereas hyperlinks are commonly used to store web addresses, you can also use them to jump to other applications. For example, you can use hyperlinks to jump to a cell in an Excel worksheet or to a heading in a Word document or a Power-Point slide. Click in the hyperlink field of the table at the appropriate record, and then click the Insert Hyperlink button in the toolbar. In the dialog box that appears (shown in Figure 44-5), click the Browse button at the top of the dialog box to locate the file that you want to link to. Then click the Browse button at the bottom of the dialog box to find a location in the other file that you want to link to (or type the location into the Named Location text box).

Publishing Access Data as HTML

Access 97 includes a Publish to the Web Wizard, a wizard that lets you convert any selection of tables, queries, forms, or reports to HTML format, so you can publish the data on the Internet or on an intranet. The Publish to the Web Wizard lets you produce static pages (these appear on web sites as fixed, unchanging data) or as dynamic pages (these change to reflect changes in the data stored in the Access tables). You can also produce a home page that ties together all the web pages you create through the use of the wizard.

You can launch this wizard through the use of the Save as HTML command on the File menu. Use the following steps to produce web-ready files based on your database objects in Access:

1. Make sure the desired database is open (the Database window should be visible).

2. Choose File➪Save as HTML. In a moment, the first page of the Publish to the Web Wizard appears, as shown in Figure 44-6.

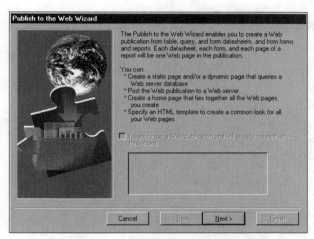

Figure 44-6: The first dialog box of the Publish to the Web Wizard.

3. If you want to use a Web Publication Profile that you created earlier using this wizard, you can turn on the option shown in this dialog box and then choose the desired profile by name in the list box. (The last step of the Web Publishing Wizard lets you save all of your template, format, and file directory choices made within the wizard to a profile, so you can reuse the profile and avoid repeatedly giving the same answers to the questions asked by the wizard.) When you are ready to proceed, click Next. In a moment, you'll see the second dialog box of the Publish to the Web Wizard, as shown in Figure 44-7.

4. Using the various tabs of this dialog box, select one or more tables, queries, forms, or reports to be published to the Web. Click the desired object and click the Select button to select it. (You can select all the objects under a given category by clicking the tab for that category, then clicking the Select All button.) When you are done selecting objects, click Next. In a moment, the third dialog box of the Publish to the Web Wizard appears, as shown in Figure 44-8.

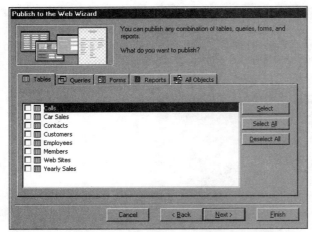

Figure 44-7: The second dialog box of the Publish to the Web Wizard.

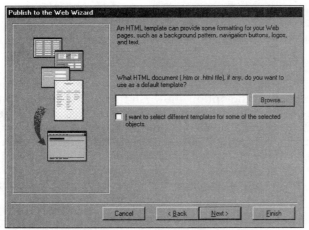

Figure 44-8: The third dialog box of the Publish to the Web Wizard.

5. You can use this dialog box to specify an optional template that you can use to provide formatting for your web pages. (You can create such templates with a knowledge of HTML programming or with a web page design utility like Microsoft FrontPage.) Enter any desired template file name in the text box, or leave the box blank if you don't want to use a template; then click Next. In a moment, the fourth dialog box of the Publish to the Web Wizard appears, as shown in Figure 44-9.

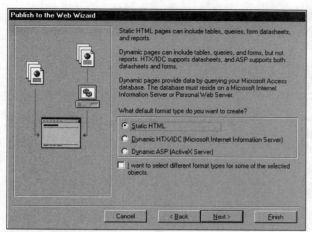

Figure 44-9: The fourth dialog box of the Publish to the Web Wizard.

6. Using the options shown in this dialog box, you can choose whether your pages should be published as static HTML files or as dynamic HTC/IDX format (for use with Microsoft's Internet Information Server) or dynamic ASP format (for use with servers that use Active X technology). The Static HTML option produces web pages that are unchanging, until you produce them again. (You can liken these to "snapshots" of the table data at a given instant in time.) The Dynamic HTX/IDC and Dynamic ASP options let you produce web pages that have dynamic links back to the Access tables so that as changes are made to the data in the tables, the web pages are updated. Note that in order to produce dynamic web pages, your Access data must be stored on a Microsoft Internet Information Server or on a Microsoft FrontPage Personal Web Server. Make the desired choice in the dialog box and click Next. In a moment, the fifth dialog box of the Publish to the Web Wizard appears, as shown in Figure 44-10.

7. This dialog box lets you specify the location where the web pages produced by the wizard should be stored. You can enter a drive and directory in the text box, or you can click the Browse button and select a drive and directory from the dialog box that appears. Also, if your data is stored on a Microsoft Internet Information Server, you can use the additional options in the dialog box to publish the web pages directly to that server. (For more specifics on publishing to the server, refer to your documentation for the Microsoft Internet Information Server.) After making the desired entry in the dialog box, click Next. In a moment, the sixth dialog box of the Publish to the Web Wizard appears, as shown in Figure 44-11.

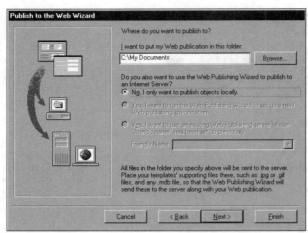

Figure 44-10: The fifth dialog box of the Publish to the Web Wizard.

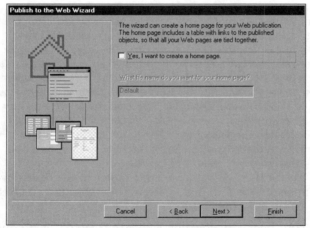

Figure 44-11: The sixth dialog box of the Publish to the Web Wizard.

8. Using the option shown in this dialog box, you can specify whether the wizard should create a home page. If you enable this option, the wizard creates a home page containing a table with the names of all the objects selected in Step 4. Each entry in the table on the home page serves as a link to the web page containing the selected object. Turn on the option if desired and click Next. In a moment, the final dialog box of the Publish to the Web Wizard appears, as shown in Figure 44-12.

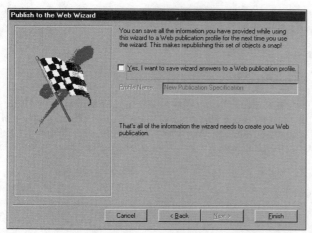

Figure 44-12: The final dialog box of the Publish to the Web Wizard.

9. This dialog box contains an option which, when turned on, lets you save all of the wizard answers to a profile name. You may find this option useful if you plan to regularly publish web pages using the same specifications you used during this session with the wizard. Turn on the option if desired and click Finish.

Once you are done answering the questions presented by the wizard, it proceeds to create the HTML files needed to produce your web pages, and they are stored in the location you specified in Step 7. You can then pass the files on to your company's webmaster, or use your own techniques to upload them to your web server.

Summary

This chapter has covered the details behind sharing your Access data with Internet/Intranet users. One of the primary uses of corporate internets is to make database information readily available to PC users, and Access 97 is a powerful tool for accomplishing that goal. Points covered in this chapter included the following:

✦ Hyperlink fields can be added to a table's design, and you can store web addresses or jump locations to other files in those fields.

✦ You can add hyperlinks to forms and reports to let users of the database easily access other file locations or web sites.

✦ You can use the Save as HTML option of the File menu to launch the Publish to the Web Wizard, for converting tables, queries, forms, or reports to HTML files for publishing on the Internet or on an intranet.

In the next chapter, you learn how to further extend the power of Access by using Visual Basic for Applications.

Where to go next...

✦ Access is just one component of the web publishing capabilities provided by Office 97. Word, Excel, and PowerPoint also offer web publishing and web interaction features. For specifics on Word and the web, see Chapter 11; for Excel and the web, Chapter 23; and for Power Point and the web, Chapter 32.

✦   ✦   ✦

Access and Visual Basic for Applications

This chapter deals with the use of Visual Basic for Applications (VBA), the programming language that is a virtual requirement for taking Access applications beyond a level of what is possible with macros alone. VBA is heavily based on Microsoft's Visual Basic programming language. Using VBA, you cannot only perform the kinds of automated operations that are possible with macros, but you can exercise a much tighter degree of control over complete custom applications. You can get an idea of the power of VBA just by looking at the flexibility of the Database Wizards: each Database Wizard is a program, written in VBA, that presents a set of dialog boxes to a user and creates a series of database objects in response to the answers.

What is Visual Basic for Applications?

Visual Basic for Applications is a full-fledged programming language that is an integral part of Access. (And as of the release of Office 97, VBA rests just beneath the surface of all the major Office products, which include Word, Excel, and PowerPoint.) You can use VBA to manipulate your database data under the control of custom applications and to customize the user interface, or the way an application looks to the person who is using it.

VBA is a structured, high-level programming language. Like other high-level languages, it includes ways to test for conditions, ways to perform repetitive operations, and ways to store information in memory or onto disk and later retrieve and use that information. If you've used Microsoft's Visual Basic programming environment, you'll find yourself on very familiar ground when it comes to using VBA. Even Access Basic, the predecessor to VBA on the Access side, has strong similarities to VBA. VBA follows a trend toward a programming methodology known as *object orientation*. In a nutshell, the user environment in an Access application that is controlled by VBA is not changed through a series of procedural statements. Instead, the control occurs in response to events that affect various objects, like text boxes, command buttons, and sections of a form or a report. With VBA in Access, the program code is attached directly to the objects, and it runs when certain events occur. As an example, making a change to existing data in a field might be the event that triggers a portion of VBA code. The code might tell the Access application to perform a specific task (such as a customized validation routine) in response to the change in the field. In this case, a certain event (changing the data) triggered a response (the execution of specific VBA code). Because all programming under Windows involves responding to a series of events, VBA provides you with the tools you need to respond to events throughout an Access application.

Why VBA? Why Not Macros?

When compared to the other primary Office programs (Word, Excel, and PowerPoint), Access is somewhat unique in one respect. While you can write custom applications in Word, Excel, or PowerPoint using VBA, only Access offers two distinct methods of building custom applications. You can use macros, or you can use VBA. Beacause you can do a great deal in Access using the power of macros, there is a lot of overlap between the use of macros and the use of VBA code. Some application designers prefer to do all or nearly all development using macros and to rely on VBA only when a task that cannot be handled by means of a macro presents itself. Other developers prefer to avoid the use of macros and depend entirely on VBA. Neither approach is necessarily incorrect; which approach you take often depends on your own comfort level with programming and on what you are trying to accomplish. Macros are generally recommended for fast prototyping of applications, for handling simple opening and closings of forms and reports, and for creating custom menus (in fact, you can only create custom menus in Access with the use of macros). Writing VBA code is recommended for tight control over how program errors are handled, for adding user-defined functions to the Access environment, and for performing applications at the operating system level (such as reading foreign data directly from a disk file).

Creating VBA Code with the Control Wizards

To see one excellent way in which you can use VBA to respond to events in the Access environment, you can take a look at what goes on behind the scenes of any button added to a form with the aid of the Control Wizards. You can use these steps to create command buttons that make use of VBA code, and you can then examine the VBA code behind those buttons:

1. Open any database containing a table of information. If you copied the Planet97 database from the IDG web site (www.idgbooks.com), you can use the Calls table in that database.

2. Select the desired table, then in the Standard toolbar, click the Autoform button. This quickly creates a default form for the table.

3. After the new form for the table opens, click the Design button in the toolbar, to switch to design view.

4. Choose View ➪ Toolbox to display the Toolbox (if it isn't already visible).

5. Make sure that the Control Wizards are turned on in the Toolbox (the Control Wizards button should be depressed).

6. Click the Command button in the Toolbox.

7. Click in a blank area of the form, to place a command button. When you do so, the Command Button Wizard dialog box appears, as shown in Figure 45-1.

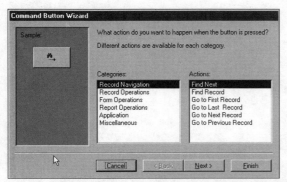

Figure 45-1: The Command Button Wizard dialog box.

8. Under Category, make sure that Record Navigation is selected. Then, under Actions, click Find Record. Finally, click Finish to add a button to the form that, when clicked, will perform a simple search.

9. Click the Command button in the Toolbox.

10. Click in a blank area of the form, just below where you placed the last button. In a moment, the Command Button Wizard dialog box again appears.

11. Under Categories, select Form Operations. Then, under Actions, select Close Form. Next, click on Finish, to add a button that, when clicked, closes the form.

12. Save the form by choosing File⇨Save from the menus. When asked for a name, call the form **Sample Code Form**. If desired, you can run the form and test the operation of the buttons.

13. Switch back to Design mode (if you are not still there) by clicking the Design button on the toolbar.

14. Choose View⇨Code, or click the Code button on the toolbar. When you do this, a window into the Visual Basic Editor opens, similar to the one shown in Figure 45-2.

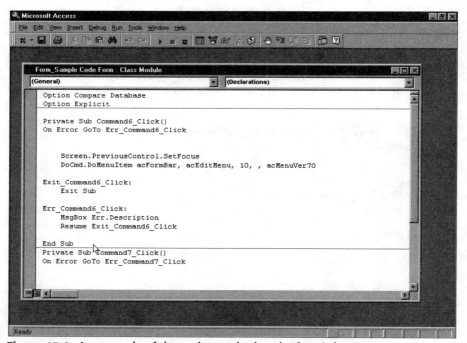

Figure 45-2: An example of the code attached to the form's buttons.

In the window, you see three portions of VBA program code: a declarations section at the top that contains some code that applies to the entire form and two sections below the top that contain the code attached to the two buttons. The first section of code attached to the Find button starts like this (but the number following the word Command may be different in your case):

```
Private Sub Command6_Click()
```

The procedure ends with the words End_Sub. The lines between these two statements make up the VBA procedure that responds to the Find button being clicked.

The line of code which performs the bulk of the work looks like this:

```
DoCmd.DoMenuItem acFormBar, acEditMenu, 10, , acMenuVer70
```

In this case, the code performs the equivalent of a menu action of choosing the Find command from the Edit menu to display the Find dialog box, allowing the user to search for a record.

Editing Visual Basic for Applications Code

When you open a VBA module, you can enter program code just like you type text in any word processor. You don't have to know the mechanics of entering text and correcting mistakes; suffice it to say that you can use the same text entry and editing techniques, including cutting and pasting, that you can use in any Windows word processor.

While you are in the Visual Basic Editor, you can also insert text from another file into your existing program code. If you want to insert text into the program code, place the insertion point at the location in the module where you want to insert the code and choose Insert⇨File. In the File dialog box, select the file that contains the text that you want to insert and click on the OK button to read the text into the file.

Learn by example

If you plan to get involved in VBA programming, one of the best ways to become familiar with what you can do with the language is to examine other tested, working applications and macros that range from the simple to the complex. You can also study the code that's attached to the command buttons you add to forms (using the Control Wizards) for performing various common database tasks.

Printing Visual Basic Code

You can print the code that is contained in your Visual Basic modules. To print the code, open the module that contains the desired code. Then choose the Print command from the File menu.

About Modules

When you work with VBA, you will do your programming within modules. In VBA, a module is nothing more than a collection of declarations and procedures, stored together as a single unit. In Access 97, you can have two types of modules: *class modules* and *standard modules*. Class modules are modules you can use to define new objects that you create under VBA, whereas standard modules are modules where you can place sub and function procedures you want to make available to objects throughout your database. (Class modules are beyond the scope of this introductory chapter.) You will often find standard modules to be quite useful because you can place general-purpose procedures in them and use them often from anywhere within your database.

About Procedures

A *procedure* is a single, definable unit of VBA code. Each procedure consists of a group of statements and methods, and together these statements and methods perform a desired operation. As an example, the following procedure is attached to the Click property of the Find button added to the form in the example described earlier in this chapter:

```
Private Sub Command6_Click()
On Error GoTo Err_Command6_Click

    Screen.PreviousControl.SetFocus
    DoCmd.DoMenuItem acFormBar, acEditMenu, 10, , acMenuVer70

Exit_Command6_Click:
    Exit Sub

Err_Command6_Click:
    MsgBox Err.Description
    Resume Exit_Command6_Click

End Sub
```

In Access 97, you can have three kinds of procedures: *event procedures*, which are procedures that are performed in response to certain events that take place; *sub procedures*, which perform one or more operations but don't return a value, and *function procedures*, which perform a calculation and return a value. You can use VBA procedures to modify the way your Access objects (tables, queries, forms, and reports) work.

Creating Event Procedures

One common use for VBA by beginning Access developers is to have certain simple to moderately complex procedures run in response to various events, such as editing a field or clicking a command button. With event procedures, the code of the procedure is attached to an event that takes place on a form, report, or a control in the form or report. The exact code you will want to use will of course vary with what you want to accomplish, but these are the overall steps needed to create an event procedure:

1. Open the desired form or report in Design view. If you want to attach the event procedure to a control, select the desired control.

2. Choose <u>V</u>iew⇨<u>P</u>roperties to open the Properties window for the form, report, or control.

3. Click the Event tab.

4. Click the event property for the event that should cause the procedure to run. As an example, if you want the procedure to run immediately after a user updates the data in a control, click the After Update property.

5. Click the Build button to the right of the property box (the button with three dots) to open a Choose Builder dialog box.

6. Double-click Code Builder in the dialog box. A window into the VBA Editor opens, and Access automatically adds the starting and ending lines for the procedure.

7. Add the desired code that you want to execute when the chosen event takes place.

Just a Beginning...

Make no mistake about it, using Visual Basic for Applications falls well into the realm of programming. (If you're completely new to programming, you should be congratulated for pressing this deeply into what, for many readers, is a subject of mystifying complexity.) You've learned how Access makes extensive use of VBA code in objects that you add with the Control Wizards, and you've learned that you can extend the power of Access macros by adding your own Visual Basic code to tightly control the behavior of the objects in your databases. Still, you've only touched the surface of what's possible with VBA in Access. VBA is a full-featured programming language that you can use to automate or customize nearly any task that can be done in Access. If you're encouraged (dare we even say excited?) by the challenges of programming, you should look into additional resources for learning about Visual Basic programming. It's a subject about which entire books have been written.

Summary

This chapter has provided an introduction to programming by using Visual Basic for Applications. The chapter covered the following points:

✦ Using VBA, you can create procedures that control how your Access objects work. These include event procedures (which respond to events), function procedures (which perform a calculation and return a value) and sub procedures (which perform operations but don't return values).

✦ Macros work well for creating menus and for handling the opening and closing of forms and reports within an application. VBA code works well for dealing with user errors, for adding customized functions, and for running other applications while under the control of an Access program.

✦ VBA programs are stored inside procedures, and one or more procedures can be placed in a module.

The next chapter will show how you can put Access to work by demonstrating how you can create and use databases for common business tasks.

Where to go next . . .

✦ Because complex applications design in Access usually involves a combination of macros and VBA, you should also be intimately familiar with the use of macros before getting deeply involved with Visual Basic for Applications. See Chapter 42.

✦ ✦ ✦

Access for Windows at Work

◆   ◆   ◆   ◆

In This Chapter

Managing mailing
lists

Tracking personnel
assignments

◆   ◆   ◆   ◆

In this chapter, you find a number of step-by-step exercises that you can follow to put Access to work quickly. The exercises in this chapter detail how you can create and manage a mailing list and a personnel assignment tracking system. As you work through the examples in this chapter, you'll have the opportunity to use common Access objects, including tables, queries, forms, and reports. You'll also have the opportunity to see how the Command Button Wizard, available as part of the form design process, lets you easily add buttons to forms to perform common tasks. By combining the various Access objects in ways demonstrated throughout this chapter, you can develop complete applications to manage business tasks, such as the management of a mailing list, an employee personnel database, a sales tracking system, or a parts inventory.

Mailing List Management

Historically, one of the most common uses for database management software is the handling of mailing lists. Mailing lists are the lifeblood of many organizations. Mailing lists in Access can be used to selectively produce mailing labels, to print envelopes on printers equipped to handle them, and to provide name and address information for use with form letters in Word for Windows.

Working Together

You can use many features in Access to manage your mailing list, including parameter queries and the Mailing Label Report Wizard. The first section of this chapter provides step-by-step instructions that you can use to build an application that manages a mailing list. Figure 46-1 shows the main form for the mailing list management system. You can use the steps outlined here to build this application, or you can copy the file Mailer.dba from the IDG Books web site (www.idgbooks.com).

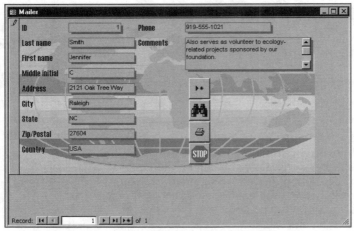

Figure 46-1: The main form used for the mailing list management system.

Creating the database and table

The first overall steps in creating the mailing list manager are to create a new database and design and save the table that will be used to store the names and addresses. You can use the following steps to create the database and table:

1. After starting Access, choose File⇨New Database, and click OK. The File New Database dialog box (Figure 46-2) appears.

Figure 46-2: The File New Database dialog box.

2. In the File name text box, enter **Mailer** as a database name and then click on the Create button to create the new database.

3. In the Database window, click on the Tables tab and then click on New.

4. In the New Table dialog box, click on Design View in the list box and then click on OK. After you do this, the Table window appears, where you can lay out the design of the new table. Fill in the Table window with these field names and data types:

Field name	Data type
Last name	Text
First name	Text
Middle initial	Text
Address	Text
City	Text
State	Text
Zip/Postal	Text
Country	Text
Phone	Text
Comments	Memo

When you're done filling out the window, your table's structure should resemble the one shown in Figure 46-3.

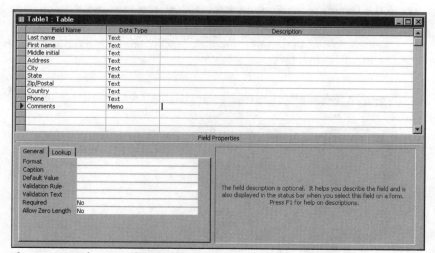

Figure 46-3: The completed table structure for a mailing list management system.

5. Choose File⇨Save to save the table. When asked for a table name, enter **Mailer** and click on OK. When Access warns you that no primary key is defined for the table, click on Yes to let Access add an AutoNumber field called ID as the first field of the table.

6. Press Ctrl+F4 to close the table and reveal the Database window that shows the new table called Mailer.

Creating the form

The mailing list application uses a single form to display records and provides a user interface where you can add and edit data and print reports by pressing command buttons. To create this form, perform these steps:

1. In the Database window, click on the Forms tab and then click on New.

2. In the New Form list box that appears, click on AutoForm: Columnar, click in the list box of tables and queries, and choose the Mailer table from the list. Then click on OK to create the form.

3. When the new form appears, press Ctrl+F4 to close the form. Access asks if you want to save the changes to the form; answer Yes in the dialog box. When prompted for a name for the form, accept the default name of **Mailer** as the desired name and click on OK.

Creating the query

You use the following steps to create a parameter query that will support a report that enables the production of mailing labels for a given state. Perform the following steps to create the query:

1. In the Database window, click on the Queries tab, and then click on New. The New Query list box appears.

2. Click on Design View and then click on OK. The Show Table dialog box (Figure 46-4) appears.

Figure 46-4: The Show Table dialog box.

3. Select Mailer from the list of tables that you can add, click on Add, and then click on Close. This process adds a list box for the Mailer table to the query grid.

4. Double-click on the title bar of the list box to select all the fields in the box.

5. Click on and drag any of the selected fields to the first row of the first column of the query grid.

6. Scroll the query grid to the right until the State field comes into view.

7. Click in the Criteria: row of the State column and type the following parameter:

   [Enter the desired state:]

   At this point, your query's design should resemble the example shown in Figure 46-5. (In the figure, the State column has been widened so that you can see the text of the entire parameter.)

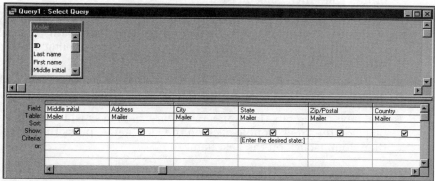

Figure 46-5: The completed query design for a parameter query.

8. Press Ctrl+F4 to close the Query Design window. When Access asks if you want to save the query, click on Yes. When Access prompts for a name, call the query **By State**.

Creating the mailing labels

Next, you can perform the following steps to create the mailing labels that you will use with the query that you just saved:

1. In the Database window, click on the Reports tab and then click on New. The New Report dialog box (Figure 46-6) appears.

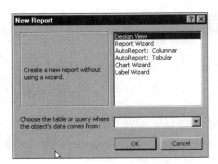

Figure 46-6: The New Report dialog box.

2. Click on Label Wizard. Then choose By State from the list box of tables and queries and click on OK.

3. In the first Label Wizard dialog box (Figure 46-7) that appears, click on 5160 (or choose a different label size if you need to use a different size for your printer) and then click on Next.

When working with mailing labels in this or any database application, make sure you use mailing labels that are designed to work with your particular printer. In some cases, the use of the wrong type of mailing labels can damage the printer.

4. In the next dialog box that appears (Figure 46-8), click on Next to accept the default font and color values for the labels.

5. The next dialog box that appears (Figure 46-9) asks which fields you want to place on the label. Double-click on the First name, press the spacebar, and then double-click on the Last name.

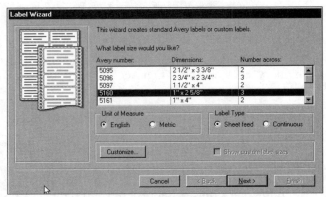

Figure 46-7: The first Label Wizard dialog box.

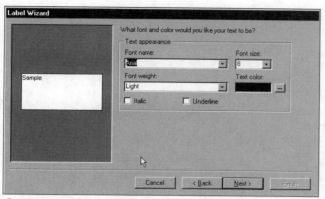

Figure 46-8: The second Label Wizard dialog box.

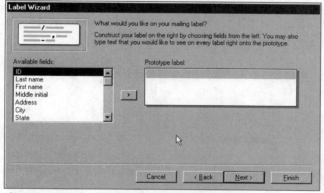

Figure 46-9: The third Label Wizard dialog box.

6. Click on the second line of the Prototype label area (at the right side of the dialog box) to move to the second line and then double-click on the Address field in the list box at the left.

7. Click on the third line of the Prototype label area to move to the third line, double-click on the City field, type a comma and a space, double-click on the State field, add a space, and then double-click on Zip/Postal.

8. Click on the last line of the Prototype label to move to the fourth line and then double-click on the Country field. At this point, your label's design should resemble the example shown in Figure 46-10.

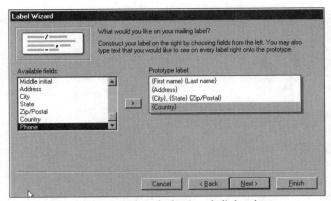

Figure 46-10: The fourth Label Wizard dialog box.

9. Click on the Next button. In a moment, you'll see the dialog box shown in Figure 46-11, asking which field or fields should be used to sort the labels. Double-click the State field and click Next.

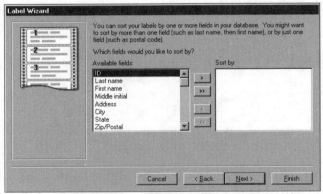

Figure 46-11: The fifth Label Wizard dialog box.

10. Click on the Finish button in the next dialog box to complete the design of the mailing label. When the label opens, you see a prompt for a parameter value requested by the query that you saved earlier. Click on Cancel in the dialog box, click on OK twice in the next dialog boxes that appear, and then close the report's window by pressing Alt+F4.

Finishing the form

Now, all that you need to add to the form are the buttons that perform common operations, such as adding new records, finding records, printing the labels, and exiting the system. Use these steps to add the buttons:

1. Click on the Forms tab. Make sure that Mailer is the selected form in the Database window, and then click on Design to open the form in Design View.

2. If the Toolbox isn't visible, choose View⇨Toolbox to turn it on.

3. Make sure that the Control Wizards are turned on (the Control Wizards button at the upper-right corner of the Toolbox should be depressed).

4. Click on the Command Button tool in the Toolbox, and click in the form just below the Comments field, to add a command button there.

5. When the Command Button Wizard dialog box (Figure 46-12) appears, choose Record Operations in the Categories list box, and then choose Add New Record in the Actions list box. Then click on Finish.

6. Click on the Command Button tool in the Toolbox and click in the form just below the button that you just placed to add a command button there.

7. When the Command Button Wizard dialog box appears, choose Record Navigation from the Categories box, and in the Actions box, choose Find Record. Then click on Finish.

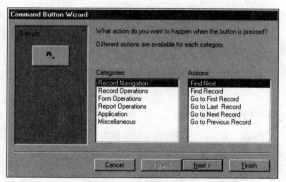

Figure 46-12: The Command Button Wizard dialog box.

8. Click on the Command Button tool in the Toolbox and then click in the form just below the button that you just placed to add a command button there.

9. When the Command Button Wizard dialog box appears, choose Report Operations from the Categories list box and choose Print Report from the Actions list box. Then click on Next.

10. In the next dialog box that appears (Figure 46-13), make sure that Labels By State is selected as the desired report to print and then click on Finish.

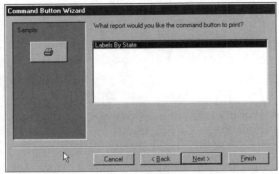

Figure 46-13: The second Command Button Wizard dialog box.

11. Click on the Command Button tool in the Toolbox and click in the form just below the button you just placed to add a command button there.

12. When the Command Button Wizard dialog box appears, choose Application from the Categories list box and then choose Quit Application in the Actions list box. Then click on Finish.

13. Choose File⇨Save to save the form with the new buttons.

Using the application

You can now switch from Design View to Form View (choose View⇨Form); the form's appearance should resemble the form shown earlier in Figure 46-1. You can use the buttons that you added for common tasks such as adding new records, locating records, and printing the labels.

You can easily add further enhancements to this application; for example, you can create parameter queries to select records based on a country name or a city name, and you can add reports that use those queries as a data source. You can also create an Autoexec macro that automatically launches and maximizes the form whenever the database is opened, presenting users with a working application screen.

More Info Chapter 42 discusses techniques for creating Autoexec macros.

Personnel Assignment Tracking

Another common business application is the tracking of assignments or tasks performed by the employees of an organization. In many organizations (especially service-oriented organizations), keeping up with employee task assignments is a vital administrative task. Managers need to know how much time employees must spend on given tasks, precisely what those tasks involve, and whether the tasks are completed. The personnel assignment tracking system highlighted here keeps track of this information with tables for employees and assigned tasks and relational queries, forms, and reports to manage the data. In the Employee database (available at the IDG Books web site — www.idgbooks.com), you can find the Access objects used in the personnel assignment tracking system outlined in this chapter, or you can use the steps that follow to duplicate the system.

Creating the database and tables

The personnel assignment tracking system requires two tables: one named Employees, which contains a record with statistics for each employee, and one named Assignments, which contains records detailing the assignments given to each employee. To create the database and the required tables, perform these steps:

1. Choose File⇨New Database to open the New dialog box. Select Blank Database. Enter **Employee** in the File name text box, and then click on Create to create a new database under this name and display the Database window.

2. In the Database window, click on the Tables tab and then click on New. In the New Table dialog box that appears, click on Design View and then click on OK to open a Table window where you can define the structure of a new table.

3. Fill in the Table window with the field names and data types for the fields as follows:

Field name	Data type
Social Security	Text
Last name	Text
First name	Text
Address	Text
City	Text
State	Text
Zip code	Text
Phone	Text
Date of birth	Date/Time
Comments	Memo

4. Click anywhere in the Social Security field and then click on the Key button in the toolbar to make this field the primary key. At this point, your table's definition should resemble the example shown in Figure 46-14.

5. When you're done defining the fields, choose File⇨Save to save the table. When Access prompts you for a name, enter **Employees** as the name and then click on OK. Press Ctrl+F4 to close the Table window. The new table, Employees, now appears in the Database window.

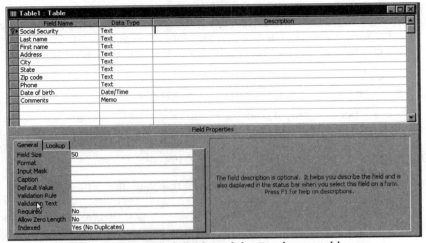

Figure 46-14: The completed definition of the Employees table.

6. In the Database window, click again on New. In the New Table dialog box that appears, click on Design View, and click on OK. The Table window appears again. Fill in the Table window with the field names and data types for the fields as follows:

Field name	Type
Social security	Text
Date assigned	Date/Time
Date due	Date/Time
Hours projected	Number
Client	Text
Task description	Text
Completed?	Yes/No
Record ID	AutoNumber

While the insertion point is in the last field (Record ID), click on the Key button in the toolbar to make this field the primary key. At this point, the table's definition should resemble the example shown in Figure 46-15.

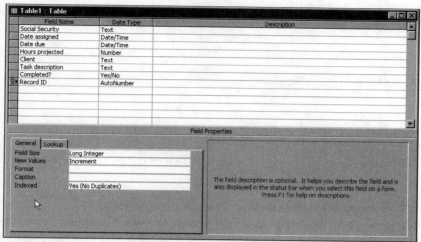

Figure 46-15: A completed definition of the Assignments table.

7. After you've defined all the fields, choose File⇨Save to save the table. When Access prompts you for a name, enter **Assignments** as the name and then click on OK. Press Ctrl+F4 to close the Table window. The new table, Assignments, now appears in the Database window.

Establishing a relationship

You need to establish a default relationship at the database level so that the Form Wizards can build the type of relational form that the application needs later. (The form will be used to display an employee, along with all assignments for that employee.) Perform the following steps to do this task:

1. Choose Tools⇨Relationships. The Show Table dialog box appears, as shown in Figure 46-16.

2. Double-click on Assignments, double-click on Employees, and click on Close.

3. Click on and drag the Social Security field from the Employees list box to the Assignments list box.

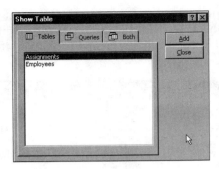

Figure 46-16: The Show Table dialog box.

4. In the Relationships dialog box that appears, click on Create.

5. Press Ctrl+F4 to close the Relationships window. Answer Yes to the prompt that asks if you want to save the changes to the relationship's layout.

Creating the forms

The personnel tracking system requires three forms. One form is used for adding and editing employees, the second for adding and editing assignments, and the third for viewing an employee name along with selected details of each assignment for that employee. To create the necessary forms, perform these steps:

1. In the Database window, click on the Forms tab and click on New. Select AutoForm: Columnar in the list box, choose Assignments in the Tables/Queries list box, and click on OK. The form you will use for adding and editing assignments appears, similar to Figure 46-17.

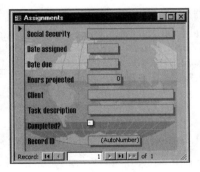

Figure 46-17: You use this form to add and edit assignments.

2. Press Ctrl+F4 to close this form. Answer Yes when Access asks if you want to save the form; when Access prompts for a name, call the form **Assignments**.

3. In the Database window, click on New again. Select AutoForm: Columnar in the list box, choose Employees in the Tables/Queries list box, and click on OK. The form you will use for adding and editing employees appears, similar to Figure 46-18.

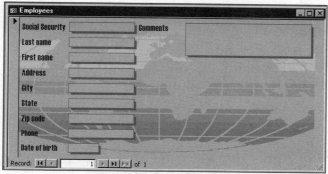

Figure 46-18: You use this form to add and edit employees.

4. Press Ctrl+F4 to close this form. Answer Yes when Access asks if you want to save the form; when Access prompts you for a name, call the form **Employees**.

5. In the Database window, click on New again. Select Form Wizard in the list box, choose Employees as the table that provides the data, and then click on OK.

6. In the first Form Wizard dialog box that appears (Figure 46-19), Access asks which fields you want on the form. Double-click on the Social Security, Last name, and First name fields in the Available Fields list box to add them to the Selected Fields list (but don't close the dialog box yet).

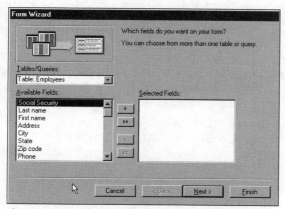

Figure 46-19: The first Form Wizard dialog box.

7. In the Tables/Queries list box, choose Assignments. In the Available Fields list box, double-click on the Date assigned, Date due, Hours projected, and Task description fields, and then click on Next.

8. The next dialog box to appear (Figure 46-20) asks whether you want to view your form by employees or by assignments. Choose by Employees and then click on Finish.

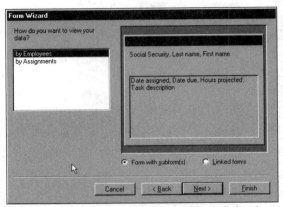

Figure 46-20: The second Form Wizard dialog box.

9. When the form appears, press Ctrl+F4 to close it. (Access saves the form under a default name, Employees1.)

Creating a relational query

To produce a report used by the system, you need to create a relational query. The query will provide relational data, in the form of each employee and that employee's assigned tasks. That information can then be provided by the report. Perform the following steps to create and save the needed query.

1. In the Database window, click on the Queries tab and then click on New. In the New Query dialog box that appears, click on Design View and then click on OK. After you perform this task, the Show Table dialog box (Figure 46-21) opens over a new Query Design window.

2. In the Show Table dialog box, click on Assignments and then click on Add. Next, click on Employees, and click on Add. Finally, click on Close to close the Show Table dialog box and reveal the new Query Design window containing list boxes for both tables.

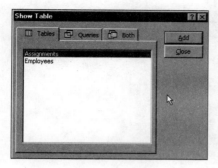

Figure 46-21: The Show Table dialog box.

3. If a join line automatically appears between the Social Security fields of both tables, skip to Step 4. If a line does not appear between the fields, click on and drag the Social Security field in the Assignments list box to the Social Security field in the Employees list box.

4. In the Employees list box, click on Last name. While holding down the mouse button, drag the field to the first column of the Field: row. Using the same technique, click on First name and drag it to the second column of the Field: row.

5. In the Assignments list box, click on Date assigned. While holding down the mouse button, drag the field to the third column of the Field: row. Using the same technique, click on Date due and drag it down to the fourth column of the Field: row. Next, click on Hours projected drag it down to the fifth column of the Field: row, and then click on Client and drag it down to the sixth column of the Field: row.

6. Use the scrollbars to scroll the query to the left so that additional columns are visible. Then, click on Task description and drag it to the next empty column of the Field: row.

7. Choose File⇨Save. Access asks you for a name for the query; enter **Relational Info** and click on OK. Press Ctrl+F4 to close the Query Design window.

Creating the report

Next, perform the following steps to design and save the report that will use the query you just constructed:

1. Click on the Reports tab, and then click on New. The New Report dialog box appears (Figure 46-22).

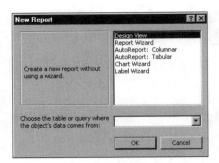

Figure 46-22: The New Report dialog box.

2. Click on AutoReport: Tabular, choose Relational Info in the list box of tables and queries, and click on OK.

3. When the new report appears, press Ctrl+F4 to close the window. When Access prompts for a name for the report, call the report **Assignments**.

Creating a main menu

The final step in building the personnel assignment tracking system is creating a blank form and adding command buttons to it. This form will serve as the main menu for the application, making it easy for users of the application to perform common tasks such as adding and editing records and producing reports. Perform the following steps to create the main menu:

1. In the Database window, click on the Forms tab, and then click on New. The New Form dialog box appears.

2. Leave Design View selected and click on OK.

3. When the blank form appears in a Design window, extend its size so that it measures at least 3 × 6 inches, as shown in Figure 46-23.

4. If the Toolbox isn't visible, choose View⇨Toolbox to turn on the Toolbox.

5. Make sure that the Control Wizards are turned on (the Control Wizards button at the upper-right corner of the Toolbox should be depressed).

6. Click on the Command Button tool and click near the center of the form, about 1 inch below the top of the form to place a Command button.

7. In the Command Button Wizard dialog box that appears (Figure 46-24), click on Form Operations in the Categories box. In the Actions box, click on Open Form. Then, click on Next.

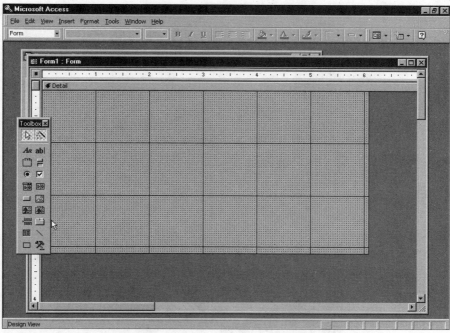

Figure 46-23: The blank form shown in a Design window.

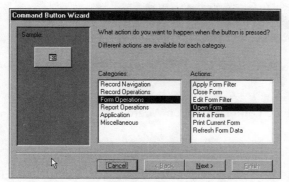

Figure 46-24: The first Command Button Wizard dialog box.

8. The next dialog box to appear (Figure 46-25) asks which form the button should open. Choose Employees from the list and then click on Next.

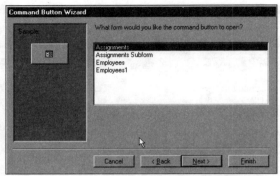

Figure 46-25: The second Command Button Wizard
dialog box.

9. The next dialog box (Figure 46-26) asks if you want the button to find
   specific information. Click on Next to accept the default option Open the
   form and show all the records.

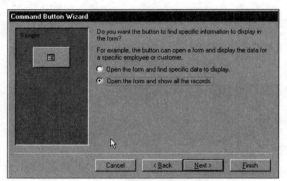

Figure 46-26: The third Command Button Wizard
dialog box.

10. The next dialog box that appears (Figure 46-27) asks if you want a picture or
    text on the button. Choose Text, and change the default entry of Open Form
    in the text box to **Add/Edit Employees** and then click on Finish.

11. Click on the Command Button tool, and click just below the lower left corner
    of the button you just placed to add a new button underneath it.

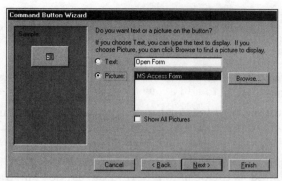

Figure 46-27: The fourth Command Button Wizard dialog box.

12. In the Command Button Wizard dialog box that appears (shown earlier in Figure 46-24), under Categories, click on Form Operations. Under Actions, click on Open Form. Then click on Next.

13. The next dialog box that appears (shown earlier in Figure 46-25) asks which form the button should open. Choose Assignments from the list and then click on Next.

14. The next dialog box (shown earlier in Figure 46-26) asks if you want the button to find specific information. Click on Next to accept the default option Open the form and show all the records.

15. The next dialog box that appears (shown earlier in Figure 46-27) asks if you want a picture or text on the button. Choose Text, change the default entry of Open Form in the text box to **Add/Edit Assignments**, and then click on Finish. (When the button appears, it may not be the same size as the one placed previously, but you can ignore this. Later, you'll size all buttons to make them the same size.)

16. Click on the Command Button tool and click just below the lower left corner of the button you just placed to add a new button underneath it.

17. In the Command Button Wizard dialog box that appears (shown earlier in Figure 46-24), under Categories, click on Form Operations. Under Actions, click on Open Form. Then, click on Next.

18. The next dialog box that appears (shown earlier in Figure 46-25) asks which form the button should open. Choose Employees1 from the list and then click on Next.

19. The next dialog box (shown earlier in Figure 46-26) asks if you want the button to find specific information. Click on Next to accept the default of Open the form and show all the records.

20. The next dialog box that appears (shown earlier in Figure 46-27) asks if you want a picture or text on the button. Choose Text, and change the default entry of Open Form in the text box to **View Staff Assignments** and then click on Finish.

21. Click on the Command Button tool and click just below the lower-left corner of the button you just placed to add a new button underneath it.

22. In the Command Button Wizard dialog box that appears (shown earlier in Figure 46-24), click on Report Operations in the Categories list box. In the Actions list box, click on Print Report. Then click on Next.

23. In the next dialog box that appears (Figure 46-28), make sure that Assignments is selected as the desired report in the list box and then click on Next. (Unless you've created other reports on your own, it should be the only available report.)

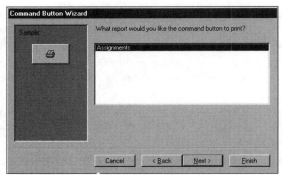

Figure 46-28: The fifth Command Button Wizard dialog box.

24. In the next dialog box that appears, click on Text and then click on Finish.

You can now perform a few aesthetic steps to improve the appearance of your menu.

1. Click above and to the left of the first button and drag down and to the right of the last button. When you release the mouse button, all the buttons you added to the form should appear selected at the same time.

2. Choose Format⇨Size⇨to Widest to make all buttons the same width.

3. Click on the Label tool in the Toolbox and then click roughly ¹/₂ inch above the top button.

4. Type **Personnel Tracking System** into the text box. If desired, you can right-click on the text, choose Properties from the pop-up window, and use the properties in the window to change the size and font of the text.

5. Choose File⇨Save to save the form. When Access prompts you for a form name, enter **Main Menu** and click on OK.

Using the application

You can run the form and try the buttons to accomplish the various tasks that you have assigned to them. When you run this form (choose View⇨Form View), a main menu for the form appears such as the one shown in Figure 46-29.

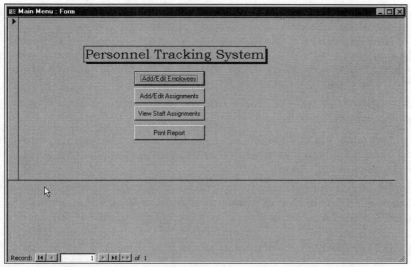

Figure 46-29: The completed main menu for a personnel tracking system.

You also can create an Autoexec macro that automatically launches and maximizes the main form whenever a user opens the database, presenting the user with a working application screen. You can enhance the system further by using the Command Button Wizard to add buttons for common data management tasks, such as adding new records and finding records to the forms of the application. You can create additional reports as needed.

More Info Chapter 42 discusses techniques for creating Autoexec macros to start applications.

If you've followed the examples detailed in this chapter, you have an idea of how Access can serve as a powerful tool to help manage your database applications. The mailing list and personnel management applications are just two examples of common database management tasks that can be handled with Access. Others include inventory, sales tracking, order entry, time and billing, and payroll, just to name a few. If you have a common application in mind and you're unsure of how to design your needed tables, you may want to consider trying one of the ready-made databases possible through the use of the Database Wizard in Access.

More Info You'll find more specifics on the use of the Database Wizard in Chapter 35.

Summary

This chapter provided you with a step-by-step look at what is involved in creating typical applications in Access. The following points were covered:

✦ The mailing list application makes use of a single form to display records and to provide a user interface where you can add and edit data and print reports by pressing command buttons.

✦ You can use the Mailing Label Wizard to quickly create mailing labels for any mailing list application.

✦ The personnel assignment tracking application uses two tables, three forms, and one report, and it uses a form with command buttons that acts as a main menu.

✦ As demonstrated with both applications, you can use the Command Button Wizard to add command buttons that perform common data management tasks.

The next chapter answers common questions that arise when using Access.

Where to go next...

✦ Queries are an important part of any application. You can find complete details on how to effectively construct your queries in Chapter 36.

✦ Forms are the way to get information into an application. To learn all about creating forms, look in Chapter 37.

✦ Application output is usually in the form of a report. To learn how to create effective reports, read Chapter 38.

✦　✦　✦

The Access Top Ten

It turns out that different users often have the same
questions about using Access. This chapter answers the
ten most common Microsoft Access questions, based on
inquiries to Microsoft Technical Support and the Microsoft
forums on CompuServe.

1. I'm attached to tables outside of Access. I can open and view the data in the tables, but why can't I make any changes to the data?

Some attached tables are read-only, which means you cannot
update them. You can update attached tables from Access
only if the attached table has a unique index.

If you are attaching to Paradox tables, they lack primary
keys; you can go into Paradox and add primary keys using
appropriate Paradox techniques. By performing this task, you
can later attach to the tables from Access and make changes
to the table's data.

If the attached tables are Microsoft SQL Server views, you
can create a data-definition query in Access that uses the
`CREATE INDEX` statement as part of the query's SQL statement, which allows you to update the data from Access.

2. How can I prevent an Autoexec macro from running when I open a database?

Hold down Shift while you open the database.

3. How can I create a calculated field?

One way to create calculated fields is to place them in queries. Open a query in Design View and enter an expression for the calculation in the Field row of the query grid. You can also create calculated fields in forms and reports by adding a text box control to the form or report and typing the expression directly into the control.

4. How can I change the initial value of an AutoNumber field to a value other than 1?

You can do this by performing these steps:

1. Create a temporary table containing a single Number field having the same name as the AutoNumber field in the other table.

2. Enter a value in the Number field of the temporary table. The value should be one less than the initial value you want for the AutoNumber field.

3. Use an append query to append the record containing the Number field value you entered to the table whose AutoNumber field you want to change.

4. Delete the temporary table.

5. Delete the record containing the Number field value you entered from the table whose AutoNumber field you want to change.

5. How can I see my table data in sorted order?

By default, Access stores data in the order in which you entered it and displays the data by the primary key order when a primary key exists. (If no primary key exists, Access displays the data in the order in which you entered it.) You can display the data in a different sort order by clicking the Sort Ascending or Sort Descending button on the toolbar, or by choosing Records⇨Sort from the menus. Alternatively, you can create a query containing a specified sort order and apply it to the table.

6. How can I refer to a subform or a control of a subform in an expression on the main form?

In the expression, include the identifier for the form or report property that represents the subform or subreport, followed by the ! operator and the name of the control, as in:

```
=Forms![main form name]![subform name].Form![subform control
    name]
```

For example, you can use the following expression in the Orders form to indicate the value of a Total Cost control on the Order Details subform:

```
=Forms![Orders]![Order Details].Form![Total Cost]
```

7. How can I customize the toolbars in Access?

Access lets you add and remove buttons from the toolbars to suit your needs. To perform this task, right-click on any blank space in the toolbar and choose Customize from the shortcut menu that appears. In the Customize dialog box that opens, click the Commands tab. Click the desired category, in the Commands portion of the dialog box move the cursor over a button you want to add, and drag it to any toolbar. To remove a button from the toolbar, drag it off the toolbar and onto any blank portion of the dialog box.

8. How can I make copies of objects (such as forms and reports) and save them under different names?

Click on the object you want to copy in the Database window to select it. Next, choose Edit⇨Copy and choose Edit⇨Paste. In the dialog box that appears, enter another name for the object.

9. How can I create and add graphics to my forms or reports?

While you're in Design View for the form or report, click on the Unbound Object Frame tool in the Report Controls toolbar, click at the starting location in the form or report for the graphic frame, and drag until the frame reaches the desired size. In the Insert Object dialog box that appears, click on the desired object type and click on OK to launch the program in which you can create the graphic. After you've created the graphic, choose File⇨Exit from the application's menus to return to Access, and click on OK to insert the graphic.

10. Why is every other page of my report blank?

When the width of the design surface in your report is wider than the printable width of the paper you are using, the printer prints blank pages for every other page. To change the width of your report's design surface (and eliminate the blank pages) open the report in Design View and pull in the edge of the design surface until it is narrower than the printable width of the page. (You can use the Print Preview button on the toolbar to check for this problem before printing the actual report.)

Summary

This chapter covered the top ten Access questions and their answers. This chapter also concludes the Access section of this book. The section that follows deals with Microsoft Outlook and Microsoft Binder, applications that are also provided with Office 95.

Where to go next...

✦ As you progress beyond using the Form Wizards and the Report Wizards, you quickly run into the complexities of manually constructing forms or reports within Design View. For specifics on manually designing forms in Access, see Chapter 37.

✦ For details on the mechanics of manual report design, take a look at Chapter 38.

✦   ✦   ✦

Office Works Together

◆   ◆   ◆   ◆

◆   ◆   ◆   ◆

Using Outlook

CHAPTER

48

Outlook is a user-friendly information management tool that you can use alone or as part of a group. Outlook combines e-mail, a calendar, group scheduling, contact management, a task list, and a journal into one complete package. Outlook can facilitate the organization of your life because it has the capability to track your appointments, meetings, tasks, contacts, and events and manage your e-mail. Outlook can literally be your planning, scheduling, and messaging assistant. It can help you keep track of your various tasks and projects. Outlook has a Task Pad, which you can see from most of its different calendar views, where you can group your various tasks by category: by project, by priority, or by due date. By viewing the Task Pad as part of the Calendar, you can see whether you should be working on a particular project on a given day or what your upcoming workweek looks like.

In addition to organizing your task list, Outlook also provides a contacts list to let you maintain information about your personal and business contacts, including notes about phone conversations and action items. For those of you who are connected to a mail server on a network, you will be able to organize meetings, send requests, and track the replies by using Outlook. You will also be able to make your schedule available to others while maintaining privacy where needed.

If you grew accustomed to using Schedule or Schedule+ (the information management program provided with earlier versions of Office), you should not assume that Outlook is just a glorified version of Schedule. While all of the tasks performed using Schedule can be managed with Outlook, you can do far more in Outlook. The appearance and operation of Outlook is significantly different than that of Schedule or Schedule+. Figure 48-1 shows the appearance of Outlook. In this case, the Calendar is visible in the Outlook window.

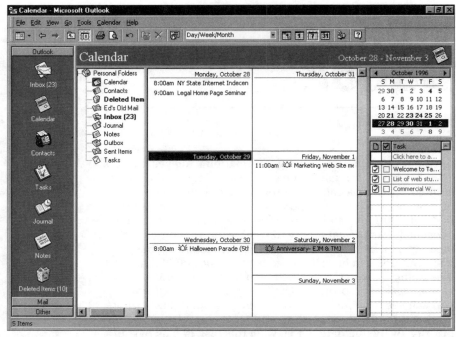

Figure 48-1: The Outlook window with the Calendar visible, and the Folder List displayed.

Outlook includes the following components:

✦ **Calendar** — offers a complete day, week, or month-based scheduling and appointment tracking system.

✦ **Inbox** — provides the capability to send and receive messages by means of network e-mail servers, through the Internet, or through commercial online services like the Microsoft Network and America Online.

✦ **Contacts** — provides a personal and business address book. You can view and sort contacts in different ways, and you can use the names and addresses stored here in Word documents like letters, or in other views within Outlook.

✦ **Tasks** — provides a to-do list that you can use for personal or business tasks. You can use Tasks to prioritize your to-do items, and if you are using Outlook on a network, you can assign tasks to others (perhaps the ultimate way to reduce on-the-job stress).

✦ **Journal** — can track the history of activities that you want to record on a time-line basis. You can set Journal to automatically record many activities, such as e-mail messages from certain contacts. Also, you can manually add any activity you wish to the Journal.

✦ **Notes** — provides an electronic equivalent to those yellow sticky notes that are so common in many offices.

In addition to these categories which are clearly visible at the left side of the Outlook window, you can also use the Other category (accessed by clicking the Other button at the lower left) to view files and directories on your hard drive or on your network. From within Outlook, you can copy and delete files, view network directories, and launch other Windows applications.

About the Outlook Window

You can think of the Outlook window as providing a view to all the major components of Outlook. The window can be divided into three sections: the *Outlook Bar*, the *Folder List*, and the *Information Viewer*. (If you can't see the Outlook Bar or the Folder List, don't panic, just read on. The Folder List is not on by default, unless you turned it on during an earlier session with Outlook.) The Outlook Bar, located at the far left, contains the icons for each of the Outlook components. Click on an icon, and the Outlook window changes to reveal that particular aspect of Outlook. For example, you can click on the Inbox icon to view and read your e-mail, or you can click on the Contacts icon to view the names and addresses stored under Contacts. You can also open the Go menu and choose any Outlook component from the menu: Inbox, Calendar, Contacts, Tasks, Journal, or Notes.

The Folder list, located immediately to the right of the Outlook Bar, shows all of the folders available in Outlook. In Outlook, you can create folders to store various Outlook items, including mail messages, contacts and journal entries, appointments, notes, and tasks. While the Outlook Bar and the Folder List are visible by default, you can hide either of these, and they will remain hidden until you choose to display them again. To display or hide the Outlook Bar, choose View⇨Outlook Bar from the menus. To display or hide the Folder List, choose View⇨Folder List from the menus.

The Information Viewer typically comprises most of the right half of the Outlook window. (Technically, you can resize any of these window sections to occupy as little or as much of the screen as you wish.) In the Information Viewer, you see the actual Outlook data you are working with, such as the names and addresses in the Contacts portion or the e-mail messages in the Inbox portion.

In Outlook, the toolbar icons change, depending on which section of Outlook you are in. Keep in mind that you can reveal the purpose of any toolbar button by holding the mouse stationary over the desired button. When you do this a window (called a ToolTip) appears, describing the purpose of the toolbar button.

It's worth learning more...

Outlook has grown so far beyond the scope of the old Schedule program it replaced that it's impossible to cover more than the basics and still keep this book to a comfortable size. If you'd like to learn the full details on Outlook, we recommend a good book devoted entirely to Outlook. One such text is IDG Books' *Discover Outlook*.

Starting Outlook

You can start Outlook by opening the Windows Start menu, choosing Programs, and then choosing Microsoft Outlook. Once Outlook loads, you see the Outlook window, as shown earlier in Figure 48-1.

Using Inbox

Inbox is the messaging component of Outlook. It's probably obvious that you can use Inbox to read and answer your e-mail, but Inbox has several capabilities worth exploring. You can format messages using a variety of fonts, styles, and colors. You can address messages based on your personal e-mail lists or based on directories stored on your company's mail servers, and you can preview the first few lines of incoming mail without opening the entire message. Clicking the Inbox icon at the left reveals the Inbox, as shown in Figure 48-2. Note that if you are using Outlook on a stand-alone PC, you must have a modem, and you must have Windows 95 Dial-Up Networking installed to send and receive mail through Outlook. (See Windows 95 Help for specifics on installing Dial-Up Networking.) If you are using Outlook on your company's network, see your Network Administrator for help in configuring Outlook to work with your company's e-mail servers. (Outlook can be configured to work with many popular network mail servers, including Microsoft Mail and Lotus cc:Mail.)

As the figure shows, when you are using Inbox your messages are displayed in the Information Viewer portion of the window. If View⇨AutoPreview is turned on, any new messages that you have not read will display the first three lines of the message text.

Reading Messages

To read a message that you've received, just double-click the message in the Inbox. In a moment, the message appears within a message window, like the one shown in Figure 48-3.

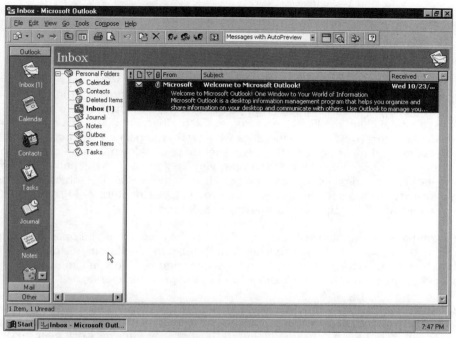

Figure 48-2: The Outlook window, with the Inbox visible.

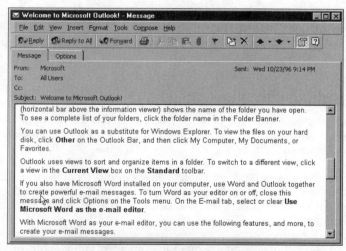

Figure 48-3: An existing mail message in the message window.

As with any good mail system, you have many options here besides just reading your mail. You can print the message by choosing File⇨Print or by clicking the Print icon on the toolbar. You can save the message as a file by choosing File⇨Save As and entering the desired name in the Save As dialog box that appears. (You can save the file under a number of file formats, including Word for Windows, Rich Text Format [(RTF)], and plain ASCII text.) You can reply to the message by clicking the Reply button in the toolbar and typing a reply in the message window that appears. And you can forward the message to another person by clicking the Forward button in the toolbar and filling in a recipient's address in the To box of the message window that appears. Also, note that the message window used by Outlook is a slightly scaled-down version of Word for Windows. Thus, while editing messages, you have most of the capabilities of Word, including cut-and-paste, the capability to insert pictures and graphics, a full range of formatting, and spelling and grammar tools. (See Chapters 2–4 for more details on using Word's editing and formatting capabilities.)

Hot Stuff If you have several messages in your Inbox to be read, once you open one, don't close the window and open another. You can use the Next Item button in the toolbar to read the next message in the same window, and you can use the Previous Item button in the toolbar to read the previous message.

How Outlook retrieves mail depends on whether you are using it with a mail service installed on a local-area network or through a dial-up connection over a modem. If Outlook has been configured to work with your network mail servers, you don't need to do anything specific to retrieve your mail: Inbox displays the mail as it is received from your mail server. However, if desired you can force Outlook to check for new mail by choosing Tools⇨Check for New Mail. If you are retrieving mail from one or more of different information services over a dial-up connection, you can choose Tools⇨Check for New Mail On, and in the dialog box that appears, choose the desired information service from the list. Windows Dial-Up Networking will contact your information service, and Outlook will retrieve your e-mail from that service.

Addressing and sending messages

To create and send a message, click the New Message button in the toolbar, or choose File⇨New⇨Mail Message. With either method, a new message opens in the message window, as shown in Figure 48-4.

If you know the names of the recipient, you can type them directly into the To: box. Recipients who are to receive copies can have their names entered in the Cc: box. If you don't know the e-mail addresses, you can click the To: or the Cc: button to reveal a Select Names dialog box (Figure 48-5).

In the dialog box, you can enter a name or select it from a list you've entered previously. You can use the Show Names From list box at the upper right to cause the list to display names from within Outlook's own Contacts list or from your company's mail server if you are on a network. Once you locate the desired name in the list, double-click the name to move it to the Message Recipients portion of the dialog box. Repeat this step for every person you want to send the same message to, and click OK to close the dialog box.

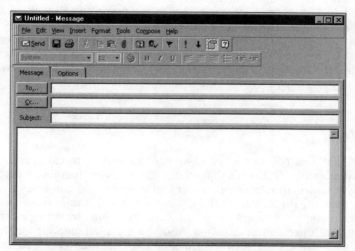

Figure 48-4: A new mail message in the message window.

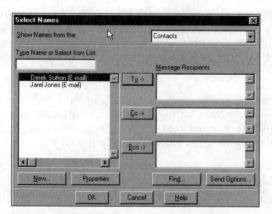

Figure 48-5: The Select Names dialog box.

Once you've entered the recipients in the To: and Cc: boxes, you can enter a desired subject in the Subject box, and click in the text box and type the text of the message. After completing the message, click the Send button on the toolbar (or choose File⇨Send) to send the message. Outlook automatically closes the mail window once you send the message.

Deleting Messages

To delete messages you've already read, just select the unwanted message and press the Del key, or click the Delete button in the toolbar. You can select a group of messages for deletion by clicking the first message in the group and holding down the Shift key while clicking the last message in the group to select them all; then press the Del key or click the Delete button in the toolbar. If you want to delete a number of messages that are not grouped together, select the first message, and hold the Ctrl key down as you click each additional message to select it. After you've selected the messages, press the Del key, or click the Delete button in the toolbar.

Using Calendar

The Calendar portion of Outlook can serve as an efficient way of tracking and planning your daily schedule. Outlook's Calendar is much more than just a display of dates with a way to store appointments under those dates. You can track events and enter tasks by jumping directly from the Calendar to the Tasks portion of Outlook. You can create appointments based on incoming e-mail by dragging the mail messages from the Inbox to the Calendar. And you can plan meetings with others who are using Outlook on a network. Clicking the Calendar icon reveals the Calendar, as shown in Figure 48-6. In the Calendar shown in the figure, the Folder List has been enabled, and the weekly view of dates has been selected.

Using the Calendar, you can work directly with three different items: appointments, meetings, and events. Appointments are any happenings you block time for in your calendar that don't involve others. You can attach reminders to appointments, and you can schedule recurring appointments. The appointments appear as text in the days of the Calendar window, and you can view the appointments by day, week, or month.

Meetings are appointments that others are invited to. You can use the Meeting Planner feature of Calendar to block out time for meetings and to invite others to those meetings via e-mail. The Meeting Planner feature uses Outlook's integrated e-mail to send reminders automatically to others whom you invite to your meetings.

Events are activities that last for 24 hours or more. (Examples of typical events include vacations, seminars, anniversaries, and birthdays.) Events do not appear as blocks of time within the days of the Calendar. Instead, they appear as banners.

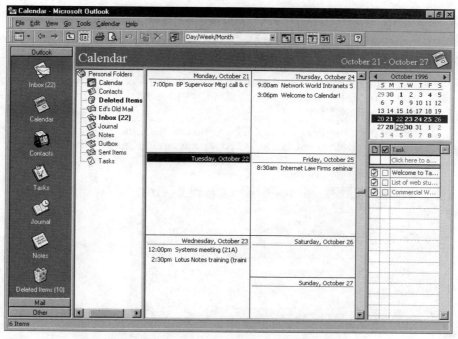

Figure 48-6: The Outlook window with the Calendar visible.

Moving around in the Calendar

As you view the Calendar, you can view the days and move around in many ways. You can view the Calendar by day, week, or month. To change the view, choose Day, Week, or Month as desired from the Current View list box in the toolbar, or select Day, Week, or Month from the View menu. In any view, the easiest way to jump to a specific date is to click on that date, either in the main portion of the Calendar or in the monthly calendar that appears at the upper right when you are viewing by the day or by the week.

If you are viewing the Calendar by the week or the month, you can use the cursor keys to move between different days. (If you're viewing the Calendar by the day, the cursor keys move you between the hours of the day.) While viewing by the day or week, you can also click any day shown in the small monthly calendar (at the upper right) to jump directly to that day, and you can jump to any date by choosing Go⇨Go to Date. This command opens a Go To Date dialog box, where you can enter the desired date to go to in any acceptable date format.

Creating appointments and events

You can add appointments or events to the Calendar by performing these steps:

1. Locate the desired day in the Calendar. (Note that if you're viewing the Calendar by the week and you are at the wrong week, one way to move around is to use the PgUp and PgDn keys to move forward or backward a week at a time.)

2. Double-click the desired day. When you do this, a new Event window appears with the Appointment tab selected, as shown in Figure 48-7.

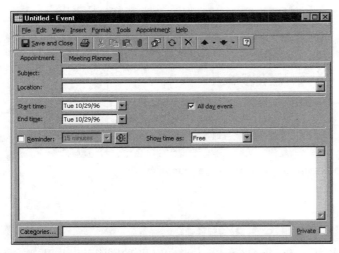

Figure 48-7: The new Event window of the Calendar.

1. Enter a subject for the entry in the Subject box and a location in the Location box.

2. If you are entering an appointment, turn off the All Day Event check box. If you are entering an event, leave the All Day Event check box turned on.

3. If desired, change the Start and End times.

4. If you want a reminder of the appointment, turn on the Reminder check box and choose the delay time between the appearance of the reminder and the appointment.

5. Make any other desired entries in the Show Time As, Comments, and Categories boxes.

6. Click Save and Close to save the appointment and put away the dialog box.

Opening an appointment

To open an appointment or an event, simply double-click it. Alternately, you can select the entry by clicking it and then choose File⇨Open.

Creating appointments by dragging mail messages

If you are using Outlook as your e-mail manager, one extremely useful feature is its capability to create appointments based on incoming mail messages. (For specifics on managing your e-mail, see the Inbox section of this chapter.) You can create appointments based on mail messages with these steps:

1. At the Inbox, click and drag the desired message onto the Calendar icon in the Outlook Bar (the far left of the Outlook window). When you do this, a new appointment window opens with the text of the message already entered into the Comments window of the message.

2. Enter the location in the Location box.

3. Enter your desired starting and ending times for the appointment.

4. Choose any additional options desired and click Save and Close.

Scheduling calendar time by dragging tasks

Outlook lets you schedule time in your calendar for tasks that you have previously entered in the Tasks portion of Outlook. (For specifics on creating tasks, see the Tasks section of this chapter.) You can create appointments based on existing tasks with these steps:

1. In the Tasks portion of Outlook, click and drag the desired task onto the Tasks icon in the Outlook Bar (the far left of the Outlook window). When you do this, a new appointment window opens with the fields of the task already entered into the Comments window of the message.

2. Enter the location in the Location box.

3. Enter your desired starting and ending times for the appointment.

4. Choose any additional options desired and click Save and Close.

Moving and deleting calendar items

You can move appointments around in the Calendar (which is far easier than deleting and reentering them), and you can delete unneeded appointments. To move an appointment, use these steps:

1. In the Calendar, place the mouse pointer at the left side of the appointment you want to move.

2. When the pointer takes the shape of a cross with arrows on each end, click the appointment.

3. Choose Edit⇨Cut from the menus.

4. Click the new date or time for the appointment.

5. Choose Edit⇨Paste.

To delete any appointment, first select the unwanted appointment by clicking it. Then press the Del key, or choose Edit⇨Delete. Also note that you can delete multiple Calendar entries by holding the Ctrl key and clicking the unwanted items, then pressing the Del key.

Scheduling meetings and inviting attendees

Calendar includes a Meeting Planner feature, a real time-saver when you work with others on a network. You can quickly set up meetings, check the free time of others who are using Outlook to manage their calendars, and send meeting reminders via e-mail. You can use these steps to plan a meeting:

1. In the Calendar, select the desired day of the meeting.

2. Click the Plan a Meeting icon in the toolbar. In a moment, the Plan a Meeting dialog box appears (Figure 48-8).

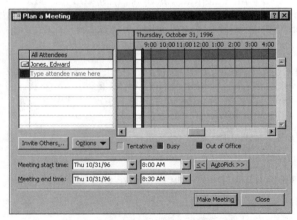

Figure 48-8: The Plan a Meeting dialog box.

3. Click Invite Others to open the Select Attendees and Resources dialog box (Figure 48-9).

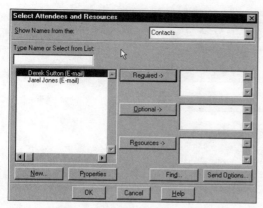

Figure 48-9: The Select Attendees and Resources dialog box.

4. In the Show Names From list box, choose the desired contact list or e-mail server containing the names of the people you want to invite. When you do this, the names appear in the list box at the left.

5. Click each desired name to select it, and click Required (if the persons' attendance will be mandatory), or click Optional (if the persons' attendance is optional). When done selecting the names, click OK. If the people you selected are also using Outlook on your network, you will see their busy and free times in the scheduling portion of the Plan a Meeting dialog box (the upper right portion of the box).

6. Choose a desired start and end time for the meeting. You can use the list boxes near the bottom of the dialog box to do this, or you can drag the colored vertical bars in the scheduling portion of the dialog box. If your workgroup is using Outlook on a network and the people you've invited have conflicting amounts of free and busy time, you can click the AutoPick button, and Outlook will choose a time to accommodate the highest available number of attendees.

7. Click Make Meeting to close the Plan a Meeting dialog box. When you do this, a new Meeting message window appears with the attendees' e-mail addresses automatically entered in the To box, as shown in Figure 48-10.

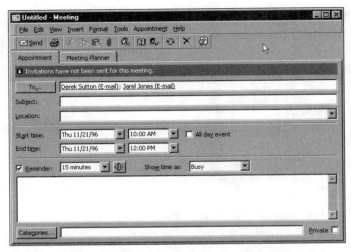

Figure 48-10: The new Meeting message window containing attendees' e-mail addresses.

8. Enter a subject for the meeting in the Subject: box and enter a location for the meeting in the Location: box.

9. Enter any desired comments in the Comment window near the bottom of the dialog box.

10. Click Send to send the invitations to your meeting.

Using Contacts

You can use the Contacts portion of Outlook to display all of your business or personal contacts and if you have a modem attached to your computer. (You can dial phone calls directly from within Outlook using the phone numbers stored in Contacts.) Clicking the Contacts icon at the left reveals the Contacts portion of Outlook, as shown in Figure 48-11.

You can display your contacts using a number of different views: as address cards (shown in the figure), as detailed address cards (similar to the figure but with additional information displayed for each contact), as a phone list, by categories, by companies, or by location. You choose the desired view by selecting it from the Current View list box in the toolbar. As an example of a different view, Figure 48-12 shows the contacts when viewed as a phone list.

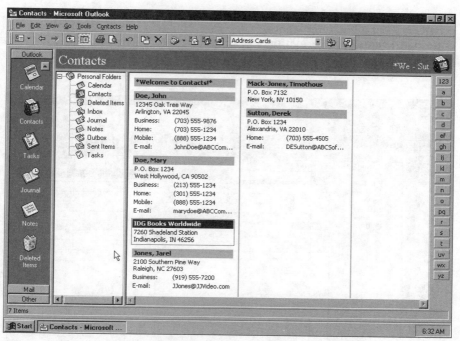

Figure 48-11: The Outlook window, with the Contacts entries visible.

Adding a contact

To create a new contact, click the New Contact button in the toolbar. (You can also choose File⟹New⟹Contact, but clicking the button is easier.) When you do this, a new Contact window appears, as shown in Figure 48-13.

You can enter the desired information into the fields of the window. In the Full Name box, you enter the person's name in the format of first name, followed by a middle initial (if desired), and the last name. (Outlook automatically discerns where the first name ends and the last name begins when it sorts your data.) The remainder of the fields are fairly self-explanatory; you can fill in the company name (if any), and the address and phone numbers. Outlook even includes fields for e-mail and web page addresses. Note that with all the phone numbers, you can click any of the down arrows and change the category. For example, you could change a phone number's category from "Business" to "Car," or from "Home 1" to "Home 2." In the Comments portion at the lower half of the dialog box, you can enter any comments to help you remember what's important about this contact, and you can use the Categories button (at the lower left) to bring up a list box of categories you can choose to add to the field to the right of the button. (This proves helpful if you later want to view your contacts by category.) When done entering the contact information, click the Save and Close button in the toolbar to save the contact and close the window.

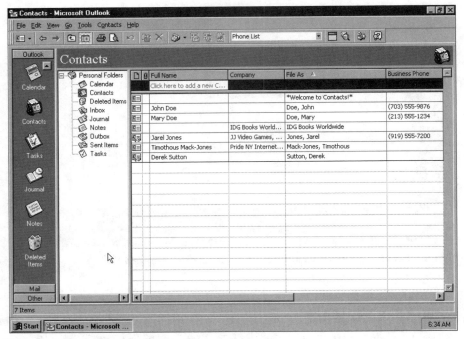

Figure 48-12: The contacts viewed as a phone list.

To create a new contact with the same company name as an existing contact, first select any contact with the company name you want. Then, choose Contacts⇨New Contact from Same Company from the menus. In a moment, a new contact window appears, with the company information duplicated from the selected contact. You can then enter the remaining needed information.

Opening and editing a contact

You can open any contact for viewing or editing by double-clicking that contact or by highlighting it with the cursor keys and pressing Enter. Using either method, the contact appears in a Contact window, like that shown in Figure 48-14.

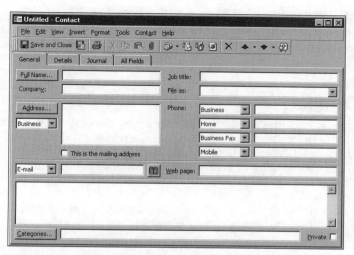

Figure 48-13: A new Contact window.

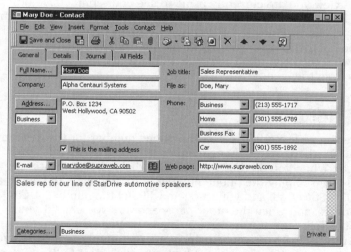

Figure 48-14: An existing contact shown in the Contact window.

You can edit any of the desired fields; when you click the Save and Close button in the toolbar, the changes will be saved.

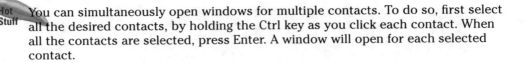

You can simultaneously open windows for multiple contacts. To do so, first select all the desired contacts, by holding the Ctrl key as you click each contact. When all the contacts are selected, press Enter. A window will open for each selected contact.

Deleting a Contact

To delete a contact, first click the header of the contact to select it. Then, press the Del key, or click the Delete button in the toolbar. Keep in mind that you can remove a number of contacts at once by selecting all the unwanted contacts (hold the Ctrl key as you click the header of each contact). With all the unwanted contacts selected, press the Del key.

Note   Deleting a contact does not cause any journal entries added for that contact to be deleted. For more on journal entries, see the Journal section of this chapter.

Printing a List of Contacts

To print a list of your contacts, click the Print icon in the toolbar, or choose File⇨Print from the menus. Keep in mind that your contacts will print in a format that's similar to the view you are currently using to see your contacts. In other words, if you have Phone List selected in the Current View list box of the toolbar, your contacts will print as a phone list. If you have Address Card selected in the Current View list box of the toolbar, your contacts will print as address cards. You can get an idea of what the printout in any view will look like by choosing File⇨Print Preview from the menus.

Dialing the Phone

To dial the phone using your modem, select the phone number for the desired contact by clicking anywhere in the phone number. Then click the AutoDialer button in the toolbar. When you do this, the New Call dialog box appears, as shown in Figure 48-15. Assuming the phone number you selected is the one that you want to call, click Start Call, and your modem will dial the number. A Call Status box also appears, and when the other party answers you can lift your receiver and click the Talk button. You can also click the Hang Up button at any point to disconnect the call. If you want to dial a different number for the same contact, you can choose it in the Number list box, and click Start Call.

When done using the Call Status dialog box, click Close to put it away.

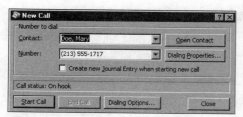

Figure 48-15: The New Call dialog box.

Using Tasks

The Tasks component of Outlook lets you organize and keep track of your business and personal tasks. As you work, you can visually get an idea of the progress you've made on your tasks. You can set reminder messages for tasks so that Outlook reminds you of the tasks at a certain date and time. You can create multiple categories for different projects, and you can group your tasks by the various categories. And you can even assign tasks to others who are using Outlook on your network. Clicking the Tasks icon at the left reveals the Tasks portion of Outlook, as shown in Figure 48-16.

In the Tasks portion of Outlook, you see a list of your tasks. However, one important point to note is that this is not the only place in Outlook where you can view your tasks. Because tasks you perform are by nature time-related, Outlook also provides an easy way to see them in the Task Pad that is a part of Calendar. Whenever you are viewing the Calendar by day or by week, the Task Pad appears at the right side of the window. Figure 48-1, shown at the start of this chapter, shows the Calendar view of Outlook. In that figure, the Task Pad is visible at the right. If you prefer to view your tasks from the Calendar portion of Outlook, keep in mind that the Task Pad does not appear if you are viewing the Calendar by month. You should also note that when you start Outlook for the first time, the Calendar shows your tasks for the current day only. To make all the tasks appear in the Calendar, choose View⇨TaskPad View, and select All Tasks from the submenu which appears.

Creating a task

To create a new task from the Tasks portion of Outlook, click the New Task button in the toolbar, or choose File⇨New⇨Task. From the Task Pad of the Calendar, double-click at the left of the area that reads "click here to add a new task." With either method, a new Task window appears like the one shown in Figure 48-17.

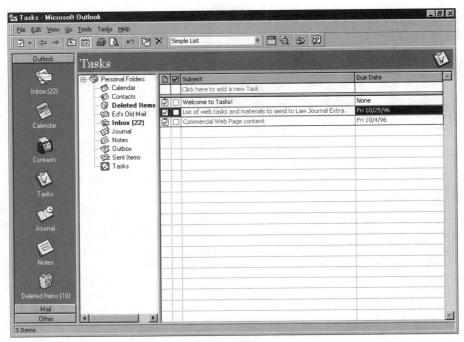

Figure 48-16: The Outlook window with the Tasks entries visible.

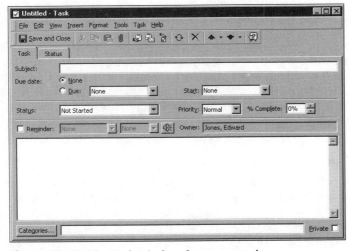

Figure 48-17: The Task window for a new task.

In the Subject box, enter a subject for the task. If the task has a due date, click Due and use the arrow to the right of the Due field to open a calendar where you can choose the desired due date. You can click Start Date and use the same technique to enter a starting date for the task, if desired.

The remaining options in the dialog box can be used to enter a status, a priority, and a percentage completed for the task. You can turn on the Reminder check box and choose a date and time in the entry boxes to the right of the Reminder check box to turn on an audible reminder for the task. In the Comments text box (which occupies most of the lower half of the window), you can enter any desired comments for the task, and you can use the Categories button (at the lower left) to bring up a list box of categories you can choose to add to the field to the right of the button. (This proves helpful if you later want to view your tasks by category.)

Creating tasks based on mail messages

You can create a task based on a mail message by going to the Inbox, and dragging the desired message onto the Tasks icon in the Outlook bar. Doing so causes the Task window to appear, with the text of the message in the Task window. You can then make any desired changes to the options in the window, and click Save and Close to save the changes.

Opening and Editing Tasks

You can open tasks from the Tasks component of Outlook or from the Calendar. To open a task, find the desired task in the task list of Tasks or in the Task Pad of Calendar and double-click it. When you double-click a task, it appears in a Task window, like the one shown earlier in Figure 48-17.

While the task is open in the Task window, you can edit any of the entries for the tasks. These include the subject, due date, start date, status, priority, and percentage of the task that's been completed. Make the desired entries in the window and click Save and Close to save any changes.

Deleting a task

To delete a task, select the task in the Tasks portion of Outlook, or in the Task Pad of the Calendar. Then press Del, or click the Delete button in the toolbar. Note that if you have assigned a task to someone else on a network and you then delete it, the task is deleted from your task list only. It does not get removed from the task list of the person who received the task.

Assigning tasks to others

You can assign tasks to others by sending the other person a task request. (The person who receives the request can then accept it, decline it, or assign it to someone else.) Use these steps to assign a task to another:

Choose File⇨New⇨Task Request from the menus.

1. In the To box, enter the name of the person you want to assign the task to, or click the To button and choose a name from the list.

2. Enter a name for the task in the Subject box.

3. Choose the due date and remaining status options desired.

4. If you want to keep an updated copy of the task in your task list, turn on the Keep an updated copy of this task on my task list check box. If you want to receive a status report when the task is complete by return e-mail, turn on the Send me a status report when this task is complete check box.

Using Journal

The Journal component of Outlook is precisely what its name implies: an electronic version of a journal, that can be used to record the variety of activities that make up your business day. Journal tracks all of your activities on a time line, so you can easily obtain a visual representation of where you are spending your time. You can record many activities automatically, and you can make manual entries into the Journal. Figure 48-18 shows the Outlook window when the Journal icon has been selected.

As with its paper based counterpart, most of what you do with Journal is to record activities, and view those activities. Journal lets you set options to automatically record Office documents that you create and revise, so you have a time-line record of when you worked with what documents. This feature goes beyond just proving to the boss that you've been working; because Office documents recorded in Journal serve as shortcuts, you can use it as a handy way to open documents. For example, if you want to open a Word document you worked on last Thursday but you can't remember where you saved it, you can find the record of the document in the Journal and click it to launch Word and open the document. Journal can also automatically keep a record of all e-mail sent to and received from specific persons. While Outlook tasks and appointments can't be recorded automatically, you can easily add manual Journal entries of these by simply clicking and dragging the task or appointment to the Journal icon in the Outlook Bar.

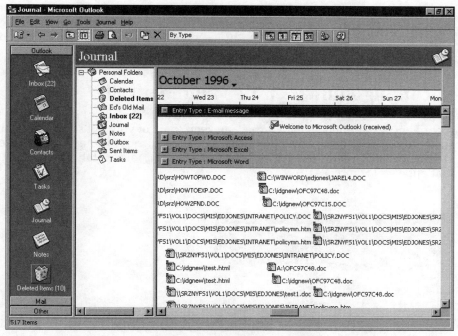

Figure 48-18: The Outlook window with the Journal visible.

Opening, viewing, and jumping to Journal entries

Journal displays the entries in groups called *Entry Types*. When you start Journal for the first time, all the Entry Types (visible in the Information Viewer portion of the Outlook window) are closed. You can open any Entry Type by clicking on the small icon with the plus or minus symbol to the left of the words "Entry Type." A plus symbol indicates the group is closed, and a minus symbol indicates the group is open. In Figure 48-18, the groups for e-mail messages and Word Documents are open.

To open any journal entry, right-click the item, and choose Open Journal Entry from the shortcut menu which appears. Alternately, you can select the item in the Journal and choose File⇨Open.

All Outlook items and Office 97 documents that you see in any open groups are hotlinks, and this fact is one of Journal's most notable and useful features. You can double-click on any of the icons to open that journal entry, and go directly to that Outlook entry or Office 97 document. For example, if you have a record of an e-mail stored in Journal under a certain date, you can double-click on that e-mail in

Journal to jump directly to a message window containing that e-mail. If you are automatically recording all your edits to Word documents, you can double-click any of the documents shown in the Journal's time line to jump to that document within Word.

Recording Journal entries automatically

To use Journal most effectively, you'll want to take advantage of its capability to record entries automatically. Journal can keep track of your activities behind the scenes as you perform your daily work. To record entries in Journal automatically, choose Tools⇨Options from the menus and click the Journal tab in the dialog box that appears (Figure 48-19).

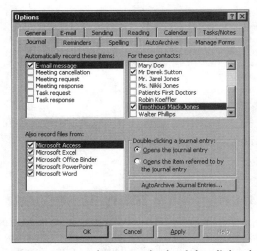

Figure 48-19: The Journal tab of the dialog box.

In the upper half of the dialog box, you can choose the Outlook items you want recorded for any person in your Contacts list. (For details on adding individuals to your Contacts list, see the Using Contacts section of this chapter.) At the left side, turn on the check boxes for the items you want recorded. (You can enable e-mail messages, meeting cancellations, meeting requests, meeting responses, task requests, and task responses.) At the right side, turn on the check boxes besides the contacts you want events recorded for.

In the lower half of the dialog box, you can choose any or all Office 97 files that you want journal entries recorded for, including Access, Excel, Word, PowerPoint, and the Office Binder.

At the lower right, you will need to choose whether a double-click on a journal entry opens the entry, or opens the actual item that the entry refers to. Once you make all the desired selections in the dialog box, click OK.

Hot Stuff When you add a new contact to your Contacts list, you can easily set items you want automatically recorded for that contact by selecting the Automatically Record Journal Entries for this Contact check box on the Journal tab of the contact.

Recording Journal entries manually

For those Outlook tasks and items that can't be recorded automatically, Journal provides the capability to manually add entries. You can manually add an Outlook item to the Journal by performing these steps:

1. Open the Outlook item you want to record in the Journal.

2. Choose Tools⇨Record in Journal. When you do this, a new Journal Entry window appears for the item, like the example shown in Figure 48-20.

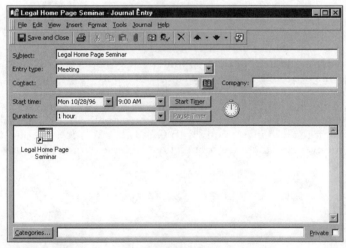

Figure 48-20: The new Journal Entry window.

3. Enter any desired options for the journal entry, and click Save and Close to save the entry.

If you want to add an entry to the Journal that's not based on any Outlook or Office 97 item (such as a phone call from Mom), you can do this by using these steps:

1. While in the Journal, click the New Journal button in the toolbar, or choose File⇨New⇨Journal Entry. In a moment, a blank Journal Entry Window appears.

2. Enter any desired options for the journal entry, then click Save and Close to save the entry.

Moving and deleting Journal entries

You can move items to different locations along the timeline in the Journal. To do this, first open the journal entry (right-click the item in the Journal and choose Open Journal Entry from the shortcut menu). In the Journal Entry window which appears, enter the new desired date and time, and click Save and Close.

To delete any journal entry, click the entry to select it. Then press Del, or click the Delete icon in the toolbar, or choose Edit⇨Delete from the menus.

Using Notes

Notes are the electronic equivalent of those popular sticky paper notes commonly used in many offices. Figure 48-21 shows an example of a note. You'll find notes handy for ideas, questions, details of phone conversations, assorted bits of information, or any other item might put on a paper note. You can leave notes open and on the screen as you work with other Windows applications. (Pressing Alt+Tab will bring the notes into view, along with your other Windows applications that are running. Windows considers each open note to be a separate running application.)

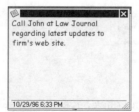

Figure 48-21: An example of a note in Windows.

Creating notes

To create a note from anywhere in Outlook, choose File➪New➪Note. Alternately, you can click the down arrow to the right of the New button in the toolbar and choose Note. The note appears with the cursor flashing within it, and you can type the text of the note. To close the note, double-click the icon at the upper-left corner of the note.

If an existing note is already open on the screen, you can easily create a new note by clicking the icon at the upper-left corner of the note and choosing New Note from the shortcut menu which appears.

Opening existing notes

To open an existing note, click the Notes icon in the Outlook Bar (this displays all your notes). Then double-click the desired note to open it. You can resize the note, if desired, by dragging the lower-right corner of the note.

Deleting Notes

To delete an existing note, click the Notes icon in the Outlook Bar. Click the desired note to select it, and press the Del key, or click the Delete icon in the toolbar.

You can also delete notes that are open. To do this, click the note icon at the top of the note. Then choose Delete from the shortcut menu that appears.

Printing notes

You can print the text of your notes. To do so, first open the note, using the technique described previously. Then click the icon in the upper-left corner of the note and choose Print from the shortcut menu that appears.

Saving notes as text

Normally, you don't have to do anything special to save notes. They are saved automatically, along with all the other entries that you make in Outlook. If you want to save the text contained in a note to a text file, you can do so. Open the note, using the steps described in the section "Opening Existing Notes." Then click the icon in the upper-left corner of the note, and choose Save As from the shortcut menu which appears. In the Save As dialog box that opens, choose the desired file format (RTF or plain ASCII text), enter a desired filename and click Save.

Managing Files from Outlook

You can use Outlook as a substitute for Windows Explorer or My Computer. Without leaving Outlook, you can browse files located on your computer's disk drives or on a network attached to your computer (and while viewing files, you can quickly open, copy, print, or delete them). You can even perform searches, to find files you are looking for.

To view or open files on your PC or on the network, click the Other button in the Outlook bar, then click My Computer in the Outlook Bar. (You can also choose Go⇨MyComputer from the menus.) When you do this, Outlook displays your computer's resources, as shown in Figure 48-22.

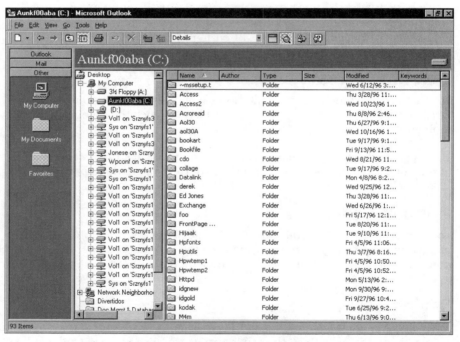

Figure 48-22: Files and folders viewed within Outlook.

You can view your files in different ways: as icons, by file details (as shown in the figure), by author, by file type, or along a time line. To change the way Outlook displays your files, choose View⇨Current View, and select the desired type of view from the next menu that appears.

Working with Files

You can open files from Outlook by using the following steps:

1. Click the Other icon in the Outlook Bar.
2. Click My Computer in the Outlook Bar.
3. Find the desired drive, and double-click it.
4. If the desired file is in a folder, double-click the folder.
5. Double-click the file you want to open. The file will open in an appropriate Windows application.

When a file is visible in Outlook, you can perform a number of common tasks by right-clicking the file and choosing a desired option from the shortcut menu that appears. Figure 48-23 shows the shortcut menu which appears when you right-click a file in Outlook.

Figure 48-23: The shortcut menu for files in Outlook.

The menu offers the most commonly used options of Open With (to open the file using an appropriate Windows application), Cut and Copy, Rename to change the name of the file, and Delete to delete the file. In addition to these options, you can also choose Add To Zip to add the file to a compressed ZIP file, or Send To to copy the file to a diskette or to send it to an e-mail recipient on the network. Finally, the Properties option opens a dialog box that displays the properties for the file.

Finding Files in Outlook

For those times when you are working in Outlook and you suddenly need to locate a file, there is no need to close Outlook and go to Windows Explorer or (horrors!) a DOS window. You can use the Find window of Outlook to search for files, and you don't need to be viewing files to do this. You can search for files from any component of Outlook. Here's how to find files from Outlook:

From any component of Outlook, choose Tools⇨Find Items to open a Find dialog box.

In the Look For list box, choose Files. The Find dialog box now takes on the appearance shown in Figure 48-24.

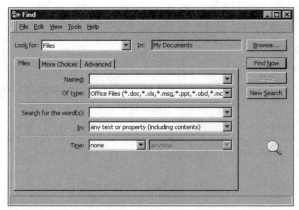

Figure 48-24: The Find dialog box used for searching for files.

If the folder you wish to search does not appear in the In box (or if you wish to search more than one folder), click Browse to select the desired folder or folders. In the Folders list box which appears, turn on the check boxes beside the folders you wish to search, clear the check boxes besides the folders you don't wish to search, and click OK.

If desired, enter a file name or a search pattern to look for and choose any other desired options in the Find dialog box.

Click Find Now. When the search is complete, the Find dialog box will expand to show all files located in the lower portion of the box.

Hot
Stuff   If you want to save the search so you can use the same search at a later time, choose File⇨Save Search from the menus and enter a name for the search in the dialog box that appears. To later run the saved search, choose File⇨Open Search and double-click the search you want to use.

Using the Timex Data Link Watch Wizard

Believe it or not, Outlook can export its data to a Timex Data Link watch. The Timex Data Link watch is a wristwatch that works with Windows software to store phone numbers, a tasks list, appointments, and multiple alarms. The watch receives data from Windows through an infrared sensor built into the watch. The watch reads data sent off the screen through software that comes with the watch or through Outlook. With this watch, you can carry much of your appointment data, phone numbers, and task list information with you. (The Data Link watch software is not installed with Outlook by default. If you want to use it, you will need to install the software. You can find the software in the Timex folder of the ValuePack folder on the Office 97 CD-ROM, or you can download it from the Microsoft web site—www.microsoft.com.)

To export data to a Timex Data Link watch, follow these steps:

1. From the Outlook window, choose File⇨Import and Export, choose Export to Data Link Watch in the dialog box that appears, and click Next. In a moment, you see the first Timex Data Link Watch Wizard dialog box, as shown in Figure 48-25.

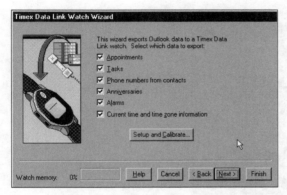

Figure 48-25: The first Timex Data Link Watch Wizard dialog box.

2. Turn on the desired options for the data that you want to export. You can choose whether you want to export appointments, tasks, phone numbers from contacts, anniversaries, alarms, or current time and time zone information. After activating your choices, click on the Next button to reveal the second Timex Data Link Watch Wizard dialog box, as shown in Figure 48-26.

3. In the second dialog box, choose how many days of appointments you want to send, whether the subject text of the appointment should be included, and whether reminder alarms for the appointments should be set. (If you turned off the Appointments option at the first dialog box, you won't see this dialog box.) When you are finished setting the options, click on the Next button to reveal the third Timex Data Link Watch Wizard dialog box, as shown in Figure 48-27.

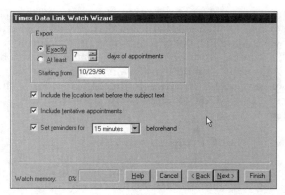

Figure 48-26: The second Timex Data Link Watch Wizard dialog box.

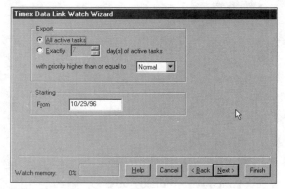

Figure 48-27: The third Timex Data Link Watch Wizard dialog box.

4. In the third dialog box, choose how many days of tasks to export to the watch and a starting date for the tasks that you want to export. Exported tasks appear in the To Do list of the watch. (If you turned off the Tasks option in the first dialog box, you won't see this dialog box.) When you are finished setting the options, click on the Next button to reveal the fourth Timex Data Link Watch Wizard dialog box, as shown in Figure 48-28.

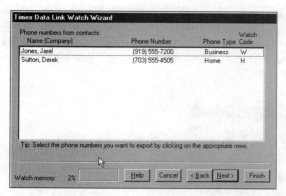

Figure 48-28: The fourth Timex Data Link Watch Wizard dialog box.

5. In the fourth dialog box, select the phone numbers that you want to export by clicking on the appropriate rows in the dialog box. If you've used the Timex software supplied with the watch, you should be aware of a difference between the way that software works and the way the Timex Data Link Watch Wizard works in Outlook. The Timex software sends all phone numbers to the watch by default. By comparison, in this dialog box, you must choose the phone numbers that you want to send each time you export. (If you turned off the Phone Numbers option in the first dialog box you won't see this dialog box.) When you are finished setting the options, click on the Next button to reveal the fifth dialog box for the Timex Data Link Watch Wizard, as shown in Figure 48-29.

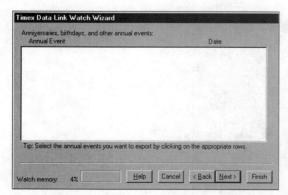

Figure 48-29: The fifth Timex Data Link Watch Wizard dialog box.

6. In the fifth dialog box, select the anniversaries, birthdays, and other annual events that you want to export by clicking on the appropriate rows in the dialog box. When you are finished selecting the desired entries, click on the Next button to reveal the sixth dialog box for the Timex Data Link Watch Wizard, as shown in Figure 48-30.

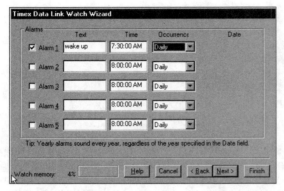

Figure 48-30: The sixth Timex Data Link Watch Wizard dialog box.

7. In the sixth dialog box, you can specify up to five alarms that should be set for the watch by turning on the check boxes and entering the dates and times. When you are done specifying any desired alarms, click on the Next button to reveal the seventh dialog box for the Timex Data Link Watch Wizard, as shown in Figure 48-31.

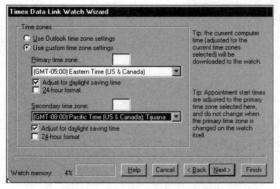

Figure 48-31: The seventh Timex Data Link Watch Wizard dialog box.

8. In the seventh dialog box, choose your desired time zone settings. You can use those already used by Outlook, or you can turn on the Use Custom Time Zone Settings option and then choose your desired time zones from the list boxes shown in the dialog box. When you are finished selecting the options, click on the Next button. A dialog box appears that tells you to put the watch into its Comm Ready Mode.

9. Put the Timex Data Link watch into Comm Mode by pressing the Mode button until Comm Mode and then Comm Ready appear on the face of the watch.

10. Hold the watch so that it's facing the screen about a foot away and click on the OK button. Outlook proceeds to download the data into the watch. When the process is over, you can click on the yes button in the dialog box to return to Outlook. If for some reason the watch did not successfully receive all of the data (for example, you moved it wildly during the transmission), you can click on No in the dialog box to resend the data.

Summary

This chapter covered Outlook, an electronic daily organizer and message center, and the use of the Timex Data Link watch. The following topics were covered in relation to these two items:

✦ You can start Outlook by opening the Windows Start menu and choosing Programs⇨Microsoft Outlook. Once Outlook opens in its window, you can click on any of the icons visible at the left (in the Outlook Bar) to view the different Outlook components.

✦ To make an appointment, double-click the desired day in the Calendar and fill in the desired options in the appointment window that appears.

✦ To add to the Tasks list, from the Task view in Outlook click the New Task button in the toolbar. When the New Task window appears, enter the desired task information.

✦ To add to the Contacts list, from the Contacts view in Outlook, click the New Contact button in the toolbar. When the New Contact window appears, enter the desired task information.

✦ To create notes from anywhere in Outlook, choose File⇨New⇨Note. You can place notes anywhere on the screen and leave them open as you work with other Windows applications.

✦ To print any of the information stored in Outlook, open the desired information and choose File➪Print, or click on the Print button in the toolbar. In the Print dialog box which opens, select the desired options, and click on OK.

The next chapter will cover the Binder, a useful utility that you can use to organize a group of different Microsoft Office documents into a single project.

✦　　✦　　✦

Using the Binder

The Binder is a utility provided with Microsoft Office that you can use to organize different types of documents into a single container. The Binder gives you easy access to all of your documents for editing or printing.

What is the Binder?

The Binder lets you combine documents that are created with Microsoft Office applications. You combine documents into units that are also called *binders*; and you can drag Word, Excel, and PowerPoint documents into the binder. You can also create new documents from within the binder. When you've stored documents in a binder, you can edit and print them as though you were working with a single file. You can create as many binders as you want: each binder is saved under its own file name.

Note Don't be confused by *Binder* and *binder*. When we write uppercase-*B Binder*, we mean the program. When we write lowercase-*b binder*, we mean one of the document containers that the Binder program creates.

You can store any combination of Microsoft Office documents inside a binder. For example, a single binder may contain two Word documents, three Excel workbooks, and a PowerPoint presentation. Figure 49-1 shows an example of a binder document that contains documents from Word, Excel, and PowerPoint.

The Binder gives you a central location where you can get quick access to all the documents that you have created within Office without having to launch each of the applications separately. In Binder, all you do is click on an icon representing a document, and its source application launches automatically. Binder is also quite useful for printing a project composed of different types of Microsoft Office documents; you can print the entire contents of the project with a single command.

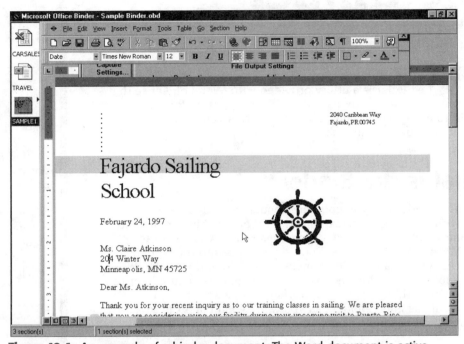

Figure 49-1: An example of a binder document. The Word document is active.

Note By nature of what it does, the Binder runs multiple Office programs as needed. Hence, performance of the Binder is less than spectacular on machines running minimal hardware requirements for Office 97. (According to Microsoft, the minimum recommended hardware is a 486 or better with 8MB of RAM, but we personally find a 486 with 8MB to be unacceptably slow when using the Binder.) During the writing of this book, we tested Binder extensively on two systems:

✦ a Pentium 60 with 8MB RAM

✦ a Pentium 133 with 16MB of RAM

Binder ran acceptably on the second machine and unpleasantly slow on the first. If you plan on making regular use of the Binder, your computer should be equipped with 16MB or more of RAM for acceptable results.

Using the Binder

You can start the Binder from the Windows 95 menus or from the Microsoft Shortcut Bar. If you use the menus, choose the Programs command from the Start menu. From the menu of programs which appears, choose Microsoft Binder, or if the Office Shortcut Bar is visible, just click on the Binder button in the toolbar. With either method, a blank binder page appears, like the one shown in Figure 49-2.

Figure 49-2: A blank binder page.

Adding existing documents to a binder

You can add existing documents to a binder in either of two ways. You can use drag-and-drop, or you can choose the Add from File command from the Binder's Section menu. To use the drag-and-drop technique, open My Computer or Explorer under Windows 95, find the desired document, and click and drag the document into the left pane of the Binder window.

To add an existing document by using the menus, choose Section⇨Add from File. In the Add from File dialog box that appears (Figure 49-3), click on the drive and folder that contain the file that you want to add. Then click on the desired file to select it and click on the OK button. (You can select multiple files in the dialog box by holding the Ctrl key as you click on each desired file.)

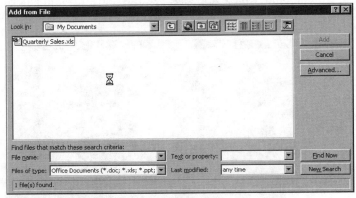

Figure 49-3: The Add from File dialog box.

Adding new documents to a binder

To add a new document to a binder, choose Section⇨Add. In the Add Section dialog box that appears (Figure 49-4), click on the type of document that you want to add and click OK.

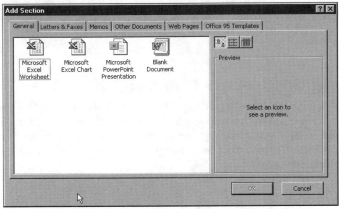

Figure 49-4: The General tab of the Add Section dialog box.

A new, blank document of the chosen type appears in the binder, similar to the example shown in Figure 49-5. In this example, a new PowerPoint document has been added to the binder. You can click on the document's icon at the left side of the binder to change to the menus of the source application so that you can edit the document as desired.

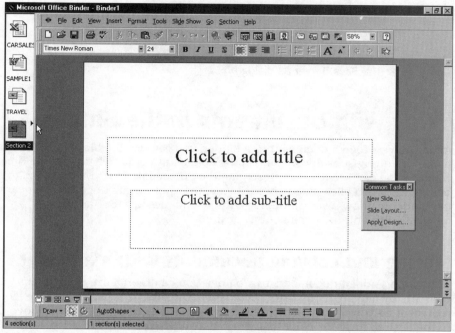

Figure 49-5: An example of a binder with a new PowerPoint document added.

Saving a binder

To save a binder, choose File⇨Save Binder. If you're saving the binder for the first time, you'll be prompted for a filename for the binder. Enter a file name in the Save Binder As dialog box (Figure 49-6) and click on the Save button.

To save a binder under a new name, choose File⇨Save Binder As. In the Save Binder As dialog box that appears, enter the desired file name for the binder and click on the Save button.

Opening an existing binder

To open an existing binder, choose File⇨Open Binder. In the Look In list box inside the Open Binder dialog box, click on the drive and folder that contain the desired binder and double-click on the desired binder name to open the binder.

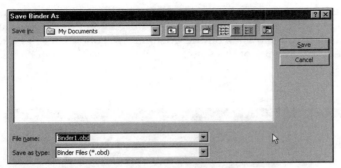

Figure 49-6: The Save Binder As dialog box.

Working with Documents in the Binder

After you've added a document to a binder, you can use the binder as a central point for editing your documents. In the column at the far left side of the Binder window, you can see icons representing the documents that you've added to the binder. After you click on any of the icons, the appropriate document appears in the binder window. You can then use the techniques appropriate to the application to edit the document as desired.

Moving and copying documents within a binder

After you've added documents to a binder, you can reorganize the binder's contents by moving around the documents as needed. Click and drag the icons representing your documents in the left pane of the Binder window to move them to the desired location. Note that you can also drag documents between the left pane of the Binder window and windows of Explorer or My Computer. (If the Binder doesn't have separate left and right panes, click on the button to the left of the File menu.)

To make a copy of an existing document, right-click on the icon of the document and choose Duplicate from the shortcut menu that appears. In the dialog box that appears, indicate which existing section you want the copy added after.

Renaming documents

To rename a document within the binder, double-click on the name of the desired document in the left pane of the Binder window. When you do so, the insertion pointer appears within the name. You can then edit the name and then press Enter to finish renaming the document.

Deleting documents

To delete a document from a binder, right-click on the desired document in the left pane of the Binder window. From the shortcut menu that appears, choose Delete.

Previewing a binder

You can print preview the entire contents of a binder. To do this, choose File⇨Binder Print Preview. In a moment, the entire contents of the binder will appear in a Print Preview window, and you can use the Next Section and Previous Section buttons that appear at the upper left to move between sections in the preview window. When done, click Exit Preview at the upper left to exit the print preview mode.

Printing binder documents

You can print the entire contents of a binder, you can print selected documents, or you can print a single document. To print the entire contents of a binder, choose File⇨Print Binder to open the Print Binder dialog box, as shown in Figure 49-7. In the Print What area of the dialog box, choose the All Sections option. Make any desired changes to the Number of Copies option and turn on the Collate option, if you want. Then click on the OK button to begin printing.

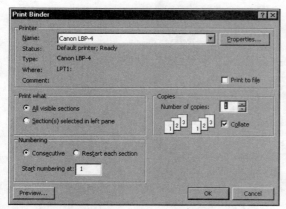

Figure 49-7: The Print Binder dialog box.

To print multiple documents in a binder, first select the desired documents in the left pane of the Binder window by holding down Ctrl as you click on each document that you want to print. Then choose File⇨Print Binder. In the Print Binder dialog box, turn on the Selected Section(s) option and then click on the OK button.

To print a single document, first select the desired document in the left pane of the Binder window. Then choose Section⇨Print. In the Print dialog box, specify the desired range of pages, make any changes to the Number of Copies option, and turn on the Collate option, if desired. Then click on the OK button to begin printing.

Printing headers and footers for a binder

One feature added to binders in Office 97 is the capability to print the same header and/or footer for a group of sections in the binder or for all sections in the binder. This feature can save time when you have to print common headers or footers for complex reports that comprise documents created in different Office programs. You can use the following steps to add headers and footers to some or all documents in a binder:

1. Choose File⇨Binder Page Setup. The Binder Page Setup dialog box appears, as shown in Figure 49-8.

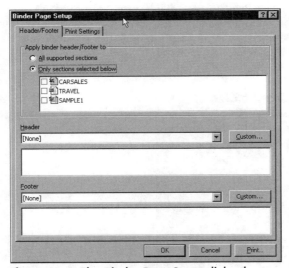

Figure 49-8: The Binder Page Setup dialog box.

2. In the lower half of the dialog box, choose a desired header and/or footer from the list boxes, or click the Custom button for the header or the footer to open a text box where you can type a header or footer of your own choosing.

3. In the upper half of the dialog box, click All Supported Sections if you want the header and/or footer to print with all sections of the binder, or click the Only Sections Selected Below option and click the desired sections in the list box.

4. Click OK to apply the header and footer to your binder documents.

Note   If you add binder headers or footers for selected sections only, sections that you did not select will print with any headers or footers specified within that section (by the program that created the section).

Summary

This chapter has detailed the use of the Binder. If you work with projects that use different types of Office documents, you'll find the Binder to be a useful organizational tool. The chapter has detailed the following points:

✦ Using the Binder, you can combine documents that you created in different applications of Microsoft Office into a single unit.

✦ To start the Binder, click on the Binder button in the Microsoft Office toolbar. Alternatively, choose the Programs command from the Start menu. From the first submenu, choose Microsoft Office and from the next submenu, choose Microsoft Binder.

✦ You can add existing documents to a binder by dragging them from My Computer or from Explorer or by choosing Section➪Add from File.

✦ You can create new documents in a binder with Section➪Add.

✦ You can move documents in a binder to different locations, and you can copy, rename, or delete documents in a binder.

✦ You can print all of a binder's contents or just selected documents in a binder by using File➪Print Binder.

✦ You can print a single document in a binder by using Section➪Print.

In the next chapter, you'll learn how you can use Object Linking and Embedding (OLE) to share information between applications.

Where to go next...

✦ The Binder is a tool that, by nature, helps you manage large and complex projects in Office. Projects of this nature often comprise complex documents (meaning binder documents that contain documents from different Office applications) and compound documents (or documents that make use of OLE objects). See Chapter 50 for more information.

✦ If you need to create complex documents and you are unfamiliar with any of the major Office applications, see Appendix B for an introduction to Word, Appendix C for basic Excel information, Appendix D for a start in PowerPoint, and Appendix E for the basics of Access.

✦   ✦   ✦

Sharing Data between Applications with OLE

Working Together

This chapter explains object linking and embedding (OLE) and shows how you can put OLE to work with the different applications

Defining OLE

If you've ever pasted a picture from Windows Paint into a Word document, if you've ever inserted charts into a Word document or into a PowerPoint presentation, or if you've ever used sound or video with any of the Office applications; you've used OLE. OLE is a *protocol* (an established set of communications rules) under Windows. This protocol enables objects that are created by one Windows application to be stored by means of *linking* or *embedding* in the documents of another Windows application.

Figure 50-1 shows an example of OLE at work. In the figure, a Word document contains an Excel worksheet and a Windows Paint drawing. Both items have been inserted into the document as OLE objects. In OLE terminology, *objects* are selections of data that you insert into your documents. An object may be a part of a Word document, an organizational chart from PowerPoint, a portion of an Excel worksheet, Windows data from another program like CorelDRAW! or Microsoft Visual FoxPro, or a sound or video clip.

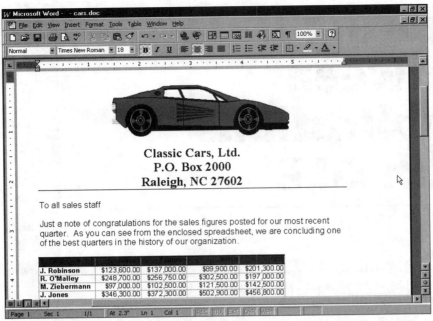

Figure 50-1: A Word document containing an Excel worksheet and a Paint image.

The only common requirement for using OLE is that the Windows software that you are using must support it. All of the Office applications support OLE. Windows applications can be OLE servers, OLE clients, or both.

✦ Some Windows packages (including Windows Paint) are OLE *servers* (also called *server applications*). An OLE server can provide data to other Windows software, but it can't accept data from other packages.

✦ Some Windows packages are OLE *clients* (also called *client applications*). An OLE client can accept OLE data from other Windows software, but it cannot supply OLE data to other software. When you work with OLE, the client application is the application where you are inserting the OLE data, and the server application is the application that is providing the data.

✦ Some Windows packages (including all that are provided with Microsoft Office) can act as both OLE clients and as OLE servers.

If you work with OLE, you'll also hear the terms *source document, destination document,* and *compound document.*

✦ A source document is the document that contains the object that you want to link or embed in the document that you are working on.

✦ The destination document is the document where you are inserting your OLE objects.

✦ Compound documents contain the OLE objects that you insert. For example, a Word document that contains an embedded Excel worksheet is a compound document, and a PowerPoint presentation that contains rows of data inserted from an Access table is a compound document.

You may also hear the term *OLE2*, which refers to Microsoft's newer standard for object linking and embedding. Both OLE and OLE2 let you move data among applications. Windows applications that support OLE2 make using OLE easier by allowing you to work with OLE data while remaining inside the current application. For example, with previous versions of Word and Excel that supported OLE, if you put an Excel worksheet inside a Word document as an OLE object and then double-clicked in the worksheet to change the worksheet data, a copy of Excel was automatically loaded, and you made the desired changes within Excel. With OLE2, if you double-click an Excel worksheet that has been inserted into a Word document, you remain in Word for Windows, but the menu choices and toolbar options change to reflect the choices appropriate to Excel.

You may have noticed this OLE2 behavior if you ever created a graph in Access, Word, or PowerPoint. If you double-click the graph, the toolbars and menu options change to those of Microsoft Graph, while you remain in the program you were working in. Figure 50-2 shows a graph that's active in a Word document with the toolbar and the menu options for Microsoft Graph visible. You don't do anything to make this change take place: it happens automatically, thanks to OLE2.

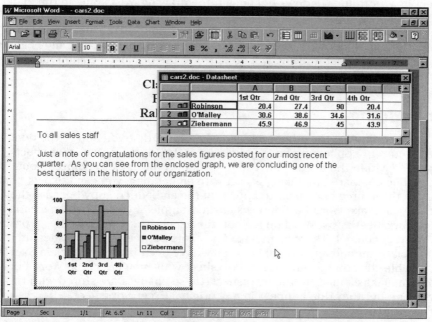

Figure 50-2: An active graph in a Word document with new menu and toolbar visible.

Applications for previous versions of Windows (versions 3.11, 3.1, and 3.0) usually support OLE, but they rarely make use of OLE2. Windows applications written for Windows 95 generally support OLE2. (Note that Windows Paint, supplied with Windows 95, is an exception because it supports OLE, but not OLE2.)

Linking Versus Embedding

Before you become deeply involved with using OLE, you should be familiar with the differences between linking and embedding. The two are often confused by new users of OLE, and they don't mean the same thing. Each offers advantages and disadvantages over the other. As their very names imply, one method involves establishing a *link* to the existing data, while the other involves *embedding* or inserting a copy of the existing data that maintains a link to the source application.

Linking

When you insert an OLE object in a document that is *linked* to existing data in another Windows application, the data remains stored elsewhere, and the current document (where you put the linked object) will be automatically updated whenever you make any changes to the data in the source document. For example, if you create and save a drawing in Windows Paint and you later add it as a linked object in a Word for Windows document, the drawing exists only in the folder where you originally saved it by using Windows Paint. If you open the document containing the drawing in Word and double-click on the drawing, the file that opens through Windows Paint's use of OLE is the original file, and any changes that you make to that drawing will be saved to the original file and reflected in the Word document.

Embedding

With embedding, on the other hand, an OLE object that you add to the document in your current application becomes a part of that document; it is, in effect, *embedded* within the document. The most important thing to realize about embedding compared to linking is that with embedding, you can't expect changes made in the source document to appear in the embedded copy because they won't. Again, take Word for Windows as an example. If you embed an existing Excel worksheet into a Word document, the Excel worksheet becomes a part of the Word document. There is no link of any sort between the worksheet in the Word document and any worksheet it may have been based on back in Excel. So if you double-click on the embedded worksheet while you are in the Word document and then make changes to the worksheet, those changes are stored with the Word document, but they don't appear in any original Excel worksheet.

Why can't I just use the Copy and Paste commands to add OLE objects?

If you've tried using the Copy and Paste commands from the Edit menu to move data from one Windows application to another, you may have noticed that the data generally is *not* automatically updated if you go back and change the source data. (Some older Windows applications will insert "live" data with these commands, but they usually do so by using an older Windows technology known as *DDE*, for Dynamic Data Exchange.)

Using the Copy and Paste commands in Windows applications generally results in the transfer of "static" data that is converted into the format of the destination document.

For example, if you select a range in Excel and choose the Copy command, and then you switch to Word and choose the Paste command, what you get is a Word table containing a copy of the Excel data because a Word table is how Word best understands the layout of the incoming data. To be assured of getting an OLE object of the type that you want, don't use the regular Paste command to insert the data in the destination document. Use the Paste Special command from the Edit menu or the Object command from the Insert menu.

When to use linking and when to use embedding

Linking is the only method to use when, for any reason, you need to maintain a link to the original data, and you want the OLE object in the destination document automatically updated when changes are made to the data in the source document. A good example of linking may be a newsletter produced in Word that contains an Excel worksheet showing monthly sales. You would want the worksheet to update each month based on the new sales, so you would add the worksheet as a linked object. Linking also takes up considerably less disk space than embedding because your document with the link doesn't have to store a complete copy of the data. This point is particularly important with sound or video, which consumes large amounts of disk space.

Embedding is generally advantageous when it's not important to keep the destination data updated based on the source document, and you need *portability* (the capability to move your documents from PC to PC). Therefore, linking depends on your software knowing where to find the source of the data. Moving documents containing linked OLE objects to other PCs can be very troublesome because the other PCs probably don't have the same objects stored in the same folders.

Establishing Links in Your Documents

After you decide to use links to include data (as opposed to embedding data), you can proceed in either of two ways: you can use the Edit⇨Paste Special command, or you can use the Insert⇨Object command. After you've established a link, you can change its update settings, and you can break and later restore the link.

Linking with the Paste Special command

When you need to add a selection of data (as opposed to an entire file) and you want to have it automatically updated when the source data changes, you want to use linking with the Paste Special command. Follow these steps to create a link with the Paste Special command:

1. Start the server application and open (or create) the document that will provide the data to which you want to establish the link. If you create a new document, you need to save it before you can link to the data from the other application.

2. Select the object that you want to place in the other application's document.

3. Choose Edit⇨Copy.

4. Start the other application, if it isn't already running.

5. Open the destination document (the document where you want to insert the OLE link).

6. Place the cursor where the linked object should appear.

7. Choose Edit⇨Paste Special to open the Paste Special dialog box, as shown in Figure 50-3. In the As list box, you'll see the different data formats that you can use to paste the data.

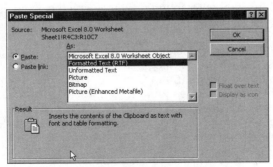

Figure 50-3: The Paste Special dialog box.

I don't see any Paste Special command!

Before trying to establish any OLE links, note that the menu options used by some Windows applications may differ from those that are described in this chapter. The steps outlined in this chapter will work for all the Microsoft Office applications, but some other Windows applications (especially older ones) may use a Paste Links command rather than a Paste Special command. If you can't find a Paste Links command or a Paste Special command anywhere on the menus, the Windows application that you are using probably doesn't support OLE. If in doubt, check the documentation or the online help for the package that you are using to see how (and if) you can use OLE.

8. Choose the desired format. (Typically, you'll want to use a choice that is an object of some type. The types will vary, depending on what software packages are installed on your system.)

9. Turn on the Paste Link option in the dialog box.

10. Click on the OK button to paste the linked object into your document. The object appears at the cursor location, and any changes you later make to the data in the source document are automatically reflected in the destination document.

Linking with the Object command

When you want to add an entire file (as opposed to just a selection of data), and you want to keep the destination document updated from any changes in the source document, you can use Insert⇨Object. Follow these steps to create an OLE link by using the Object command:

1. Start the client application (if it isn't already running) and create or open the destination document.

2. Place the cursor where the inserted object should appear.

3. Choose Insert⇨Object to open the Object dialog box, as shown in Figure 50-4.

4. Click on the Create from File tab. When you do so, you see the options shown in Figure 50-5.

5. Click on the Browse button to display the Browse dialog box (see Figure 50-6).

6. Use the Look In list box and click on the Up One Level button to navigate to the folder that contains the file to which you want to link. Then select the file in the File Name list box and click on the OK button to close the Browse dialog box.

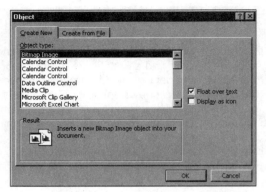

Figure 50-4: The Create New tab of the Object dialog box.

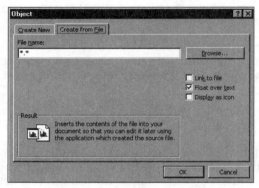

Figure 50-5: The Create from File tab of the Object dialog box.

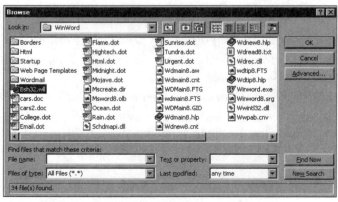

Figure 50-6: The Browse dialog box.

7. Turn on the Link to File option in the Create from File tab of the Object dialog box.

8. Click on the OK button to close the dialog box and to insert the linked file into the destination document.

Changing a links update settings

By default, linked OLE objects that you insert in the destination document are automatically updated when you make changes to the data in the source document. You can change this situation so that the data is updated only upon your command. Use the following steps to change the update settings for the links to your OLE object:

1. Open the destination document that contains the OLE object whose link you want to change.

2. Choose Edit➪Links. (In some Windows applications, this choice is called Link Options.) The Links dialog box appears, as shown in Figure 50-7. In the Source File list box, you see the name for all linked objects in the document along with the path of the source data.

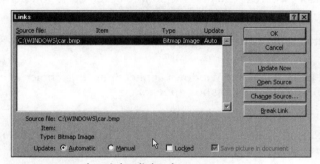

Figure 50-7: The Links dialog box.

3. Select the link that you want to update.

4. Change the Update setting to Manual.

5. To update the link with the latest data from the source document, click on the Update Now button.

6. Click on the OK button to close the dialog box.

7. Save the document in the usual manner.

After you have changed a link's update status from Automatic to Manual, you will need to open the Links dialog box (by choosing the Links command from the Edit menu) and click on the Update Now button every time that you want to update the OLE object with the latest data.

Breaking and restoring links

At times, you may want to break a link intentionally between an OLE object and the source data. For example, when you are sure that you will never need updates in the linked object, you can break the link so that the data becomes a "static" or unchanging copy of the original data. You can break an existing link by performing the following steps:

1. Open the destination document that contains the OLE object whose link you want to change.

2. Choose Edit⇨Links. (In some Windows applications, this choice is called Link Options.) The Links dialog box appears.

3. Select the link that you want to break.

4. Click on the Break Link button. (In some Windows applications, this button may be named Delete Link.) In the confirmation dialog box that appears, click on the Yes or the OK button to break the link.

If you accidentally break a link (which usually happens when you move a document containing a linked object to another PC), you can re-create the broken link by telling Windows where it can find the source of the data. You perform the following steps to re-create a link that has been broken:

1. Open the destination document that contains the OLE object whose link is broken.

2. Choose Edit⇨Links. (In some Windows applications, this choice is called Link Options.) The Links dialog box appears.

3. In the dialog box, select the broken link.

4. Click on the Change Source button to open the Change Source dialog box, as shown in Figure 50-8.

Figure 50-8: The Change source dialog box.

5. Use the Look In list box and click on the Up One Level button to navigate to the folder that contains the file to which you want to reestablish the link. Then select the file in the File Name list box.

6. Click on the OK button to close the Links dialog box and to re-create the link to the destination document.

Embedding Objects in Your Documents

When you decide to embed OLE data (as opposed to establishing links to it), you can use the Edit⇨Paste Special command (with the Paste Link option turned off), or you can use the Insert⇨Object command to embed the data.

Embedding with the Paste Special command

You want to use embedding rather than linking when you don't need a connection to the source data but you want to be able to edit the inserted object. When you want to embed a selection of data (as opposed to an entire file), use the Paste Special command in most Windows applications *but leave the Paste Link option turned off*. Follow these steps to embed data by using the Paste Special command:

1. Start the server application and open (or create) the document that will provide the data that you want to embed in the destination document.

2. Select the object that you want to place in the other application's document.

3. Choose Edit⇨Copy.

4. Start the other application, if it isn't already running.

5. Open the destination document (the document where you want to embed the data).

6. Place the cursor where the embedded object should appear.

7. Choose Edit⇨Paste Special to open the Paste Special dialog box. In the As list box, you'll see the different data formats that you can use to paste the data.

8. Choose the desired format (typically, you'll want to use a choice that is an object of some type). The types will vary, depending on what software packages are installed on your system.

9. If there is a Paste Link option in the dialog box, make sure that it is turned off.

10. Click on the OK button to embed the object in your document. The object appears at the cursor location. You can later edit the object by double-clicking to bring up the original application (if it supports OLE) or to change to the toolbars and menus of the application (if it supports OLE2).

Embedding with the Object command

When you want to embed an entire file (as opposed to just a selection of data), or if you haven't yet created the object that you want to embed, you can use Insert⇨Object to embed an object in your destination document. Follow these steps to embed an object by using the Object command:

1. Start the client application (if it isn't already running) and create or open the destination document.

2. Place the cursor where the inserted object should appear.

3. Choose Insert⇨Object to open the Object dialog box.

4. If you are embedding an object that you haven't yet created, click on the Create New tab, choose the desired object type in the list box, and click on the OK button. (If you want to create the object based on an existing file, skip to Step 8.)

5. After you've clicked on the OK button in the dialog box, a window appears in your destination document that contains a new version of the desired object, and (depending on what software you are using) the other program is launched or the menus and toolbars change to reflect the appropriate choices of the other program. You can now use the usual techniques of the other program to create the desired object.

6. When you are finished creating the object, click on any part of the destination document's window to change back to the destination application. (If you are using a very old Windows application, you may have to choose File⇨Save Changes and then choose File⇨Exit to get back to the destination application.)

7. Save the destination document.

8. If you are embedding an object based on an existing file, click on the Create from File tab in the Object dialog box.

9. Click on the Browse button to open the Browse dialog box.

10. Use the Look In list box and click on the Up One Level button to navigate to the folder that contains the file that you want to embed. Then select the file in the File Name list box and click on the OK button to close the Browse dialog box.

11. Turn off the Link to File option in the Object dialog box.

12. Click on the OK button to close the dialog box and to embed the file as an OLE object into the destination document.

Why can't I find the object I want in the Object dialog box?

In a few (fortunately rare) cases, you won't be able to find the type of object that you want to insert in the list box in the Object dialog box. This missing object type is not a sign that you've done something wrong (unless you're the type to go around randomly deleting important files that Windows needs). The missing object type is a sign that the *Registry*, a bit of hocus-pocus that Windows 95 uses, has somehow become incomplete or corrupted.

Each time that you install software that supports OLE, that software's own installation routine updates the Registry. When you choose Insert ➪ Object in any Windows program, the list of possible object types in the Object dialog box is based on what Windows knows from the registry database. If you have installed a program that you know supports OLE, and the program doesn't appear as a valid type in the dialog box, the only easy way to correct the problem is to reinstall the program so that the registry database is updated. (From a technical standpoint, there are *harder* ways to fix an incorrect Registry, but they get so into the realm of the technical that we're not about to delve into them here.)

Brian Livingston's *Windows 95 SECRETS* (IDG Books, 1995) tells you all about the Registry.

Editing embedded OLE objects

To edit embedded OLE objects, just double-click on the object. Depending on whether the applications that you are using support OLE or OLE2, one of two things will happen:

✦ If you're using OLE2, the object will become active in a window, and the menus and toolbars will change to reflect choices available in the source application.

✦ If you're using OLE, a copy of the source application will be launched containing the object.

In either case, you can make the desired changes to the object. When you are finished editing the object, click on any part of the destination document's window to change back to the destination application. (If you are using an older Windows application, choose File➪Save Changes and then choose File➪Exit to get back to the destination application.)

If your OLE object is a link to existing data in another document, you can also launch the source application, open the document containing the data, and edit the document from within the source application. When you save the changes, however, the data will be automatically updated in the destination document.

Converting file formats of embedded objects

One problem occasionally arises when you move documents containing embedded objects from PC to PC: what if you want to edit the embedded object, but you don't have the source application installed on your PC? Suppose that a co-worker or a client sends you a disk with a Word document that contains an embedded spreadsheet created in Corel's Quattro Pro for Windows. You want to edit the spreadsheet data, but you don't have Quattro Pro for Windows; instead, you're using Excel as your preferred spreadsheet. With all the Microsoft Office applications, you can use a Convert option that is available through the Edit menu to convert the embedded object to a format that your Microsoft Office application can work with.

Follow these steps to convert an embedded object to another file format:

1. Open the document that contains the embedded object and select the object.

2. From the Edit menu, choose the last command shown on the menu. (The name of this command will vary, depending on what type of object you've selected.)

3. From the submenu that appears, choose Convert to open the Convert dialog box, as shown in Figure 50-9.

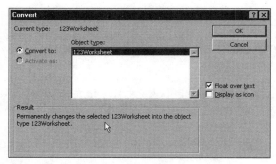

Figure 50-9: The Convert dialog box.

4. Turn on the Convert To option in the dialog box. (The other option, Activate As, enables you to activate temporarily an object that uses a different file format.)

5. In the Object Type list box, choose the type of file format to which you want to convert the object.

6. Click on the OK button to perform the conversion. After you've converted the object, you can double-click on it in the document to edit it.

Adding Sound and Video to Office Documents

You can insert sound and video clips into the various documents that you create in the different Microsoft Office applications by using Insert⇨Object, just like you do to insert other types of OLE objects. If your machine doesn't have Windows sound or video drivers already installed, you won't be able to use sound or video on your system. Sound drivers are usually installed when you add a sound card to your system, and video drivers are usually installed by programs that use video, such as many of the CD-ROM encyclopedias on the market.

To add sound or video to a document, start the destination application, open the destination document, and place the cursor where the sound clip or video clip should appear. Then choose Edit⇨Object. In the Object dialog box, choose Video Clip or Wave Sound if you want to add the clip by using the toolbar and menu options of Windows Media Player. You can also click on the Create from File tab in the Object dialog box if you want to insert the object based on an existing sound (.WAV) or video (.AVI) file. If you choose the Create from File tab, you can enter the file name in the text box or you can click on the Browse button to open a Browse dialog box, where you can find the desired sound or video file. Then you click on the OK button to insert the sound or video.

You can play the sound or video by selecting the object, choosing the last menu option on the Edit menu and then choosing Play from the submenu that appears.

Creating an OLE Example

The best way to get an idea of the usefulness of OLE is to try creating and working with compound documents. Assuming that you have at least the Word and Excel components of Microsoft Office installed on your system, you can duplicate the following example to demonstrate how you can use OLE to add an Excel worksheet to a Word for Windows document.

Working Together

To create an OLE link in an example, follow these steps:

1. Start both Word and Excel in the usual manner.

2. In Word, open any document containing two or more paragraphs of text.

3. Switch to Excel (click its icon in the taskbar or use Alt+Tab to switch to it) and open an existing worksheet containing data.

4. Select a range of the worksheet that you want to insert into the Word document (click and drag from the upper-left corner to the lower-right corner of the desired range). Then choose Edit⇨Copy.

5. Switch back to Word (with the taskbar or Alt+Tab) and place the insertion point on a blank line between two existing paragraphs.

6. Choose Edit➪Paste Special.

7. In the Paste Special dialog box, click on Excel Worksheet Object to select it.

8. Turn on the Paste Link option and then click on the OK button.

In a moment, the worksheet appears in the Word document. It should look something like the example shown in Figure 50-10.

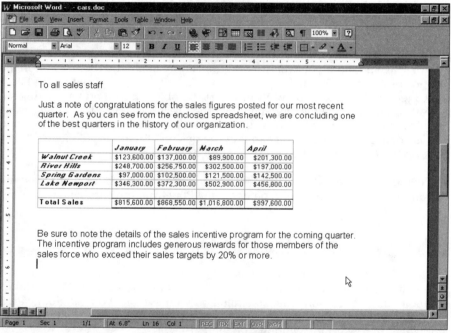

Figure 50-10: Excel data added as a linked OLE object in a Word document.

You can try switching back to Excel and changing the worksheet data in the range that you originally selected. When you switch back to Word, you will see that the Excel data in the Word document changes accordingly.

Summary

This chapter has covered the use of object linking and embedding, and it has provided details concerning how you can put OLE to work with the different applications of Microsoft Office and with other Windows applications. The chapter covered the following points:

✦ Linking involves inserting an OLE object in a destination document that maintains a link to the source data.

✦ Embedding involves inserting an OLE object that does not maintain a link to any source data, but it exists independently in the destination document.

✦ In most Windows applications, you can use the Paste Special command to insert OLE objects containing portions of data from other Windows applications.

✦ In most Windows applications, you can use Insert⇨Object to insert OLE objects as entire files or to add new OLE objects to a destination document.

✦ You can edit OLE objects by double-clicking on the object in the destination document.

✦ You can change the update settings for linked objects, and you can break and restore links to objects by using Edit⇨Links.

Where to go next...

Much OLE work is visual in nature: Often, you're adding Excel graphics to a Word document, or perhaps you are putting Word or Excel data into a PowerPoint presentation.

✦ For thoughts on integrating visual elements into a Word document, see Chapter 10.

✦ If you're working in Excel, Chapter 18 gives useful tips on working visual elements into Excel worksheets.

✦ You can also add Excel worksheets and Word tables to PowerPoint presentations; Chapter 28 has the details.

✦   ✦   ✦

Appendixes

Installing Microsoft Office

Microsoft Office 97 comes either in the form of a CD-ROM or as a (rather large) collection of floppy disks. As far as hardware requirements are concerned, any system that will run Windows 95, Windows NT Workstation, or a higher version of Windows than either of these will run Microsoft Office 97.

Beginning the Installation

You can perform the following steps to install Microsoft Office 97 on your hard disk:

1. Put the Office CD-ROM into the CD-ROM drive and close the door. Windows starts the installer, or if you are installing the product from diskette, insert Disk #1 in the drive. Open the Start menu, choose Run, and enter **A:\SETUP** in the dialog box that appears.

2. Select Install Microsoft Office from the window that appears. A welcome screen appears, as shown in Figure A-1. Click Continue to proceed.

3. The Name and Organization Information dialog box (Figure A-2) appears next. It asks for your name and the name of your organization. Enter the data and then click on the OK button. You will then see another screen asking you to confirm your name and organization name; again, click OK to proceed.

4. The next dialog box to appear shows the product ID number for your version of Microsoft Office. You may want to make a note of this number because it may come in handy if you ever need to contact Microsoft Customer Support for any reason. When you are finished, click on the OK button to proceed.

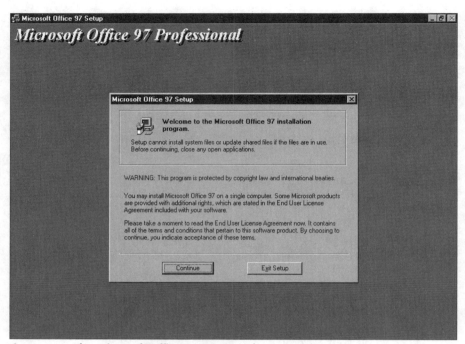

Figure A-1: The Microsoft Office 97 Setup welcome screen.

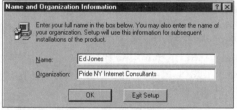

Figure A-2: The Name and Organization Information dialog box.

5. The first Microsoft Office 97 Setup dialog box (Figure A-3) appears next. It asks you to choose the folder in which Microsoft Office should be installed. By default, the program is installed in C:\Program Files\Microsoft Office. If the default location suits you, click on the OK button to proceed. If you want to install Office into a different directory, click on the Change Folder button to display the Change Folder dialog box, shown in Figure A-4. Choose the desired folder, and click on the OK button.

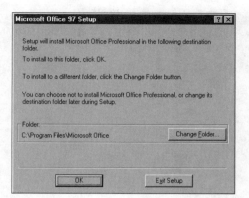

Figure A-3: The first Microsoft Office 97 Setup dialog box.

Figure A-4: The Change Folder dialog box.

If you have an older version of Microsoft Office, and you want to keep using the older applications along with the current version, you should choose a different folder for storing the newer version of Microsoft Office. If you accept the default, you may overwrite any earlier version of Microsoft Office that is installed on your system.

6. After a brief period of time (during which the Setup program scans your hard disk), you'll see the second Microsoft Office 97 Setup dialog box. It displays options of Typical, Custom, and Run from CD-ROM options, as shown in Figure A-5.

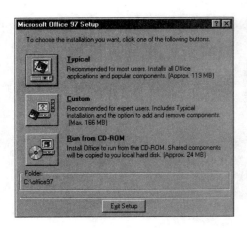

Figure A-5: The second Microsoft Office 97 Setup dialog box.

7. Choose the Typical, Custom, or Run from CD-ROM option from the dialog box, as desired. The Typical option results in what Microsoft calls a "typical" installation, with the options used by most users of Office added to your hard disk (this option takes 119MB of disk space). The Custom option enables you to specify which applications will be added, as detailed in the next section. If you choose the Custom option and install all the features of Microsoft Office, you will need 166MB of disk space. The Run from CD-ROM option installs Office to load programs from the CD-ROM as needed, but see the note that follows (this option takes 24MB of disk space). If you choose the Typical or the Run from CD-ROM option, the installation process will begin.

When the installation process is complete, Setup displays a dialog box that says so. Click on the OK button to return to Windows 95 or Windows NT Workstation.

Note The measly 24MB of disk space consumed by the Run from CD-ROM option may appeal to many who don't have a lot of disk space to begin with, but you should be aware of drawbacks to this method. CD-ROM drives move data considerably slower than do hard disks, so you'll notice slower general operation as the programs load into memory when you use the Run from CD-ROM option. (We recommend that you have a relatively fast CD-ROM, six speed or better, for acceptable performance if you choose this option.) Secondly, having to leave the Office CD-ROM in the drive while you are using the different Office components is a problem if you want to use another CD, like Microsoft Bookshelf, an encyclopedia, or that favorite Pet Shop Boys album. Listening to music through your computer's CD-ROM drive while running Office from the CD-ROM is out of the question, and you can use other CD-ROM–based Windows programs, but you'll have to put up with a horrendous amount of disk swapping. In general, we recommend this method of installing Office only for those who are very short on disk space.

About the Custom Installation Options

When you choose the Custom installation, the dialog box in Figure A-6 appears. It lists the different groups of components for Microsoft Office, which vary depending on whether you purchased the Standard or the Professional Edition:

✦ The Office Binder

✦ Microsoft Excel

✦ Microsoft Word

✦ Microsoft PowerPoint

✦ Microsoft Access (Professional Edition only)

✦ Microsoft Outlook

✦ Web Page Authoring (HTML) tools

✦ Microsoft Bookshelf Basics

✦ Data Access

✦ Office Tools

✦ Converters and Filters

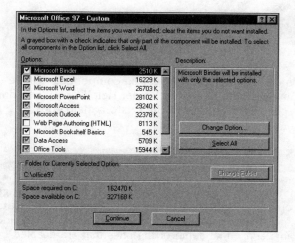

Figure A-6: The Microsoft Office 97 Custom dialog box.

By default, check boxes are turned on for all these applications, with the exception of Web Page Authoring. You can turn off a check box for any application that you don't want to install. Also, while a particular option is highlighted, in most cases you can click on the Change Option button in the dialog box to reveal individual features for that option that you can turn on and off. (Some options, such as Web Page Authoring, don't offer any individual features; they install as a complete group.) Selecting an option means it will be installed. If an item is turned off, it won't be installed. These options are further noted in the paragraphs that follow. Also, note that the purpose of each option appears in detail at the right side of the dialog box when you have the option selected at the left side.

Office Binder and Shortcut Bar options

If you select the Microsoft Binder option in the Custom dialog box and then click Change Option, you see the Microsoft Binder dialog box, as shown in Figure A-7.

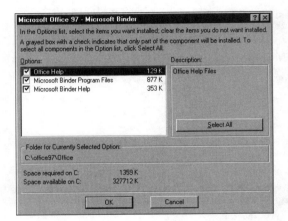

Figure A-7: The Microsoft Binder and Shortcut Bar dialog box.

In the dialog box, you can turn on or off any of the desired components: Office Help, Microsoft Binder Program Files, and Microsoft Binder Help Files. When done choosing the desired options, click OK to return to the Custom dialog box.

What should I install?

When you use the Customize options as part of the installation process, a natural question that arises in every case is which Office options you should consider installing, and which ones you can omit. The answer is going to vary for every individual — after all, what you should install depends on your needs. One point to keep in mind is that it may be worth your time to use the Change Option button in the Custom dialog box to examine each of the options. You may find that some of the ones that are enabled by default aren't really needed in your case, while others that aren't turned on by default will make your life easier if you have them.

Excel options

If you select the Microsoft Excel option in the Custom dialog box and then click Change Option, you see the Microsoft Excel dialog box, as shown in Figure A-8.

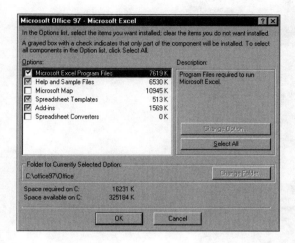

Figure A-8: The Microsoft Excel dialog box.

In the dialog box, you can turn on or off any of the desired components: Microsoft Excel program files, Help and sample files, Microsoft Map, Spreadsheet Templates, Add-ins, and Spreadsheet Converters. When done choosing the desired options, click OK to return to the Custom dialog box.

Word options

If you select the Microsoft Word option in the Custom dialog box and then click Change Option, you see the Microsoft Word dialog box, as shown in Figure A-9.

In the dialog box, you can turn on or off any of the desired components: Microsoft Word Program Files; Help; Wizards and Templates; Proofing Tools; Address Book; WordMail; and Text Converters. When done choosing the desired options, click OK to return to the Custom dialog box.

PowerPoint options

If you select the Microsoft PowerPoint option in the Custom dialog box and then click Change Option, you see the Microsoft PowerPoint dialog box, shown in Figure A-10.

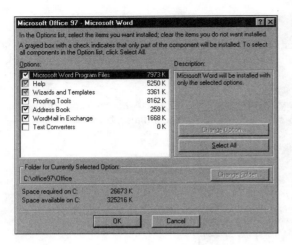

Figure A-9: The Microsoft Word dialog box.

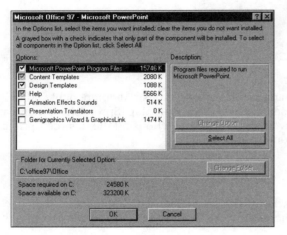

Figure A-10: The Microsoft PowerPoint dialog box.

In the dialog box, you can turn on or off any of the desired components: Microsoft PowerPoint Program Files, Content Templates, Design Templates, Help, Animation Effects and Sounds, Presentation Translators, and Genigraphics Wizard & GraphicsLink. When done choosing the desired options, click OK to return to the Custom dialog box.

Access options

If you select the Microsoft Access option (provided with Office Professional only) in the Custom dialog box and then click Change Option, you see the Microsoft Access dialog box, as shown in Figure A-11.

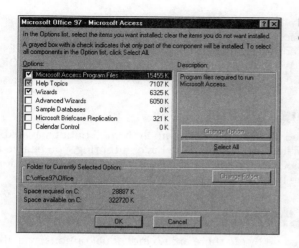

Figure A-11: The Microsoft Access dialog box.

In the dialog box, you can turn on or off any of the desired components: Microsoft Access Program Files, Help Topics, Wizards, Advanced Wizards, Sample Databases, Microsoft Briefcase Replication, and Calendar Control. When done choosing the desired options, click OK to return to the Custom dialog box.

Outlook options

If you select the Microsoft Outlook option in the Custom dialog box and then click Change Option, you see the Microsoft Outlook dialog box, as shown in Figure A-12.

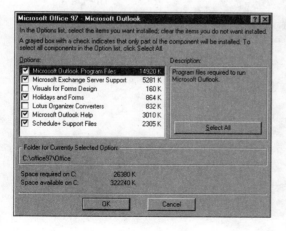

Figure A-12: The Microsoft Outlook dialog box.

In the dialog box, you can turn on or off any of the desired components: Microsoft Outlook Program Files, Microsoft Exchange Server Support, Visuals for Forms Design, Holidays and Forms, Lotus Organizer Converters, Microsoft Outlook Help, and Schedule+ Support Files. When done choosing the desired options, click OK to return to the Custom dialog box.

Web Page Authoring option

This option can only be turned on or off; there are no individual options available under Web Page Authoring. When you turn on Web Page Authoring, you enable a set of tools within the various Office programs that help you publish information to the World Wide Web on the Internet or to a corporate intranet.

Microsoft Bookshelf Basics option

This option can only be turned on or off; there are no individual options available under Microsoft Bookshelf Basics. When you turn on Microsoft Bookshelf Basics, you enable a help system that aids you with the use of Microsoft Bookshelf. (Microsoft Bookshelf is a separate reference product on CD-ROM that includes a thesaurus, dictionary, encyclopedia, atlas, and other reference works.)

Data Access options

If you select the Data Access option in the Custom dialog box and then click Change Option, you see the Data Access dialog box, as shown in Figure A-13.

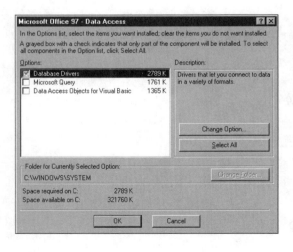

Figure A-13: The Data Access dialog box.

In the dialog box, you can turn on or off any of the desired components: Database Drivers, Microsoft Query, and Data Access Objects for Visual Basic. When done choosing the desired options, click OK to return to the Custom dialog box.

Office Tools options

If you select the Office Tools option in the Custom dialog box and then click Change Option, you see the Office Tools dialog box, as shown in Figure A-14.

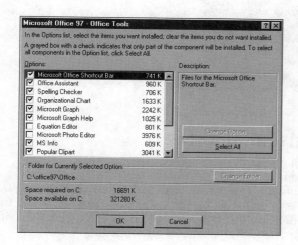

Figure A-14: The Office Tools dialog box.

In the dialog box, you can turn on or off any of the desired components: including Microsoft Office Shortcut Bar, Office Assistant, Spelling Checker, Organizational Chart, Microsoft Graph, Microsoft Graph Help, Equation Editor, Microsoft Photo Editor, MS Info, Popular Clip Art, Clip Gallery, Find Fast, Microsoft TrueType Fonts, Lotus VIM Mail Support, and Find All Word Fonts. When done choosing the desired options, click OK to return to the Custom dialog box.

Converters and Filters options

If you select the Converters and Filters option in the Custom dialog box and then click Change Option, you see the Converters and Filters dialog box, as shown in Figure A-15.

In the dialog box, you can turn on or off either of the desired components: Text Converters, or Graphics Filters. When done choosing the desired options, click OK to return to the Custom dialog box.

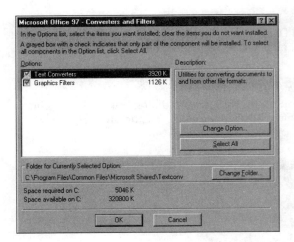

Figure A-15: The Converters and Filters dialog box.

Completing the installation process

When you are finished choosing your desired options, click on the Continue button to proceed. The Setup program checks your system for the necessary disk space and then begins installing the options you selected. If you are installing from floppy disks, the system will ask you to insert the next disk, as needed. When the installation process is finished, Setup displays a dialog box that says so. Click on the OK button to return to Windows 95 or Windows NT Workstation.

✦   ✦   ✦

Word Basics

APPENDIX

In This Appendix

Starting Word

Understanding
Word's screen

Opening new and
existing documents

Navigating
documents

Editing documents

Saving documents

Using File⇨Save All

Printing documents

This appendix provides a fast-paced overview of Word for Windows basics. If you've never used Word, start here.

Starting Word

You can start Word in at least three ways. The simple way is to click on the icon that looks like a *W* in the Microsoft Office Manager. You can use the Start menu: choose Programs and then Microsoft Word. If you like to stick to the keyboard: First press Alt+S to open the Windows Start menu. Then use the arrow keys to navigate to the Word item, and press Return to start it.

About the Screen

More Info When Word starts, you're placed in a blank document where you can begin to enter text. Figure B-1 shows the different parts of the screen. Title bars, menu bars, toolbars, and scroll bars are common to all Windows applications. The Ruler lets you use the mouse to change paragraph indents, adjust page margins, change the width of columns, and set tab stops. See Chapters 2, 3, and 5 for more information. When you're working with a document, the document area contains the document. When you're not working with a document, the document area contains nothing but a white background. The status bar gives you information about your document. These elements are discussed in more detail throughout this appendix.

More Info Figure B-2 shows the toolbars that, by default, appear when you start Word: the Standard and Formatting toolbars. Table B-1 describes the Standard toolbar's buttons. Table B-2 briefly describes the Formatting toolbar's buttons; for detailed information, see Chapter 3.

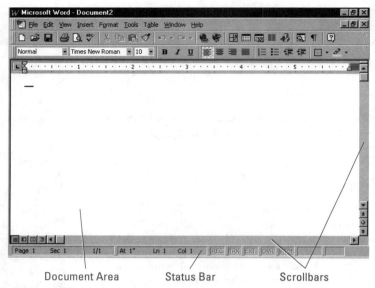

Document Area   Status Bar   Scrollbars

Figure B-1: The Word window.

Figure B-2: The Standard and Formatting toolbars.

Table B-1
Standard toolbar buttons

	Name	Description
	New	Opens a new document using the default page settings.
	Open	Opens an existing document.
	Save	Saves the current document under its present name; if no name exists, the Save As dialog box appears so you can provide one.
	Print	Prints one copy of all pages in the current document.
	Print Preview	Lets you see what your current document will look like when printed and to make layout changes.

	Name	Description
	Spelling	Checks the spelling of the current section (see Chapter 3 for an explanation), or of the entire document if no section exists.
	Cut	Removes a section of highlighted text and places it into the Clipboard.
	Copy	Makes a copy of the current section of text and places it into the Clipboard.
	Paste	Pastes the contents of the Clipboard into the document at the insertion pointer.
	Format Painter	Copies formatting characteristics from one selection of text to another.
	Undo	Reverses the last action.
	Undo Arrow	Lets you choose the action that you wish to undo.
	Redo	Redoes the last action that was undone.
	Redo Arrow	Lets you choose the undone action that you wish to redo.
	Insert Hyperlink	Inserts a link to a URL or another file in Word.
	Web Toolbar	Activates the Web Toolbar (See Chapter 11 Word and the Web)
	Tables and Borders	Activates the Tables and Borders Toolbar, and allows creation of tables. (For more information see Chapter 5.)
	Insert Table	Inserts a table in your document. (Chapter 5 tells you all about tables.)
	Insert Microsoft Excel Worksheet	Inserts a Microsoft Excel Worksheet in Word for Windows.
	Columns	Formats the current section into columns.
	Drawing	Shows or hides the drawing toolbar.

(continued)

Table B-1 (*continued*)

	Name	Description
	Document Map	Activates the Document Map pane. (For more information see Chapter 5)
¶	Show/Hide	Shows or hides all nonprinting characters.
?	Help	Gives help on a command, a screen region, lets you examine text properties. To activate general help, double-click on the Help button. To get help on a specific area of the screen or some text properties, click on the Help button once to make a question mark appear. Then move it to the region of the screen and click on again. If help is associated with that area, it appears.
	Zoom Control	Lets you scale the editing view. This lets you get a closer or less close look at the screen. If text is particularly small, use this button to make it appear larger. If text is particularly large, use this button to make it appear smaller. This doesn't affect the *actual* characteristic of the text — only its appearance on the screen. 8-point Arial, zoomed so it's larger, is still 8-point Arial.

Table B-2
Formatting toolbar buttons

Name		Description
Normal	Style	Lets you choose a style for your text
Times New Roman	Font	Lets you choose a font for your text
10	Font Size	Lets you choose a size for your text's font
B	Bold	Applies or removes boldfacing from text
I	Italic	Applies or removes italics from text

Name		Description	
U	Underline	Applies or removes underlining from text
	Align Left	Aligns text to the left margin
	Center	Centers text
	Align Right	Aligns text to the right margin
	Justify	Aligns text to both the left and the right margins
	Numbering	Creates a numbered list from a selected set of items
	Bullets	Creates a bulleted list from a selected set of items
	Decrease Indent	Indents a paragraph to the previous tab stop
	Increase Indent	Indents a paragraph to the next tab stop
	Borders	Lets you apply borders and shading to your text
	Highlight	Applies or removes highlighting from text

Starting from the left side of the Formatting toolbar, you'll first see the Style list box. This lets you apply any of Word's styles to a section (a paragraph where the insertion point is placed). Next comes the Font list box, which lets you change the appearance of characters by choosing different typefaces. Near the center of the Formatting toolbar, you'll find the Font Size list box; this lets you change the size of a document's characters. Next are the three character-formatting buttons: **Bold,** *Italic,* and Underline. Next, you'll see the Highlight button, which lets you highlight text in a color.

The four alignment buttons come next — Align Left, Center, Align Right, and Justify. Following those are the Numbering, Bullets, Decrease Indent, and Increase Indent buttons. Finally, you'll find the Borders button, which lets you place various types of borders and shading on sections of a document.

Each component of the Formatting toolbar is discussed in detail in the corresponding section.

Opening New or Existing Documents

You can create new documents from a blank document screen in either of two ways. You can start Word in the usual manner by clicking on the Word icon, or by choosing Programs from the Start menu and then using the arrow keys to select Word from the list of programs. Or, from within Word, you can choose File⇨New. If you don't use a template when creating a document, the document screen appears resembling a blank sheet of paper, and formatting takes on a standard appearance, with default margins and text style controlled by the default template, Normal.dot.

To open an existing document, choose File⇨Open and enter the filename in the File name text box that appears in the Open dialog box.

You insert text into a document either by typing it or by pasting it from the Clipboard. If you're completely new to Word for Windows, practice by typing the following text. Humor me on this — I'll use this example again later, and it'll help if you've already typed it in:

Bungee Jumping

Bungee jumping is considered by many a high-risk sport. The sport entails tying a giant rubber band to your legs and jumping from a high object, usually a crane of some kind. The sport has become increasingly popular over the years since its introduction. At present you can take vacations that include trips to practice these high-risk sports. Bungee jumping has become so popular that it is now a sport at the Extreme Games. There are now professionals that make their living much like platform divers do. There are many similarities to platform diving and bungee jumping. The grading is much the same and the tricks that the jumpers do are very reminiscent of diving.

Basic Navigation

Now that you have some text in your new document, you can practice some basic navigation skills. Table B-3 lists keystrokes that move you around your documents.

Table B-3
Navigation keystrokes

Keystroke	Function
Arrow keys	Move around in your document.
Ctrl+Up Arrow	Move up one paragraph.
Ctrl+Down Arrow	Move down one paragraph.
Alt+Left Arrow	Move the cursor one word to the left.
Alt+Right Arrow	Move the cursor one word to the right.
Page Up	Move up one screen.
Page Down	Move down one screen.
Home	Move the cursor to the beginning of the current line.
Ctrl+Home	Move the cursor to the beginning of the document.
End	Move the cursor to the end of the current line.
Ctrl+End	Move the cursor to the end of the document.

The scroll bars will move you through a document, too. There are four ways to scroll with the scroll bar: click on the arrows incrementally, hold down the mouse button on the scroll arrow, drag the scroll bar box, or click on the scroll bar.

Basic Text Editing

Text editing is also relatively simple in Word. You can do it in several ways.

Return to the second line of the "Bungee Jumping" document that you typed earlier and now type the letter **R**. As you can see, the letter is added to the line of text. But if you press the Insert key and then type something, what you type replaces the text that was there. You can delete letters by using the Delete key: Place the cursor at the beginning of your second line in front of your *R* and then press Delete. Presto, the *R* is removed. The Insert key is a toggle key. The first time you press it, text you type replaces existing text (Overtype mode); the second time you press it, text you type is inserted into the existing text (Insert mode). The status bar at the bottom of the Word window tells you which mode you're using. Look for the REC, MRK, EXT, OVR, and WPH boxes. If OVR appears in black letters, then you're in Overtype mode. Otherwise, you're in Insert mode.

If you want to replace a paragraph or a large section of text, there are two methods that you can use. One is to press the Insert key until you are in Overtype mode and to then begin typing. This replaces all text until you stop typing, so be careful not to overwrite what you want to keep. If you happen to find something that you do want to keep, press the Insert button again and Overtype is turned off.

The second method is to highlight a word, sentence, or paragraph and then press Delete to remove it from your document. Make sure that Overtype is off if you replace an area of text; otherwise, when you begin to type again, you'll overwrite the text that was moved as a result of the deletion.

Saving

Saving documents is a basic but important operation that you can do with any word processor. Word provides a variety of options. You can save a file either under a new name or an existing one. You can save files in Word's own file format, or you can do it in the formats of other popular word processors. And you can save all open files with a single command.

Saving a document

To save a file, either choose the Save icon from the Standard toolbar or File⇨Save. If the file has been saved previously, Word saves the file without prompting you for any information; the document remains on the screen. If you want to leave Word, you must also use the File⇨Exit command, or its equivalent, Alt+F4.

If you use the File⇨Save command to save a document that has never been saved, Word displays the Save As dialog box (Figure B-3) asking for the name for the file. Enter the filename that you want. Word ordinarily assigns an extension of .DOC to all files saved in its normal file format. Since Word assumes that files have this .DOC extension, you need not include it when entering names for saving and loading files. You can assign your own extension by typing the period and the extension that you want along with the filename; however, if you do this, you'll have to type the extension whenever you later open the file with the File⇨Open command.

If you created the example document "Bungee Jumping," save it now by performing these steps:

1. Choose File ⇨ Save. Because you have never saved this file, the Save As dialog box appears.

2. In the File name field, type **Bungee Jumping**.

3. Click on OK. Word saves the document under the name Bungee Jumping.doc.

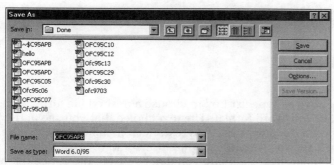

Figure B-3: The Save As dialog box.

Word also provides an easy way to save files to other directories or to floppy disks, with the File⇨Save As command (see the following section, "Using File⇨Save As").

Note If you want to save a document and exit from Word, the Alt+F4 (File⇨Exit) hot key is useful. When you press Alt+F4 to exit, Word automatically prompts you to save any changes made to the document. Click on Yes, and your changes are saved. If the document has not been saved before, you are prompted to supply a filename in the Save As dialog box. Enter a file name, click on OK, and the document is saved.

Using File⇨Save As

You can use the File⇨Save As command to save files to other directories or to a floppy disk. You can also use this command to save a copy of your file in the format of another word processor or as ASCII text. When you choose File⇨Save As, the same dialog box appears as the one shown earlier in Figure B-3.

The name of the file appears in the File name field (if the document has ever been saved). If you want to save the file under a different name, you can type a new name, and that name will replace the existing one. If the document has never been saved, this field is blank; you can type in an original filename for the file.

To save the file to a different directory or drive, tab to or click on the list box beside the Save in field and select the drive or directory that you want. You can navigate up and down within subdirectories by using the list box. To move to a subdirectory, select it by name.

You can also use the File⇨Save As command to save a document in the format of another word processor. To do this, choose File⇨Save As and then click on the arrow of the Save as type list box. When you do this, the dialog box expands to show additional formats that you can save your document in (as shown in Figure B-4).

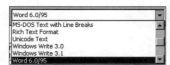

Figure B-4: The Save as type list box.

Tab to or click on the Save as type list box to choose a desired file format other than the standard Microsoft Word format. The text choice that you see in the list box can be used to save a document as ASCII text. Keep in mind that the other available formats you'll see will depend on what formats were installed along with Word. If you need a popular file format and you don't see it in the list box, it may not have been added during the installation process.

To look at the options for saving a file, open the Save As dialog box and choose Options. A list of options will appear: Always Create Backup Copy, Allow Fast Saves, Prompt for Document Properties, Prompt to Save Normal Template, Save Native Picture Formats Only, Embed True Type Fonts, Save Data Only for Forms, and Automatic Save Every x Minutes. The following sections cover the most basic options for saving files.

Note When the Always Create Backup Copy option is on, Word will create a backup file every time you save. The backup file will have the .BAK extension.

Allow fast saves

Some of Word's behavior when saving files depends on how much editing you've done to the file since it was saved last.

Word saves files using either of two methods: a *fast save* or a *full save*. When you choose File⇨Save, Word saves your file using the method indicated by the circumstances.

Normally, Word performs a fast save, where your changes are appended onto the end of an existing file. With a full save, Word saves the entire document, including unchanged parts, as if you were saving the file for the first time.

The first time a document is saved, Word performs a full save. After that, Word usually performs a fast save whenever you save updates to your document. (If you make massive changes, Word may perform a full save automatically.)

Operationally, you'll see no difference between the two methods other than in speed. Full saves take somewhat longer than fast saves; exactly how much longer varies greatly depending on the speed of your hardware. To turn fast saves on or off, go to the Save Options list box in the Options dialog box by choosing File⇨Save As, click on Options, and turn off the Allow Fast Saves check box by either clicking on it or pressing Alt+F.

Prompt for Document Properties

The Prompt for Document Properties option will show the Summary tab of the Properties dialog box. This tab lets you store general information about the document, such as title, subject, author, and so on.

Automatic Save Every *x* Minutes

You can set the Automatic Save option for whatever time period you want, depending on your preference and work speed.

Using File⇨Save All

You can use the File⇨Save All command to save all open documents. Choose File⇨Save All, and Word will then display a dialog box for each document and ask if the document should be saved. Choose Yes from the dialog box, and a similar dialog box for the next document will appear. To save all documents, continue choosing Yes. If any of the documents were not saved previously, Word will prompt you for filenames as necessary.

Note   In addition to saving all open documents, File⇨Save All will save any open global macros, templates, or glossaries.

Printing

You'll want to print most of the documents that you create. Printing is covered in detail in Chapter 4; this section shows how to print one copy of a document.

To print a document, choose File⇨Print (or press Ctrl+P). The Print dialog box appears, as shown in Figure B-5.

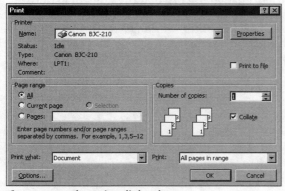

Figure B-5: The Print dialog box.

Assuming that the printer name that appears at the top of the dialog box matches the printer connected to your PC, you're ready to print. The default options in the dialog box assume that you want one copy of the document and that you want all pages in the document printed. You can change the defaults by changing the number of copies in the Number of copies field or by changing the beginning and the ending page numbers in the Pages field.

After selecting the options that you want, choose OK to begin printing your document. If you have difficulty printing — or if the printer name in the Print dialog box doesn't match the printer that's actually connected to your PC — the problem may lie with how Windows is set up on your system. If you can't print from any Windows application (for example, Cardfile or Notepad), you won't be able to print from Word, either. Make sure that the correct printer chosen is on the Printer name field. See Chapter 4 for more information on Print Setup.

Printing part of a document

Keep in mind that you can quickly print specific pages of a document by entering beginning and ending page numbers in the Print dialog box. Just enter the starting and ending page numbers in the Pages field of the Page range area of the dialog box.

To print a selected portion of a document, first highlight the selection and then choose File⇨Print. In the Print dialog box, choose Selection (Alt+S). After you click on OK, only the selected text is printed.

Opening Existing Documents

To open a document, either click on the Open icon on the toolbar, choose File⇨Open, or press Ctrl+O. The Open dialog box appears. From there, either choose the name of the document that you want to open by scrolling to its name or type the name of the document in the File name field and then press Enter. If the document is on another drive, change the drive in the Look in list box.

This appendix provides just an overview of the workings of Word. Each of the topics touched on here is covered in detail in the Word section of this book.

Summary

This appendix covered topics related to the basics of Word. All of these topics are covered in more depth in their respective chapters. Here are some of the topics that we covered.

✦ You start Word by clicking on the *W* icon in the Microsoft Office Manager, or by using the Start menu in the taskbar.

✦ You can use Word's Standard and Formatting toolbars to open, close, print, and save documents; to cut and paste text; to insert objects such as graphics and Excel worksheets; to get help; and to apply formatting to text.

✦ You can create a new document by starting Word; a blank document automatically appears. If you're already in Word, create a new document with File⇨New. Then insert text by typing.

✦ Several keystrokes and commands are available for navigating your document.

✦ You can use Overtype mode (press the Insert key until OVR appears in the status bar) to replace text. Click on where you want to replace text, turn on Overtype mode, and type. Alternatively, you can select text you want to replace, press Delete, make sure you're in Insert mode (press the Insert key until OVR does *not* appear in the status bar), and type the new text.

✦ You save a document with File⇨Save. To save a document under a new name, use File⇨Save As.

✦ Print your document with File⇨Print.

Where to go next...

✦ Part II describes all of Word's features. Start in Chapter 2.

✦   ✦   ✦

Excel Basics

After you installed Excel, you were returned to the Windows 95 desktop. To start Excel, choose Programs from the Windows 95 Start menu and then choose Microsoft Excel.

Understanding Spreadsheets

A spreadsheet is an electronic version of old bookkeeping tools: the ledger pad, pencil, and calculator. Excel spreadsheets, called *worksheets* in Microsoft terminology, can be likened to huge sheets of ledger paper. Each worksheet measures 65,536 rows by 1,024 columns — realistically, more size than you should ever need on a single page. Each intersection of a row and column comprises a cell, and cells are identified by their row and column coordinates. A1 is the cell in the upper-left corner of the worksheet.

Data that you enter in a worksheet can take the form of *constant values* or of *variables* that are based on formulas. Constant values, such as a number (81.5) or a name (Timothous Mack), do not change. Values derived from formulas often refer to other cells in the worksheet. For example, a cell might contain the formula C5+C6, which adds the contents of two other cells in the worksheet, C5 and C6.

Excel's worksheets can display data in a wide variety of formats. You can display numeric values with or without decimals, currency amounts, or exponential values. You can also enter text, such as the name of a month or a product model name. And you can store and display date and time-of-day data in worksheet cells.

Besides storing your data, in most cases you will want to perform calculations on that data — after all, calculations are what nearly all spreadsheet models are about. Excel helps you in this regard by providing a rich assortment of *functions*, which are special built-in formulas that provide a variety of calculations (the average of a series of values, for example, or the square root of a number). Excel provides functions for mathematical, statistical, financial, logical, date and time, text, and special-purpose operations.

As a product, Excel appeals to numbers-oriented PC users who must manage numbers on a day-to-day basis. Thanks to its extensive built-in graphics support, Excel also works well for those who need to highlight numeric data with presentation graphics.

Understanding the Excel Screen

When you look at the Excel screen, you'll see some buttons that may be unfamiliar to you although you may be a regular user of Microsoft products. This section describes Excel's toolbars.

Figure C-1 shows what Excel looks like when first opened; you'll see a new workbook with the title Book1.

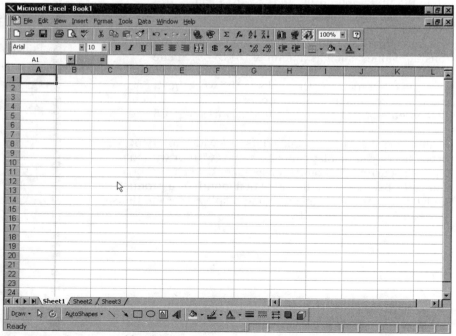

Figure C-1: A new workbook in Excel.

Figure C-2 shows Excel's Standard toolbar. Table C-1 shows its buttons.

Figure C-2: The Standard toolbar.

<table>
<tr><td colspan="2" align="center">Table C-1
Toolbar buttons</td></tr>
<tr><td>*Name*</td><td>*Function*</td></tr>
<tr><td>New Workbook</td><td>Opens a new workbook.</td></tr>
<tr><td>Open</td><td>Opens a workbook file.</td></tr>
<tr><td>Save</td><td>Saves a current workbook; if it has not been saved before, you are prompted to enter a name for the workbook.</td></tr>
<tr><td>Print</td><td>Opens the Print dialog box for printing.</td></tr>
<tr><td>Print Preview</td><td>Shows you what the workbook will look like when printed.</td></tr>
<tr><td>Spelling</td><td>Checks the spelling for the current sheet or the selected section.</td></tr>
<tr><td>Cut</td><td>Cuts the selected information and places it on the clipboard.</td></tr>
<tr><td>Copy</td><td>Copies selected text and places it on a clipboard.</td></tr>
<tr><td>Paste</td><td>Pastes selected text in the document at the insertion pointer.</td></tr>
<tr><td>Format Painter</td><td>Copies text formatting from one area to another.</td></tr>
<tr><td>Undo</td><td>Reverses last action.</td></tr>
<tr><td>Undo Arrow</td><td>Lets you choose the action that you wish to undo.</td></tr>
<tr><td>Redo</td><td>Redoes the last action that was undone.</td></tr>
<tr><td>Redo Arrow</td><td>Lets you choose the undone action that you wish to redo.</td></tr>
<tr><td>Insert Hyperlink</td><td>Inserts a link to another file or to a web site on the Internet or on an intranet.</td></tr>
<tr><td>Web Toolbar</td><td>Displays the Web Toolbar, which can be used for various web-related tasks.</td></tr>
<tr><td>AutoSum</td><td>Invokes the sum function, which adds a column of numbers.</td></tr>
<tr><td>Paste Function</td><td>Activates the Function Wizard, which quickly locates a desired function for use in a formula.</td></tr>
<tr><td>Sort Ascending</td><td>Sorts list information in ascending order.</td></tr>
</table>

(continued)

Table C-1 (*continued*)

Name	Function
Sort Descending	Sorts list information in descending order.
ChartWizard	Activates the Chart Wizard, which creates a chart based on worksheet data.
Map	Activates the Map Wizard, which inserts a map into a worksheet.
Drawing	Displays the Drawing toolbar, which contains various tools which can be used to draw graphic shapes in a worksheet.
Zoom Control	Controls the size of a document's appearance on-screen.
Office Assistant	Activates the Office Assistant help system.

Figure C-3 shows Excel's Formatting toolbar. Table C-2 explains its buttons.

Figure C-3: The Formatting toolbar.

Table C-2
Formatting toolbar

Name	Function
Font	Displays list of fonts
Font Size	Displays available font sizes
Bold	Changes the selected text to boldface
Italic	Changes the selected text to italics
Underline	Underlines the selected text
Align Left	Left-aligns cell entries
Center	Centers cell entries
Align Right	Right-aligns cell entries
Merge and Center	Centers cell entries across the columns
Currency Style	Applies currency formatting to the current selection

Name	Function
Percent Style	Applies percent formatting to the current selection
Comma Style	Applies comma formatting to the current selection
Increase Decimal point in the selection	Increases the number of digits shown after the decimal
Decrease Decimal point in the selection	Decreases the number of digits shown after the decimal
Decrease Indent	Reduces the amount of indentation of the selection
Increase Indent	Increases the amount of indentation of the selection
Borders	Displays a Borders palette, which can be used to apply a border to the current selection
Fill Color	Displays a Color palette, which can be used to apply a color choice to the current selection
Font Color	Displays a Font Color palette, which can be used to apply a font color choice to the current selection

Understanding the Workbook Concept

The concept of workbooks may be new to Excel users who haven't upgraded since the dark ages (specifically, before version 5.0). In a nutshell, a *workbook* is a collection of worksheets. Each of the worksheets consists of columns and rows that form cells. There are tabs at the bottom of each of the sheets; you can click on each of these tabs if you want to change to a different sheet.

The advantage of using workbooks is that you can keep more than one spreadsheet in a file. This is especially useful when you have a series of worksheets that track time-related data, such as sales or expenses for a series of months. Instead of having to open several files, you can place all the worksheets in the same workbook and look at each of them with a click of your mouse.

Opening an Existing Workbook

To open a previously saved workbook, choose File⇨Open. In the Open dialog box that appears (see Figure C-4), you can choose the file that you want.

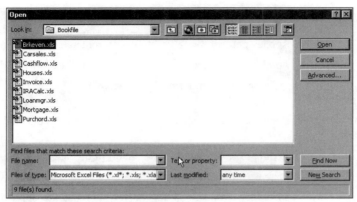

Figure C-4: The Open dialog box.

If the file is in a folder, you can double-click on the folder to open it. You may need to navigate within the folders to find your file; you can click on the Up One Level button in the dialog box to see higher-level files and folders.

Workbook and Worksheet Navigation

This section teaches the basics of navigation in a worksheet and a workbook. As always, you can use either the mouse or the keyboard, depending on preference.

Navigating in the workbook window

When Excel starts, you see a workbook with the current worksheet in front. All workbooks consist of three worksheets by default, so you need a quick, convenient way to move from worksheet to worksheet.

Keyboard users can do this by pressing Ctrl+PgDn to move to the next sheet or Ctrl+PgUp to move to the preceding sheet. If you prefer the mouse, click on the desired worksheet's tab at the bottom of the window. Figure C-5 shows the worksheet tabs in an Excel workbook. (If you can't see the needed tab, use the scroll buttons at the lower left to move it into view.)

Figure C-5: The tabs of an Excel workbook.

Navigating in a worksheet

After selecting the worksheet that you want, you need to be able to move about in it. Keep in mind that the part of the spreadsheet you see on-screen is but a small section of the entire worksheet. Table C-3 shows the key combinations that move you around in an Excel worksheet. (The key combinations are especially beneficial for those who customarily keep their hands on the keys for quick text entry.)

Table C-3 Keys and key combinations for navigating in a worksheet	
Keys	**Function**
Arrow keys	Move the insertion point in the direction of the arrow
Ctrl+Up Arrow or Ctrl+Down Arrow	Moves to the top or bottom of a region of data
Ctrl+Left Arrow or Ctrl+Right Arrow	Moves the insertion point to the left-most or right-most region of data
PgUp or PgDn	Moves up or down one screen
Home	Moves to the first cell in a row
Ctrl+Home	Moves the insertion point to the top left corner of the worksheet
Ctrl+End	Moves to the first cell of the last row in a worksheet
End+Enter	Moves the pointer to the last column in a row

If you like using the mouse, it's also easy to navigate in a worksheet that way. You can use the scroll bars to move to the screen area containing the cell that you want to work with and then click in any cell to make it active. There are four ways to scroll with the scroll bar: click on the arrows incrementally, hold down the mouse button of the scroll arrow, drag the scroll bar box, or click on the scroll bar.

If you are using Microsoft's IntelliMouse (or a compatible mouse equipped with a mouse wheel), you can scroll the worksheet up and down by rolling the mouse wheel, and you can scroll the worksheet horizontally or vertically by clicking once on the mouse wheel to enter the scrolling mode, and then dragging in the desired direction. When done scrolling, click with any mouse button to exit the scrolling mode.

Yet another option for moving about in Excel is with the Go To command. If you want to move to a specific cell on a worksheet, either choose Edit⇨Go To or press F5. This opens the Go To dialog box, as shown in Figure C-6. Here you can enter the cell address that you want to see and then click on OK to go directly to that cell.

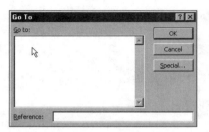

Figure C-6: The Excel Go To dialog box.

Entering and Editing Data

You can enter combinations of numbers and letters. Just move to any cell and start typing. When done with your entry, press Enter to store it in the cell.

As you enter text, you'll sometimes want to edit it. You can use the following steps to edit existing data in worksheet cells:

1. Move the cursor to the cell containing the data that you want to edit.

2. Move the mouse pointer over the Formula bar. (As you do so, the mouse pointer takes on the shape of an I-beam.)

3. Place the mouse pointer at the location where you want to start editing, and click. A flashing insertion point in the Formula bar indicates where your editing will occur, and you can proceed to make the necessary edits. You can press Enter when done.

If you haven't completed your entry and decide that you want to change it, click on the Cancel button in the Formula bar (the button with the red *X* in it, as shown in Figure C-7) or press Esc. If you've already entered the text by pressing Enter, you can erase the entry by clicking on the Undo button on the Standard toolbar.

Cancel

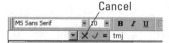

Figure C-7: The Cancel button of the Formula bar.

Two kinds of data can be entered into a worksheet: *values* and *formulas*.

✦ Values are data such as dates, time, percents, scientific notation, or text; values don't change unless the cell is edited.

✦ Formulas are sequences of cell references, names, functions, or operators that will produce a new value based on existing values in other cells of the worksheet.

Figure C-8 shows a typical worksheet containing both values and formulas.

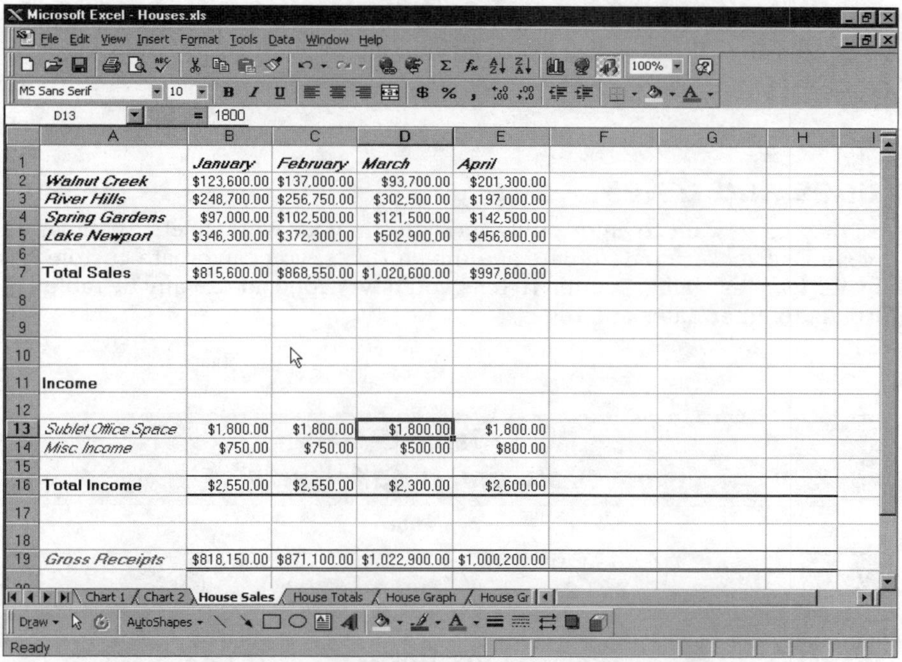

Figure C-8: A typical worksheet with values and formulas stored in cells.

Numbers

When you begin a new worksheet in Excel, the cells are formatted with the General Number format. This causes Excel to display numbers as accurately as possible using the integer, decimal fraction, and — if the number is longer than the cell — scientific notation.

In most cases, Excel automatically assigns the correct format for your number as you enter it. If you enter a percent sign before your number, the number is assigned the percent format; if you enter a dollar sign before the number, the number is assigned a currency format. In cases where the number is too large to fit in the column, Excel displays a series of # symbols. To see the entire number, simply widen the column by double-clicking on its right border.

Entering numbers as text in Excel can be useful at times; for example, when you want to enter zip codes or other numbers that should appear as text. To do this, you must tell Excel by entering a single quotation mark (') before the number. This tells Excel to format the numbers as text and left-align them.

You can enter numbers in your worksheet using any of the numeric characters along with any of the following special characters:

+ - ( ) , / $ % . E e

Times and dates

You may often want to enter times and dates in your worksheets. Whereas Table C-4 shows Excel's standard date and time formats, you can create custom formats of your own, as well. (Chapter 16 tells you how.) You can use any of Table C-4's formats to enter dates and times.

Table C-4 Date and time formats	
Format	**Example**
D/M	3/5
D/M/YY	3/5/95
DD/MM/YY	03/04/95
D-MON	3-Apr
D-MON-YY	3-Apr-95
DD-MON-YY	03-Apr-95
MON-YY	Apr 95
MONTH-YY	April 95
MONTH-D-YYYY	April-5-1995
HH:MM	10:30

HH:MM AM/PM	02:30 PM
HH:MM:SS	10:30:55
HH:MM:SS AM/PM	02:30:55 PM
HH:MM.n (with tenths)	02:30.7
HH:MM:SS (24-hour)	14:30:55
D/M/YY H:MM	3/4/95 2:30
D/M/YY H:MM AM/PM	3/4/95 2:30 PM

To enter a date or time, simply enter it in one of the acceptable formats and press Enter.

Text entry

To enter text in Excel, type the text in the cell where you want it. You can type no more than 255 characters into a cell. Entries can include text and numbers and, as mentioned earlier, numbers can also be entered as text.

You may want to format large amounts of text in a way that presents an attractive display. To do this, choose Format⇨Cells; you'll see the Format Cells dialog box shown in Figure C-9.

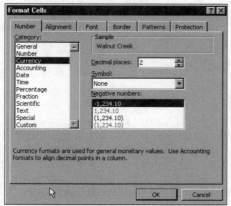

Figure C-9: The Format Cells dialog box.

If you'll be entering a long display of text, you can activate the Wrap Text check box; this prevents long strips of text from overflowing into other cells. First, though, be sure that your columns are the width that you want them.

To activate text wrap, click on the Alignment tab in the dialog box and turn on the Wrap Text check box. This lets you have multiple lines of text in your cells.

Building Formulas

The whole point of spreadsheets is to manipulate the numbers. Add them. Multiply them. Calculate their cosines, if you're trigonometrically inclined. You use *formulas* to do this. You build a formula by indicating which values should be used and which calculations should apply to these values. Formulas always start with an equal sign.

For example, if you wanted to add the values in cells B1 and B2 and then display the results of that calculation in cell B5, you could place the cursor in cell B5 and enter the simple formula **=B1+B2**.

A formula calculates a value based on a combination of other values. These other values can be numbers, cell references, operators (+, -, *, and /), or other formulas. Formulas can also include the names of other areas in the worksheet, as well as cell references in other worksheets.

More Info   Math operators produce numeric results. Besides addition (+), subtraction (-), multiplication (*), and division (/) symbols, Excel accepts as math operators the exponentiation (^) and percentage (%) symbols. A number of other types of characters can be used in formulas for manipulating text and numbers; Chapter 14 covers them in detail.

Printing the Worksheet

To print an Excel worksheet, choose File⇨Print. A Print dialog box appears, as shown in Figure C-10. You can press Enter or click on OK to begin printing; this selects the default values for the options shown. If you want an option other than the default options, click on the option you want and then click on OK to start printing. If you want to print one copy of all the data that is in the currently selected worksheet, just click on the Print button on the Standard toolbar.

More Info   Chapter 20 covers printing options in detail.

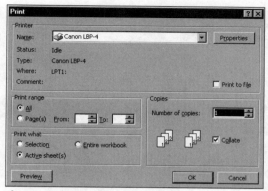

Figure C-10: The Print dialog box.

Saving the Worksheet

It's a good practice to save your worksheet on disk periodically, even if you plan to continue working on the worksheet later. Doing so reduces the possibility of losing large amounts of information because of a power failure or system crash. The commands used for saving worksheets — Save, Save As, and Save Workspace — are found in the File menu.

The Save and Save As commands save worksheets to disk. Save As prompts you for a new filename; Save saves the worksheet under the existing name (after it has been saved once).

Save As saves files in different formats from Excel's normal one. Worksheet data can be saved as ASCII text (a format that virtually all word processors can read), in Excel for Windows 95 format, in the formats of older versions of Excel, in Lotus 1-2-3 format, as HTML for publishing on the Internet or on an intranet, and in many other database and spreadsheet file formats.

To save your worksheet, choose File⇨Save. When you do this the first time, the dialog box shown in Figure C-11 appears.

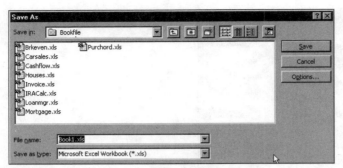

Figure C-11: The Save As dialog box.

Here you can enter a title for the worksheet in the File name text box. When you press Enter, the worksheet is saved on disk.

Summary

This appendix provided an overview of Excel basics for those who have never worked with the program. This appendix covered these points:

✦ Excel stores information in worksheets.

✦ Excel provides several toolbars to help you enter and format worksheet entries.

✦ Excel lets you store related worksheets in a workbook.

✦ You can use either the keyboard or the mouse to navigate a worksheet and a workbook.

✦ You enter data just by clicking in a cell and typing away; and you edit data by clicking in a cell and retyping the value, or by modifying the value in the Formula bars.

✦ You can format entries as numbers (the default), as times and dates, and as straight text.

✦ Excel lets you create formulas to manipulate the data you enter into a worksheet.

✦ You can save and print your worksheets and workbooks.

Where to go next...

✦ Part III tells you the whole Excel story. Start with Chapter 15.

✦   ✦   ✦

PowerPoint Basics

This introduction to PowerPoint provides details regarding basic PowerPoint skills. It is designed to familiarize readers who have never worked with PowerPoint before with the basics of the package. In this introduction, you'll learn how to create presentations with and without the aid of the wizards, how to enter and edit text, how to add clip art to slides, and how to print your slides. You'll also learn some basic terminology that applies to using PowerPoint. When you feel familiar with the basics, you'll find the more advanced details of PowerPoint in Chapters 27 through 34.

Understanding PowerPoint Terminology

As you work with PowerPoint, you'll often encounter some common terms. Being familiar with these terms will maximize your effectiveness in using PowerPoint. Check over the following list to familiarize yourself with these common PowerPoint terms:

✦ **Presentation** — In PowerPoint, a *presentation* is the container holding all the individual slides, text, graphics, drawings, and other objects that make up your presentation in its entirety. PowerPoint stores each presentation in a separate file on your hard disk.

✦ **Template** — A *template* is a kind of *formatting model* in PowerPoint. You use templates to apply a chosen group of styles, colors, and fonts to the slides that you are working with. PowerPoint comes with over 150 different templates; you can see examples of the style and layout of each of these by referring to Appendix F of the *PowerPoint User's Guide*.

✦ **Slides** — *Slides* are the individual screens or pages that you see within your presentation.

✦ **Slide masters** — *Slide masters* are master documents that control the appearance and the layout of the slides that you create. If you make a design change to a slide master, the same change is reflected in all the new slides that you create based on that master.

✦ **Layout** — The term *layout* refers to the overall appearance of a single slide. You can change the layout for any slide on an individual basis without affecting other slides in the presentation.

Creating Presentations

To create a new presentation, choose File⇨New to open the New Presentation dialog box shown in Figure D-1. When the New Presentation dialog box opens, the General tab is displayed along with the Blank Presentation icon. Choose from among these options:

✦ **General** — This tab contains the Blank Presentation icon. Use it to create a presentation that contains no preformatted slides. Next you will see the New Slide dialog box. Choose the layout for the first slide of your presentation.

✦ **Presentation designs** — This tab contains templates that you can use for the presentations that you create. PowerPoint contains 27 template designs that you can use to design your presentations.

✦ **Presentations** — This tab contains 20 different presentations that you can use for different subjects. You will also see the AutoContent Wizard that will help you create a presentation if those listed do not meet your needs. The AutoContent Wizard produces six styles of presentations, including strategy, sales, training, progress report, and bad news.

✦ **Web Pages** — This tab contains presentations that can be used for web pages on the Internet or on an intranet. After creating the presentation, you can use the techniques described in Chapter 32 to produce web pages written in HTML, the common language used by web browsers.

After you choose the way in which you want to create the new presentation, click on the OK button. If you chose a Wizard, you may be asked additional questions to help determine the layout and content of your presentation. When you are finished answering the questions, the basis of your presentation appears on-screen, and you can edit it as you see fit.

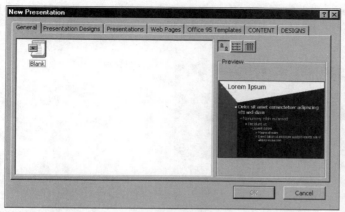

Figure D-1: The General tab of the New Presentation dialog box.

Using the AutoContent Wizard

When you start a new presentation with the AutoContent Wizard option, the first AutoContent Wizard dialog box appears explaining the purpose of the wizard. After you click on the Next button, the second AutoContent Wizard dialog box appears, as shown in Figure D-2.

Figure D-2: The second AutoContent Wizard dialog box.

The second text box asks you to choose the type of presentation you want to create. You have choices divided into several categories. Clicking on the button corresponding to the desired category makes all the choices for that category appear. The default is all, which shows all the listings from all the categories.

After you choose the type of presentation you want to create, click on the Next button; you see the third AutoContent Wizard dialog box, as shown in Figure D-3.

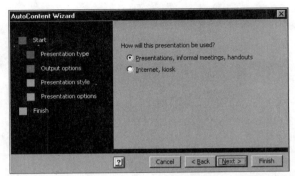

Figure D-3: The third AutoContent Wizard dialog box.

In this dialog box, you can select the manner in which your presentation will be used. Your choices are Presentations, Informal meetings, handouts and Internet, and Kiosk. After you choose an option, click on the Next Buttons to show the Fourth dialog box (Figure D-4).

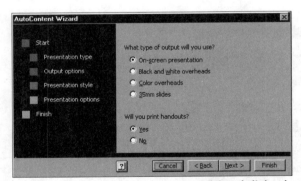

Figure D-4: The fourth AutoContent Wizard dialog box.

The fourth dialog box is used to choose the desired style of your presentation. Under the type of output section, you will want to select the way you will be presenting your slides. You can choose from on screen, black and white overheads, color overheads, or 35mm slides. Also you can tell the wizard whether you will be printing out the slides. After you have made your selections click next to go to the fifth window of the AutoContent Wizard (Figure D-5).

This fifth dialog box to the AutoContent wizard is used to set up your title slide. Here, you will enter a title for your first slide. After entering a title you may want to include your name. If so, enter it in the name field. The wizard also allows space for any additional information that you wish to add to the title slide of presentation. After you have completed making your choices, click next to go to the final dialog box of the AutoContent Wizard. This dialog box asks for confirmation before creating the presentation, and you can click Finish to complete the presentation.

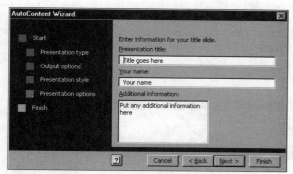

Figure D-5: The fifth AutoContent Wizard dialog box.

Using a template

To use a template, choose File⇨New, and then select the Presentations tab. Now choose the template on which you want to base your presentation. Choose the desired template and click on the OK button. Next, you see the New Slide dialog box, as shown in Figure D-6.

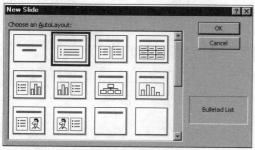

Figure D-6: The New Slide dialog box.

After you choose one of the layouts shown in the dialog box, click on the OK button. PowerPoint creates a presentation containing a single slide that uses the style and layout that you have specified. You can then add text and graphics to the slide and insert additional slides into the presentation.

Starting a blank presentation

The Blank Presentation option is suited to PowerPoint users who are familiar with the package. This option assumes that you want to handle all the design and content decisions on your own. After you choose the Blank Presentation option from the General tab of the New Presentation dialog box, the New Slide dialog box appears. After you select the layout that you want, click on the OK button. The result is a blank presentation containing a single slide, like the one shown in Figure D-7. You can add text and add slides as desired.

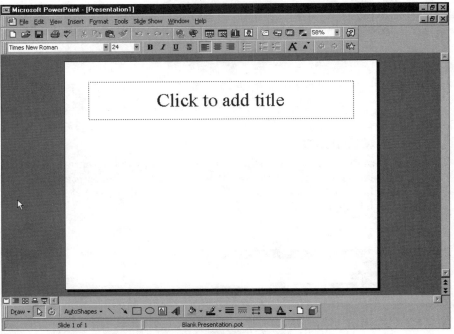

Figure D-7: The result of selecting the Blank Presentation option.

Opening a Presentation

You can open an existing presentation by choosing File⇨Open or by clicking on the Open button on the Standard toolbar. Either method results in the appearance of the Open dialog box. Choose the presentation that you want and click on the OK button. You can open and work with multiple presentations simultaneously. As you open each presentation, its name is added to the bottom of the Window menu. You can switch among presentations by clicking on the presentation name from the Window menu or by pressing Ctrl+F6.

Saving and Closing a Presentation

PowerPoint uses the standard Windows methods to save files. When you choose File⇨Save or click on the Save button on the Standard toolbar, PowerPoint saves the presentation to a file. If you are saving the presentation for the first time, a Save As dialog box appears, where you provide a filename for the presentation. You can save an existing presentation under a different filename by choosing File⇨Save As and entering the new name for the presentation.

To close a presentation that you are finished working with, choose File⇨Close or double-click on the close box in the presentation's window.

Understanding PowerPoint's Views

As you work with your presentations, you can switch between any one of five different views: Slide, Outline, Slide Sorter, Notes Pages, and Slide Show. Each of these views provides you with a different way of looking at the same presentation. To switch between the available views, you can click on the appropriate View button at the lower-left corner of your screen. You can also choose the corresponding view from the View menu. For example, choosing View⇨Outline switches you to Outline view.

Slide view fills the window with a view of the current slide. In this view, you can add and edit text and graphics or change the layout of the slide. Figure D-8 shows an example of a presentation in Slide view.

Outline view provides a view of the overall organization of the text in your presentation. In this view, it's easier to see a large portion of your presentation's contents. Although you can't change the slide layouts or modify graphics in this view, you can add and edit the slide titles and the main text. Figure D-9 shows an example of a presentation in Outline view.

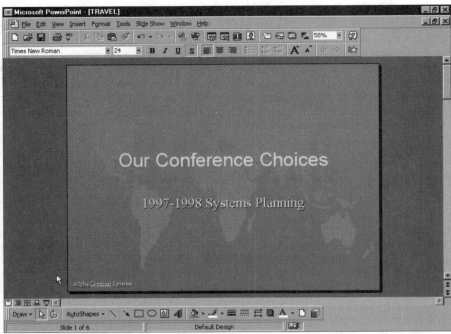

Figure D-8: An example of a presentation in Slide view.

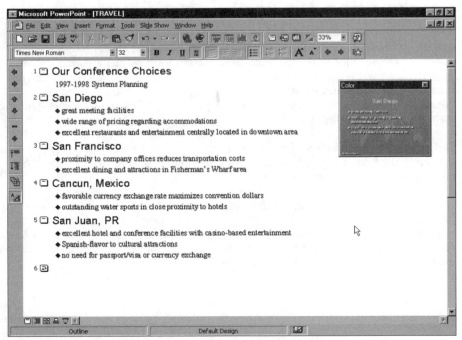

Figure D-9: An example of a presentation in Outline view.

More Info Slide Sorter view provides a window containing up to 12 slides, each in reduced form. This view is best when you want an overall view of your presentation or when you want to see the overall appearance of the text and the graphics. You can't edit text or graphics in this view, but you can reorder the slides. When you are working with electronic slide shows, you can also add transitions between slides and set the timing in this view (see Chapter 30). Figure D-10 shows an example of Slide Sorter view.

Notes Pages view provides a view where a single slide is placed in the top half of a page, and the bottom half of the page is reserved for the typing of notes. This view is useful when you want to add speaker's notes that you can refer to during your presentation. PowerPoint lets you print the notes pages separately from the slides or overheads that you produce for your presentation. Figure D-11 shows an example of Notes Pages view.

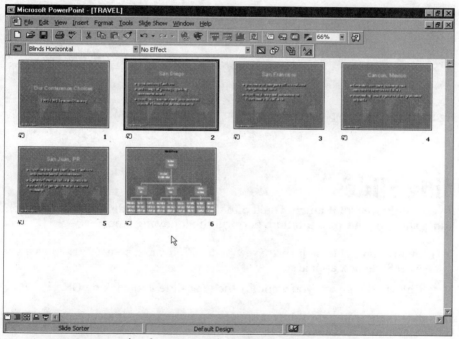

Figure D-10: An example of a presentation in Slide Sorter view.

Slide Show view fills the screen with a view of one slide at a time. In this view, you also see the effects of any transitions and timing that you have added to the presentation.

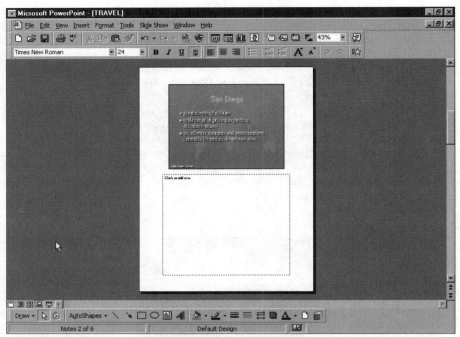

Figure D-11: An example of a presentation in Notes Pages view.

Adding Slides

If you use PowerPoint much, you'll often find yourself adding slides to presentations. To add a slide to your presentation, perform the following steps.

1. In any view, choose Insert⇨New Slide. (You can also use Ctrl+M as a shortcut.) The New Slide box appears.

2. Choose the layout you want for the new slide and click on OK.

The slide is then added to the end of your presentation. It has the same design as the other slides in your presentation.

Moving among Slides

Most presentations have more than one slide, so you must be able to move among slides to work on your whole presentation. How you move among slides depends on which view you're in. Table D-1 shows the different methods for moving around within the different slide views.

Table D-1 **Methods of moving among slides**	
View	*How to move among slides*
Outline view	Drag the scroll box to display the desired slide. Click on the slide icon to the left of the slide's title to select the slide. Click anywhere within the slide's text to edit it.
Slide view	Drag the scroll box until you reach the desired slide number or click on the Previous Slide or Next Slide button at the bottom of the vertical scrollbar.
Slide Sorter view	Click on the desired slide.
Notes Pages view	Drag the scroll box until you reach the desired slide number or click on the Previous Slide or Next Slide button at the bottom of the vertical scrollbar.

Editing a Slide's Contents

If you've created a presentation based on a blank slide, you must enter all the required text. If you used an AutoContent Wizard, you've got a fair amount of text in your presentation already, but it's probably not precisely what you want. In either case, you need to add or edit the text that you want in your presentation. This section details how you can add or edit text in Slide view or in Outline view.

Editing text in Slide view

In Slide view, you see your text along with any graphics that you have added to the slide, and you can edit any object in the slide by clicking on the object. To add text, click in the placeholder labeled *Click to add title* and type the text, as shown in Figure D-12. To edit existing text, click on the text to select it and then edit it as you normally would. If you're working with a bulleted list of topics, you can add a new topic by placing the insertion point at the end of an existing topic and pressing Enter.

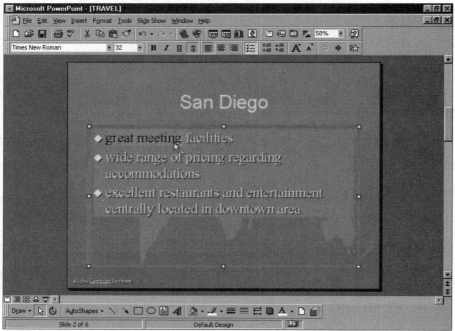

Figure D-12: Editing text in Slide view.

Editing text in Outline view

Outline view provides an easy way to edit text because you can view a lot of your presentation at one time. To edit text, just click to place the insertion point where you want it and type the desired text, as shown in Figure D-13. You can use the Delete or Backspace keys to remove unwanted text.

As you work with text in Outline view, keep in mind that you can use the Promote, Demote, Move Up, and Move Down buttons on the Outlining toolbar to the left of the screen to change the levels or the locations of the items that you are working with. Simply place the insertion point anywhere inside the desired entry and then click on the appropriate button. The Outlining buttons perform the following tasks:

✦ **Promote (Indent less)** — Click on this button to remove an indent and to move the entry one level higher (in importance) within the list. The item moves to the left, and in most cases, the font size increases.

✦ **Demote (Indent more)** — Click on this button to add an indent and to move the entry one level lower (in importance) within the list. The item moves to the right, and in most cases, the font size decreases.

✦ **Move Up** — Click on this button to move the entry up in the list by one line.

✦ **Move Down** — Click on this button to move the entry down in the list by one line.

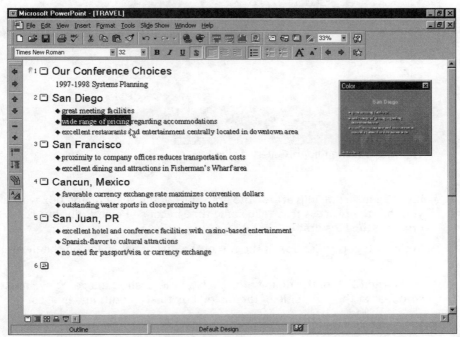

Figure D-13: Editing text in Outline view.

Adding Clip Art to a Presentation

PowerPoint comes with hundreds of clip art images that you can easily add to your presentations to add pizzazz to your slides. Note that before you can insert clip art, you must have installed the ClipArt Gallery along with PowerPoint. You can add clip art by performing the following steps:

1. Switch to Slide view and display the slide where you want to add the clip art.

2. Choose Insert⇨Picture, then Clip Art or click on the Insert Clip Art button on the Standard toolbar to open the ClipArt Gallery dialog box, as shown in Figure D-14.

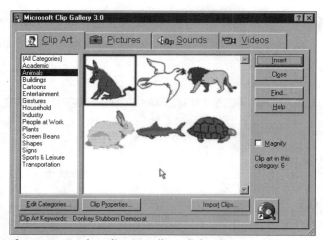

Figure D-14: The ClipArt Gallery dialog box.

Note

If you're inserting clip art for the first time, you'll see a dialog box warning you that the process may take some time because PowerPoint has to organize the files first.

3. In the Categories list box at the top of the dialog box, click on the desired category.

4. In the right half of the dialog box, click on the desired image. You can use the scrollbar at the right side of the dialog box to see additional images.

5. Click on the OK button to place the clip art in the slide.

After the clip art appears in the slide, you can click on it to select it. Then hold down the mouse button while you drag it to the location that you want. You can resize the clip art by clicking on one of the sizing handles (the small rectangles that surround the clip art when you select it) and dragging it until the clip art reaches the desired size.

Hot Stuff

You may often want to add clip art to the same area as existing text, but by default, any clip art that you add covers the existing text. To solve this problem, go into Slide view and select the clip art by clicking on it. Then choose the Send to Back command from the Draw menu to place the clip art underneath the text, which makes the text visible.

Printing Your Presentation

You can print various parts of your presentation or all of your presentation. To print your presentation, choose File⇨Print or click on the Print button on the Standard toolbar. The Print dialog box appears, as shown in Figure D-15.

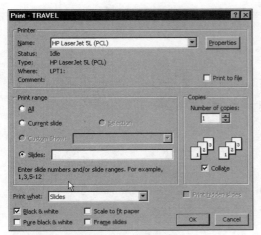

Figure D-15: The Print dialog box.

More Info You will learn more about the Print dialog box in Chapter 30, but for now, the most important point is to remember to select exactly what you want to print. In the Print What list box, you can choose Slides, Note Pages, Handouts, or Outline View. Then choose a range of slides by selecting the desired options in the Slide Range area of the dialog box (the default option is All). Select any other desired options in the dialog box and click on the OK button to begin printing.

This appendix has provided an introduction to the basics of PowerPoint with the goal of getting you up and running quickly. The PowerPoint section of this book provides you with much more detail about what you can accomplish with all the features of PowerPoint.

Summary

This appendix covered topics relevant to quickly getting started in PowerPoint. All of the topics that were considered are considered in more depth in their respective chapters. These are some of the topics we covered.

✦ To work effectively with PowerPoint, you must understand these terms: Presentation, Template, Slide, Slide Master, and Layout. (They're explained at the beginning of the chapter.)

✦ Use File⇨New and the New Presentation dialog box to create a presentation. This dialog box gives you several options. You can use the AutoContent wizard to customize one of several presentations. You can use a template to start with a basic structure for your presentation. Or, you can start with a blank presentation, and design it from the ground up.

✦ PowerPoint has five *views* in which you can create and edit your presentation: Slide, Outline, Slide Sorter, Notes Pages, and Slide Show.

✦ Use Insert⇨Slide to insert a slide into a presentation. This command works from any view.

✦ You can edit slide text in either Slide view or Outline view.

✦ Use Insert⇨Clip Art to insert clip art into a presentation.

✦ Use File⇨Print to print your presentation.

Where to go next...

✦ Part IV describes PowerPoint in detail. Start with Chapter 27.

✦   ✦   ✦

Access Basics

Welcome to Access, the database management component of Microsoft Office that you can use for various data management tasks. This appendix is designed to give you a fast introduction to the basics of Access by quickly demonstrating how you can put Access to work. The appendix provides a step-by-step exercise you can follow to create a typical database used to track sales contacts at a business. By following the steps in this appendix, you learn how to create a new database, design a table, use a form to add records to the table, search for specific records, and produce reports. After completing the exercise in this appendix, you can refer to the chapters in the Access section of this book for full details on working with Access.

Creating the Database and the Table

By design, Access stores your tables, queries, forms, and reports that you work with in a *database*. Tables contain your data; queries retrieve specific data that you need; and forms and reports help you edit, display, and print your data. Before you create any tables, you need to create a database in which to store your tables and other Access objects such as forms and reports.

The database you create in this example contains one table, which will be used to record names, phone numbers, and other details of the sales contacts. To create the database and the required table, first start Access in the usual manner (double-click on the Access icon on your Windows desktop). When Access loads and the Access desktop appears, perform these steps:

1. Click Blank Database in the dialog box that initially appears and click OK, or, if you closed the dialog box that initially appears, choose File⇨New Database to

open the New dialog box, select Blank Database, and then click on OK. (If you want to store your sample database in a different directory, use the Directory list box to locate the desired directory now. Double-click on the desired directory, and Access will store the new database in that directory.)

2. Enter **Contacts** in the File name text box as a name for the database, and then click on the Create button. Access creates the database file on your network drive or your hard disk, and the Database window appears, as shown in Figure E-1. The Database window is divided into tabs, each of which is used to display the common Access objects stored in a database: Tables, Queries, Forms, Reports, Macros, and Modules.

Figure E-1: The Database window.

3. In the Database window, click on the Tables tab, and then click on the New button. In the New Table dialog box that appears, click on Design View, and then click on OK. In a moment the Table window appears, as shown in Figure E-2.

4. With the cursor flashing in the first Field Name column, enter **Contact ID** as the first field name, and then press Tab to move the cursor to the Data Type column.

5. In the Data Type column, type **A** to change the field type from the text (the default) to AutoNumber. In this type of field, Access stores a numeric value that is automatically incremented for each new record that is stored in the table. You can click on the arrow at the right side of this column to open a menu showing your choices of field types; the choices include AutoNumber, Text, Number, Date/Time, Currency, Memo, Yes/No, Hyperlink, and OLE Object.

More Info

For more details on field types, see Chapter 35.

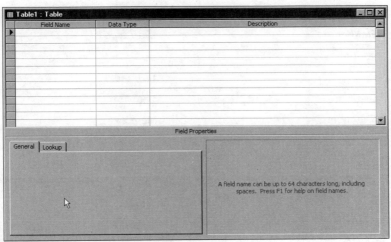

Figure E-2: The Table window.

6. Press Tab twice to move past the Description column (descriptions are optional) and back to the Field Name column.

7. Using the Tab key, enter the remaining field names and field types as shown below. To select each field type, click on the arrow at the right side of the Data Type column, and choose the desired field type from the menu that appears.

8. Click anywhere in the first field (titled Contact ID), and choose Edit⇨Primary Key (you can also click on the Key button in the toolbar at the top of the screen) to make this field the primary key. At this point, your table's structure should resemble the example shown in Figure E-3.

Field name	Data type
Last name	Text
First name	Text
Company	Text
Address	Text
City	Text
State	Text
Zip code	Text

(continued)

(continued)

Field name	Data type
Phone	Text
Fax	Text
Last contact	Date/Time
Comments	Memo

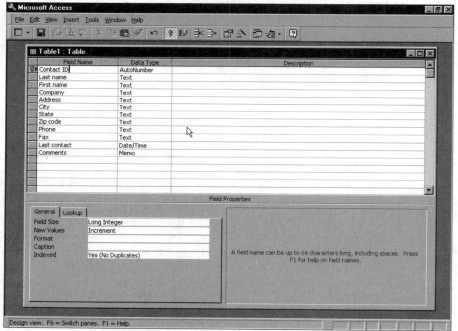

Figure E-3: The completed table's definition.

9. Choose File⇨Save to save the table. When asked for a table name, enter **Sales Contacts** as the name and click on OK.

10. Press Ctrl+F4 to close the Table window. The new table, Sales Contacts, now appears in the Database window. At this point, both the database and the table exist; you can, if desired, create additional tables and store them in this database. (For this example, only one table is needed; however, you can have over 32,000 different tables in any one database.)

In this example, for some fields that will store numbers (such as the Zip code and Phone fields) we suggested text fields as the data type rather than number fields. In Access, you should only use number fields when you intend to perform calculations on the contents of the fields; otherwise, use text fields (which can store letters, numbers, or a combination of both). For more on this subject, refer to Chapter 35.

Creating a Form

The most common way that you will use Access is to enter data and edit records in a table. With Access, you use forms to add and edit the records in a table. Access makes creating forms easy with a feature called the Form Wizard. To create a form that you can use with the table you just created, perform the following steps:

1. In the Database window, make sure that the table you just created is selected; if not, click on it to select it.

2. Click on the arrow to the right of the New Object button in the toolbar (it's the second button from the right), and choose AutoForm from the menu that appears to create a default form for the selected table. The form should resemble the example shown in Figure E-4.

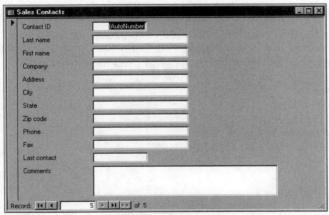

Figure E-4: The completed example of a new form.

Adding and Editing Data

Before you can experiment with queries and reports, you need to add data to the table by using the form you created in the last step. You add data to tables by typing the desired entries into the fields of the form and pressing Tab after each entry. (You can use Tab to move to any successive field, and you can press Shift+Tab to move backward to previous fields.) You can correct any mistakes that you make during data entry by clicking in the field where you made the mistake and using the Backspace or Delete keys to delete the entry. Enter the following new record in the table with the form now, using the following data (remember to press the Tab key after each entry).

Contact ID: **1** (automatically entered by the AutoNumber field)
Last name: **Johnson**
First name: **Mary**
Company: **Acme Fibers, Inc.**
Address: **1700 La Costa Mesa Drive**
City: **Hayward**
State: **CA**
Zip code: **94542**
Phone: **408-555-2330**
Fax: **408-555-2328**
Last contact: **3/22/97**
Comments: **Expressed high level of interest in our Premier line of #10 envelopes.**

After completing the entry in the Comments field, press Tab again, and the cursor moves to the first field of a new, blank record. Enter the three additional records that follow, using the same techniques that you used for the first record:

Last name: **Benson**
First name: **Terry**
Company: **Swift Technology**
Address: **2100 Stanford St.**
City: **Santa Monica**
State: **CA**
Zip code: **90404**
Phone: **310-555-2000**
Fax: **310-555-2020**
Last contact: **3/25/97**
Comments: **Wants full pricing information on our Standard line of #10 envelopes.**

Last name: **Alvarez**
First name: **Maria**
Company: **Image Systems, Ltd.**
Address: **9090 Telstar Drive**
City: **El Monte**
State: **CA**
Zip code: **91731**
Phone: **818-555-4050**
Fax: **818-555-4068**
Last contact: **3/23/97**
Comments: **Wants to know current discount on bulk envelope orders.**

Last name: **O'Malley**
First name: **Sandy**
Company: **Corporate Support**
Address: **1111 Lincoln Ave.**
City: **Hayward**
State: **CA**
Zip code: **94545**
Phone: **510-555-2985**
Fax: **510-555-3121**
Last contact: **3/26/97**
Comments: **Did not need pricing info we sent on Standard-line envelopes. Is interested in pricing on interoffice-mail envelopes.**

After you've entered all of the data, you can move between the existing records using the PgUp and PgDn keys, or by clicking on the navigation buttons that appear at the bottom of the form. You can use the cursor keys (or the mouse) to move between the different fields on the form.

Saving a Form

After you create a form, you must save it for future use. Saving a form is a simple task; first, make sure that the form is the active window. (You can click anywhere inside the form to make it active.) While the form is active, choose File⇨Save. (If you are following the example, do this now to save the form you just created.) If this is the first time you've saved the form, Access displays a dialog box that asks you for a name for the form.

Enter a name for the form, and then click on OK. (For this example, call the form **Contacts**, and then click on OK.) You can give your form any name of 64 characters or fewer, and you can use spaces in the name. When you click on OK, Access saves the form as a part of the database, and the form name appears when you click on the Forms tab in the Database window.

Opening an Existing Form

If you want to use an existing form to add records to a table, start Access in the usual manner and follow these steps:

1. Open the desired database by choosing File⇨Open Database, click on the name of the desired database, and click on OK.

2. Click on the Forms tab in the Database window to display all forms in the database.

3. Click on the desired form to select it, and then click on the Open button. (You can also double-click on the form to open it.)

After the form opens, you can add or edit records, or perform searches using the steps outlined in the following section.

Note You can close a form after you are done using it by pressing Ctrl+F4 or by double-clicking on the X button in the upper-right corner of the form. (Don't do this yet if you are following the example because you want to have the form open to perform the search in a later exercise.)

Finding Records

A natural part of the editing process is finding what you need to edit. In Access, you can use the Edit ⇨ Find menu option, or the equivalent Find button on the toolbar, to display the Find dialog box. You then fill in the dialog box options and click on OK to search for the data that you want to edit. If you created the table and added the records described in the previous sections of this chapter, you can use the following steps to find a specific record in the table:

1. Click anywhere within the field that you want to search, unless you want to search all fields. (Generally, the faster method is to search within a single field rather than to search all fields within a table.) For this example, you want to search the table for a specific entry in the Company field, so click anywhere within the Company field now.

2. Next, choose Edit⇨Find. When you choose this option, the Find dialog box appears, as shown in Figure E-5.

Figure E-5: The Find dialog box.

3. In the Find What box, enter the text that you want to find. For this example, enter **Swift**.

4. Click on the arrow at the right edge of the Match list box to open the drop-down list box, and choose the Any Part of Field option to search for text located somewhere within the field.

5. The Search Only Current Field check box should already be selected. If not, click on the option to restrict the search to the current field.

6. Click on the Find First button. (This causes Access to find the first match of the search term.) When Access finds the record, you see the words "Search succeeded" at the bottom left corner of the window.

7. After the search is finished, you must click on the Close button in the dialog box to close it and reveal the desired record.

To find the next match of the search term and any additional matches, you choose Edit ⇨ Find from the menu, and click on the Find Next button. (For more on searches and the options in the Find dialog box, see "Finding data" in Chapter 35.)

If you are following the example, press Ctrl+F4 now to close the form. (In any Windows application, pressing Ctrl+F4 always closes the active window.)

Using Datasheet View

For this exercise, you entered your data into Access using a form, but this method is just one of the two ways in which you can add and edit data. The other way is through a Datasheet View. In this view, Access shows your data in the familiar row-and-column format, similar to that of a spreadsheet.

Note   Although you can use Datasheet View to add and edit records, you probably will prefer to use a form because it is easier to see the full contents of your fields when editing with a form.

If the table or form is not open (that is, if you're in the Database window), you can click on the Tables tab to display all tables in your database, and then click on the desired table and the Open button to open the table in Datasheet View. If you are already viewing data through a form, you can switch to the Datasheet View at any time by choosing View ⇨ Datasheet from the menu (or by clicking on the Datasheet button on the left side of the toolbar). Figure E-6 shows the Datasheet View for the table created in this section.

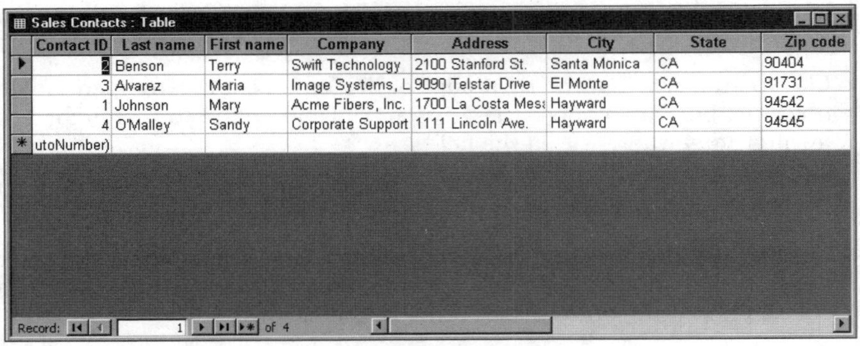

Figure E-6: The Datasheet View for the sample table.

While you're in Datasheet View, notice that the left edge of the table contains *record selectors*. Click on any of the record selectors to select a record. After you select a record, you can delete it by pressing Delete, or you can print it by choosing File⇨Print and clicking on the Selection button in the Print dialog box.

You can select several records at once by clicking on and dragging over the record selectors. For example, if you click on and drag from the record selector for the second record to the record selector for the fifth record, records 2 through 5 are selected. Alternatively, you can click on the record selector for the first record you want, press and hold down Shift, and click on the record selector for the last record you want to select multiple, adjacent records.

In Access, every table contains a blank record at the end of the table. You can add data by clicking in the blank record and typing the desired data, and then pressing Tab to move to each successive field. If you are entering data into a memo field, you can press Shift+F2 while in the memo field to open a small window that allows you to see the field's contents more clearly. When done with the table, you can close it by pressing Ctrl+F4 or by clicking on the X button in the upper-right corner of the table.

Working with Queries: An Example

In Access, you make use of *queries* to obtain specific data that you want. Queries provide you with a way to obtain specific fields and records from one or more tables, to form a subset of your overall data. Suppose that you want to see all the records of companies located in Hayward, California. Additionally, you only need to see the company name, the name of the contact, and the phone number; the other fields aren't needed. You can perform the following steps to create and run the desired query.

1. Click on the Queries tab in the Database window, and then click on the New button. When the New Query dialog box appears, click on Design View, and then click on OK. In a moment, the Show Table dialog box appears over a Query Design window.

2. Select the Sales Contacts table in the list box, and click on Add. Finally, click on Close. At this point, you see the new Select Query window, such as the one shown in Figure E-7. In Access, you use Query Design windows such as this one to design your queries.

More Info

See Chapter 36 for more details about the use of the Select Query window.

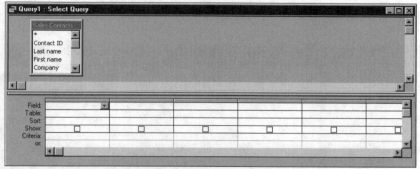

Figure E-7: A new query within the Query window.

3. In the Sales Contacts list box, click on the Last name field and drag it to the first empty column of the Field: row in the query. Click on the First name field and drag it to the next empty column of the Field: row in the query. Click on the Company field and drag it to the next empty column of the Field: row in the query. Scroll down in the list box, click on the City field and drag it to the next empty column of the Field: row in the query. Finally, click on the Phone field and drag it to the next empty column of the Field: row in the query.

4. Click in the Criteria: row under the City column, and enter **Hayward**. At this point, your query should resemble the one shown in Figure E-8.

5. Choose Query⇨Run (or click on the Run button shown near the center of the toolbar) to run the query. If you are using the sample data that you typed in according to the instructions earlier in this section, the results will resemble those shown in Figure E-9. If you want a printout of these records, you choose File⇨Print from the menus to print the results of the query.

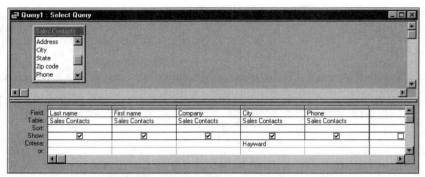

Figure E-8: A completed version of a query.

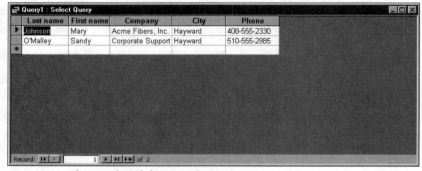

Figure E-9: The results of the sample query.

6. Press Ctrl+F4 now to close the window containing the query results. When Access asks if you want to save the query, click on No in the dialog box; you will not need this example query. When you are using Access for your actual work, you can save queries, so you can reuse them later.

More Info

Chapter 36 contains details on saving and reusing queries.

Creating a Report

Access provides a feature called the Report Wizard that helps you create reports. The Report Wizard asks a series of questions about the report you want to create, and it uses the answers that you provide to automatically design a complete report. You can use the Report Wizard to create different styles of reports, including columnar reports, tabular reports, summary reports, and mailing labels. You will use the Report Wizard to create a sample report in the following list. Chapter 38 covers the Report Wizard in greater detail. For now, perform the following steps to create a sample report for the Sales Contacts table.

1. In the Database window, click on the Reports tab, and then click on the New button. When you perform this task, the New Report dialog box appears, as shown in Figure E-10.

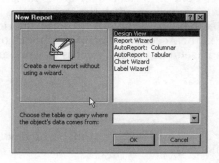

Figure E-10: The New Report dialog box.

2. Choose AutoReport: Columnar in the list of available report types. Then, click on the arrow to the right of the list box near the bottom of the dialog box, and click on Sales Contacts in the drop-down list. Finally, click on OK, and the Report Wizard proceeds to create the report. If you are using the sample data that you typed in earlier in the exercise, your new report should resemble the example shown in Figure E-11.

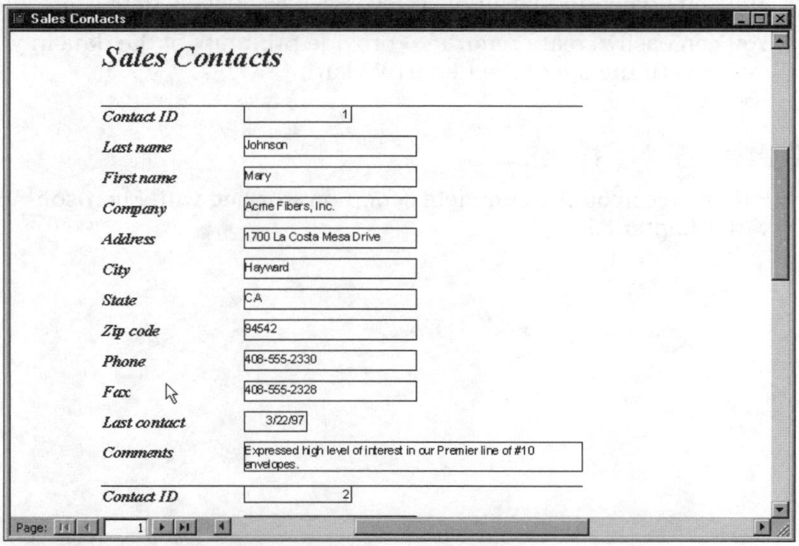

Figure E-11: A completed report.

3. Press Ctrl+F4 to close the new report. Access asks if you want to save the report; click on Yes in the dialog box that appears. When prompted for a name, call the report **Sales Contacts**.

This completes the exercise. If you are done with Access for now, choose File⇨Exit to exit the program. Assuming that you've performed all the steps in this appendix, you now have a basic understanding of the use of tables, queries, forms, and reports in Access. The chapters in the Access section of this book contain detailed information that you will find useful as you put Access to work to meet your own database needs.

Summary

This appendix provided an overview of Access basics for those who have never worked with the program. The appendix covered these points:

✦ In Access, you create tables with the fields that you want to store your data.

✦ You can use the Form Wizard to quickly create forms that you can use to add and edit data in a table.

✦ While editing data in a form, you can use the Edit⇨Find command to locate a specific record.

✦ You can view your Access data through forms or Datasheet View.

✦ You can create queries in Access to retrieve specific data from your tables.

✦ You can easily create reports to provide printouts of the data in your Access tables with the aid of the Report Wizard.

Where to go next...

✦ Part V gives you the complete scoop on working with Microsoft Access. Start with Chapter 35.

✦   ✦   ✦

Index

Symbols and Numbers

A

C

D

E

G

M

P

Q

X

Y

z

IDG BOOKS WORLDWIDE REGISTRATION CARD

Visit our Web site at http://www.idgbooks.com

Title of this book: Office 97 Bible

My overall rating of this book: ❑ Very good [1] ❑ Good [2] ❑ Satisfactory [3] ❑ Fair [4] ❑ Poor [5]

How I first heard about this book:

❑ Found in bookstore; name: [6] _____   ❑ Book review: [7]

❑ Advertisement: [8]   ❑ Catalog: [9]

❑ Word of mouth; heard about book from friend, co-worker, etc.: [10]   ❑ Other: [11]

What I liked most about this book:

_____
_____
_____

What I would change, add, delete, etc., in future editions of this book:

_____
_____

Other comments:

_____

Number of computer books I purchase in a year: ❑ 1 [12] ❑ 2-5 [13] ❑ 6-10 [14] ❑ More than 10 [15]

I would characterize my computer skills as: ❑ Beginner [16] ❑ Intermediate [17] ❑ Advanced [18] ❑ Professional [19]

I use ❑ DOS [20] ❑ Windows [21] ❑ OS/2 [22] ❑ Unix [23] ❑ Macintosh [24] ❑ Other: [25]_____

(please specify)

I would be interested in new books on the following subjects:

(please check all that apply, and use the spaces provided to identify specific software)

❑ Word processing: [26] _____   ❑ Spreadsheets: [27] _____

❑ Data bases: [28] _____   ❑ Desktop publishing: [29] _____

❑ File Utilities: [30] _____   ❑ Money management: [31] _____

❑ Networking: [32] _____   ❑ Programming languages: [33] _____

❑ Other: [34] _____

I use a PC at (please check all that apply): ❑ home [35] ❑ work [36] ❑ school [37] ❑ other: [38] _____

The disks I prefer to use are ❑ 5.25 [39] ❑ 3.5 [40] ❑ other: [41]_____

I have a CD ROM: ❑ yes [42]   ❑ no [43]

I plan to buy or upgrade computer hardware this year: ❑ yes [44]   ❑ no [45]

I plan to buy or upgrade computer software this year: ❑ yes [46]   ❑ no [47]

Name: _____   Business title: [48] _____   Type of Business: [49] _____

Address (❑ home [50] ❑ work [51]/Company name: _____)

Street/Suite# _____

City [52]/State [53]/Zipcode [54]: _____   Country [55] _____

❑ **I liked this book!** You may quote me by name in future
IDG Books Worldwide promotional materials.

My daytime phone number is _____

IDG
BOOKS
WORLDWIDE

THE WORLD OF
COMPUTER
KNOWLEDGE®

 # YES!

Please keep me informed about IDG Books Worldwide's World of Computer Knowledge. Send me your latest catalog.